SAFETY, NUTRITION, AND HEALTH

in Early Education

4TH Edition

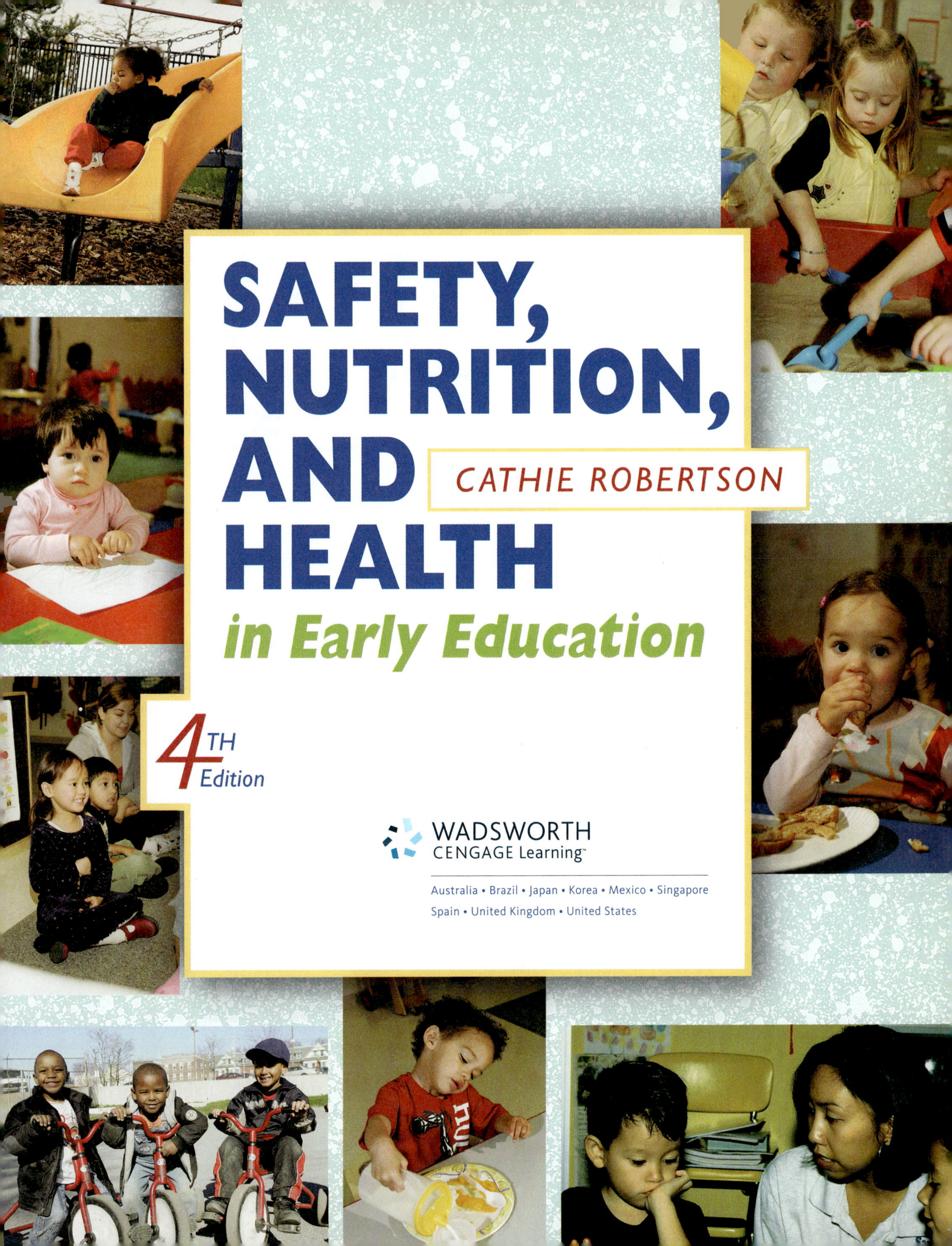
SAFETY, NUTRITION, AND HEALTH
in Early Education
CATHIE ROBERTSON
4TH Edition
WADSWORTH
CENGAGE Learning™
Australia • Brazil • Japan • Korea • Mexico • Singapore
Spain • United Kingdom • United States

Safety, Nutrition, and Health in Early Education, Fourth Edition
Cathie Robertson

Acquisitions Editor: Chris Shortt

Development Editor: Robert Jucha

Assistant Editor: Caitlin Cox

Editorial Assistant: Linda Stewart

Associate Media Editor: Ashley Cronin

Marketing Manager: Kara Parsons

Marketing Assistant: Ting Jian Yap

Marketing Communications Manager: Martha Pfeiffer

Project Manager, Editorial Production: Cheri Palmer

Creative Director: Rob Hugel

Art Director: Maria Epes

Print Buyer: Linda Hsu

Permissions Editors: Tim Sisler and Mandy Groszko

Production Service/Composition: Macmillan Publishing Solutions

Text Designer: Marsha Cohen

Copy Editor: Jill Pellarin

Illustrator: Macmillan Publishing Solutions

Cover Designer: Lee Friedman

Cover Image: Cover Images from top to bottom, clockwise: © Veer; Stockbyte Photography/Getty/Veer; Photosindia collection/Getty Images; © Veer

Library of Congress Control Number: 2008933931

ISBN-13: 978-1-4283-5293-3

ISBN-10: 1-4283-5293-7

Wadsworth
10 Davis Drive
Belmont, CA 94002-3098
USA

Cengage Learning is a leading provider of customized learning solutions with office locations around the globe, including Singapore, the United Kingdom, Australia, Mexico, Brazil, and Japan. Locate your local office at **international.cengage.com/region.**

Cengage Learning products are represented in Canada by Nelson Education, Ltd.

For your course and learning solutions, visit **academic.cengage.com.**

Purchase any of our products at your local college store or at our preferred online store **www.ichapters.com.**

Printed in the United States of America
1 2 3 4 5 6 7 12 11 10 09 08

BRIEF CONTENTS

CONTENTS

SECTION III
Nutrition in Early Childhood Education | 211

PREFACE

Working with children in today's world can be challenging. There has been a societal shift, and the daily lives of children are not the cultural images of a perfect childhood that have been popularized in the media and on children's websites. *Safety, Nutrition, and Health in Early Education* includes vital information for those who work with children and addresses the challenges they will encounter in today's diverse world. Adequate preparation in the areas of safety, nutrition, and health is imperative because even the best child development knowledge for learning and the teaching of early education to children will not be useful if the children are unhealthy, in unsafe environments, or malnourished.

This text focuses on the safety, nutrition, and health of children in early childhood education settings, including centers, early elementary schools, family child care homes, and in-home care. The audience for this text is students of child development or early childhood education who are or are preparing to be teachers, paraprofessionals, nannies, family home child care providers, or workers in other jobs that directly relate to young children. My experience teaching a variety of students who became preschool teachers, elementary teachers, family home care providers, and nannies has helped me understand that, although they will have many similar experiences, there will also be differences. This text is organized so that both the similarities and the differences are recognized and discussed.

ORGANIZATION

The whole child is addressed with respect to safety, nutrition, health, and special topics. All areas of the environment are examined to create policies that emphasize children's status and minimize any risk to children's well-being. *Safety, Nutrition, and Health in Early Education* combines basic information and theory with practical applications, resources, and caregiving skills needed today for working with children, families, and staff. Because the purpose of this book is to help prepare people for a variety of occupations working with children in early education, I have chosen to use the term "teacher," which will apply to all. Regardless of the specific job, all people who work with young children are their teachers. That term seems relevant because more children will be entering early education sites as states offer "preschool for all" or "universal" preschool. I have chosen the term "early childhood education" because it relates better today with the circumstances surrounding the early education of children. This includes infant and toddler care, preschools, day care, family child care, state preschools, and the early elementary years.

This book is divided into four sections: safety, nutrition, health, and current issues in early childhood education. This text serves courses that may include all of those subjects, but it was meant to stand alone for each of the subjects as needed. Every college and every instructor has a unique way of organizing the

HEALTH

Strategies for maintaining a healthy early childhood education environment are covered in this section of the text. Tools are provided for observation, assessment, and screening of physical and mental health. One focus in this area is how to use technology to observe and record information.

Information on staff health, infection control, and health care will help teachers manage good care in early education with minimum health risks. Methods and strategies for using education, cultural competence, role modeling, and supervision are highlighted for the student to reinforce understanding of the health needs of children in care.

This section includes new information on head lice/nits, the effects of a child's disposition on his mental health, and the importance of having a medical home for children with disabilities and special needs. Information on secondhand smoke and lead poisoning has been expanded, and this section now includes information on norovirus, cryptosporidium infection, and methicillin-resistant staph aureus, which all can greatly affect the early childhood education environment.

CURRENT ISSUES

This section covers topics of special interest to teachers. These chapters have been included due to demand from students and many reviewers who say that the information found in this area is vitally important to students, especially if they have not previously studied the topics. The chapter on Child Maltreatment includes the latest in statistics and strategies for working with children who have been maltreated. It also includes information on how to work with families that are abusing substances, with an expanded section on foster and kinship families who might take on the family role for children of substance abusers. The newest information on the "Period of Purple Crying" explains shaken baby syndrome and what to do about it. A chapter on children with disabilities or special needs in early education environments reflects the growing number of children that fit the description. It now includes a graphic entitled Cultural Dimensions in Families that provides specific information about cultural differences in dealing with disabilities and special needs. This chapter was included in the last edition because of requests from reviewers and students stating that it is information that they need and appreciate. The chapter on linkages that a teacher needs to be successful in the areas of safety, nutrition, and health is included to give teachers the tools they need to be successful. These linkages and strategies include communication skills, cultural competence, accessing resources, using advocacy for improved early childhood education, creating a caring community for families to maximize the environment for children, and supporting families. This chapter now has information on the Internet and how it can be used as a resource tool. Two new Reality Checks, based on expressed needs, focus on creating linkages for children's challenging behaviors and the positive effects of relationship-based care that is critical to infant and toddler programs. Information on creating caring communities for families has been expanded as the importance of including families has been recognized. As in previous sections, reinforcement is provided through discussion of methods and strategies in education, cultural competence, and supervision.

SPECIAL FEATURES

Reality Checks address current issues that have an impact on the well-being of children. They bring an *in-depth* approach to some of the more critical areas that are affecting children and early childhood education environments today. Reality Checks include information that is often absent in the popular cultural images found in many textbooks and the media regarding children's development. At the end of each Reality Check, a Checkpoint question encourages critical thinking about the information that has been covered. Following are some of the issues discussed in **Reality Checks:**

- Effects of war and terrorism on children
- Toy safety in a changing world (NEW)
- Kids and guns
- Bullying
- Neighborhood violence
- Dealing with natural disasters in early childhood education environments
- Dealing with human-caused disasters in early education environments
- Sudden infant death syndrome
- Secondhand smoke
- Effects of lead poisoning
- Effects of poverty on children
- How Americans are eating: Do we fulfill our nutritional needs?
- Effects of electronic media on diet and exercise (NEW)
- Peanut allergy effects of advertising on children's food choices
- Children of the fast-food generation
- How elementary school nutrition really rates (NEW)
- Helping vulnerable children to become resilient
- Lice in early childhood education environments
- Special care for mildly ill children
- Shaken baby syndrome
- Domestic violence and its effects on children's lives
- Children and attention deficit/hyperactivity disorder
- Autism (Expanded)
- Linkages for challenging behaviors
- Relationship-based care

More Reality Checks

More Reality Checks can be found at www.cengage.com/education/robertson and include:

- Child custody and its impact on early childhood education environments
- Otitis media in early childhood education environments
- Fetal alcohol syndrome

Vignettes are located throughout each chapter so that the student can "observe" stories based on real-life events. These have been expanded and at least two vignettes are found in every chapter.

Pause for Reflection allows the student time to reflect on how the information might pertain to his or her own life.

Case Studies are placed at the end of each chapter to allow an opportunity for critical thinking on one or more of the subjects covered therein. These have been expanded to reflect early elementary education environments.

PEDAGOGY

The chapters are organized for ease of use, beginning with an outline of expected outcomes. This outline format is used so the student can easily assimilate the information. In the beginning of each chapter, research findings are cited that support the need to learn the information provided in that chapter. Each section of a chapter ends with **Key Concepts,** which summarizes the important points of that portion of the chapter.

Case Studies, Pause for Reflection, Checkpoints, and Vignettes reflect practical applications and help the teacher apply the information. Reality Checks enhance the chapter information with an in-depth look at subjects that are affecting children today.

Important terms are highlighted in color in the text and defined on the page where they first appear. There is also a comprehensive glossary found on the website www.cengage.com/education/robertson.

Chapters 2 through 15 include **Implications for Teachers.** These sections reinforce the information given and reflect the responsibilities of the teacher to perform the practices, strategies, and methods discussed in each chapter. The information on cultural competency and families has been expanded in most chapters to reflect the information teachers have requested. Chapter 16 is devoted to issues that directly relate to the teacher's ability to provide the best environment possible for all children in care. In this edition, information related to curriculum development is dispersed throughout the text. At the end of Chapter 1, a brief discussion on Building Curriculum provides an introduction to how this can be achieved. The complete information for ***Building Curriculum,*** including an overview of how to build curriculum, with lesson plans and topic map curriculum on safety, nutrition, health, and current issues, is placed on the website www.cengage.com/education/robertson. There are specific examples of how curriculum for a topic might be built. This curriculum is an important feature of the website because, although teachers can find curriculums for other subjects, these rarely pertain to issues concerning safety, nutrition, and health. Also included under ***Building Curriculum*** on the website is an expanded list of appropriate children's books for that topic, offering the student or teacher some excellent resources.

The final section of each chapter is entitled **To Go Beyond.** This section gives the instructor ideas for classroom discussion, individual and group projects, assignments, and case studies. Also in this section are questions for chapter review. Chapter references are now located on the website www.cengage.com/education/robertson.

Tables, graphs, checklists, figures, and photographs throughout each chapter present information in an organized manner, reinforcing important concepts. For example:

TABLE 7-7
Educational Methods for Nutrition and Nutritional Risk

• Telling	Explaining and providing information
• Showing	Role modeling good nutritional habits
• Providing resources	Offering handouts and website addresses for parents
• Questions	Ask children questions to assess their understanding
• Practicing	Engaging in physical activity, making healthy food selections

Source: Adapted from Story, M., Holt, K., Sofka, D., & Clark, E. (Eds.). (2002). *Bright Futures in practice: Nutrition-pocket guide*. Arlington, Va.: National Center for Education in Maternal and Child Health.

LEARNING AIDS FOR THE STUDENT

Book Companion Website

The book-specific website at www.cengage.com/education/robertson offers students a large variety of study tools and useful resources such as chapter references, Internet exercises, reflection activities, web quizzes for each chapter, frequently asked questions, glossary and flashcards, case studies, and links to related websites for each chapter as well as general links the teacher might use while on the job. There is also a section for building curriculum, which includes lesson plans, topic maps, and lists of children's books to go with the different subjects that are covered in the text. In the section for tables and forms, there are many tables from the text as well as forms that are very helpful to the teacher and which can be printed out to use in an early childhood education environment.

Professional Enhancement Booklet

This booklet for Safety, Nutrition, and Health, part of the Early Childhood Education Professional Enhancement series, focuses on key topics of interest to future early childhood directors, teachers, and caregivers. Students will keep this informational supplement and use it for years to come in their early childhood practices.

TEACHING AIDS FOR THE INSTRUCTOR

Book Companion Website

The instructor area of the book companion website at www.cengage.com/education/robertson offers access to password-protected resources such as the Instructor's Manual, PowerPoint slides, and more.

Instructor's Manual with Test Bank

The Instructor's Manual contains resources designed to streamline and maximize the effectiveness of your course preparation. The contents include objectives, grading suggestions, an outline guide, a test bank, applications, enhancement activities, case studies, a video and film list, and other resources for each chapter. The enhancement activities offer ideas for meaningful projects that include many community links. The case studies will provide opportunities for critical thinking and practical application of the information provided in the text. ISBN 14128352953

PowerLecture CD-ROM

This one-stop digital library and presentation tool includes preassembled Microsoft® PowerPoint® lecture slides by Cathie Robertson. In addition to a full Instructor' Manual and Test Bank, PowerLecture also includes ExamView® testing software with all the test items from the printed Test Bank in electronic format, enabling you to create customized tests in print or online. ISBN 1428352761

WebTutor Toolbox

WebTutor™ Toolbox for WebCT™ or Blackboard® provides access to all the content of this text's rich Book Companion Website from within your course management system. Robust communication tools—such as course calendar, asynchronous discussion, real-time chat, a whiteboard, and an integrated e-mail system—make it easy for your students to stay connected to the course.

ACKNOWLEDGMENTS

I wish to extend my gratitude to a number of people who continue to make this text a valuable tool for child development professionals. I really appreciate the effort of Philip Mandl, my Delmar/Cengage development editor through the first draft. After the first draft, Wadsworth/Cengage became the publisher, and my present development editor, Robert Jucha, finished the task and helped to make this edition as it was envisioned. Christopher Shortt, my acquisitions editor for Cengage Learning, has been very supportive throughout this edition, including during the transition process and I appreciate that. I would like to thank Jill Traut, project editor for Macmillan Publishing Solutions, and Jill Pellarin, who provided the actual copy editing, for making sense of everything. Cheri Palmer and Janice Bockelman were the necessary liaisons for all components of the text and helped things run smoothly. And finally, I thank Caitlin Cox and Ashley Cronin, who provided the expertise needed to put together the ancillary materials and the website.

I want to extend my heartfelt thanks to the following reviewers for sharing their expertise with me. Their constructive suggestions and recommendations were very helpful in shaping the final product. I especially appreciate Nancy Beaver's extra help in reviewing and discussing information that should be included for early elementary education. I consider her critiques and suggestions throughout this edition and the previous one as an important component of the changes that were made.

Nancy H. Beaver, M.Ed.
Eastfield College of the Dallas County Community College District
Dallas, TX

Teresa Frazier, Ph.D.
Thomas Nelson Community College
Hampton, VA

Jennifer M. Johnson, M.Ed.
Vance-Granville Community College
Henderson, NC

Ithel Jones, Ed.D.
Florida State University
Tallahassee, FL

Laura Manson, M.A.
Santa Monica College
Santa Monica, CA

Elizabeth Tarvin, M.S.
Orange County Community College
Middletown, NY

I would also like to acknowledge the faculty and staff at Grossmont College for the excellent job they do in our center. Amy Obegi, Maura Mehring and Kathryn Ingrum, in particular, have been advocates for family-centered, culturally competent and relationship based care. I have seen the positive effects of these practices on the children and families present and have included many of these practices in this text.

DEDICATION

I would like to dedicate this book to my husband, Dan, and my daughter Madilyn. Dan's loving and constant support has allowed me the time, energy, and effort to complete this ongoing project. Madilyn's recent entrance into the elementary school environment has helped me realize that this information is equally valuable to teachers of her age group. I also appreciate her ability to constantly learn more about the world around her, including those issues involving safety, nutrition, and health. My observation of what she has learned reinforces for me the need for the education and training this text promotes.

I would like to thank my grandchildren Zarli, Tatiana, Jacob, Jessica, Daniel, Frankie, Hannah, and Emily—who are all works in progress and who have continued to help me remember the importance of childhood and how good care and early education can affect its outcome. Having young children in my life was an important part of the decision to write this text in the beginning and to continue in my quest to see that all children have what I expect for the children in my life. This expectation includes a good start through quality early childhood education that emphasizes caring about the safety, nutritional, and health needs of children. I would also like to thank my older children, Matt, Annie, and Tara, whose lives have enriched mine in many ways. I fully appreciate the fact that Annie, as a preschool teacher and child care supervisor, has used this text to aid her in her own work.

THE AUTHOR

Cathie Robertson received her B.S. and M.S. degrees from San Diego State University. She is a professor of Child Development and Family Studies at Grossmont College near San Diego, California. She has taught child development, family studies, and food and nutrition courses, specializing in childhood nutrition, for a number of years and is now semi-retired and teaches online. She is the former president of the International Nanny Association and presently serves on several committees for issues that involve early childhood education. Ms. Robertson has made numerous national, state, and local professional presentations.

Ms. Robertson has been the recipient of a number of grants, including one for a curriculum and resource guide for working with prenatally substance-exposed children and their families and another to create an intergenerational program where senior volunteers were trained to work with preschool children. She volunteers regularly in several early elementary classes to keep current. Ms. Robertson is married, the mother of three adult children plus one elementary school-age child, and grandmother to eight.

SECTION I
Introduction

This section discusses the holistic approach to safety, nutrition, and health in quality early childhood education environments.

1. A Holistic Environmental Approach to Safety, Nutrition, and Health in Quality Early Childhood Education Environments

Wadsworth/Cengage Learning

CHAPTER 1

A Holistic Environmental Approach to Safety, Nutrition, and Health in Quality Early Childhood Education Environments

After reading this chapter, you should be able to:

1.1 Holistic Approach

Define a holistic approach to the safety, nutrition, and health of children.

1.2 The Environment

Describe an ecological perspective and explain how the environment may affect the safety, nutrition, and health of a young child.

1.3 Health Promotion, Protection, and Disease Prevention

Describe and discuss the differences between health promotion, protection, and disease prevention as they apply to early childhood education.

1.4 Risk and Risk Management of Children's Well-Being

Define risk and discuss how risk management is crucial to the safety, nutrition, and health of children in early childhood education.

1.5 Providing High-Quality Early Childhood Environments for Safety, Nutrition, and Health

Discuss how a teacher can provide high-quality early childhood education for safety, nutrition, and health.

1.6 Building Curriculum for Quality Early Childhood Education in Safety, Nutrition, and Health

Design and construct quality curriculum for early childhood education in the areas of safety, nutrition, and health.

1.1 HOLISTIC APPROACH

It can no longer be assumed that all of the safety, nutritional, and health needs of children are met at home by parents. The U.S. Department of Labor estimates that more than 13 million children younger than age 6 have mothers in the workforce, and it is expected that these numbers will continue to increase. It is estimated that between 50 and 76 percent of children younger than 5 years are in some form of early childhood education, dependent on age and income level (U.S. Department of Health and Human Services [USDHHS], 2006). More than 50 percent of infants are in some form of early childhood education environment on a regular basis (Lucarelli, 2002; Goldstein, Hamm, & Schumacher, 2007). By age 6, a minimum of 82 percent of children in the United States have received supplemental early childhood education (Mulligan, Brimhall, & West, 2005), and approximately 6.5 million children over age 5 participate in afterschool care (Little, 2007). Public and private center-based early childhood education programs, family child care homes, afterschool programs, and nanny care are providing nonparental care for the majority of children while their mothers are working. A new trend is growing where there is round-the-clock child care available for parents who work the second and third shifts (Negley, 2007). These nonparental **teachers** must help parents meet the health, safety, and nutritional needs of the children in their care. Throughout this text, general reference will be made to "parents." The author recognizes that families have many different compositions, such as dual working parents, single parents, grandparents raising grandchildren, same-sex couples, immigrant families, and foster families. The term "parents" will be used to refer to the primary caregivers who have the responsibility of raising the children. The term "teacher" will be used to describe all those who work in early childhood education, whether they are teachers at the infant, toddler, preschool, or elementary school level; family child care providers; or nannies.

- **teachers** *persons who provide care for children; instructors, family child care providers, nannies.*

Teachers, family child care providers, nannies, and other nonparental caregivers spend their days working with children to provide intellectual stimulation, social and emotional support, and physical care. Good physical care is of primary importance to support the health, safety, and nutritional well-being of children. Children who are unhealthy or whose physical well-being is **at risk** may have difficulty performing cognitive tasks and relating to others in terms of social and emotional development. Cognitive, social, and emotional deficits as well as physical difficulties may result in poor health. Health should be defined in terms of a person's physical, mental, social, and emotional well-being. These areas are interrelated, and a **holistic** approach considers the development of all these areas necessary for health and well-being.

- **at risk** *exposed to chance of injury, damage, or hazard.*
- **holistic** *concerned with the whole being.*

Good health is the result of reducing unnecessary risk, preventing illnesses, providing sensitive and stimulating care, and promoting the well-being of an individual child. Teachers must create an atmosphere that provides this protective type of environment for children. To accomplish this task, teachers should focus on three basic areas: safety, nutrition, and health. Lack of good health practices, an unsafe environment, or providing poor nutrition may all contribute to failure in protecting children. The interrelationship of the areas of health, safety, and nutrition will be easier to understand if a holistic approach is used.

- **environment** *all of the conditions, circumstances, and influences that surround and affect the development of an individual.*

The **environment** of children's safety, nutrition, and health in early childhood education is the focus of this text. It is important to remember that early childhood education programs mirror the diversity in society. So, when we look at this ecological interrelationship of health, safety, and nutrition, we must also consider culture, families, and the teachers themselves. A lead-in paragraph at the beginning of each chapter poses an issue concerning risks to children in early childhood education programs, family child care, and nonparental at-home care; next, current research findings are presented. Each chapter provides teachers with the information and strategies needed to deal with these issues.

The following research findings support the need for dealing with safety, nutrition, and health in a holistic manner:

- "The whole child has been fragmented"; early childhood educators must have the knowledge, training, and skills to support the development of the whole child (Hyson, 2001). To be effective in dealing with the whole child, we must work with families (Christian, 2006).
- Good quality early childhood education where families are involved can help reduce the magnitude of the effects of problems children may encounter such as poverty, violence, and the ability to achieve their whole potential (American Academy of Pediatrics [AAP], 2005; Bronfenbrenner, 2005; LoCasale-Crouch et al., 2007).
- Good-quality early childhood education should meet the standards that protect the basic health and safety of all children (AAP, 2005). Health and safety quality improvement is needed for early childhood education programs (Healthy Child Care Pennsylvania, 2007). Elementary schools should promote a healthy and safe environment by adopting policies that do so (Jones et al., 2007).
- "The reality is that only 10 to 15 percent of day care is of high quality . . ." (Greenspan, 2003). Only 8 percent of infant/toddler classrooms were found to be what is considered good quality (Kreader, Ferguson, & Lawrence, 2005). Low-income parents who thought their children's care was of good quality were proven wrong in half the cases that were studied (Morris, 2005).
- Children in this country are experiencing a greater number of at-risk difficulties than previously reported. These include psychological problems, emotional disorders, and chronic physical conditions (USDHHS, 2006). High-quality early childhood education is likely to have a more positive outcome for these children (Hungerford & Cox, 2006; Bradley & Vandell, 2007).
- A holistic approach is required to address the needs of children who are at risk for severe health problems and school failure (Wilson, 2006).
- Issues of nutrition and feeding children can affect a child's well-being in both the short term and the long term. We can help to facilitate good nutritional habits (Briley & Roberts-Gray, 2005).
- Excellence of early childhood education is directly related to compliance with a high standard of care (Bassok et al., 2005). Early childhood teachers with more professional training provide more nurturing and responsive care (National Association for the Education of Young Children [NAEYC], 2006; Smith, 2007). An increasing number of policymakers are requiring public preschool teachers to have at least a bachelor's degree in early childhood education (Early et al., 2007).
- Early childhood education programs can be seen as second homes, and teachers face the task of creating safe environments in these

Research findings support the need for dealing with safety, nutrition, and health in a holistic manner.

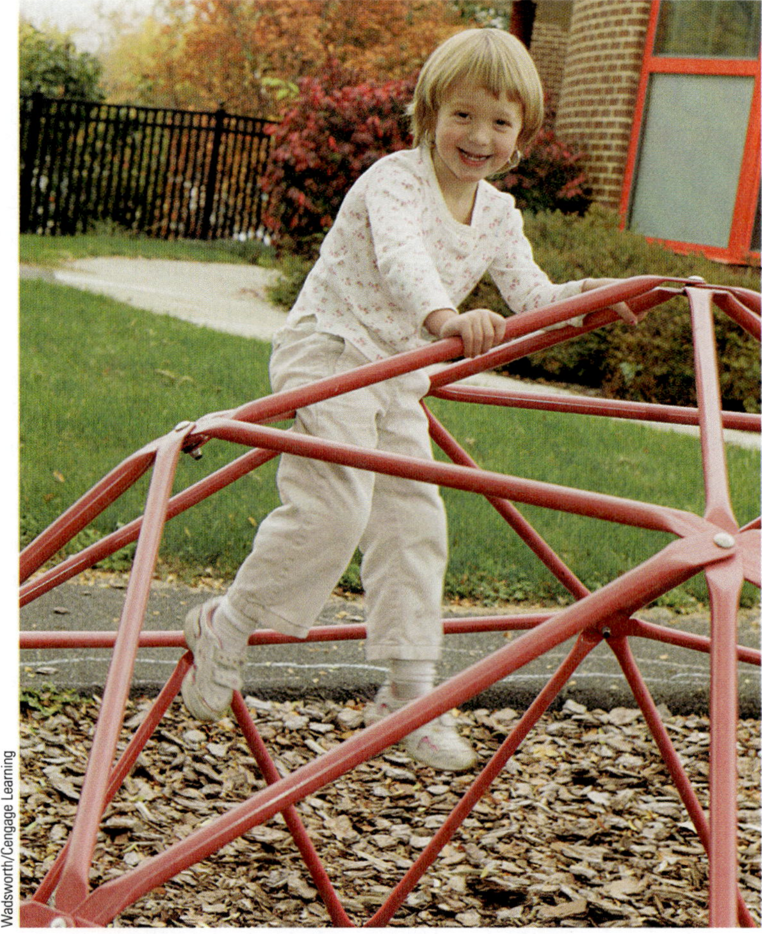

Wadsworth/Cengage Learning

challenging times (Gaines & Leary, 2004). Today, teachers need the knowledge to promote children's health and nutrition, establish and sustain mutual relationships with families, and use community resources to help children and families (Freeman & Feeney, 2006).

- We must understand that we are partners with the families of the children in our care. Early education programs are steadily becoming family-centered organizations (Hamilton, Roach, & Riley, 2003). There should be written policies for family involvement (Halacka Ball, 2006).

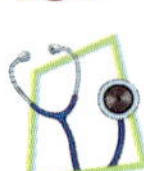

Key Concept 1.1

Holistic Approach

A holistic approach is the sensible way to deal with the interrelationship of safety, nutrition, and health in the well-being of young children. Those who provide nonparental early childhood education should consider the environment of every child in care. Growth, health, development, and safety are a result of each child's environment.

1.2 THE ENVIRONMENT

- **ecological** *pertaining to the relationship of the individual to the environment.*

Environment includes all of the conditions, circumstances, and influences that surround a person. All of the complex factors in the environment can be simplified by using an **ecological** point of view (Figure 1-1). The ecological perspective examines the physical, social and emotional, economic, and cultural environments that affect a child. It relates all of the factors that might influence children's lives in terms of growth, health, safety, development, and well-being. Early childhood education is an essential part of the environment for those children who receive nonparental care. Those who are teachers should be aware of all of the environmental factors. The ecological point of view allows teachers to work with the child, the family, and the community to help provide the best environment possible. Children are best supported and understood when all of these contexts are looked at in the holistic perspective. Bronfenbrenner (1979, 2005) uses the term "bioecological model" to describe how to study the development of the whole child. This is similar to the Holistic Ecological Approach shown in Figure 1-1.

The Physical Environment

For a child, the physical environment begins in the mother's womb. A child born to a mother who had regular prenatal checkups and proper nutrition

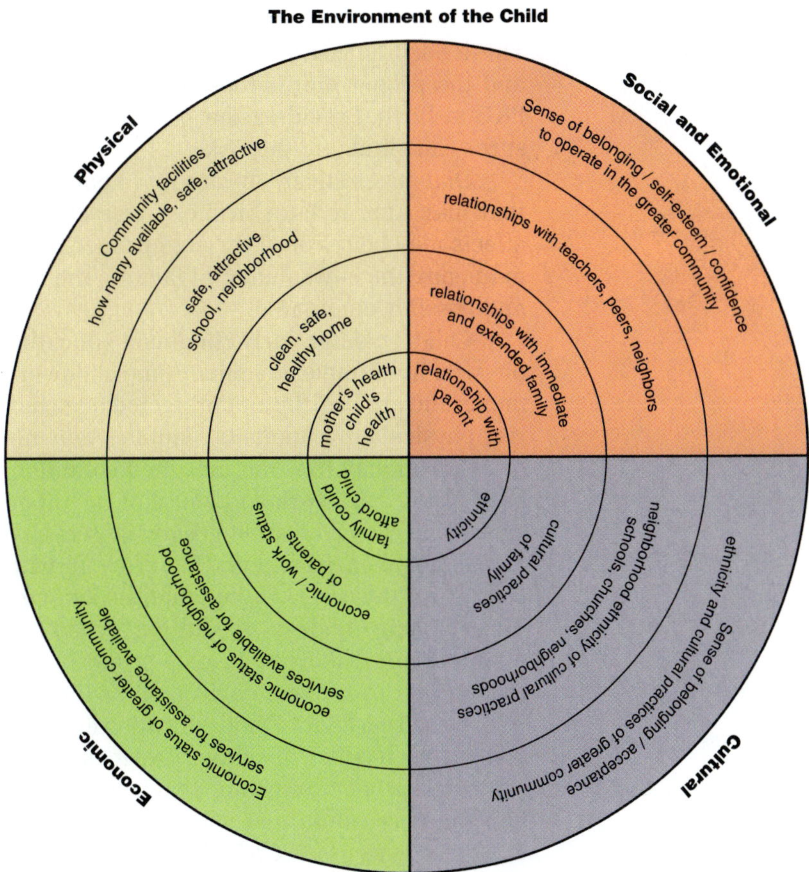

FIGURE 1-1
Holistic ecological approach.

during pregnancy is less likely to have physical complications at birth and more likely to experience good health later in life than a child born to a mother who had no prenatal care (USDHHS, 2006). A child whose mother had no prenatal care is more likely to be born at a low birth weight and is far more likely to have physical problems at birth and health difficulties later in life.

- **genetics** *the study of the origin of features of an individual.*

Beyond **genetics** and the health of the mother, the physical environment encompasses a number of things. The child's temperament, physical health, and attributes are genetic in nature but can be affected by environment. Environmental factors include the family, home, school, neighborhood, and greater community. Children who are raised in poor circumstances are more vulnerable to inadequate nutrition, family violence, and exposure to environmental toxins *and are likely to have diminished physical health* (Zenah et al., 2005). Children who live in neighborhoods where they are protected from harm and are carefully watched are less likely to become injured or victims of violence than children who live in unsafe neighborhoods (Wilson, 2006). This is significant because in recent years violence, poverty, physical illness, and family stress have increased in the United States.

- **heredity** *the transmission from parent to child of certain characteristics.*
- **metabolize** *change occurring by chemical and physical processes in living cells.*

Another factor in the physical environment is **heredity**. Heredity plays a key role in the health and nutrition of children. In addition to body type and temperament, the propensity for certain diseases may be inherited. The disease may show up at birth or appear later in life.

An example of a disease that shows up at birth is phenylketonuria (PKU). It causes an inability in the child to **metabolize** one type of protein. Left untreated, this condition can cause brain damage and mental retardation. These harmful effects can be prevented if PKU is diagnosed in early infancy and the proper diet is followed. Hospitals in many states routinely test for PKU at birth. Providing the proper environment through correct diet measures can eliminate the risk.

Diabetes, cancer, obesity, and heart disease are inherited family factors that may appear later in life. These conditions may be prevented or their effects may be reduced through proper diet and exercise throughout life. By managing the environmental factors, the associated risks can be diminished and possibly eliminated.

Children enter early childhood education programs from many different physical home environments. Some children have had good physical environments and are healthy and protected from harm. Other children come from at-risk physical environments. Families may not provide good health practices, or children may have an inherited condition or disease. Some children may be at risk for safety due to abuse or neighborhood violence. Access to quality early childhood education greatly increases the likelihood that children from at-risk home environments will grow up without behavior problems and will contribute to society rather than becoming violent teens or adults (Zero to Three, 2005). Children who attend a good early childhood education environment are more likely to develop properly even if they are considered to be at risk in their own home environments (Foster et al., 2005).

A good early childhood education environment using the holistic approach screens for health difficulties, provides good health and safety practices, and promotes proper nutrition. Teachers integrate health, safety, and nutrition into the curriculum and value them as highly as social skills, language, or any other aspects of curriculum. This means that teachers include all of these areas in the program every day.

Andrea was 10 months old when she was diagnosed with diabetes. Her family struggled to control the disease through diet and insulin. Even though several members of the extended family had the disease, none had been as young as Andrea at its onset. At age 2½, her disease was finally managed with insulin in the morning and careful diet control. When Andrea was 3, her mother went back to work part-time, and she put Andrea in a family child care home. Andrea's teacher worked closely with her mother to make sure Andrea's diet was carefully monitored. Today, Andrea is a healthy 17-year-old high school senior. The cooperation of her early childhood education teacher contributed to maintaining a positive environment for Andrea so that she could be healthy and grow.

Early childhood teachers should be professionals who possess this specialized knowledge in health and nutrition and can promote healthy habits (Freeman & Feeney, 2006). By providing this instruction to children in care, a high-quality early childhood education environment can provide the foundation for good health and well-being in adulthood. Early childhood education may offer many children a better chance for an improved physical environment for at least part of the day.

The Social and Emotional Environment

The social and emotional environment of a child begins with the parent–child relationship. As the child grows, this environment expands to include the family, neighbors, teachers, peers, and other members of the community. Children's mental health and sense of well-being are very important factors in overall health. A family that provides a stable environment and creates the opportunity for a secure **attachment** for a child is more likely to raise a happy, cheerful child. A family that exposes a child to a high-risk situation, such as homelessness or child neglect, and fails to form a secure attachment is more likely to produce a child who is at risk for many social and emotional problems (Goldstein, Hamm, & Schumacher, 2007). Children raised in healthy, functional families are more likely to retain good mental health and be well adjusted than those raised in dysfunctional, violent households (Bowlby, 1988; Osofsky, 1999). Children may also be impacted by the absence of a parent due to deployment, separation, divorce, or prison.

- **attachment** *the bond that develops between a child and another person as a result of a long-term relationship.*

The consistency of caregiving and emotional investment on the part of a teacher has a direct relationship to the healthy development of children (AAP, 2005; Zenah et al., 2005; Christian, 2006). Quality care contributes to children's sense of well-being. A good early childhood education environment is one in which there are good one-on-one relationships between teachers and children in care. Larger early childhood education situations up to kindergarten may have to provide a **primary caregiver** for each child to accomplish this optimal type of relationship (USDHHS, 2003). The teacher who relates to the children in care is more likely to be alert and observant. A teacher who has noticed any social or emotional effects of nonparental care can help the child adjust (Shonkoff & Meisels, 2000; Zenah et al., 2005). The teacher can also work with families to offer them strategies for providing a

- **primary caregiver** *the person who takes care of a child most of the time and with whom, hopefully, he or she will form a positive attachment bond.*

Mary Elizabeth is a 4-year-old girl with a healthy appetite, a hearty laugh, and the ability to move from activity to activity with little need for transition. When she was born to a cocaine-addicted mother, the doctors were not sure of her prognosis for growth or behavior. She was briefly removed from her mother's custody and then returned when her mother went into a parent-supportive recovery program. Her mother, Ellen, received help for her addiction as well as help in learning how to parent, including the importance of early bonding in the mother–child relationship. Ellen studied to be a computer operator at a local community college and has been working for the past two years. Mary Elizabeth has been in the same early childhood education program since she was 11 months old.

The staff at the early childhood education program was supportive of Ellen and understood that Mary Elizabeth might need some special help as a result of prenatal substance exposure. When Mary Elizabeth exhibited a high degree of frustration in certain types of play, the staff was able to provide emotional assurance and reduce the stimulation around her while redirecting her behavior. Mary Elizabeth is a good example of what early intervention and a good environment can do for the healthy development of a child at risk. Studies that have followed substance-exposed children from birth have concluded that, in many cases, a secure and supportive environment can overcome most of any possible side effects of prenatal exposure to drugs (Robertson, 1993).

home environment that makes a child feel more secure and mentally healthy (Christian, 2006).

The quality of peer relationships may be a good indicator of a child's mental and emotional health status. A child's ability to cope with new situations, her sense of self-esteem, and her level of confidence affect how she deals with her peers. The observant teacher will notice these things. A child's sense of self affects how he grows and develops into a member of the greater community as an adult. It is widely recognized that early intervention by a teacher provides a more secure environment for children who are at risk for adjustment difficulties (American Public Health Association [APHA] & AAP, 2002; Robinson, McIntyre, & Officer, 2005).

The Economic Environment

- **economic** *pertaining to the material needs of people.*

A child's **economic** environment is established in the home and is influenced by the parents' work history and the economic health of the neighborhood, the community, and the nation. Low income is the primary factor for the majority of childhood health and nutritional risks in this country (Reid, 2006). Census data in 2006 showed that 78 percent of poor children had at least one parent who worked. (*America's Children,* 2007). Approximately 13 million children live in poverty today (Reid, 2006). Many children who are economically at risk are in child care situations.

Forty percent of the homeless are families. Children in homeless families are at high risk for mental health difficulties (National Mental Health Association, 2005). More children who are economically at risk are now in early childhood education situations than ever before, due to the welfare policy shift that encourages mothers to work outside the home (Loeb et al., 2004; Foster et al., 2005). One in every six young children in the United States lives below the poverty level, and the number of children living in poverty has increased 9 percent since 2000 (Reid, 2006). More than three out of four poor children live in a home where at least one family member is employed. This implies that many families with a working parent may still be in economic situations where the basics of life are difficult to come by. The impact of financial stress on the home environment can affect children's emotions and behavior (Zenah et al., 2005; USDHHS, 2006). Financial limitations, including lack of good medical care, poor nutrition, and an environment in which parental attention is limited, can affect children's well-being. Another effect of low income may be the inability to afford quality early childhood education. Poor children are more at risk for serious illness and death. Some childhood health problems related to poverty are:

- Low birth weight
- Accidental death
- Lead poisoning
- Asthma
- Lack of immunizations; death due to childhood diseases
- Iron deficiency anemia
- Socio-emotional difficulties

Economic factors that include lack of preventive care and lack of access to care seriously impair the potential of many children in this country for maximum growth, healthy development, and protection from harm.

The person who provides early childhood education needs to be aware of the impact that the economic environment of families has on the health, safety, and well-being of children. Teachers may be able to improve the effect of the economic environment on children by providing good nutrition and preventive health and safety measures. Teachers can also help families access resources, and they can create community linkages and advocate for children. These efforts and collaborations may provide families with critical information on health, safety, and nutritional issues. Teachers who collaborate with the greater community on these issues can improve their community environment.

How can an at-risk environment where parental attention is limited negatively affect a child's well-being?

Wadsworth/Cengage Learning

The Cultural Environment

• **cultural**
related to traits and ascribed membership in a given group.

The child's **cultural** environment includes the framework of beliefs, perspectives, and practices of the family, the neighborhood, and the greater community. It has been estimated that by the year 2050, for children under the age of 5 years, Hispanics and blacks will outnumber non-Hispanic whites. Today, one in four poor children have at least one foreign-born parent (Collins & Ribeiro, 2006). The United States has become a multiethnic society. With so many cultural traditions, practices, and values present, there may be value conflicts among different cultures. There may be bicultural conflict within families that represent several generations of values. One outcome of these conflicts may be the reinforcement of cultural values within families. This may be due to the changing culture of some of today's families. Biracial/bicultural families are increasing in number. These parents may need support to resolve their differing cultural views on child rearing, including safety, nutrition, and health issues. A number of military families that are bicultural/biracial have an additional factor to deal with—the absence of one parent. This may bring another level of conflict.

Practices for maintaining traditional cultural values in daily life, such as food choices and child care practices, are seen as meaningful declarations of family heritage. For example, the cultural perspective of a family may have an impact on the type of early education that is chosen for a child (Johnson et al., 2004; Collins & Ribeiro, 2006; Obeng, 2007). It is important that the professional early childhood education teacher support the family cultural values of the children in care (California Association for the Education of Young Children [CAEYC], 2005; Bradley & Kibera, 2006). In instances where these cultural values put children at risk, cultural differences and legal practices will have to be addressed.

Characteristics of family health attitudes may relate directly to culture. For example, some Latin American families may appear to have lower expectations for their children's health and therefore may be less likely to use preventive services (Carballo & Nerukar, 2001). This may be due in part to health practices and lack of access in their native countries. This does not mean that these families do not value the health of their children and want them cared for. They just may not understand the system or have easy access to preventative health care. The combined impact of social problems due to culture and economic hardship may cause harm to children. Children from these environments are more likely to experience social, emotional, and behavioral problems and to suffer from poor mental health (Duarte & Rafanello, 2001).

It is important for the teacher to be aware of the diversity of the children and families in care (Obegi & Ritblatt, 2005). In 2006, this diversity of children was apparent. Twenty percent of American children were Hispanic, 15 percent were African American, 4 percent were Asian/Pacific Islander, and 1 percent was Native American (*America's Children,* 2007). These numbers are expected to increase in the next three decades, especially in the Hispanic and Asian/Pacific Islander categories. Teachers must go beyond cultural sensitivity or awareness, because these call for responsiveness but go no further. Teachers must practice **cultural competence** in interactions with the children and their parents so that relationships are mutually beneficial, even though all may have diverse cultural heritages and practices (Obegi & Ritblatt, 2005). This will allow teachers to look at the way families from diverse backgrounds differ in their values and beliefs about raising children

• **cultural competence**
demonstration of behaviors, attitudes, and policies that allow for cross-cultural effectiveness and valuing of diversity.

and their attitudes toward seeking help (Bradley & Kibera, 2006). This type of competence will help teachers to better understand ways to communicate information on issues concerning safety, nutrition, and health.

The National Association for the Education of Young Children (NAEYC) makes specific recommendations to address cultural competency in early education. For children, teachers should (1) recognize and ensure the connection children have to the culture of their language and of their home, (2) be aware that children demonstrate their capabilities in many ways, and (3) realize that learning a second language is not easy and that children should be supported in this as well as given support for their home-language usage. For families, teachers should (1) actively involve families in the early education program, (2) provide support and encouragement for the learning of another language while at the same time valuing the home or first language, and (3) try to honor and support the culture of the children, including the values and norms present in the home (CAEYC, 2005).

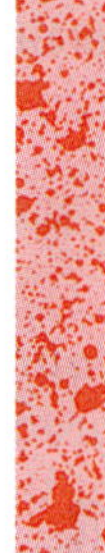

Pause for Reflection

Consider your own childhood environment. What was the physical environment? What was the social and emotional environment? What was the economic environment? What was the cultural environment? What factors of these influences from your childhood led you to want to work with children? What positive factors from your childhood influences will you have to contribute to the children you work with?

Key Concept 1.2

Environment

An ecological perspective allows one to view the environment of a child. A risk factor in the health and well-being of children can come from any area of the environment. The physical, social and emotional, economic, and cultural environments all influence children's growth and development. Negative conditions from any part of a child's environment may place that child at risk. Poor physical and mental health, injury, or an impaired sense of well-being and self-esteem may prevent the maximum growth potential and development of a child. Using an ecological perspective, the teacher can approach the safety, nutrition, and health of children by considering their total environment.

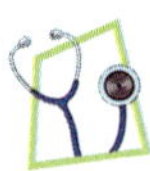

1.3 HEALTH PROMOTION, PROTECTION, AND DISEASE PREVENTION

This text deals with the developmental aspects and issues that can help promote and protect children's well-being. The text also illustrates ways to prevent childhood illness, disease, or accidents. It has been found that

- **health promotion** *the improvement of health conditions by encouraging healthful behavior and habits.*

health promotion in preschools can improve child health (Gupta et al., 2005). Teachers should establish and maintain a healthy environment using health promotion. Teachers promote health by checking for immunization and encouraging the use of proper hand-washing and diapering techniques. They provide adequate nutrition and arrange for hearing, vision, and dental screening tests. Teachers protect children in care by promoting safety practices such as using child safety seats in travel, checking toys and other equipment for hazards, and providing a low-risk environment. In the early elementary years, health promotion includes requiring immunizations, and teaching about and monitoring for injury prevention and nutrition education.

The holistic approach includes other measures to promote the health, safety, and well-being of children outside the early education environment. The idea of a whole child focus includes families and community linkages (UMOS, 2007). Awareness of the necessity to include others in a partnership may help clarify the role of a teacher in providing good health, safety, and nutrition practices in the early childhood education environment. This knowledge may also help the teacher understand the importance of family and community linkages and of advocacy for children. The following sections present several examples of how others are trying to ensure the health and well-being of children.

Healthy People 2010

The report *Healthy People 2010: National Health Promotion and Disease Prevention Objectives* is a product of a national process that has set health objectives for the year 2010. The major purpose of the program is to improve the health and well-being of Americans (Tate & Patrick, 2000). Here are some of its objectives that affect children:

- Consider the environmental risks that cause emotional, physical, psychological, and learning problems.
- Provide culturally appropriate educational and support programs for parents in high-risk environments to help reduce child maltreatment and other health problems.
- Increase the proportion of children whose intake from snacks at school (in the early childhood education environment) contribute proportionally to overall diet quality.

A teacher can help improve the health and well-being of children in care by addressing these issues. Topics in this text provide the teacher with a base of knowledge to consider the issues effectively.

National Health and Safety Performance Standards for Child Care

The American Public Health Association (APHA) and the American Academy of Pediatrics (AAP) collaborated and produced *National Health and Safety Performance Standards: Guidelines for Out-of-Home Child Care Programs* (APHA & AAP, 2002). The Maternal and Child Health Bureau of the Department of Health and Human Services provided funding for this project and its in-process update. These guidelines recognize the need for some consistency and guidance to help teachers provide the optimal environment for child health, safety, and nutrition (USDHHS, 2003).

National Association for the Education of Young Children

The National Association for the Education of Young Children (NAEYC) is another organization concerned with the well-being of children. Although in agreement with many of the standards set by the APHA and AAP, NAEYC encourages teachers to make decisions based on information from several points of view. Teachers must first have the information and an understanding of specific procedures before making any decision regarding the health, safety, and nutritional needs of children in early childhood education environments. Teachers need training to do this (Caulfield & Kataoka-Yahiro, 2001). Another contribution to early education by NAEYC is their Code of Ethical Conduct and Statement of Commitment. This holistic approach includes all areas of responsibility. The principal responsibility of a teacher to a child is to provide a safe, healthy, and nurturing environment with responsive care. The foremost commitment a teacher has to a family is to bring about collaboration between the school and the home to maximize the potential development of the child. To colleagues, the main responsibility is to provide supportive relationships and productive environments. The teacher's primary responsibility to the community (and to society) is to provide programs that meet its needs and to advocate for children (NAEYC, 2005). A full reference to this document may be found by searching for Code of Ethical Conduct at http://www.naeyc.org. This text was written to help teachers acquire training in the areas of health, safety, and nutrition.

Early Childhood Environmental Rating Scales

The Early Childhood Environment Rating Scales (Harms, Clifford, & Cryer, 2005) (Table 1-1), or ECERS as it is commonly known, was originally created in 1980 to measure quality in early childhood environments up to kindergarten. The scales rate how a program meets the three basic needs of children: protecting their health and safety, building positive relationships for them, and giving them opportunities for stimulation and learning through their experiences. These scales measure items in seven categories that reflect a holistic approach to determine the quality of a program. Within these subscales are many items related to health, safety, nutrition, children with special needs, and families (see bulleted list below). In the years since the original development of the ECERS, there have been three additions to these scale-type measurement tools. These include the Family Day Care Rating Scale (FDCRS) in 1989, the Infant/Toddler Environment Rating Scale (ITERS) in 1990, and the School-Age Care Environment Rating Scale (SACERS) (Harms, Jacobs, & Romano, 1995) in 1995. There have been updated revisions in 1998 and 2005 of the original ECERS, now called ECERS-R (Harms, Clifford, & Cryer, 2005); in 2003 a revised ITERS-R (Harms, Cryer, & Clifford, 2003); and in 2007 the renamed, revised FDCRS, now called Family Child Care Environment Rating Scale (FCCERS-R) (Harms, Cryer, & Clifford, 2007). These revisions used data collected from research and frequent users to make improvements that reflected changes in the knowledge about the early childhood field that have occurred in the ensuing years. These rating scales are widely used in the United States and in other countries. Users include the Head Start and Early Head Start programs and the accreditation program of NAEYC. These scales with their use of a holistic approach are important tools for all types of early childhood education environments.

TABLE 1-1
Some ECERS-R Items That Reflect a Holistic Approach

ECERS-R Rating Scales Categories That Apply to Safety, Nutrition, and Health
• Indoor space and its arrangement
• Furniture for routine care
• Space for privacy
• Meals/snacks
• Diapering/toileting
• Health and safety practices
• Promoting acceptance of diversity
• General supervision of children
• Staff-child interaction
• Discipline
• Provisions for children with disabilities
• Provisions for parents
• Provisions for personal needs of staff

Other Efforts

Many federal and state programs, such as Project Head Start, Early Head Start, WIC (Women, Infants, and Children; a supplemental food program sponsored by the U.S. Department of Agriculture [USDA]), Project Healthy Start in Hawaii (El-Kamary et al., 2004), and Team Nutrition from the USDA for all child nutrition programs including elementary schools, are promoting good health and nutrition habits. Groups such as the Consumer Product Safety Commission (CPSC) and the National Program for Playground Safety (NPPS) promote safety measures that improve the safety of children of all ages.

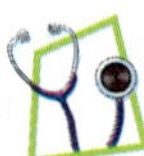

Key Concept 1.3

Health Promotion, Protection, and Disease Prevention

Health promotion, protection, and disease prevention are ineffective if teachers fail to understand the effects of the environment. Clearly, some programs and initiatives try to help parents and teachers promote and protect the health and well-being of children. Teachers play an essential role in the holistic approach to early childhood education environments. They should be able to provide good nutrition and healthy environments that are safe from harm for the children in their care. By modeling this environment, teachers can help children feel secure and help parents recognize the value of quality care and good early childhood education.

Many of the initiatives that fund health promotion, protection, and disease prevention operate at all levels of government. There is a clear indication of the need for all entities involved in caring for young children to work together. There are implications for teachers from these governmental efforts. Teachers should be prepared to perform the preceding tasks. They also must understand how to communicate with families and collaborate with others in the community.

1.4 RISK AND RISK MANAGEMENT OF CHILDREN'S WELL-BEING

Risk is defined as a chance or gamble that is often accompanied by danger. Risk management is a way to minimize the chance that danger may occur. Risk management takes on specific meaning when it is applied to taking care of children. Results of health risks include illness, infection, disease, mental illness, developmental difficulty, disability, and death. Results of safety risks include accidents, disability, and death. Nutritional risk results include developmental delay, growth retardation, poor health, and lack of resistance to infection or disease.

The opposite of risk in relation to health is well-being. Well-being is measured by wellness, degree of activity, resiliency, proper growth, at-level development, and general vitality. Children who are at risk for problems will display one or more of the risk factors previously discussed.

Proper risk management strategies remove risk factors from children's health, safety, and nutrition. For the teacher, the strategies of health promotion, safety protection, and nutritional education are necessary risk management tools. Children's curiosity can involve experiences that help them to learn about their world and it may lead to risk-taking behaviors. If the early childhood education program has precautions in place, children's safety is better protected and their ability to learn is improved (Curtis & Carter, 2005). Modeling good health, safety, and nutrition practices is a positive risk management strategy. So is careful supervision of children. When children are well supervised, their risk for unintentional injury is lessened (Schwebel & Gaines, 2007). Supervision of children at all times is one of five major criteria

Joey, a bright, happy 2-year-old boy, was small for his age and seemed not to have grown in the six months that he had been at the child care center. Occasionally, he was listless. His teacher was concerned and spoke to Joey's mother, who had noticed the same thing. Joey's mother took him to the doctor for a checkup. The doctor inquired about Joey's diet and discovered that the mother was giving Joey large amounts of fruit juice and not enough milk and other foods. The doctor put Joey on a balanced diet. The mother explained that she had had a problem of being overweight when she was a child and did not want to feed him foods that had too much fat in them. The doctor explained that too much fruit juice may hinder growth and promote snacking on sweets in the future and that Joey needed some fat and more milk in his diet. To stay healthy and grow properly, children need a variety of food sources (Bittman, 1994; Briley & Roberts-Gray, 1999).

for NAEYC accreditation (NAEYC, 2006). It has been found that children who spent more time in child care have a reduced risk for unintentional injury (Schwebel, Brezausek, & Belsky, 2006). The key to managing risk in relation to the well-being of children is to set thorough standards and guidelines for early childhood education environments, including training and staffing. When child care is regulated and directors are required to have more education, the occurrence of unintentional injuries is reduced (Currie & Hotz, 2004). Licensing laws for child care are a key means for reducing risk for children (Colbert, 2005).

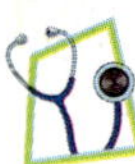

Risk and Risk Management

Risk management is an effective way to protect, promote, and prevent difficulties regarding children's health, safety, and nutrition. A number of strategies, such as modeling good practices and complying with standards and guidelines, are good risk management tools for teachers.

1.5 PROVIDING HIGH-QUALITY EARLY CHILDHOOD EDUCATION ENVIRONMENTS FOR SAFETY, NUTRITION, AND HEALTH

According to Bredekamp and Copple (1997), high-quality early childhood education programs should provide "a safe and nurturing environment that promotes the physical, social, emotional, and cognitive development of young children while responding to the needs of families" (p. 1). In terms of the health, safety, and well-being of children, the teacher must have six basic goals in mind to ensure a high-quality early childhood education program (Figure 1-2):

1. Maximize the health status of the children.
2. Minimize risks to the health, safety, and well-being of the children.
3. Utilize education as a tool for health promotion and risk reduction for both children and adults.
4. Recognize the importance of guidelines, standards, and laws as they apply to the health, safety, and well-being of children.
5. Practice cultural competence.
6. Develop partnerships with families to provide a caring community.

Goal One: Maximizing Children's Health Status

- **health status** *the condition of an individual's health.*

A person's **health status** reflects the condition of health of that person. Teachers have the opportunity to provide optimal conditions to maximize the health and sense of well-being of the children in their care. To accomplish this goal, a set of objectives for health promotion and the prevention of illness and disease should be planned, carried out, and monitored through the creation of health policies (Table 1-2). It has been suggested that collaboration

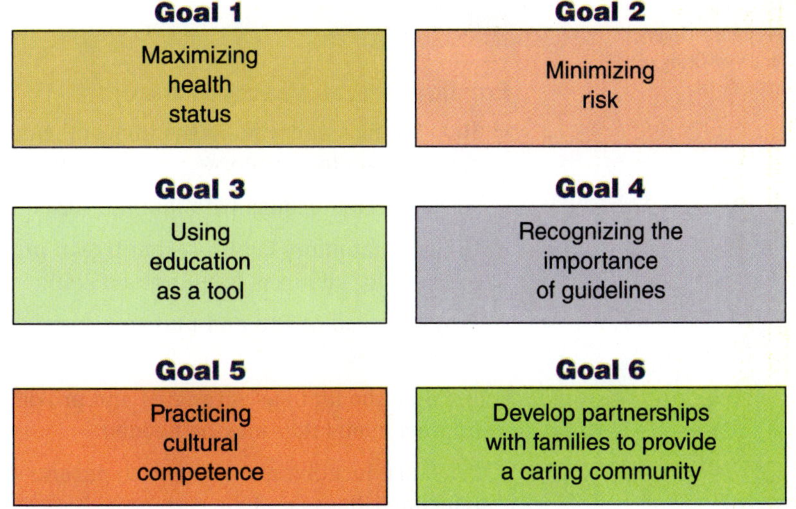

FIGURE 1-2 Six major goals of high-quality early education for children.

between early childhood educators and people from the medical field could further improve the effectiveness of health promotion education (Gupta et al., 2005). Regardless of whether care takes place in an early childhood education program, a family child care home, or the child's own home, many of the objectives are the same. In some instances, the objectives may apply more specifically to the type of setting in which the care is performed.

TABLE 1-2 *Objectives for the Optimal Health and Well-Being of Children*

For children, all teachers should:

- Respect the developmental needs, characteristics, and diversity of each child.
- Support a child's development based on current knowledge of the general health and unique characteristics of the individual child. This includes emotional support as well as attention to physical needs.
- Provide and maintain healthy, safe, and nurturing environments.
- Reduce and prevent the transmission of infectious and communicable diseases.
- Understand the management of ill children, including exclusion policies.
- Use universal health procedures for toileting, diapering, maintaining toys, and handling and storing food.
- Utilize the health status of the staff as an important component of job performance.
- Ensure good nutrition and food safety by following the requirements of the USDA child care component, the Child Care Food Program, and the Code of Federal Regulations.

(continues)

TABLE 1-2 *(Continued)*
Objectives for the Optimal Health and Well-Being of Children

For families, all teachers should:

- Help families understand the importance of developing care routines that contribute to children's sense of well-being.
- Develop relationships with families based on mutual trust.
- Utilize community health and nutrition professionals to create helpful linkages for children, families, and staff.
- Promote good health and nutrition through education for children, families, and staff.
- Build on the families' strengths and provide support for any improvements that may be needed.
- Provide education and support to parents for the management of infectious illness and disease.
- Respect each family in regard to culture, language, customs, and beliefs.

For early childhood education programs, all teachers should:

- Provide a primary caregiver for each child.
- Provide someone to communicate in the children's and parents' first language.
- Provide an atmosphere of mutual respect, trust, and cooperation for everyone involved.

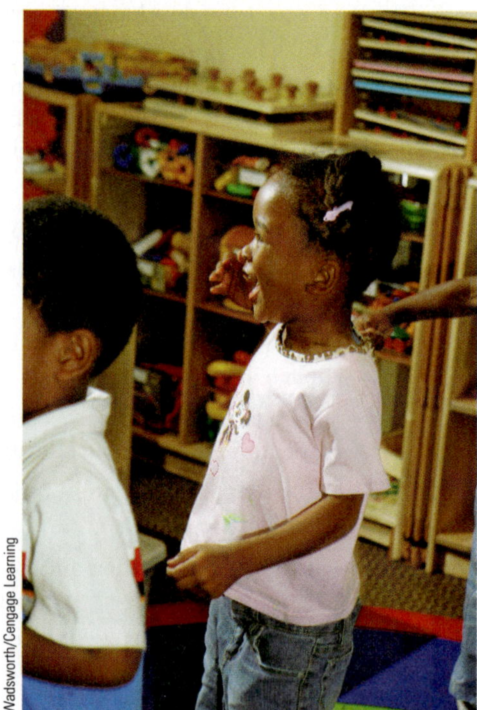
Wadsworth/Cengage Learning

This happy, healthy child shows us that we need to be aware of the importance of optimizing conditions for health, safety, and nutrition in the early education environment.

Goal Two: Minimizing Risks for Childhood Safety, Nutrition, and Health

Proactive planning to reduce risk for children is an essential element in providing quality early childhood education. The vulnerability of children places them at risk for many problems that can be prevented. Historically, infectious diseases have been perceived as the major risk associated with childhood. The threat of many childhood diseases has been lessened or eliminated with the availability of widespread immunizations to eliminate those diseases. However, these immunizations are effective only if they are administered to children. Other risks for spread of disease could decrease through proper sanitation practices.

Today, in reality, the major risks to children are unintentional injury, child maltreatment and neglect, homicide, lead poisoning, and developmental difficulties. Age, cognitive development, motor skills, and the home environment all influence the vulnerability of children at risk for unintentional injuries (Centers for Disease Control and Prevention, 1999; Boles et al., 2005). Many injuries happen in situations where anticipation could have deterred the risk. The danger of child maltreatment and neglect and homicide has become a major issue in the health and well-being of children in America. Children are more at risk for violence when substance abuse, poverty, and family violence are present in the home environment.

This text includes a number of Reality Checks to help the reader understand the significance of current issues that affect the health, safety, or nutrition of children. The first Reality Check indicates an overview of issues that often go unnoticed due to lack of awareness.

REALITY *Check*

Early Childhood Education and Child Care in America: The Reality

Historically, the care, protection, and supervision of children have been performed within families. The shift from family care to nonparental care has taken place mostly in the last half of the last century. Today, at least 82 percent of children who reach kindergarten age have participated in some form of nonparental early childhood education (USDHHS, 2006). Seventy-three percent of infants and toddlers are in nonparental care at least part of the time (Ehrle, Tout, & Adams, 2000). Enrollments in early childhood education programs will continue to rise as more mothers enter the workplace for economic reasons (Loeb et al., 2004; Bassok et al., 2005). One reason for increased workplace entry is the change in the welfare system referred to as the Personal Responsibility and Work Opportunity Reconciliation Act of 1996 (PRWORA), which compels people formerly on welfare to enter the workforce. Considering the number of children in care, early childhood education is no longer an option but a necessity for most families. The majority of families must rely on others to provide for the care, protection, and supervision of their children at least part of the time (Elias, 2007).

Because early childhood education before kindergarten is such an important part of most young

(continues)

REALITY *Check* (continued)

children's lives, one would assume that quality care would be the norm. There are 1.2 million early education teachers in this country who are responsible for the health, safety, and well-being of the children in their environments (Smith, 2007). Of children in nonparental care, approximately 33 percent are in center-based care, 23 percent are in family child care, and 5 percent are at home with a nanny or babysitter. Ninety percent of parents rated the early childhood education programs that their children are in as very good. However, trained observers rating the same programs noted that the great majority of care was poor to mediocre (Cost, Quality, and Outcomes Study Team, 1995). In fact, many studies on the same subject lead us to believe that quality center-based care is not the norm, but is available in only 10 to 15 percent of the licensed early childhood education programs in this country (Greenspan, 2003). In addition, many parents cannot afford good-quality early childhood education and must settle for substandard programs in terms of health and safety (Lucarelli, 2002; Sugiyama & Moore, 2005). Many parents assume people who take care of their children in day-care situations have had background checks and training, but that is often not the case (Riggs, 2007).

In a study of state preschools, it was found that not one state program met any of 10 quality standards (Report on Preschool Programs, 2004). The Cost, Quality, and Outcomes Study also found that the quality at most early childhood education centers does not meet children's needs for health, safety, and secure attachments. A report that reviewed several studies on family child care showed that these early education environments reported good quality in only 10 percent of the cases (Morrisey & Banghart, 2007). Another study on infant care in family child care homes found that only 12 percent of these homes were rated as good quality. This study also found that 13 percent of the infant care in these homes was rated inadequate (Kreader, Ferguson, & Lawrence, 2005). Operating a family child care home without a license and with no training are predictors of low quality. Another study added that in family child care settings where there were more children, both the provider behavior and child function were generally poorer (Kryzer et al., 2007). There are approximately 3 million child caregivers in this country who work in 102,458 licensed early childhood education centers and 290,000 regulated family child care homes (Child Care Aware [CCA], 2001). The remainder work in nonregulated family child care homes and as nannies in families where no supervision is provided for them. In this country, there is no formal system in place to oversee family child care homes (Shallcross, 1999) or nanny care, and no consistent federal regulations for center-based care. Many states have marginal licensing laws for child care and nine states have no licensing laws for child care at all. Regardless of the age or family income of the children in care, consistent state and federal policies for child care would help children receive the quality care they deserve (Capizzano, Adams, & Sonenstein, 2000). Quality does matter for the best outcomes for children (Bradley & Vandell, 2007).

If we were to have the quality of prekindergarten childhood education that children deserve, what would it look like? Many people in the fields of child development, health education, and safety education, and others that support children have their opinions. Here are some of the best of these considerations:

- Teachers would have adequate training in the areas of child development, health, safety, and what provides for the well-being of children (Caulfield and Kataoka-Yahiro, 2001; AAP, 2005; Bassok et al., 2005; Morrisey & Banghart, 2007).
- Teachers who have healthy behaviors and good health status themselves are more likely to provide a quality environment that promotes good health (Baldwin et al., 2007).
- Teachers must provide sensitive, responsive care that allows for secure attachment (Honig, 2002; Bassok et al., 2005; Lally & Mangione, 2007; Goldstein, Hamm, & Schumacher, 2007).

(continues)

REALITY *Check* (continued)

- Teachers who have knowledge of culturally informed teaching can create learning environments that welcome children from diverse cultures (Im, Parlakian, & Sanchez, 2007; Lee & Johnson, 2007).
- Teachers must have skills to engage families in communication and promote parental nurturing for the well-being of the children (DiNatale, 2002; AAP, 2005; Greenberg, 2006; Halacka Ball, 2006).
- Teachers should be competent with diverse cultural and language backgrounds of children (Derman-Sparks, 1999; Obegi & Ritblatt, 2005; Chang, 2006).
- The environment should allow for good health and safety in early childhood education and provide good working conditions for teachers (Greenspan, 2003; Bassok et al., 2005, Wilson, 2006).
- Teachers should be adequately compensated (Cost, Quality, and Outcomes Study Team, 1995; Greenspan, 2003, Goldstein, Hamm, & Schumacher, 2007) so that they will remain on the job and be a stable part of the children's lives.
- There should be an adequate teacher-to-child ratio (Gordon, 2000; Child Care Bureau [CCB], 2000; Shonkoff & Phillips, 2000; CCA, 2001; Greenspan, 2003, Goldstein, Hamm, & Schumacher, 2007).
- For care that includes meals and snacks, caution should be taken to provide adequate nutrition and food safety (Hispanic PR Wire, 2004; Briley & Roberts-Gray, 2005).
- An environment in which toys and equipment are age appropriate and developmentally appropriate should be an integral part of the program (Shonkoff & Phillips, 2000; NICHD, 2003; Curtis & Carter, 2005; Zamani, 2006).

The importance of the need for quality early childhood education environments prior to kindergarten in the United States is overlooked by many people, including legislators and some families who utilize this care and by some of the people who are performing this care. *It is critical to the development of young children who are in care to be in high-quality early childhood education environments. This type of care best can provide a stable, safe, and consistent environment.* This would allow children of all incomes, ethnic and cultural backgrounds, and family circumstances to have equal opportunities for good child development. This has been proven by several recent studies (Bassok et al., 2005, LoCasale-Crouch et al., 2007; Belsky et al., 2007).

There are many ways that high-quality early education and child care can be accomplished (AAP, 2005; NAEYC, 2006; Morrisey & Banghart, 2007). It was best summed up by a teacher, Peggy Haack of Madison, Wisconsin, who said, "The key to quality is the person providing it" (Winik, 1999). It is the responsibility of teachers to be caring, consistent, well educated, and well trained so that they can support the children in their care with the best quality care available. But, beyond that, we must educate parents as to what quality care looks like. The public should be made aware that these changes will require legislative guidelines, standards, and regulations, as well as funding to ensure that quality early childhood education is a reality for all children in care. There are several areas that are testing child care ratings systems, including one in the St. Paul–Minneapolis area (Boldt, 2007). The Department of Human Services will rate day care providers on a point system that includes staff experience and qualifications, family education, adult-child interactions, and how well the children do in care.

CHECK*point:* **Imagine you have a 3-year-old whom you want to place in a quality early education program. How would you go about finding one in your local area? What five things would top your list as to what to look for in a quality program? See Table 1-3 for some questions you might ask.**

TABLE 1-3
Questions for Quality

Questions to Help Determine Whether Early Childhood Education Environment is Good Quality

- Does the environment look safe and sanitary?
- What health practices are used?
- Are developmentally appropriate practices used?
- Does the environment look child-friendly and stimulating?
- What is the quality of relationships between teachers and children?
- What are the teacher's qualifications?
- Are there predictable routines for the children? Is there a daily schedule posted?
- What is the adult-to-child ratio and size of the group in the classrooms ?
- Is it licensed by local authorities?
- Is it accredited by the NAEYC?
- Can you drop in any time?
- What type of discipline, if any, is used?

Prevention, recognition, protection, and early intervention are the major tools that teachers can use to reduce risks to children in their care. Table 1-4 lists some risk management objectives for child care safety, nutrition, and health.

TABLE 1-4
Risk Management for Early Childhood Education

All teachers should:

- Require proof of immunizations before admitting children to care.
- Meet immunization requirements personally.
- Follow health and safety licensing guidelines.
- Provide a safe staff-to-child ratio.
- Develop good observational skills.
- Use health appraisals and assessment as risk management tools.
- Follow sanitary guidelines for hygiene and food handling.
- Protect the facility from neighborhood violence.
- Recognize and manage mild childhood illnesses.
- Provide backup or substitute teachers to replace ill teachers.
- Develop an inclusion/exclusion policy for ill children.
- Communicate by written notice about exposure to communicable disease.
- Provide a hazard-free environment.

(continues)

TABLE 1-4 *(Continued)*
Risk Management for Early Childhood Education

- Prevent accidents in the indoor environment by following safety guidelines and practices.
- Prevent accidents in the outdoor environment by selection and placement of equipment and by following safety guidelines and practices.
- Create a safety plan for the facility.
- Create a disaster preparedness plan for fire and other dangers.
- Prevent fire by following local fire code standards and practices.
- Post and be ready to follow emergency procedures.
- Have knowledge of pediatric first aid and be able to practice it in case of an emergency.
- Be able to perform cardiopulmonary resuscitation (CPR).
- Detect, prevent, and report child maltreatment.
- Understand and utilize acceptable methods of discipline.
- Arrange the facility so there is no opportunity for isolation or privacy of individual teachers with children.
- Develop a written plan for nutritious meals and snacks.
- Provide nutritious foods.
- Provide relief time for all staff.

Family child care providers and nannies should:

- Organize the home for child care.
- Organize for mixed-age child care.

Goal Three: Education as a Tool for Children's Health Promotion and Risk Reduction

A holistic approach to health promotion and illness and disease prevention is required because health and well-being cannot be achieved without awareness. An educational component must be present in order to create a safe and nurturing environment for children. The educational component must impact the staff, the children, and the parents involved in the early childhood education program or relationship.

Education and training for quality early childhood education are essential (Whitebook et al., 2006; NAEYC, 2006; *The Science of Early Childhood Development*, 2007; Early et al., 2007). The teacher should be educated in promotional, preventive, and protective practices to provide the maximum environment and minimum risk for the child (Table 1-5). A fundamental role of the teacher is to pass along knowledge. Modeling good health and safety measures and good food choices teaches children by example. Role modeling also allows children and their parents to see the teacher put this knowledge to practice.

Teaching children about good health and proper nutrition helps them contribute to their own health. Instructing children in preventive and protective measures permits them to participate in their own well-being. The

TABLE 1-5
Educational Tools for Teachers

A teacher should have knowledge of:

- Health promotion and the importance of modeling health promotion behavior
- Observational skills
- Immunizations and when they are to be given
- Health appraisals and use of assessment tools
- Mechanisms of communicable diseases and how they are spread
- Universal sanitary practices
- Common childhood illnesses, including management and exclusion policies
- Environmental health and safety hazards
- Safety standards and practices for both indoor and outdoor equipment
- Disaster preparedness
- Emergency response procedures
- Cardiopulmonary resuscitation (CPR) and first aid
- Detection and reporting of child maltreatment
- Prevention of child maltreatment
- Nutritional needs of children
- Good feeding practices for children
- Any special health or nutritional needs of children in care
- Communication skills
- Diversity and how it can affect health, safety, and nutrition
- Advocacy for children
- Access to community resources
- Development of family and community coalitions for improved safety, nutrition, and health

children can pass that information on to others by modeling and through discussion. This may motivate parents to be more receptive to the teacher's modeling and information.

Teachers educate parents by discussing health, safety, and nutrition directly with them and by providing handouts and holding workshops. Teachers can access the help of community groups to aid with this task. Parents who are supported through continual contacts with teachers and educational assistants are better at providing holistic health for their children (USDHHS, 2003; Wilson, 2006).

Knowledgeable teachers who work with children, parents, and the community contribute to a team effort to promote good health, safety, prevention, and nutrition. Creating these linkages allows the teacher to effect a holistic approach to ensure a quality environment for the children.

Goal Four: Recognizing the Importance of Guidelines, Standards, and Laws for the Health, Safety, and Well-Being of Children

- **guidelines** *statements of advice or instruction pertaining to practice.*
- **standards** *statements that define a goal of practice.*
- **laws** *rules of conduct established and enforced by authority.*

Guidelines, **standards**, and **laws** affecting early childhood education environments have been created for the purpose of protecting children and promoting quality environments for them. Programs in states where there are stringent regulations tend to provide higher quality care than those in states that have less stringent regulations (CCB, 2000). When teachers in all settings comply with standards, there is a lower turnover rate, more sensitive care, and staff with better training, resulting in better-quality early childhood education. NAEYC's position on licensing and regulation states, "The fundamental purpose of public regulation is to protect children from harm, not only threats to their immediate physical health and safety, but also threats of long-term development impairment" (1997). Compliance with minimum standards can affect environmental practices, relationships with parents, and the general attitude of teachers (Goldstein, 2006; Goldstein, Hamm, & Schumacher, 2007).

Whenever a child is injured or dies in the care of a teacher, the media are quick to report it. Although the sensationalism may hurt the profession at the time, good may come from these unfortunate accidents or poor care. Quality early childhood education seeks to improve health and safety standards as well as provide education for families (Caulfield & Kataoka-Yahiro, 2001; Wilson, 2006). Some legislators in this country are more receptive to recommendations from organizations such as the NAEYC, Children's Defense Fund, the AAP, The National Center for Clinical Infant Programs, The American Dietetic Association, and The American Public Health Association. Those organizations have developed standards and recommended guidelines for teachers to follow concerning the safety, nutrition, and health of young children. These and other groups are helping to effect legislation that originates **regulations** or enacts laws that protect children's well-being. For example, the **staff-to-child ratio** is an issue covered by regulations.

- **regulations** *recommendations that are made a requirement by law.*
- **staff-to-child ratio** *the number of staff required to provide proper care for the number of children of a certain age group.*

The AAP and the APHA believe that standards and guidelines should be established for all nonparental early childhood education programs. The USDHHS oversees federal regulations that have been enacted to help children. Individual states can enact legislation that creates regulations for early childhood education programs. Many states have strict licensing regulations for child care settings, although some states have few, if any, licensing requirements and nine states have none. These licensing requirements basically relate to center-based care, schools, and family child care. There are virtually no regulations for nannies.

Guidelines, standards, and regulations affect the teacher. They exist to support and promote the health and well-being of children. If guidelines, standards, and regulations exist, they should be followed. In a center-based facility, it is up to the director to ensure that the staff complies with and understands the guidelines, standards, and regulations. In a family child care home, it is the provider who monitors guidelines, standards, and regulations to ensure compliance. A teacher who cares for a child in the child's own home must use common sense and form guidelines based on information from classes and available support such as this text or a network of community resources.

If the state in which the early childhood education environment is located has no regulations, it is imperative that the teacher follow guidelines and standards suggested by the organizations previously discussed in this introduction. NAEYC accreditation gives clear steps and expectations of what is expected by a program seeking to obtain it. Today to achieve this accreditation in their new system, an early childhood education environment must meet all 10 NAEYC program standards. The use of ECERS-R and other measurement tools like quality rating systems are also helpful and provide a framework for making program improvements. Quality Rating Systems (QRS) "are a method to assess, improve and communicate the level of quality in early care and education settings" (National Child Care Information Center [NCCIC], 2006). These QRSs with their systematic approaches can be used by states and linked to local licensing bodies. By 2006, 12 states were using these QRSs for guidelines and standards for quality (NCCIC, 2006).

Local districts, states, and the federal government regulate the early childhood education environment. Programs have to comply with certain guidelines and standards in order to get funding.

Many of the guidelines and standards for good quality early childhood education environments for health, safety, and nutrition are reflected in this text. It is basic good early childhood education practice to follow them. The teachers who use them will be able to provide a healthy, protective environment for the children they teach.

Goal Five: Practice Cultural Competence

The United States is becoming more and more diverse, and this diversity is especially noted in the numbers of children. The 2000 census reflected a 63 percent increase in immigrant families since 1990 (Daniel & Freidman, 2006). In that same time period, the Latino population grew by 50 percent and now represents the largest portion of diversity in our country. A teacher would be remiss if he or she did not consider the cultures of the children present when planning for the safety, health, and well-being of those children. For quality early childhood education, the best practice in relation to culture would be that the teacher's practices and the environment reflect the language and culture of the children in care (Duarte & Rafanello, 2001; Obegi & Ritblatt, 2005; National Center for Cultural Competence [NCCC], 2007). It is thought that quality early childhood education is reflected in practices that consider cultural differences (Burchinal & Cryer, 2003). For example, Head Start performance standards for care require a multicultural perspective or approach to the children and families in their program.

By displaying behaviors, attitudes, and policies that allow for cross-cultural effectiveness, teachers are more competent to deal with the diversity found in their early childhood education programs. The National Center for Cultural Competence (NCCC) believes that cultural competence "is achieved by identifying and understanding the needs and help-seeking behaviors of individuals and families" (NCCC, 2007). This may not always be easy to do because caregiving practices are a reflection of the culture beliefs and history of those performing the care. In order to become culturally competent, a teacher must first examine his or her own cultural background, beliefs, and practices (Obegi & Ritblatt, 2005; Greenberg, 2006; Im, Parlakian, & Sanchez, 2007). This self-assessment can help determine whether there are any biases that should be addressed. These might include beliefs about what a child is capable of at a particular age, what behaviors are acceptable, what is the best way to support children, and how each gender should be treated

(Im, Parlakian, & Sanchez, 2007). Teachers should also understand that the beliefs and practices of families might be quite different from their own. This is why open and reciprocal communication and respect for each family is vital. Teachers should encourage families to discuss their cultures in an open manner and should be open to different approaches in caregiving practices. We must accommodate and help empower children from diverse cultures (Obegi & Ritblatt, 2005; Okagaki & Diamond, 2000). Chang (2006) suggests asking parents the following questions as a child enters the program:

- "How would you like us to recognize your child ethnically?"
- "What family traditions would you like for our program to acknowledge?"
- "What can we learn about your culture to help us to be as respectful as possible?"
- "What language or languages does your family speak?"
- "What holidays do you celebrate?"

Cultural values often are reflected in the early childhood education choice of the families prior to kindergarten (Johnson et al., 2004; Collins & Ribeiro, 2006). The ease with which a child and his family adapt to care will be accelerated if the caregiving practices in the early childhood education environment are similar to those of the home environment. Collaboration or partnering between the teacher and the family are more likely to occur when care is taken to understand the child's cultural background. If inquiry is made to parents as to the family's beliefs, values, and practices, the teacher can help to create a more complementary environment for the child (Chang, 2006). Cultural competency is more likely to lead to quality early childhood education programs that help keep children safer and healthier

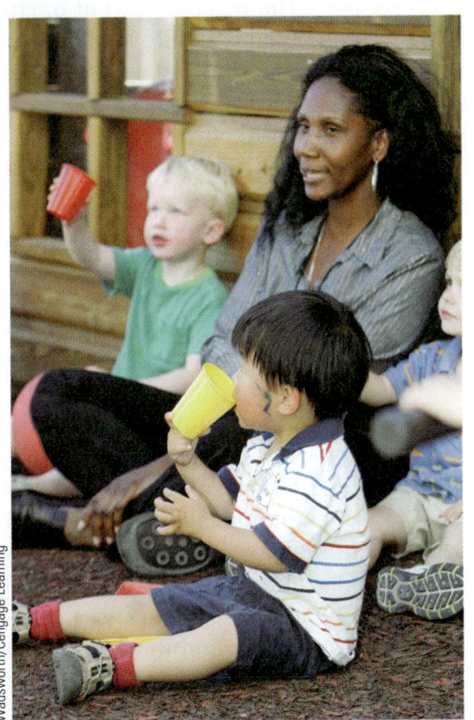

Wadsworth/Cengage Learning

Quality in early childhood education is reflected in practices that consider the needs of children from many backgrounds; this teacher is sitting quietly meeting the needs of her charges at the moment.

and promote a greater sense of well-being. In the case of elementary school early childhood environments, cultural competency is equally important. The same questions presented above can be asked, collaboration can occur, and cultures can be discussed. Teachers at this level have a schedule of competencies children must learn and doing so in a culturally competent manner would be of great assistance.

Goal Six: Develop Partnerships with Families to Provide a Caring Community

The number of women with young children who work outside the home has continued to increase (USDHHS, 2006), and demand for nonparental care is expected to rise another 12 percent by the end of this decade (Neugebauer, 2002). In part, this has been caused by a shift in family policy (Loeb et al., 2004). As a result, more families are using out-of-home care prior to kindergarten (Greenspan, 2003) and are depending on that care for the benefit of both the children and the family. The NAEYC standards for teachers have given high priority to building family and community relationships (Hyson, 2002). The NAEYC suggests that well-prepared professionals should value, respect, and involve families in order to help a child reach his or her greatest potential. Early childhood education environments that have meaningful family involvement are more likely to reflect quality (DiNatale, 2002). Teachers who invite families to partner for the success of the child and are aware of the families' circumstances and needs are able to be more effective in establishing a caring community for the child (Baldwin, DaRos-Voseles, & Swick, 2003; Knopf & Swick, 2007). A caring early childhood education community is especially important for the health, safety, and well-being of the child at all age levels. Teachers and principals in elementary schools should do what they can to increase family involvement (Michael, Dittus, & Epstein, 2007).

The teacher–parent partnership is established in numerous ways. First, the families should be offered a real orientation to the early childhood education program regardless of where it occurs. A good orientation for families can relieve concerns and confusion that they may have about what takes place in their children's particular program and can make them feel really welcome. This is especially true for "first-time" families that have never accessed the use of early childhood education in any form. An orientation allows the family to know the people involved in the program. Quality early childhood education programs are likely to offer a parent handbook that includes much important information, such as policies and practices and even the program philosophy or mission statement (DiNatale, 2002). An orientation may even include home visits (Baldwin, DaRos-Voseles, & Swick, 2003; Greenberg, 2006), during which the teacher can gain insights into the child's home environment. This is true for all education environments throughout the early childhood period.

The parent and the teacher should establish a clear and open channel of communication. Any prejudice on the teacher's part about the superiority of his or her knowledge of early childhood education should be dispelled if a relationship is to be established (Ahnert & Lamb, 2003; Greenberg, 2006). The teacher should show respect and a willingness to communicate sincerely. The parent and the teacher should talk often and begin to know each other. It is important for the teacher to remember that, no matter what the culture, composition of the family, or economic status, each family is unique

(Christian, 2006). Discussing such topics as parenting practices, child-rearing perspectives, and family interactions can help both parent and teacher understand each other. Sending home weekly notes can encourage conversations (Greenberg, 2006). A regularly scheduled parent conference should occur several times a year for more in-depth discussion. One of these should be early in the year to establish goals for the child. These various ways of communication help to establish respect and reciprocity between the family and the early childhood education program. Good communication can enhance parenting and create a balance between the home and early education programs for children. Another benefit is that, as parents become involved, they become educated about best practices for their children.

Families can also be actively involved by volunteering to help with activities such as field trips or special events or by helping out at home in a number of appropriate ways. This invitation doesn't have to stop with parents; other family members such as grandparents, aunts, uncles, or older siblings should also be encouraged to participate and should be given a number of options to choose from. These might include helping with a newsletter, repairing a book, sewing, or computer work. Parents might also be asked to visit the classroom and share information about their home life, culture, or work (Halacka Ball, 2006). Many elementary schools encourage family involvement directly in the classrooms.

Special events that involve families and children can also be scheduled. A yearly picnic, an open house for families once or twice a year, and other events such as "nacho" parties, story parties, or ice cream socials can give families a chance to get to know each other and the teachers better in a less formal setting. Vary the time of day that these events take place so that more family members can attend depending on their schedules. When everyone is involved, a caring community is the result.

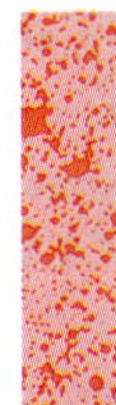

Pause for Reflection

Why are the six goals so important to creating a caring environment for children and families in early education programs? What could you specifically do to prepare to help create this type of environment for the children you work with or will be working with?

REALITY *Check*

The Reality of War and Terrorism for Young Children in the United States

As we look at safety, nutrition, and health in a holistic manner and think about providing a quality environment for children, we have a new reality to deal with. We are providing early education and care to children who are living in a country that has been attacked by terrorism for the first time on its own soil and, as a result, has been involved in a lengthy war on terrorism. Terrorism is about putting potential victims in a state of terror that has psychological and emotional repercussions (Schonfeld, 2002). This is especially true if the child has experienced the trauma or loss firsthand (National Center for

(continues)

REALITY*Check* (continued)

Children Exposed to Violence [NCCEV], 2003). Children express grief from a tragic event in different ways. Some withdraw or become clingy and fearful. Others act out and become more aggressive (Brodkin, 2004). A range of behaviors that may be expressed include the ones listed here (North Carolina State University [NCSU], 2003):

- Irritability
- Inability to be calmed
- Sadness
- Fearfulness, including talking about scary things
- Anticipation of another bad event
- Developmental regression
- Anger
- Aggressive behavior
- Changes in sleep patterns
- Clinging behavior
- Physical effects such as stomachaches or headaches
- Change in eating habits
- Hypersensitivity

When children are fearful, they often want to know all about whatever it is that they are afraid of (Perry, 2003). Many children have fantasies that do not reflect reality. They may ask questions, or they may hesitate to ask questions. Part of each child's reaction to the issue of war and terror depends on his or her age, developmental level, and personality (NCCEV, 2003). Children who have had trauma in their lives before may be more vulnerable than others who have not experienced trauma (National Association of School Psychologists [NASP], 2003). Children who have been actually involved in a terrorist attack in some manner are three times more likely to suffer from posttraumatic stress disorder than if exposed to some other type of trauma (Mental Health Weekly, 2004).

As teachers, it is important to be truthful with children. On the other hand, teachers should not offer more information than they need. Listen carefully to what they are asking. Give the best possible answer that deals only with the question. Do not go beyond the simple question they ask. A simple answer is best. Children may also exhibit nonverbal cues. These might include changes in their normal facial expressions, play behavior, or how they talk (LifeCare, 2003).

One of the things that young children want to know is that everything is okay and that they are safe. War is a concept that children do not fully understand, and part of that lack of understanding may be the fear that war is closer than it really is and that it may come to where the child is. To help children better understand the situation can be difficult because we do not know what will happen, but we can reassure them that we are doing as much as we possibly can to keep them safe and secure. Teachers can let the children know that they are there for the children and they can be counted upon.

War may be a greater reality to a young child if either or both of her parents are deployed to the war zone. Besides the factor of war, the child is dealing with separation from her parent(s). This can cause major changes, such as moving, a change in income for family necessities, or even living with others if both parents have left (Myers-Walls, 2003). These children may need the extra reassurance and familiarity that a teacher can provide. Keeping an open line of communication with these families will help teachers be aware of the circumstances that they are going through (Allen & Staley, 2006). The knowledge gained from this type of communication can help the teacher to better understand the issues with individual families and help the children accordingly. Providing a safe and caring environment can help children learn the coping skills they may need at this time of deployment.

Children look to teachers for stability and security. Teachers are very important in their lives, and children need their help to deal with scary and fearful feelings about what is happening in our world today. The most important thing you as a teacher can do is to provide routine and structure that is familiar in the environment you have created. A simple hug or two might be just enough to reassure a fearful child when he is thinking about war or terrorism.

Teachers can help children by letting them deal with some of their fears in their own ways. One of

(continues)

REALITY *Check* (continued)

the things that Fred Rogers used to tell children was to look for the "helpers" in any scary situation (Mister Rogers' Neighborhood, 2004). That would have been easy to do on 9/11, with all the firemen and policemen helping. Today, while we are in a war situation, it is easy to find the soldiers, both men and women, who are helping the United States. Finding the helpers can lead to discussions about how these people help to keep the world a safer place.

Play is one way that children are able to deal with things they do not understand (AAP, 2003). Unfortunately, much of the play that comes out of the issue of war and terror may be violent play (Levin, 2003a). There has been an increase in play with weapons, which is not surprising considering the circumstances (Perry, 2003). This type of play may lead to unsafe conditions or aggressive behaviors by some children. If the play gets scary or dangerous, intervention may be needed. Play behavior may need to be redirected, and discussions might take place about how people can help or support each other instead of hurting one another. As children play, watch to find out what they are thinking or feeling and what they are worried about. If toys such as rescue vehicles or doctor's kits are available, children might be led into more positive play (Levin, 2003a). Talking about the importance of peace and conflict resolution might lead children into a different mode of thinking (Levin, 2003b). Another consideration is to spend more time outdoors doing gross motor activities; this will help children be active and less involved in thinking about the issues surrounding war and terrorism (Perry, 2003). The use of a "Huggy Puppy" doll as a toy to help calm children has been very successful in several countries where children actually observed a war environment. This type of intervention allowed the children to attach and be involved with the doll and helped reduce stress (Sadeh, Hen-Gal, & Tikotzky, 2008).

Children may feel anger toward a group of people who may be seen as causing this war on terrorism. Children can become prejudiced at a young age. Cultural competency is something a teacher should strive for, and it would be especially important here. An early childhood education environment should model respect for diversity. Provide activities that help children appreciate differences among cultural groups. Help children to learn tolerance and nondiscrimination.

It is also very important to involve families as part of the early childhood education program to deal with the turbulent times we all live in. Be involved with the families of children in your work. Talk often with them. If there are concerns in this area, it might be wise to hold a deeper discussion about what is happening with the child at home in dealing with the unease over war wherever it may be occurring and the threat of terrorism that is lived with on a daily basis. Work closely with the family to provide consistency between home and the early childhood education environment when it comes to discussions or feelings on this subject. This is especially important if a family member is deployed in the military or other services.

In all, it appears that what a child needs from a teacher in this instance, as in many others, are five fundamental things (Tylenda, 2004):

- Structure
- Consistency
- Predictability
- Nonpunitive limit setting
- Nurturance

The teacher's job is not an easy one. Trying to maintain the stability of children's lives can be difficult after watching the nightly news reports on deaths of our soldiers or terror attacks around the globe. The task may be even more formidable if we have a loved one in another country fighting for our protection. Teachers should remember to take care of themselves so they can take care of the children in their care (Tyson, 2003). They should also provide a good role model for coping. One way to do this is to make sure that teachers talk about their feelings with others such as family, friends, and coworkers (Stephens, 2003).

CHECK*point:* **What would you specifically do to support a family that has a parent away at war? What protective measures might you offer to the child in your program from this family?**

Key Concept 1.5

Providing High-Quality Early Childhood Education

High-quality care should be the objective of every teacher. For good safety, nutrition, and health in early childhood education, the teacher should have six basic goals: maximizing the health status of children; minimizing risks to children; utilizing education as a tool for health promotion and risk reduction; recognizing the importance of guidelines, standards, and laws as they apply to early childhood education; practicing cultural competence; and developing partnerships with families to provide a caring community.

1.6 BUILDING CURRICULUM FOR QUALITY EARLY CHILDHOOD EDUCATION

- **curriculum** *course of study that relates to the subject being examined.*

Curriculum provides the mechanism for teaching children. Teachers provide instruction in safety, nutrition, and health to children every day by role-modeling behaviors and actions. However, role modeling does not provide enough information for children so that they can understand, change their actions, and practice healthy and safe behaviors. Other methods are needed to properly inform children and to involve families. The author realizes that students get instruction in curriculum in other classes; however, some students may enter the course for which this text is used without experience in creating curriculum. For elementary school teachers, curriculum is an essential and they may already have had a whole course in it. Students have requested that this text contain particular ideas for curriculum in safety, nutrition, and health because, even if they have had some experience with curriculum or attended a course on it, these subjects are rarely covered. Because this information may not be needed by all students, the curriculum section and materials are available on the companion website found at www.cengage.com/education/robertson. The curriculum area of the website contains the rest of Building Curriculum for Quality Early Childhood Education, and in addition, has a number of specific lessons plans and topic maps to go with the areas of safety, nutrition, health and special topics.

CHAPTER SUMMARY

A holistic approach allows the teacher to view the interrelationships of safety, nutrition, and health for young children. An ecological perspective views the total environment of the child. The physical, social and emotional, economic, and cultural environments all have an effect on the growth and development of children. Risk factors for safety, nutrition, and health for children may come from any or all of these environments.

Awareness of efforts on national, state, and local levels may help clarify the role of the teacher concerning practices that involve safety, nutrition, and health. The ability to recognize signs and symptoms of at-risk issues is key to early intervention.

(continues)

CHAPTER SUMMARY *(continued)*

Quality early childhood education involves maximizing the health status of children and minimizing risks to safety, nutrition, and health. Using education for health promotion will reduce risk. A teacher who recognizes the importance of guidelines, standards, and laws has the tools to create the best possible learning environment.

Practicing cultural competence affords the tools needed to address diversity in early education. Teachers who collaborate with parents and develop a caring community will offer the optimal environment for healthy development of the children they work with. When teachers carefully construct curriculum to meet the needs and developmental levels of children, they can offer the children tools of their own to maintain safety, good nutrition, and a healthy lifestyle.

TO GO BEYOND

Additional resources for this chapter can be found by visiting the book companion website at www.cengage.com/education/robertson. This supplemental material includes chapter objectives, internet exercises, reflection questions, quizzes, web links, glossary and flash cards, case studies, frequently asked questions, downloadable forms and tables, curriculum supplements, more reality checks, additional key concepts, references, and more.

Chapter Review Critical Thinking Applications

1. Discuss the holistic approach to children's safety, nutrition, and health. Why do you suppose so many people who work with young children fragment or select one portion to look at and do not view the whole child? Does the interrelationship between safety, nutrition, and health affect issues regarding any one of them when applied to early childhood education?
2. Describe the ecological perspective of the total environment. Consider a child whom you know. How does each of these areas affect this child's safety? Nutrition? Health?
3. Discuss the changes in diversity in this country. How might these changes affect early childhood education programs or elementary education in the early years? What could be done to minimize the impact?

As an Individual

1. Look at your own environment at home. What risks do you see in it? What could you do to minimize those risks? What can be done to maximize the health and safety of your environment? What if your environment were used for an early childhood education environment—would it be a safe and healthy place for children?
2. Look at either a preschool or elementary school classroom. What risks do you find there? What might a teacher do to minimize these risks? If it is an elementary classroom, how might the elementary

school environment pose challenges to health and safety that might not be present in preschools?

3. Write down everything you have eaten for one typical weekday and one typical weekend day. How could you improve your own nutritional status?
4. Observe an early childhood education situation. Look at it with a holistic approach. What are the teacher and the facility doing to contribute to the children's safety, nutrition, and health? How would you improve the program by thinking of the whole child?
5. What are the health and safety standards or licensing regulations for early childhood education programs in your community? Your state? If possible, obtain a copy. If you plan on teaching the early elementary years, what are the health and safety standards in the local district? What are the state elementary health and safety standards?

As a Group

1. Examine the health promotion activities on your own campus. Are you aware of them? Are they adequate? What suggestions for improvement do you have? Remember to consider the whole person.
2. Obtain and analyze the local licensing requirements for health and safety measures in early childhood education environments. Would you consider them adequate? How would you change these requirements to improve the health, safety, and well-being of children? Are those changes practical? As an alternative, find out the policies for health and safety measures for a local elementary school district and ask the three questions above in relation to their policies.
3. Assess your community's environment. Be sure to consider all the elements: physical, social, emotional, economic, and cultural. How would you rate your community in relation to safety, nutrition, health, or a place to raise children? What might be done to improve it? List 10 things that could be done to improve your community.
4. Analyze the quality of early childhood education on your campus. If you do not have a program on-site, choose an off-campus site or local elementary school to evaluate. Compare the quality in relation to items reported in the Reality Check on Early Education and Child Care in America.
5. Design a quality early childhood education environment considering both a holistic approach and the total environment. You may do this for an infant, toddler, preschool, or early elementary education environment.

Case Studies

1. Tilda is about to have a baby and is thinking about finding child care before she has to go back to work, when the baby will be about 4 months old. She wants to look for a place convenient to her work and one she can afford. What are the items she should look for to make sure it is a quality place for her baby?

2. Evelyn has been taking child development classes for several years and has worked in a child care center. She is thinking about opening a family child care so that she can stay home with her children more. What types of steps should she take before opening a family child care?
3. Ellen just began teaching in a kindergarten class close to a military base. Four of her students have a parent who is deployed overseas. What protective measures can she offer to these students? What might she do to involve the families of these students in a more meaningful way?

SECTION II
Safety in Early Childhood Education

This section discusses elements of safety in early childhood education.

2. Creating Safe Environments for Early Childhood Education
3. Indoor Safety
4. Outdoor Safety
5. Emergency Response Procedures for Early Childhood Education Environments

Wadsworth/Cengage Learning

CHAPTER 2

Creating Safe Environments for Early Childhood Education

After reading this chapter, you should be able to:

2.1 Safety Policies

Define and discuss safety policies and their use as tools for safety, risk prevention, protection, and promotion.

2.2 Structuring Safe Environments

Discuss the importance of safe environments and describe a safe environment for all types of early childhood education.

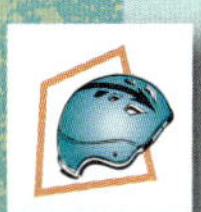

2.3 Management for Injury Prevention

Discuss the factors involved in childhood injury and describe strategies for use in injury prevention.

2.4 Constructing a Safety Plan for Early Childhood Education Environments

Explain the development of a safety plan for a child care setting.

2.5 Implications for Teachers

Describe the importance of and strategies for education, working with families, supervision, and observation for maintaining a safe environment.

2.1 SAFETY POLICIES

Developing safety policies for the teacher to manage risk, provide protection, and promote safety in early childhood education environments is important. Some factors that indicate the need for these safety policies are listed here.

- Unintentional injury is now the leading cause of death in childhood (*America's children: Key national indicators of well-being, 2007*). Injury is the leading cause of death and disability for children in the United States and Canada (Schwebel & Gaines, 2007). To ameliorate this fact, safety intervention strategies are needed (Schnitzer, 2006).
- In 1997, about 31,000 children under age 4 were treated in U.S. hospital emergency rooms for injuries that occurred in early childhood education or school settings. At least 56 children have died in early childhood education environments since 1990 (Shepard, 2002). Falls are the leading cause of injuries to children of all ages (Schnitzer, 2006).
- Sixty-seven percent of parents believe that children's serious injuries are "random acts of fate or accidents" and therefore do not think in terms of prevention (Ontario Early Years [OEY], 2004).
- Children who spent more time in nonparental care such as early education environments were at a slightly reduced risk for unintentional injury (Schwebel, Brezausek, & Belsky, 2006). Risk for injury can be ameliorated with good adult supervision (Schwebel & Gaines, 2007).
- Playground design, lack of attention, falls, and choking are common hazards in early childhood education environments (Aronson, 2001).
- Sudden infant death syndrome (SIDS) as a hazard in early childhood education environments can be decreased if babies are put to sleep on their backs and educational efforts for care providers are increased (Moon, Sprague, & Patel, 2005). The "Back-to-Sleep" campaign has helped reduce cases of SIDS (SIDS Network, 2008).
- Children's sense of safety may be at risk as a result of what they observe in their world (Levin, 2003a).

Teachers should realize that most injuries to children are preventable. An accident infers a chance occurrence that is accompanied by no control or responsibility. Many injuries that children suffer can be prevented and do carry with them the need for a degree of control for prevention and responsibility for protection. Because of developmental factors that limit children's physical, cognitive, and emotional abilities, they are more vulnerable than adults to injury. Children are natural risk takers who attempt actions for which they may lack skills. Children want to test and master their environments, but they need a sense of trust and security that their environment is friendly and safe. Depending on their developmental level, children may lack the capacity to judge the safety of their environment. Good, constant quality supervision of children in early childhood education environments has been shown to reduce unintentional injury risk to children (Schwebel & Gaines, 2007).

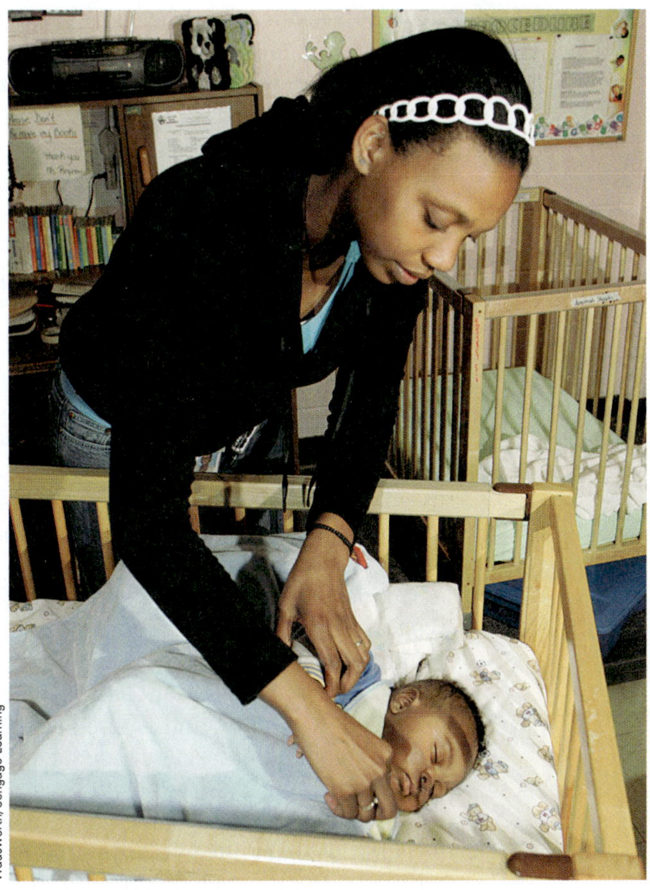

Wadsworth/Cengage Learning

One very important safety measure for early childhood education environments with infants is making sure they are put down for naps on their backs, to help prevent SIDS.

Designing a Safety Policy

Safety policies should be developed and directed toward the children and staff. They should promote safe practices for the child, the teachers, and the family. Basic safety policies lay the foundation for quality early childhood education.

Policies establish a process, assign responsibility, and offer guidance for action. Safety policies may take the form of checklists, injury reports, guidelines, practices, or strategies to decrease risk. When policies are being developed, the following questions should be asked (Aronson, 2002).

- What should be done?
- What process will be followed?
- Who is responsible for making sure the process is followed?
- Are there any time parameters or limitations?

The question "What should be done?" provides the teacher with information needed to create a specific safety policy for each particular safety hazard that might be present in the early childhood education environment. The teacher should know what hazards the local licensing regulations and fire board address. An example is a state mandate that teachers must report any suspected maltreatment. The teacher then creates a policy for dealing with how, when, and where to make a report of suspected maltreatment. Some local areas have county or city fire regulation and zoning codes that may affect the design of safety policies.

Addressing the process involved in a safety policy helps the teacher understand how the policy should be carried out. The process explains when, and perhaps where, an action should be performed. The teacher should be aware of what safety hazards exist in both the indoor and outdoor environments. Viewing the environment through the eyes of a child will help the teacher find safety hazards and create safety checklists and other policies that offer maximum protection. It is essential that the teacher have knowledge of the developmental abilities of children in early childhood education programs. Developmental level safety checklists are important tools that may be used to manage the environment for risk. An example of this could be the safety items in the ECERS-R, FCCERS-R and ITERS-R ratings scales or the safety checklists found on the University of North Carolina, Frank Porter Graham School website, http://www.fpg.unc.edu/~ECERS/.

Knowledge of environmental hazards will help the teacher create specific policies for early childhood education. For each type of safety hazard, there should be a process of actions to be followed to avoid risk. For example, if field trips are to be taken, there should be a definite policy for travel with children. This policy would include actions to be taken before the trip as well as actions needed during the trip. Or, for example, if pesticides are used, the type and method used should be researched and clearly spelled out. Time limitations or parameters may be a critical factor in some areas of safety in early childhood education. This is especially true for emergency situations. A child who has fallen and is unconscious for more than a few seconds should have immediate emergency medical care.

The setting determines who is responsible for carrying out the policy. In an early childhood education environment, responsibility may fall to the director, primary teacher, principal (see Chapter 5), or to an assigned safety advocate. In family child care, the responsibility usually falls to the provider. For in-home care, the nanny will probably share the responsibility with the parents. It is important to define the responsible party so that the policy does not go unenforced. At the elementary school level, it is the district and even the states that dictate what safety policies should be in place. A good safety policy will have checks and balances for responsibility built into it. All staff should be encouraged to understand all safety precautions required in the early childhood education environment. Every teacher should be encouraged to carry out actions that provide for the greatest degree of safety. Of foremost importance in those teachers' actions is good supervision of children in the early childhood education environment.

Safety policies should be clearly written and should include guidelines, limitations, and suggested methods of communication to be used. Safety policies help the teacher develop proper practices based on the knowledge of safety, risk prevention, protection, and promotion. Basic policies should be created for safety, nutrition, health, and special topics, and should incorporate the six major goals of high-quality early childhood education. See page 19 Figure 1-2 for those six goals.

A responsible teacher helps to encourage safety and safe behaviors. Educating the children and their families so that they also know how to recognize dangers in any setting will ensure further protection. There should be several policies addressing the educational aspects of safety.

General early childhood education safety policies should cover the following issues.

- **Creating Safe Environments:** practices for creating and managing safe facility-specific environments.
- **Injury Prevention Management:** understanding of injury and practices for preventing injury and protecting children.
- **Developing a Safety Plan:** strategies for developing guidelines for prevention and protection in early childhood education environments.
- **Implications for Teachers:** methods and practices for conducting education, observation and supervision, and working with families to provide safety and minimize risk.

Safety Policies

Safety policies should be planned and executed to prevent unintentional injury; protect the children from harm; and promote the use of safety practices for the teacher, the child, the family, and the people in the environment of the greater community. These policies should be clearly written and should be based on standard safety practices and licensing regulations. The policies should consider developmental stages of the children and should be applicable to the specific early childhood education environment. These safety policies guide the teacher in methods of practicing safety prevention, using protection and promotion to maximize the environment and minimize the risk to children.

2.2 STRUCTURING SAFE ENVIRONMENTS

- **injury prevention** *forestalling or anticipating injury risk.*

The teacher should use all the risk management and **injury prevention** tools available in order to create the safe environment children need to grow to their greatest potential. Knowledge of the ABCs of potential for injury helps the teacher be aware of what is required to create a protective and secure environment. As Schwebel and Brezausek (2007) stated, "A child does not develop in a vacuum, but rather in the presence of places, people, and situations that influence how the individual child thinks, behaves, and acts." It is important that the teacher keep this in mind. Knowing that a child acts and reacts in response to the environment makes planning for safety especially crucial. Safety policies for modifying the environment, modifying behavior, monitoring children, and teacher injury-preventive behaviors help the caregiver to provide more safety, protection, and prevention in every situation in the early childhood education environment. Most of the practices and behaviors that create a safe environment can be applied to all early childhood education environments. See Table 2-1 for a guide to safe practices and injury prevention. Safety policies can be created from the list.

There may be some variations in early childhood education safety policies that depend on several considerations. How these policies apply to specific safety protection, prevention, and promotion practices may relate to the following questions:

- In what type of environment are you applying these safety practices?
- What are the ages of the children in care?

TABLE 2-1
A Teacher's Guide to Safe Practices and Injury Prevention for a Safe Environment

- Know all applicable safety practices for the early childhood education environment.
- Screen environment for hazards and remove, where possible.
- Use safety devices, where applicable.
- Monitor environment for hazards that are part of the environment.
- Know developmental levels of the children, including capabilities and limitations.
- Promote safety through action, word, and deed.
- Promote safety in the children's home environments through safety precaution handouts for families.
- Role model safety practices to children and parents.
- Be aware of conditions that contribute to injury.
- Closely observe children, giving special consideration during at-risk conditions.

- What is the greater community surrounding the early childhood education environment like?
- What is the child's family environment?

The Type of Environment

The type of early childhood education environment has a definite impact on the degree of safety the teacher is able to provide. Protective and preventive measures may differ depending on the type of environment. Early childhood education centers may be able to control for safety more than a family child care home. Early education environments on elementary school campuses may pose challenges for safety for the younger children who attend. By the time a child is 8 years old, he or she may be less at risk for injury, due to coordination and brain development. Afterschool care may be performed at a wide variety of sites, many of which may pose risks. The level of injury in an in-home care situation may vary widely, depending on the home and conscientiousness about safety on the part of the parents.

Early Childhood Education Programs. Early childhood education environments are different from homes. In most states, they must follow certain licensing safety codes and practices (AAP & APHA, 2002). These basic codes and practices help the teacher lay the foundation for normal safety practices for that environment. Early childhood education environments generally are not **multiuse facilities**. A major purpose of early education programs in child care centers is to perform care and to provide a safe environment for the children in care. One advantage that this type of early childhood education environment may have is that it may be able to better ensure a child's personal safety by using a buzzer or keyless entry pad, as shown in Figure 2-1.

- **multiuse facilities** *child care sites that are used for other functions.*

FIGURE 2-1
These two types of keyless pin entries for the early childhood education environment help to provide an extra measure of safety.

Wadsworth/Cengage Learning

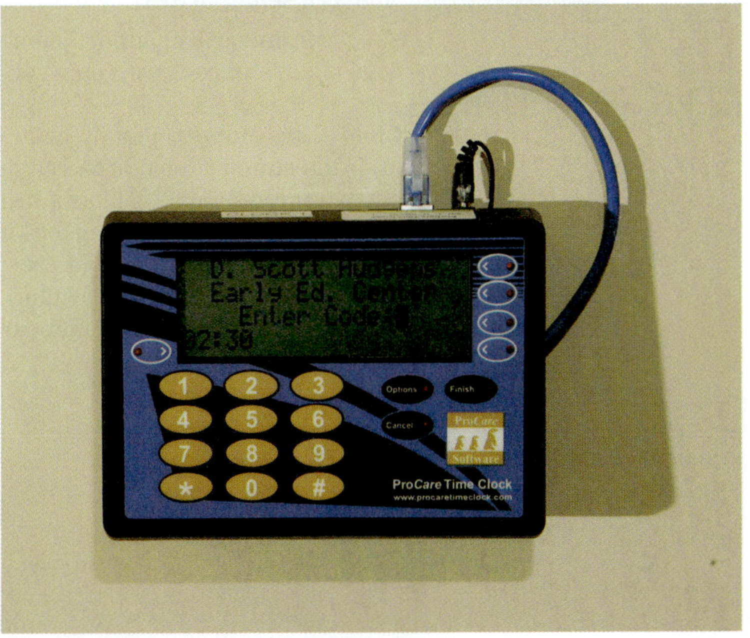

Wadsworth/Cengage Learning

Some early education programs are very different due to the location of the center where the programs are held. An early education program in a church-related environment may not be subject to the same safety rules and guidelines as those in the public sector. In addition, the church facility may be used by a number of different groups for different activities, thus introducing a greater degree of safety risk factors.

The same hazardous situation may exist for early childhood education environments that are located in public facilities. Ski resorts, fitness centers, community centers, and elementary schools may have early childhood education centers on site. These sites may not be subject to the same licensing safety codes or regulations and may be used for other purposes at other times. Modifying the environment in these unregulated, multiuse facilities can be a challenge for the teacher. Modification is a constant, ongoing process. Environments that are unregulated may make it even more imperative that teachers know safety practices, act as role models, and promote safety through actions, words, and deeds. Teaching the children about these safety risk factors may help provide an added level of monitoring for these environments. The responsibility for maintaining a safe environment rests with the teachers. Some examples of shared space are listed here.

- A college or university preschool used in the evenings for classroom space
- A ski lodge that uses a corner of its lounge for early childhood education while parents ski
- A church preschool room, used as a Sunday school and meeting room
- A fitness center with an area set aside for multiple-age child care
- A community center that is used for afterschool care in the afternoons and as a senior activity center in the mornings or evenings
- A corporate early childhood education center that is used for meetings and training classes on weekends

Family Child Care Homes. Family child care homes are multi-purpose by definition. If the state or local area requires licensing, the home must pass certain safety requirements, such as a fire code. Some states and local jurisdictions do not require any licensing for family child care homes. Other states may license only larger family child care homes with 12 or more children. This puts the responsibility of providing safety and protection directly on the provider in whose home the child care takes place. Self-regulation and

Wadsworth/Cengage Learning

Depending on the environment, different degrees of protective and preventive measures must exist.

monitoring of the environment are vital for the prevention of injuries and protection of the children.

There may be local programs available through resource and referral services that help to support the family child care provider. The use of rating scales such as FCCERS-R (Harms, Cryer, & Clifford, 2007) that have been specifically created for this environment would be a very useful tool to maximize safety. These types of support can help the teacher create a safe environment using specific safety policies that are similar to licensing regulations in other areas. Another source of help for the family provider is the National Family Child Care Association. This organization offers a program for accreditation that includes safety standards, policies, and practices.

Elementary Schools. As the trend toward universal preschools continues, many of these are and will continue to be located on elementary school campuses. A feature of the universal preschool idea is to have the teachers be prepared with a bachelor degree within a few years. As this develops, we may find that early education teachers may go back and forth from prekindergarten to the elementary years with seamless ease. Regardless, more children are getting early education on elementary campuses. For the younger children there may be real safety issues on elementary school campuses that may not be able to meet standards for younger children that other sites do. In these cases, good supervision is critical. Children should be old enough to be taught many more safety measures for themselves and others. Bullying may be even more of an issue at these schools, so interpersonal safety should be monitored carefully. Seventy-seven percent of elementary schools participate in programs to prevent bullying (CDC, 2007). Keeping the school environment safe and secure is a priority for the majority of elementary schools in the United States, and the following examples are indicative of that:

- Ninety-two percent of school districts have a safety policy that assigns staff or volunteers to monitor the playground when in use, and 47 percent of districts nationwide use the safety checklist and equipment guidelines in the *Handbook for Public Playground Safety* by the CPSC (Jones et al., 2007).
- Seventy-five percent of all school districts have an emergency preparedness, response, and recovery plan and two-thirds of the districts have a policy on the inspection/maintenance of fire extinguishers, smoke alarms, and sprinkler systems.

In-Home Child Care. An in-home situation in which the nanny comes to the child's home presents different challenges. In both the family child care home and the early childhood education center, the teacher is the person responsible for creating and monitoring the environment for safety. An in-home teacher shares this responsibility with the parents. It would be easy to assume that this is a fairly straightforward task. Unfortunately, this is not always the case. Some parents do not understand the need for making the environment as safe as possible. The environment is the home they have carefully selected and decorated for comfort and style, and it meets their needs.

When an infant arrives in the home, that child makes no demands on the home environment other than a place to sleep. As the child grows older and goes through the developmental stages, the need for modifying the home environment becomes important. Some parents are intent on making these

Damon was a quiet, curious toddler. Mary Ann, his nanny, was concerned that as he was becoming more mobile, Damon would get into unsafe situations. Mary Ann asked Damon's parents to remove the cleaning chemicals from under the sinks in the kitchen and bathroom. She asked that they remove small decorative objects from his reach. Some of these objects had sharp edges, and others were small enough for him to choke on if he put them in his mouth. The parents did not see the need. They felt that Mary Ann should rely solely on monitoring the child and not worry about the environmental hazards.

Mary Ann served her two-week notice when they refused to cooperate. The following weekend, while in the care of his aunt, Damon got under the sink and drank some cleaning solution. He was rushed to the hospital and had his stomach pumped. He was very lucky that the cleaning product he swallowed did not do permanent damage. The aunt felt terrible, the parents realized their mistake, and Damon had to go through a very scary situation. The family begged Mary Ann to stay and offered their full cooperation for childproofing their home.

modifications, but others do not see the need because they believe their child is "just going through a phase." It is on the shoulders of the nanny or in-home teacher to make sure the parents participate in modifying and monitoring the home environment for safety. If the parents choose not to childproof the home environment, it is recommended that the teacher not stay in this situation.

Not all situations like Damon's turn out so well. A home environment should be just as safe as any early childhood education environment.

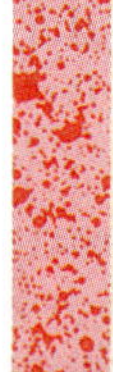

Pause for Reflection

Take a minute to think about the safety of your own home environment. Is it a place that might pose risk to children if they were to come visit you? What steps would you have to take if a toddler came to visit? What types of things might you have to anticipate, monitor, and modify to make your home safe?

The Age of Children in Care

Because of the developmental stages children go through (Table 2-2), the age of children in care affects the type of safety policies that are needed (AAP & APHA, 2002). If the environment is planned for a particular age group and the children are all at about the same developmental level, as is true in most large early childhood education environments, the safety modifications that the teacher makes will be standardized to fit that age range.

Jean Piaget explained the four cognitive developmental stages that children go through from birth to age 18 (Smith, 1997). The first three stages are referred to in the following developmental categories of infant, toddler and preschooler.

TABLE 2-2
Piaget's Sensorimotor Developmental Stages

Stage	Age	Actions
1	0–1 month	Mostly sucking and looking.
2	1–4 months	Making interesting things happen repeatedly with the body, like kicking legs or sucking a finger. Pleasure from repetition.
3	4–8 months	Repeated actions focusing on objects and events, for example, picking up a rattle and shaking it over and over. Pleasure from repetition.
4	8–12 months	Combining actions to reach a goal.
5	12–18 months	Experimenting to find new and different ways to solve problems or reach a goal. This stage is often referred to as the "little scientist."
6	18–24 months	Beginning of thought using symbols or language to solve problems mentally.

Infants. Some early childhood education environments involve caring for infants. This may be a center at which infant care is available, a family child care home that specializes in infants, or a nanny caring for one or two infants. Infants are totally dependent and therefore very vulnerable to injury if not carefully monitored. Infants develop their motor abilities in the

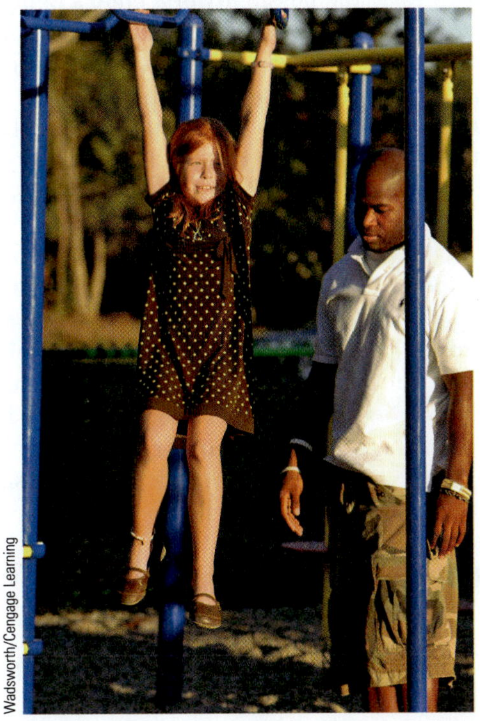
Wadsworth/Cengage Learning

All children should be provided with a safe environment that accommodates their developmental stage. This girl exhibits her developmental level by hanging on the bars, which are well padded underneath.

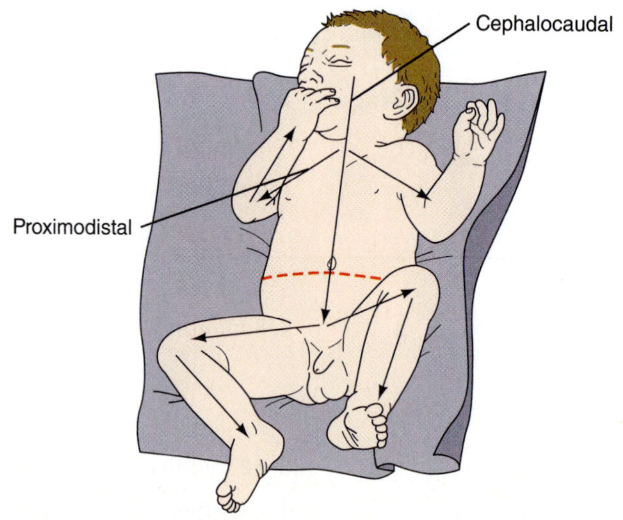

FIGURE 2-2
An infant showing proximodistal and cephalocaudal development.

- **cephalocaudal** *development from the top to the bottom of the body or from the head down toward the toes.*
- **proximodistal** *development of the body from the inside toward the outside or the torso through the arms and out to the fingers.*
- **gross motor skills** *physical skills using large body movements such as running, jumping, and climbing.*
- **fine motor skills** *physical skills related to small body movements, particularly of the hand and fingers. These skills include using scissors, holding a crayon, or working a puzzle.*
- **sensorimotor cognitive development** *first stage of cognitive development that utilizes motor abilities and senses.*

cephalocaudal and **proximodistal** directions. Development in the cephalocaudal direction moves from head to toe. As a child grows, development progresses down the body. For example, one of the first milestones for an infant is the ability to lift the head. One of the last infant milestones is the ability to walk. These **gross motor skills** develop earlier than **fine motor skills**. Proximodistal direction motor development works from the center of the body to the outside. An infant can roll over and use her arms long before she can reach and grasp (see Figure 2-2).

During the first few months of life, infants are not mobile and do not encounter many risks. The major risk that infants of all ages encounter is SIDS. The teacher should use protective and preventive measures to reduce the possibility of a child's being at risk for SIDS (see Reality Check, page 53).

Once an infant rolls over, mobility and thus risk increases. A child could turn over and fall from a changing table or infant seat set on a counter. As the cephalocaudal motor direction develops, skills and thus mobility increase. Children who creep and then crawl are apt to get into more and more territory that may pose risk to them. The need for safety devices increases at this stage. This is the time for safety gates on stairs, closed doors to bathrooms, and so forth.

Proximodistal motor development allows children to become more agile when using their hands and arms to reach for and pick up things. Combined with **sensorimotor cognitive development** (see Table 2-2), this can lead to danger. Children who are able to pick up objects usually explore those objects by placing them in their mouths. The agile infant can get into practically any cabinet and may also be able to open containers in those cabinets. Safety latches should be used for cabinets, doors, and so forth. Any cleaning solutions or other chemical hazards should be removed to a high, locked cabinet. All electrical sockets should have safety plugs blocking inspection by curious infants.

Toddlers. Once a child has begun walking, both his skills and his ability to access dangerous situations increase. Cephalocaudal development progresses to abilities that include running and climbing. At the beginning of this stage, the balance of the toddler is somewhat unsteady. Being mobile allows the toddler different ways to look at the environment. It can also give the

REALITY *Check*

Sudden Infant Death Syndrome

Sudden infant death syndrome (SIDS) describes the sudden death of an infant younger than one year of age that cannot be explained even after thorough investigation by medical and police authorities (Stubbs-Wynn et al., 2004; American Heart Association, 2005). It is the most common case of death in infants who are four weeks or older (Hunt & Hauck, 2006). One of every 2,000 infants between the ages of 2 and 4 months dies of SIDS (Desmon, 2007). SIDS claims more child deaths between the ages of 1 month and 1 year than cancer, child maltreatment, AIDS, cystic fibrosis, muscular dystrophy, and heart diseases combined (SIDS Network, 2008). It is estimated that there are as many as 2,500 deaths per year from SIDS ("States Seek Ways," 2003). SIDS strikes without warning to children of all racial, ethnic, and economic groups. It has been found that SIDS rates are higher for American Indian and African-American infants than for white infants (National SIDS/Infant Death Resource Center [NSDRC], 2004). The hours that children are in care in early education programs or facilities are the hours when SIDS strikes most commonly (Aronson, 2003). SIDS can occur at any time of the day and it can happen relatively quickly (Blair et al., 2006). About 17 percent of deaths due to SIDS occur in nonparental child care. Of these deaths, 37 percent occurred in family child care, 18 percent occurred in a child care center, and 18 percent occurred with a nanny at home (Moon, Sprague, & Patel, 2005).

The medical community still cannot explain what causes SIDS. Speculation includes a vulnerability period early in infancy, a birth defect, stress caused by infection and/or failure to develop (SIDS Network, 2008). One new study links SIDS deaths to an inner ear abnormality in infants, (Desmon, 2007). This is an avenue of research that has not been previously explored.

Several risk factors that contribute to SIDS have been previously identified. These risk factors include:

- Sleeping on the stomach in the prone position
- Pre- and postnatal exposure to cigarette smoke
- Sleeping materials that are too soft
- The baby overheating

In October 2005, the AAP came out with additional, specific recommendations to reduce the risk of SIDS that had been supported by research (Saririan & Hauck, 2006). These new recommendations for risk reduction include:

- The infant should not share a "family bed."
- Side sleeping (putting a child to bed on its side) is no longer acceptable.
- Pacifiers should be used at nap time and bedtime for the first year of life except for a breastfeeding child, who needs to establish the breastfeeding routine. The use of a pacifier for those babies is recommended at one month.

Further studies have shown infants who shared beds with their parents were more likely to have risk for SIDS due to bedding environment and sleep position (Ostfeld et al., 2006). These two aspects are being studied internationally to see to what extent they present risk (Mitchell, 2007).

In addition, the AAP recommends that parents not use commercial devices marketed to reduce the risk of SIDS, nor count on monitors as a deterrent to SIDS (Schnitzer, 2006). The teacher can help reduce risk by offering protective measures for the majority of these risks.

A major discovery has revolutionized how parents, teachers, and other caregivers should put babies down to sleep. Studies in Europe in the 1980s found that babies who were put to sleep on their stomachs in the prone position, were twice as likely to die from SIDS as children placed on their sides. Since 1992, the AAP has recommended that all babies be put down to sleep on their backs or sides and not on their stomachs. More recently, it has been found that children placed on their sides are likely to roll onto their stomachs, thus increasing risk, so the AAP removed their suggestion to place babies on their sides (AAP, 2005a). It was also found that the combination of

(continues)

REALITY *Check* (continued)

infection and being put to sleep on their sides greatly increases the risk.

Today, only 24 percent of American infants sleep on their stomachs, compared with 70 percent in 1992. This change alone has contributed to as much as a 48 percent reduction in SIDS deaths (Mitchell, Hutchison, & Stewart, 2007). This reduction applies to full-term and preterm babies, as well as low birth weight babies. It is hoped that not putting babies on their sides will further decrease risk and contribute to a reduction in numbers of deaths due to SIDS.

Despite this success, it has been found that people in early childhood education centers continue to place infants in the prone position. It is estimated that 20 to 25 percent of early childhood education centers continue to place infants on their stomach (Moon & Oden, 2003). One reason cited for the discrepancy was that as many as 43 percent of teachers were unaware of the relationship between prone sleep and SIDS. To help ameliorate this discrepancy, the Healthy Child Care America "Back to Sleep" campaign was launched in 2003 (NSDRC, 2004). Another reason cited for why many teachers did not put children to sleep on their backs is that they believed it was more likely to increase illness, cause trouble sleeping, or cause choking problems if infants vomited while on their backs. These excuses have been proved wrong (Aronson, 2003). It has been found that infants who are placed on their backs for sleeping until the age of 6 months actually have fewer reports of illness or doctor's visits. Since the Back to Sleep campaign began, many states have changed regulations about putting children to sleep on their backs and about restricting soft bedding in cribs (Moon, Kotche, & Aird, 2006). However, there are still some states that have no regulations for these recommendations.

Cigarette smoke is considered to be the second greatest risk factor for SIDS. It is believed that this risk factor may account for 20 to 40 percent of SIDS cases (DiFranza & Lew, 1995). An infant exposed to cigarette smoke may be at 200 percent increased risk for SIDS (Wisborg et al., 2000). If babies are also exposed in utero, they are three times more likely to die of SIDS (Anderson & Cook, 1998). In some places there are increases in rates of women smoking during pregnancy. Exposure to smoke may lead to a complex range of effects upon anatomical and physiological development both in the fetus and in postnatal life (Fleming & Blair, 2007). Smoking is still not prohibited in 15.6 percent of early childhood education care centers in 45 states (Moon, Weese-Mayer, & Silvestri, 2003). An interesting study has found that in areas where cigarettes are priced higher and indoor smoking is prohibited, the number of SIDS-related cases goes down (Markowitz, 2008). This study recommended that stronger restrictions be put on smoking in child care environments.

Babies should sleep on firm, flat mattresses to lessen the risk of entrapment or heavy covering (Saririan & Hauck, 2006). Parents, teachers, and other caregivers should avoid placing infants on beanbags, sheepskins, synthetic pillow and foam pads, either alone or covered with a comforter. All stuffed animals should be removed from the crib or sleeping area (Schnitzer, 2006).

Overheating is another important factor. Too much bedding, clothing that is too heavy, and an environment that is too warm can contribute to SIDS (Saririan & Hauck, 2006). Overheating may occur when babies have a cold and efforts are made to keep them warm. Babies who are overheated exhibit sweating, damp hair, heat rash, rapid breathing, and fever. It is recommended that the indoor temperature be kept at 70 degrees Fahrenheit or less (SIDS Network, 2008).

Several recent studies have found that bed sharing increases risk in infants under 11 weeks of age (Tappin, Ecob, & Brooke, 2005; Ostfeld et al., 2006). This risk is increased if there are multiple bed sharers, a smoker who shares the bed, or a bed sharer that has had alcohol before going to bed. Room sharing, without being in the same bed, has appeared to reduce risk because of the proximity (AAP, 2005b; Saririan & Hauck, 2006). Further studies of bed sharing indicate that infants who shared beds with their parents were more likely to be at risk for SIDS due to bedding environment and sleep position (Ostfeld et al., 2006).

(continues)

REALITY *Check* (continued)

Another factor that appears to reduce risk is the use of a pacifier (Arnestad et al., 2001; AAP, 2005a). The use of a pacifier during nap time and bedtime is recommended after one month in breast-fed babies and from birth for bottle-fed babies. The use of a pacifier has been further studied, and there is good evidence that this lessens risk for SIDS, but the mechanism as to why it does still remains unknown (Mitchell, Blair, & L'Hoir, 2006). To further reduce risk, the AAP also recommends checking for foreign objects by sweeping the child's mouth with clean hands when placing a child to sleep. Pacifier use and bed sharing are being studied internationally to see to what extent they prevent risk (Mitchell, 2007). Research has also shown that SIDS cases are more likely to be reported in the fall and winter than at any other time of year and that boys are more likely to die of SIDS than are girls (NSDRC, 2004). A more recent suspected factor has been dispelled. The relationship between multiple doses of vaccines and SIDS was investigated, and the conclusion was that the evidence was insufficient to link the two (Stratton et al., 2003; Mitchell, 2007). The use of preventive measures can reduce risk, but nothing can guarantee that SIDS will not strike. Parents and teachers should remember this. A SIDS death disrupts the sense of normalcy and security regardless of where it occurs.

CHECK*point:* **What are the four most protective factors for preventing SIDS in early childhood education environments? How would you pass this information on to parents?**

toddler the ability to overcome obstacles that may have previously prevented action.

Proximodistal development leads to greater manipulative abilities. Sensorimotor development presents cognitive abilities in children that will challenge any teacher to keep one step ahead. Children at this stage are perhaps most at risk for dangerous situations. Piaget referred to this time as the "little scientist" stage. Children are exploring and trying to master their environments, but they do not have the cognitive abilities to understand cause and effect. This can be a deadly combination.

Children in the toddler stage must be supervised very closely. Their physical abilities and cognitive limitations will have them performing dangerous acts, so they must be carefully watched. All physical and environmental hazards must be examined. Safety devices should be in place, and all hazards that can be removed should be.

- **preoperational stage** *second stage of cognitive development, in which logic is limited.*

Preschoolers. Preschool children have mastered most of their gross and fine motor skills. They are capable of most physical tasks. Cognitive abilities of children of this age have also developed. They are in the **preoperational stage** (Table 2-3), which offers some limitations in their thought processes. These limitations cause preschool children to see the world from their point of view. Children of this age may not perceive risk when it is present. For example, a 4-year-old may be certain that she can climb to the top of playground equipment, jump off it, and land on the ground without getting hurt because she saw her favorite cartoon character do this very thing. Risk-taking behavior may be dependent on a number of factors such as gender, socioeconomic status, and ethnicity (Schwebel & Gaines, 2007). This is one

TABLE 2-3
Limitations of the Preoperational Stage

Limitation	Meaning
Egocentrism	World is centered around "me." Nothing else exists. Sharing is hard. All toys seem to be "mine."
Centration	Child focuses only on one aspect of a situation or object. Child sees a toy and heads for it, regardless of what is in the way.
Fantasy	Children love to make-believe and role-play.
Irreversibility	Inability to reverse a situation or an action. Difficult for child to retrace steps of thoughts or action.
Animism	Everything is "alive" and all objects are capable of human feelings or actions.
Transductive Reasoning	Children cannot relate general to specific or a part to the whole. They only relate specific to specific. For example, if Sparky, the dog, is friendly, any dog that is encountered is friendly.

reason that supervision is important at this stage also, even though it may appear children need less supervision than they previously did.

The preschooler age group responds well to role modeling and education. They are less likely to need safety devices such as stair gates and plastic plugs in electrical sockets because they understand the perceived risk from these items. Preschool children can be trained to understand many of the risks in their environment. They will need good, constant monitoring, but perhaps not at the intense level of the older infant and toddler.

School Age. School-aged children are at far less risk for safety because they have cognitive abilities that can help keep them out of danger. Children of this age are at the **concrete operational stage** of cognitive development and have the ability to understand most situations that involve safety risks or hazards. Children of this age like to test their abilities to perform. Accidents and injuries involving this age group are often from sports activities such as bicycling, skating, or organized sports such as soccer and baseball. Another area of concern for this age group is the curiosity about firearms. Guns are objects that provide great risk to children of any age, but this age group is more likely to be able to access them (Jackman et al., 2001).

- **concrete operational stage** *third stage of cognitive development in which logical ideas can be applied to concrete or specific situations.*

School-aged children respond well to education and role modeling. The issue of firearms and the risk they pose should be discussed with these children (Eller, 1998). School-aged children can be excellent examples when they role model safety to other children. Although school-aged children need some monitoring, they can also be their own monitors for safety if they are armed with safety knowledge.

Multiage Groups. If the children in an early childhood education program are of varying ages and thus different developmental levels, the teacher will need to take a different approach when planning for safety in the environment. If the environment must be designed for multiage groups, then it should be modified as closely as possible to fit the youngest child's developmental abilities. This may cause some frustration for older children, but safety issues must come first. Role modeling and talking with the older children about the need for safety can help buffer their frustration and lead to greater understanding. Depending on their ages, older children may even help the teacher monitor the potential risks in the early childhood education environment and observe unsafe behaviors that younger children exhibit.

The Community Surrounding the Early Childhood Education Environment

The safety of the children in early childhood education environments can no longer be taken for granted. It is wrong to consider the environment of early childhood education as only the premises and the surrounding yard or outdoor play area. Early childhood education takes place in the middle of cities, in suburbs, and in rural areas. The holistic approach for child care safety must consider the community area that surrounds the site (Earls & Buka, 2000). No matter where the early childhood education takes place, there are safety hazards, conditions, and behaviors that may affect the situation. In a national survey on the health and well-being of children in the United States, it was found that in about 13 percent of cases neighborhoods are only sometimes safe, and in 3 percent of cases neighborhoods were found to be totally unsafe (USDHHS, 2006).

It is the teacher's responsibility to be aware of the safety aspects or **liabilities** of the area surrounding the premises. In some inner-city areas, violence may be a liability; in other areas, traffic may be the key liability. Rural and suburban areas may be isolated, and distance may be a liability in case of an emergency. Rural areas may be more likely to have hazards such as animals.

- **liabilities** *safety risks or hazards.*

It is the teacher's responsibility to understand the risks and liabilities of the surrounding neighborhood. The children should be taught safety and prevention strategies that apply to the surrounding community. The promotion of safety should not end at the door of the early childhood education environment. It is important for teachers to assist families by providing information that can help keep children safe from harm while at home.

Wadsworth/Cengage Learning

In addition to violence and traffic, discarded drug paraphernalia may be a potential hazard and liability for providers using inner city public playgrounds with their children.

The Child's Family Environment

A child's family environment may affect the early childhood education environment. If the child's home environment is safe and secure, the child trusts that the teacher's is also. A child who is free to explore and master a safe environment at home will also explore the early childhood education environment. It is essential that the teacher teach the child the rules and limitations that will help keep the child safe while in the early childhood education environment.

A child who comes from an environment that is less safe and secure will also need consideration. As previously discussed in Bronfenbrenner's bioecological model on page 7, experiences that a child has at home can affect the child care environment (Schwebel & Brezausek, 2007). Low income or poverty can affect the home environment. Abraham Maslow (1968) tried to explain basic human needs to help us understand why people act as they do. He came up with five levels of need (see Figure 2-3). The first level is physiological needs, which include shelter, food, and clothing. The second level of needs involves safety and security. The third level is the need for love and the feeling of belonging. The fourth level involves a human being's desire for self-esteem. And finally, at the fifth level is the need for self-actualization, which a person reaches upon achieving his or her potential. If a lower need is not met, it is difficult to go beyond that need. For example, if a family is poor, the parents may try to meet the basic needs of the first level and may not have the time or energy to think much about safety and security as an important issue. Ninety percent of Native American children, one-half of African-American children, one-third of Hispanic-American children and one-fifth of Caucasian (white) children live in poverty. These children are at increased risk for injury due to their hazardous environments (National SAFE KIDS Campaign [NSKC], 2007). Forty percent of homeless people in the United States today are children (NMHA, 2005). Because of their poverty and homelessness, the basic needs of these children for safety and security may be almost completely unfulfilled, and their environments may challenge their first-level needs. Families with children represent the fastest growing segment of the homeless population.

The number of children living in poverty is significant considering the safety risks that may be present. Children from low-income families may require help understanding the need for safety and protective measures. In this case, role modeling and safety promotion will be important tools. Some of these children may also be unfamiliar with a secure environment that allows them to explore and develop a sense of independence. These children

FIGURE 2-3
According to Maslow's Hierarchy of Human Needs, a person's needs for such basics as food, shelter, and clothing must be met before higher-level needs can be addressed.

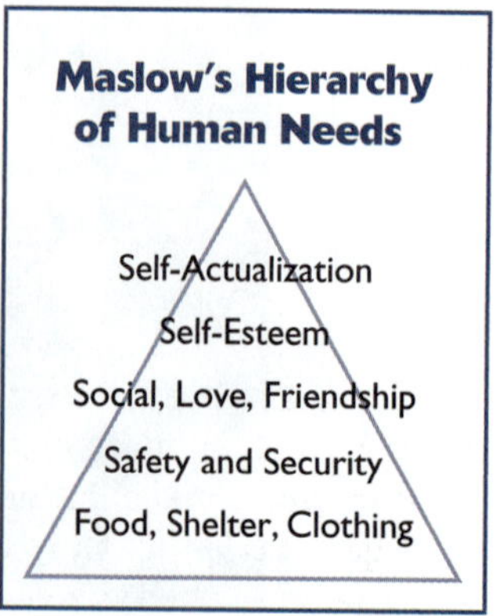

Children living in poverty situations may be unaware of the potential safety and health risks their environment presents.

Wadsworth/Cengage Learning

will need a predictable, supportive environment so that they can develop a sense of trust.

Violence and child maltreatment are also safety risks that can occur in the home environment of some children.

Key Concept 2.2

Creating a Safe Environment

Creating a safe environment by using safe practices allows the teacher to provide a sense of security and protection from harm so that children are free to develop, learn, and grow. Developing safety policies should directly relate to the type of early childhood education that is being provided. Understanding the developmental needs, capabilities, and limitations resulting from the age of children in care helps the teacher to lay a foundation of safety and protection. Knowing about the community and the family will enable the teacher to more adequately prepare the safest environment possible for the children in the early childhood education environment.

2.3 MANAGEMENT FOR INJURY PREVENTION

A safe environment for a child is one that provides freedom from harm and offers a sense of security in which to play, develop, and learn. The teacher is responsible for providing this type of environment for the children in care. A major goal for a teacher is to manage the early childhood education environment for injury prevention. Injury prevention promotes safety, protects the child, and minimizes risk. Injury prevention also offers a plan to manage injuries as they occur, with the least distress to everyone concerned. The early childhood education environment should be prepared for reducing

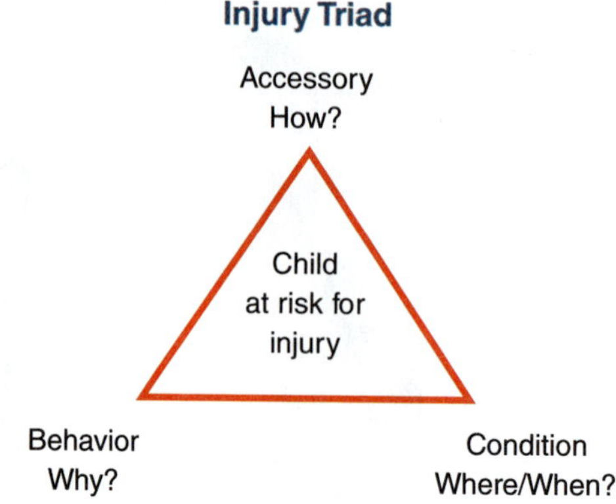

FIGURE 2-4
The injury triad is used to understand the circumstances surrounding an injury and to help prevent future injuries.

risk, protecting children from harm, and planning for occurrence of injury. Injury prevention offers children the sense of safety and security they need to develop to the fullest potential.

ABCs of Childhood Injuries

Every accident has a cause. Accidental injuries generally occur when a risk is taken or a hazard is present in the environment. To avoid unintentional injuries, causal factors must be understood and anticipated.

The injury triad is a valuable tool for injury prevention (Figure 2-4). When an injury occurs, certain questions can be asked to understand the circumstances.

- What type of injury occurred?
- How did the injury happen?
- Why did the injury occur?
- Where did the injury occur?
- When did the injury happen?

As these questions are explored, a clearer picture may form as to what could have been done to prevent the injury to the child. Table 2-4 provides common factors for childhood injury.

TABLE 2-4
The ABCs of Injury Risk to Children

A	=	**Accessory = How**
		Physical and environmental hazards
		Lack of safety devices
B	=	**Behavior = Why**
		By Child:
		Developmental level
		Mastery/Exploration
		Don't know/understand

(continues)

TABLE 2-4 *(Continued)*
The ABCs of Injury Risk to Children

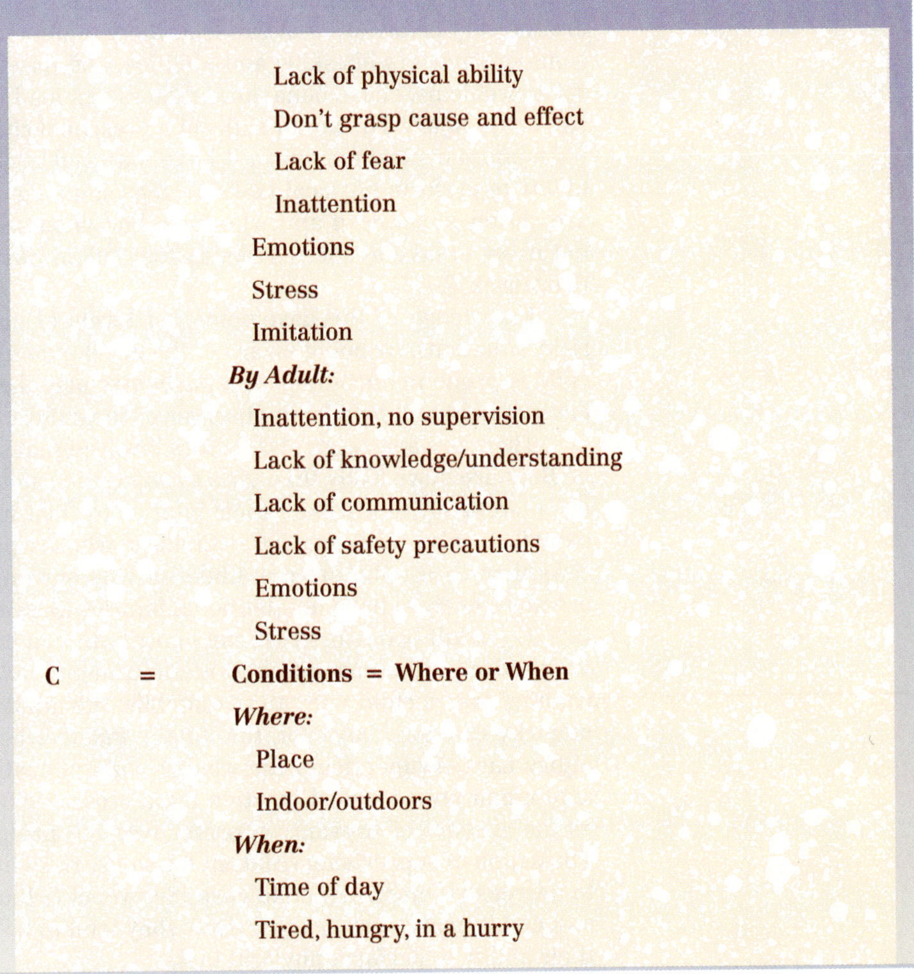

		Lack of physical ability
		Don't grasp cause and effect
		Lack of fear
		Inattention
		Emotions
		Stress
		Imitation
		By Adult:
		Inattention, no supervision
		Lack of knowledge/understanding
		Lack of communication
		Lack of safety precautions
		Emotions
		Stress
C	=	**Conditions = Where or When**
		Where:
		Place
		Indoor/outdoors
		When:
		Time of day
		Tired, hungry, in a hurry

Accessories. Accessories that are involved in injuries include physical and environmental hazards and lack of safety devices. Accessories help explain how the injury happened. An accessory is a known factor. A physical hazard could be an object such as a penny on the floor, a cleaning solution stored under a sink, or a piece of equipment such as a jungle gym. Environmental hazards might include a swimming pool or traffic around the early childhood education environment. Lack of safety devices might include an open electrical outlet without a plug cap or a car without a proper safety seat.

The most effective risk management tool to remove accessories as a risk factor in the injury triad is to use preventive and protective strategies and practices. Because accessories are known factors, the teacher can modify the environment to remove risk caused by them. Modifications might include moving cleaning solutions to a high, locked cabinet, placing safety impact materials around a jungle gym, or installing electrical outlet plug covers. These environmental modification strategies help to prevent and control injury.

Behavior. Either through action or inaction, behaviors can lead to an injury. Behavior is also the leading cause of injury. Action of a child is the most common behavior in the injury triad. The majority of behaviors children display are related to their developmental level (Bredekamp & Copple, 1997). The common developmental tasks children perform as they go from stage to stage are the very behaviors that can lead them to injury. A child explores his environment, masters his skills and abilities, and uses his cognitive processes to solve problems. These behavioral factors can lead a child into situations that can cause injury. The motor skills of a preschool child may be developing, but his impulse control may not yet have matured. A child may overestimate his ability to perform physical tasks such as stepping or reaching. Children who are closely supervised and who have had good safety modeled to them are not likely to take as many risks as they might have previously (Schwebel & Brezausek, 2007).

Knowledge of the developmental levels of children can help alleviate risky situations. By being aware of the developmental stages and situations a child is prone to encounter at a particular age, the teacher can monitor the environment and be a keen observer of the child.

There are also other risk factors involved that a teacher should be aware of. Boys are more likely than girls to engage in safety risk behaviors, and they are more likely to attribute their injuries to "bad luck" instead of poor judgment (Schwebel & Barton, 2005). Children who are poor are more likely to take risks than those who are not. Children who are impulsive in their behaviors are more likely to have unintentional injuries (Schwebel & Gaines, 2007).

The adult behaviors that can contribute to a child's injury can be active or inactive. In the case of child maltreatment, violence, or an accident like running over a child with an automobile, the adult behavior is active. In the majority of cases, however, the adult's inactive behavior contributes to an injury. Lack of supervision, knowledge, communication, and understanding of a situation are causes of inaction (Shallcross, 1999). Inaction presents itself as the absence of preventive, protective, and promotional safety measures. The action of supervising children for safety risks has been positively related to decreased injuries in child care (Schwebel & Barton, 2005). When impulsive children are closely supervised, they tend to be more cautious in judging their ability to perform physical tasks.

Inaction on the part of the teacher can lead to a legal term called negligence. The general standard used by courts in the United States requires that a person use prudent, reasonable behavior (Crosser, 2007). This assumes that a teacher will perform the assigned duties of supervision for whatever activity for which supervision is necessary, in close proximity and with the children in clear view. If a risky situation should occur, the teacher should do whatever is reasonable to try and prevent the injury from happening. Therefore, the younger the children in the environment, the more close supervision is required. Activities for children should be developmentally appropriate and not present risk in and of themselves (Crosser, 2007).

The same risk management tools for children's safety also apply to adult behaviors. A full knowledge of safety practices through education is critical to provide the necessary supervision for a safe and secure environment for children (Aronson, 2001; Schwebel & Brezausek, 2007). Teachers should also be aware of how stress and emotions can affect the care they give to children. Through education, promotion, and good role modeling, teachers can help children learn more safe practices. The teacher should be practical and use good judgment. These risk management tools may also lead children to an earlier understanding of cause and effect and provide them with preventive strategies to protect them from harm in dangerous situations. Using education, role modeling, and communication, the teacher can also help parents lay the foundation for a safer, more secure environment in the home.

- **condition** *circumstance or situation in which safety is at risk.*

Condition. The **condition** factor of the injury triad indicates the circumstances around an injury. Questions as to when and where the injury took place are answered as conditions are explored (Smith, 2001). The place, time, and situation in which an injury takes place may have contributed to the injury. Injuries take place in early childhood education environments, in homes, on playgrounds, and in many other places.

Certain types of injuries are more likely to happen in certain places (Figure 2-5). For example, falls from equipment such as climbing structures are more likely to occur on playgrounds or in early childhood education environments than in a home environment because this type of equipment is more likely to be found at a center than in a private home. A child is more likely to have a bicycle accident in the street than on a sidewalk because streets have automobile traffic as well as pedestrians, whereas only pedestrians are on sidewalks. Certain types of injuries are more likely to happen indoors, and others more commonly occur outdoors.

Time can be a critical factor contributing to injury. Children are more likely to be injured in the late morning or late afternoon, when they are tired. Children who have had less sleep the night before are more likely to be injured than those who had a good night's sleep. (Valent, Brusaferro, & Barbone, 2001).

FIGURE 2-5
Pie chart with common conditions for childhood accidents.

If a child or adult is in a hurry, an injury is more likely to occur. A shift in environment or routine can present distractions or conflicts that are stressful and may lead to accidents. Developing an awareness that certain conditions in the early childhood education environment contribute to injury can help the teacher be more alert when those conditions are present. The teacher should keep an open line of communication with parents to obtain and pass along any information that could affect how a child might act in relation to safety risk.

Table 2-5 applies the causal factors from the injury triad to specific situations that may be found in early childhood education environments.

TABLE 2-5
Factors in Childhood Injury

Who = Children of all developmental stages and ages

What	How	Why	Where	When
Motor vehicle accident	Lack of seat belt or safety seat Inattention of driver	Inattention to importance of using safety device	In automobile	Any time
Riding bicycle near cars	Darting in front of car	Inattention Doesn't grasp cause/effect Lack of fear In a hurry	Near home, school, neighborhood	Any time Unsupervised
Fall	Unsafe equipment Mastery Exploration	Lack of safety knowledge Lack of ability Doesn't grasp cause/effect Imitation	Outdoor playgrounds Indoor climbing	Late morning Late afternoon Unsupervised Tired
Collision with objects	Mastery Exploration	Hazards in environment Lack of ability Doesn't grasp cause/effect In a hurry Imitation	Anywhere	Any time Tired Unsupervised
Poisoning	Exploration Mastery	Hazards in environment Doesn't grasp cause/effect Imitation Inability to read	Kitchen, bathroom, bedroom, garage, living room, yard	Unsupervised Any time

(continues)

TABLE 2-5 *(Continued)*
Factors in Childhood Injury

Who = Children of all developmental stages and ages

What	How	Why	Where	When
Choking	Exploration	Hazards in environment Doesn't grasp cause/effect	Anywhere	Unsupervised Any time
Burns	Lack of safety devices Mastery Exploration	No smoke detector Water too hot Doesn't grasp cause/effect Imitation Access to fire device	Anywhere Bathroom Kitchen	Unsupervised Any time
Drowning	Exploration Mastery	Lack of ability Imitation Lack of safety precautions Doesn't grasp cause/effect Hazards in environment	Bathtub Pool Any body of water	Unsupervised Any time
Child Maltreatment	Parent Someone child knows Stranger	Repeat of cycle of abuse Poverty Dysfunction	Anywhere	Any time Under stress
Violence	Lack of safety precautions Firearms available	Guns and other hazards Inattention to safety	Neighborhood Home School	Any time Unsupervised

Rodney was a teacher for 2-year-olds at an inner-city day-care center. The 2-year-olds shared a large room with the 3-year-olds and often played together during free time. Rodney was well aware of the differences between his children and those in the older group. He carefully monitored the free playtime. One morning he stopped Joshua from putting a small toy part in his mouth. Kelley, a 3-year-old, had brought a small car from home. One of the wheels had fallen off, and Joshua picked it up and attempted to put it in his mouth. Although Rodney had no choice about his group playing with the older children and their toys, he was careful in what he watched for, because he knew the developmental level limitations of his two-year-olds.

Wadsworth/Cengage Learning

Regardless of the cause, when an injury occurs it must be taken care of properly by a teacher or nurse.

When Injury Does Occur

Even in the safest environments, injuries do happen. How the teacher handles the injury can contribute to keeping the early childhood education environment as secure as possible. Careful planning prepares the teacher to handle accidents and injuries as they occur with as little stress as possible. This can help reinforce the trust of the children present in an early childhood education environment. Safety policies should include injury response methods and practices to help provide good injury management. Some subjects for these policies are covered in Chapter 5 on page 167.

Key Concept 2.3

Injury Prevention Management

Injury prevention is a major responsibility of the teacher. To prevent injury and protect children, the teacher must first understand how injuries occur. A teacher who understands how accessories, behaviors, and conditions contribute to injury will have the ability to anticipate injury. Monitoring the children and modifying the environment allows the teacher to prevent injury and promote safety.

2.4 CONSTRUCTING A SAFETY PLAN FOR EARLY CHILDHOOD EDUCATION ENVIRONMENTS

The safety policy designed for each type of early childhood education environment includes the construction of a safety plan. This plan prevents risk and promotes safety. It consists of the guidelines the teacher develops to promote safety in the early childhood education environment (Aronson, 2002). The guidelines address the areas in which risks are anticipated, and the environment is modified and monitored for safety. These applications lessen risks due to accessories, behaviors, and conditions.

Anticipation

The anticipation process begins with a room-by-room indoor inspection and an overall outdoor inspection for safety with checklists that the teacher creates for that particular early childhood education environment. These checklists apply to the type of early childhood education environment, child care, the ages of the children in care, the surrounding community, and the family environments the children represent.

Teachers should search for the accessories, behaviors, and conditions that affect injury prevention. The teacher should anticipate these factors based on both the cognitive and the motor skills developmental levels of the children who are present in the early childhood education environment. Seeing the environment room by room from a child's eye view helps the teacher to identify risks that an adult-only point of view might miss.

The next step is to anticipate the behaviors leading to injury that might occur in the teacher's type of early childhood education environment. To best meet the needs of the children, the teacher must consider the factors of age, community, and family. Knowledge of behaviors that contribute to injury helps the teacher prepare to promote safety through education and good role modeling. Children who learn safe practices and preventive strategies are less at risk for behavior factors that contribute to injury. A program called the "Stamp-in-Safety" intervention program has been created to help early education environments reduce behavioral risks for playground injury because it has been proven that this type of preventive strategy works well (Schwebel et al., 2006).

Conditions that contribute to injury must be anticipated next. Creating a plan for safety and carefully observing children during times when they are more likely to be injured will help to reduce the possibility of injury. The teacher who understands the common conditions and times associated with injuries will be especially alert when faced with those circumstances.

Children who come to early childhood education from conditions that place them at greater risk for injury can especially benefit from efforts to help them understand safety and prevention. Children need a supportive and caring environment in which they can explore yet be protected from harm. Children from at-risk environments may not feel this protection at home. Children in violence-prone neighborhoods may feel especially vulnerable. For these children, the early childhood education environment or school may serve as a safe haven. Giving these children tools of safe practices and a sense of security in the early childhood education environment may help them to be more resilient in their home environments (Levin, 2003b; Schwebel & Brezausek, 2007) and more alert in their community environment.

Communicating with parents about conditions such as stress that contribute to injury may help them avoid situations that can lead to injury. Providing literature or newsletters with reminders on injury prevention may help lessen risk at home. Role modeling for safety under stressful conditions delivers the message to the parent that injury can be prevented and that a safer environment can be created for children.

Modifications

Carefully screening the environment for hazards, removing the hazards, and placing safety devices where needed are simple tasks that a teacher can

REALITY*Check*

Bullying in the Early Childhood Education Environment

Bullying and its effects on children have been a topic of discussion since the shootings at Columbine High School in 1999; Santana High School in 2001; Red Lake High School in 2005; and at Virginia Tech, a university, in 2007. These shootings that ended in the deaths of other students have made educators take a better look at the causal factors involved. One major conclusion has been that bullying and the victimization that occurs as a result of bullying were contributing factors. It is estimated that 10 percent of children are bullied on an ongoing basis, and 50 percent of children have the experience of being bullied at some point during their school years (Huston, 2003). Bullying is considered a major public health and safety issue. Bullying can be defined as ongoing physical or verbal abuse or persecution between two or more people where the power is unequal (Olweus, Limber, & Mihalic, 1999). Basically, bullies abuse their power by teasing and taunting others (Walls, 2004). Bullying can be very serious and can affect the physical health, mental well-being, and learning of young children who become victims (StopBullyingNow, 2007). A child does not have to be a direct victim to feel threatened. Just observing bullying can upset young children.

Bullying doesn't begin in high school, nor does it necessarily have its roots in elementary school. Bullying can begin as early as toddlerhood. Young children may push others, bite, grab toys away, or make up rules so that they are in charge (Ucci, 2004). Some of us might think of the character "Angelica" on the Nickelodeon cartoon *Rugrats*. She constantly takes advantage of the power she has as the oldest child in the group.

Very young children whose parents have difficulty in social experiences and are coercive or verbally abusive may have little positive reinforcement or social skills in their lives (Goleman, 1995). Some children who bully may be victims themselves or may have watched intimate partner violence (Bauer et al., 2006). Parental involvement and warmth may not be present (Huston, 2003). Another reason for bullying in young children is that parents may not set limits or clear expectations for behavior, and any behavior on the part of the child may appear to be acceptable to the parent. Children may also be overwhelmed in their lives by a loss or change, such as the divorce of their parents or a move from familiar surroundings. Young children who bully may also have higher levels of depression, anger, and impulsivity (Garakani, 2006; Clock, 2007). In addition, a recent study found that preschoolers who watch 3½ hours of television per day are 30 percent more likely to exhibit bullying behaviors than children who watch no television (Zimmerman et al., 2005).

One way a child can feel better is to display her anger at her circumstances and find someone who is less powerful, so as to feel powerful in that child's presence (Walls, 2004). Bullying behavior is apt to attract attention, and a child may feel more important when attention is paid to her. This type of showing off may get the child exactly what she wants. In addition, a scared, insecure, or angry child may also feel more powerful when she is being abusive to other children (North Carolina Child Care Health and Safety Resource Center [NCCCHSRC], 2004). In an elementary school situation, older children may tend to bully younger children.

Some gender differences are evident in bullying. Boys are far more likely to bully, and their victims are more likely to be boys than girls. Boys are likely to use both direct physical and verbal bullying and an indirect, relational form of bullying. Girls are less likely to engage in physical bullying and much more likely to engage in relational bullying toward another girl, such as gossiping about her, slandering her, or engaging in actions to exclude her from her social peer group (Smith & Myron-Wilson, 1998; Townsend-Butterworth, 2007). This can begin at a very young age.

Victims tend to be the more vulnerable children in the group (Bosch, 2003; Perren & Alsaker, 2006). They may be sensitive or quiet, or they may stand out in some way, such as having a disability or being a child with special needs. Children who are annoying or appear to be occasionally aggressive due to lack of social skills might also be targeted as victims. Another

(continues)

REALITY *Check* (continued)

reason for victimization in preschool is that the bully is jealous of the child or children targeted. In general, those who are targeted as victims may be those less likely or able to defend themselves in this type of situation (Huston, 2003). Children who are being bullied often say that they have a stomachache or other reasons not to go to school. This is especially noteworthy if a child has previously enjoyed school.

Bullying can begin as early as preschool, and teachers who work in early childhood education environments must anticipate bullying actions and monitor and modify those behaviors immediately. Sixty percent of states and 95 percent of school districts have a policy against bullying. Many elementary school teachers may have an anti-bullying or peacemaking program in place that they can rely on for help. Adults sometimes underestimate the importance of bullying, but it is a matter of great significance for children, parents, and teachers. Teachers can watch for early signs of bullying and being bullied in the environment. If there is unacceptable behavior, it is important for teachers to intervene so that this type of behavior stops before the problem escalates (parenting.org, 2005; Garakani, 2006). They must set behavior limits and ensure that there are consequences for unacceptable behavior. Teachers can create an early childhood education environment that is safe and developmentally appropriate (Ucci, 2004). Adults can be role models for positive, warm relations and can help children by mediating disputes at any age. Teachers can also take opportunities for talking about bullying, giving children an opportunity to discuss it and sharing the ideas of empathy, compassion, and caring (Holland, 2006).

CHECK*point*: What are some of the reasons a child may become a bully at a young age? Name three preventive measures that a teacher might take when faced with bullying behavior.

Rechelle, the teacher, knew that Cedric had always been a little aggressive in his play. But lately she had noticed that this generally happy child had begun displaying bullying behavior to several children who were smaller than he was. Rechelle felt the first step for helping him was to talk with his mother. Crystal, Cedric's mother, explained that circumstances at home had changed. Her sister and two children, a 2-year-old girl and a 6-year-old boy, had moved in with them while her sister recovered from knee surgery. Crystal explained that the little girl was always getting into Cedric's things and that the older boy, Ethan, was jealous of Cedric and constantly taunted him. She herself was at her wit's end. Rechelle and Crystal devised some strategies to help Cedric both at home and at school. Crystal arranged to set aside some time every day for Cedric to play and talk just with her, and she spoke with her sister about Ethan's behavior. As a result, her sister enrolled Ethan in a soccer league to help him. Crystal also got several containers so she could place Cedric's special toys out of reach of the 2-year-old. Rechelle explained to Cedric that the younger, smaller children in class were not his 2-year-old cousin, and he did not have to be afraid that they would mess up his work or play with the things he was playing with. She also counseled him about not making other children feel like his cousin Ethan made him feel. Rechelle also decided to put a rocking horse that Cedric could ride hard when he felt angry or upset into a corner of the room, away from other items. In about two weeks, both Rechelle and Crystal noticed that Cedric was happier and back to being himself again. Involving Cedric's family was a key to this solution.

perform to ensure a safe and secure physical environment for children. The use of checklists can assist the teacher in this process.

Behaviors can be modified through teaching and exhibiting safe, protective, and preventive practices. The teacher's safety plan should use the most applicable and suitable models of communication for the early childhood education environment. Injury prevention can be taught at all levels, to some extent. Preschool children are more receptive and have greater capabilities than toddlers or infants. School-aged children are very receptive to safety behaviors and practices. There are several steps that the teacher can use to help children of all ages modify their behaviors to protect themselves and prevent injury. The three most important teaching tools for promoting behavior change are

- Feedback
- Modeling
- Role playing through practice drills

- **feedback** *a technique for encouraging desired behaviors in children through communication.*
- **positive reinforcement** *reward given in response to a particular behavior that increases the chance of that behavior occurring again.*
- **diversion** *something that changes the focus of attention.*

Feedback about safety can include **positive reinforcement** for good safety behavior practices, **diversion** away from unsafe situations and practices, and two-way communication about both safe and unsafe practices.

Modeling can include role modeling by the teacher; the use of safety posters and signs; and the use of videos, stories, and other modes of communicating about safety and how it is achieved.

Role playing helps prepare children to act in unsafe or dangerous situations. It is a preventative tool that allows children to be better equipped in a real emergency. Drills for fires, earthquakes, and other types of disasters are practiced on a regular basis in many early childhood education environments. Role playing is often recommended for other types of dangerous situations, such as prevention of child maltreatment, gun safety, and neighborhood safety.

Modification works well when it is applied to the factor of condition. The teachers cannot change the time of day when injuries are most likely to happen. However, they can teach children to avoid certain activities when they are tired. Teachers can also modify activities at times when children are more prone to injuries, such as making a climbing apparatus off limits during high-injury times such as late morning. The teacher might also make that a time when children gather together to relax over stories instead of playing outside. If a

Teachers can role model safe behaviors, and they can talk with the children about how to be safe in particular situations.

mixed age group is present, while younger children nap, older children might play with toys that are not appropriate for the younger children. These would be put away once the younger children awakened (Blythe-Saucier, 2000).

Role modeling and communicating about safety conditions offer children greater protection. Older children who are able to learn safety practices and understand certain conditions that can lead to injury can have a greater sense of safety and security.

Monitoring

Monitoring the physical environment of the early childhood education environment for accessories is an ongoing process. Change is a constant process. A teacher should develop an intuition for the changes, but the monitoring process should be formalized. The use of checklists allows the teacher to evaluate changes and check for hazards.

Monitoring the early childhood education environment for behaviors includes observing whether safety practices have changed. This involves keeping track of whether injuries have decreased or increased and examining the behaviors present in the environment. Regularly scheduled weekly examination of injury reports is a good idea because it helps the teacher to recall any incidence of lack of safety precautions in the environment while they are still fresh in mind. The early childhood education environment should be reviewed for changes on a monthly basis. Changes can occur with the arrival of new children, in the developmental levels of the children in care, in the community, or in family situations. Monitoring helps the teacher to manage change by once again anticipating and modifying the environment.

Careful observation and supervision under conditions that lead to injury is the foremost activity of monitoring. Mishaps can be prevented through observation. Ongoing evaluation for conditions that lead to injury will help identify changes. Use of monitoring tools such as convex mirrors on corners to increase visibility and baby monitors to listen for safety might lessen risk (Aronson, 2001). If changes in conditions occur, this type of evaluation can lead to early intervention to prevent injury and protect the child. Evaluation of conditions is accomplished through observation, active listening, and communication.

Key Concept 2.4

Constructing a Safety Plan for Early Childhood Education Environments

Constructing a safety plan for early childhood education environments is a process that involves anticipation, modification, and monitoring. The three-step process considers the accessories, the behaviors, and the conditions that lead to injury or lack of safety and protection of the children in care. Some of the tools for the process include checklists, feedback, modeling, practice drills, education, and other promotional techniques. Other effective tools include careful observation, active listening, and communication.

2.5 IMPLICATIONS FOR TEACHERS

The teacher should use preventive and protective measures to prepare and maintain a safe early childhood education environment. The risk-management tools that will help the teacher to provide a good measure of safety include role modeling, education, observation, and supervision.

Role Modeling

Children like to imitate the adults in their lives. Teachers who role model good safety practices and create a safe, secure environment can influence safety and protect children from harm.

A safety policy for role modeling should reflect those behaviors the teacher wishes to instill in the children. Some of the knowledge and practices the children should be able to observe the teacher role model are listed in Table 2-6.

Education

Safety education should involve the teacher, the children, and the parents. To provide safety in the early childhood education environment, the teacher must be aware of strategies and methods to reduce risk (Aronson, 2001). The teacher must develop a keen awareness of the risks posed by the accessories, behaviors, and conditions of the particular early childhood education environment.

Children can learn safe practices as they watch the teacher model safe practices and behaviors. The teacher can talk to the children about safety and share books and videos that promote safety and safe behaviors.

Educational materials provided for the parents can help them understand the importance of safe practices and behaviors for children in all environments. A parent who is aware of conditions or behaviors that may put

TABLE 2-6
Role Modeling Behaviors for Safety

- Verbalizing safety actions to the children
- Teacher safety actions in the early childhood education and community environments
- Presence of safety devices such as smoke alarms and electrical outlet plugs
- Teacher being attuned to unsafe conditions
- Teacher safety behaviors during practice drills and role playing
- Good teacher/parent communication level about safety measures
- Daily routines for safety checklists
- Removal of hazards to ensure a safe physical environment
- Promotion and education on safety issues and practices
- Teacher predictability and support given the importance of safety in the early childhood education environment

a child at risk for safety is able to offer an extra measure of protection and prevention.

For Families

One item that teachers could provide for families is a checklist to examine the early childhood education environment for safety. The checklist would include these points:

- For early childhood environments prior to kindergarten, the staff-to-child ratio is safe and in compliance. These ratios are available from the licensing agency in the state in which the early childhood education program is located.
- Teachers have training and continue to educate themselves about issues of safety in early childhood environments.
- There is careful supervision of all children, and teachers focus on the children, not on other adults.
- Teachers act in a way that is developmentally appropriate for the children they are with.
- Teachers avoid conflict between children and create a peaceful classroom.
- Toys are safe and developmentally appropriate.
- Extra precautions are taken in multiage environments
- All equipment is maintained for safety.
- All cleaning materials are locked away.
- Outdoor areas are safe, developmentally appropriate, and well maintained.
- Emergency numbers and an emergency exit plan are posted.
- There is an "open door" policy that welcomes parent visits. Some parents may prefer a "nanny cam" at the facility so that they can watch their children from work.
- The facility is licensed and maintains licensing standards, if applicable.

When parents have a list to check for safety in the early childhood education environment, it might cause them to think about their own home safety situation. The teacher might want to have a brief discussion about safety when handing the checklist to the parent, before the decision is made to sign the child up for the program. It is critical that parents understand the entire issue of safety that teachers are trying to provide.

Observation

A teacher can use observation to protect children from safety risks. Observing for accessories, behaviors, and conditions keeps the teacher aware of all areas of injury risk management. The teacher should watch for safety risks from hazards and equipment. He or she should observe for the need for safety devices. Behaviors of both children and adults should be observed for safe practices and risk of injury. The teacher should observe the conditions in the environment that are known to lead to risk of injury and reduction of safety.

Supervision

Using the ABCs of injury risk management helps the teacher offer the greatest degree of constant supervision in order to maintain the safest possible early childhood education environment. Supervision can also help ensure that all strategies and practices that promote safety, prevent risk, and offer protection are used.

Key Concept 2.5

Implications for Teachers

The teacher should use all tools at her disposal to help promote safety, prevent injury, and offer protection. Role modeling, education, observation, working with families, and supervision provide the practices, strategies, and methods needed to protect the children in care.

CHAPTER SUMMARY

Safety policies that manage risk and prevent injury promote and protect the safety of the early childhood education environment. Teachers should be aware of environmental hazards such as accessories, behaviors, and conditions in their particular early childhood education program. It is most important that children's developmental levels be understood and considered when addressing safety in the environment. Teachers should learn to anticipate, modify, and monitor the environment for injury prevention. Role modeling is a key to promoting safe practices. Education for both the children and the parents helps the teacher to maintain a safer environment. Supervision adds another level of safety to early childhood education programs.

TO GO BEYOND

Additional resources for this chapter can be found by visiting the book companion website at www.cengage.com/education/robertson. This supplemental material includes chapter objectives, internet exercises, reflection questions, quizzes, web links, glossary and flash cards, case studies, frequently asked questions, downloadable forms and tables, curriculum supplements, more reality checks, additional key concepts, references, and more.

Chapter Review Critical Thinking Applications

1. Discuss the interrelationship of accessories, behaviors, and conditions of safety applied to early childhood education environments.

2. Describe how the anticipation, modification, and monitoring processes occur in a typical early childhood education environment before kindergarten. Compare that to a family child care home. Compare it to an in-home care situation. Compare it to an elementary school. What are the commonalities? What are the differences? Select the five most important elements for any early childhood education situation.
3. How does developmental level affect the risks for injury? What are some common injuries in infancy? In toddlerhood? For a 4-year-old? For a 6-year-old?
4. Why is bullying a problem even with young children? How might it be different with children prior to kindergarten and kindergarteners through third-graders.

As an Individual

1. Interview a teacher in your community, preferably at an early childhood education program. Ask the person how risk and injury prevention are managed in the program. Is the teacher aware of developmental levels? How are these applied to risk management? Are any modifications made to the early childhood education environment in relation to developmental levels? How might you personally improve your own risk management in relation to early childhood education?
2. Go to a local park and observe the community surrounding the park. Would you consider this a safe environment for children? Would there be any risk to an early childhood education program or family child care home if the park were nearby? Record your observations and conclusions.
3. Go to the local elementary school district website. Is there any indication on the website about what the safety policies are for that district? If so, what are they? If not, call the school district and ask about the particular safety policies that the district has. Do you think these are adequate? Why or why not?

As a Group

1. Watch *Setting Up for Health and Safe Care,* an AAP video. What safety measures were observed? If you do not have access to this video, go as a group to an early childhood education environment and observe for safety. Discuss two indoor and two outdoor risk management measures that were promoted. Compare those measures to the measures from other groups in your class. Have the entire class select the two most important indoor and outdoor safety measures that will lessen risk in the early childhood education environment.
2. In a small group of four to five people, create a safety checklist that could be used in an early childhood education environment. Compare the lists. Select the 10 most important items.

3. Divide the class into three smaller groups. Have one group write a safety policy for indoor safety; one group, a policy for outdoor safety; and one group, a policy for SIDS. Review the policies with the whole class and make any suggested changes.
4. Survey a local early childhood education program for the diversity of its population. Estimate the largest non-English-speaking group at the site. Obtain the three safety policies that are considered most important in that program. Enlist the help of parents from that program who represent the population to help translate the three center safety policies. Present these translations to the early childhood education program.
5. Survey a local elementary school for a policy regarding bullying. Explain what you found, and if you found a policy or program, discuss it. If there was no policy for bullying, find out from the local district why not. Then create your own policy for that school district. How might this bullying policy be different for younger children?
6. As a class, discuss sudden infant death syndrome. List the major risk factors. Design a safety policy that would work for an early childhood education environment from this list.

Case Studies

1. Late on Monday morning, because of special morning activities, Luwanda and Kelly are sharing the outdoor play area with their two classes. Luwanda is the teacher for the 4-year-olds, and Kelly is the teacher for the 2-year-olds. They are good friends, and both had exciting weekends that they want to share with each other. What risks for accessories, behaviors, and conditions might an observer find in this scenario? What might Luwanda and Kelly do to reduce the potential risk?
2. Kyle is the first teacher to arrive at the church preschool on Monday morning. Since the last preschool session, the activities room that he teaches in has hosted a number of events including a quilting bee, preparation for a wedding, Sunday school, Bible study, and babysitting for attendees of the evening service. How should he proceed before the children arrive? What types of accessories might he find left in this shared space?
3. Mary Ellen is the director of an early childhood education program in the downtown area of a major city. It is a convenient site for many parents who either live or work in the local area. The center is very near to a city park and an inner-city high school. She is concerned about the safety of the neighborhood surrounding her early childhood education environment. What steps might she and her teachers take to maximize the safety of the children in care?
4. Graciella is a teacher of 4-year-olds in a state preschool. Henry is a robust 4-year-old boy who just started school a few weeks ago. It appears that he is trying to intimidate Marcus and Leon when they go out to play. Henry is trying to make up rules and coerce the

other boys into playing what he wants to play. How should Graciella handle this potential bullying? What direction should she take?

5. Reyna is a kindergarten teacher and is on a committee to help design a new playground for the site she works at. About the time the playground will be finished, several portable classrooms for a new universal preschool site will also be added. Reyna has the opportunity to have input about the safety of the younger children on the campus, including the kindergartners she teaches. What are some of the things she might point out about considerations for the younger children's safety in the construction of this new playground?

CHAPTER 3

Indoor Safety

After reading this chapter, you should be able to:

3.1 Indoor Safety Policies

Describe and discuss safety policies for indoor environments as tools for risk prevention, protection, and promotion.

3.2 Indoor Safety Guidelines

Indicate and discuss specific guidelines for making any indoor early childhood education environment free from risk and protected for safety.

3.3 Indoor Equipment Safety

Relate and discuss the safety hazards of indoor equipment in early childhood education environments.

3.4 Toy Safety

Describe and discuss the importance of safe, risk-free toys for infants, toddlers, and preschoolers.

3.5 Interpersonal Safety

Describe and discuss clear rules for consequences of behavior and appropriate methods of conflict resolution.

3.6 Poison Control

Indicate the methods and means of poison control and risk prevention in early childhood education environments.

3.7 Fire and Burn Prevention

Describe and discuss methods of fire and burn prevention in early childhood education environments.

3.8 Implications for Teachers

Indicate the need for education, observation, and supervision to maintain a safe indoor environment.

3.1 INDOOR SAFETY POLICIES

The safety risks of indoor and outdoor environments vary widely. Because the variation is so widespread, we will look at these environments separately. The indoor early childhood education environment can include many physical hazards that pose risk through choking, interpersonal violence, poisoning, burns, lead poisoning, and other means. The following factors indicate the need for policies to cover indoor safety:

- If children learn safe behaviors in child care, those behaviors can be carried back into the home (Schwebel & Brezausek, 2006).
- Two-thirds of early childhood education programs were reported as unsafe in a study conducted in 300 centers throughout the United States (Shepard, 2002; Colbert, 2007). Injury prevention strategies require actions including education and environmental modifications (Schnitzer, 2006; Jones et al., 2007).
- Toys and equipment provided for children should be checked and maintained to prevent toy-related injuries (Hood & Smith, 2005; NCCCHSRC, 2008). This is especially important due to all the toy recalls the United States has experienced (Shin, 2007; U.S. Public Interest Research Group [U.S. PIRG] Education Fund, 2007).
- Falls are the most common source of injury in the early childhood education setting (Zavitkovsky & Thompson, 2000). Children under the age of 4 are at the greatest risk for falls (NSKC, 2007).

Wadsworth/Cengage Learning

Because children may lack the capacity to judge whether an activity is safe, they must be provided with a secure, safe environment to ensure their well-being and protection.

- In 2001, 1.2 million poisonings occurred in children younger than 6 years of age. Preventing poisoning is a critical component in making early childhood education environments safe (Sutton, 2004; Zamani, 2007).
- Approximately 210,300 toy-related injuries were treated in U.S. hospital emergency rooms in 2004. Children 5 years of age and younger accounted for 72,800 of toy-related injuries in 2005, and young children choking to death accounts for more than one-half of all toy-related deaths (U.S. PIRG Education Fund, 2007).
- Sixty percent of the products used in fall zones for indoor equipment in early childhood education environments do not meet national standards (AAP, 2003a).
- Using violence to solve interpersonal problems has become common for children (Levin, 2003b).
- "Biting causes more upset feeling than any other behavior in child care" (Oku, 2002). Biting is a highly charged issue for all concerned in the early childhood environment (Ramming, Kyger, & Thompson, 2006) and can cause health risks (Conlon, 2007).
- Teachers should model the values of compassion and kindness to children for interpersonal safety skills (Moore et al., 2007; Lamm et al., 2006).

The indoor environment includes a multitude of risks. Hazards come from household items, toys, animals, stoves and other kitchen equipment, children's furniture, foods, firearms, fireplaces, paint, ceramics, medications, plants, and electrical outlets and cords, among others. Other indoor risks include unsafe teacher practices, unmonitored conditions, and children's behavior based on developmental levels, physical abilities, and emotional health. The teacher must have an awareness of all accessories, behaviors, and conditions that may lead to an accident or injury. The teacher must also be in compliance with all regulations affecting the safety in care, such as those from licensing and fire boards (Colbert, 2007). Teachers should keep up on the latest hazards to equipment and toys by checking the Consumer Product Safety Commission website at http://www.cpsc.gov/. Routine inspection and maintenance of equipment can prevent injuries (Jones et al., 2007). Many early childhood education environments are already doing their best to promote safety, and it has been noted that children in early childhood education settings are safer than at home (Schwebel, Brezausek, & Belsky, 2006). Indoor environment risk management should include the following:

1. *Indoor Early Childhood Education Environments:* understanding indoor safety practices and applications for risk management as they apply to specific early childhood education environments
2. *Indoor Equipment Safety:* practices for preventing injuries and managing safety on indoor equipment
3. *Toy Safety:* practices for preventing injuries, removing unsafe toys, and managing selection of toys for children in care
4. *Interpersonal Safety:* strategies for developing guidelines for interpersonal safety and conflict management for the children in care
5. *Poison Control:* strategies for developing guidelines for poison prevention and protection in early childhood education

6. *Fire and Burn Prevention:* educational and promotional strategies to model good fire and burn prevention behaviors and practices
7. *Implications for Teachers:* methods and practices of conducting education, supervision, observation, and use of outside resources

Key Concept 3.1

Safety Policies

Safety policies should be planned as a tool for prevention of injuries, the protection of children, and the promotion of safe practices in the early childhood education indoor environment. These policies should consider the specific environment and should be applicable to the accessories, behaviors, and conditions present indoors. Use of these policies minimizes risk to children and maximizes the early childhood education environment for safety.

3.2 INDOOR SAFETY GUIDELINES

Some hazards are common to all early childhood education environments. The most common indoor childhood accidents are related to

- Falls
- Choking
- Burns
- Drowning
- Poisoning

Screening the environment for these risks to safety should be done in an organized fashion. In 1999, the U.S. CPSC conducted a national study of safety hazards in 200 licensed early childhood education settings. They were looking for safety hazards in these product areas: cribs, soft bedding, playground surfaces, surface maintenance, window-blind cords, drawstrings in children's clothing, and recalled children's products. This investigation found that two-thirds of these settings had at least one safety hazard present. Applying the ABCs of injury risk (see Table 2-4) allows the teacher to anticipate, modify, and monitor the early childhood education environment. This chapter provides indoor safety checklists that can be used as a basis to help prepare to minimize risk.

Environmental Hazards

The great majority of children's time is spent indoors, including in early childhood education programs. Indoor screening should include environmental hazards such as secondhand smoke, lead, asbestos, chemicals, and anything else that might be a risk in the environment, even though it may not be within a child's reach. Children are more susceptible to toxins in their environments than are adults. Infants and toddlers who are low to the ground may spend more time playing on or near the floor, and if the surface has something on it, it could get into the children's mouths via toys or hands. A child's size, behaviors, and habits affect his or her risk for exposure to environmental toxins (NCCCHSRC, 2005).

Several recent studies of children's environments have shown that pesticide residues have entered the bloodstream of children through breathing and ingestion (Rose, 2006). Nearly one-third of centers who were sampled had three to four pesticide residues detected in floor wipe samples, and 38 percent of centers detected pesticide residues in soil samples (Healthy Child Care Pennsylvania, 2007b). Children are also exposed to toxins from household chemicals (Zamani, 2007). Children can consume these and other toxins when they put fingers or toys into their mouths, or these toxins can pass through children's skin or be breathed into their lungs.

It is important to keep the environment as free of these toxins as possible. All surfaces that children might come into contact with should be made of nontoxic materials. Frequent wiping of surfaces with a damp cloth and vacuuming helps to keep the environment at a decreased risk. Another way to reduce pesticide residue from reaching children is to wash all fresh fruits and vegetables that come into the environment for their consumption. Other irritants to a child's air quality environment should also be thought through. Examples of irritants may include air fresheners, plug-in fresheners, and perfumes used by teachers. All environmental hazard risks should be removed or modified wherever possible.

Ventilation. Inadequate ventilation is a safety risk that is considered an environmental hazard. Air should move sufficiently so there is no gathering of fumes, germs, or other safety risks to children. Children inhale two to three times more air than adults, so adequate ventilation is necessary (Rosenblum, 1993). APHA and AAP standards can be found in *Caring for Our Children: National Health and Safety Performance Standards: Guidelines for Out-of-Home Child Care Programs* published by the APHA. Air quality can be polluted from a number of sources including molds, secondhand smoke (see Chapter 10), and carbon monoxide (NCCCHSRC, 2005; *America's Children: Key National Indicators of Well-Being, 2007,* 2007). Cleaning air ducts is also a consideration. If the air ducts have mold, are clogged with dust, or have droppings from insects or rodents, they should be cleaned (Calder, 2006). It may be best to have this done professionally.

Carbon monoxide is a deadly gas that cannot be smelled, tasted, or seen. It is important that all gas appliances such as furnaces and water heaters be installed professionally and checked regularly. A carbon monoxide detector should be placed in each room on every level in the early childhood education environment. The symptoms of CO poisoning often are similar to the flu, with aches, nausea, and tiredness, to name a few (Cowling, 2007). If the carbon monoxide detector goes off, quickly move everyone to the outdoors if possible or to another source of fresh air. These detectors should be maintained with a regular schedule of checks and battery replacements.

Radon is another gas that can seep into buildings and get into the air. This is a radioactive, toxic gas that is odorless and colorless. The Environmental Protection Agency estimates that elevated radon levels can be found in one in every fifteen homes (Holland, 2007a). It has been recommended that early child care environments be tested for this. This can be done professionally or with a kit that should have "meets EPA requirements" on the label (Holland, 2007a). It is important for the health, safety, and well-being of children that the environment be radon free.

Pets or Animals. Pets or animals in the environment can also provide safety risks through injury, infection, and allergic reactions. The Centers for Disease Control and Prevention (CDC) has recommendations at their website Healthy Pets–Healthy People at http://www.cdc.gov/healthypets/. Their recommendations include these:

- An adult should directly supervise children younger than 5 years while they are interacting with animals.
- Children under the age of 5 years should avoid contact with the following animals *and their habitats:* reptiles, amphibians, and poultry. This includes lizards, snakes, turtles, frogs, baby chicks, and ducklings.
- If the elementary school classroom has a science project with eggs hatching, the children should be carefully monitored when holding baby chicks, and should wash their hands properly and thoroughly afterward.
- Children should not be allowed to kiss pets or put their hands or other objects in their mouths if they have handled an animal. They should always properly wash their hands afterward.
- Children must wash their hands thoroughly (see Chapter 12, page 463, for details). Using a hand wipe or sanitizer is not sufficient.

Children can contract serious or fatal illnesses when they do not follow the above guidelines. Teachers who ignore the CDC guidelines could be liable if children in their care become ill (Healthy Child Care Pennsylvania, 2006a).

Any acceptable animal that is present should be friendly and healthy. The American Society for the Prevention of Cruelty to Animals (ASPCA) has reported that half of all children are bitten by a dog by the time they are 12 years old, usually by a familiar male dog (AAP, 2003b). For young children, most bites occur around the neck and head (Schalamon et al., 2006). Children under age 10 are at the highest risk for dog bites, with children under 1 year at the greatest risk. Any animal bite should be reported to the authorities because of the possibility, if only slight, of transmission of rabies (Palmer, 2003).

Some diseases carried by cats and dogs are cat scratch fever, salmonella, scabies, and ringworm. Puppies and kittens can carry infections that cause a variety of serious diseases in children. Dogs and cats should be fully

Wadsworth/Cengage Learning

Pets, though clean and friendly, may still be a conceivable safety and health risk to children in the early childhood education environment. Children who play with animals should be supervised and monitored to avoid unpleasant incidents.

immunized and under a veterinarian's care for flea, tick, and worm control. Flea collars for either dogs or cats may pose risk to children and their developing nervous systems (Colino, 2003).

Do not allow other wild or aggressive animals such as ferrets to be present in any early childhood education environment (Zamani, 1999). If pets are present, they should be kept in a supervised and confined area of the facility and regularly checked for disease by a veterinarian. Pet living quarters should be cleaned often, and animal waste should be kept to a minimum. Another risk factor that pets may present is allergic reactions. Some children may be allergic to certain pet hair or dander. Parents may be unaware of the allergy if there are no pets in the home environment. The teacher should observe children for any reactions to the pets in the early childhood education environment.

Cleaning and Other Supplies. Cleaning supplies are a risk to children whether or not they are poisonous. These items can cause burns or rashes and other possible problems. When purchasing cleaning products it is best to buy those that are labeled as nontoxic, natural, citrus based, or biodegradable (Zamani, 2007). These "green products" also help the environment. All cleaning supplies that are not so labeled and chemicals that might present danger to children should be kept at a level where children cannot reach them. These more dangerous products should not be used on surfaces where very young children crawl or sit. Using cleaning products while children are present is not advised; use these materials when children are not around.

FIGURE 3-1
Teachers should teach children the meaning of the poison sign.

Paints and some craft supplies may present a risk if a child ingests them. Anything that might be poisonous should be kept at a high level in a locked cabinet. These items should be well labeled with the poison sign. The teacher can instruct the children that danger is present when they see the sign (Figure 3-1). This may not help the toddler or crawling infant, but it will help older children. Written safety policies for storage of these items and cleaning supplies are a must (Crosser, 2007).

Safety Devices

Safety devices should be present wherever applicable in the indoor early childhood education environment. All wall sockets should be covered with difficult-to-remove plastic plugs. All drawers that can be pulled out and fall onto a child's head or upper body should have childproof safety latches. All doorways that might lead to danger should be shut and lockable. Safety gates should be installed where doorways without doors may lead to danger or

Safety latches and electric outlet covers are just two of the numerous safety devices available. As with any device, these must be properly installed and used to be truly effective.

Wadsworth/Cengage Learning

Wadsworth/Cengage Learning

risk. All stairways where infants and toddlers are present should have safety gates to prevent children from crawling up or falling down the stairs. The teacher should check local hardware stores, the Internet, and early childhood education catalogs for sources of safety devices.

Developmental Level

Prevention is the single most significant factor in risk management for safety. The teacher begins this process by defining the boundaries for indoor safety and screening the environment for hazards with the developmental levels of the children in care in mind (Schnitzer, 2006). Safety hazards can be broken down by developmental age and vulnerabilities associated with that particular stage, as shown in Table 3-1.

Infants. Young infants are relatively helpless and must be carefully watched to protect them and prevent risks. Older, more mobile infants rapidly develop new motor skills at a rapid rate that lead them into an increasing number of hazardous situations. Children at this stage are particularly at risk for choking on small

TABLE 3-1
Indoor Safety Hazards

Age	Hazards	Prevention Tips
0–6 months	Scalds	Set hot water temperature to 120°F or less and always test bath water before immersing baby.
	Falls	Never leave infant alone on bed or table.
	Choking/Suffocation	Buy toys larger than two inches in diameter. Keep crib free of plastics or pillows. Crib slats should be less than 2⅜ inches apart, and space between mattress and slats should be less than 2 fingers wide.
	Toys	Toys should be larger than 1½ inches in diameter and should have smooth round edges and be soft and flexible.
	Drowning	Never leave child in bath unattended.
6 months–1 year	Burns and scalds	Check water temperature (see above). Keep hot foods and liquids out of reach. Put guards around hot pipes, radiators, and fireplaces.
	Poisons	Store household products, cosmetics, and medicines in high, preferably locked cabinets. Post poison control number by phone.
	Choking	Check floors and reachable areas for small objects such as pins, coins, and buttons. Avoid raw vegetables, nuts, hard candy, popcorn, and other foods that are difficult for child to properly chew and swallow.
	Toys	Toys should be large, unbreakable, and smooth.
	Drowning	Always supervise child's bath.

(continues)

TABLE 3-1 *(Continued)*
Indoor Safety Hazards

Age	Hazards	Prevention Tips
1–2 years	Falls	Put toddler gates on stairways and keep any doors to cellars, attics, and porches locked. Remove sharp-edged furniture from child's frequently used area. Show child proper way to climb up and down stairs using handrails.
	Burns	While cooking, turn pot handles to back of stove. Keep electric cords out of reach. Use shock stops to cover used and unused outlets. Teach child the meaning of the word *hot* and talk about different types of hot.
	Poisons	Keep poisons locked in high cabinets. Have child tested for lead poisoning during regular checkup.
	Drowning	Always supervise child's bath.
	Choking	Remove small objects.
2–3 years	Poisons	Teach child about the difference between food and nonfood and what is not good to eat. Watch child during art projects so he does not put art supplies in mouth. Keep poisons locked in high cabinets.
	Burns	Keep matches, lighter, and cigarettes out of reach and sight of children. Put screen around fireplaces and wood stoves. Reinforce the meaning of *hot*.
	Toys	Check for sharp edges, hinges, and small parts that could be swallowed. Remove toy chest lids.
	Drowning	Always supervise.
	Guns	Keep any firearms unloaded and locked away out of reach.
3 years and up	Burns	Teach child "drop and roll" to prepare for clothing catching fire. Practice fire drills with escape route, meeting place, and sound of smoke alarm. Train to bring found matches to adult.
	Tools and equipment	Teach child safe use of scissors. Keep sharp knives out of reach.
	Guns	Keep firearms unloaded and locked. Teach safety precautions about guns, by telling an adult immediately when they see a gun and not to touch! Discourage use of toy guns or violent play.

objects that they can mouth. The environment should be constantly and carefully monitored for small objects if infants are present, and expanding hazards should be anticipated. Another particular area of concern for infants is suffocation. Most injury-related deaths for infants result from suffocation (Schnitzer, 2006).

Infants should not be put to sleep in child swings, child seating devices, or on couches or cushioned chairs. All soft bedding and soft sleeping surfaces should be avoided. An infant should never be put to sleep where his or her body could become wedged between a mattress and a wall.

Falls are also a concern with infants. Common falls for infants include falling down the stairs when using an infant walker and falls from windows. A tiny baby can wiggle and move and push. An older baby can roll over, crawl, and creep. Another type of fall is from changing tables. Changing tables vary greatly and an infant can fall if left unattended, even if the safety strap is used. To further prevent falls, an early childhood environment should also have safety devices such as window guards and safety gates. The early childhood education environment should frequently be updated and checked for any CPSC recalls of toys or infant equipment that might pose risk (CPSC, 2004).

Toddlers. Toddlers probably are the developmental group with the most potential for unsafe practices. They are at a cognitive level that allows them new ways of thinking and solving problems, but they do not understand cause and effect. Toddlers try to stretch their limits and test their environment, which they now have the physical ability to accomplish. Toddlers like to explore places that may not be in view. Poisons and chemicals that are kept in cabinets, drawers, or on shelves are a major risk for this age group. Falls and poisonings are the leading cause of nonfatal injuries that require hospitalization for toddlers (Schnitzer, 2006). They can climb to get to places that were formerly inaccessible. Discouraging climbing on furniture and other equipment helps prevent risk. Falls from windows injure more than 4000 children per year (Smith & Hendricks, 2005). Using a safety device such as a window guard helps to prevent falls. These should be checked regularly to make sure they are working properly. If windows are low enough for children to reach them, a barrier should be put in front of them.

Fires and burns also contribute to injury-related deaths in children of this age. Toddlers require careful, constant monitoring and potential hazards should be constantly anticipated. Therefore, the environment should be modified as needed (Figure 3-2).

FIGURE 3-2
Common indoor hazards.

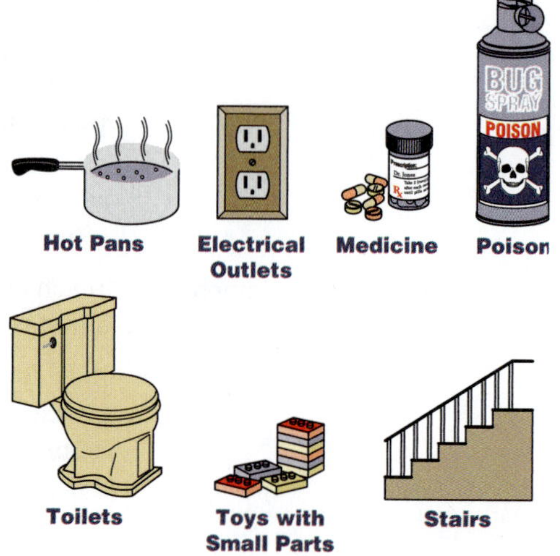

The Preschooler. Preschool-aged children have more physical and cognitive abilities and are beginning to understand cause and effect. Indoor falls pose risk to these children. Although they know about cause and effect, physical mastery often takes precedence over thought processes. Preschoolers are coordinated enough and fast enough to do almost any physical activity. Children of this age often feel their abilities are greater than they are in reality. This age group may also lack impulse control. Using only safe, sturdy equipment that is in good repair and practicing good supervision helps protect children from falls. Table 3-2 presents a list for checking indoor equipment to help prevent falls.

Besides monitoring conditions and safety risks, the teacher can teach preschool children preventive measures and help them to anticipate hazards. Children of this age can be good helpers to monitor the indoor environment for hazards.

School Age. School-aged children are much less prone to indoor safety hazards than children who are younger. Firearms may be the greatest threat to school-aged children. This age group has intense curiosity about things they see in movies and on television. They may not understand the danger guns pose. It is important, if guns are present in an early childhood education environment, such as a family child care home, that they be stored unloaded and locked up. Another indoor risk factor that applies to these children is fires and burns. Children may play with matches or lighters or even fire in a

TABLE 3-2
Checklist to Prevent Falls in the Indoor Environment

✓ **CHECK FOR:**

- ☐ Use infant and child equipment that is in good repair and inspected for safety.
- ☐ Use durable, balanced furniture that will not tip over easily.
- ☐ Do not allow climbing on furniture, stools, or ladders.
- ☐ Place safety gates at stairways.
- ☐ Remove all objects from stairs.
- ☐ Repair or remove frayed carpeting or other flooring.
- ☐ Install window guards on upstairs windows.
- ☐ Secure all window screens.
- ☐ Clean up spills quickly.
- ☐ Avoid highly waxed floors and stairways.
- ☐ Do not use loose throw rugs.
- ☐ Keep toys picked up as often as possible.
- ☐ Never leave a baby alone in a high place.

Most children younger than 3 years old are not developmentally ready to use scissors. Even children who are 3 years or older should be regularly monitored for safety reasons.

Wadsworth/Cengage Learning

fireplace. They may also try to cook for themselves in the case of a family child care or in-home care. Children of this age can learn preventive measures and can help the teacher monitor the environment and the younger children.

Space

Specific early childhood education environments present unique conditions and circumstances that can lead to environmental hazards. There should be adequate space to move around the equipment and not have to compete for space with other children. Most early childhood education centers, Head Start programs, and state preschools are licensed and do comply with spacing required by the licensing agencies.

Recommended indoor space is 35 square feet of play space per child, which does not include kitchen, bathroom, closet, laundry, or staff facilities (APHA & AAP, 2002). This space usually translates to 50 square feet per child when furnishings are included. Family child care homes that are informed try to keep to this standard. Unlicensed or license-exempt sites also must follow this standard for space. Some states have this as a requirement in licensing standards, whereas many others do not.

Adequate floor space is essential. How the teacher sets up the environment in the space available is a critical factor in prevention of injury. Enough space should be provided for crawling, keeping separate play areas for infants/toddlers and older children. The indoor space in early childhood education environments other than elementary schools should allow areas for children to engage in climbing, jumping, and swinging to help develop their strength and sense of competency. This should be enough space so that children can safely engage in these risk-taking activities with precautions and protective surfaces in place (Curtis & Carter, 2005). Barriers should not impair teachers' ability to watch all the children at the same time. These considerations should be taken into account as the early childhood education environment is planned and organized. Exceptions to this are elementary school classrooms that focus on learning, not on play; because they are public facilities, classroom space may be a factor. Planning in any case should include the arrangement of areas of interest in the classroom with safety in mind (Figure 3-3).

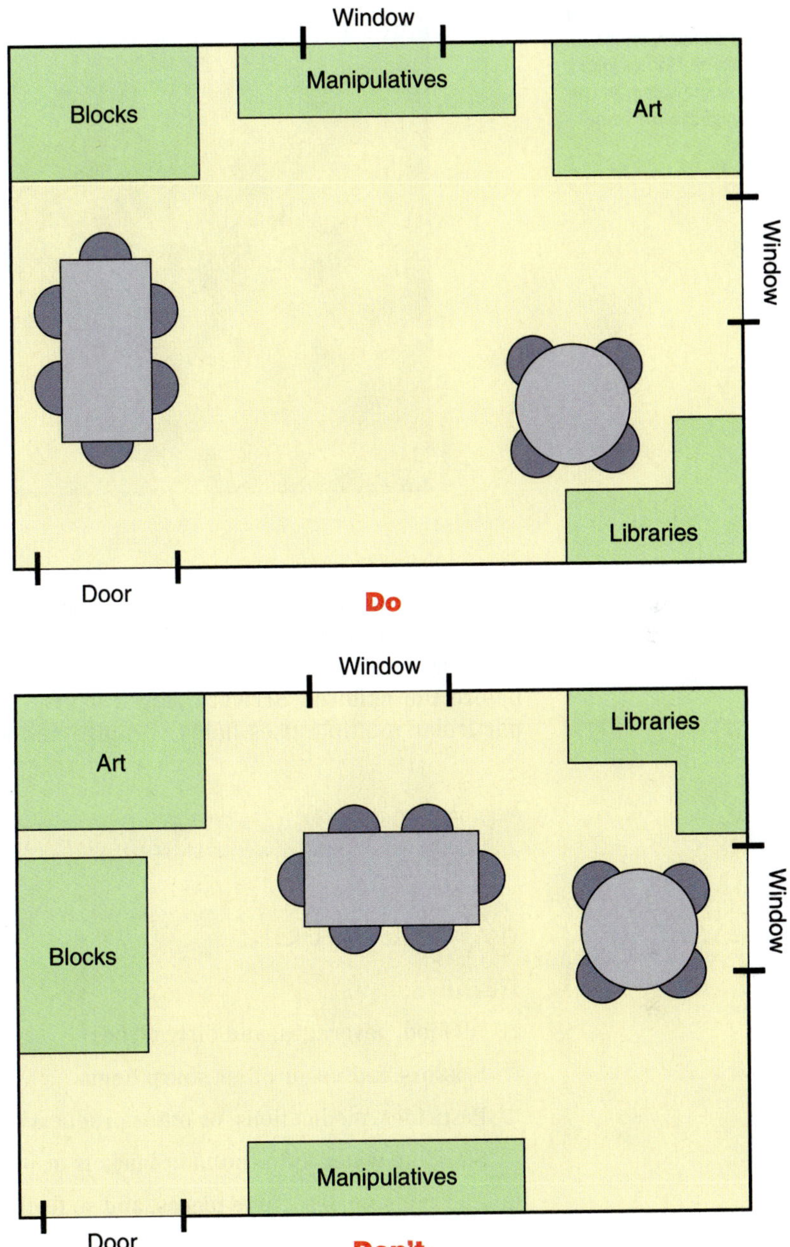

FIGURE 3-3
How to set up an early childhood education environment.

Shared Space

Another indoor environmental hazard for early childhood education may be shared space. Some early childhood education environments are located in areas that have multiple uses. These shared spaces may carry risks that the teacher must anticipate, continually assess, and be prepared to eliminate (see Table 3-1).

Whenever spaces are shared, safety risks can occur. Multiple-use facilities require thoughtful anticipation for possible hazards, and the environment

Wadsworth/Cengage Learning

Adequate floor space in a clear and organized environment aids in the prevention of injury. Do you see some things in this room that might cause some safety issues?

should be carefully screened before resuming early childhood education in a shared space that has been used for another purpose.

Screening a shared space may require coming to the site 15 to 30 minutes before the children arrive. Using a shared facility checklist created for the particular multiple uses helps organize and speed up this process. Table 3-3

TABLE 3-3
6 A.M. Checklist

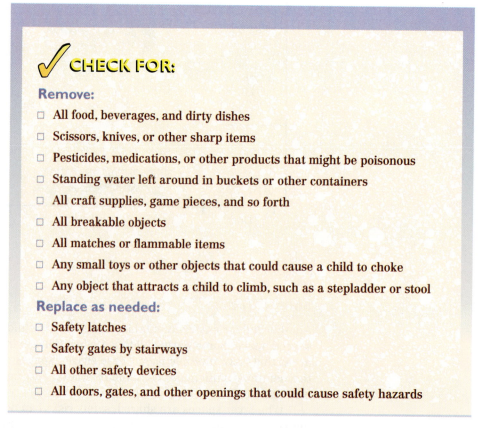

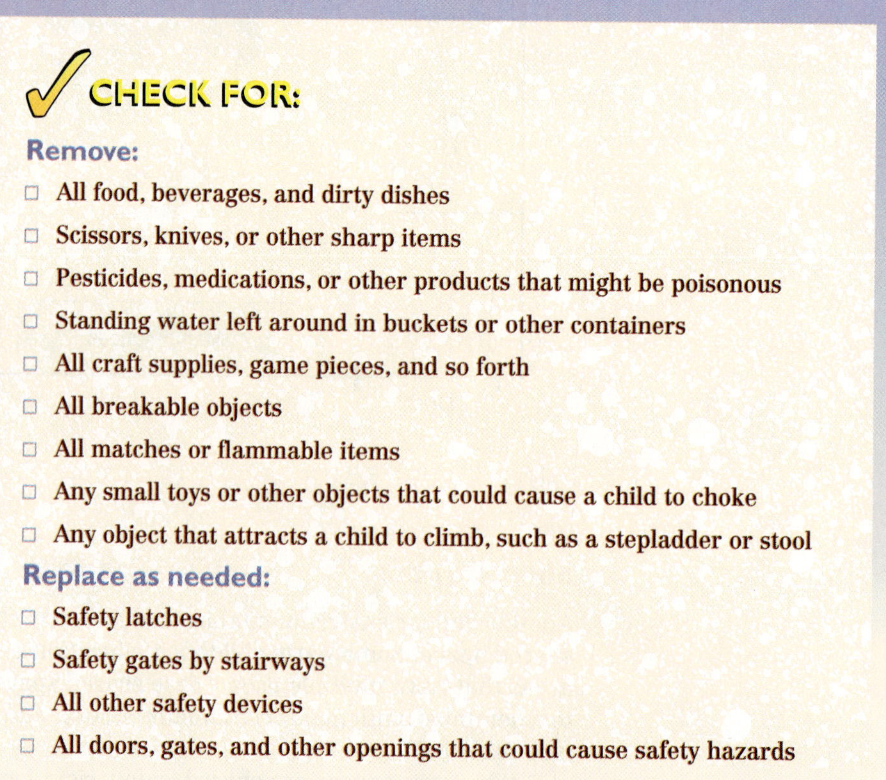
✓ **CHECK FOR:**

Remove:

- ☐ All food, beverages, and dirty dishes
- ☐ Scissors, knives, or other sharp items
- ☐ Pesticides, medications, or other products that might be poisonous
- ☐ Standing water left around in buckets or other containers
- ☐ All craft supplies, game pieces, and so forth
- ☐ All breakable objects
- ☐ All matches or flammable items
- ☐ Any small toys or other objects that could cause a child to choke
- ☐ Any object that attracts a child to climb, such as a stepladder or stool

Replace as needed:

- ☐ Safety latches
- ☐ Safety gates by stairways
- ☐ All other safety devices
- ☐ All doors, gates, and other openings that could cause safety hazards

FIGURE 3-4
Sign for shared use facility.

Please Remember
Child Care Takes Place Here!

- Pick up all small objects.
- Put any dangerous objects out of reach.
- Check electrical outlets for safety covers.
- Lock all cabinets that contain nonchildproof objects.

contains a checklist for a family child care home's morning check that could also be used by a nanny on arrival at a child's home.

It is also helpful to post signs in the shared facility about hazards so that others who use the facility are aware of safety risks to the early childhood education environment (Figure 3-4). Speaking with the person in charge of the other uses helps to keep the risks at a minimum. People who are responsible for cleaning and care of the facility should be encouraged to cooperate and watch for possible safety hazards in order to keep the children from undue risks. Parents should also be trained and utilized as environmental scanners whose extra eyes can help check for risks when they drop off their children.

Another example of a shared space might be an elementary school site that includes a universal preschool in it. The indoor and outdoor equipment may be geared to older children and may have to be adapted as much as possible to the younger children who attend.

It was Monday morning at the church preschool. Monica, the teacher, was pleased to see that someone had filled the juice pitchers for her and had them ready in the refrigerator. The children had come to school either tired or still excited from a busy summer weekend, so Monica really appreciated the extra help. Lorraine, the director, had a habit of taking time to sit with the children at their morning snacks on Mondays to see how they were doing and to hear about their weekends. She sat down after the snacks had been handed out and the juice had been poured. Lorraine took one sip of the juice and commented to the children, "You know this juice doesn't taste quite right—let's all throw it out and get some new juice." Lorraine had a very organized reaction to drinking punch with alcohol that had been left over from a wedding at the church over the weekend.

It turns out that the people cleaning up didn't want anything to go to waste, so they saved the punch in the only containers available—the preschool pitchers. Monica should have checked to see what it was first, and fortunately Lorraine had the presence of mind to solve the problem before anyone had a chance to take more than a sip of juice.

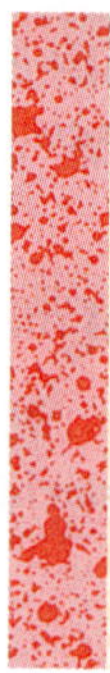

Pause for Reflection

Have you ever considered that indoor space might be a safety issue? Consider the early childhood education facilities you have seen or worked in. Was care taken to make the area as safe as possible and to meet the standards discussed? Shared space is even more likely to present risk. Have you experienced a shared-space early childhood education program that had particular risks that would not have been there if the space had not been shared?

Key Concept 3.2

Indoor Safety Guidelines

Examining the indoor environment for safety hazards allows the teacher to provide protection for the children and may help prevent unnecessary accidents. Indoor environmental hazards include ventilation, cleaning and other supplies, and pets. Safety devices can be used to prevent risk. The environment should be screened for risk in relation to the developmental levels of the children in care. Adequate space and setup for indoor early childhood education are factors that should be considered to prevent undue risk. Shared spaces pose many risks and require extra supervision to promote safety and prevent risk.

3.3 INDOOR EQUIPMENT SAFETY

Equipment used in early childhood education environments must be sturdy and free of sharp points or corners, pinch points, splinters, protruding nails or bolts, loose rusty parts, hazardous small parts, or paint that contains lead (APHA & AAP, 2002). Furniture should be durable, easy to clean, and, where appropriate, child-sized. A child's changing abilities to move about and manipulate the environment are major contributors to causing safety risks with indoor equipment. Falls are one of the most common injuries related to indoor equipment. Childhood falls account for 2.3 million emergency room visits per year (NSKC, 2007). Equipment should be placed so that children have enough freedom of movement to prevent accidents and collisions with equipment and each other, and precautions to prevent falls with the equipment should be taken. Refer to Figure 3-3 for improper equipment placement and proper placement of the same equipment. Other indoor equipment such as computers may also pose risk for musculoskeletal injuries (see Reality Check, page 97).

Some infant equipment is regularly tested and must comply with certain standards (APHA & AAP, 2002). Cribs, high chairs, strollers, and safety gates fall into this category. For information regarding the specifications of the standards, the teacher can write to:

The American Society for Testing and Materials
1916 Race Street
Philadelphia, PA 19103

Wadsworth/Cengage Learning

Wadsworth/Cengage Learning

Safety gates and latches should be routinely used.

Cribs should be made of wood, metal, or plastic and should have nonleaded paint. Cribs should also have

- Slats that are no more than $2\frac{3}{8}$ inches apart.
- A mattress that is fitted so that no more than two fingers can be wedged between the mattress and the crib side.
- A minimum height of 36 inches between the top of the mattress and the top of the crib.
- Secure latches, which, when the sides are up, hold the sides in the raised position. The latches should be inaccessible to the child in the crib.

Never leave a large stuffed toy in a crib. Children can use such toys to climb out of the crib. Never place a crib near a window because children can fall out of windows, hurt themselves on broken glass, or get caught up in cords from window shades or curtains. It is suggested that bumper pads not be used. Make sure that blinds or curtains do not have a looped cord, as the cord could cause strangulation.

When high chairs are used in early childhood education environments, they should have a safety strap that goes between the legs and around the waist. The legs should have a wide enough base so the high chair will not tip over. If paint is used on the high chair, it should be lead free. Strollers should clearly display the American Society for Testing and Materials (ASTM) seal of compliance with the number F833. Safety gates should display the seal with the number F406 (APHA & AAP, 2002).

If the teacher is using a changing table, it should have a lip around it to prevent a child from rolling off. The changing table should have a safety strap, and the strap should always be used. The child should never be left unattended when being changed.

Infant walking devices should not be used. They contribute to a large number of falls for infants. Nearly 80 percent of children who suffer baby walker injuries are being supervised. Three out of four children who fall in these walkers also fall down stairs (NSKC, 2007). The AAP has recommended that these devices not be used, even though they are tested by the CPSC.

Infant seating devices should be used sparingly in child care, and never for long periods of time as they might have an impact on the orthopedic and motor development of infants. It is better to have children on the floor or to hold them whenever possible (Myers, Yuen, & Walker, 2006). In some cases, parents have requested that their children be allowed to sleep and be fed in their infant seating devices. Teachers should explain to these parents that doing this is not in the best interest of the child's physical and motor development. Child swings and care seats are not meant to be used as devices in which children sleep. Infants who sleep in these devices can have their blood oxygen drop to an unsafe level. Strangulation can also occur when infants slip into positions that trap them against hard surfaces of these devices (Healthy Child Care Pennsylvania, 2007a).

Indoor Water Safety

Water safety is also a consideration in the use of indoor equipment. Drowning is the second major cause of death to children under age 5 (American Heart Association, 2005). Under any condition, direct adult supervision is necessary any time water play is introduced into the early childhood education environment (Sutton, 2003). Drowning can occur in a relatively small amount of water, such as a bucket of standing water that someone forgot to clean up and put away. A curious infant or toddler could look into the bucket, fall in, and drown. Toilets, tubs, and sinks also pose risk for drowning. Toilet lids should always be closed. Some early childhood education environments do not have lids for toilets, in which case, the toilet area should have a door that shuts and should be carefully monitored. Water should never be left standing in tubs or sinks.

Hot water faucets also pose risk. Hot water can cause burns by scalding. All hot water heaters should be set at 120°F. Children should never be left unattended near hot water faucets. When turning on water for children, always turn on the cold water first.

Toilets and water tables may also carry germs that put children at risk. To promote indoor water safety, the basic rules in Table 3-4 should be followed.

TABLE 3-4
Indoor Water Safety Guidelines

- Any equipment that uses water, such as toilets, sinks, tubs, and buckets, should be carefully monitored and cleaned often.
- Keep hot water temperature at 120°F.
- Never leave standing water unattended.
- No child should ever be left unattended in a tub or other device used to bathe a child.
- Where toilet lids are present, keep them down, if possible.
- In a family child care home, keep the door to the bathroom closed when not in use, if very young children are present. Keep a set of jingle bells on the door so that it can be heard opening and closing.
- Keep lid on diaper pail securely fastened.
- Keep lid on water table when not in use.

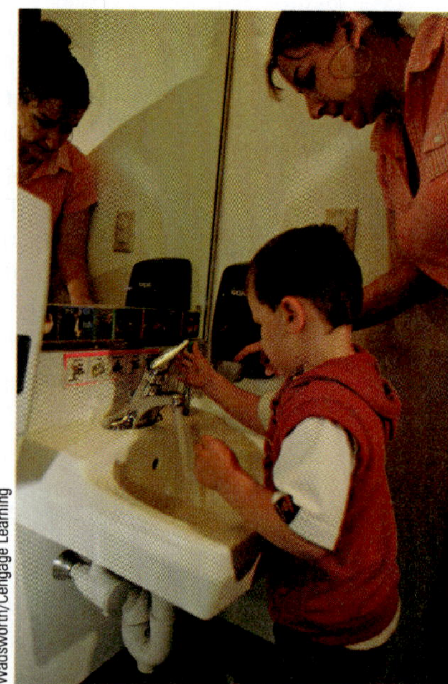

Equipment that uses water, such as toilets and sinks, should be carefully monitored and cleaned often, and children and staff should be encouraged to wash hands often.

REALITY *Check*

Safety Issues with Computers in the Early Education Environment

Computer use in the early childhood environment is becoming a norm. When used appropriately by children, computers can be beneficial learning tools (Holland, 2007b). Computer use by young children can also present some safety issues. Zamani (2004) suggests that there are five possible hazards associated with the use of computers by children: (1) musculoskeletal injuries, (2) vision problems, (3) lack of exercise, (4) social isolation, and (5) other long-term hazards.

The musculoskeletal issues are similar to those of adults with carpal tunnel syndrome. A child's body is developing at a rapid rate during the first years of life. A child who spends too much time on a computer might damage the developing bones, muscles, nerves, and tendons. Frequent computer use may also result in a strain on a child's visual development. A child that spends too much time on a computer could have blurred vision, headaches, and eye irritation as a result (Holland, 2007a). Children may not always indicate they are having problems looking at a screen, but if they have an awkward posture, it could be a clue that the child is having a hard time seeing the computer. The computer should be placed in an appropriate position for a child's use. If this equipment is ergonomically correct, a child is less apt to squint or assume an awkward posture in order to use the computer. Children should also be taught how to correctly position their arms and bodies so they can be comfortable and not cause strain to arms, necks, shoulders, and hands. The computer area should be designed specifically for use by children because they cannot comfortably adapt to adult computer stations (Holland, 2007a).

When a child spends too much solitary playtime on the computer, it can lead to both lack of exercise and lack of social interaction. Children should be actively engaged in play and be having positive interactions with other children and adults. Other issues that may result from too much time spent on a computer are that a child may have a lack of self-discipline, might not be as motivated to do other types of play, and may feel emotionally detached from others in his sphere. It is important that a child have a balance of exercise and playtime with others if he is to be using a computer for part of his day.

Researchers who have investigated the issue of computer use by children have recommended that children under the age of 3 not use computers. The AAP has a set of recommendations for the amount of media use by children (Vandewater et al., 2007). It is known that young children spend a great deal of time using media such as television, videos, and DVDs, and now they are using computers for more than just games on purchased software. Many websites are especially designed to capture young children's attention—even those who cannot yet read. One study on the impact of television viewing (Certain & Kahn, 2002) revealed that there is a correlation between attention difficulties and time spent viewing electronic media. Attention deficit may result from too much computer time. Another consideration for computer use is the fact that children may be commercially exploited or exposed to violence and other inappropriate materials online. To accommodate these safety issues, children should be closely supervised when using the computer and should have their computer time limited to short periods so that they do not isolate themselves from the rest of the children and adults in the environment.

In addition to computer use, the area around computers may also present some safety hazards. The area where computers are used should not be near any water such as a water table, sink, or art activities where liquids may be used. Children who are around computers should be taught some basic electrical safety precautions. They should be discouraged from playing around the area where the computer plugs into the wall outlet. If a computer is donated to the early childhood education facility, it should be thoroughly checked for signs of wear and fraying cords (Holland, 2007a). Correct lighting and ventilation

(continues)

REALITY*Check* (continued)

are also considerations. When there is glare, it may cause the child to squint. The area around the computer should provide good light, but not too much in front of or behind the computer. If there is a window in front of or behind the computer, a blind may be required to help cut down on glare. The computer should not be off in a corner where ventilation may not be as good as in another part of the room.

Less of an issue in most early childhood environments, but an issue in some, is the presence of a paper shredder. In family child care homes and in in-home situations, there may be a paper shredder near a printer close to the computer. Paper-shredding injuries can pose great risk to young children (Warren & Foltin, 2006). A child could seriously injure or even amputate her finger(s) by sticking her hand in a paper shredder. Most of these devices are used in offices and therefore do not have child safety devices as commonly as they should. If there is a paper shredder in the early childhood environment, it should be kept out of the reach of children, in a locked cabinet if that is appropriate.

Key Concept 3.3

Indoor Equipment Safety

Using safe, sturdy indoor early childhood education equipment can help eliminate some risk. Safety devices, safety practices, and good supervision will help the teacher add a greater degree of protection for the children. Some indoor equipment that involves water poses risks. The risk of drowning and of burns from scalding water can be reduced through safe practices and supervision.

3.4 TOY SAFETY

Toy-related accidents cause more than 202,000 children to be injured each year, and at least 36 percent of those injured are children under 5 years of age (U.S. PIRG Education Fund, 2007). Toys and other children's products (CPSC, 2005) cause approximately 70 percent of deaths for children 4 years of age and younger. Other typical toy-related accidents involve choking on or inhaling balloons or small balls, toy chest lids falling on or pinching a child, projectile toys piercing the body, and strangulation on toys with ropes or strings. These accidents may be avoided if the toys are examined for **age appropriateness** for the children playing with them (Child Health Alert [CHA], 2003a). Art supplies may also pose risk to children and should be checked for safety and age appropriateness. Separate toys by age group so that younger children are not exposed to toys that may endanger their safety, and inspect them for any small parts, broken pieces, or sharp surfaces. They should also be checked for cords or strings that could cause strangulation or entanglement (Walsh, 2005). Projectile toys should be eliminated from early childhood education programs if they pose risk for eye injuries. The number of recalls for toys made in China more than doubled from 2000 to 2007. It is very important that all toys should be carefully checked for hazards before

- **age appropriateness** *consideration of the developmental abilities of a particular age group in the selection of toys, materials, and equipment.*

use. It is a good idea to go to the CPSC website at http://www.spsc.gov and check for the latest recalls (see Reality Check: *How Safe Are America's Toys?*, page 103).

Choking and Suffocation Hazards

Choking and suffocation are major hazards to very young children who still mouth toys, foods, and small objects in their environment. The developmental level for that mouthing, along with new cognitive abilities to master the environment, can lead children to risk their safety (Table 3-5).

Ensuring that small toys and other objects are too large for mouthing is important to prevent choking and suffocation hazards (Figure 3-5). As consumers, we are probably more conscious of foods and small objects causing choking hazards than we are of toys. We purchase a toy and expect that

TABLE 3-5
Choking and Suffocation Hazards for Young Children

Toys	
Marbles	Game tokens
Balloons	Game pieces
Dress-up jewelry	Jacks
Plastic bags	Toy chests with no air holes
Doll pacifiers	Toys with strings or cords long enough to encircle a child's neck
Any toy less than 1½ inches in diameter	
Food	
Hot dogs	Popcorn
Cheese "cubes"	Marshmallows
Grapes	Olives and cherry tomatoes
Gum	Dried fruits such as apricots or raisins
Lollipops	Spoonfuls of peanut butter
Carrots, celery, and other raw vegetables	Hard and gummy candies, jelly beans, caramels, and cough drops
Peanuts, other nuts, sunflower and pumpkin seeds	
Small Objects	
Pins and safety pins	Nails and screws
Toothpicks	Pencils, pens, and erasers
Tacks	Staples
Jewelry	Damaged or loose nipples on pacifiers
Coins	Small cuplike objects such as spray can lids, measuring cups, and small bowls
Crayons	

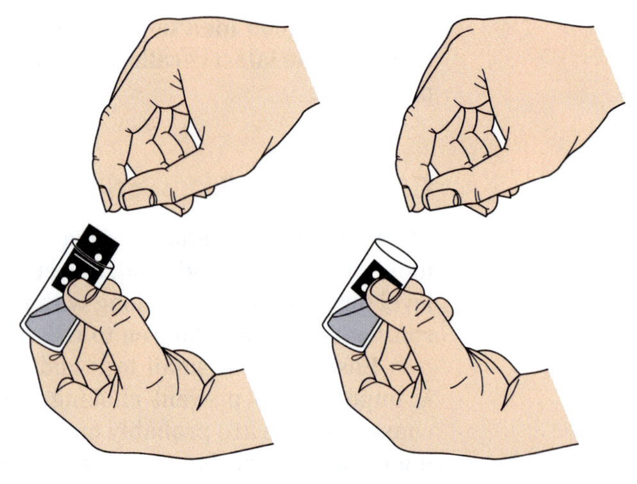

FIGURE 3-5
Device for measuring small parts to prevent choking. Notice that the domino gets caught in the tube, but the die passes through the tube, indicating a choking hazard.

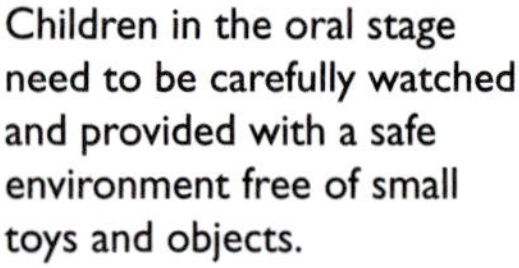

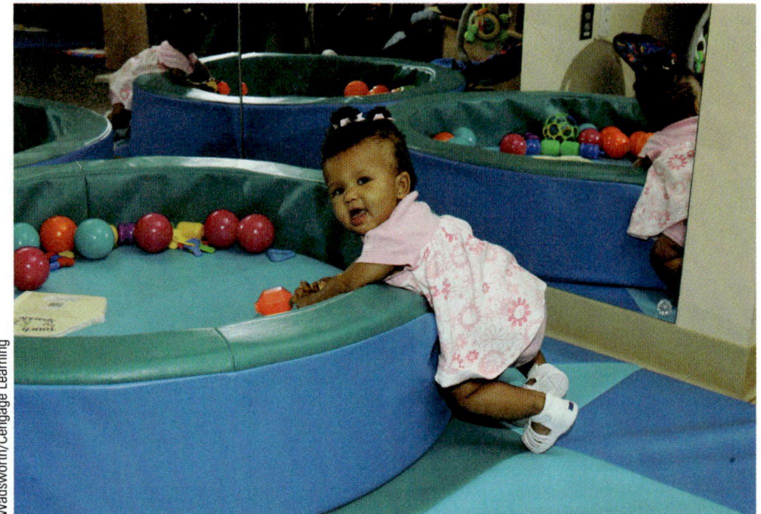

Wadsworth/Cengage Learning

Children in the oral stage need to be carefully watched and provided with a safe environment free of small toys and objects.

Marty had been a family child care provider for about six months. She had children in care from 4 months old to 5 years old. The older children were very active and helpful. Diana, the older 4-year-old, and Holly, the 5-year-old, really liked to do grown-up things. They especially enjoyed helping Marty. Marty appreciated their help and liked to give them little tasks to do. One of those tasks was to help her go through the child care setting looking for any safety risks. The girls often caught things that Marty might have missed because they explored the environment from a child's viewpoint.

One day Ramsey, a toddler, was chewing something. Holly went to Marty and brought her to Ramsey right away. Even though they had all searched for hazards that morning, they had missed a playing piece from a Monopoly game. The safety consciousness in this early childhood education environment helped save Ramsey from a hazard that could have caused a real problem.

toy to be safe. However, what is safe for a 5-year-old may be very dangerous to a 2-year-old. The CPSC has a small-parts standard that prohibits manufacturers from marketing toys with small parts to children younger than 3 years of age. Their toll-free telephone number is 1-800-638-2772.

Age Appropriateness

The age group for which a toy is intended is often included on the package. However, contents of the package, including small parts, are not always listed, and safety precautions are often not included in the packaging or instructions. If a teacher fails to see the package, or if she does not understand other safety precautions that should be taken with the toy, she may put the children in care at risk for injury. She could also be at risk for negligence (Crosser, 2007).

Consumer awareness of toy safety is imperative, especially in early childhood education environments where there is a population of children of mixed ages. Age appropriateness is one of the most important tools for removing hazardous toys from the environment. Table 3-6 shows age-appropriate toy suggestions.

The teacher must check the environment for the age appropriateness of toys, because different developmental levels affect the way children play with toys. Table 3-7 gives teachers a checklist for toy safety.

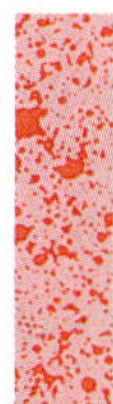

Pause for Reflection

Have you ever had a toy that broke easily or posed risk for children in your life? What measures did you take?

What further measures should be taken to make toys safer?

TABLE 3-6
Age-Appropriate Toys

Age	Toys
Up to 6 months	Squeeze toys, colorful mobiles, large pictures of faces or simple patterns, and nonbreakable mirrors
6 months to 1 year	Cradle gyms, sturdy books, drums, manipulative toys, toys that make noises, and busy boards
1 year to 18 months	Stacking toys, balls, large blocks, pounding toys, push-pull toys, books, simple puzzles, and tapes with simple stories or music
18 months to 3 years	Large blocks, crayons, puzzles, trucks, dolls, dramatic play toys, musical instruments, outdoor climbing equipment, sandboxes, sand toys, and water toys
3 to 6 years	Dramatic play toys, puppets, playhouses, art materials, chalkboards, tricycles, bicycles, balls, simple games, books, simple board games

TABLE 3-7
Toy Safety Checklist

✓ CHECK FOR:

- ☐ Age appropriateness for the children playing with the toy.
- ☐ Set safety rules for mixed-age groups to keep toys for older children out of younger children's reach, and secure a place in the care environment where the older children can use these toys.
- ☐ No toys or toy parts smaller than 1½ inches.
- ☐ Check for sharp parts, points, rough edges, pinch points, and loose small parts.
- ☐ Check toys for durability—if a toy is easily broken, it is dangerous.
- ☐ Examine toys for construction, including stuffed animals that might have seams that could open easily or eyes that could be pulled off and swallowed.
- ☐ Throw out all broken pieces of toys, crayons, and games.
- ☐ Regularly check pacifiers that children use to ensure that nipples resist pulling and guards cannot fit inside a child's mouth.
- ☐ Check instructions for art and craft supplies and make sure that they are nontoxic, washable, and environmentally safe.
- ☐ Make sure toys that are mouthed but too large to be swallowed are washed after use.
- ☐ Check paint on toys to make sure it is lead free.
- ☐ Make sure that toys with projectile parts are not present.
- ☐ Ensure that toy chests with lids are not present.
- ☐ Make sure all toys are flame resistant.
- ☐ Check that mobiles and other hanging crib toys are not used after infants are able to sit up.
- ☐ Make sure that toys are cleared and put away when not in use.
- ☐ Make sure that toys with pull strings are restricted to use when an adult is present.
- ☐ Set up play areas away from electrical cords and other cords such as telephone wires.

Art Supplies

Art supplies present some potential hazards. The hazards may be from inhaling lead or other dangerous substances or from mouthing the various materials used for art. The Federal Arts Materials Labeling Act took effect in 1990. Products that are potentially toxic should carry a health label that indicates caution or a warning. Labeling has been improved to determine whether an art product is safe for children. The Art and Creative Materials Institute (ACMI) conducts a program that certifies products as being safe and nontoxic or

REALITY *Check*

How Safe Are America's Toys?

Almost 3 billion toys are sold every year in the United States (ToyInfo.org, 2008). Less than 1 percent of these toys are recalled each year. The Consumer Product Safety Commission has been monitoring toy recalls for the public since 1974. Many of the recalls are voluntary, instigated by the toy manufacturers themselves. These recalls are listed at http://www.cpsc.gov. Approximately half of the toy recalls since 1974 have occurred since 2000. In 2007, there were 61 toys recalled, which was 30 percent more than in the year 2006 (Williamson, 2008). Many in the toy industry are referring to 2007 as "the year of the recall" (U.S. PIRG Education Fund, 2007). These recalls were not all for "cheap" toys found at thrifty dollar-type stores. Major manufacturers such as Mattel, Playskool, Disney, Fisher-Price, Battat, and Gund all recalled toys. Stores that sold these toys included Target, Wal-Mart, Lakeshore, Land's End, Tiffany and Company, and ToysRUs. Familiar toys that were recalled have included Barbies, Polly Pockets, Winnie-the-Pooh play sets, Thomas the Tank Engine toys, Easy Bake Ovens, Cookie Monster and Curious George dolls, and other products related to these toys. In addition, over the past few years other toys such as magnets, blocks, puzzles, drums, rattles, cars, plush toys, and wagons have all had recalls posted. The toys were recalled for a number of reasons, including these:

- Lead paint or excessive lead in the toy
- Sharp edges
- Choking hazards
- Intestinal hazards
- Entrapment hazards
- Thermal burn or chemical hazards
- Finger amputation
- Strangulation
- Noise hazards that can cause hearing impairment

Somehow, seeing all the above items listed by manufacturer, familiarity, type, and hazard, it makes one wonder about the safety of the toys that the children in America are being exposed to at home, in schools and in fast-food restaurants. In 2005 alone, more than 20 toy-related deaths were reported (NCCCHSRC, 2008). Every year the U.S Public Interest Research Groups publishes a survey of toy safety, entitled *Trouble in Toyland*. They reported that toys are safer than ever before because of the diligence of parents, product safety advocates, and legislation from Congress. These recalls are occurring because today most toys are imported, and many of those come from China, which does not have the same standards for toy safety or other product safety inspections. This is an issue because the Consumer Product Safety Commission has a budget equivalent to half the size of its start-up budget in 1974; has less than half the employees of the 1980 level (U.S. PIRG Education Fund, 2007); had only one toy tester, who recently retired; and has only 15 on-duty full-time port inspectors for all the imported products.

The U.S. Public Interest Research Group sites that four categories of toys are the most dangerous: choking hazards, magnetic toys, loud toys, and toys containing lead. Between 1990 and 2005, 166 children died after choking or asphyxiating on a toy or toy part. Nine children died of this circumstance in 2005 alone. This group recommends that testing for small parts for toys used by children under age 3 be more protective than current standards. The under-3 age group is the most vulnerable for the majority of hazards. Several young children have died in the past few years by swallowing powerful magnets that can cause intestinal perforation or blockage. The U.S. PIRG suggests there be strong guidelines for the labeling of magnetic toys so parents know to seek immediate medical attention if a child swallows one.

Approximately 15 percent of children from ages 6 to 17 years are showing signs of hearing loss. In 2003, the American Society for Testing and Materials embraced the voluntary standard of no more than 90 decibels for toys. Some toys that have been tested more recently have topped 100 decibels. Lead in toys can be a hidden hazard. Some toys and children's jewelry have been found to contain high levels of lead. One piece of jewelry tested by U.S. PIRG was found

(continues)

REALITY*Check* (continued)

to be 65 percent lead by weight. Lead paint can also be a problem. Some toys were found to exceed lead paint standards by 50 to 500 percent. Lead has been found in plastic, wooden, and metal toys and on lunch boxes and children's bibs. In addition to these four areas, U.S. PIRG found toxic chemicals in children's play cosmetic kits (U.S. PIRG Education Fund, 2007).

The Consumer Product Safety Commission works with toy manufacturers, retailers, and importers to make sure toys are safe. Toys are consistently listed as one of the safest of the 15 most common consumer product categories for the home (ToyInfo.org, 2008). In response to the large numbers of toy and other product recalls, the Consumer Product Safety Commission is planning several revamps. First, Congress passed a bill providing the CPSC with an additional $20 million for 2008. During this time, the CPSC placed more full-time staff at some of the nation's busiest ports (Yen, 2008), where they will work to implement an important tracking system (Williamson, 2008). In addition, the CPSC is working with the toy industry to put together a program that will test and certify all toys imported into the United States, regardless of where they were made. The CPSC will also create an "early warning" system to identify and respond to safety hazards for children's products. In regards to Chinese goods, if a faulty product is identified as being manufactured in China and the name of the manufacturer is known, the CPSC will notify the Chinese government agency responsible for consumer product regulation (CPSC, 2008). It will provide the Chinese government with a press release regarding the recall. In turn, the manufacturer will be notified of the recall. The Chinese government appears to be cooperative due to a "memorandum of understanding" between their government regulatory body and the CPSC. It appears that Congress will take even further measures to strengthen the regulation of imported goods, including toys.

The toy industry follows federal toy safety standards to test toys that are on shelves. That is how they discover many of the recalled toys. Even if all elements are in place, toy safety may still be at risk. Here are some recommendations for consumers to help ensure increased safety in the purchase of toys (Shin, 2007; U.S. PIRG Education Fund, 2007, NCCCHSRC, 2008):

- Examine toys for potential hazards.
- Look for toys' small parts, see whether there is a federal warning label reading "not for children under 3 years of age," and test all small toy parts with the choke-test cylinder (as seen in Figure 3-5).
- Look for toys with sturdy parts that are well secured at joints.
- If a toy is for a baby, it should be washable and should have no strings attached.
- All finishes should have lead-free paint.
- If possible, examine the item for quality construction and check for hazards before purchase. This includes listening to the sound the toy emits for loudness. If unsure of the loudness, a sound meter could be used to test it.
- If already purchased, test toys by trying to pry or pull to loosen small objects, and look for sharp corners.
- *Consumer Reports* suggests using a lead test kit such as LeadCheck®, whereas CPSC is unsure if they are reliable. It is suggested that although these lead test kits may be a "rough test," they may also find lead hazards.
- Avoid buying soft plastic toys or metal jewelry.
- Check toys with magnets to see whether they could fall out.
- If purchasing a toy with batteries, make sure they are firmly attached and that children cannot get to them easily.
- Avoid purchasing toys on the Internet from unknown sources as the toys may have been recalled and are being resold. Well-known retailers follow recalls and take toys off shelves.
- If a hazard is found, report it immediately.

CHECK*point:* **What are the four major safety hazards concerning toys? What measures are and should be taken to ensure greater toy safety? What things should one look for when purchasing toys for children?**

indicates that they are potentially harmful and toxic (Allen, 2005). This ACMI certification ensures compliance with the Federal Arts Materials Labeling Act as well as state regulations. Hazard-free art products should be labeled "AP," and the hazardous products should be labeled "CL," indicating caution should be taken. For example, there are nine safe glitter products that have been evaluated for inhalation and ingestion hazards and skin contact problems (Healthy Child Care Pennsylvania, 2006b).

Table 3-8 will help the teacher lessen risk to safety when using art supplies. If there is any question regarding art supplies, contact the manufacturer and ask for a copy of the Material Safety Data Sheet. This will give information about ingredients and toxicity.

Common household products are often used to make art materials. Examples of these are play dough, cornstarch clay, and goop. If these items are used in the early childhood education environment, children should be instructed in how to use them. Children should not mouth these materials, and toddlers should be well monitored when these materials are used.

Other products such as beans and seeds may be dangerous to children. Kidney beans, apple seeds, morning glory seeds, and four-o'clock flower seeds are toxic (Sutton & Slattery, 2004). It is also important to choose a well-ventilated area for indoor art and craft projects. Fumes from

TABLE 3-8
Keeping Art Safe

- Avoid using any art supplies that are dry and could be easily inhaled, such as tempera paint and clay.
- Avoid using any materials that contain lead or other hazardous substances that can cause poisoning if ingested.
- Use poster paints, liquid paints, and water-based paints that are nontoxic.
- Do not use rubber cement, epoxy, or instant glue. Use glue sticks, double-sided tape, paste, or school glue. These should have the AP label. Use only water-based glues, glue sticks, and paste.
- Do not use permanent markers. Use only washable markers, and avoid using scented markers that tempt children to put them in their mouths.
- Avoid using empty film canisters for art projects, as the lids can be mouthed and have the potential hazard for choking.
- Avoid organic solvents or products containing them.
- Avoid using aerosol spray cans or air brushes.
- When using small items such as beans, rice, or small Styrofoam shapes for projects, always keep special watch, because children may mouth their art materials and might choke on them. It is better to use these items only with older children.
- Avoid the use of glitter, which is metallic and can cause eye damage if it gets into the eye.

certain safe art supplies can build up. Cleaning up as you go in art projects is a good safety measure to avoid needless injuries such as a fall caused by spilled paint.

Other Factors

Reports indicate that children can suffocate other than from choking (CHA, 2003a). A condition called "cupping" can occur when the child puts a small cuplike object over the mouth and nose. When the child's breathing creates a vacuum, the object attaches tightly enough to cause suffocation. Another issue that has caused concern about children's toy safety is the use of polyvinyl chloride (PVC) in toys that children may mouth. There can be chemicals called phthalates that are toxic in PVC. Although most toy manufacturers are removing this from teething toys, it may still be present in other toys. For a list of toy products that are unsafe, go to http://www.toysafety.net/.

Wadsworth/Cengage Learning

The computer area should be safely set up so that children don't have to lean forward like the child on the right.

Key Concept 3.4

Toy Safety

The teacher should supply toys and other play materials that are safe and as risk free as possible. Toys should be examined for hazards. By using such tools as the choking hazard checklist and the toy safety checklist, the teacher can eliminate those toys that may present risk. Knowledge of age-appropriate toys will help the teacher select toys that are safe for the care environment. If the environment is mixed age, supervision and safety practices should be used to make certain younger children are not playing with toys that may present risk to them. Art materials may pose risk. The teacher should be aware of these risks and do whatever is necessary to minimize them.

3.5 INTERPERSONAL SAFETY

Injuries to children by other children such as biting, kicking, scratching, and fighting are common in early childhood education settings. Teachers should be prepared to intervene when these challenging behaviors that threaten interpersonal safety occur. They must understand the background for such behavior and know strategies for eliminating that behavior and utilizing conflict resolution. Focused intervention to help aggressive children with their social skills and interactions can have long-term benefits. The NAEYC's position statement on violence reflects this.

Of all the aggressive behaviors, biting is the most upsetting. It upsets the hurt child and the parents of both the biter and the child who was bitten. It is also common for children younger than 3 years of age. There are a number of reasons why children bite. Among these are using their mouths to explore, not having language to express themselves, teething, and attention getting. Children may also bite when they feel insecure, stressed, anxious or threatened. Many teachers ask parents whether a young child has had a biting problem before entering care. If so, they can be alert. It is important that quick, proper action be taken when biting occurs, because it is disturbing to the child who is bitten and may be dangerous (Oku, 2002; "Biting, bullies, and other bad behavior," 2005) (Table 3-9). A human bite can be the source of infection, exposure to transmission of communicable diseases, and exposure to body fluids. A child who has a bite that has broken the skin should be sent to his physician. If this occurs on an elementary school site, the child should be sent to the school nurse or health clerk first and then referred to a physician (Conlon, 2007).

A teacher also needs other tools because biting can be frustrating for teachers too. Ramming, Kyger, and Thompson (2006) suggest that teachers consider biting from an oral sensory developmental level. When a child transitions from one feeding level to another in his oral development, she goes from being able to suck liquids, to gum pureed foods, to munch soft foods, to crunch hard foods, and then to chew on foods that take more chewing than most such as raw vegetables and meats. As children transition through these stages, it is important that a teacher provide a variety of textures in foods and toys that a child can chew on if needed. If a child appears to have these issues with feeding levels, it is suggested that an oral stimulation brush be provided to the child to chew on; this helps the transition and also helps the development of the molar teeth, which can help the child chew better. Provision of this brush should be for one child and not a shared item.

Lucarelli (2006) suggests that all behavior has meaning and that when a child acts out, he is communicating that something is wrong or that a need is unmet. Children's aggressive behavior may be caused by poor health or nutrition or developmental issues (Garakani & Leonard, 2006). If an aggressive child doesn't seem to have any of those conditions present, then a teacher might have to take a further look at the child's whole environment. A child may have issues in the home environment such as a new baby, job stress for a parent, or a move. There may be issues in the early childhood environment such as a friend moving away, a beloved teacher leaving, or the child having to relate to circumstances and being from a different culture. A significant number of children who show aggressive behaviors have sleep disturbances that do not allow for a good night's sleep (Sakimura et al., 2007). Gender

TABLE 3-9
Biting in Child Care

Develop a policy for biting, and inform parents on entry of the child into care. Try to create an atmosphere that reinforces positive behaviors, to avoid biting in the first place.

If biting does occur, find out:

- When (under what conditions) did it happen?
- Who was involved?
- Why did the child bite? (Is there a pattern?)
  —Teething
  —Exploring
  —Inability to express frustration or anger verbally
  —Overstimulation
  —Jealousy
  —Insecurity
  —Recent changes in child's life
  —Asserting independence
  —Oral development issues

Immediately after biting occurs:

- Intervene.
- Never bite the child back.
- Talk to the child who bit.
  —Tell the child that biting is not okay.
  —Explain that food is for biting, not friends.
  —Encourage the child to help the child she bit.
- Talk to the child who was bitten and give her reassurance.
  —Encourage the child to tell the biter, "That hurt me."
- Give immediate first aid (see Chapter 5).

Follow-up

- Alert the staff.
- Fill out an injury report.
- Tell the parents of both children what happened.
- If it is not the first incident, sit down with the parents of the biter and work out a plan for changing the behavior, and review the biting policy that has been established for the early childhood environment. Using this plan as a basis, establish a "no biting" plan for the child, and involve everyone in the early childhood education environment to help carry out and monitor the plan. If all information has been gathered, the plan is in place, and there still seems to be an issue, involve the child's medical home or a child health care consultant.
- Examine the early childhood education environment for any actions, behaviors, or conditions that might be modified to lessen risk. Discuss with the parent practices to use at home so that there is consistency from one environment to the other.

may have an impact on aggressive or challenging behaviors. Studies have shown that boys are four times more likely to show aggressive behaviors than girls (Brault & Brault, 2005). Temperament may also play a role. A feisty or difficult child is more likely to show aggressive behaviors than a shy, slow-to-warm child (Sakimura et al., 2007).

In addition, a child's disposition may be the reason behind a behavior. Disposition indicates ways of thinking and action that are frequent and voluntary (Da Ros-Voseles & Fowler-Haughey, 2007). A child's disposition is acquired and either supported or weakened in his or her environment. Watching violent television during the preschool years can cause a child to become more aggressive later (Christakis & Zimmerman, 2007; Mistry et al., 2007). What is considered aggressive behavior may differ from culture to culture, and a teacher has to be aware of this (Gonzalez-Mena & Shareef, 2005). What might be thought of as assertive behavior in one culture may look like aggressive behavior to another. A teacher searching for the source of aggression would look at the individual, family, culture, and other sources.

Once the origin of aggressive behavior has been established, it is easier to help the child deal with the feelings that may be causing the aggressive reactions. It is important for everybody in the early childhood education environment that clear limits for acceptable behaviors be set. When a child acts out, the teacher should respond to the child in a calm, consistent manner and should not ignore the aggressive behavior. She can help a child by giving him coping skills for dealing with his anger or teach the child other culturally acceptable ways to be assertive. The teacher can help the child to problem solve and redirect him to another activity that is more calming. She can also help the child learn to identify the warning signals or what might trigger anger and how to express it in acceptable ways (Lucarelli, 2006). One way to accomplish this is to keep a log of the child's behaviors and what instigates the child's aggressive behavior (Rose, 2007). The teacher can become attuned to look for these conditions and change circumstances to avoid the aggression. She can help children use their words to describe how they feel and what they want. She can ask the parents what they do to comfort their child when he is in distress. The teacher can include an area in the environment that is peaceful and calm to send the child to until the anger or aggression he is feeling is under control.

A good way to prevent aggressive behaviors and to reduce the risk to interpersonal safety is to organize the environment to have a positive effect on how children function (Burdette, 2006). When the early childhood education environment is well organized in the use of space, rules, routines, and appropriate schedules, it can help reduce problem behavior. Another key to reducing problem behavior is to develop positive relationships with everybody in the environment. This includes the teacher monitoring the environment for his own negative comments. Although a teacher should never engage in negative comments, he may not realize that a child may hear a direct instruction comment and perceive it as a negative comment (Funk, 2006). When the teacher is aware that an affirmative request has a more positive impact than does a direct order, it can shift the atmosphere and encourage children to act in a more helpful manner. Another tactic is to "catch" children being good and to compliment them on positive behavior or accomplishments. Constructive comments and positive reinforcement can help the child gain confidence. Modeling positive behaviors helps to create a more positive base for all relationships in the early education environment. If the child is old enough to understand the idea of conflict resolution, where discussion takes place, this is another positive way to make change in the environment (Heydenberk & Heydenberk, 2007).

If the environmental precautions and strategies do not work for helping a child control his challenging behavior, the parents should be contacted. In children about the age of first-graders, as many as one in three parents are contacted due to challenging behaviors in their children (Blanchard, Gurka, & Blackman, 2006). A third party such as a health consultant may have to be called in to work with the situation (Lucarelli, 2006; Rose, 2007). If a child loses control quickly and often, and no solution has been found or behavior changes have taken place over a period of time, a child may have to be expelled from a program. This does occur throughout the country, with an average of 6.7 students per 1000 preschool children having to be permanently terminated from their early education environments (Brault & Brault, 2005). This would be done if there were a constant threat to the other children or teachers present, and it is only fair to all concerned to do so. This expulsion rate is three times that of school-age children; in kindergarten through 12th grade, the expulsion rate is around 2.1 students (Lewin, 2005). There may be several reasons for this. In many public districts throughout the United States there are school psychologists who may help children and there are special classes for emotionally disturbed children. There is no funding for this on the preschool level, but it has been found that when mental health professionals are consulted, the risk of expulsion is reduced (Perry et al., 2008). Mental health consultation is a positive strategy for reducing the risk of expulsion for children with challenging behaviors.

Have you been around a child who had aggressive behavior or was "out of control"? What did the parent or teacher do when this child acted out? What temperamental, dispositional, or other characteristics did this child display? What strategies might be used to help get that child "under control" for aggressive behavior?

Exposure to Violence

Violence as a means of handling conflict has filtered down into early childhood. It cannot be assumed that children are being raised in a gentle environment where they experience only love and kindness (Renshaw, 2006). Children are seeing violent behavior modeled on television, on the streets, in their neighborhoods, and even in their homes (Levin, 2003a; Holland, 2007b; Moore et al., 2007). This is especially true when war and terrorism are being talked about and shown on television or when children watch cartoons where violence is an integral part of the story. When children or angry, tired, or upset, they may resort to behaviors that reflect their exposure to violence in our society. They may also act out their need to feel strong and powerful in ways they have seen portrayed in the media. There are a number of toys today that are linked to violent media (Levin, 2003a). Action figures, guns, and video games can depict or recall violent stories or violent behavior.

Interpersonal behaviors that threaten safety include biting, fighting, kicking, hitting, stealing, screaming, spitting, hard pushing, and threatening violence. These behaviors show aggression that may indicate a child has personal problems that may have to be addressed if the behavior continues.

Research has shown that children who have witnessed or been direct victims of violence can suffer from posttraumatic stress disorder. This disorder can be displayed by reliving the violence in play (Groves et al., 2000). Children who display especially violent behavior may need special help, including psychological referrals. A conscientious teacher can often handle violent behavior by observation, communication, and redirection (Poole, 2004).

The amount of violence shown on television is increasing. It can be harmful to children and may cause children who watch it to be more aggressive with other children (Thornburg, 2002; Wilson, 2006). The use of guns has escalated even among young children. Real firearms, not just toy guns, are a threat to many young children in their neighborhoods and their homes. Thirty-four percent of U.S. children, or 22 million children, live in homes with at least one firearm (Rand Corporation, 2001).

In Texas, teachers have created a holistic curriculum that deals with this specific issue. Called Connect4Success, it is a joint effort by children, teachers, families, and the greater community. This training focuses on child development and practical classroom strategies to promote peaceful problem solving (Lamm et al., 2006). Training participants learn about the impact of television and other media exposure and how to limit its negative effects. The basics of this program include three strategies to implement in order to improve interactions in the early childhood environment. The first is to make sure the environment is positive both in how the classroom is set up and the interactions conducted by all involved. The second is to help children recognize their feelings and respond in a positive way to those feelings. The third is to learn how to peacefully resolve conflicts. This involves examining the problem and finding solutions, which can then be tried one at a time to see which ones might work. This curriculum would work well for children over the age of 3 or 4 years because at that age they are beginning to have a greater understanding of themselves and the world around them. It gives a sense of connection with this issue to the children, the families, and the teachers, and helps create a more peaceful community within and outside the early childhood education environment.

Fox and colleagues (2006) designed a teaching pyramid model to describe practices that are both preventive and supportive of the social and emotional development of children (see Figure 3-6). This model begins with creating positive relationships and then moves on to using preventive practices in the early childhood education environment. Next, it focuses on teaching strategies that promote healthy social and emotional skills. The top of the pyramid deals with inventive intervention strategies for the child who needs extra help.

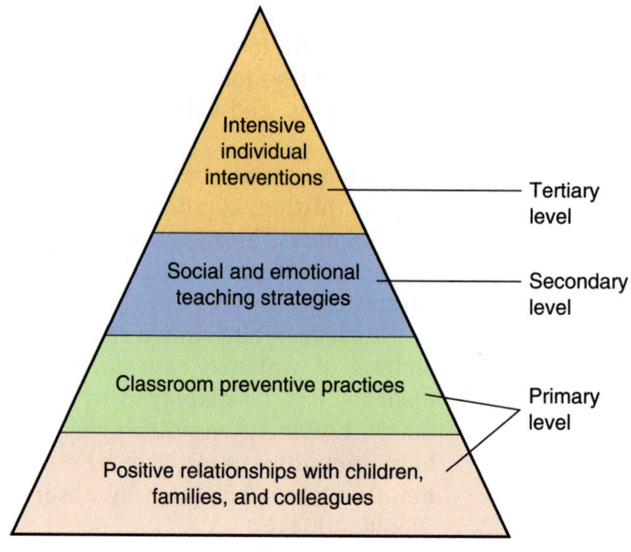

FIGURE 3-6
The Teaching Pyramid Model. (From Fox, L., & R.H. Lentini. 2006. "You got it!" Teaching social and emotional skills. *Young Children* 61 (6): 36–42. Reprinted with permission from the National Association for the Education of Young Children.)

Kevin lived in a neighborhood where he saw much violence. His early childhood education center was in an inner city. Jacob, Kevin's primary teacher, noticed that Kevin seemed to become more and more aggressive in his play. One day Jacob decided to track Kevin's behavior. He counted four physical confrontations with friends, two biting incidents, and several threats. Jacob did not know what might have occurred to change Kevin's usually good behavior. Jacob spoke to Kevin's mother, Mona, and found that Kevin's older brother had been beaten up and Kevin had witnessed it. Jacob decided to try several things to help Kevin deal with his emotions.

First, Jacob talked to Kevin about his brother and what had occurred. He explained to Kevin how violence did not solve problems and that talking out feelings was better than acting on them. Jacob knew that this was not always easy. He decided to bring in a punching bag and placed it in a corner of the early childhood education center so that using it would not put children at risk.

Jacob showed Kevin how to use the bag and instructed Kevin to come and use it whenever angry feelings started to grow. Kevin began using it the next day. In fact, he spent a lot of time punching the bag. After a week or so, Kevin's behavior was noticeably improved, as was the interpersonal safety of the other children. Jacob noticed an interesting result in helping Kevin. Without discussing it, many of the children began using the punching bag when they were angry.

REALITY *Check*

Kids and Guns

Kids and guns cause a serious safety issue for this country. Approximately 1.69 million children older than age 6 have access to guns in their homes. One in every three households contains a gun (Okoro et al., 2005). Forty-four million Americans own a total of 192 million guns. More than 60 percent of these guns do not have trigger locks. In homes with children and guns, 8 percent of the guns are unlocked and loaded, and 22 percent of guns are unlocked (Johnson et al., 2006; Connor, 2005). It is estimated that only one-third of firearms in homes are stored safely (Durant et al., 2007). Having children in the home did not increase the likelihood of safe storage (Connor, 2005). Approximately one-third of the guns owned are handguns (Eller, 1998). In the United States, about half of the children who die from gunshot wounds are under 5 years old (NSKC, 2001). In 1998, more children died from gunshot wounds than from a combination of HIV-AIDS, cancer, asthma, influenza, and pneumonia. Gun-related injuries in the United States are more than twice those of any other industrialized nation in the world (American Heart Association, 2005). More children and teens are lost to gun violence in America than servicemen are killed in combat in Afghanistan and Iraq (Children's Defense Fund [CDF], 2007).

The majority of families that own guns feel their guns are hidden and stored safely. A study showed otherwise. As many as 80 percent of children whose families had guns knew where those guns were by the time they were in the first or second grade (NSKC, 2001). A more recent study revealed that 73 percent of children younger than age 10 know the location of guns in their homes, and about half of those children had handled the guns (Geller, 2006). Twenty-two percent of the parents of these children who handled guns reported that their children never touched guns. Parents appeared to believe that their children were either "too smart" or that they "knew better" than to handle guns (Connor & Wesolowski, 2003). Fifty-eight of those killed by guns in 2004 were preschool-aged children. It seems that parents have an unrealistic view of children's developmental levels when it comes to guns (Baxley & Miller, 2006).

A revealing study whose subjects were 8- to 12-year-old boys found that even though 90 percent of these boys had had gun safety training, when they found a handgun in a safe environment, all of them picked up the gun and played with it, and many pulled the trigger (Jackman et al., 2001). It appears that parents of adolescents are less likely to keep a gun that is unlocked and loaded than they are with younger children. Many firearm injuries to children involve adolescents (Johnson et al., 2006).

Children are witnessing violence in increasing numbers on the streets, in their homes, and on television. Even very young children who see a violent act are deeply affected by it (Adults and Children Together [ACT], 2001). Because children's minds develop rapidly in these early years, behavior learned at this time can affect development and adult personality (Palmer, 2000). Witnessing violence may threaten a child's basic sense of trust in people. Some children who witness violence may turn their feelings outward toward others (Groves et al., 2000; Holland, 2007b).

Often, witnessing violence occurs while viewing television. By the time a child completes elementary school, she has witnessed some 8000 murders on television. Commercial television for children is 50 to 60 times more violent than adult prime-time television (Osofsky, 1999). Children may learn that handling violence with aggression is acceptable. Violence and the use of firearms are often treated humorously in cartoons. Some cartoons average 80 violent acts per hour.

Children need a sense of trust and safety so they can grow and develop to their potential. Children are witnessing the fact that they may not be safe or protected in many of their life situations. They need

(continues)

REALITY *Check* (continued)

to feel that they can have some direction over their lives, but children who live with violence learn that they have little say in what happens to them. Beginning with the restrictions on autonomy when they are toddlers, this sense of helplessness continues as they reach school age (Wallach, 1994). As they grow up, many children exposed to violence may begin to carry guns in order to feel safe and protected.

Children's curiosity about guns and how they work is encouraged by the violence they see on television. In the nightly news, they can view terrorism and war (Levin, 2003a). They are also tempted by manufacturers of children's toys. Guns are everywhere. They are in poor neighborhoods as well as middle-class schools. The events at Columbine and other schools reinforce this fact. Many children are at risk for safety because of guns.

The teacher can do several things to protect children from guns. The best thing would be to have no guns in the environment so that no children are at risk (AAP, 2000). However, some family child care homes and some early childhood education centers in high-risk neighborhoods may have guns. The teacher can ensure that any firearm present is kept out of sight, locked away, and separate from the ammunition (Health and Human Services Agency [HHSA], 2004). Teachers can provide children with alternative forms of handling disagreements in a prosocial manner by teaching them to resolve their conflicts (Levin, 2003b). Teachers can insist on a peaceable classroom, with no toy guns and no pretending other toys such as Legos or blocks are guns. Teachers can also provide a sense of community in their early childhood education environment so that children learn that contributing toward peace in a community is valuable (Levin, 2003a). They can also educate parents about the dangers of guns and tell them that no child is immune from playing with a firearm if it is around. If television is available in the early childhood education environment, programs may be monitored and violent programs should be turned off. Teachers should also model appropriate behaviors in how they handle conflict, anger, and stress (Poole, 2004).

CHECK*point:* **Under what situations might guns be available in an early childhood education program? What could a teacher do to educate a child about how to prevent violence in the home and community?**

Strategies to Promote Positive Interaction

Teacher awareness of unsafe behavior is the primary tool for safety promotion and prevention of injury in interpersonal relations among the children. Children learn best when appropriate behavior is modeled for them.

Strategies that the teacher can use to promote positive social interaction and conflict resolution are listed in Table 3-10. The use of these strategies will be helpful to ensure a greater degree of interpersonal safety in the early childhood education environment.

TABLE 3-10
Strategies for Promoting Interpersonal Safety

- Help children recognize the difference between appropriate and inappropriate behaviors.
- Help children recognize that violence and antisocial behavior cause problems.

(continues)

TABLE 3-10 *(Continued)*
Strategies for Promoting Interpersonal Safety

- Provide limits and consistent behavior.
- Acknowledge needs, fears, and wants of children.
- Realize negative behavior may indicate unmet needs of a child.
- Verbally redirect children's behavior.
- Model a full range of emotions in acceptable ways.
- Allow, identify, and react to a child's expression of emotion.
- Label expressions of emotions so that children learn to identify those emotions.
- Help children find acceptable ways to express their emotions.
- Use play, role playing, conversation, books, and pictures to explore and help children express a range of feelings.
- Help children find calming strategies that work, such as taking deep breaths.
- Do not allow the use of toy guns.
- Avoid storing firearms in the early childhood education environment, if possible. If present, the guns must be locked up with ammunition stored in a separate location.
- Support and encourage cooperation among the children during play.
- "Catch them being good" by acknowledging positive behaviors.
- Encourage those behaviors that promote conflict resolution.
- Develop a behavior support plan to help the problem child throughout the early childhood education environment and with all teachers so there is consistency.

Key Concept 3.5

Interpersonal Safety

The early childhood education environment may have situations involving behaviors that put interpersonal safety of those present at risk. Biting, kicking, and other aggressive behaviors can pose threats to other children and the teacher. The effect that television and other media have on how children behave in relation to violence should be addressed. Some types of early childhood education environments may have guns present that would pose great risk if children were to gain access to them. It is very important that the teacher use all strategies for positive social interaction to resolve conflict and protect the interpersonal safety of those present in the early childhood education environment.

3.6 POISON CONTROL

The most common emergency involving children is accidental poisoning. Ninety percent of poisonings occur in the home, and of these more than two-thirds involve children younger than 4 years (*America's children: Key national indicators of well-being, 2007*, 2007). Children younger than 2 years old are especially at risk. Family child care and nanny care operate out of a home environment, so these places are more likely to pose risk than center-based care. Regardless of the type of early childhood education environment, the teacher must employ prevention as the primary means of poison control. A strategy suggested by some is to use the "Mr. Yuk" warning sticker on products that contain poison in order to deter children, but this has not proven to be effective at all (Schnitzer, 2006). The first order of prevention is vigilance in monitoring the children in care. This is effective only if the environment has been modified for safety. Removing all hazards and risks for exposure to poisons is the only way to provide a protected environment.

Examining the Environment

Poisoning occurs from many common items found in a household or early childhood education environment. Cleaners, medicines, laundry supplies, cosmetics, plants, pesticides, garden supplies, automobile fluids, and certain foods can poison a child who ingests them. The teacher should make a room-by-room inspection for poisons in the early childhood education environment. If the care is performed in a home, special care should be taken to inspect the entire environment. Bathrooms, bedrooms, kitchens, and garages are full of poisonous substances that may go unnoticed in daily life if children are not present. Table 3-11 gives the teacher a list of common substances that are poisonous to children and are found in the home. For more information contact the American Association of Poison Control Centers at 1-800-222-1222 or visit their website at http://www.aapcc.org/findyour.htm.

Wadsworth/Cengage Learning

Knowledge of poisonous substances could prevent a dangerous situation here. Apple seeds can be poisonous, so this innocent-looking art project could actually put children at risk.

TABLE 3-11
Common Hazardous Substances Found in the Home

Bathrooms	
Prescription drugs	Antacids
Over-the-counter medicines, creams, and lotions	Hair care products
Peroxide, alcohol, Mercurochrome, and other medications for injuries	Makeup and skin care products
Vitamins, iron pills, and other dietary supplements	Nail products such as polish and polish remover
Cleaning solutions	Hair removal products
	Electric blow dryers, curling irons, and radios
Bedroom	
Birth control pills, foams, and so forth	Hair care products
Body lotions	Makeup and skin care
Kitchen	
Cleaning products	Alcoholic beverages
Detergents	Bleach
Polishes for silver, brass, chrome, and so forth	Oven cleaning products
Baking sprays and oils	Waxes and other appliance care products
Insecticides	Floor care products
Kidney beans, apple seeds	
Garage	
Gasoline	Insecticides and pesticides
Motor oil, lubricants, and other engine care products	Laundry products
Waxes, detergents, and other car care products	Solvents
	Paint and paint removal products
Home Office	
Printer or copy machine toner	Permanent marking pens
Glue	

Pause for Reflection

Use Table 3-11 to think about what poisons might be in your own home environment. In your mind's eye, go through your home room by room, as the table indicates. What items did you think of? Were there more than were in the table? What could you do to make your own home safer from poisons?

Strategies for Removal of Risk from Poisons and Toxins in the Early Childhood Education Environment

The teacher who anticipates, modifies the environment, and monitors children carefully should be able to avoid risk due to poisoning. Poisonings can occur in five ways.

1. Ingestion
2. Contact
3. Inhalation
4. Animal, insect, or reptile bites
5. Injection

Ingestion is swallowing the poison. Children are attracted to bright, colorful packages, pills, and odd shapes. They often encounter containers that have been previously used for food or drink and that now contain poisonous substances.

Contact occurs when poisonous substances or plants come in contact with the skin. This type of poisoning is indirect; the poison is absorbed through the skin into the bloodstream. In a study on children in day care centers and homes, it was found that when dust samples were taken from carpets, surfaces, and the indoor air, there was residue of pyrethroid insecticides, also know as permethrins, in almost all aspects of the environment (Morgan et al., 2007).

Inhalation occurs when children breathe fumes from pesticides, certain types of art materials, or dust that may contain lead. The exchange of air in the lungs allows the poison to come in direct contact with the lungs, after which it enters the bloodstream. In another study with dust samples in day care environments, pentachlorophenols (PCPs) were detected in more than 50 percent of the cases. The potential exposures to PCPs were found to be mostly through inhalation (Wilson et al., 2007).

Animal and insect bites can cause allergic reactions in children. Some allergic reactions are very toxic and can lead to death. Certain insect bites can cause health and safety risks. These include tick bites, which can transmit Lyme disease or Rocky Mountain spotted fever. Reptiles such as rattlesnakes and copperhead snakes can bite children, and their poison enters the bloodstream. Other diseases such as cat scratch fever, rabies, and salmonella can come from bites or other types of direct contact with animals.

Injection occurs when there is a puncture wound. The danger may come from the substance that was injected or remnants of tetanus on the item that caused the puncture. Today there is an extra threat of children finding needles that have been used to inject drugs. An accident like this can expose the child to human immunodeficiency virus (HIV).

Table 3-12 includes teacher strategies for promoting poison control protection in the early childhood education environment.

Some common indoor plants such as the philodendron are poisonous. To protect the children in their care, teachers need to know which plants are poisonous and keep them out of the children's reach. (Courtesy of Interior Plantscape division of ACLA.)

Plants that Pose Risk

Plants are another poisonous hazard found in the indoor environment. The teacher should be familiar with the types of plants that may be present. All plants should be out of reach of children. Any plants that are potentially hazardous to children should be removed from the early childhood education environment. Table 3-13 lists indoor plants that pose risk for poisoning. In the past, it was recommended that syrup of ipecac be given to a child who swallowed poisonous material. That policy changed in 2003, and the AAP is no longer recommending that syrup of ipecac be used at all (Sutton, 2004).

TABLE 3-12
Strategies for Promoting Poison Control

- Always supervise children in care.
- Keep poisons in a locked cabinet out of sight and reach of children.
- Keep medicines, household cleaners, and laundry products in their original containers. Never store nonfood items in food containers.
- Use childproof safety caps.
- Use safety latches or locks on all storage cupboards.
- Never call medicine "candy," and do not take medicine in front of children—they love to imitate.
- Inspect the early childhood education environment location from a child's-eye view—on your hands and knees—to check the environment for poison risks.
- Wipe surfaces and vacuum carpets on a regular basis to keep dust down from PCPs and other potentially harmful agents.
- Mop floors often to keep surfaces free of PCPs and other potentially harmful agents.
- Determine that all the plants in your environment are nonpoisonous.
- Keep pets in a regulated environment.
- Keep the environment free of insects.
- Teach poison prevention to the children and the teachers who are in the early childhood education facility.
- Keep the local poison control center number on your phone.
- Keep parents informed about poison control.
- When prevention fails, learn to act immediately in an educated manner.

TABLE 3-13
Common Indoor Plants that Pose Risk for Poisoning

Plant	Reaction
Philodendron Schefflera Pothos	Burning and irritation of the lining of the mouth, tongue, and lips. Can be fatal. May also cause skin reaction.
Diffenbachia Elephant ear	Intense burning and irritation of the lining of the mouth and tongue. If tongue swells, it may cause blockage to air passage and result in death.
Hyacinth Narcissus Daffodil	These bulbs are often found indoors in late winter and early spring. Nausea, diarrhea, and vomiting. Can be fatal.
Castor bean Rosary pea	Fatal. A single pea or bean is enough to kill a child.
Poinsettia	Nausea, skin reactions.

Key Concept 3.6

Poison Control

Poison control is an essential task of the teacher. The environment should be examined for poisons. Safety risks from poisons in the early childhood education environment can be reduced through removal, proper storage, supervision, and by using as few poisonous products as possible. Good safety practices and supervision help prevent accidents involving poisoning. Plants in the environment should be nonpoisonous and should be kept away from children.

3.7 FIRE AND BURN PREVENTION

Children are very susceptible to fires and burns because they are so curious and do not yet recognize dangers. The sense of touch is important for children when they are learning to explore their world. The most common injury from fires and burns comes from touching (Sailors, 2006). Injuries from burns and accidents with fire are the third leading cause of death among American children (CDC, 2001a). About 80 percent of the deaths result from house fires and smoke inhalation. Thirty-five percent of all burn injuries happen to children; scalding is the chief cause of burns to children of preschool age. Fires caused by playing with matches and lighters are the number one cause of fire-related deaths among young children. Burns range in severity from first degree to third degree (Figure 3-7). Burns to children can happen in numerous ways. Dry heat from fires and wet heat from steam are the most common, but burns can also come from electricity, chemicals, and hot objects. The concept of cause and effect is not enough to help children protect themselves unless they are repeatedly taught fire and burn prevention and safety. One of the best preventive measures is to install smoke detectors because 70 percent of deaths from fire and smoke inhalation happen in places without one (American Heart Association, 2005).

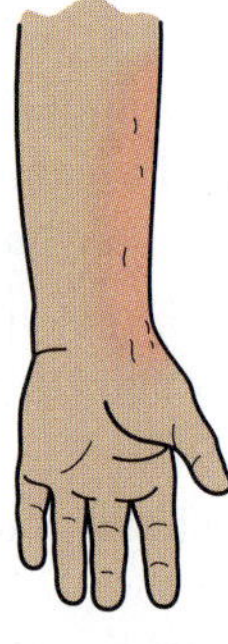

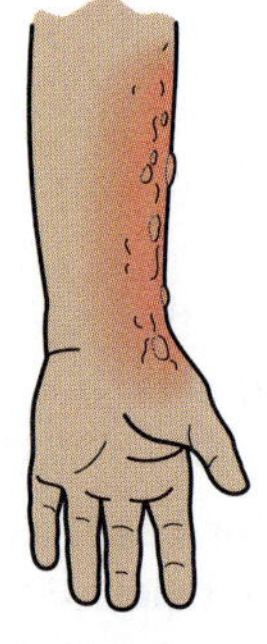

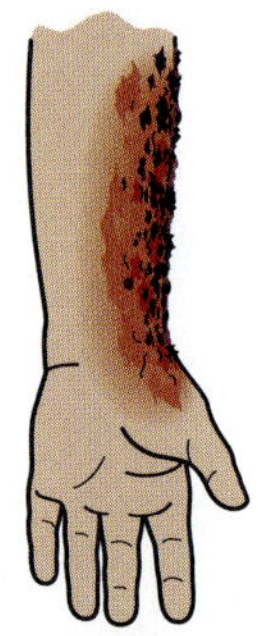

FIGURE 3-7 First-, second-, and third-degree burns.

Environmental Hazards

The teacher must be aware of everything in the early childhood education environment that can present hazards and fire and burn risks. Table 3-14 gives an overview of typical environmental hazards that may be present.

TABLE 3-14
Environmental Hazards for Burns

Scalding

- Boiling liquids or food on or off stove
- Steam
- Hot coffee or cocoa
- Hot bath water or tap water hotter than 120°F

Electrical

- Sticking a foreign object into an electrical outlet
- Touching a live wire
- Water contact with an electrical appliance

Contact

- Hot pan on stove
- Touching fire in fireplace
- Candles or candle wax
- Cigarettes, cigars, or pipes
- Matches, lighters
- Flammable clothing or sleeping materials

Chemical

- Strong household chemicals
- Automobile chemicals
- Lawn and garden chemicals

Strategies for Fire and Burn Prevention

It is up to the teacher to help children be aware of hazards that can cause fires or burns. Children should regularly be taught to avoid matches and lighters. These items should be stored out of sight and not used unless necessary. Children should also have regular practice drills for fire evacuation. They should be familiar with "Stop, Drop, Roll, Cool, and Call," "Go Tell a Grown-up," and "Crawl Low under Smoke" (Cole, Crandall, & Kourofsky, 2004). Safety devices such as fire extinguishers and smoke alarms should be present and in working condition. It has been recommended that irons not be used in early childhood environments and that heat-resistant screens should be place around heat sources so children cannot reach them (Sailors, 2006). As with any safety hazard, the teacher is ultimately responsible for keeping children safe. One of the best things that can be done is to lower the hot water heater to 120°F or less so that there is no chance for scald burns in the sink. Modeling preventive behaviors will reinforce fire and burn accident prevention. Table 3-15 gives teachers some strategies that will help prevent fires and burns in the early childhood education environment.

TABLE 3-15
Strategies for Fire and Burn Prevention

- Use only correct size fuses in the fuse box.
- Install and regularly check smoke detectors. Change batteries frequently.
- Teach children to "Stop, Drop, Roll, Cool, and Call." Be sure to tell them to keep their faces covered with their hands during the Roll portion.
- Keep a fire extinguisher on hand, know how to use it, and refill it immediately after use.
- Place and maintain barriers around fireplaces, heaters, radiators, and hot pipes.
- Try not to use matches or lighters around children. If matches are present, store them out of sight in a locked cabinet or drawer.
- Teach children to bring you any matches they find. If they find a lighter, have them immediately tell you so that you can pick it up.
- Use safety devices to cover electrical outlets.
- Inspect and clean heating systems, including stoves and fireplaces, once a year.
- Make sure there are sufficient outlets for all appliances to prevent overloading electrical wiring.
- Keep extension cords exposed; do not run them under furniture or rugs.
- Keep all flammable liquids stored in safety cans and out of reach of children.
- Keep furnaces, heating equipment, and chimneys and flues cleaned regularly.
- Never allow children in the food preparation area without supervision.
- Do not drink or carry anything hot when close to a child.
- Test hot food before giving it to a child.
- Never warm a bottle in the microwave.
- Set water heaters to no higher than 120°F.
- Never bathe a child in water you have not tested.
- Never leave children unattended in the bath or near a faucet. They might turn on the hot water.
- Turn pot handles in toward center or rear of stove, and only cook on rear burners when possible.
- Never use portable, open-flame, or space heaters.
- Never smoke around children.
- Never store flammable liquids such as gasoline near the child care environment.

Key Concept 3.7

Fire and Burn Prevention

The teacher should actively practice fire and burn prevention. Burn hazards to children come from many areas. Children can be burned from scalding hazards, electrical hazards, hazards that are directly contacted with heat, or fire and chemical hazards. The teacher should use all strategies available to protect children in early childhood education environments from any hazards that might cause fires or burns.

3.8 IMPLICATIONS FOR TEACHERS

The teacher should use observation, supervision, and education to provide a safe indoor environment. These risk management tools provide preventive and protective measures for the early childhood education environment (Schwebel & Gaines, 2007).

Table 3-16 shows a safety policy for the teacher to prevent choking and suffocation. This measure uses all of the risk management tools previously mentioned.

Observation

Observation for accessories, behaviors, and conditions offers the teacher the awareness needed to prevent risk in the indoor environment. Knowledge of hazards in equipment, toys and craft supplies, and poisons helps the teacher

TABLE 3-16
Preventing Choking and Suffocation in Early Childhood Education

- Remove loose parts from toys.
- Use a choke-testing device on small toys. Always do this before adding a questionable toy to the environment.
- Keep diaper and other pins, toothpicks, and nails out of your mouth.
- Do not wear dangle-type jewelry such as necklaces and earrings.
- Check toys, games, and art supplies for broken pieces and throw them away.
- Teach children not to run with anything in their mouths.
- Teach children to chew well, and do not allow playing when eating.
- Never prop a baby bottle.
- Never use Styrofoam cups—children like to chew them.
- Regularly hand out consumer toy alerts as you find them. Newspapers and magazines carry this information, particularly around Christmas.

remove these items and reduce risk. Observation adds another layer of protection. The teacher must also be aware of unsafe interpersonal behavior practices. This may help the teacher to stop or redirect action before it causes injury. The early childhood education environment should also be inspected for fire and burn hazards. Children should be carefully observed to avoid burns or fires.

Supervision

The greatest concern for supervision is constantly monitoring children for safety in all situations. In addition, the teacher should monitor all safe practices, methods of prevention, and means of promoting safety (Aronson, 2001). This will ensure that every measure possible is being used to provide a safe environment. Careful observation, anticipation, monitoring, and modifying is necessary at all times. Never let conversation or anything else distract from the safety of children in care. Checking for compliance with licensing standards, local fire safety guidelines, and other safety-related ordinances is another way the environment must be monitored for safety. Through communication, the teacher can make sure all adults in the early childhood education environment are using safe practices.

Education

Preventing safety risks is promoted through education of teachers, children, and their parents. The more tools everyone has for becoming aware of hazards, developmental limitations, and the early childhood education environment, the greater the opportunities that are available to prevent accidents and injuries.

Children can be taught many safe behaviors through a number of methods and curriculum. Visitors such as firefighters and police officers can show children how to keep safe. Teachers can be role models of safe behaviors every day. They can read books and provide videotapes that will help children become aware of the need for safe practices. Teachers can conduct regular drills for fire and other safety threats. They can practice "Stop, Drop, Roll, Cool, and Call" with children on a regular basis. Teachers can talk with children about appropriate and inappropriate interpersonal behaviors.

For Families

Teachers can provide families with information about safety by handing out information sheets or handouts supplied by agencies such as fire departments, poison control centers, and police departments. They can request parents and children to practice fire drills at home on a regular basis. Teachers can also provide indoor information on a bulletin board, in a newsletter, or by having workshops on safety for families. They can point out safety measures that are being used and help families to understand the importance of safety.

If a child is having a particular problem such as biting or aggressive behavior, the teacher can work with the family to develop a plan to modify the child's behavior.

Key Concept 3.8

Implications for Teachers

The teacher should use all measures possible to protect the children and prevent injury. Tools such as observation, supervision, education, and working with families can provide practices for the teacher to ensure safety through promotion, prevention, and protection.

CHAPTER SUMMARY

There are a number of threats to indoor safety, including indoor equipment, toys, interpersonal behaviors, poisons, and fires and burns. Safety policies are necessary for the teacher to monitor and protect the environment. An understanding of the developmental levels of the children present is essential. The teacher should use checklists to monitor and modify the early childhood education environment. All items, including cleaning supplies, pets, computers, plants, and art supplies, should be examined for safety and removed if they present risk. Through the use of observation, supervision, education, and working with families, teachers can promote and practice safe behaviors in the early childhood education environment.

TO GO BEYOND

Additional resources for this chapter can be found by visiting the book companion website at www.cengage.com/education/robertson. This supplemental material includes chapter objectives, internet exercises, reflection questions, quizzes, web links, glossary and flash cards, case studies, frequently asked questions, downloadable forms and tables, curriculum supplements, more reality checks, additional key concepts, references, and more.

Chapter Review Critical Thinking Applications

1. Compare and contrast the safety policies for the indoor environment found in an early childhood education center and a family child care home. How are these policies affected by the ages of children?
2. Discuss the need for safe, risk-free toys.
3. Relate how age appropriateness affects toy selection for early childhood education. What are some of the potential risks if inappropriate toys are selected?
4. Discuss how an indoor environment for an infant/toddler program would be different than one for 4-year-old preschool children.

5. Discuss the importance of conflict resolution for interpersonal safety in the early childhood education environment.
6. Discuss the importance of fire and other drills for children.

As an Individual

1. Visit an early childhood education center and survey it for indoor safety. Make a list of the risks observed and bring it back to class to share. Compare your list with what others observed.
2. Take the list of indoor plants found in this chapter to a local nursery or flower shop and identify poisonous indoor plants that you find there. Have you seen any of these plants in a household that has children? Share your results in a discussion in class.
3. Search the Internet for two sites that directly relate to kids and guns. Write a synopsis of the sites. Share these sites with your classmates in class.
4. Call a local fire department and find out the types of programs it offers to educate young children about fire safety. Compare this to what others found in different fire jurisdictions.
5. Visit the local toy or discount store after having looked at the U.S. Consumer Product Safety Commission website about recalled toys. Make a list of the latest recalls from the past six months. See whether you can find any of the latest recalls on the shelves. Also, look for signs in regards to recalls. Next, choose a couple of toys to scrutinize for safety. Report your findings to the whole class.

As a Group

1. List the developmental-level risks for an 18-month-old toddler in an indoor environment at an early childhood education center, then a family child care home. Compare and contrast the two lists.
2. In groups of four or five students, design an early childhood education room for 2-year-olds that includes all the amenities, while being low risk.
3. In groups of four or five students, have the group choose among the following topics and design a safety policy.
   - Fire safety
   - Play dough
   - Art projects
   - Interpersonal safety
   - Poison control
   - Indoor water safety
   - Toy safety
4. In groups of four or five students, choose three early childhood centers for each group and find out what, if any, safety policy they have regarding use of computers. Compare information. If no safety policies for computers were found, have the entire class create one.

5. Visit a fire station and have the firefighters give the class the same demonstrations they would give to preschoolers. Assess the presentation for developmental appropriateness. Have students discuss what they learned from this demonstration.

Case Studies

1. Travis is a gregarious, feisty 3½-year-old who has been at the early childhood education center for about six weeks. He has two much older brothers, one of whom may be in a gang. Mallory, his teacher, has been concerned about Travis's behavior. He seems to have a number of disagreements with his classmates, and now he has started biting other children. What actions should Mallory take? What supportive measures could she offer to Travis, while still protecting the other children in her care? How should she approach Travis's mother about this problem?
2. Marnie has worked as a nanny for the Wilson family for ten months. The Wilsons have two children Josh, 6 years old, and Jocelyn, 14 months old. They have a two-story house, and it took Marnie several weeks of begging to get them to install a safety gate for the stairs. Her concern now is the kitchen and the bathroom, where there are hazardous substances within Jocelyn's reach. The Wilsons' answer to her plea to remove these items was, "Josh lived through this stage and never bothered a thing." They don't seem inclined to reduce the risk factors. What should Marnie do?
3. Madelyn is a family child care provider who has generally specialized in infant care. She has decided to continue with the three infants she now cares for, as they grow older. One of them is approaching 12 months, and Madelyn feels that she must safety-proof her home to allow for the change in developmental levels of the children she is caring for. You are a friend who provides early childhood education for a multiage group of children. What advice would you give her to inspect her environment, to anticipate actions and behaviors, and to monitor and modify her child care environment for safety risks to toddlers?
4. Jennifer is a first-grade teacher who just received three "new" computers in her classroom. She is very excited about this but wants the children to use them safely. What type of setup for the computers should she have? What rules should she make for using the computers in a safe manner?
5. Erika is a director of a community college child care center. A new center building is about to be finished, and she has been given a budget for equipping it with furniture, toys, and other items. What safety measures should she look for in furnishing the infant classroom? What toy safety features should she focus on for toys for children under age 3?

CHAPTER 4

Outdoor Safety

After reading this chapter, you should be able to:

4.1 Safety Policies for the Outdoor Early Childhood Education Environment

Describe and discuss safety policies for outdoor environments as tools for risk prevention, safety protection, and safety promotion.

4.2 Examining Early Childhood Education Environments for Outdoor Hazards

Indicate and discuss specific guidelines for making the early childhood education playground environment free from risk and protected for safety.

4.3 Playground Equipment Safety

Relate and discuss the safety hazards of outdoor equipment as they relate to early childhood education situations and general safety.

4.4 Traffic and Transportation Safety

Relate the guidelines for safe transportation and traffic involved in early childhood education environments.

4.5 Water Safety

Describe and discuss the water safety hazards in outdoor early childhood education.

4.6 Implications for Teachers

Indicate the need for education, observation, cultural competency, working with families, and supervision to maintain a safe outdoor environment.

4.1 SAFETY POLICIES FOR THE OUTDOOR EARLY CHILDHOOD EDUCATION ENVIRONMENT

Unintentional accidents and risks to safety are more likely to occur in the outdoor environment than indoors. Some risks are incurred by the child, such as drowning, falling, choking, and poisons. Other hazards, such as automobiles and bicycles, are responsible for a large number of childhood injuries and deaths each year. The following factors indicate a need for outdoor safety policies:

- Falls from playground equipment are the leading cause of injury in early childhood education environments. Head injuries cause most of the disabilities and fall-related deaths (NCCCHSRC, 2005a; NSKC, 2007a).
- Playgrounds should provide both play value and safety for healthy development (Frost, 1994; Sutterby & Thornton, 2005).
- In child care centers, children played on playground equipment without adult supervision 5 percent of the time, and on elementary school playground equipment children played without supervision 32 percent of the time (NSKC, 2007c). The most promising way to reduce playground injuries is through better quality and quantity of supervision by adults (Schwebel, 2006; Schwebel & Brezausek, 2008).

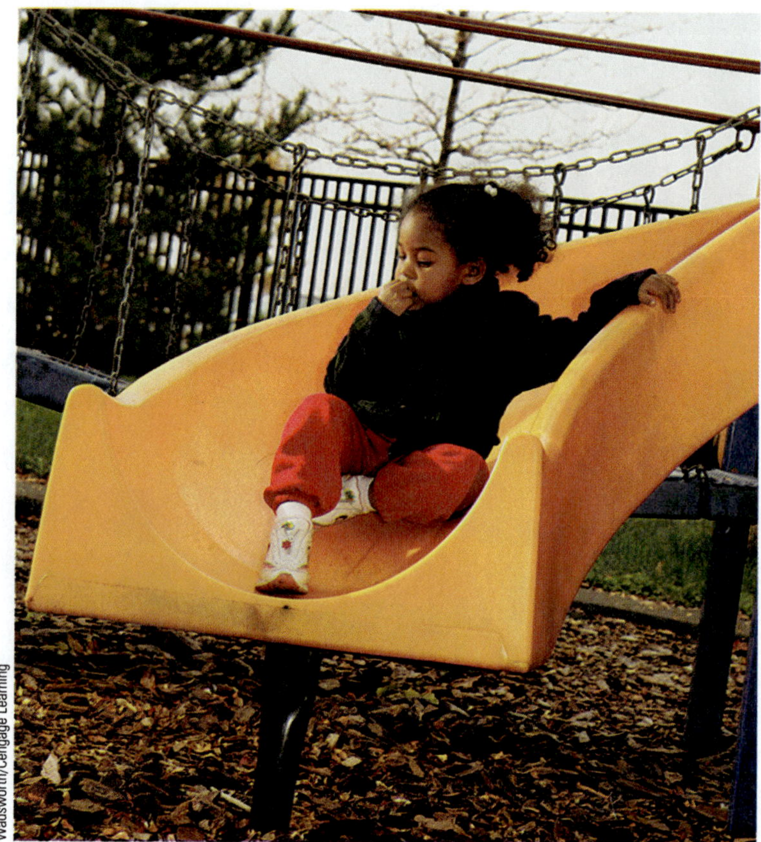

Wadsworth/Cengage Learning

Lack of attention is one of the reasons children may be at risk in outdoor situations. The child looks contemplative, but there may be another child ready to come down the slide, and she might not realize it and could be hurt.

- Early excessive exposure to the sun can cause serious damage to the skin and could later lead to malignant melanoma, and this is especially true for children (Knight, 2006; Mathe, 2007). Only 2 percent of elementary school districts require that outdoor activities be scheduled to avoid the times when sun intensity is at its peak (Jones et al., 2007).
- Approximately 3 million thefts and violent crimes occur near public schools each year (Levin, 2003). Many early childhood education centers and family child care homes are close to schools and therefore are at risk for safety. Feeling a lack of safety in a child's own neighborhood may impact him even if he is in a safer environment in school (Pachter et al., 2006).
- Motor vehicles are the most common cause of accidental deaths of children (Schnitzer, 2006; *America's children: Key national indicators of well-being, 2007,* 2007). More than 70 percent of the fatalities could be prevented with the use of a safety seat restraint (NSKC, 2004b).
- Almost 300,000 children each year are treated in an emergency room for bicycle-related injuries (NSKC, 2004a). Bicycle injuries are one of the leading causes of injury and death in children (Lipman, 2006).

Safety policies for the outdoor environment need to cover a wide range of areas. Not all the policies in this chapter will apply to all early childhood education environments. Vulnerability to injury involves a number of risks that may come from playground equipment, travel, traffic, bicycles, bodies of water, and the nearby neighborhood. Some of the hazards are related to accessories such as improper equipment or lack of proper cushioning under equipment. Behaviors such as lack of attention or a child trying a physical act she is not capable of performing may present risks. Conditions such as the child being tired or the teacher talking to another adult can cause risk.

Policies should cover monitoring accessories, conditions, and behaviors. They should comply with local licensing regulations and suggestions for accreditation, if applicable. Planning and promoting safe practices should be based on children's physical and developmental abilities as well as their emotional needs. Safety policies should include the following:

1. *Outdoor Early Childhood Education Environments:* understanding outdoor safety practices for the early childhood education environment and applications for risk management as they apply to the type of outdoor environment
2. *Playground Equipment Safety:* practices for preventing injuries and managing safety on playground equipment
3. *Travel and Traffic Safety:* practices for preventing injury, promoting safety, and strategies for developing guidelines for travel and traffic as it applies to early childhood education environments
4. *Water Safety:* practices for removing hazards, promoting safety, and preventing injury as it applies to water in the early childhood education environment
5. *Implications for Teachers:* methods and practices for conducting education, supervision, and observation and working with families for safety in the outdoor environment

Outdoor Safety Policies

The outdoor environment offers a large degree of risk for early childhood education environments. Outdoor safety policies should begin with examining the care environment. Policies should be created for playground equipment, traffic and travel safety, and water safety, and implications for teachers should be included.

4.2 EXAMINING EARLY CHILDHOOD EDUCATION ENVIRONMENTS FOR OUTDOOR HAZARDS

Outdoor environments may vary greatly from one early childhood education environment to the next, but they all have common features that contribute to outdoor childhood accidents, relating to these:

- Falls
- Motor vehicle and other transportation accidents
- Poisons
- Equipment

The environmental screening for safety should address the ABCs of injury risk (refer to Table 2-4). The teacher must anticipate problems, modify the environment, and monitor the children in care for unsafe practices. The teacher must also be aware of conditions and behaviors that lead to injury in the outdoor environment. A teacher must always supervise children in the outdoor environment.

Outdoor Environmental Hazards

The early childhood education outdoor environment should be free of hazards. Protective measures and preventive practices can help reduce the risk that accessories may provide in the outdoor environment. General environment hazards include lack of barriers, poisons, insects, and extremes of temperature. Other considerations may also present risk in the outdoor environment.

Barriers. The play area should have a fence or other barrier that surrounds it and is at least four feet high. A fence should separate the play area from all automobile traffic and any hidden corners of the outdoor area that could go unobserved if a child wandered into that corner. Fences should be constructed of safe materials and kept intact and in working order. Gates should fasten securely and should have latches high enough to be out of the reach of children or a safety latch that is childproof.

Poison Control. Poison control in the outdoor environment is essential. Toxic plants are the most common hazard for poison in the outdoors. Table 4-1 has a comprehensive listing of toxic outdoor plants.

TABLE 4-1
Common Outdoor Poisonous Plants

Flowers	
Azaleas	Hyacinth
Bleeding heart	Iris
Calla lily	Jonquil
Daffodil	Larkspur
Delphinium	Lily-of-the-valley
Foxglove	Lobelia
Four o'clock	Rhododendron
Shrubs and Trees	
Black locust	Oak
Chinaberry	Oleander
Elderberry	Poison hemlock
Holly berries	Pencil tree
Jerusalem cherry	Wild cherry
Mistletoe	Wisteria
Night blooming jasmine	Yellow jasmine
Nightshade	
Vines	
Boston ivy	English ivy
Devil's ivy	Morning glory
Vegetable Plants	
Potato sprouts and leaves	Rhubarb leaf
Tomato vines and leaves	

Other poison hazards include pesticides, insecticides, other gardening materials, and barbecue supplies. If these are in the environment, they should be placed up high in a locked cabinet (NSKC, 2004c). If a garage or workshop is present on the site, where automobile repair fluids and gasoline are stored, this area should be off limits and fenced off, or a locked door should serve as a barrier to this area.

Keep the outdoor area as free from pollutants as possible. Use insect sprays sparingly and only when children are not present. If lawns are sprayed with weed killers or fertilizers, wait several days before allowing children to play on them (Fournier, 2004).

Also, keep the environment free of poison ivy, poison oak, and sumac, which can cause rashes that may spread on contact. One of the most common poisonous plants throughout much of the United States, in elevations from sea level to 5000 feet, is poison oak. Contact with this plant can cause a mild to severe rash that can be spread easily by touching the affected area. Children and staff should be educated as to what it looks like and what to do if contact is made (Walsh, 2006). This is also true of poison ivy and sumac. Remove these plants from the environment, but do not burn them either

Wadsworth/Cengage Learning

Children need an environment where they are safe from poisonous plants and other outdoor hazards.

indoors or outdoors because the fumes can damage the lining of a child's lung. You would not burn *anything* outdoors with children present, but the fumes from burning these plants can linger.

Insects. Insect safety is important (AAP, 2004a). Although bites and stings do not normally cause serious harm to a child, some children may be especially sensitive. If the teacher knows that a child is sensitive to bee stings, he should be prepared to deal with this situation (Knight, 2007; Rose, 2007) (see Chapter 5). The outdoor environment should be inspected and rid of insect infestation such as wasp nests and anthills. Wasps live in trees or have nests on buildings or wooden playground equipment. Yellow jackets have underground nests and bees construct hives in trees. Ants nest underground with a small dirt mound above the ground. If any of these are spotted, keep children from this area until the pest problem is taken care of (Knight, 2007). The U.S. Environmental Protection Agency (EPA) suggests that places where children gather, such as early childhood education environments, should rely less on spraying for insects and more on what is referred to as insect pest management or IPM (Fournier, 2004; Rose, 2006). This method has the teacher doing a thorough investigation of the outdoor area of the early childhood education environment and managing it for pest control. For example, getting rid of standing water is especially critical for keeping down the population of mosquitoes that can carry the West Nile virus; young children are especially at risk (AAP, 2002; Healthy Child Care Pennsylvania, 2006a). Checking for standing water includes flower pots, buckets, old tires, water tables, and bird baths (Palmer, 2004). Those things that hold water, such as bird baths and water tables, should be changed frequently to avoid giving mosquitoes the opportunity to breed. If pest access to water, food, and shelter is removed, it is much less likely that they will habitate the area. Another consideration is inspecting buildings for structural gaps where wasps could gather. Another way to use IPM is to choose the least toxic alternatives to control pests. This may mean restricting food consumption to only one outdoor area, storing food in containers with tightly fitting lids, and cleaning garbage cans regularly. If food is consumed outside, it should be covered. Bees and other flying insects can land in food and drink and cause a sting to the mouth of an unsuspecting child. IPM can also include keeping vegetation at least one foot away from structures and using physical traps for pests, placed out of reach of the children (Rose, 2006). If chemicals must be used, it is important to use a licensed professional who understands IPM and the risks that chemicals can have to young children.

To keep children as protected as possible from stings and bites, there are several things the teacher can do:

- Do not use scented soaps, perfumes, hairspray, or lotions.
- Make sure children wear shoes and socks. Closed toe shoes are best.
- Teach children what wasps' and bees' nests look like.
- Have children wear light-colored, long-sleeved clothing.
- If eating outside, cover the food and beverages.
- Reduce outdoor activities in the early morning and late afternoon hours, when pests are more likely to gather, especially in spring and summer.

Some recommend the use of DEET, which is effective against mosquitoes. However, there are several drawbacks. These products should not be used with children younger than 3 years old, and, if used with children, they should contain no more than 30 percent DEET or they can be harmful to children (AAP, 2002). Palmer (2004) recommends using a DEET product that has a concentration of 10 percent, which he says is effective. The AAP recommends that DEET should be applied to the clothing rather than skin (Colino, 2003; Healthy Child Care Pennsylvania, 2006a). DEET should never be applied to a child's hands (NCCCHSRC, 2005b). Regardless, before a teacher would ever apply insect repellent with DEET in any way, the parents should give permission; in some states, a physician's permission is also needed. If the child appears to develop a rash or reaction to the repellent, wash it off with milk, soap, and water.

Some areas of the country have problems with ticks that can transmit Lyme disease. In these areas, children should be dressed in high socks, and their clothing should be checked for ticks before they come indoors. In fact, it is recommended that children wear light colors and long sleeves for greatest protection (Bush, 2003). Another recommendation is to avoid sitting on the ground. Remind parents to check children during bath time. If pets are in the early childhood education environment, inspect them daily and remove any ticks that are found.

Temperature. Extremes of temperature are potential hazards for children. Protection from heat stroke or heat exhaustion is a major consideration for outdoor play areas. Infants are especially susceptible to heat rash if they get too warm (Leonard, 2007). Shade should be present in the outdoor area. Try to schedule your outdoor activities before 10 A.M. and after 4 P.M., because the midday hours are when the sun exposure is the most damaging or the heat is at its hottest (Mathe, 2007). If it is not naturally available, provide a shade structure. Children need relief from the sun and heat to prevent overheating. All facilities should also have a safe outdoor source of drinking water to protect children from overheating or becoming dehydrated. Some early education environments provide a self-help thermos with cups. This cuts down on germs that children may pick up and spread while using a water fountain (Calder, 2006). It is a good idea to make sure children drink water before they go outside and that they drink some water every 20 minutes while they are outdoors to keep well hydrated (Colino, 2003) (for more information see Reality Check: *Sun Safety*).

Freezing temperatures and snow on outdoor equipment may result in slippery surfaces that cause children to fall more easily. Before going outdoors in these conditions, check equipment surfaces to make sure they are safe and not slippery. Children can go outside in temperatures as low as 20–32°F. Older children can safely go outdoors several times a day for 30 minutes or less. For toddlers and infants who are not walking, the time should be limited to less than 15 minutes several times a day (NCCCHSRC, 2005b). Children should be dressed warmly when playing outdoors in the cold. Ask parents not to dress their children with bulky clothing, but instead to layer lighter clothing on cold days. This allows warm air to be trapped and keeps the child from getting chilled sooner (Koontz, 2003). Children should go outside during the warmest part of the day and should be engaged in active play to keep warm. Their hands should be checked to see whether they are cold, and if they appear to be, it would be wise to go back inside. Even though the weather is cold, children need fresh air, and playing outside for a limited time while dressed warmly is a good way to see that they get it. Monitoring them for being cold is a good way to reduce the risk.

Other Considerations. Other safety considerations for the outdoor area include keeping bushes and trees trimmed so that children do not run into branches and injure themselves. Trimming trees also discourages or prevents climbing. If there is dirt in the environment, make sure it is not so fine that it

Wadsworth/Cengage Learning

Outdoor areas should have a good source of shade to prevent risk from the sun.

REALITY*Check*

Sun Safety

Skin cancer from sun exposure begins in early childhood. Scientists believe that two things can predispose a person to skin cancer: (1) a lifetime exposure and (2) severe sunburns (Norris Cotton Cancer Center [NCCC], 2002; NCCCHSRC, 2005). It may take only one severe sunburn as a child to cause melanoma in adulthood (Knight, 2006). Children have skin that is more easily damaged by the sun than is the skin of adults. Because children do play so much outdoors, and the outdoor environment in early childhood education is so important to children's development, it is critical that children be kept sun safe (Mathe, 2007). It is important that children be taught why and how they should protect themselves from ultraviolet rays. Instead of focusing on "skin cancer," it is felt that teachers should focus their sun safety education to children in terms of discomfort (Mathe, 2007). It is important to include sun safety in the policies created for the early childhood education environment. This includes elementary schools, where only 2 percent of districts have adopted procedures to minimize sun exposure during the peak times of the day, and only 4 percent of districts require that students use sunscreen before going outside (Jones et al., 2007).

Protecting children from the hazards of the sun on hot and sunny days is very important. It is recommended that the teacher access the climate prediction center (http://www.cpc.ncep.noaa.gov/) and find out the degree of ultraviolet exposure for that day (U.S. Environmental Protection Agency [EPA], 2001). On days when the ultraviolet exposure is highest, plan activities that keep children out of the sun.

Other suggestions to help keep ultraviolet exposure for children at a minimum include these:

- Keep infants out of direct sunlight (AAP, 1999).
- Avoid exposing children to the sun between the hours of 10 A.M. and 4 P.M., if possible (Mathe, 2005, 2007).
- If that is not possible, make sure children play in a shady area, such as under a tree, a permanent shade structure, or a cloth canopy. Teach children how to seek out these areas for themselves (EPA, 2001).
- Make sure children wear protective clothing if going out into the sun, such as hats, long-sleeved shirts, pants, and socks. Sheltering the eyes should be part of a sun protection program (Knight, 2006). It has also been suggested that children wear sunglasses that provide 100 percent UVA and UVB protection (Mathe, 2007). Teachers should model this behavior. Explain to parents that on hot sunny days, dressing children in lightweight clothing that will cover their body offers more protection. Even infants should be dressed in lightweight clothing to prevent overheating because they are very susceptible to heat rash (Leonard, 2007).
- When taking children out into the sun, use a sunscreen of SPF 15 or higher for children over the age of 6 months, and apply 30 minutes before going outside (Mathe, 2007). Staff should also do this. The AAP has recommended that, if there is no shade for infants under 6 months, a sunscreen could be used (AAP, 1999). You may want to ask parents to provide the sunscreen for their child or children. Some states require a physician's statement allowing the use of sunscreen. Be sure to check on the requirements for child care facilities and elementary schools in your state so you are compliant with its laws.
- If planning field trips for sunny days, make sure there is shade available (Buller & Farina, 1999).
- It is essential to educate parents and children about sun safety in order to develop sun safe behavior patterns (Boe & Tillotson, 2006).

CHECK*point:* **Why is it important to keep children sun safe? What do you do on a regular basis to keep yourself protected from the harmful rays of the sun? How could you be a better role model for children?**

will cause breathing problems for some children. Always check the outdoor environment after storms, high winds, and heavy rains. There may be fallen branches, twigs, and other debris on the ground.

Sand in a sandbox is another outdoor safety issue. The best type of sand to use is play sand or "natural sand" that is specifically made for use by children and has been sterilized. It does not contain any harmful materials such as asbestos that is found in some other types of sand. Sand in an outdoor area should be replaced every two years (Sutton, 2003). When playing in sand, children should always be well supervised to make sure they are not eating or throwing sand. Follow the same steps for sand toys as for indoor toy safety. Plastic toys are best; wooden or metal toys should be avoided because they can splinter or rust with time. When feasible, sandboxes should be covered, especially if there is an animal present in the environment. These sandboxes should be checked on a regular basis. In some cases, it would not be feasible to be cover large sand boxes and those on elementary school campuses, which are usually very large. Sandboxes should be kept clean and raked at least once a week. If the sandbox is in a shared-use facility, it should be carefully checked and raked daily for broken glass and other sharp objects. Surfaces around the sandbox should be swept often to prevent falls. If standing water remains in the sandbox after a rain, it should be removed as soon as the rain stops.

Some family child care backyards or shared facilities may have barbecue equipment present. This implies potential for harm from lighter fluid, barbecue utensils, and the grill itself. Other common hazards in these two environments are gardening tools and equipment. All of these hazards should be kept in a garage, barn, or out of the reach of children.

Items such as toxic fumes, gases, and air conditioner units should not be present in the outdoor environment. Early childhood education environments should not be less than 30 feet from high-voltage power stations, railroad tracks, or electrical substations. The facility should be maintained in a safe condition by removing any sharp rocks, building supplies, or dilapidated structures. The outdoor area should be free of unprotected ditches, cesspools, wells, and utility equipment (APHA & AAP, 2002). Abandoned appliances should not be present in the early childhood education environment. It is also important to check for the degree of air pollution in the outside environment. Some cities and states have air pollution alerts in compliance with the Clean Air Act (*America's children: Key national indicators of well-being, 2007,* 2007) and these are readily available by phone, Internet, or radio.

Limit children going barefoot to areas where the surfaces are safe. An example would be allowing infants or toddlers in an infant/toddler room to crawl or walk around where there is carpeting on the floor. Confine pets to certain areas during child care, and remove animal feces often. Treat the feces as you would diaper disposal (see Chapter 12), as in Table 12-6 on page 468.

Pause for Reflection

After reviewing the section on environmental hazards in the outdoor environment, what do you think you could do to improve an early education environment you have worked in or observed? Would it be the same for a family child care home?

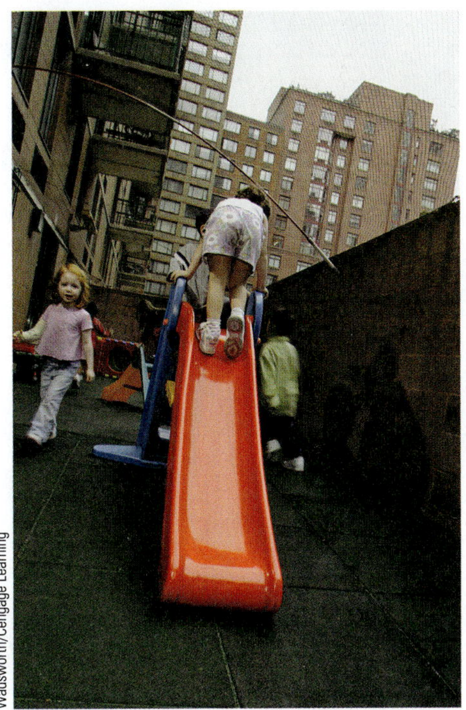

Wadsworth/Cengage Learning

Children should always be carefully observed in the outdoor environment. Many times, children are overconfident about their abilities and can get in situations like this that present a safety risk.

Developmental Level

The impact that development and behavior have on risk for safety is especially crucial in an outdoor environment. The majority of accidents happen outdoors. Children's developmental behaviors such as lack of fear, curiosity, inattention, poor impulse control, and going beyond physical capabilities can easily put them at risk for injury. A child's stage of developmental ability may make equipment a risk if it is not chosen for its age appropriateness (NCCCHSRC, 2005b). Teachers may not be paying adequate attention or may not properly communicate the risk of certain outdoor hazards. It has been shown that child care is actually safer than a child's own home (Schwebel, Brezausek, & Belksy, 2006; Schwebel, 2006), and this may well be because the majority of teachers are paying close attention to the environment for risk.

Using developmental levels to define the boundaries of the outdoor environment will help the teacher screen for accessories, behaviors, and conditions that lead to injuries. Prevention is the key to risk management. Planning and evaluating the environment based on the vulnerabilities of the children in care will help increase protection. Developmental levels of the children in care should be used as the starting point for screening the outdoor environment for hazards. Table 4-2 indicates the relationship of outdoor safety hazards to the developmental levels by age. This chart also indicates the greatest threats to safety at particular ages.

When the teacher realizes the hazards that put children at risk by age level, it will be much easier to carry out safe practices, appraise risks, and avoid potentially dangerous situations.

As the teacher inspects the outdoor environment, age appropriateness should be kept in mind. If there are children of different ages and they play at the same time, the teacher will need to provide low barriers that prevent

TABLE 4-2
Outdoor Safety Hazards by Developmental Levels of Age

Age	Hazards	Prevention Tips
0–6 months	Motor vehicle	Infant should always be in rear-facing infant safety seat in backseat.
6 months–1 year	Motor vehicle	Continue using safety seat; switch to toddler seat when child is able to sit up by self; keep child in backseat.
	Poisons	Watch child for mouthing of objects.
		Check area for poisonous plants.
	Choking	Watch child for mouthing of objects.
	Drowning	Keep pool covered, fenced, and lock gate.
1–2 years	Motor vehicle	Continue using safety seat; keep child in backseat.
	Falls	Carefully watch while climbing on outdoor equipment. Teach child safe play practices.
	Equipment	Check playground equipment for rough edges, rust, loose parts.
		Wood chips or soft sand are best ground coverings under play equipment.
	Poisons	Place all outdoor chemicals and hazardous substances in a high place, preferably locked.
		Check area for poisonous plants.
	Drowning	Cover, fence, and lock gate to pool.
		Always supervise a child playing near a pool or any body of water.
2–3 years	Motor vehicle	Keep child away from streets and driveways, using supervision, fences, and firm discipline.
		Role-model pedestrian behavior such as crossing street.
		Role-model wearing seat belt; use safety seat for child; keep child in backseat.
	Falls	Carefully supervise a child playing on equipment.
		Reinforce safe behavior on equipment.
	Poisons	Keep poisons up high and locked.
		Check for poisonous plants.
	Drowning	Always supervise a child near any body of water.
		Begin to teach water safety, including role modeling.
		Cover, fence, and lock gate to pool.

(continues)

TABLE 4-2 *(Continued)*
Outdoor Safety Hazards by Developmental Levels of Age

	Equipment	Check equipment for hazards.
		Supervise and role-model safety.
3 years and up	Motor vehicle	Use safety seat or seat belt; keep child in backseat.
		Teach pedestrian and traffic safety rules.
		Role-model this behavior.
	Equipment	Reinforce safe play habits.
		Supervise a child who is using tools.
		Check equipment for hazards.
	Drowning	Children should have swimming lessons if they are in care near a body of water.
		Teach water safety.
	Violence	Teach children neighborhood safety, including safe houses and familiarity with law enforcement.

infants and toddlers from using equipment intended for older children. These barriers provide the teacher more time to watch the children for safety and less time for worry.

Infants and Toddlers. The outdoor play area for infants and toddlers should consist of flexible materials that offer no hazards, due to the common "mouthing" of children of this age. The emphasis for this age group is sensory motor activity, so the outdoor equipment for them should reflect that need. These children will be exploring and mastering their environment, so it is imperative that there be a safe place for them to investigate.

Wadsworth/Cengage Learning

There are many interesting ways to create a safe space for infants and toddlers in the outdoor area.

Preschool. As the teacher looks at the environment with preschool children in mind, the task is to see whether space has been provided for the children to be as active as this age group is likely to be. Are there areas for exercise play, construction play, and dramatic play, as well as solitary play? Are the climbers and swings at appropriate heights, or are they too high or too low? Does this inappropriate height level provide risk? The APHA & AAP standard for children 6 years old and younger is that no structure shall be more than 5½ feet tall. When structures are taller than that, research indicates that injuries are more serious. Do the climbers, swings, and slides have appropriate cushioning materials under them? Are these structures free of loose or rusty parts? A complete checklist for these pieces of equipment is found in Table 4-3 later in this chapter. The teacher should ensure that the children have been given guidelines for the use of swings, slides, and climbing equipment, and should remind them on a constant basis of proper use.

Children who are taught safety guidelines for outdoor play are much less likely to get injured. A teacher should also remember that even if these children are more capable than younger children, they are also more likely to overestimate their abilities, so they should still be closely supervised (Schwebel & Barton, 2005). Supervision of children causes them to behave differently and reduces the risk (Schwebel, 2006).

School Age. Children of this age have good coordination and are physically capable of most activities. The teacher should provide equipment that will offer children the ability to use their skills. Is there enough equipment available so that children do not become bored and find inappropriate activities to engage in that may pose risks? Does the equipment provide options for degree of difficulty for children of different ability levels? For example, does the climbing structure provide different heights, a number of exits, and areas that challenge skills yet do not threaten the safety of a child with less physical ability? Managing risks by age appropriateness minimizes the risk and provides greater protection. Even though children of this age are very capable, there should be some degree of supervision because some of these children are more likely to take risks. This is especially true for boys, who are a significantly higher risk because of their patterns of rougher play and risk taking (NSKC, 2007b).

Space

Early childhood education facilities vary greatly. Each facility's outdoor area is unique and presents conditions that may be unsafe or lead to risk. Adequate outdoor space is important to prevent crowding of children and equipment. Space must also be provided to allow safety zones around large equipment so there is no encroachment by other equipment or potential for collision with other children playing in the area. The rule of thumb is a clearance of 9 feet around stationary equipment and 15 feet around equipment with moving parts, such as swings.

The outdoor play area should provide 50 square feet of space for each child. If equipment areas are figured in, this generally translates to about 75 square feet per child (APHA & AAP, 2002). There may be further local or state codes that can affect this recommended space requirement. If this is not possible in some early childhood education environments, but these pass local or state codes, there should be a large local indoor activity area available, such as a gym, or outdoor areas such as a park. These can be used for some outdoor types of activities, and space is less likely to be a risk factor.

The total outdoor play area may not be utilized by all the children at once, so the total area need not reflect space for all children present. The general standard in that situation is that there should be enough space for one-third of the children in care to play at any one time and that the outdoor scheduling should accommodate all children over a period of time without space being an issue. If the entire play area is utilized at the same time, then space becomes a more critical issue.

The outdoor space should be arranged so that all play areas are visible to the teacher at all times. This allows for prevention of injury and abuse and gives children a more secure feeling. Bathrooms should be close enough to the outdoor play area so that the teacher can keep an eye on the children in the outdoor area as well as the child who is using the toilet facilities. The challenge is to create a safe outdoor space without it looking like a cookie cutter to all other early childhood education environments, but instead have it reflect the children in it and the community that serves it (Curtis & Carter, 2005).

Shared Space

A shared space facility can present a distinctive set of dangers that must be managed for risk. The outdoor environment of these facilities may not meet early childhood education safety standards. Close inspection and constant observation are vital to children in care under these situations.

Using a list similar to Table 3-2, the outdoor environment should be inspected every morning before it is used. Remove all debris, trash, and anything else that may have been discarded in the play area. Inspect the area for animal droppings.

For public multiuse facilities in inner-city areas, particular caution should be taken to inspect for sharp objects such as broken glass, razors, and needles from syringes. Also inspect the area for discarded condoms, clothing, and so on that may pose risk for infectious diseases.

In cases where the facility includes a swimming pool or other body of water, particular care should be taken to make sure that all safety devices are in place, including shutting the gate to this area of the facility before children are allowed outside to play.

When the multiuse facility is a family home in the evenings and on the weekends, the provider should routinely inspect the outside for hazards that might remain after normal family use. For example, if there are pets, a check for animal feces should be a regular morning event, or if someone barbecued the night before, a check for matches and lighter fluid would be necessary.

Time of Day

Many outdoor accidents can occur at any time of day. Poisoning, choking, drowning, and burns occur because of the potential hazards in the environment. Many accidents and injuries occur because children cannot understand cause and effect. This may relate to developmental level.

Maureen and Sara were two teachers at an inner-city early childhood education center. One Monday morning they decided to take the children to the park next door. Several of the children were excited and really wanted to get on the slide, the swings, and the climbing structure. The children had seen their teachers go through an inspection process before, but they rarely found any hazards. Several of the children voiced displeasure about the inspection, but Maureen and Sara insisted that the children wait. On this morning, they were very surprised to find razor blades placed on the slide. The teachers showed the children this hazard and explained what might have happened. The children never complained about the safety inspection again.

Some accidents seem to occur at particular times of day, when children are tired or hungry and are not concentrating on what they are doing. The teacher should be aware of the times in the early childhood education environment when a child appears to be tired or indicates that she is hungry. For example, more active play injuries occur in summer and fall during mid-morning and mid-afternoon (Aronson, 2001). Monitoring can help prevent risk. The teacher can modify the environment by changing the schedule to avoid the outdoor environment at the times of day that seem to pose a higher risk.

The Neighborhood

The neighborhood contributes to the early childhood education environment. It may offer conditions that support the care of the children, or it may offer risks to them. The neighborhood can effect how a child behaves (Pachter et al., 2006). The teacher should be aware of the neighborhood surrounding the early childhood education environment and plan for safety accordingly.

A supportive environment is one that has little traffic and no noise pollution and poses little risk for the safety of children. It may be a neighborhood where people know and support each other and the safety of the area. There may be community resources such as a park or recreation center that pose no risk for violence or injury. These neighborhoods with a sense of community, neighborhood cohesion, and collective efficacy can offer the social capital to support healthy outcomes of the children who live and play there (Zolotor & Runyan, 2006).

Many neighborhoods do not offer an environment that supports safety (Shonkoff, Phillips, & Keilty, 2000). Sixteen percent of parents have reported that they do not feel safe in their own neighborhoods (USDHHS, 2006). A number of risks may come from the neighborhood where the early childhood education environment is situated. There may be traffic, people who do not belong coming in and out of the area, and noise pollution. There may be community resources that are not safe areas for children. It is up to the teacher to determine what the risks are in the neighborhood. Once these risks are determined, the teacher should do everything possible to minimize the risk to the children in care.

REALITY *Check*

Neighborhood Violence

Someone is raped, murdered, assaulted, or robbed every 16 seconds in the United States (Moyers, 1995). Children are often victims of violence and may react by being instruments for violent behaviors themselves (Osofsky, 1999). Many children are finding that the world is no longer a safe place (Renshaw, 2006). It is dangerous and people use violence to hurt other people (Groves, 2003). Poor neighborhoods, where violence may be a way of life, can have severe impacts on a child's and a family's well-being (Shonkoff, Phillips, & Keilty, 2000; Leventhal & Brookes-Gunn, 2003; Pachter et al., 2006). Neighborhoods that have safety concerns such as exposure to violence can be a potential barrier to children's physical activity; these conditions can limit the time spent outdoors playing because it might not be safe to do so (Carver, Timperio, & Crawford, 2008). Exposure to neighborhood violence is particularly common in low-income inner-city areas. In New Orleans, it was found that 90 percent of elementary children surveyed had witnessed violence in their community, and 40 percent of those children had seen a dead body. It is estimated that children witness 10 to 20 percent of homicides in Los Angeles (Groves, 2001).

Exposure to neighborhood violence can put children at risk for safety as well as for good mental health. Neighborhood violence can have indirect effects on development if mothers feel they must restrict their children's ability to interact with their environment (Shonkoff & Phillips, 2000; Benson, 2004; Pachter et al., 2006). Even very young children may remember and have been known to play out traumatic events they witnessed as infants. Some children may be exposed to so much violence that they become desensitized to it (Linares, 2001). Children may lose perspective on what is right and what is wrong. When neighborhood violence is the norm, children may be at risk for performing violent crimes themselves later in life (Groves et al., 2000; Groves, 2003).

Violence is becoming a standard in our society (see Figure 4-1). Although known to permeate neighborhoods in the inner cities, it has reached the suburbs and rural areas as well (*America's children: Key national indicators of well-being, 2007*, 2007). Neighborhood violence is severely affecting the children in this country (CDC, 2000). More children than ever before are reported to have posttraumatic stress disorder (Groves et al., 2000). Many of the victims and perpetrators of violence may be the parents of young children (Osofsky, 1999). If children perceive a threat from the people around them, they are less likely to interact with them (Haberman, 1994; Moore et al., 2007).

Children's ability to cope with violence and the resulting trauma may depend on several factors: (1) age, (2) developmental stage, (3) the availability of resources to help them, and (4) the ability of the children to use those resources (Groves et al., 2000).

Teachers can offer children a safe haven from neighborhood violence (Osofsky, 1999). They can monitor their neighborhood environment for safety on a constant basis. They can access resources such as police and public help to offer children a greater degree of protection. Teachers can encourage children to become less violent and gentler (Haberman, 1994; Levin, 2003). A good teacher can help children recognize and acknowledge their feelings (Meltz, 2004). When children become angry, teachers can show them appropriate ways to express their anger (Fox & Lentini, 2006). Teachers can offer children a person they can trust and relate to (Zenah et al., 2005, Brault & Brault, 2005). Teachers can also help to create a peaceful classroom where a child feels safe (Lamm et al., 2006).

When an early childhood educational environment teaches a child to understand emotions, solve problems, and develop relationships with peers, social skills for getting along improve (Fox & Lentini, 2006). For a part of every day, in a peaceful and harmonious early childhood education environment, neighborhood violence can be eliminated from children's lives. A child with good social skills can better handle the world outside.

CHECK*point:* **How could you as a teacher create a more peaceable community in your early childhood education environment? What might your early childhood education program do to encourage a more peaceable community in the neighborhood or the surrounding locality?**

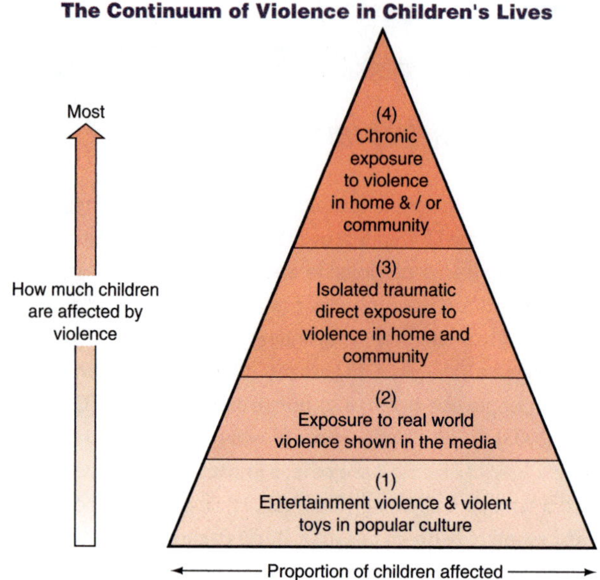

FIGURE 4-1
Continuum of Violence in Children's Lives. Reprinted with permission from *Teaching Young Children in Violent Times: Building a Peaceable Classroom,* by Diane E. Levin © 1994. Published by Educators for Social Responsibility. (For more information, call 800-370-2515.)

Key Concept 4.2

Examining the Outdoor Environment for Safety

The outdoor environment should be examined for safety on a regular basis. Hazards that pose risk include poisons, insects, temperature, lack of barriers, and others. Developmental behaviors and mixed-age play may pose risk. Lack of space or space not properly organized can pose risk through collisions and falls. Shared space allows certain conditions such as debris or trash that may cause danger to children. The neighborhood may pose risk for outdoor safety and should be carefully monitored.

4.3 PLAYGROUND EQUIPMENT SAFETY

Playground equipment is a major source of childhood accidents. Falls are responsible for 70 percent of playground injuries (Scott, 2004). The greatest numbers of these injuries are the result of falls to the ground, onto other children, or onto other equipment. Thirteen percent of injuries to young children on playgrounds occur during early childhood education programs (Tinsworth & McDonald, 2001). Recent trends have all but removed swings from public playgrounds because they have been the source of the greatest number of falls. It is important to balance safety with the need for physical activity for children. A playground should offer a number of opportunities for children to use and develop their motor skills (Sutterby & Thornton, 2005).

SAFE Playgrounds

The National Program for Playground Safety (NPPS) has surveyed a number of playgrounds and has identified four components for a "SAFE" playground.

Supervision, the first component, begins with the design of the playground so that all areas of safety are considered. Play areas should be divided into zones that reflect the type of activity involved in order to promote safety and reduce accidents (Olsen, Hudson, & Thompson, 2004). These areas might include a playground zone, a gross motor zone, a quiet play zone, and a sand zone. There might also be an area for riding, such as a blacktop zone. These areas should be free of visual barriers. There should be an adequate child–staff ratio outdoors as there is indoors (Hull, 2007). Staff should work together to keep all children within at least one member's field of vision. The supervision that takes place by any staff member should be vigilant because it reduces the risk of negligence on his or her part (Crosser, 2007).

Appropriate developmental design is the next component. It has been found that playgrounds that are designed for age appropriateness reduce the number of playground accidents (NPPS, 2001). Playground equipment for 2- to 5-year-olds should be designed closer to the ground. Playgrounds for children of this age could include the following:

- Low platforms with a few access points
- Crawl areas
- Ramps with pieces for grasping
- Low tables for water, sand, and manipulation
- Tricycle paths
- Sand area with covers
- Shorter slides
- Play areas to play alone or with other children
- If swings are included, they should be low to the ground

- **shock absorbers** *materials that lessen the force of a fall.*

Falls are the third component to consider. The major consideration for falls is the surfaces where falls may occur. The first factor to consider is suitable materials that will be used under equipment. All playground equipment should have energy-absorbing, resilient surfaces under and around them to cushion falls and prevent serious injury. Materials such as soft, loose sand; pine or bark mulch; or pea gravel are **shock absorbers** and should have a minimum depth of 12 inches. Asphalt, grass, and dirt are more dangerous and should not be used around play equipment. The surface material should be raked every few days to keep it from getting compacted that and therefore losing some of its shock absorbency. Even with safe impact areas, there should be a playground emergency plan in place should a fall that causes injury occur (Hull, 2007).

The final component of SAFE playgrounds is **equipment** maintenance. This should be a consideration when equipment is purchased. Equipment made with wood may dry out over time and begin to splinter. A recent concern about wood equipment is the use of pressure-treated wood to create outdoor structures. This green-tinted wood has been found to contain arsenic, which can leech out onto the surface and wash down into the materials beneath when it gets wet (Dolesh, 2004). It has been recommended that structures

FIGURE 4-2
Potentially harmful areas on a playground:
A. The end of the slide is too close to the border.
B. The slide faces south and will get hot during the warm months. Locating the slide in a shaded area will minimize the risk of burns for children wearing shorts.
C. The structure is built on asphalt, whereas rubber, sand, pea gravel, wood chips, bark, or turf cushions falls.
D. Decks above 3 feet need a safety barrier to prevent falls.
E. The climbing net and posts are too close to the main structure and maximize the risks of collisions and injury during accidental falls.
F. The border is too close to the swing area; children jumping from the swings are likely to fall against the border.
G. Openings such as in rails or between ladder rungs should be less than 3.5 inches or more than 9 inches in order not to trap children. Guardrails should surround elevated platforms and should be at least 29 inches high for preschoolers.

built with pressure-treated wood before 2003 be immediately disposed of because of the poisoning hazard they pose. Pressure-treated wood treated after 2003 no longer contains arsenic in the treatment. Metal equipment can rust and may cause serious cuts if it breaks. Plastic equipment has been found to be the safest over time. Equipment must be safe and in good repair so that teachers are considered reasonable and prudent in terms of avoiding negligence (Crosser, 2007). In addition to being inspected for general hazards, climbing equipment, slides, and swings, if they are present, must meet standards set by the U.S. CPSC. Figure 4-2 shows areas to check on this equipment. ECERS-R would be a good source of checklists for safety issues involving playgrounds.

Play equipment that is properly designed, well maintained, and correctly placed can help minimize risk and provide greater protection from serious injury. It is a good idea for the teacher to use a general inspection list when reviewing the safety of the playground equipment. The list in Table 4-3 is suggested as a tool for regular inspection. If an accident does occur, it is important to be prepared by having a first aid kit available in the outdoor environment so that any injury can be tended to immediately.

In addition to creating a SAFE playground, access to the playground by children with disabilities and other special needs should be considered. Children should be able to get to the playground area and enter it easily (Sutterby & Thornton, 2005). Surfaces should be accessible and able to support wheelchairs, if they are present. A child who is disabled or has special needs also must be able to use at least some of the equipment. This means that an assortment of equipment needs to be at ground level and there must be access to ramps or climbers so that these children may use the play structure.

Riding Toys

Toys that children ride should be sturdy, have a low center of gravity, and be well balanced. These toys should also be age appropriate. There should be no sharp edges, and pedal and hand grips should be in good condition. The area for riding should have a flat, smooth surface and not be slippery.

TABLE 4-3
General Inspection for Outdoor Equipment

✓ CHECK FOR THE PRESENCE OF THE FOLLOWING HAZARDS:

- ☐ Lack of supervision; children cannot be seen at all times
- ☐ Inadequate fall zone
- ☐ Protrusion and entanglement hazards
- ☐ Insufficient equipment spacing
- ☐ Age-inappropriate activities
- ☐ Platforms with no guardrails
- ☐ Equipment not recommended for public playgrounds, such as swinging exercise rings and trapeze bars
- ☐ Broken, cracked, bent, or warped surfaces
- ☐ Sharp parts or edges
- ☐ Squeaky parts in need of lubrication
- ☐ Loose nuts and bolts
- ☐ Rotting wood, splinters
- ☐ Defects in moving parts
- ☐ Broken or missing parts
- ☐ Peeling paint, rust
- ☐ Tripping hazards
- ☐ Too little depth of loose fill under equipment
- ☐ Too small a zone of loose fill or shock-absorbent surface around equipment
- ☐ Worn-out parts
- ☐ Open tubes or pipes that must be capped
- ☐ To get a playground safety report card that you can use to rate your playground, go to http://www.idph.state.ia.us and search for the report card.

Adapted from U.S. Consumer Product Safety Commission, 1997, *Handbook for public playground safety,* Publication 35, Washington, DC: Author.

There should be barriers protecting this space from other play areas as well as from traffic and walkways.

Other Hazards

Seesaws and trampolines are not recommended as regular equipment in early childhood education environments. All equipment, including equipment assembled or made at home, must meet the basic criteria of the standards set for manufactured equipment. Close inspection and adaptation to U.S. CPSC standards will lessen risk. If someone donates equipment to an

Beacon Farms Elementary School had gotten a grant to add new playground equipment. They still had the old equipment including swings, monkey bars, and a climbing structure. The children were very excited about the new equipment and the school had to schedule the use of the new equipment by grade so that all the children would not try to use it at once and cause safety concerns. Before children were allowed on the new equipment, the way to use it safely was demonstrated to the children, grade by grade, because this equipment was totally unlike what they already had. The thinking was that the minor accidents that had occurred previously on the old equipment were due to so many children using it. It soon became apparent with fewer children using the old equipment, that there were some safety risks around the equipment that they had not noticed before. In order to keep the children safe, several of the teachers and their classes videotaped the proper and improper way to use the old equipment. During one morning the video was shown on a local school broadcast system, and all children were able to see how to use the old equipment properly. Everyone was surprised how that simple act of demonstration cut down on the frequency of accidents on the playground for both the new and the old equipment.

early childhood education facility, follow the same procedure. Proceed with caution, because you can never assume that playground equipment is safe. One risk factor that should always be carefully observed with outdoor equipment is that children should never wear hoods or drawstrings that could get caught on equipment and cause a choking hazard (National Safety Council, 2004). Perhaps one of the biggest hazards is the lack of good supervision. Lack of supervision is correlated with 40 percent of playground injuries to children (NSKC, 2007c).

Wadsworth/Cengage Learning

This school provided a different type of equipment that might appear dangerous, but it is well-cushioned underneath and not high enough to cause a hazard.

Playground Equipment Safety

Playground equipment safety is essential in the early childhood education environment. Risk is posed if the equipment has not met national safety standards. Climbing equipment, swings, and slides should be properly placed to prevent accidents. There should be shock-absorbing material beneath this equipment. Riding toys should be sturdy and not tip over easily. Proper supervision of children in outdoor play areas is the most effective ingredient in playground safety. All equipment should be regularly inspected to keep the playground safe.

4.4 TRAFFIC AND TRANSPORTATION SAFETY

In 2002, 227,000 children under age 14 were involved in motor vehicle accidents (NSKC, 2004b). Of those, 1579 died from their injuries. In the United States, motor vehicle accidents are the number one killer and crippler of children younger than 4 years. Motor vehicle injuries to children occur in three ways:

1. When children are pedestrians and are hit by an automobile
2. When children are riding in a car that stops suddenly or crashes
3. When children are riding bicycles and crash into or are run into by a car

To protect the children in care, safety policies should be developed for each case.

Pedestrian Safety

Children being let off at and picked up from school account for the great majority of pedestrian accidents. Pedestrian injury is the second leading cause of death (after cancer) for children ages 5 to 9 years ("Childhood pedestrian injuries," 2002). There should be a plan devised for safely dropping off and picking up children. Observe how the families and children arrive and leave. Pickup and drop-off points for children should be located in an off-street area or directly at a curb near the early childhood education facility under an adult's supervision. If children must cross a street, there must be some type of traffic control (Healthy Child Care Pennsylvania, 2006b). In the majority of cases, this would be the parent bringing the child to school or taking him home. Parents should be reminded of the importance of closely supervising their children in a traffic situation. Their lack of impulse control and fear, in addition to their curiosity, puts children at risk for pedestrian injury (NSKC, 2007b). If possible, some person in the early childhood education environment should be available to help families who have more than one child to supervise during the drop off and pick up time. The outdoor play area should be as far away from traffic as possible and should be fenced. The Head Start program is required to provide pedestrian safety to children and their parents who participate in their program (AAP, 2007).

Motor Vehicle Safety

Transporting children involves major safety concerns for early educators and for the families of the children in care (NAEYC, 2002). Most fatal injuries of children ages 1 to 14 years involve motor vehicle accidents (*America's children: Key national indicators of well-being, 2007,* 2007). All drivers, chaperones, and assistants should receive instruction in safety precautions. If buses or minibuses are used, all drivers should have a commercial driver's license and undergo a criminal background check (AAP, 2007). At least one of the adults who either drives or accompanies the children must have training by a professional who is knowledgeable in safety and child development (USDHHS, 2003). Car travel and field trips are likely to be special events, not common occurrences, in most early childhood education situations. Planning for these events should be well organized and teachers should use accessories, behaviors, and conditions as the guidelines for safety. Some early childhood educators regularly transport children to and from home and pick up older children after school. If this is the case, as much risk management as possible should be considered. Head Start provides an example. Beginning in January, 2004, any transportation service involving Head Start vans must ensure that all vehicles used to transport children are equipped with child restraint systems that consider the height and weight levels of children (AAP, 2007). Any child weighing less than 65 pounds must use a child restraint system. Another example of safety precautions for early childhood education transportation is the Tennessee law that requires child safety monitoring systems in all early childhood education vans ("Tennessee Lawmakers," 2004). The National Highway Traffic Safety Administration (NHTSA) has available a curriculum for child passenger safety including how to properly use child safety restraints (AAP, 2007).

The Vehicle. The accessories in motor vehicle travel are the vehicle itself and the safety seats utilized. Vehicles should be in good working order and should be cleaned and inspected inside and out on a regular basis. Special care should be taken to see that brakes, lights, and other safety features of the car are working properly. It is suggested that SUVs are more likely to roll over in motor vehicle accidents. Children who are not safely buckled into a car seat or booster seat may be 25 times more likely to be injured (Leonard, 2006).

Vehicles should have heating and air conditioning in locations where temperatures go below 50°F and over 75°F. Children are susceptible to cold and heat and need a climate-controlled vehicle. Several children have been unintentionally left in vans and have died due to the heat (Tomlin, 2008).

Safety Seats. Safety seats are very important to the prevention of serious injury in motor vehicles. Children are safest when they ride in age/weight-appropriate safety seats. Although there are laws in every state that require a child riding in a car to be safely restrained, many drivers still do not follow the "buckle up" rule. About 14 percent of children younger than age 14 ride unrestrained, and of those children who are restrained, about 82 percent are riding in safety seats that are either not correctly installed or used incorrectly. When safety seats are used correctly, they can reduce deaths of children from ages 1 to 4 by 54 percent and deaths of infants by 71 percent (NSKC, 2004b). The AAP recommends that schools provide age- and weight-appropriate safety seats and restraint systems for all preschool-age children (AAP, 2007).

Drivers should become familiar with the manufacturer's installation instructions for each safety seat used by children in care.

Each child should be in an appropriate safety seat, harness, or seat belt that corresponds to the child's weight and age. These features should be approved in accordance with federal safety seat standards and used in compliance with the manufacturers' directions. All children younger than 1 year and weighing 20 pounds or less should ride in the backseat in a rear-facing safety seat (NHTSA, 2002). Children who are more than 1 year old or weigh more than 20 pounds may ride forward facing and should ride in a safety seat with full harness until they reach the weight of 40 pounds. Booster seats can be used for children who weigh more than 40 pounds but are younger than age 8 unless they are more than 4 feet 9 inches tall (NHTSA, 2002). Finding a correct safety seat for obese children may be more difficult because they are usually over 3 years old and weigh far more than 40 pounds, which is more than the upper weight for height limit currently available (Trifiletti et al., 2006). Seat belts must be provided for all children who are too old for safety seats. If a small bus or van is used, seat belts shall be provided for all children.

The teacher should always model safety by using a seat belt. She should also provide a child safety seat law poster in a visible area and discuss child passenger safety so parents understand that teachers are concerned. Another valuable tool would be to schedule a car seat checkup with a passenger safety expert from a local automobile club so that parents can get their children's car seats checked (Leonard, 2006).

Pretravel Guidelines. Safety behaviors are necessary in the preplanning stage as well as in actual travel in the motor vehicle. In planning for the field trip or other reason to travel, make sure the destination itself is safe (Walsh, 2005). A good way to make sure is to visit the site before the trip is even planned. This will provide an opportunity to look at the site to check for all safety hazards before trip planning continues. Begin pretravel planning by using the guidelines in Table 4-4.

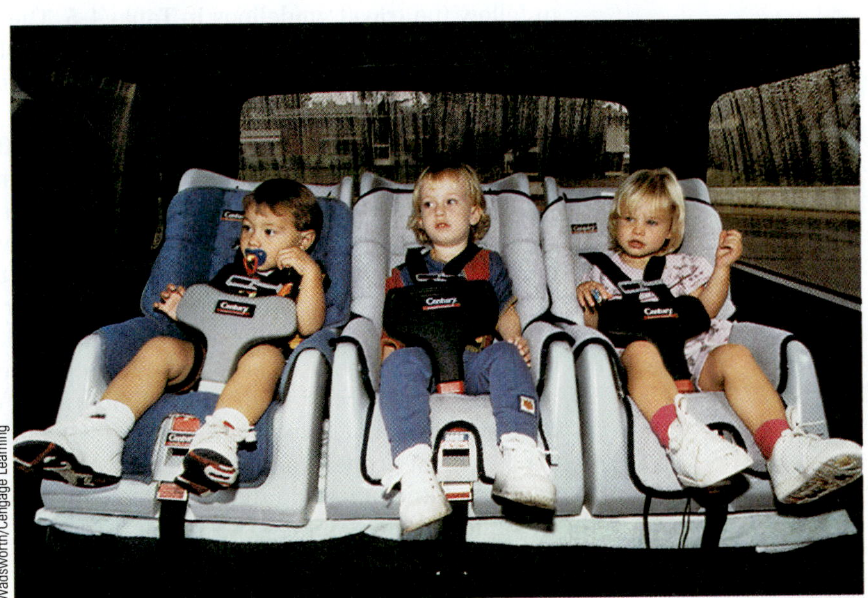

The safest place for children in a motor vehicle is riding in the backseat and in an approved, secured car seat.

TABLE 4-4
Pretravel Safety Guidelines

Teacher:

- Obtain permission slips for all children participating in travel. Check your insurance coverage.
- Make sure driver is licensed and familiar with the vehicle, and knows how to drive defensively.
- Carefully plan out the route, including placement of emergency care facilities along the way.
- Explain the route to children and point out highlights.
- Prepare children for travel by explaining why buckling up and safe passenger behavior are important.
- Arrange for a backup vehicle in case of car emergency.
- Understand safety precautions and child supervision for travel.
- Bring a second set of emergency contact forms on any excursion.
- Know how to handle emergency situations, and be certified in pediatric first aid and CPR.
- Make sure the vehicle is in good working condition. This includes checking the gas, oil, and tires.

Children:

- Understand the importance of travel safety, including buckling up.
- Practice safe travel behaviors, including hands inside the car.
- Understand rules for play in car, including no yelling or screaming.

Travel Guidelines. If the pretravel guidelines have been met, the next step is to follow the travel guidelines in Table 4-5. These guidelines are to help the teacher be prepared for all contingencies and offer a greater degree of protection for a safe journey for the children in care.

Travel Conditions. Try to plan any travel with the children for a time when the conditions are optimal. Avoid high traffic times or times when children will be most tired or hungry and less alert. If the weather is bad, it is best to postpone the trip until it improves. Prepare a backup activity that will excite the children to lessen the disappointment if the trip is postponed.

Make sure children are constantly under supervision during travel. At a minimum, keep to the proper adult–child ratio, but it is a good idea to ask for volunteers to accompany the teacher and children. If travel is by walking and away from the neighborhood or across streets, the ideal ratio would be one adult for three to five children, depending on age. The teacher must prepare any volunteers with the rules for supervision by giving them handouts and talking to them several days before the trip so that they understand what is expected of them. It is also helpful to remind them of basic travel safety before leaving, so that this will be fresh in their minds when the trip begins.

TABLE 4-5
Early Childhood Education Travel Safety Guidelines

Teacher:

- Have trip authorization forms in your possession for all children present.
- Keep a passenger log, with each child's name for each trip.
- Whenever loading or unloading, use the log for a roll check of each passenger.
- Provide the proper ratio of adults to children and assign specific children to each adult.
- Do not allow loud music or tapes.
- Stop and pull off the road to calm children down if they are unruly and noisy.
- Do not be under the influence of drugs or alcohol, including prescription or over-the-counter medications that could make you drowsy.
- Provide soft books or toys and conversation and songs for children so the driver can concentrate on traffic safety.
- Provide a first aid kit to carry in each vehicle.
- Make sure everybody buckles up, and never allow children out of seat restraints while car is moving.
- Pay special attention to traffic and the children when exiting and entering the vehicle.
- If the trip is more than a few minutes, have juices and snacks for children; this will allow you to keep your focus on safety, not on their being hungry or thirsty.
- Do not allow children to ride up front in vehicles that have passenger airbags.
- If a child is being released to a parent or guardian, this should be noted in the passenger log.
- When you have returned to the early childhood education site, have a designated person carefully go through the vehicle and inspect it. This is especially important because there have been cases where children who have been transported by early childhood programs have been inadvertently left in a vehicle and died as a result of accumulated heat.

Children:

- Observe car safety rules.
- Buckle up.
- Ride quietly, keeping hands to yourself.
- Be extra alert for traffic when exiting and entering the vehicle.

- **travel information sheet** *An information sheet that monitors conditions for travel safety.*

The teacher should always leave a **travel information sheet** with a responsible person left at the early childhood education site. This sheet should include the following:

- Date and time of trip, including approximate return time
- Destination, including address, telephone number, and contact person

- Planned route; be specific: "Main Street to Laurel Ave., left on Center Circle, right on Pine, two miles to Fourth"
- Names of children participating
- Names of teachers and parents providing supervision

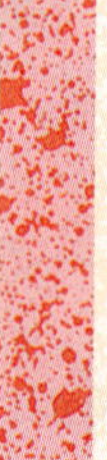

Pause for Reflection

Do you remember taking a field trip as a child? Do you remember any safety precautions taken before or during the trip? Have you ever taken a field trip with children as an adult? What was the experience like? What might have been done to make it a more safe and pleasant experience?

Bicycle Safety

School-aged children in family home child care, nanny care, or after-school care should be taught about bicycle safety. Every year more than 20,000 injuries and nearly 150 deaths to children occur in bicycle-related crashes (American Heart Association, 2005). The majority of these crashes involve head trauma. Using bike helmets can reduce the risk of injury by more than 80 percent (American Heart Association, 2005) and the risk of brain injury by 88 percent (NSKC, 2004a). Unfortunately, it is estimated that only 25 percent of children between ages 5 and 14 wear helmets. If all children used helmets, 75 percent of fatal bicycle head injuries could be averted.

Helmets. Practicing safety by using bike helmets for children riding tricycles and small bicycles in the early childhood education environment can reduce risk when children ride the vehicles in an outdoor environment. It can also

These boys look like they are having a good time on sturdy bikes, but they would be safer if they were wearing helmets.

Wadsworth/Cengage Learning

help prepare children for a future of greater safety by teaching them the habit of wearing a helmet. A December 2006 study by the Centers for Disease Control and Prevention reported that preschool children who wear helmets have fewer injuries and would be more likely to wear helmets in the future (Healthy Child Care Pennsylvania, 2007). In February 2007, the AAP recommended that all children wear approved safety helmets while riding tricycles, bicycles, and other riding toys and that the helmets meet the mandatory standards of the U.S. CPSC (National Resource Center for Health and Safety in Child Care and Early Education, 2007). A review of studies shows that when a community-based program promoting helmet use is offered to children, it is more effective than legislation that states children must wear helmets (Royal, Kendrick, & Coleman, 2008).

The Consumer Product Safety Commission sets mandatory standards for helmets, so the teacher must make sure the helmets provided meet these standards. There should be at least one helmet per riding toy at the early education environment. Helmets should be pre-fitted to various sizes and have a label such as a colored sticker so that a child can identify the helmet that best fits (Lipman, 2006) (Figure 4-3). Some staff should be trained on how to check and adjust for proper fit. Lipman (2006) suggests that early childhood education environments with inadequate budgets might use community partnerships, grants from local service clubs, or funding from safety programs in the local area as sources for funding for the helmets. Helmets should be sanitized as needed due to the prevalence of lice in early childhood education environments. When a child learns how to ride bikes safely in an early childhood education environment, she is more likely to exhibit bicycle safely at home and in the community.

Riding Safety. Helping children learn proper tricycle behaviors can begin in the early childhood education environment, using the same rules as for the riding toys. The skills and precautions in Table 4-6 will help the teacher set guidelines for teaching children bicycle safety.

The riding safety guidelines will help the teacher set up the early childhood education environment to minimize risk. If children all ride in the same direction, the number of crashes or collisions with other riders will be reduced. Keeping non-riders out of the area also reduces the number of collisions. A teacher who observes the children for speed, reckless riding, and two hands on the handlebar can prevent accidents and ensure a safer experience for them. Checking the riding toys for proper working order will also reduce risk.

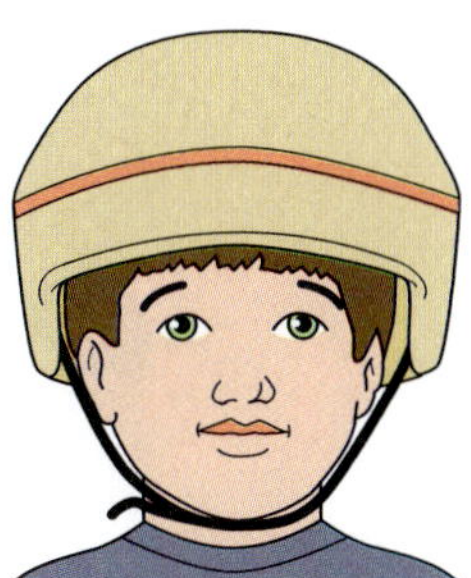

FIGURE 4-3
Bicycle helmets are available in various sizes.

TABLE 4-6
Guidelines for Safe Bicycle Riding

- Always ride in the same direction so all traffic goes the same way and not against each other.
- Always be careful of other people and other traffic in the riding area.
- Keep hands free to hold handlebars with both hands. Never carry anything with your hands.
- Never show off, fool around, or ride recklessly.
- Do not ride too fast, so if you do see someone in your path or other traffic, you can slow down or stop to avoid a collision.
- The tricycle, bicycle, or other riding vehicle should be appropriate for the age of the rider.
- The riding vehicle should be in good working order.
- Stay clear of pedestrians.

Other Riding Conditions. Optimizing the conditions in the outdoor environment should not be too difficult. Creating a riding area in which riders have a flat, nonslip surface is important. Enforcing the rule that riders go in only one direction will be a matter of changing habits; most children will readily adapt and will change direction when reminded, but others may require more effort.

Setting the time of day when children are most alert for outdoor riding activity decreases risk. Providing necessary and active supervision will also help offer greater protection to the children in the outdoor environment.

Key Concept 4.4

Traffic and Travel

Traffic and travel pose risk for children in and out of the early childhood education environment. Children should be protected and learn good travel safety practices. Pedestrians, motor vehicles, and bicycles are the three areas where there should be safety promotion and prevention from risk. Checklists, guidelines, use of safety devices, travel information sheets, and using optimum conditions will help the teacher set up the environment for travel and traffic safety. For more information on transportation, bicycle, and traffic safety go to http://www.nhtsa.dot.gov/.

4.5 WATER SAFETY

Water safety presents its own set of challenges to the early childhood education environment. Bathtubs pose the biggest drowning hazard to infants, and pools are the greatest drowning hazard to toddlers, preschoolers, and school-aged children (Zavitkovsky & Thompson, 2000). Adults are supposedly supervising 88 percent of children who drown (Sullivan, 2004). Two-thirds of

Even this water table can be a water safety hazard and should be closely supervised, especially with children this young.

Wadsworth/Cengage Learning

all drownings occur in the outdoor environment in standing bodies of water such as swimming pools, wading pools, hot tubs, ponds, and ditches. Covers for some of these items that are left with standing water after a rain become potential drowning hazards even though originally they may have been meant to protect. Drowning rates are highest in children from ages 1 to 3 years. Many of the drownings in this age group are due to a momentary lapse of supervision (Schnitzer, 2006). Popular belief is that a child in danger of drowning screams for help. In reality, drowning can be a silent event, which means that constant adult supervision is necessary whenever there is any body of water around children. The AAP recommends that whenever children are in or around water, adults supervise children from within an arm's length and not allow distractions to occur (Brenner, 2003). These same bodies of water such as pools and ponds also present the potential risk for germs and the spread of disease.

Water Hazards

Safety precautions must be taken to keep the water in the early childhood education environment as risk free as possible (NCCCHSRC, 2004). Any body of water can pose a threat, so screening the outdoor environment for hazards that may lead to the risk of drowning should be thorough. Young children can drown in as little as one or two inches of water. Children who are playing with water tables or buckets of water, as well as those who are in child-size restroom stalls or near a bathtub, should be closely supervised. It is also important to remember that even small standing bodies of water make good breeding grounds for both mosquitoes and germs. Children who play in water tables should have previously washed their hands and should wash them again when they finish playing at the water table (Healthy Child Care Pennsylvania, 2006c).

Water hazards in the outdoor environment must be secured to prevent children from reaching them (NCCCHSRC, 2004). Drownings occur in surprisingly short periods of time. Children have been seen playing indoors or outdoors away from a water source, and adults have been present nearby, yet these children have still drowned. Table 4-7 lists ways to childproof the early childhood education environment from the hazards that may lead to drowning. Other hazards may include furniture outside the fence that children could climb on and having riding and other non-water toys around a pool.

TABLE 4-7
Water Safety Guidelines

- Any hazard should be enclosed with a fence that is at least five feet tall and made of material that is not easy to climb. A door or sliding glass door is not a safe substitute for a fence.
- Gates should have locks that are at least 55 inches high and should be self-closing. Keep gate keys in a safe place away from children.
- Remove chairs and objects children can use to climb over fences or gates or into spas.
- All bodies of water that are man made, such as swimming pools, hot tubs, and cesspools, should have rigid covers to protect children from falling in, if they get past the gate.
- If an inground pool is present in the early childhood education environment, a nonskid surface should surround the pool to prevent slipping and falling.
- Always drain standing water from pool or spa covers.
- Do not use floating spa or pool covers. Children can slip underneath and out of sight.
- Avoid the use of floating devices that can give children a false sense of safety.
- Remove all toys from pool after children are out of pool.
- If a portable wading pool is used in the early childhood education environment, it should be filled with water, used immediately, and drained and put away as soon as children leave the pool.
- Always carefully supervise children if there is a body of water present in the outdoor environment. *Never leave children without adult supervision, even for a few seconds.* Maintain visual contact with children.
- Keep a rescue device such as a long pole right next to the pool.
- Have telephone access to pool for emergencies.

Reprinted with permission of Children's Hospital of San Diego.

Children's Behavior Around Water

Children themselves pose a threat when a body of water is present in the outdoor environment. They move fast, are curious, and do not understand cause and effect. They may lack fear or overestimate their physical abilities. Adults may underestimate children's abilities to manipulate their environment and therefore get into trouble. The majority of drownings occur within a very short period of time after an adult has seen a child (Schnitzer, 2006). It is imperative that the teacher *never* leave a child alone, even for a moment, when there is a body of water in the outdoor environment. Make sure that the teacher who is observing the children is responsible and knows how to help if it is needed (Healthy Child Care Pennsylvania, 2006d).

The children should be taught safe practices for swimming and playing in the water to further protect them if they will be using the pool or wading pool. When outdoors and near the water, always reinforce safety for the children. If the children are allowed to play in water, plan the time of day for this activity for when they are least tired and most alert. Always be sure there is adequate supervision, and maintain a sufficient ratio of adults to children. *Anyone attending children in the water should know how to swim and be competent in CPR.*

Key Concept 4.5

Water Safety

Water in many forms poses risk for children in the outdoor environment. Swimming pools, ponds, or any type of standing water may cause safety concerns. The teacher must understand water hazards and how to eliminate them, if possible. Children's behavior poses risk, and teachers should be prepared to promote and teach children water safety behaviors.

4.6 IMPLICATIONS FOR TEACHERS

Outdoor spaces pose a number of risks to children in the early childhood education environment. The risks may come from different areas of hazards, such as environmental hazards, playground equipment, traffic and travel, and water. The risk may come from specific hazards, behaviors, and conditions. The teacher should provide observation, supervision, and education to promote safe behaviors and prevent risks.

Observation

There are many areas of outdoor safety for which observation is the best method of preventing accident and injury. Learning to use the ABCs of safety as it applies to outdoor accessories, behaviors, and conditions can help the teacher. A teacher who understands specific risks can be on guard for those risks.

Supervision

Children must be constantly supervised in the outdoor environment. The teacher should supervise all aspects of the environment for risks posed by accessories, behaviors, and conditions. These are effective tools for managing outdoor risks to children (Schwebel, & Brezausek, 2008).

Supervision also supplies the teacher with methods and practices that provide a checks-and-balances system where there is more than one teacher. This is especially important to remember, because a teacher may view outdoor time as "break time," and it is essential to avoid that mentality. Communication about outdoor safety should be a regular occurrence between the teachers. Constant supervision can also ensure that outdoor safety training and promotion take place on a regular basis.

Education

Teachers, children, and parents can be educated for outdoor safety. The teacher should access training that will provide the knowledge and awareness needed. The teacher who has a knowledge base of outdoor safety can maximize the environment to protect the children.

Children can be taught safe behaviors and items or conditions to look for that may pose risk. The children can be encouraged to use safety devices that will protect them. Having signs around that spell out cautions such as "Stop," "Danger," "Walk," and "Ride in One Direction" can help children learn; even though they might not be able to read the signs, they can remember the warning the sign poses (Smith, 2002). Communicating with children on a regular basis and reminding them about outdoor safety can offer a greater degree of protection both in and out of the early childhood education environment. The teacher can use educational methods such as reading books, showing videos, and circle time to reinforce safety measures and methods.

For Families

Teachers can help parents understand the safety risks present in the outdoor environment. Methods such as an outdoor safety awareness week with handouts, videos to borrow, and a group meeting that families attend allows the teacher to provide education. Another valuable tool would be to schedule a car seat checkup with a passenger safety expert from a local automobile club so that parents can get their children's car seats checked (Leonard, 2006). These types of educational strategies will provide families with greater awareness about the importance of outdoor safety, which in turn can lead to more protective outdoor environments at home for the children.

Key Concept 4.6

Implications for Teachers

The teacher can promote and protect for outdoor safety in a number of ways. Looking out for safety risks can prevent injury. Supervising to make sure safe practices are followed can promote safety and provide protection. Education for teachers, children, and families can provide extra measures of security.

CHAPTER SUMMARY

Risks for accidents are great in the outdoor environment even though less time is spent there than indoors. Risks can occur on playgrounds, in backyards, on bicycles, in cars, on streets, and in water. Teachers should monitor both the environment and the children for safety and make modifications using checklists. Safety devices such as helmets and safety car seats should always be used. Teachers can use observation, supervision, and education to protect and promote safety in their environment. They can work with families to ensure a higher degree of awareness of the importance of safety in the outdoor environment.

TO GO BEYOND

Additional resources for this chapter can be found by visiting the book companion website at www.cengage.com/education/robertson. This supplemental material includes chapter objectives, internet exercises, reflection questions, quizzes, web links, glossary and flash cards, case studies, frequently asked questions, downloadable forms and tables, curriculum supplements, more reality checks, additional key concepts, references, and more.

Chapter Review Critical Thinking Applications

1. Discuss the relationship between outdoor activities and risk to safety.
2. Describe some of the safety hazards that might be found in a shared space environment. How do these differ from those in an early childhood education environment that does not share space? Compare and contrast the two types.
3. How would developmental stages between infancy and toddlerhood affect how the outdoor environment is set up?
4. How can SAFE concepts improve playground safety in the early childhood education environment?
5. Compare playground safety between a local center-based early childhood program and an elementary school.
6. You are organizing a field trip to a pumpkin patch. Describe the steps you will follow and some of the hazards you may encounter.

As an Individual

1. Find an early childhood education setting in the local area that reflects shared space, such as a church preschool, an early childhood education program at a gym, or a community center. Observe the environment and record your observations.
2. Visit an elementary school playground. Observe the equipment and the surface under it. Do these meet the safety standards discussed in the text? For a further look, visit a local child care center. Ask the same questions, then compare the two environments. Why do you think you might find such a difference, if you did?
3. Locate a park in your area. Assess it for the degree of shade it would provide for children on a hot day. What might you do to improve it?

As a Group

1. In groups of four to five people, make a safety checklist for a shared-space environment at a church preschool. Use the information collected as individuals to compile this list. Compare the lists of the whole class.
2. Collect handouts from community resources that deal with outdoor safety. These might include an auto club, a poison control center, and the American Red Cross.

3. Think of a local neighborhood that is often in the news for the violence that occurs in it. What are the characteristics of that neighborhood? Research what might be done to make the neighborhood safer for children. List the local agencies that might be enlisted to help with this project.
4. View the video *S.A.F.E. Surfaces* from the National Program for Playground Safety, which describes the proper selection of safety surfacing for playgrounds. After watching it, break the class up into groups, with each discussing the pros and cons of different surfaces. Come together toward the end of class and come to a conclusion about what the best surface would be for a new preschool and an existing elementary school.
5. Break the class up into several groups, and have each group find a different type of early childhood education environment that transports students in the local area. You could include a corporate-type day care, a family child care provider, and an elementary school district that offers bus transportation. Compare and contrast the safety rules/policies that each of these have with those found in this chapter. What might be done to improve the ones you found?

Case Studies

1. A teacher, Dan, notices that there appear to be a number of bees in the outdoor play yard. On further inspection, he comes upon a beehive. What course of action should he take to protect the children and eliminate the risk of bees?
2. Deborah is a family child care provider who has been in business for ten years. Her family has saved for many years to put in a pool so that her own children can enjoy the swimming and other water sports they love. The pool has been installed, and she has put up a 7-foot fence around it. What else should she do to protect the toddlers and young children in her care?
3. Marilou is in the process of setting up an early childhood education program, with limited funds. A friend offers to donate his children's home-built play equipment because they have outgrown it. Should she accept this gift? How should she proceed to check for the safety of this equipment?
4. Greg wants to have a helmet policy at the corporate child care center where he is the director. The center cares for school-age children before and after school, and it has bicycles for these students to use. Survey the local area for bicycle helmet regulations for children under age 5 and over age 5. Are they the same or different? Find a local child care center and ask about helmet use. How do the elementary schools in the local area encourage or enforce these regulations? Give Greg the five most important suggestions that you found.

CHAPTER 5

Emergency Response Procedures for Early Childhood Education Environments

After reading this chapter, you should be able to:

5.1 Safety Policies for Emergency Response

Describe and discuss safety policies for response to childhood accidents and injuries.

5.2 Identifying an Emergency

Define and discuss the differences between what constitutes an emergency and what necessitates only basic first aid.

5.3 Basic Emergency Response Procedures

Indicate the steps to go through in addressing the proper responses to a real emergency and how they are to be performed.

5.4 Basic Cardiopulmonary Resuscitation and First Aid

Define, discuss, and summarize the methods of basic cardiopulmonary resuscitation and first aid to infants and children.

5.5 Emergency Planning for Children with Special Needs

Discuss methods and practices for emergency care of children with special needs.

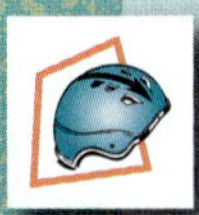

5.6 Disaster Preparedness

Define, discuss, and summarize the basic methods of disaster preparedness for early childhood education.

5.7 Implications for Teachers

Indicate the need for supervision, observation, education, cultural competence, and working with families for basic response procedures for childhood injuries and accidents.

5.1 SAFETY POLICIES FOR EMERGENCY RESPONSE

Emergencies occur in many situations. Automobiles, playground equipment, and natural disasters all pose risk for accidental injury that might be classified as an emergency. A chronic illness or a childhood disease might manifest as an emergency situation. It is important that the teacher in any early childhood education situation be prepared to handle emergencies. The following points show the need for preparedness for emergency response in early childhood education:

- In a survey of more than 300 early education environments, two-thirds were considered to be at risk for safety (Shepard, 2002).
- Teachers of young children should be prepared to treat bleeding, poisoning, convulsions, sprains and fractures, head injuries, and dental and mouth injuries (Reeves, 2003).
- Broken bones, often the result of falls, are the fourth most common injury in preschool-aged children (NCCCHSRC, 2005c).
- Early childhood education teachers should be able to recognize and deal with anaphylaxis that may occur in children with severe allergies (Patel, Bansal, & Tobin, 2006).
- During a disaster, teachers should be able to provide safe, competent care to the children in care for several days, regardless of whether it is the regular early childhood education setting or an evacuation site (LeMay, 2004).
- A plan for emergency including security and communication should be put in place in early childhood education environments (Calder, 2007)
- Parents of children in early education environments expect that their teachers should be able to handle emergencies (Gaines & Leary, 2004).
- When emergencies do happen in early childhood education environments, it is necessary to know how to take proper action (Reeves, 2006).
- It is essential that at least one teacher in an early childhood education program be trained for emergency, life-threatening situations such as breathing difficulties, head injury, or poisoning (Hooper, 2006).
- Early education environments should be prepared for all levels of disaster alerts (Federal Emergency Management Agency [FEMA], 2002).
- Children need help healing after a disaster occurs (NAEYC, 2005; Ippen, Lieberman, & Van Horn, 2005)

Teachers should avoid unnecessary emergencies by providing prevention and protection in the care environment. They do this with constant supervision and by anticipating, modifying, and monitoring for accessories, behaviors, and conditions that pose risk. These proactive behaviors reduce risk.

To provide the maximum protection in the early childhood education environment, the teacher should be prepared for the possibility that an emergency may occur. The teacher must plan for emergencies, be prepared to handle emergencies, and be equipped with the training necessary to deal with life-threatening emergencies as they occur. Having a plan and being prepared ahead of time can help the teacher to respond correctly and quickly should an emergency take place.

In order to carry this out, the teacher must plan for policies in the following areas:

1. *Defining an Emergency:* understanding what constitutes an emergency situation
2. *Basic Emergency Response Procedures:* understanding methods and practices for response to emergencies in early childhood education environments
3. *Basic CPR and First Aid:* understanding when and how to use basic CPR and first aid to handle emergencies in early childhood education environments
4. *Emergency Planning for Children with Special Needs:* methods, practices, and understanding of how to handle emergencies for children in care with special needs
5. *Disaster Preparedness:* methods and practices for preparing for disasters such as fire, weather disasters, and earthquakes
6. *Implications for Teachers:* methods and practices for preparing the early childhood education environment to deal with emergencies through education, observation, and supervision

Key Concept 5.1

Safety Policies for Emergency Procedures

Even though much risk may have been reduced, accessories, behaviors, and conditions can cause situations that constitute an emergency. The teacher has to be prepared to respond to any emergency in the early childhood education environment. The preparation includes defining an emergency, learning how to respond to an emergency, acquiring basic CPR and first aid skills, and finding out how to prepare for disaster. The implications for the teacher to carry out these preparations are providing for education, observing, working with families, and supervising in the early childhood education environment.

5.2 IDENTIFYING AN EMERGENCY

To understand how to prepare for an emergency, the teacher must first understand what constitutes an emergency. Webster's dictionary defines an emergency as "a sudden, urgent, and usually unexpected occurrence requiring immediate action." There are common factors that indicate an emergency exists. The teacher should be able to identify these factors in order to determine whether an emergency is occurring. Three major factors have been used to indicate that an emergency is taking place.

Breathing, Bleeding, and Poison

The three basic factors that always indicate an emergency exists are difficulty breathing, bleeding, and poison. These emergencies are fairly easy to recognize. They are also rapidly life threatening and must be acted upon quickly. There may not even be time to call 911 right away if there is only one person present besides the victim. Any of these three factors could occur in the early childhood education environment, and the teacher should be prepared to recognize them and act immediately and appropriately.

- **profusely** *pouring forth freely or abundantly.*

A person who is bleeding **profusely** may die if the bleeding is not stopped. Stopping the bleeding is of foremost importance, and first aid is needed immediately. If someone else is present, that person can call the emergency number (usually 911).

- **rescue breathing** *the process of steps to help a person who is not breathing resume normal breathing.*

If a person has difficulty breathing, brain damage can occur in a matter of a few minutes and the heart may stop, with death following. Anything that interferes with a child's breathing is life threatening (Aronson, 2001). Offering **rescue breathing** may be the only alternative. Calling an emergency number is also vital, if possible.

When someone has ingested poison, contacted it directly through the skin, or inhaled it, emergency procedures should begin immediately. Call Poison Control Central (800-222-1222) to get help for the victim. In most cases, the person who answers will walk the rescuer through the exact method of treating the particular poison. Be aware that the use of syrup of ipecac to make a victim vomit up poison that has been swallowed is no longer recommended (Sutton, 2006).

Other Emergency Indicators

There are a number of other indicators that show when an emergency may be present. The American Red Cross (ARC) suggests that using one's senses is a good tool to help recognize when an emergency may exist. Hearing, seeing, smelling, and feeling can all be tools of recognition, as listed in Table 5-1.

When any of the conditions in Table 5-1 are present in the early childhood education environment, an emergency may exist and the teacher should act

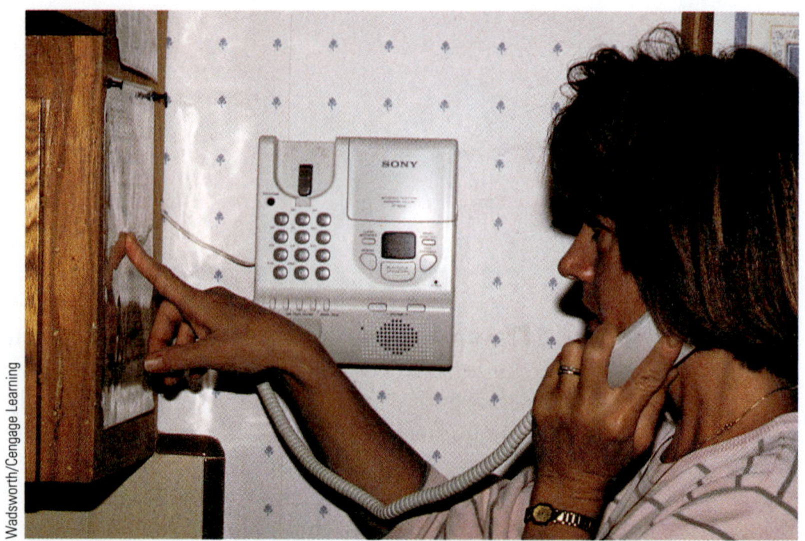

Emergency numbers, such as the local poison control number, should be located next to the phone for immediate use.

TABLE 5-1
Indicators of Emergencies

Your senses may help tell you whether an emergency exists. Below are some examples of emergency indicators that may be ascertained through the senses of hearing, smelling, seeing, and feeling.

Unusual Sights

- Stopped vehicle on the roadside
- Broken glass
- Overturned pot in the kitchen
- Spilled medicine container
- Downed electrical wires
- Sparks, smoke, or fire

Unusual Appearances or Behaviors

- ☐ Unconsciousness
- ☐ Confused or unusual behavior
- ☐ Trouble breathing
- ☐ Clutching chest or throat
- ☐ Slurred, confused, or hesitant speech
- ☐ Unexplainable confusion or drowsiness
- ☐ Sweating for no apparent reason
- ☐ Uncharacteristic skin color
- ☐ Inability to move a body part

Unusual Odors

- ☐ Odors that are stronger than usual
- ☐ Unrecognizable odors
- ☐ Inappropriate odors

Unusual Noises

- ☐ Screaming, yelling, moaning, or calling for help
- ☐ Breaking glass, crashing metal, or screeching tires
- ☐ Sudden, loud, or unidentifiable sounds
- ☐ Unusual silence

From the *American Red Cross First Aid/CPR/AED for Schools and the Community Participants Manual* (copyright 2006).

promptly (Figure 5-1). The teacher should follow through with investigating any unusual sights, sounds, or smells. The follow-up may prove that nothing was out of order; on the other hand, it may establish that an emergency is taking place. The teacher should remain calm, act quickly, and follow emergency procedures.

There are a number of human-caused and other risks that regularly contribute to childhood injuries and must be prepared for. These risks can be found in Table 5-2.

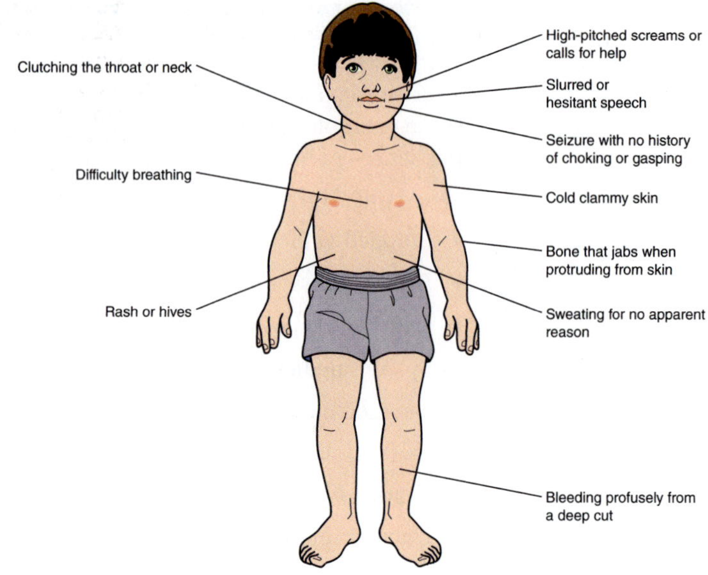

FIGURE 5-1
Illustration of indicators of emergencies.

TABLE 5-2
Contributors to Early Childhood Education Emergencies (From American Red Cross First Aid/CPR/AED for Schools and the Community Participants Manual. *Copyright © 2006. Courtesy of the American National Red Cross. All rights reserved in all countries.)*

- Garage door injuries (family child care)
- Choking from toys and other hazards
- Falls from playground equipment
- Firearms, poisons, and bodies of water
- Burns from fires, scalding, or electric wires
- Natural disasters such as floods, earthquakes, hurricanes, and tornadoes
- Human-caused disasters such as hostage taking, bomb threats, terrorism, and random acts of violence

Key Concept 5.2

Identifying an Emergency

The teacher must be able to identify what constitutes an emergency. Difficulty breathing, profuse bleeding, and ingestion or direct contact with poison always indicate emergency conditions that require prompt action. Other emergency indicators may be observed through the use of the senses of sight, hearing, smell, and touch. Once the teacher has observed a questionable condition, follow-up can eliminate or determine the need for emergency response procedures.

5.3 BASIC EMERGENCY RESPONSE PROCEDURES

The teacher should be ready for an emergency at all times. To lessen risk as an emergency occurs, the teacher should be prepared with proper planning, organizing, and responses based on knowledge and training. It is suggested that all teachers have an emergency response plan (Bright Horizons, 2003; Hooper, 2006). This plan should define the procedures and policies to respond to and recover from any type of emergency or disaster (Riopelle et al., 2004). Here is a list of emergencies that should each have a response plan with procedures to follow:

- Medical emergencies
- Severe allergic reactions
- Evacuation procedures and process
- Survival mode sheltering/sheltering in place
- Natural disasters (hurricane, tornado, severe storms)
- Utility disruption
- Fire/smoke emergencies
- Hazardous materials
- Bomb threat
- Suspicious articles
- Potentially violent situations
- Random acts of violence
- Disgruntled impaired parents/guardians or parent's/guardian's authorized representatives
- Hostage situations
- Missing child

Organization for Emergency

When an emergency occurs, the teacher should remain calm and act immediately. This is hard to do under normal conditions, but even more difficult in emergencies if you are not prepared to follow emergency procedures. There are a number of ways to prepare for the possibilities of emergencies and organize the early childhood education environment to cope with them.

The procedures in Table 5-3 should be followed to prepare the environment for emergencies.

Basic Training. All teachers should have basic training for and certification in first aid for infants and children, including how to offer help to a choking victim. This training should be updated as required by certification and a record should be kept of follow-up training (American Heart Association, 2005). Any new teachers should have this training before they start. At all times one teacher at the early childhood education site should be trained in basic CPR and should renew that certification yearly. All other teachers should know how to perform basic rescue breathing.

Every teacher should be familiar with the procedures to be followed for first aid and rescue breathing for both infants and children. Keep reminders of this training in a notebook or on the wall, readily available. Posting pictures

TABLE 5-3
Emergency Preparedness Procedures

- Make sure all teachers have had basic training and certification for first aid for children, including how to offer help to a choking victim. One teacher on site in the early childhood education environment should be certified in basic CPR, and all other teachers should be trained in rescue breathing.
- Have all emergency information forms and health records readily available for each child and teacher in the early childhood education environment. It would be helpful to have a second set in a box that is easy to carry in case of evacuation. A Rescue Registration form for everyone in the early childhood education environment should be filled out and turned in to the nearest fire rescue department.
- Post emergency numbers next to each phone. In addition, post a list of vital information that the emergency operator will need.
- Have a list of backup helpers in case the teacher must accompany a child to the hospital, away from the early childhood education environment.
- Prepare an evacuation plan to use in case of fire, natural disaster, or other major human-caused emergency. Predetermine an evacuation place such as a local school or a place the American Red Cross has designated as a shelter-in-place for evacuations. If the designated spot is not available at the time of the evacuation, other shelters in the local area should be considered. The shelter should be considered accessible and safe under all conditions. Develop a transportation plan for this.
- Prepare a survival mode or shelter-in-place plan to use in case of natural disaster, chemical spill, or other human-caused disaster.
- Have available a first aid kit that is comprehensive enough for most emergencies.
- Place copies of the emergency response plans throughout the early childhood education environment.
- Designate one person to be a "team" leader for emergencies.
- Check all emergency supplies on a monthly basis.
- Have regular fire drills and other evacuation practices.
- Post a map that includes emergency exit routes and locations of all utilities that might have to be turned off, such as water, electricity, gas, furnace, and control panels for the telephone and any alarm controls. Clearly label all emergency exits and utility shut-off areas.
- Develop a code word or words for use in human-caused emergency situations. Make sure all teachers understand the meaning of the words so that if they are said, the person who hears the words will understand that an emergency exists.
- Notify families of the evacuation procedures you have planned and prepare a list of family phone numbers, including cell phone numbers, so the families can be notified when a large-scale emergency exists. Keep these numbers current by checking them three or four times a year.

Wadsworth/Cengage Learning

A

Wadsworth/Cengage Learning

B

A. Emergency and first aid kits should be readily available. This one is located above the fire alarm, so it is easily seen and convenient.
B. Emergency response plan posted at an early childhood education program.

that depict emergency responses are helpful as reminders. These reminders can be invaluable in a real emergency. Reference books for this training should also be available for the teacher to look at on a regular basis to keep current, and updates should be added as changes in these procedures occur.

Emergency Information. All emergency information forms and health records should be readily available in a file for each child in care. These forms include:

- Emergency information forms filled out by parents, including health information; the parents' work, cell, and home phone numbers; emergency phone numbers of other people listed by the parents in case of an emergency; the physician's phone number; the name of the hospital that has a treatment release on file; and any allergic reaction information. This information should be updated on a regular basis every four or five months because phone numbers or emergency contacts may change.
- A parental release form to treat the child in case of an emergency
- All "ouch" or injury reports filled out for the child
- All health records, including immunizations
- A master log of injuries that occurred in the early childhood education environment

Another part of organizing emergency information would be to submit a "Rescue Registration Form" (see Figure 5-2) to the local or closest fire rescue department, so that if an emergency does occur, they have adequate information to help them in arriving as quickly as possible. It would also help them to have knowledge of the early education environment where the children are located (Shallcross, 1999). Although these forms were intended for family child care, they would work equally well for any early education environment.

Emergency Numbers. Emergency numbers should be posted next to each telephone. In addition, a list of vital information that the emergency operator

Wadsworth/Cengage Learning

It is important to have all emergency medical treatment authorizations in one easily accessed folder.

will need should be posted as a reminder of what the teacher must provide. This emergency information includes

- Teacher's name and address of early childhood education or family child care site
- Type of emergency (e.g., burn, fall)
- Where and how the accident occurred
- Child's (or children's) name, sex, age, and condition
- Directions to the early childhood education site
- Assistance already given to the child

The teacher should always stay on the line until the emergency operator hangs up and should be informed about the local area emergency system. Knowing where the emergency care is coming from, how it is dispatched, and the location of the nearest hospital emergency room are helpful pieces of information that may prove crucial in an actual emergency.

A list of emergency contact numbers for all children in care should also be posted by each phone. These will be readily available and can be grabbed if an evacuation takes place or a field trip is planned. Again, it is necessary to keep this list updated in case of any changes.

Emergency Backup. A list of backup helpers should be available in case the teacher must accompany a child to the hospital, away from the early childhood education environment. The backup person could be an off-duty teacher, a substitute, a friend, a neighbor, or a volunteer to the early childhood education environment. It is essential that these people be familiar with the early childhood education environment and that they have been introduced to the children. A familiar person adds a sense of protection to children who may already be very upset. Leaving the children with a stranger would be more upsetting. If the teacher must leave with an injured or ill child, she should have the peace of mind that the children are in familiar good hands.

Shelter-in-Place or Survival Mode Plan. In case of natural disaster, or some human-caused disasters such as a chemical spill, it might be best to stay at the early childhood education site. This major issue will be discussed later in this chapter.

FIGURE 5-2
Family Child Care Rescue Registration Form. (Courtesy of Mary Ann Shallcross Smith, Ed.D. Child Care Connection.)

FAMILY CHILD CARE RESCUE REGISTRATION FORM

(Send one copy to your nearest fire/rescue station. Keep one copy for your files.)

Date of Registration ______________

Provider's Name ______________________________

Street Address ______________________________

City/Town ______________ State ________ Zip Code ________

Phone ______________________________

Licensed Family Child Care Home? Yes ________ No ________

License # (if Applicable) ______________________________

Hours of Operation ______________________________

Maximum Number of Children (Including Own Children) in Home at Any Time ______________

Age Range of Children in Child Care ______________________________

Employee(s)/Assistant(s) Present: Yes ________ No ________ If Yes, What Are Their Hours? ________

Language Commonly Spoken in Home ______________________________

Describe where exactly in your home you provide child care. Include as much information as possible, including the type of home (single, multifamily, etc.), which floors and rooms you use. Describe entrance to child care and any additional entrances, etc. ______________________________

____

____

____

____

Other important information, such as special needs children/adults, animals, etc.

____

____

____

DESIGNED AND PREPARED BY DR. MARY ANN SHALLCROSS-SMITH, CEO
25 BLACKSTONE VALLEY PLACE
LINCOLN, RI 02865
PHONE NUMBER 401-727-8982
WWW.CHILDCARECONNECT.COM

Emergency Response Plan. In case of fire, natural disasters, or other major emergencies, an evacuation plan should be ready, another topic that will be dealt with later on. A copy of this plan should be available in a number of easily accessed locations; these might include the director's office, the staff room, and the classroom. In the case of a family child care home or at-home nanny care, it should be in several easily accessible places. One person in care should be designated the "team leader" of the plan, and this person should be prepared to take charge in case of emergency in a calm manner. This person would obviously be the family child care provider or nanny in those modes of care, but in a center it might be the director, a teacher, or another designated person.

Practice Drills. Drills for fire and other evacuation emergencies should be practiced on a regular basis. Children should know what is expected of them, and teachers should be very familiar with the procedure. It might be helpful to practice evacuating to another site once a year to get the feel of how it would be. In some states it is a requirement that a disaster drill be performed at least once every six months (Hooper, 2006).

First Aid Kit. A first aid kit that is comprehensive enough for most emergencies should be available. The kit should be easy to access and at the same time should be out of reach of the children. It should include the items listed in Table 5-4. The first aid kit should accompany the teacher and children on any outings (walking) or any field trips (automobile). In addition to the kit, there should be ice or bags of frozen vegetables available for fast ice packs.

TABLE 5-4
Emergency First Aid Kit Checklist

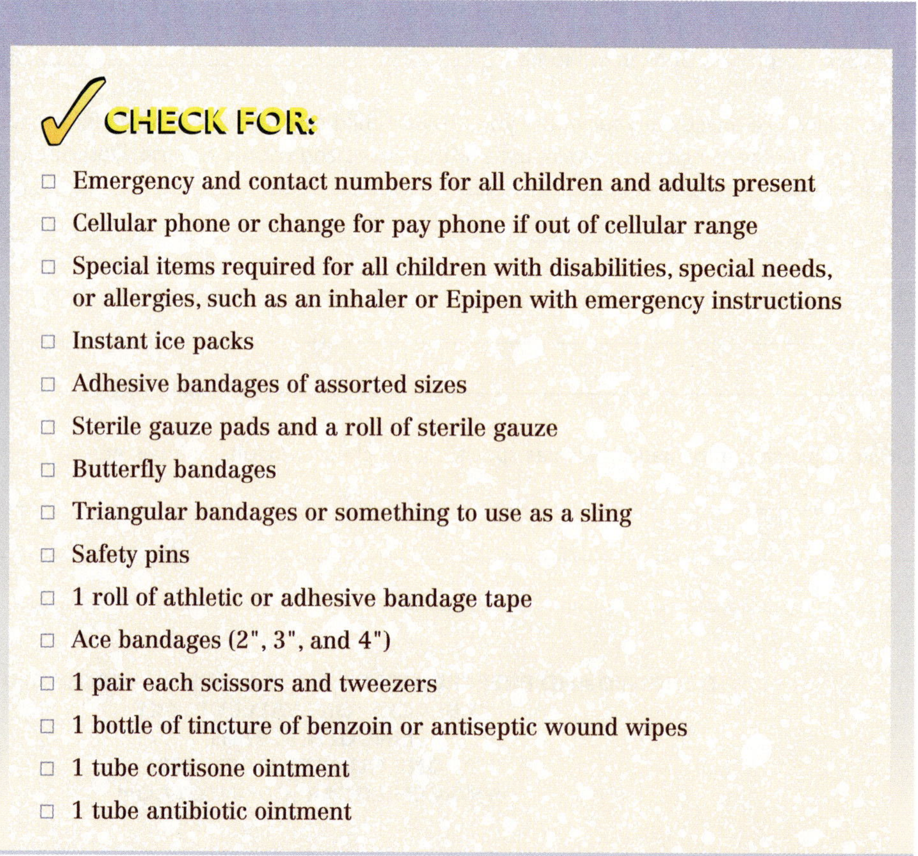

CHECK FOR:

- ☐ Emergency and contact numbers for all children and adults present
- ☐ Cellular phone or change for pay phone if out of cellular range
- ☐ Special items required for all children with disabilities, special needs, or allergies, such as an inhaler or Epipen with emergency instructions
- ☐ Instant ice packs
- ☐ Adhesive bandages of assorted sizes
- ☐ Sterile gauze pads and a roll of sterile gauze
- ☐ Butterfly bandages
- ☐ Triangular bandages or something to use as a sling
- ☐ Safety pins
- ☐ 1 roll of athletic or adhesive bandage tape
- ☐ Ace bandages (2", 3", and 4")
- ☐ 1 pair each scissors and tweezers
- ☐ 1 bottle of tincture of benzoin or antiseptic wound wipes
- ☐ 1 tube cortisone ointment
- ☐ 1 tube antibiotic ointment

(continues)

TABLE 5-4 *(Continued)*
Emergency First Aid Kit Checklist

- □ 1 micro shield for giving CPR
- □ Charcoal suspension for poisoning, used only as advised
- □ 1 bee sting kit and insect bite relief medication stick
- □ Hand sanitizer and antibacterial hand soap
- □ Pads for eye injuries
- □ Eye wash (saline wash)
- □ Unbreakable thermometer
- □ Bottled water
- □ 2 or 3 large black plastic trash bags
- □ Duct tape
- □ First aid guide and CPR instruction card

Supplies

There are also specific supplies (see Table 5-11) that will be needed in case of a shelter-in-place mode of emergency. The first aid kit and these supplies should be checked on a monthly basis to make sure that everything is in place and adequate to cover an emergency.

Signage/Maps

All exit routes out of the classroom or early childhood education environment should be clearly posted, as should the locations of all turn-off valves for water, gas, electrical panels, and the furnace. If there is a telephone control panel or alarm controls, those too should be clearly marked. An exit route and

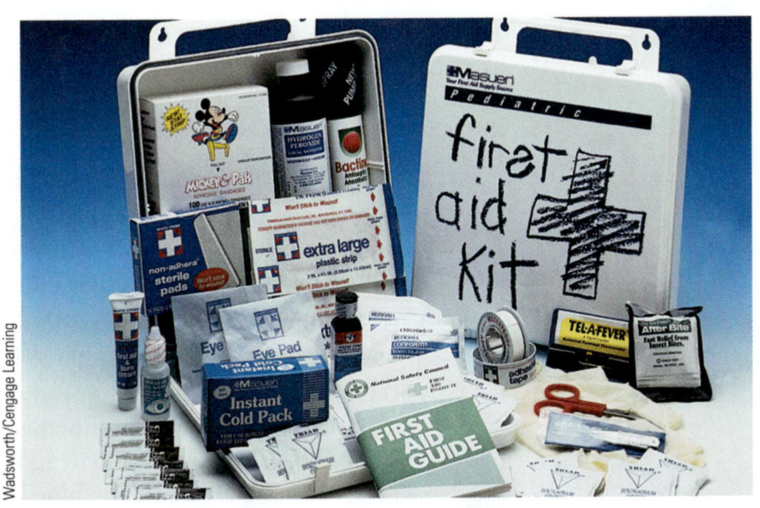

A first aid kit should accompany the teacher and children on any outings or field trips. (Photograph courtesy of Masuen.)

emergency shut-off map should be posted throughout the care facility and in the classrooms. This information should also be available in a family child care home or a home where a nanny works.

Communication

Develop an emergency communication plan for the early education environment. This includes having a list of parents' phone numbers for work, cell, and home phones. Parents should have previous notice of what type of evacuation or shelter-in-place plan you have devised and the procedures you will follow in cases of emergency. Included with this notice should be the telephone numbers of the early childhood education center, including at least one dedicated cell phone line that can be called should an emergency arise. Another essential communication piece is the selection of a code word or sentence that could be used in case of potentially threatening situations where other people are involved (Calder, 2007). If a situation arises in which a person or persons pose risk, the word or sentence could be used (for example, "Doctor Jones sent his regards"). If it is a medical emergency only, a detailed injury report should be filled out and a copy given to the parent. It is essential to communicate to the family of a child when an emergency does take place so they can feel involved and make decisions if necessary.

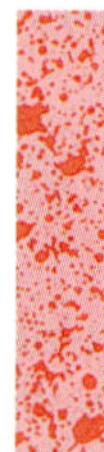

Pause for Reflection

Have you ever been in an emergency situation such as an earthquake, fire, blizzard, or hurricane? What emergency precautions were taken, and what steps were used to recover from this emergency? How was communication handled?

Order of Response

The early childhood education environment that is organized for possibilities of an emergency situation will be better prepared to respond to an emergency when it actually occurs. If an emergency does occur, the NAEYC recommends the following responses for the teacher attending to the emergency:

1. Act immediately and remain calm.
2. Stay at the scene, giving help and reassurance to the victim and other children present. If another teacher is present, assign him the task of keeping the other children calm.
3. Assess the child with a head-to-toe check, as if using Figure 5-1 and the senses check in Table 5-1.
4. Do not move a seriously injured child unless a life-threatening situation exists, such as immediate danger from fire. If you must move the child, you should drag her by the legs in order not to compromise the neck and spine if an injury is present.

5. If necessary, call for emergency help. In most areas of the country, this is accessed by dialing 911. The emergency numbers will be posted by the phone. If for some reason the early childhood education environment's phone is out, send someone to the nearest pay phone, car phone, or cellular phone. A portable or cellular phone serves as an extra precaution for emergencies in an early childhood education environment.
6. Notify parents and agree on a plan of action. If the agreement is to meet at the emergency care site because it is closer, call for backup help for the early childhood education site. If the parent is unavailable, call other emergency contacts and let the child's physician know what has happened. Call for backup teacher.
7. Treat child for **shock**, if indicated. Cover the child with a blanket and keep her warm.
8. Stay with the child until parents or emergency help arrives. Accompany child if parents are to meet the child at the emergency care site. Have backup teacher stay with children. If parents have not arrived and there is no other teacher present and the backup teacher is unavailable, the teacher must stay with the children who remain in the early childhood education environment. Try to reassure the child that he will be taken care of by the emergency technicians. If the teacher knows that a parent or other emergency contact is going to be at the emergency care site, let the child know that someone will be with him soon.
9. After the incident is over, fill out a report. Study it carefully to see whether the incident could have been avoided through better safety practices or greater compliance with health practices. Make any changes to the emergency plan as needed.

- **shock**
  an imbalance of the circulatory system as a result of injury that includes a decrease in blood pressure, a rapid pulse, and possible unconsciousness.

These procedures are easy to follow if they have been reviewed frequently and are posted in several places throughout the early childhood education site. Good planning and preparation will help the emergency situation go more smoothly and help the teacher to remain calm.

Key Concept 5.3

Basic Emergency Response Procedures

Knowledge of and training in basic emergency response procedures are essential for the teacher. All teachers should have training in basic first aid and rescue breathing, and at least one teacher per site must be certified in CPR. The teacher should organize for emergencies and plan accordingly. Emergency numbers and information should be posted and easily accessible. Every early childhood education program should have a comprehensive first aid kit that travels with the group if they leave the site for an outing or field trip. Every teacher should have an understanding of the nine steps for emergency response and be able to respond in the right order.

5.4 BASIC CARDIOPULMONARY RESUSCITATION AND FIRST AID

Breathing emergencies are always life threatening. Regular breathing is effortless and comfortable. When breathing becomes an effort, causes pain, or involves unfamiliar noises, these are indicators that a breathing emergency may be occurring. If a child is found unconscious, it probably indicates a breathing problem. Every teacher should be able to recognize the symptoms and be able to perform rescue breathing. Certification for this is available from both the American Heart Association and the American Red Cross, and certification should be renewed every three years (Reeves, 2006). When the determination is made that it is necessary to perform rescue breathing, the ABCs of rescue breathing should be put into place. This memory tool makes it easier to follow the correct steps to help someone who may need immediate assistance. The **A** stands for **airway**, the **B** represents **breathing**, and the **C** represents **circulation** (American Heart Association, 2005). If a disabling condition such as fracture or bleeding may be present, then a **D** should be added to this list.

The following illustrations are informative and are not meant to replace the needed CPR and first aid training. It must be recognized that these procedures may change before a newer edition of this text comes out. See website for updated information.

Basic CPR for Infants

For the basic procedures for CPR for infants, follow Figure 5-3 through Figure 5-6. This is the recommended procedure at the time of the preparation of this text. The illustrations give you the step-by-step process for CPR for an infant. This simplified procedure, begun in 2005, was done in response to the lack of success achieved with the formerly complicated infant CPR process. It is designed for the lay person to be more successful in saving an infant's life.

Basic CPR or Rescue Breathing for Children

For the basic procedures for CPR for children ages 1 to 8 years, follow Figure 5-7 through Figure 5-9. This is the recommended procedure at the time of the preparation of this text. The illustrations show you the procedures for CPR for a child. This simplified procedure, begun in 2005, was created to replace the formerly complicated process where there was not as much

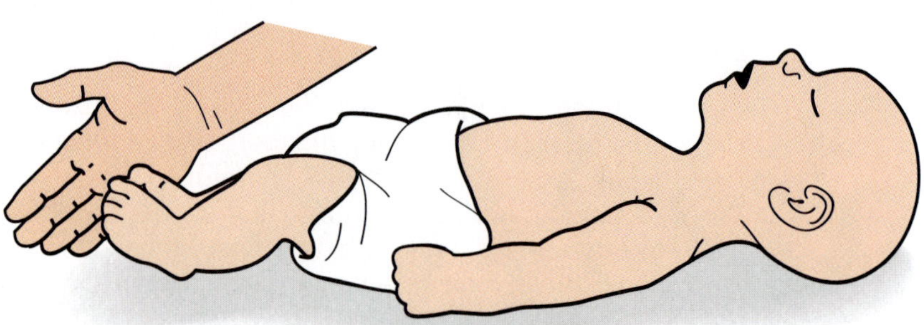

FIGURE 5-3
To see whether an infant is responsive, tap and flick the soles of her feet. If alone, shout for help and begin CPR if indicated.

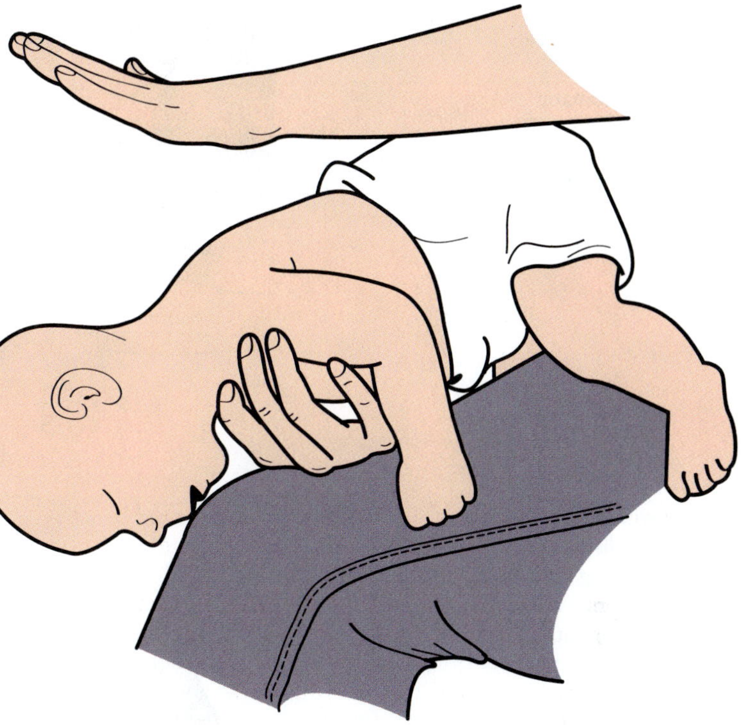

FIGURE 5-4
If the infant cannot cough or breathe and is choking, use the heel of your free hand to give the baby five rapid blows to the back between the shoulder blades. Support the infant between your arms and turn his face up, keeping his head lower than his chest. Give five chest thrusts, as in the chest compressions, but more slowly. Repeat this procedure for the five cycles of CPR until the obstruction is removed or the infant is no longer responsive.

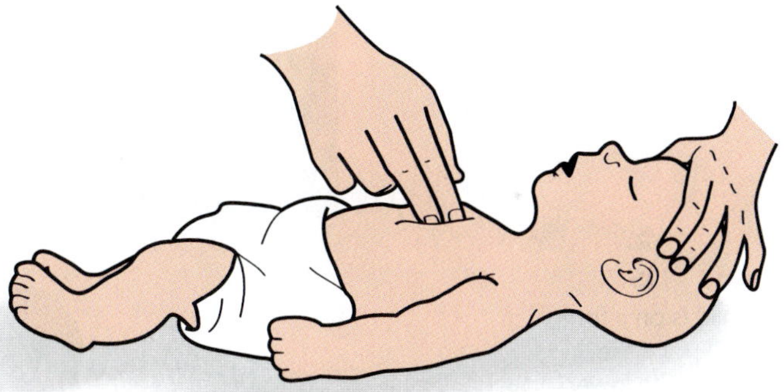

FIGURE 5-5
Place the infant on a firm, flat surface. Carefully hold the forehead with gentle pressure to keep the airway open. Using two fingers, compress the chest 30 times with a $\frac{1}{3}$ to $\frac{1}{2}$ depth of the chest at the rate of 100 compressions per minute, blow two breaths (see Figure 5-6), and continue for 2 minutes. At this time call 911, if alone.

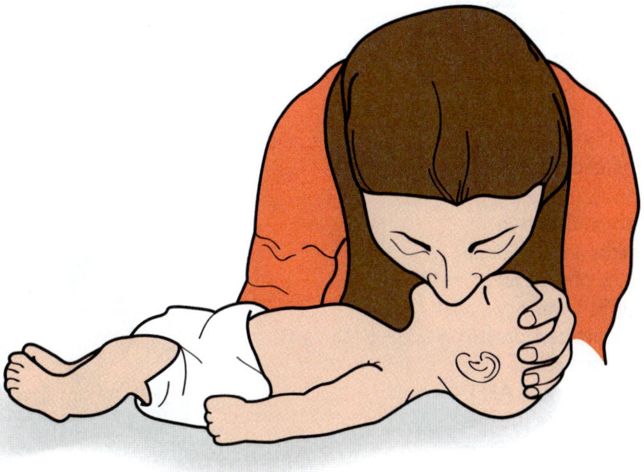

FIGURE 5-6
After 30 compressions, breathe into infant's mouth and nose for 1 second two times, enough for the chest to rise. Continue CPR as needed.

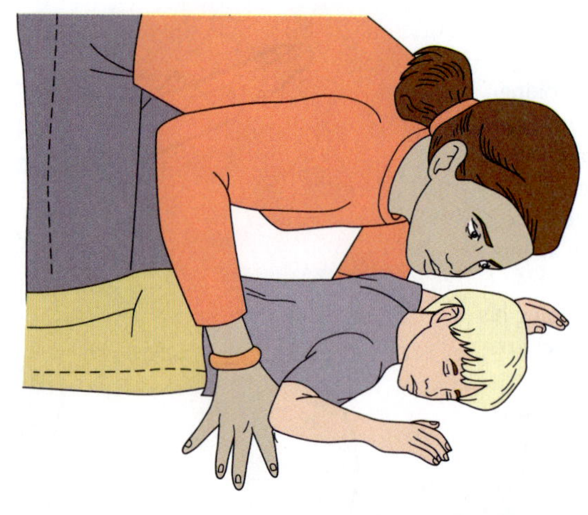

FIGURE 5-7
If the child is unresponsive, send someone to call 911 and get an automatic external defibrillator (AED), if available. If alone, shout for help and begin CPR if indicated.

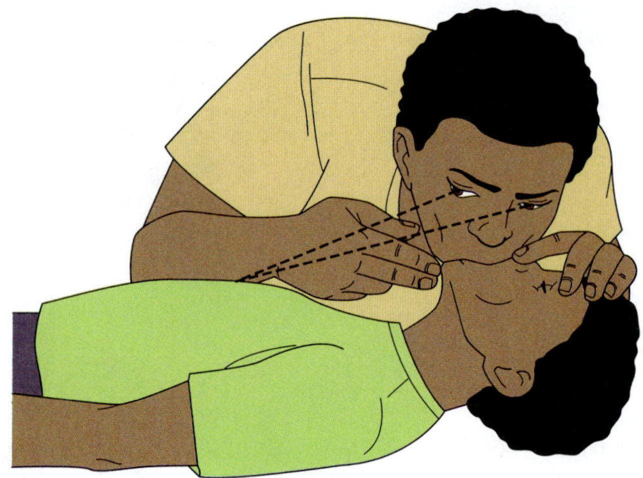

FIGURE 5-8
Open airway with head tilt/chin lift. Look, listen, and feel for breathing for 5 to 10 seconds. Pinch nose and cover victim's mouth with your mouth. Give two breaths for 1 second each and make sure chest rises. Immediately begin chest compressions.

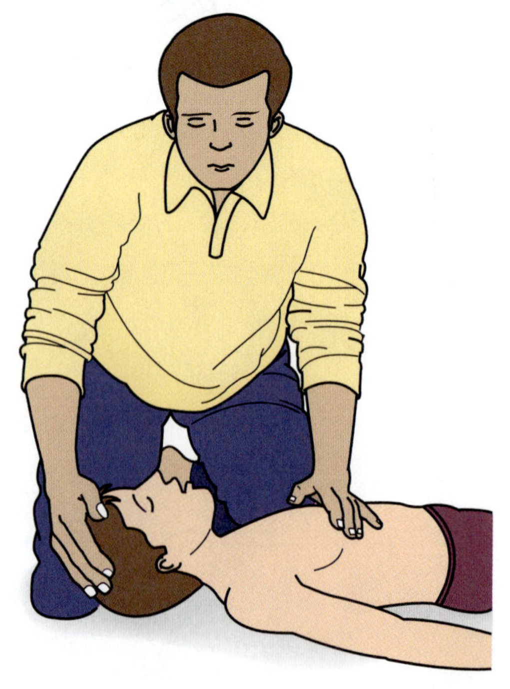

FIGURE 5-9
Ensure the child is on a firm, flat surface and place the heel of a hand on the lower half of the sternum between the nipples. Keep fingers lifted off the rib area. Keep airway open by using the other hand to give gentle pressure to the forehead. Compress the chest 30 times at a depth of ⅓ to ½ the depth of the chest at a rate of 100/minute. If necessary, use two hands. Give two rescue breaths and continue for five cycles of CPR for 2 minutes. If 911 was not previously contacted, do so know and come back as quickly as possible. If an AED is present, use it after the five cycles of CPR. If not, continue CPR as needed.

success with CPR for children as desired. This process is designed for the lay person to be more successful in saving a child's life.

Some larger early education environments such as college campuses may have an automated external defribrillator (AED) available. If that is the case, it is suggested that after the first two minutes/five cycles of rescue breathing, an AED shock should be used and then CPR should be continued. It is important to follow the instructions for the AED exactly, and it would be a good safety measure to make sure at least one person in the environment has had special training for it.

First Aid Procedures

There are many minor emergencies, such as scraping a knee or bumping a head, which can be taken care of easily by first aid. Other emergencies, such as a broken bone, a cut that requires stitches, or a burn that is beyond first degree, will need prompt first aid; then the parent should take the child to his own physician for further treatment. It is essential that the teacher know how to perform basic pediatric first aid procedures. The American Red Cross and other organizations perform a service to the community by providing this training. Following are reminders for the teacher of signs, symptoms, and responses.

Bites. There are a number of common ways that a child can suffer bites in an early childhood education environment. These include bites from insects, animals, or other children. Insects may bite or sting a child. These commonly come from bees, wasps, ants, and ticks. These bites may cause an allergic reaction in some children. The teacher should watch for those signs of allergic reaction. A mild allergic reaction might include watery eyes, itching, or hives. A parent should be called and the child should continue to be observed (Rose, 2007). If the teacher observes those more serious signs found in Table 5-5, the emergency medical services should be called immediately. Teachers in the early childhood environment should be familiar with the treatment of anaphylaxis, which can be life threatening if a child has an allergic reaction to a bite or sting. If a child has a history of reactions to stings or bites, the parent

TABLE 5-5
Signs of Allergic Reaction to Insect Bites or Stings

- Pain
- Itching
- Hives or red rash
- Swelling of the face, lips, or throat
- Flushing
- Abdominal cramps, nausea, and vomiting
- Wheezing or other difficulty breathing
- Dizziness or restlessness
- Partial loss of consciousness

Some cuts and wounds require stitches.

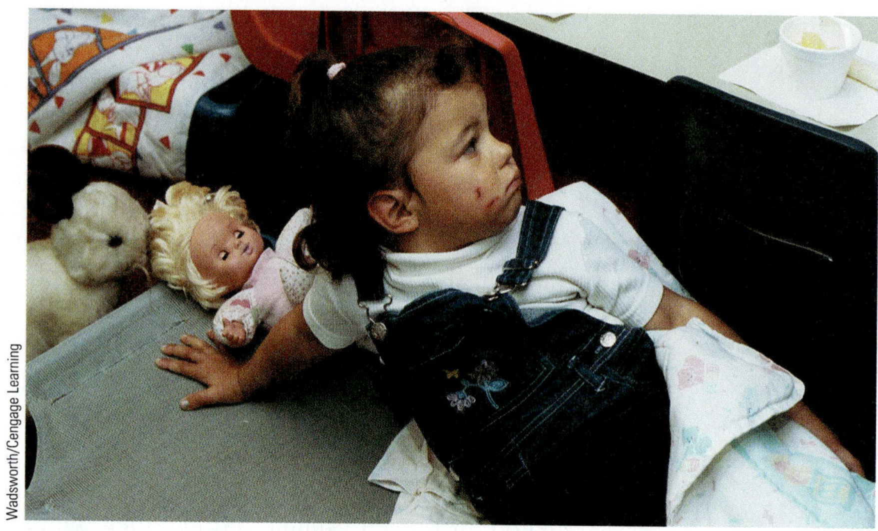

Wadsworth/Cengage Learning

may provide an Epipen, and if necessary, a teacher may have to administer the Epipen to the child. Teachers who had training in the use of an Epipen were more likely to use it properly (Patel, Bansal, & Tobin, 2006). (See Chapter 13 for the use of an Epipen in the case of a severe reaction to an insect bite or sting.)

If a child is stung and the stinger remains embedded, the teacher should try to remove it by gently scraping the area, using a credit card or gauze (Rose, 2007; Knight, 2007). The teacher must then wash the area with soap and water and apply an ice pack, a procedure that should also be followed with an insect bite that leaves no stinger. Comfort the child because a bite or sting may be surprising and cause a child to be upset. If the early childhood education program is located in an area of the United States where ticks, scorpions, black widow spiders, or brown recluse spiders live, the teacher should have first aid information regarding them. For further information on ticks, see Chapter 4. In addition to first aid, if the teacher suspects that a child was bitten by a scorpion, black widow, or brown recluse spider, the child should see a physician immediately.

There are a number of types of poisonous snakes throughout the United States and Canada. If a snake bites a child, remove the child from the area of the snake immediately. Get a good description of the snake for medical purposes. Have the child lie down, and if the child appears to be in shock, elevate the legs, if possible. Call 911 for emergency assistance.

For a bite from another child or an animal, the teacher should wash the wound immediately with soap and water and cover it with a sterile gauze bandage. If the bite breaks the skin, the child should be taken to his or her physician for a follow-up. If the wound causes heavy bleeding, emergency assistance must be called. There should be a policy for biting by children, and parents of both children should be involved in the communication about it.

If a child is bitten by a dog or cat, the incident should be reported immediately to public health officials or a physician because bites from animals could carry infection or rabies. It is important to wash the area well with soap and water and bandage it to keep it clean. If it is a serious animal bite, call 911 for emergency assistance. Animal bites can also cause emotional trauma, and this should be carefully watched for. As in the case of any bite or sting, the child should be comforted.

Cuts and Other Injuries to the Skin. Cuts and other injuries to the skin occur when children play, collide with objects, or take risks. The type of cut or degree of injury to the skin determines whether emergency assistance is necessary. If the cut is bleeding profusely or is jagged, torn, or deep, or near the eye, emergency assistance will be needed. Table 5-6 indicates the type of cut and the degree of injury.

Before emergency assistance arrives, it is important to stop the bleeding of a deep or severe cut. If possible, elevate the wound above the level of the heart. The teacher should use a clean, folded cloth to apply pressure firmly. If this cloth becomes soaked with blood, do not remove it, but instead add another cloth on top of it. Keep applying this pressure for at least 7 minutes or as long as 10 minutes. If emergency help has not yet arrived, find a pressure point that is closest to the wound and apply pressure with the heel of the hand. It is important to avoid the use of tourniquets. During the waiting time, be sure to remain calm and comfort the child.

Cuts and wounds not requiring emergency medical treatment should be washed with soap, and then clean running water should be applied for at least 5 minutes. The wound should be washed until it shows no sign of foreign matter. If the wound is an abrasion or is superficial, apply an antibiotic ointment or cream, and cover the wound with a bandage. Cuts that are more than an inch long and those that involve a large or deep wound that could cause scarring may require stitches. If there is an indication for stitches, the child should be sent to his or her own physician as soon as possible.

Injuries Involving the Head, Mouth, and Nose. Injuries involving the head are common in early childhood education because of falls from outdoor equipment and collisions with objects or other children. These injuries may be internal or external. External injuries may involve cuts or scratches; internal injuries may involve bruising of the brain or blood vessel damage to the skull (NCCCHSRC, 2005a). Head injuries may be minor or they may be more serious. Sometimes it is difficult to tell immediately whether the injury is

TABLE 5-6
Types of Cuts and Wounds

Abrasion—a scrape caused by contact with a hard surface such as pavement or carpet. Common childhood cut.

Incision—a sharp, even cut caused by glass, knives, and other sharp objects. The depth or length of wound determines the blood flow and the degree of seriousness.

Laceration—a jagged or torn cut caused by objects with uneven edges or by force. Tissue damage may be great.

Puncture—a hole in the skin caused by sharp objects such as a nail, thorn, or splinter.

Bruise—a discolored area of the skin caused by contact with an object, usually by force, such as falling or colliding with another object.

Adapted from American Red Cross.

Head injuries should be carefully evaluated before they are determined serious.

Wadsworth/Cengage Learning

serious when the child remains conscious. Table 5-7 lists the symptoms of a serious head injury. Most head injuries heal with rest, so the child should not engage in strenuous activity after the injury, even if it does not appear to be serious. It is important for the child to remain calm and for an adult to carefully monitor the child.

For many children, the result of a fall will be a bruise and swelling where contact was made. Have the child lie down for a while with an ice pack. Carefully observe the child's behavior for at least one hour.

Injuries to the mouth and nose can happen easily. Injuries to the mouth can be to the gums, teeth, tongue, or lips. If there is unusually heavy bleeding, emergency assistance must be summoned. Otherwise bleeding is controlled with direct pressure by holding a sterile piece of gauze where the injury has occurred. Once the bleeding has stopped for a while, have the child rinse out his or her mouth with water. If the injury is outside the mouth, wash the area

TABLE 5-7
Symptoms of Serious Head Injury

- Vomiting
- Shock
- Confused behavior
- Unevenly dilated pupils
- Seizure
- Dizziness
- Change in breathing rate
- Change in pulse rate
- Cold, clammy skin
- Loss of consciousness
- Bleeding or clear fluid coming from nose, ear, or mouth
- Weakness or paralysis

with soap and water. In case of swelling, apply an ice pack. If a child loses a tooth, find the tooth and clean it off with water. Place the tooth in a jar of milk and have the parents take the child to his or her dentist immediately.

Nose injuries most commonly involve nosebleeds. This is usually handled by the teacher's pinching the child's nostrils together between thumb and forefinger, while wearing gloves, for about 10 minutes. Do not tilt the child's head back. Have the child sit quietly and tilt head slightly forward. This will help keep the blood out of the child's stomach and prevent him from getting nauseated or vomiting (Leonard, 2006). Talk quietly to the child while this is being done. Explain the procedure and ask the child if he or she has any questions. It normally takes approximately 10 minutes for a nosebleed to stop. If it does not stop after 10 minutes, the child's physician or parent should be consulted. Some children have a history of nosebleeds that may take longer to stop. The physician can offer further advice or the parent can come pick up the child and take him directly to the physician.

Bones. Falls are the most common reason in the early childhood education environment for broken bones. If a broken bone is suspected, have someone call 911 and the parent. Calm the child, keep the injured limb or area in the same position it was found, and place clean pads around the area so that it does not move until help arrives (NCCCHSRC, 2005a). A teacher or other adult should stay with the child and comfort her. If there is bleeding, then treat it carefully, using gloves. When help arrives, follow the emergency plan to deal with the situation, including calming and talking to the other children.

Burns. Burns come from a number of sources, such as heat, steam, chemicals, or electrical sources. The different degrees of burns are listed in Figure 5-10.

If the burn is a third-degree burn, emergency medical assistance must be called immediately. There are three basic steps to care for burns. First, the burning must stop, which may entail putting out a fire and removing the child from the area. Never pull off clothes that are stuck to the skin. Second, cool the burn by flushing it with water. Do not use ice unless it is a very minor burn, because ice could damage the tissue. Flush the skin, or layer cool, wet cloths on the burn. Third, when the burn has cooled down, cover it with a dry, clean, sterile dressing. If the burn appears to be more serious than a first-degree burn, have the parents take the child to his or her physician. It is important to remain calm and comfort the child through all these procedures.

Temperature. Both extremes of temperature can have an effect on children in an early childhood education environment. Children can get overheated easily. They may get cramps from the heat or heat exhaustion. The cramps occur in the leg muscles and the stomach. These are usually the first warning signs of trouble with heat. Heat exhaustion involves nausea, headache, dizziness, and flushed skin. These conditions are treated by placing the child in a cool place and having him drink lots of liquids. Sometimes applying a cool cloth to the face makes the child think he feels cooler (Figure 5-11). To avoid heat exhaustion, it is important to keep a child hydrated at all times in the hot weather. An outside source of water should exist and children should be encouraged to drink water frequently, at least once every 15 to 20 minutes (NCCCHSRC, 2005d).

FIGURE 5-10
Burn Institute Burn Depth Categories. (Courtesy of the Burn Institute.)

BURN DEPTH CATEGORIES

DEGREE	APPEARANCE	PAIN LEVEL
1st	Pink Red	Uncomfortable
2nd	Pink - Pale May blister Moist	Marked discomfort
3rd	Pale - White Charred Dry	Painless Some pain

WHEN TO CALL FOR MEDICAL HELP:

- ✓ If the burn is on the face, hands or feet.
- ✓ If the victim is an infant, child, sick or elderly person.
- ✓ If swelling or infection develops.
- ✓ If there is marked discomfort or the burn is painless.
- ✓ If a third degree burn is suspected.
- ✓ If there is any doubt about how serious the burn is. Burns are often more serious than they first appear.

FOR BURN EMERGENCIES

(619) 543-6503

UCSD Regional Burn Center, 24 hours a day

or **911**

3702 Ruffin Rd, Ste.101, San Diego, CA 92123 (619) 541-2277

Exposure to cold may involve frostbite, but the normal conditions of early childhood education would preclude this from occurring. However, if the teacher observes the signs, he or she should act accordingly. Frostbite is indicated by a lack of feeling in an area where the skin is cold and may appear discolored or look waxy (Figure 5-11). To render first aid, warm the area by soaking it in warm (not hot) water. Keep doing so until the area appears red and feels warm. Bandage the area with a light sterile dressing. Have the parents take the child to her physician.

FIGURE 5-11
Heat exhaustion results from fluid loss through perspiration; frostbite results when cold temperatures freeze body cells.

Hypothermia is another winter risk for very young children. A young child usually loses heat faster than an adult, and with the larger head in proportion to the body, a child is more likely to lose heat from the head area. It may be easy for children to ignore this condition because they are cold and may not know when it is time to go inside. Hypothermia usually comes on gradually, and the first sign is shivering. Other signs include slow rate of breathing, pale skin, and slurred speech. If you see these signs, move the child out of the cold, remove any wet clothing, give him something warm to drink, and share body heat if necessary. Breathing should be monitored. Do not apply direct heat or massage/rub the child. Either of those measures can have serious or even fatal consequences. To avoid this, do not take a child younger than 1 year old out for more than 10 or 15 minutes at a time, and only twice a day. Older children should not be outside in the cold weather more than half an hour twice a day (NCCCHSRC, 2005d).

- **poison control center** *a resource available through a phone call in case of poisoning.*

Poisoning. Poisoning can occur in four ways: by ingestion, inhalation, absorption, and injection (such as snake venom). Under any poisoning circumstance, the first step in first aid is to call the **poison control center** in your area. Closely follow the instructions given. These instructions will include giving the age of the child and the evidence of poisoning that has been observed. As indicated by poison control, call for emergency assistance where applicable. Table 5-8 indicates the symptoms of poisoning by ingestion, inhalation, and absorption. The symptoms in Table 5-5 are the same symptoms that may appear after injected poisoning.

The child must not have anything to eat or drink unless instructed. If the poison has been absorbed through the skin, flush the skin with water until help arrives. If the child appears to have inhaled a poison, provide fresh air or put the child in a well-ventilated room with an open window. In cases of ingestion, do not administer syrup of ipecac (Schnitzer, 2006).

TABLE 5-8
Symptoms of Poisoning

Ingested

- Nausea and/or vomiting
- Diarrhea
- Change in breathing
- Unconsciousness

Inhaled

- Headache
- Dizziness
- Difficulty breathing
- Unconsciousness

Absorbed

- Irregular breathing
- Headache
- Abnormal pulse
- Skin or eye irritations

Key Concept 5.4

Basic CPR and First Aid

It is important for the teacher to know basic CPR and first aid techniques because they may help save a child's life. Knowing what an emergency is and when to call for help is vital. There may be other situations in which basic first aid techniques will enable the teacher to take care of the child's injury. Having information about illness or injury due to bites, cuts, head injuries, temperature, burns, and poisons allows the teacher to provide a greater degree of protection for the children in care.

5.5 EMERGENCY PLANNING FOR CHILDREN WITH SPECIAL NEEDS

Many early childhood education situations today include one or more children with special needs such as a chronic medical condition or allergy that may call for emergency response. The teacher should be very familiar with what emergency might arise for each child who has special needs. The AAP recommends that someone in the early childhood environment be trained to deal with children who have seizures, food allergies, and asthma (Hooper, 2006).

Every child with special needs should have a written emergency management plan that includes the child's diagnosis as well as routine measures that keep that child healthy and at less risk (Sokol-Gutierrez, 1999; California Child Care Health Connections [CCCHC], 2006). It should also include emergency signs to watch for, emergency procedures that should be followed, and who should be contacted when this occurs. A duplicate copy of this plan should be kept in the first aid kit, and this information should be updated regularly (AAP, 1999). Any time a child with special needs has an emergency, the parents should be called.

If medication is part of the emergency response, it should also be included in a separate first aid kit. This might include inhalers for children

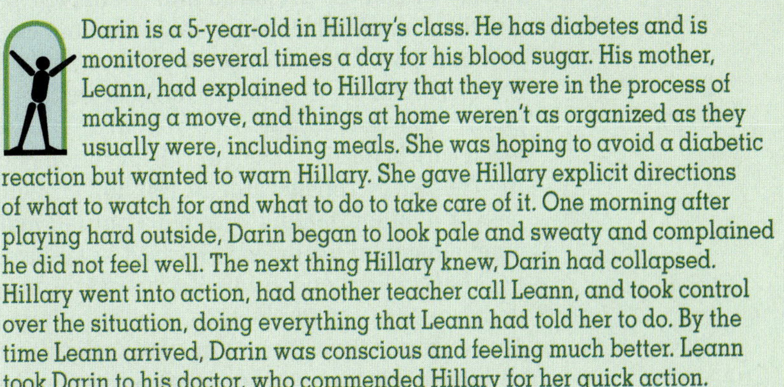

Darin is a 5-year-old in Hillary's class. He has diabetes and is monitored several times a day for his blood sugar. His mother, Leann, had explained to Hillary that they were in the process of making a move, and things at home weren't as organized as they usually were, including meals. She was hoping to avoid a diabetic reaction but wanted to warn Hillary. She gave Hillary explicit directions of what to watch for and what to do to take care of it. One morning after playing hard outside, Darin began to look pale and sweaty and complained he did not feel well. The next thing Hillary knew, Darin had collapsed. Hillary went into action, had another teacher call Leann, and took control over the situation, doing everything that Leann had told her to do. By the time Leann arrived, Darin was conscious and feeling much better. Leann took Darin to his doctor, who commended Hillary for her quick action.

with asthma, epinephrine for children with peanut or other allergies, and insulin for a diabetic child. It would be helpful for the teacher to speak to the physicians of children with special needs in order to better understand how to protect them and to be prepared to handle emergency situations that can arise when children with special needs are in care (Sailors, 2004a). Parents will have to authorize the release of this information.

Key Concept 5.5

Emergency Planning for Children with Special Needs

It is essential for a teacher to be prepared to handle emergency responses for children with special needs. An emergency management plan should be written for each child in care who has special needs. The teacher should be prepared to respond in the proper manner. These responses may include the administering of special medications that will help a child to recover from the emergency.

5.6 DISASTER PREPAREDNESS

Disaster preparedness is an essential element in addressing emergency response procedures. No teacher ever expects a disaster to occur. Disasters generally occur suddenly without warning and can cause great damage. For the safety of the children in care, disasters should be planned for, and the environment should be organized to cope with a disaster, should one occur. One way to accomplish this is to imagine a natural disaster that specifically could happen in the area where the early childhood education environment is located. Picture the type of damage and injuries that might occur, and then create a plan for the natural disaster in response to those conditions (Hooper, 2006) (see also Reality Check: *Natural Disasters* on page 199).

Disasters have normally been associated with acts of nature, such as tornadoes, floods, earthquakes, or fires. (Fires may also be caused by human carelessness.) Other potential disasters might include a gas leak or noxious fumes from a chemical spill. Procedures for a chemical emergency spill or release should be prepared and posted (Bright Horizons, 2003; ARC, 2005b). Another potential disaster might be an electric blackout, whether rolling or otherwise. Lack of electricity could affect heating, air conditioning, and refrigeration. These may be critical factors for some children with special needs. An example might be a child who has to be on a nebulizer for which electricity is needed. Lack of refrigeration could put the food that is stored in the freezer or refrigerator at risk for growing bacteria that could cause illness. A plan for dealing with blackouts should be discussed if the early childhood education program is located in an area where they are an issue.

Early childhood education programs may also be impacted by an intentional human act of violence, meant to harm. The destruction of the World Trade Center Twin Towers in New York City greatly affected the on-site early childhood education program. Quick action and an evacuation plan by teachers allowed all children in care to escape safely. The bombing of the Federal Building in Oklahoma City included an on-site early childhood education center, and there was much loss of life, including children. Early childhood education centers have also been threatened with violence involving guns. For example, an incident in the late 1990s in Granada Hills, California, occurred when a man invaded an early childhood education environment and shot a number of children. In another situation in North Carolina in 2004, a man chased a woman who was holding her 6-month-old baby through a child care facility and shot her in the leg. The baby was not hurt, but those present in the facility were upset and traumatized (NCCCHSRC, 2005b).

A planned response to violence should be talked about and agreed upon before it occurs. All teachers should know a code phrase, such as "Ground Hog Day," so that they can be alerted to danger without causing fear to the children (Sailors, 2000; Rose, 2007). If you are a family child care provider who is all alone with no one to assist you, you should respond by calling 911 or the rescue number in the local area. It is important to be familiar with the layout and locality of the early childhood education environment in terms of security. Are there places within the environment or nearby that could be dangerous hiding places? One security measure might be to install a buzzer on gates or outside doors to alert staff when somebody enters.

Just as it has been suggested to all Americans that we be vigilant in our awareness of our surroundings for terrorists, the same should hold true for an early childhood education situation. As teachers we are protectors of children and should do our utmost to keep their environment safe from any type of violent act, including terrorism. See Figure 5-12 for the Homeland Security Alert List, adapted for early childhood education environments.

The disaster most likely to occur is fire because it is more common than all of the other disasters combined. Fire can happen any time, anywhere, and under a number of circumstances. Because it is a common disaster, all teachers should prepare the environment to deal with a fire, should it take place.

The location of the early childhood education environment has an impact on the type of natural disaster that may occur. Tornadoes are more likely to occur in the mid-America sector, whereas hurricanes are more likely to occur on the southern coastal areas. Earthquakes are more apt to happen in California. Floods occur near rivers, lakes, dams, and other bodies of water. Snow, with blizzard potential, occurs throughout the country. Knowledge of the particular disasters that are likely to occur in the location of the early childhood education environment is a good way to begin preparations.

FIGURE 5-12
Recommended action for early childhood education environments.

Risk of Attack

Develop an emergency plan for the environment
Develop policies for the type of emergency
Create an emergency supply kit for shelter-in-place
Create an emergency supply kit for evacuation
Know how to turn off utilities in the environment
Have all emergency information and phone numbers of families gathered and available
Have an emergency packet for each child with a letter, picture of the family and a special toy
Make sure at least one person in the environment has first aid and CPR training
Send home emergency plan information including communication system that will be used
Have a cell phone available for emergency calls

Green
Low Risk

Review all steps at level green
Check emergency supplies and replace outdated items
Conduct emergency drills
Be alert to suspicious activity and report it to proper authorities
Send emergency information home to families
Send reminder of emergency and communication plan home

Blue
Guarded Risk

Complete recommended steps from levels green and blue
Update emergency information and phone numbers as necessary
Develop alternative routes to and from early childhood education site
Be more vigilant and alert to suspicious activity and report it to authorities

Yellow
Elevated Risk

Complete recommended steps from levels green, blue, and yellow
Review emergency plan and policies
Be prepared to handle concerns from children and families
Survey the neighborhood for emergency assistance
Be more vigilant and alert to suspicious activity and report it to authorities

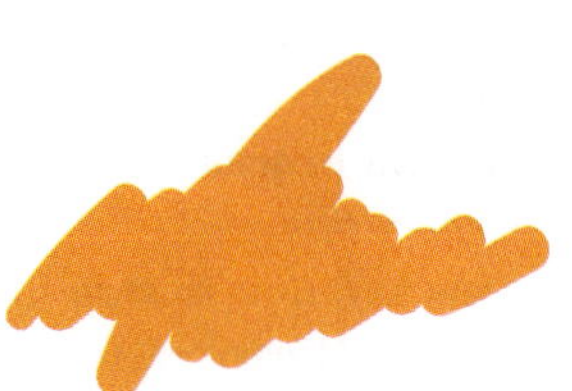

Orange
High Risk

Complete recommended steps at all other levels
Listen to emergency information and stay tuned to radio or television for instructions
Be prepared to shelter-in-place or evacuate
Close early childhood education site if recommended
Be extremely vigilant about strangers in the environment or unusual situations

Red
Severe Risk

Information Adapted from Homeland Security Advisory System

Teachers should conduct fire drills once each month. In this case, children are practicing walking out of a building through a darkened area.

Wadsworth/Cengage Learning

Evacuation Procedures

- **evacuation** *removal of persons from a site where a disaster or emergency exists.*
- **survival procedures** *preparation and steps to follow to stay in place in case of disaster or weather emergency.*

Most disasters can be divided into two categories. The first is a disaster that requires **evacuation**, and the second type of disaster calls for **survival procedures**. These survival procedures are usually referred to as "shelter-in-place"; instead of leaving the site, you would remain in place for the greatest safety. Many types of disaster such as fires, floods, tornadoes, and hurricanes may require evacuation. Evacuation procedures are basic. Because evacuation may be necessary in the case of fire, all teachers should be prepared with evacuation procedures and policies that help to reinforce them.

Every early childhood education environment should have a written plan that includes a diagram about emergency evacuation. Figure 5-13 shows a diagram of a typical early childhood education center. Included on the diagram are the exit doors and windows; location of first aid kits, daily attendance records and fire extinguishers; utility shutoff; and location of food, clothing, and tools. Each of these items may have to be accessed.

It is essential that there be an evacuation plan that everyone concerned with the early childhood education program understands. This includes teachers, children, and their parents. Teachers will need to know what emergency records might have to be accessed. It is a good idea to keep copies of all children's emergency information in a fireproof, portable file because this allows the teacher access to information about emergency contacts and so forth. If a child has a specific health challenge such as an allergy or other special needs, his or her records should be copied and placed in the portable file. A teacher should be designated in charge of this file, including keeping

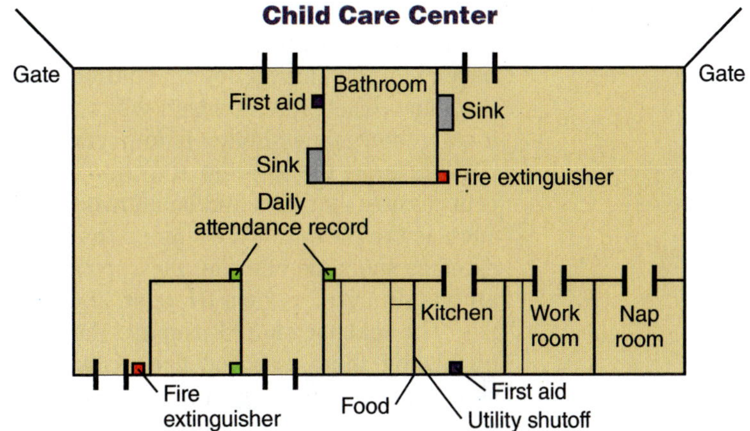

FIGURE 5-13
A diagram of the early childhood education center is an important tool to have during emergencies, particularly if the center must be evacuated.

the information current and updated. Also, if a teacher has a medical condition such as high blood pressure for which he or she needs medication, there should be an "emergency grab and go kit" that includes these medications (NCCCHSRC, 2005b). It is suggested that when preparing this kit that there be a 3-day supply of medication available.

A teacher should be responsible for keeping daily attendance checklists for the children in care. The checklist should be frequently checked throughout the day for accuracy. This information may be needed if evacuation occurs and confusion ensues. Having a checklist will help to bring order. The teacher should also be familiar with emergency phone numbers and should follow the organization for emergencies. The teacher should plan for emergency evacuation using several proactive strategies. These are included in Table 5-9.

TABLE 5-9
Proactive Strategies for Evacuation

- Plan two exit routes from the building. Post these throughout the building.
- Test smoke detectors and fire alarms once a month.
- Plan a fire drill once per month.
- Plan exit strategies for removing infants and toddlers, perhaps by using a wagon, crib, or some such conveyance that can carry several children at a time and will go through a door.
- Be familiar with and post information concerning the shut-off switches for gas, water, electricity, and other utilities that may pose a safety risk.
- Know how and when to use a fire extinguisher.
- Prepare children to handle emergencies by drills, discussion, and use of diagram.
- Teach children "Stop, Drop, Roll, Cool, and Call" techniques and practice with them.
- Keep a fireproof, portable file with emergency and health information for special needs of children in care.
- Choose a safe emergency shelter spot and prearrange for its use during an emergency.

The teacher must discuss emergency procedures with parents so they are familiar with the practice and drills the children are performing. Inform parents of the emergency evacuation plans. The teacher should let the families know where the children will be taken in case of an emergency. Having a safe emergency shelter is important, and it is equally important that the parents know the location. If a child can be picked up in an evacuation site, it is necessary that the child be allowed to leave only with an authorized person such as the parent or a designee that the parent has previously selected and listed as someone who can pick up the child. Never send the child home with an unauthorized person (Hooper, 2006).

The teacher should prepare the children for an evacuation emergency by having them practice fire drills, using and understanding exits. They should participate in group discussions about what to do and should understand about a meeting point outside if the building does have to be evacuated. These drills should be held once a month. It is also suggested that disaster drills should be practiced several times a year (Hooper, 2006).

The teacher should practice drills with infants and toddlers who may not walk or not yet walk well. These exit drills would take place in a wagon or crib, just as they would under emergency conditions. Children should also be taught several catch phrases. For fire drills these include "Stop, Drop, and Roll," "Go Tell a Grown-up," and "Crawl Low Under Smoke" (Cole, Crandall, & Kourofsky, 2004). Figure 5-14 shows an example of a sign that children could recognize and that would help them learn. They should practice the procedure regularly on the day of a fire drill.

Shelter-in-Place Procedures

Other disasters such as an earthquake or blizzard may call for everyone to remain in the early childhood education environment. This isolation may last a few hours or several days. The survival mode or shelter-in-place procedure may have to be applied in this instance. If the early childhood education site is in the type of location where the use of the survival mode may be necessary, then the teacher must be organized and properly prepared. Another reason for survival mode might be a countywide school lockdown due to

FIGURE 5-14
Stop, Drop, Roll, Cool, and Call. (Courtesy of the Burn Institute.)

gunfire, an intruder in the local area, or a chemical or radiation emergency (ARC, 2001; 2005b). Certo (1995) suggested that a "pretend" emergency day be held so that children and staff are prepared to function should that emergency occur. Table 5-10 shows a sample schedule explaining the functions that can take place when simulating an emergency due to an earthquake. Table 5-11 shows a list of emergency survival supplies that should be kept on hand in case of a survival mode emergency.

In case of an earthquake, it may be safer if the teacher carries out the survival mode outdoors. The supplies kept on hand might just be moved outside. It is important to have a designated area in which care will take place.

It is very important that the teacher do whatever possible to protect health during this time (Sailors, 2004b). Having a clean supply of water is essential. Enough bottled water should be available for drinking. To stop the spread of disease, frequent hand washing is critically important for this time. If a chemical spill or other contamination compromises the water, then use alternatives to hand washing such as antibacterial hand wash. Contaminated water can be used to flush toilets. Make sure that plenty of toilet paper, diapers, and diaper wipes are readily available to sustain a three-day shelter-in-place. If the water supply is cut off due to broken pipes, then use a plastic bucket with a lid or a child's potty chair as alternatives (Sailors, 2004b). Having plenty of bleach on hand will be important for sanitizing the environment. As discussed above, there should also be a personal kit for medication if it is required for a teacher to maintain good health.

TABLE 5-10
Sample Schedule for an Earthquake Emergency Drill

Time	Activity
8:15 A.M.	Pretend quake. Children get under tables. Staff supervises, then gets in doorways. Staff then simulates damage and blocks off some areas. Staff tries to keep children calm and quiet.
8:25 A.M.	Go to center of room. Count children, check attendance list. Discuss plan and assign every child a partner. Give first aid with masking tape. Simulate shutoffs of gas, electricity, and water.
8:35 A.M.	Gather emergency survival kit (see Table 5-11) and emergency information. Pretend cleanup, with children helping with smaller items.
8:45 A.M.	Try to resume normalcy by having children play in small groups away from windows. Simulate aftershock. Children go under tables, staff into doorways. Try to calm and quiet children again.
9:00 A.M.	Children wash up (simulate, using very little water). Have snack bar from emergency survival kit. Drink juice. Talk about quake and plans for further survival mode.
9:15 A.M.	End of drill.

Adapted from "Helping Children and Staff Cope with Earthquakes," by D. Certo, *Child Care Information Exchange*, March 1995.

TABLE 5-11
Emergency Survival Supplies Checklist

✓ CHECK FOR:

- ☐ Fire extinguisher
- ☐ First aid kit
- ☐ Flashlights and extra batteries
- ☐ Crescent or pipe wrench to turn off gas/water, if needed
- ☐ Shovel, screwdriver, 20-foot length of rope
- ☐ 1 gallon of water per child, 2 gallons per adult, and iodine tablets
- ☐ Duct tape and one package plastic sheeting
- ☐ Portable radio and batteries for emergency broadcasts
- ☐ Three- to four-day supply of dry or canned food per person, hand (nonelectric) can opener; include energy bars and juice boxes. Also include some comforting foods for all, such as tinned cookies, candies, and tea and/or coffee for the staff.
- ☐ Paper plates, plastic utensils, paper cups, and paper towels
- ☐ Alternate cooking source, matches
- ☐ Blankets and extra clothing (Most early childhood education sites already keep extra clothing for children.)
- ☐ Extra newspapers to wrap waste and trash
- ☐ Large plastic trash bags for trash and waste
- ☐ Three- to four-day supply of toilet paper
- ☐ Infant supplies—diapers, formula, food—for three to four days
- ☐ Three- to four-day supply of food and water for any pets present
- ☐ Essential medications required for children with special needs (e.g., inhaler for asthmatic)
- ☐ Safe alternate heat source (nonelectric) and fuel for it; this might be wood for a fireplace or kerosene for a room heater
- ☐ Copies of class lists, medical records, and release form for children
- ☐ Maps with evacuation exit routes if needed later, and shut-off sites for utilities, and so forth
- ☐ Large plastic bucket with lid, a child's potty chair, and toilet paper
- ☐ One gallon of bleach and a bottle of liquid soap
- ☐ Several bottles of antibacterial hand wash
- ☐ Work gloves
- ☐ Personal hygiene items
- ☐ Whistle to signal for help if needed

Fire extinguishers should be visible, and all emergency exits should be clearly marked.

Wadsworth/Cengage Learning

REALITY *Check*

Creating an Emergency Natural Disaster Plan for Your Early Childhood Education Environment

Natural disasters are more widespread than one might think. In 2000, there were 44 major disasters in 32 states in this country. These disasters included tornadoes, tropical storms, severe winter and spring storms, hurricanes, floods, and wildfires. Each area has liabilities for certain natural disasters (Riopelle et al., 2004). Floods, wildfires, severe thunderstorms, and earthquakes have occurred in every state. Hurricanes occur from Texas to Maine on the Gulf and eastern seaboard. Hailstorms happen in the Midwest, and tornadoes take place in 38 states. Weather-related disasters seem to be increasing due to changes in the weather pattern and ozone layer (Institute for Business and Home Safety, 1998).

Mitigation is the preparation to protect people and structures from risk for natural disasters (Disaster Training International [DTI], 2001). This should occur in early childhood education environments because risk is everywhere and children may be more vulnerable to injury. Lack of adequate preparation for disaster could cause the need to replace equipment or repair buildings, requiring a program to be shut down for a time. It could also mean injury or loss of life to children or teachers.

An example of an early childhood education environment using mitigation measures took place in Washington State, when Federal Emergency Management Agency (FEMA) officials helped Little Church on the Prairie Learning Center, which was in a seismic zone, prepare for earthquakes. The measures, such as bolting cribs to walls and strapping water heaters in place, prevented any children from getting injured on February 28, 2001, when a quake hit (FEMA, 2001c). The project was funded in part by FEMA Hazard Mitigation funds and the rest by local businesses.

To adequately prepare for a natural disaster in your local area, there are certain steps to consider. The first step is to identify the hazards that are typical in your area (ARC, 2001; NCCCHSRC, 2005b).

(continues)

REALITY *Check* (continued)

There are several ways to do this. You could talk with emergency management people in the local area to find out the possible hazards they have dealt with, or you could look at the history of weather for the past 100 years for that area. The American Red Cross has a list on their website that identifies the typical disaster state by state: http://www.redcross.org. FEMA's website, http://www.fema.gov/, has storm watches and other information to help determine risk in your area. The national weather bureau's site, http://www.noaa.gov/, includes a large amount of information on weather, as well as forecasts for hurricanes and tropical storms.

The next step is to develop an outline for each hazard you have found to be present in your area.

- How often does this hazard occur?
- How bad might it get?
- Where is it likely to happen?
- How long might it last?
- Is it seasonal?
- How fast might it occur?
- Will there be a warning?

You may live in an area where an earthquake has occurred once in 50 years, so it would not be a hazard for which you might develop a disaster plan. On the other hand, if you live in an area where there are severe snowstorms or tropical storms on a regular seasonal basis, you might have to be better prepared for them than you have been. An individual such as a director can draw up disaster plans, but it is more efficient if there is a group who works on the plan so that more people fully understand what might have to be dealt with in the event of a natural disaster.

The third step is to put together the information that has been gathered as to risk for each hazard and then look to the early childhood education center or family child care home for possible consequences should that hazard occur. For example, if the center or family child care home is in a valley near a river and the greatest potential risk found was flooding, the location points to greater degree of risk than if the early childhood environment were located on a hillside. To fully examine this step, the following questions should be asked:

- What are the geographical features that might put you at risk (DTI, 2001)?
- Are there any features of your property that might cause risk or offer protection? For example, are there telephone or electrical wires directly above your building?
- What are the available communication systems between your facility and the parents? Do you have a cell phone, and which parents have cell phones or pagers?
- How many children are in care, and what are their developmental levels (i.e., can they walk or do they have to be carried)?
- What local resources do you have that could help in an emergency and help you plan for one?

As those questions are answered, the information will be combined with the information gathered in the first two steps and used to prioritize risk for the local area and specifically for the early childhood education center or family child care home.

The last step is to think about possible scenarios for the risks that were found. What would the impact of each hazard be, and how would it be dealt with? At this point, make a list of the needed actions and resources that would be available to help mitigate the potential damages at the early childhood education center or child care home in order to prepare for disaster. This might be a complex preparation, or it could be simple. For example, if earthquakes were a great risk, then mitigation similar to the example in Washington state would have to be performed. Earthquakes would be discussed, earthquake drills for "stop, drop, and hold" would be conducted with children, and the "safe place" in every room would be found. Adequate preparation for survival mode should take place (ARC, 2005b).

However, if the greatest risk in your area were thunder and lightning storms, the mitigation would be to be aware that a storm might be coming and

(continues)

REALITY *Check* (continued)

to take the necessary precautions. Lightning kills approximately 100 people each year in this country, and injures another 300 (Lay, 2001). You could talk to the children about lightning and read books about how it occurs (FEMA, 2001b). You could also look at the FEMA website for kids: http://www.fema.gov/kids (FEMA, 2001a). You will know that when you hear thunder you must move children inside immediately, even before it rains (Lay, 2001).

As the plan or plans for natural disasters in the local area are created, remember that children learn a lot by seeing and talking about events. They can be better prepared to deal with natural disasters if you talk about them, read books about them, look at websites, and discuss how to keep safe. Do not scare the children, but treat these disasters as the natural occurrences that they are and help the children to understand them before they happen. Brodkin (2005) suggests taking advantage of the opportunity to let the children talk and to dispel some concerns they may have. When the teacher does not know the answer to a question that a child asks about a disaster, it is important to be honest with the children and to find the answers for them by doing some research. The more a child understands, the better prepared he will be.

At this time there are two excellent sources that deal with disaster preparedness specifically for early childhood education environments. These are the Head Start Disaster Preparedness Workbook from UCLA's Center for Public Health and Disaster, available online at http://www.cphd.ucla.edu/headstart, and the Pennsylvania Chapter of the American Academy of Pediatrics (PAAAP) Daycare Facilities Emergency Planning Guide (2003), available online at http://www.pema.state.pa.us. These are both comprehensive and would be of assistance in developing a disaster plan.

CHECK*point:* **What is the most likely natural disaster in your local area? What steps would be required to prepare for an emergency should it occur? Do you know an early childhood education program that is prepared? Do you know one that should take greater safety measures for an emergency?**

Helping Children Cope with Disaster

The first rule of any disaster is for the teacher to behave in a calm manner. If the teacher is in a total panic, the children's behavior will reflect this (ARC 2001). Therefore, although the teacher may feel upset or panicky, he should try not to show it. When disasters are planned for and practiced, physical safety is easier to cope with and handle.

Adults often tend to ignore the emotional needs of a child once safety has been established. Children often have emotional consequences as a result of being in an emergency situation. They are often very afraid and may not be able to verbalize it. This may be especially true in situations such as earthquakes, when aftershocks occur, or tornadoes, when the wind might still be blowing. The University of Illinois Cooperative Extension (UIE) has a helpful pamphlet, *Children, Stress, and Natural Disasters,* that may be useful to you as you support the children as they try to cope with any type of disaster that has occurred (UIE, 1998).

Because children need reassurance, the teacher must explain as clearly as possible, without speculation, what has occurred and the facts that are known about it. The teacher should encourage the children to talk and express their concerns and fears. Listening to what others say about their fears and about how they feel and think about what has happened can help the children realize that this shared experience affected everyone (Ippen, Lieberman, & Van Horn, 2005). When things settle down, it is important for the teacher to establish a routine. Routines give children a sense of comfort and some predictability (NAEYC, 2005).

It is important for the teacher to understand that children may go through stages similar to the bereavement process in dealing with *any* disaster. The first stage occurs during and immediately after the disaster and can bring anxiety and disbelief. The second stage can appear several days or several weeks after disaster strikes. This is when the most disturbing behavior may occur and children may need the most reassurance. Boys are more likely to take a longer time to recover and to display more aggressive behaviors, whereas girls may be more distressed and more verbal about how they feel (Saylor, Swenson, & Stokes, 1994). The last stage may occur months later, and this is the time when the children come to terms with the disaster. It is important for teachers to understand that they may feel extra stress and strain in dealing with distressed children and should take care of themselves as well as the children in care (Giosa, 2004).

Some children may act clingier or revert to an earlier stage of behavior. Very young children can get irritable and cry more than usual. Preschool-age children may feel helpless and frightened about being separated from a parent or other caregiver (ARC, 2005a). Often children are afraid of being left alone, and this may escalate because they are not with their families. Continued reassurance and physical closeness will help. In most disasters, help arrives quickly and the children are likely to be reunited with their families in a short period of time.

If the disaster that the children are reacting to is a result of an act of violence or terrorism, it is especially important that they get extra help in trying to cope with this disaster. There are crisis counselors available, through both public and private agencies, who are trained to deal with this type of traumatic event, for both children and adults. You may be having difficulty yourself, coping with your own reactions. Do not try to do this alone. Both you and the children in your care may need professional help, so do not be afraid to seek this outside support.

Once children have been through a disaster, their upset feelings, fears, and sadness may not go away quickly. It is good to provide plenty of experiences

James is an elementary teacher in an area where wildfires seem all too common in recent years. Several years ago, two students in his class lost their homes. He was unprepared to deal with the questions, emotions, and fears of the children, but learned quickly that he had to comfort these children and came up with some strategies and ideas that might help them and the entire class with recovery. This year, another wildfire came close to the area, and a student's aunt and uncle lost their home. James was prepared to deal with the children's questions and fears because he had been through this before. He was able to help the students in his class feel better about the situation by getting them involved in collecting food, toys, and articles of clothing for the children in the area that was hardest hit, as he had done two years before. This helped the children feel like they were making a difference in a situation where they had no control.

that are beneficial to healing such as water, sand, or play-dough play opportunities. Dramatic play is another helpful way for children to work through their emotions in this stressful time (NAEYC, 2005). Lots of outdoor physical activity, if it is safe, can help children release pent up emotions. Talk with children about their feelings, letting them lead the way in discussing how they feel. Children in this state of mind might really enjoy some favorite activities such as stories and songs that are special to them (Ippen, Lieberman, & Van Horn, 2005). It is also important for the teacher to take care of herself so that she can be a greater help for the children.

REALITY *Check*

Human-Generated Disasters

In Chapter 1, in a Reality Check, war and terrorism and their effects on children were discussed. Unfortunately, in the world we live today, we must be vigilant not only for natural disasters but also for those that are generated by humans. Some of these disasters may be unintentional, such as a chemical spill or a wildfire that starts with a careless camper. However, many of the human-generated disasters that teachers must think about and be prepared for are intentional. These include chemical and biological terrorism, bomb blasts, radiological releases, and hostage taking. The world was made very aware of how terrorism can affect an entire community in 2004 when terrorists invaded a school in Beslan, Russia, and hundreds of people, many of whom were children, were taken hostage. That situation ended badly, with several hundred people dying, half of them being children. This situation left the world wondering what was next. If terrorists were so motivated to make their mark there with so many children present, where would they stop? One difficulty with that situation was the lack of planning and organization on the part of the government and the community for an act of this kind. Today, many schools all over the world are thinking about preparing for this type of a human-generated disaster. Forming a plan for this type of disaster might require a group of people, such as a committee or task force (Calder, 2007).

It is much more difficult to do a risk assessment for human-generated disasters than for natural ones because they will come without warning. It is possible, though, to examine the area that you live in for the possibility of a human-generated disaster and begin preparation from there (Riopelle et al., 2004). This is best done by examining your community for risk. Is there a nuclear plant or dam nearby? Does your community have a railroad, or is it near a shipping port? Are there any military bases nearby? Are you close to a government building or other government installation? A teacher can understand what the local risks are by doing a resource assessment of local agencies to see what risks they may be preparing for. The local Red Cross, fire or police departments, or hospitals may have a plan in place and may offer specific training. Public schools may also have plans prepared. Because many early childhood education environments are privately owned and operated, there is no public plan of action in place for these facilities. It is important to partner with these public agencies to seek some help in planning for a human-generated disaster. It would be helpful for at least one teacher in each early childhood education program to be trained in disaster preparedness, and it is important that all adults in the early childhood environment know and understand the disaster preparedness plan. A teacher may also look to early childhood education organizations for information on planning for this type of disaster.

It is important to maintain awareness of what is going on in the world. The U.S. Department of Homeland Security issues a color-coded alert. Figure 5-13 presents the preparation steps adapted for early childhood education environments. Review this list to see how it applies to your particular facility. Besides including risk assessment and knowledge of

(continues)

REALITY *Check* (continued)

the potential types of disaster, it is important that plans assess the particular early childhood education environment and the possible impact that each disaster might have. The next step is to consider the possible scenarios that might exist and how they would affect an early childhood education environment. This is a good reason to have a group working on this because the synergy from group work can result in more solutions to the possible scenarios.

Vigilance is key to avoiding the effects of disaster in every community. It is important to watch for unusual persons or items, such as suspicious items left outside the early childhood education facility. If there appears to be someone loitering around the facility for no particular reason, this should be a red-flag warning. It is important to enforce the security that is present in the early childhood education environment. This is the daily signing in and out, having a record of who is and who is not allowed to pick up children, and basic awareness of who is coming and going. It is a good idea to know the neighbors and the neighborhood near the early childhood education environment. Many areas are organized for a Neighborhood Watch; it would be helpful to be part of such a group.

If someone comes into your facility and is armed, the first thing to do is call for help. This may mean calling 911 or calling out the code word or sentence so that someone else can call 911 (Calder, 2007). The children should be gotten to safety, either in an area of the early childhood education facility that can be locked or through evacuating the building and going to a safe place previously agreed upon that the parents are aware of. There should be a system in place for knowing which children and teachers are present in the early childhood environment at all times. If confronted by this situation, try to remain calm before the intruder, and do what you can to calm him or her. Pay attention and remember details (PAAAP, 2003).

Any suspicious-looking package outside the early childhood education environment should be treated as if it were dangerous. A suspicious item should be reported to local authorities immediately (NCCCHSRC, 2005b). Evacuation should take place as soon as the outside area is surveyed to see whether it is safe. A package or a bomb threat that causes evacuation could be a ploy for hostage taking. Threats from a bomb can also occur via the phone. Get the details, including the distinctive sound of the voice, the apparent age of the caller, and the threat (PAAAP, 2003).

Hazardous substances or materials include chemicals, radioactive materials, and biological agents. If chemicals are manufactured in the local area or if there is a nuclear plant nearby, local fire and other emergency departments have knowledge about the materials. When an incident occurs, there is usually a warning by local police or fire departments (PAAAP, 2003; ARC, 2005b). You may be evacuated from your facility, or it may be determined that it is better to shelter-in-place. If evacuated, before returning, authorities should give an all-clear signal. If sheltering-in-place, it may be necessary to use the duct tape and plastic sheeting in your disaster kit to close off all outside ventilation and keep the radio on for further instructions (ARC, 2005b).

Be truthful with children, but do not offer more information than they need. Children under the age of 8 years can have trouble separating reality from make-believe (Brodkin, 2005). Answer questions clearly but do not go into needless detail. The teacher should have practice drills for evacuation and shelter-in-place. Children will want to know what they are doing. Listen carefully to what they are asking. Give the best possible answer that deals only with what they are asking. Don't speculate, and be sure to tell them that preparing for unexpected events may lessen risk. Above all, remember that the main objective is to keep the children and staff safe. Whenever possible, call the emergency resources in the local area.

CHECK*point:* **Have you ever wondered what you would do in a situation that was prompted by terrorism? What do you think you might personally need to be prepared for in your local area?**

Key Concept 5.6

Disaster Preparedness

Teachers should be prepared to handle a disaster. Although chances for disasters are slim, preparation will allow for the physical safety of the children to be protected in an organized manner. Disasters come in many forms and may be natural or man-made. Regardless of the source, disasters can be prepared for by defining what type of disaster might be likely to occur in the early childhood education environment. All teachers should prepare for evacuation, because fire is the most likely disaster to occur. Children should practice fire drills and know all exits. Teachers in locations where the survival mode might be required should be prepared to handle taking care of children for several days. Teachers should also be prepared to help children with their emotions throughout the disaster, as well as protecting their physical safety.

5.7 IMPLICATIONS FOR TEACHERS

Providing prevention and protection should be a part of everyday early childhood education. The teachers should be prepared as best as possible to handle emergencies as they arise. In order to promote protection and prevention in the early childhood education environment, the teacher can act in several ways.

Education

The beginning step for the teacher is training and education to be prepared to handle an emergency. All teachers should know basic pediatric first aid and rescue breathing. At least one teacher per early childhood education site should have basic CPR training for infants and children. The teacher should know how to organize for and respond to an emergency, including disasters.

Children should be educated in evacuation procedures, should understand exit routes, and should know how to respond. The teacher should arrange for the fire department to visit several times a year to explain about fires and the procedures to respond to them.

Fire drills should be offered monthly. Evacuation and shelter-in-place drills should take place several times a year. It is important to prepare and practice. The drill should be so routine that all children and teachers can be evacuated in minutes, if necessary. Children should also be taught about falls and collisions and how to avoid them. They can also be informed about how to avoid poisons in any environment. Children in areas where survival mode may be a possibility should be given practice drills in survival mode emergency situations.

For Families

Parents and other family members should be educated in preventing and responding to emergencies as well. The teacher should provide written information to parents that details evacuation procedures, a safe place to meet, and how the early childhood education environment will respond to emergencies. The teacher can hold a workshop on how to make a family emergency plan for the household in order for children to have a more protective environment at home as well. This would include an evacuation plan that can be practiced at home every six months. Fire safety information is readily available and can be provided to families. Most fire stations are happy to provide a speaker, and it would be beneficial for families to hear about fire emergencies and evacuation plans from a professional.

Supervision

Supervision plays a major role in keeping the environment prepared to respond to emergency situations. The emergency forms should be accurate, current, copied, and ready for fast response by being in a fireproof file. Emergency information should be posted by each phone. The teacher should make sure that everyone in the early childhood education environment is prepared to make a call if necessary. Everyone should understand the information needed in an emergency. The teacher should make sure that the backup list for people to help in emergencies is updated and kept current. These backup teachers should be contacted on a monthly basis to maintain the currency of the list.

The first aid kit should be checked regularly to make sure that it is kept up-to-date. As items are used, they should be replaced. If there is a supervising teacher, he should make sure that all teachers have the basic first aid and rescue breathing procedure training, and follow up to make sure everyone is kept current in their training. The teacher should be prepared for evacuation or survival mode disasters. The evacuation plan should be regularly reviewed. The survival mode supplies should be periodically checked and replaced if needed.

Cultural Competence

Emergencies are unsettling to everyone. Emergencies require understanding and adequate preparation. The teacher should provide families of children whose first language is not English with all the written emergency information in their native language whenever possible. The teacher may have to find someone who can translate by using resources such as the local chapter of the NAEYC or the National Family Child Care Association. Arming people with knowledge can prevent panic in emergency situations. The families can reinforce the information that the teacher has given the children by discussing it at home.

If there are families who are recent immigrants or refugees, they may have left their home country environments in emergency situations. Because of the trauma they suffered, these children may need extra support during emergencies.

Key Concept 5.7

Implications for Teachers

Teachers should be prepared to handle emergencies in the early childhood education environment. This requires education for both the teacher and the children, working with families, supervision, and cultural competence to get the information across. Education takes place by training the teacher in basic first aid, rescue breathing, and organization for and response to emergencies. Teachers should prepare children for emergencies by providing training through drill and practice techniques for emergency response. Teachers also should provide written information to families and communicate with them about the emergency response procedures that will be used, if needed.

Supervision should be provided to update and keep current the emergency information for everyone in the early childhood education environment. This includes having a backup teacher list, a first aid kit, an evacuation plan, and the shelter-in-place supplies needed. Teachers should practice cultural competence by having emergency information translated into native languages so that all families are prepared to help their children respond to emergencies.

CHAPTER SUMMARY

An important part of being a teacher in an early childhood education environment is knowing how to respond in an emergency. In order to be prepared for this response, the teacher must understand what constitutes an emergency and what types of injuries will necessitate first aid. The teacher has to establish an understanding of what steps should be taken for proper action and how they are performed, and should be able to perform them if an emergency occurs. Basic CPR and rescue breathing are summarized. Disaster preparedness is explained, and the differences between evacuation procedures and shelter-in-place procedures are given. Strategies for teachers on education, working with families, supervision, and cultural competence are discussed.

TO GO BEYOND

Additional resources for this chapter can be found by visiting the book companion website at www.cengage.com/education/robertson. This supplemental material includes chapter objectives, internet exercises, reflection questions, quizzes, web links, glossary and flash cards, case studies, frequently asked questions, downloadable forms and tables, curriculum supplements, more reality checks, additional key concepts, references, and more.

Chapter Review Critical Thinking Applications

1. Describe the three factors that always indicate an emergency. Relate these to other indicators that an emergency is present.
2. Discuss the importance of preparing for an emergency. How might this preparation have helped the teachers at the World Trade Towers on-site early childhood education program?
3. Compare and contrast the evacuation and shelter-in-place modes of disaster preparedness.
4. Would the handling of a disaster be different for different sites? For example, how would an infant/toddler center handle a disaster? A family child care center? An elementary school site?
5. Compare and contrast natural disasters with human-generated disasters. How are the preparations similar, and how are they different?

As an Individual

1. Assemble a list of emergency numbers for your local area.
2. Create an emergency contact form for the early childhood education program.
3. Survey your home town or the local area of your school for the most common natural disasters. List three or four things that can be done to mitigate for that type of disaster.
4. List the items that you would have in an emergency survival mode kit for the type of natural emergency most likely to occur in your local area.
5. Using mostly local resources, choose three conditions such as diabetes, seizures, or so forth, and get pamphlets or other information from these organizations on how to handle an emergency related to that condition.

As a Group

1. Discuss the items that should be kept in the early childhood education environment to prepare for disaster.
2. Break into smaller groups and identify and list at least five things that should be done in the early childhood education environment to prepare children for an emergency.
3. Role-play different emergency situations, taking turns being the injured parties and the teacher who finds them. Have the group evaluate the actions of the teacher during the exercise.
4. Formulate a plan and safety policy that would help you deal with a gun-carrying, irate ex-husband of one of your teachers. Compare and contrast that plan to one you might have for a gun-carrying, upset parent in a child custody suit.
5. What might be done in an early childhood education environment to help children and families who do not speak English prepare for an emergency?

Case Studies

1. There is a lot of rain in your area, but lately there has been much more than normal. Your early childhood education program is located on a hill in a suburban area that is close to a river. The center would be in no danger of flooding if the river were to rise, but the lower-lying area might flood enough to isolate you and the children. How might you prepare for this possibility?
2. Mei Lee is a director for an infant/toddler center. A teacher notices smoke coming from the water heater area of the early childhood education environment and rushes to tell Mei Lee about it. Before she can investigate, smoke and flames come pouring out of the water heater closet. How should she proceed? What directions should she give her teachers? What might she have done to prepare her early childhood education environment for this type of emergency?
3. Sam and Kevin, both 6 years old, have just collided while riding their bikes on the bike path at their school. Sam scraped his knee; Kevin hit his forehead really hard, and there is swelling and some bleeding. What procedures would you take to treat both boys?
4. Ariel, a student in your class, has diabetes. You understand that she could go into a diabetic coma and want to be prepared to handle it. How would you go about finding out what to do, and what should you do to be prepared in case that emergency should arise?

SAFETY CURRICULUM SUPPLEMENT

Sample lesson plans and topic maps for subjects that concern safety are provided on the companion website to help reinforce the information that is being modeled by teachers and learned by the children in the early childhood education environment. In addition to the sample curriculum there is a list of children's books and sources for further information. Some of this information may include songs or finger plays. This sample group is presented to help the teacher design his or her own curriculum by adding to the information provided.

SECTION III
Nutrition in Early Childhood Education

This section discusses nutrition and how it impacts children:

These topics relate nutritional needs to health promotion and risk management tools that will enable the student to design nutritional policies that work well in early childhood education settings.

CHAPTER 6

Basic Nutrition in Early Childhood Education Environments

After reading this chapter, you should be able to:

6.1 Nutrition Policies

Define and discuss nutrition policies and their use as tools for the nutritional well-being of children.

6.2 Understanding Nutritional Guidelines

Describe the importance of the Dietary Guidelines for Americans, the MyPyramid Food Guidance System, Daily Recommended Intakes, and other measures that provide guidelines for nutritional well-being.

6.3 Basic Macronutrients

Define the three basic macronutrients in the diet and discuss their importance to overall well-being.

6.4 Basic Micronutrients

Define the three basic micronutrients in the diet and discuss their importance to overall well-being.

6.5 Implications for Teachers

Indicate the need for education, working with families, supervision, and role modeling for proper nutrition to promote health and well-being.

6.1 NUTRITION POLICIES

Policies that ensure proper nutrition for early childhood education are important to the overall well-being and development of children in care. Children are at risk for poor nutrition under most circumstances. Indicators of the need for nutrition policies include the following:

- There are 13 million children in early childhood education (prior to kindergarten) every day, 46 percent of whom are infants and toddlers, and these children get a significant part of their weekday nutrition from the early childhood education environment (Padget & Briley, 2005; Hayden, 2002). Meals served in early childhood environments should meet the nutritional needs of children while they are there (NCCCHSRC, 2006).
- Parents should consider the nutritional program of a center before choosing an early childhood education program. This includes meals and snacks as well as the environment for eating and the nutrition education program (Nicklas, 2001).
- Many children fail to consume enough vegetables, bread, cereal, pasta, and rice while in child care (Briley & Roberts-Gray, 2005). American preschool children do not consume enough dietary fiber and consume more sugar than they should (Kranz, Smicklas-Wright, & Francis, 2006).
- Nutrition services in many elementary schools need improvement (O'Toole et al., 2007; Knight Ridder/Tribune Business News, 2008). Contrary to popular perception, elementary school children will eat healthy lunches (Karnowksi, 2007).
- The degree of staff nutritional knowledge has a direct effect on menu planning, food selection, and role modeling (Romaine et al., 2007; Hughes et al., 2007). Children's food preferences and eating behaviors are influenced by the adults around them (Parlakian & Lerner, 2007; Kendall & Puck, 2007; Sigman-Grant et al., 2008).
- One study found that fewer than 50 percent of children ages 2 to 5 years old in early childhood education environments ate the recommended amounts of grains, fruits, and dairy products, and about 30 percent did not meet the recommended amounts of vegetables and meat in their diets. Overall, these children were lacking zinc, calcium, iron, folate, and vitamin E in sufficient amounts (Padget & Briley, 2005).
- The Dietary Guidelines for Americans, 2005 (USDHHS, 2005; Federal Register, 2004) recommends an increased intake of whole grains, fruits and vegetables, and low-fat milk and milk products (Gidding et al., 2006). Sixty percent of Americans do not eat the recommended amounts of fruits and vegetables (Guenther et al., 2006).
- Water is an important component of a child's diet, and making healthy drink choices is an important consideration for teachers (Rose, 2007b; Sprouse, 2007b).

All teachers should have a basic knowledge of nutrition. This information may be used to model proper food selection, create menus to serve the children, or teach nutrition to children and their parents. Food and nutrition should be an integral part of the promotion of health.

Teachers must create nutritional policies that will support the growth, health, and well-being of the children in their care. The six major goals for nutritional policies are similar to the policies for health and safety. They include:

1. Maximizing nutritional status
2. Minimizing nutritional risk
3. Using nutritional education as a tool
4. Recognizing the importance of nutritional guidelines
5. Practicing cultural competence
6. Developing partnerships with families to provide a caring community

Nutritional policies may include menu planning guidelines, food selection, and preparation practices. These policies should be clearly written and should reflect nutrition as part of the promotion of health.

Nutritional policies should encompass the following:

- ***Nutritional Guidelines:*** understanding nutritional guidelines for optimum nutritional well-being
- ***Basic Macronutrients:*** understanding the basic **nutrients**, their sources, and the problems related to deficiencies
- ***Basic Micronutrients:*** understanding basic micronutrients, their sources, and the problems related to their deficiencies
- ***Implications for Teachers:*** methods and practices for promoting good nutrition through education, role modeling, and supervision to provide minimum nutritional risk and maximum health

- **nutrients** *substances found in foods that provide for the growth, development, maintenance, and repair of the body.*

Key Concept 6.1

Nutrition Policy

Nutritional policies should be created for early childhood education environments. These policies should cover nutritional guidelines and basic nutrition. They should also be helpful to the teacher as regards nutrition education, working with families, role modeling, supervision, and observation.

6.2 UNDERSTANDING NUTRITIONAL GUIDELINES

Adequate nutrition during childhood is necessary to maintain overall health and provide for growth. A number of nutritional guidelines or strategies for good health have been established to help accomplish this task. In the past, the responsibility for following these recommendations fell to the parents because young children ate most of their meals at home. The past 25 to 30 years have presented major societal shifts in the number of working mothers and the number of single-parent families. As a result, the number of children in early childhood education has risen dramatically. In the United States, teachers are helping to meet at least part of the nutritional needs of 60 percent of children younger than 5 years, as well as millions of school-aged children (Briley & Roberts-Gray, 2005). The food that is provided should be nutritious and developmentally appropriate (Giosa, 2006).

Although some families of school-aged children depend on the children to care for themselves, the majority of these children are in some form of care. It is essential that the teacher understand nutrition regardless of whether the care is center based, school based, family child care, or nanny care. Because so many children are cared for by others, the transfer of responsibility for adequate nutrition has at least partially shifted from the home to the early childhood education environment. The more hours the child is in care, the greater the teacher's responsibility for providing adequate nutrition for growth and maintenance of health (NCCCHRS, 2006).

Established nutritional guidelines help the teacher plan for adequate nutrition in menu selection. These guidelines and good nutritional practices can be shared with the children and their parents.

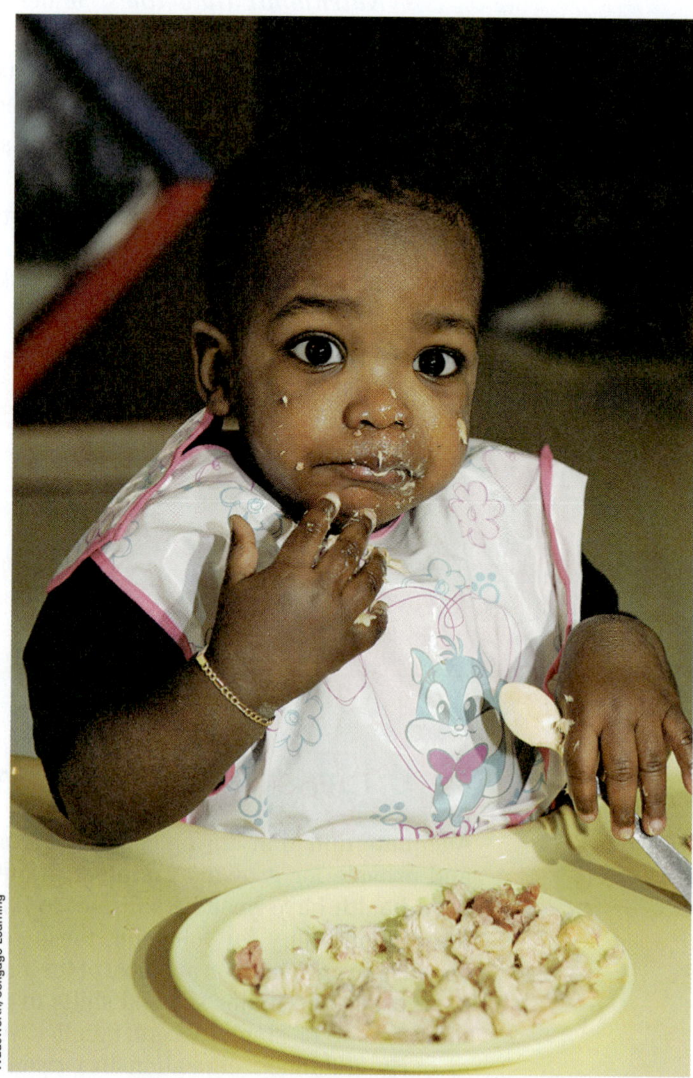

Wadsworth/Cengage Learning

Providing nutritious meals to children in the early childhood education environments can be challenging, but children can learn to develop good eating patterns that will last a lifetime.

Dietary Guidelines for Americans

Dietary Guidelines for Americans (USDHHS, 2005; Federal Register, 2004) forms the basis for nutrition policies in the United States. It is considered an important part of the standard for any federal program that deals with food and nutrition. The guidelines were completely revised in 2005. Table 6-1 highlights the basic guidelines, which should be used in planning meals for children (Kendall & Puck, 2007). The 2005 version is not without some controversy because the item about moderating intake of sugar has been eliminated. It has been found that sugar and fruit juice intakes in preschoolers have increased over the past 25 years (Gidding et al., 2006; Kranz et al., 2005). This suggests that, although the proposition for moderation of sugar intake has been removed, it is still important to consider.

TABLE 6-1
Dietary Guidelines for Americans: The ABCs of Nutritional Recommendations

Aim for fitness

- Aim for a healthy weight by balancing calories from foods and beverages with calories expended.
- Engage in at least 60 minutes of physical activity on most, preferably all, days of the week.

Build a healthy base

- Meet recommended intakes within energy needs by adopting a balanced eating pattern, such as the USDA MyPyramid Food Guidance System.
- Consume a variety of nutrient-dense foods and beverages within and among the basic food groups while choosing foods that limit the intake of saturated and trans fats, cholesterol, salt, and added sugars.
- Consume a sufficient amount of fruits and vegetables while staying within energy needs.
- Children ages 2 to 8 years should consume 2 cups per day of fat-free or low-fat milk or equivalent milk products.
- Keep foods safe to eat.

Choose sensibly

- Choose a variety of fruits and vegetables each day. In particular, select from all five vegetable subgroups (dark green, orange, legumes, starchy vegetables, and other vegetables) several times a week.
- Consume whole-grain products often; at least half the grains should be whole grains.
- Keep total fat intake between 20 and 35 percent of calories, with most fats coming from sources of polyunsaturated and monounsaturated fatty acids, such as fish, nuts, and vegetable oils.
- When selecting sources of protein, make choices that are lean, low-fat, or fat-free.
- Choose fiber-rich fruits, vegetables, and whole grains often.

MyPyramid Food Guidance System

The U.S. Department of Agriculture (USDA) (2005) introduced a tool entitled MyPyramid Food Guidance System in April 2005 (see Figure 6-1). This tool replaced the Food Guide Pyramid that had been used for more than 12 years (USDA, 2005). This system is designed to help Americans make good food choices, falling within the Dietary Guidelines for Americans, that they had not been previously making with the information presented in the Food Guide Pyramid (Britten, Haven, & Davis, 2006). MyPyramid has been designed to help people meet the nutritional standards set in those guidelines, but it is also supposed to help people make better choices in areas that relate to excess. A number of focus groups were used to test consumer response, and some of the more confusing elements of the former Food Pyramid were removed, but the original premise and pyramid shape was retained because it was thought to give continuity (Haven et al., 2006). The components or food intake patterns of MyPyramid Food Guidance System should help people to make food choices that will meet nutritional recommendations (Britten et al., 2006). In late 2005, a children's version, MyPyramid for Kids, was introduced to address obesity among elementary school–aged children (French et al., 2006). The information on this is tailored for children, and although it is specifically for children ages 6 to 11 years, it is easily adapted to very young children. Many early education programs depend on MyPyramid for Kids for guidance to ensure good nutrition (NCCCHSRC, 2006).

The entire MyPyramid system, whether for children or adults, emphasizes the consumption of fruits, vegetables, whole grains, and fat-free or low-fat

FIGURE 6-1
MyPyramid for Kids Food Guidance System: Overall view of the pyramid.

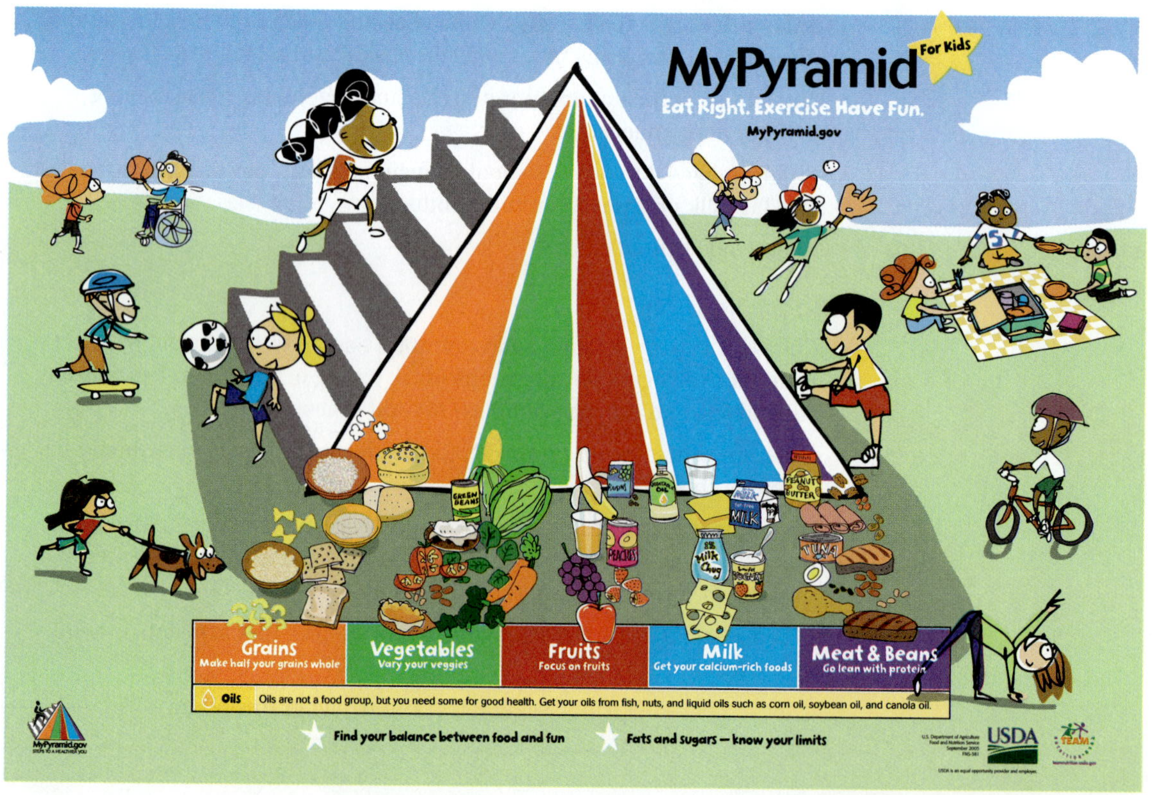

milk and milk products. In accord with the Dietary Guidelines for Americans, it focuses on low-fat or lean meats, poultry, and fish and includes beans, eggs, and nuts as acceptable sources of protein. This system also accentuates lowering saturated fats, trans fats, cholesterol, salt, and added sugar. The recommendations of the system are interrelated and direct the individual toward an increased intake of dietary fiber, vitamins, minerals, and other essential nutrients. It is hoped that this new system will help people to lower intakes of saturated fats, sugars, trans fats, and sodium, as well as increase the amounts of micronutrient-dense foods that are consumed by Americans.

MyPyramid is divided into two levels: (1) individualized daily food intake recommendations and (2) information to help individuals make better food choices. It uses Daily Food Intake Patterns that will help consumers identify suitable choices for foods and amounts to eat. These choices are based on activity level, sex, and age. MyPyramid Food Guidance System is designed to be interactive and to allow individuals to work with their own information to create their most appropriate food and activity pattern. The system for adults can be accessed at http://www.mypyramid.gov. Included on this site is a Food Tracker, where a person can fill in age, sex, and activity level into "My Plan" and get dietary recommendations that include seven days of menus for the recommended calorie intake. This would be helpful for teachers because they can also model the use of this system to children. MyPyramid for Kids can be found at http://www.mypyramid.gov/kids/index.html and includes information for parents and teachers, the My Blast Off game for kids, and coloring pages.

MyPyramid for Kids was created to help children improve their food intake choices and the amounts to eat to help them meet nutritional guidelines. This version of the food guidance system is simplified for kids to be able to understand easily. Four dominant themes are presented: variety, proportionality, moderation, and activity. *Variety* reminds children to eat from all food groups and subgroups. *Proportionality* prompts children to eat more of some foods that are healthier and to eat less of foods that are not as healthy or are full of calories but few nutrients. *Moderation* focuses on choosing foods that limit intake of sugars, cholesterol, salt, saturated fats, and trans fats. *Activity* addresses physical activity, or energy expenditure, as a way to look at food consumed and balance it with energy expended.

MyPyramid Guidance System uses Daily Food Intake Patterns to help us identify suitable choices for foods and amounts to eat (Britten, Haven, & Davis, 2006). These pattern choices for children are based on activity level and age. MyPyramid for Kids separates the list of intake patterns into five major food group categories and their subgroups: grains, vegetables, fruits, milk and milk products, and meat and beans. There is a minor category of oils, but it is not focused upon (see MyPyramid, Figure 6-1).

The MyPyramid for Kids system divides grains into two groups: refined grains and whole grains. Grains include any food made from wheat, rice, oats, cornmeal, barley, or other cereal grains. We receive our grains from breads, pastas, cereals, tortillas, and other such products. MyPyramid for kids suggests that half of an individual's intake in this area should be whole grains every day (see Figure 6-2). For children ages 6 to 11 years, the recommended daily total amount of grains is 6 ounces, with 3 ounces being whole grain. Whole grains include the entire kernel of grain, including the bran and germ. Refined grains have been milled, and the bran and germ have been removed. Milling also removes many nutrients such as iron and vitamin B and dietary fiber. Often, these products are "enriched," which means that the nutrients taken out are added back after processing. But this enrichment

FIGURE 6-2
MyPyramid for Kids Food Guidance System: Foods in the Grain group.

Grain Group
Make half your grains whole

MyPyramid.gov

What foods are in the grain group?

Any food made from wheat, rice, oats, cornmeal, barley or another cereal grain is a grain product. Bread, pasta, oatmeal, breakfast cereals, tortillas, and grits are examples of grain products.

Grains are divided into 2 subgroups, **whole grains** and **refined grains.**

Whole grains contain the entire grain kernel—the bran, germ, and endosperm. Examples include:

- whole-wheat flour
- bulgur (cracked wheat)
- oatmeal
- whole cornmeal
- brown rice

Refined grains have been milled, a process that removes the bran and germ. This is done to give grains a finer texture and improve their shelf life, but it also removes dietary fiber, iron, and many B vitamins. Some examples of refined grain products are:

- white flour
- degermed cornmeal
- white bread
- white rice

Most refined grains are *enriched.* This means certain B vitamins (thiamin, riboflavin, niacin, folic acid) and iron are added back after processing. Fiber is not added back to enriched grains. Check the ingredient list on refined grain products to make sure that the word "enriched" is included in the grain name. Some food products are made from mixtures of whole grains and refined grains.

Some commonly eaten grain products are:

Whole grains:
brown rice
buckwheat
bulgur (cracked wheat)
oatmeal
popcorn

Ready-to-eat breakfast cereals:
whole wheat cereal flakes
muesli

Refined grains:
cornbread*
corn tortillas*
couscous*
crackers*
flour tortillas*
grits
noodles*

*Pasta**
spaghetti
macaroni

FIGURE 6-2 *(Continued)* MyPyramid for Kids Food Guidance System: Foods in the Grain group.

whole grain barley
whole grain cornmeal
whole rye
whole wheat bread
whole wheat crackers
whole wheat pasta
whole wheat sandwich buns and rolls
whole wheat tortillas
wild rice

Less common whole grains:
amaranth
millet
quinoa
sorghum
triticale

pitas*
pretzels

Ready-to-eat breakfast cereals:
corn flakes

white bread
white sandwich buns and rolls
white rice

*Most of these products are made from refined grains. Some are made from whole grains. Check the ingredient list for the words "whole grain" or "whole wheat" to decide if they are made from a whole grain. Some foods are made from a mixture of whole and refined grains.

Some grain products contain significant amounts of bran. Bran provides fiber, which is important for health. However, products with added bran or bran alone (e.g., oat bran) are not necessarily whole grain products.

does not include the dietary fiber many people are missing from their diets. By looking at the list and reading labels, children and the adults providing their food can make better food choices on a daily basis (Sprouse, 2007a).

Under the Vegetable section, MyPyramid for Kids suggests that children eat more dark green and orange vegetables and have dry peas and beans on a regular basis (see Figure 6-3). For children ages 6 to 11 years, it is suggested that they eat 2½ cups of vegetables from the five different areas listed: dark green vegetables, orange vegetables, dry beans and peas, starchy vegetables, and "other" vegetables, which includes tomatoes, onions, and celery. Any vegetable or 100 percent vegetable juice counts as a member of this group. Vegetables can be cooked, raw, frozen, canned, or dehydrated.

In the Fruit group section, MyPyramid for Kids suggests that children ages 6 to 11 years focus more on fruit and eat a variety of fruits on a daily basis (see Figure 6-4). It also cautions kids to go easy on fruit juice, and if it is consumed, to make sure it is 100 percent juice. MyPyramid emphasizes that a better choice than juice is fresh, frozen, canned, or dried fruit. All fruits and only 100 percent juices are considered part of this group. The list of commonly eaten fruits includes everything from apples, to melons and citrus, to berries. The suggested consumption amount of fruits for children is 1½ cups.

Milk is the next major group on MyPyramid for Kids (see Figure 6-5). Children ages 6 to 11 years are encouraged to eat calcium-rich food and to choose low-fat or fat-free types. The recommendation for lower fat intake would not apply to children younger than 2. It is suggested that children drink 3 cups of milk or its equivalent every day. MyPyramid for Kids also suggests that children who cannot or do not consume milk should choose lactose-free products or other sources of calcium. The milk group includes all fluid milk products and many foods that are made from milk. This would include milk-based desserts such as pudding or ice cream, cheese, and yogurt.

FIGURE 6-3
MyPyramid for Kids Food Guidance System: Foods in the Vegetable group.

What foods are in the vegetable group?

Any vegetable or 100% vegetable juice counts as a member of the vegetable group. Vegetables may be raw or cooked; fresh, frozen, canned, or dried/dehydrated; and may be whole, cut-up, or mashed.

Vegetables are organized into 5 subgroups, based on their nutrient content. Some commonly eaten vegetables in each subgroup are:

Dark green vegetables
bok choy
broccoli
collard greens
dark green leafy lettuce
kale
mesclun
mustard greens
romaine lettuce
spinach
turnip greens
watercress

Orange vegetables
acorn squash
butternut squash
carrots
hubbard squash
pumpkin
sweetpotatoes

Dry beans and peas
black beans
black-eyed peas
garbanzo beans (chickpeas)
kidney beans
lentils
lima beans (mature)
navy beans
pinto beans
soy beans
split peas
tofu (bean curd made from soybeans)
white beans

Starchy vegetables
corn
green peas
lima beans (green)
potatoes

Other vegetables
artichokes
asparagus
bean sprouts
beets
Brussels sprouts
cabbage
cauliflower
celery
cucumbers
eggplant
green beans
green or red peppers
iceberg (head) lettuce
mushrooms
okra
onions
parsnips
tomatoes
tomato juice
vegetable juice
turnips
wax beans
zucchini

FIGURE 6-4
MyPyramid for Kids Food Guidance System: Foods in the Fruit group.

Fruit Group
Focus on fruits

MyPyramid.gov

What foods are in the fruit group?

Any fruit or 100% fruit juice counts as part of the fruit group. Fruits may be fresh, canned, frozen, or dried, and may be whole, cut-up, or pureed. Some commonly eaten fruits are:

Apples
Apricots
Avocado
Bananas

Berries:
strawberries
blueberries
raspberries
cherries

Grapefruit
Grapes
Kiwi fruit
Lemons
Limes
Mangoes

Melons:
cantaloupe
honeydew
watermelon

Mixed fruits:
fruit cocktail

Nectarines
Oranges
Peaches
Pears
Papaya
Pineapple
Plums
Prunes
Raisins
Tangerines

100% Fruit juice:
orange
apple
grape
grapefruit

The last major category on MyPyramid for Kids is Meat and Beans (see Figure 6-6). MyPyramid for Kids suggests that children ages 6 to 11 years go lean on protein and eat 5 ounces of it daily in some form. Children are encouraged to make low-fat or lean choices of meats and poultry. Preparation of meats for everybody should focus on broiling, grilling, or baking. MyPyramid for Kids also suggests that protein choices should include more fish, beans, peas, nuts, and seeds. One reason for this is to include healthy oils from these products in the diet. The recommendation to consume more fish ties directly in with the recommendations of the American Heart Association (Giddings et al., 2006). The Meat and Beans category is divided into six areas: meats, poultry, eggs, fish, dry beans and peas, and nuts and seeds.

A minor category, but an important one in the MyPyramid Food Guidance System, is Oils (see Figure 6-7). In this category, it is suggested that children know sources of fats so that they can make healthier choices from fish, nuts, and vegetable oils. The system suggests that children limit their

FIGURE 6-5
MyPyramid for Kids Food Guidance System: Foods in the Milk group.

MyPyramid.gov

What foods are included in the milk, yogurt, and cheese (milk) group?

All fluid milk products and many foods made from milk are considered part of this food group. Foods made from milk that retain their calcium content are part of the group, while foods made from milk that have little to no calcium, such as cream cheese, cream, and butter, are not. Most milk group choices should be fat-free or low-fat.

Some commonly eaten choices in the milk, yogurt, and cheese group are:

Milk*
All fluid milk:
- fat-free (skim)
- low fat (1%)
- reduced fat (2%)
- whole milk

flavored milks:
- chocolate
- strawberry

lactose reduced milks
lactose free milks

Milk-based desserts*
Puddings made with milk
ice milk
frozen yogurt
ice cream

Cheese*
Hard natural cheeses:
- cheddar
- mozzarella
- Swiss
- parmesan

soft cheeses
- ricotta
- cottage cheese

processed cheeses
- American

Yogurt*
All yogurt
- Fat-free
- low fat
- reduced fat
- whole milk yogurt

***Selection Tips**

Choose fat-free or low-fat milk, yogurt, and cheese. If you choose milk or yogurt that is not fat-free, or cheese that is not low-fat, the fat in the product counts as part of the discretionary calorie allowance.

If sweetened milk products are chosen (flavored milk, yogurt, drinkable yogurt, desserts), the added sugars also count as part of the discretionary calorie allowance.

For those who are lactose intolerant, lactose-free and lower-lactose products are available. These include hard cheeses and yogurt. Also, enzyme preparations can be added to milk to lower the lactose content. Calcium-fortified foods and beverages such as soy beverages or orange juice may provide calcium, but may not provide the other nutrients found in milk and milk products.

FIGURE 6-6
MyPyramid for Kids Food Guidance System: Foods in the Meat and Beans group.

Meat & Bean Group
Go lean with protein

MyPyramid.gov

What foods are included in the meat, poultry, fish, dry beans, eggs, and nuts (meat & beans) group?

All foods made from meat, poultry, fish, dry beans or peas, eggs, nuts, and seeds are considered part of this group. Dry beans and peas are part of this group as well as the vegetable group.

Most meat and poultry choices should be lean or low-fat. Fish, nuts, and seeds contain healthy oils, so choose these foods frequently instead of meat or poultry. (See Why is it important to include fish, nuts, and seeds?)

Some commonly eaten choices in the Meat and Beans group, with selection tips, are:

Meats*
Lean cuts of:
- beef
- ham
- lamb
- pork
- veal

Game meats:
- bison
- rabbit
- venison

Lean ground meats:
- beef
- pork
- lamb

Lean luncheon meats
Organ meats:
- liver
- giblets

Poultry*
- chicken
- duck
- goose
- turkey
- ground chicken and turkey

Eggs*
- chicken eggs
- duck eggs

Dry beans and peas:
- black beans
- black-eyed peas
- chickpeas (garbanzo beans)
- falafel
- kidney beans
- lentils
- lima beans (mature)
- navy beans
- pinto beans
- soy beans
- split peas
- tofu (bean curd made from soy beans)
- white beans

bean burgers:
- garden burgers
- veggie burgers
- tempeh
- texturized vegetable protein (TVP)

Nuts & seeds*
- almonds
- cashews
- hazelnuts (filberts)
- mixed nuts
- peanuts
- peanut butter
- pecans
- pistachios
- pumpkin seeds
- sesame seeds
- sunflower seeds
- walnuts

Fish*
Finfish such as:
- catfish
- cod
- flounder
- haddock
- halibut
- herring
- mackerel
- pollock
- porgy
- salmon
- sea bass
- snapper
- swordfish
- trout
- tuna

Shellfish such as:
- clams
- crab
- crayfish
- lobster
- mussels
- octopus
- oysters
- scallops
- squid (calamari)
- shrimp

Canned fish such as:
- anchovies
- clams
- tuna
- sardines

(continues)

FIGURE 6-6 *(Continued)*
MyPyramid for Kids Food Guidance System: Foods in the Meat and Beans group.

***Selection Tips**

Choose lean or low-fat meat and poultry. If higher fat choices are made, such as regular ground beef (75 to 80% lean) or chicken with skin, the fat in the product counts as part of the discretionary calorie allowance.

If solid fat is added in cooking, such as frying chicken in shortening or frying eggs in butter or stick margarine, this also counts as part of the discretionary calorie allowance.

Select fish rich in omega-3 fatty acids, such as salmon, trout, and herring, more often.

Liver and other organ meats are high in cholesterol. Egg yolks are also high in cholesterol, but egg whites are cholesterol-free.

Processed meats such as ham, sausage, frankfurters, and luncheon or deli meats have added sodium. Check the ingredient and Nutrition Facts label to help limit sodium intake. Fresh chicken, turkey, and pork that have been enhanced with a salt-containing solution also have added sodium. Check the product label for statements such as "self-basting" or "contains up to __% of __", which mean that a sodium-containing solution has been added to the product.

Sunflower seeds, almonds, and hazelnuts (filberts) are the richest sources of vitamin E in this food group. To help meet vitamin E recommendations, make these your nut and seed choices more often.

FIGURE 6-7
MyPyramid for Kids Food Guidance System: What are "oils"?

MyPyramid.gov

What are "oils"?

Oils are fats that are liquid at room temperature, like the vegetable oils used in cooking. Oils come from many different plants and from fish. Some common oils are:

- canola oil
- corn oil
- cottonseed oil
- olive oil
- safflower oil
- soybean oil
- sunflower oil

Some oils are used mainly as flavorings, such as walnut oil and sesame oil. A number of foods are naturally high in oils, like:

- nuts
- olives
- some fish
- avocados

FIGURE 6-7 *(Continued)*
MyPyramid for Kids Food Guidance System: What are "oils"?

Foods that are mainly oil include mayonnaise, certain salad dressings, and soft (tub or squeeze) margarine with no *trans* fats. Check the Nutrition Facts label to find margarines with 0 grams of *trans* fat. Amounts of *trans* fat are required on labels as of 2006. Many products already provide this information.

Most oils are high in monounsaturated or polyunsaturated fats, and low in saturated fats. Oils from plant sources (vegetable and nut oils) do not contain any cholesterol. In fact, no foods from plants sources contain cholesterol.

A few plant oils, however, including coconut oil and palm kernel oil, are high in saturated fats and for nutritional purposes should be considered to be solid fats.

Solid fats are fats that are solid at room temperature, like butter and shortening. Solid fats come from many animal sources and can be made from vegetable oils through a process called hydrogenation. Some common solid fats are:

- butter
- beef fat (tallow, suet)
- chicken fat
- pork fat (lard)
- stick margarine
- shortening

intake of solid fats such as butter, stick margarine, shortening, and lard. One reason for this focus on limiting solid fats is to limit trans fats. Since 2006, USDA regulations require that dietary food labels reveal the amount of trans fats in foods. In addition to these measures, MyPyramid for Kids suggests that children know their limits on fats and sugars and that they get facts on these selections from reading nutrition facts on food labels.

MyPyramid Food Guidance System was intended to simplify the original USDA Food Guide Pyramid information in order to help people make better choices. One major difference is the focus on an individual's needs. This system fosters several key recommendations by the AAP in 2003 to help control the epidemic of overweight children that the United States is experiencing today (AAP, 2003). In the past three decades, the number of overweight 2- to 5-year-olds has more than doubled, to more than 10 percent of children (Nicklas & Johnson, 2004). The number of overweight children ages 6 to 11 has tripled in that same period, to more than 15 percent of that age group. The AAP recommendations include dietary practices that emphasize moderation in energy-dense foods and encourage making healthy food selections along with getting regular physical activity. Physical activity is a major focus of MyPyramid for Kids. The tagline for MyPyramid for Kids reads: "Eat Right. Exercise. Have Fun." It is suggested that children aim for at least one hour of physical activity per day on most days. This component will be more thoroughly covered in Chapter 7 on page 265.

Shortly after the MyPyramid Food Guidance System was introduced, the American Heart Association came out with even more stringent recommendations. These guidelines address the changes in nutritional behaviors in children that have led to increased overweight in children and prevalence for cardiovascular risk issues (Gidding et al., 2006). The general recommendations cover children ages 2 years and older. The recommended diet primarily consists of whole grains, low-fat and nonfat dairy products, fruits and vegetables, beans, fish, and lean meat. The recommendations also include a physical activity component. Their website at http://www.americanheart.org/presenter.jhtml?identifier=3034000 shows the specific recommendations to lower cardiovascular risk and decrease weight among children so they can be heart healthy. Note that in addition to dietary recommendations, they advise limiting television viewing and computer and video game use.

The American Dietetic Association (ADA) published a position paper that deals with the nutritional intakes of children ages 2 to 11 years in the United States (Nicklas & Johnson, 2004). They found that there has been an increase in the consumption of foods that are high in sugar content, such as fruits, fruit juices, and sweetened beverages, while a decrease in the consumption of foods such as milk, vegetables, and grains and breads has been reported. The ADA concluded that the food choices of most children in the United States do not meet the recommended nutritional guidelines. The ADA also introduced a position paper on nutrition in early childhood education programs (Briley & Roberts-Gray, 2005). The basic premise of this position is that children's nutritional needs must be met, and done so in ways that model healthy dietary patterns. In 2007, the ADA published a position paper on using a total diet or holistic approach to dispensing food and nutrition information for a healthy lifestyle (ADA, 2007a). Use of the MyPyramid for Kids will help children and teachers meet the recommended guidelines on all three of these ADA positions, as well as address the concerns of the AAP and the position of the American Heart Association. In the years since the publication of MyPyramid, the system has been analyzed for its literacy and its linguistic and cultural factors as they relate to consumers. Although the website is already available in Spanish, other improvements in this system have been recommended for the future (Neuhauser, Rothschild, & Rodriguez, 2007). It has been found that in order for the MyPyramid Food Guidance System to reach its potential to improve the diet quality and health of Americans, it must be understood

Wadsworth/Cengage Learning

Nutrition education includes having graphics around the classroom, as well as providing dramatic play materials for the children to play what has been modeled to them.

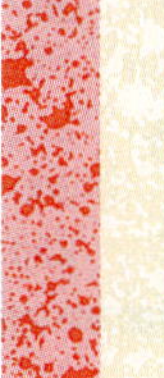

Jessica was a nanny for a family with three young children, ages 2, 4, and 6 years. The parents were both professionals and led a very busy life, including lots of lunches and dinners out with clients. They rarely had time to grocery shop, and there were times when Jessica went to the house and found only some cheese and a bottle of champagne in the refrigerator. There were times when she had to go shopping with her own money to buy food for the children and then get reimbursed. Jessica decided it was time for action. She gathered up all the information from MyPyramid for Kids and created a menu for the children based on this. She estimated food costs and then asked the family for a weekly budget to buy the children's food. The parents were happy to oblige and even suggested that she do some of the shopping at a large warehouse store. They purchased a membership for her and bought gift cards so she could purchase many of the items she needed there, and did this in addition to providing money for the budget she had already given them. The parents were particularly pleased at this arrangement because the menus were planned and food was available for them to feed their children a healthier diet even when they had to prepare it themselves.

by professionals and the information must be widely dispersed to the public (Krebs-Smith & Kris-Etherton, 2007). A suggestion for the early childhood education environment is to display MyPyramid for Kids so that children and adults begin to understand the importance of good diet quality balanced with exercise.

Pause for Reflection

How do your dietary habits hold up to this MyPyramid Food Guidance System? For a real look at your own habits, go to MyPyramid Plan at http://www.mypyramid.gov and find out. What could you do to improve your dietary habits to better fit MyPyramid? Why do you think modeling good nutrition on your part will influence your work with children?

Daily Reference Intake

The U.S. Daily Reference Intake (DRI) values are the suggested amounts of essential nutrients such as protein, vitamins, and minerals that should be consumed in foods daily to ensure good health (Baylor College of Medicine, 2004). The Daily Reference Values (DRVs) have been established for **macronutrients**: cholesterol, sodium, and potassium.

• **macronutrients** *major nutrients needed for the body, such as fats, protein, and carbohydrates.*

DRIs are most commonly found on food labels (Figure 6-8) of packaged products where manufacturers are required to list nutrition facts. The information is broken down on a per-serving basis. Calories; amounts of fat, including trans fat, saturated fat, and unsaturated fats, and cholesterol; carbohydrates, including fiber and sugars; protein; vitamins, including vitamin A, vitamin B (thiamine, riboflavin, and niacin), vitamin C, vitamin D, sodium; and

FIGURE 6-8
Sample nutrition facts label for macaroni and cheese. As of 2006, the amount of trans fat has been included on the label.

Sample label for Macaroni & Cheese

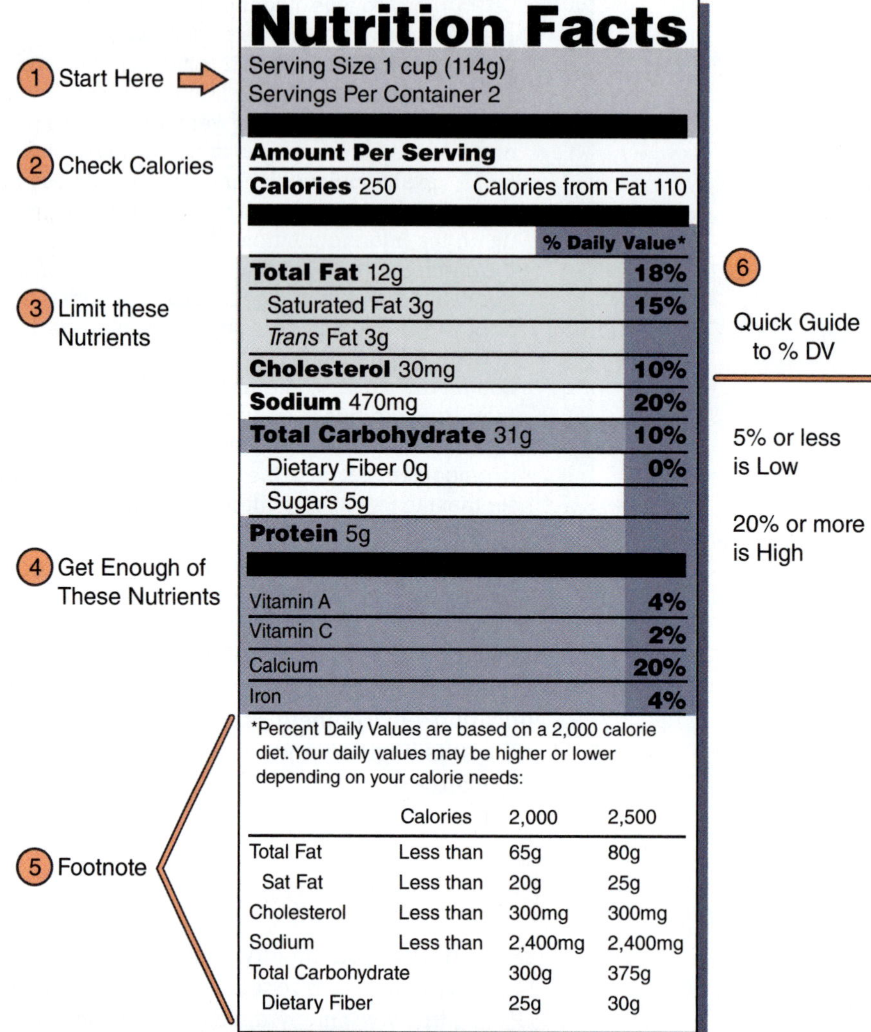

Nutrition Facts
Serving Size 1 cup (114g)
Servings Per Container 2

Amount Per Serving
Calories 250 Calories from Fat 110

	% Daily Value*
Total Fat 12g	**18%**
Saturated Fat 3g	**15%**
Trans Fat 3g	
Cholesterol 30mg	**10%**
Sodium 470mg	**20%**
Total Carbohydrate 31g	**10%**
Dietary Fiber 0g	**0%**
Sugars 5g	
Protein 5g	
Vitamin A	**4%**
Vitamin C	**2%**
Calcium	**20%**
Iron	**4%**

*Percent Daily Values are based on a 2,000 calorie diet. Your daily values may be higher or lower depending on your calorie needs:

	Calories	2,000	2,500
Total Fat	Less than	65g	80g
Sat Fat	Less than	20g	25g
Cholesterol	Less than	300mg	300mg
Sodium	Less than	2,400mg	2,400mg
Total Carbohydrate		300g	375g
Dietary Fiber		25g	30g

1 The Serving Size

Serving Size 1/2 cup (114g)
Servings Per Container 4

(#1 on sample label)
The first place to start when you look at the Nutrition facts is the serving size and the number of servings in the package. Serving sizes are standardized to make it easier to compare similar foods; they are provided in familiar units, such as cups or pieces, followed by the metric amount, e.g., the number of grams.

other essential minerals such as calcium and iron are listed. The daily values shown on the label help one to understand the general contribution of nutrients that particular food makes toward the daily diet. More than 80 percent of consumers look at the label sometimes, and more than 44 percent look always or almost always at this information (Borra, 2006). Most consumers could identify fat, calories, carbohydrates, fiber, serving size, protein, sugars, and Daily Value without seeing a label. This label appears to be a help strategy for improving health and weight for adults.

Diet Quality Index for Preschoolers

Recently a new intake index has been added, called the Diet Quality Index for Preschoolers, developed with a grant from the USDA. This dietary intake recommendation includes a component for energy balance in order to measure whether a child is getting adequate nutrition for growth, development, and disease prevention (Kranz et al., 2006). The recommendations for children's diet quality index, referred to as the RC-DQI, is used to help differentiate preschool children's diets by level of diet quality. The components of this index include added sugars, excess fruit juice, dairy, total fats, fatty acids, total and whole grains, fruits, vegetables, and iron. The energy component that interacts with diet measures sedentary activities, such as watching television. The points given reflect whether a diet is either deficient or adequate in each area. Total scores could range from 0, which would indicate a totally deficient diet, to 100, which would indicate a completely adequate and favorable diet. In applications to date, the range found has been from 28 to 93, with an average score of 64 (Kranz et al., 2006). As total scores increase to reflect a favorable diet quality, results have shown that the consumption of sugars and juices decreases and the intake of essential fatty acids, fruits, and vegetables increases. This index will shed light on the diet quality of young children and give information that may lead to improvement in their diets.

Healthy People 2010

Many of the objectives included in Healthy People 2010 are aimed at decreasing the prevalence of overweight in both adults and children; increasing intake of fruits and vegetables; and decreasing intake of sodium, sugar, and fat. It also addresses reducing growth retardation and iron deficiency in children (Nicklas & Johnson, 2004).

Child and Adult Care Food Program

The Child and Adult Care Food Program (CACFP) of the USDA enables family child care homes as well as nonprofit early childhood education centers to be reimbursed for creating menus and serving meals that meet dietary guidelines established by this program. These dietary guidelines are based on the DRIs and the Dietary Guidelines for Americans. Recommended meal patterns are provided by CACFP.

Early childhood education programs and regulated family child care homes that participate in the CACFP are required to follow meal pattern guidelines (see Table 9-1 in Chapter 9), engage in some training, and utilize food and nutrition handbooks. Investigations in the past have shown that as many as 90 percent of observed participating centers fell short of the recommended CACFP standards (Briley, Roberts-Gray, & Rowe, 1993). More recent studies have found early childhood education centers falling short of nutrients compared to those recommended by the Food Guide Pyramid, which has been used until recently (Padget & Briley, 2005). ADA has stated that no extensive evaluations have been done to assess the effectiveness of CACFP; however, they have issued a position statement regarding the fact that all children should have access to food and nutrition programs that ensure a safe and adequate food supply for optimal growth and development (ADA, 2006).

National School Lunch Program

The National School Lunch Program, begun in 1946, is a federally assisted meal program. It operates in more than 100,000 public and nonprofit private schools and provides lunches to more than 30 million children every school day (Food and Nutrition Services, USDA, 2007). Today, this program has been expanded to include reimbursement for snacks served in afterschool programs for children under the age of 18 years. This program is administered by the Food and Nutrition Services arm of the USDA at the federal level, and at the state level by the education agency of each state. School districts that opt to participate in this program get cash subsidies and donated commodities from the USDA for each meal served. In order to participate, the schools must serve lunches that meet the nutritional standards and federal requirements. Also, they must offer free or reduced-price meals to children who are eligible for them. The USDA provides technical assistance and training to schools via Team Nutrition. This group also helps with nutrition education for children. Federal legislation mandating a local school wellness policy was enacted in 2005 and took effect in July 2006 (School Board Notes, 2005). In order for districts to receive federal funding for their school lunch programs, they must have this policy, which should include goals for nutrition education and physical activity. In addition, nutrition guidelines for all foods selected by the district must be at each school site.

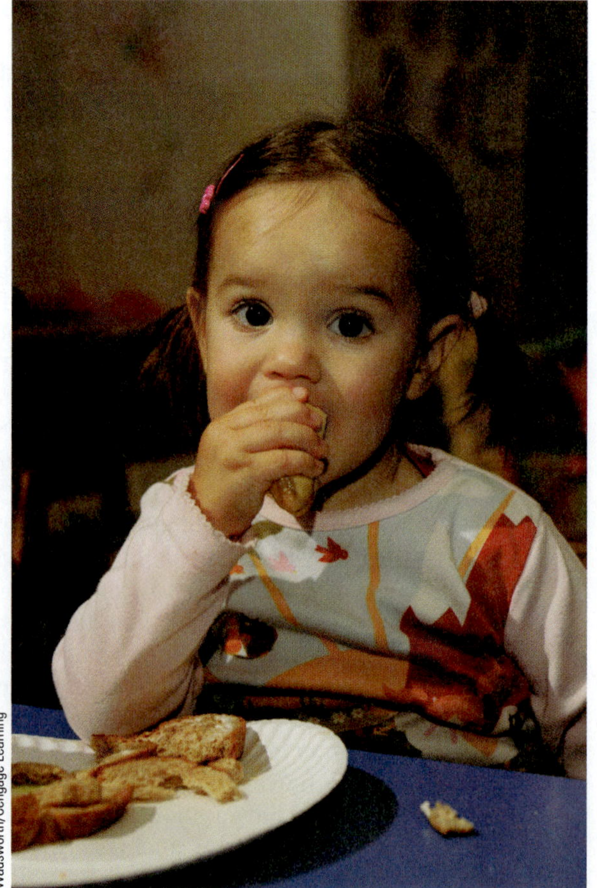

Wadsworth/Cengage Learning

Even at a young age, children can be taught good nutritional habits for eating and selecting foods.

REALITY *Check*

How is America Eating: Do We Fulfill Our Nutritional Needs?

There has been a great deal in the news recently about how obesity has taken hold in all ages of the population in the United States. Almost 60 percent of the country is overweight (Cox, 2003). Americans are eating too much saturated fat, sodium, and added sugar, but too few fruits, vegetables, and whole grains (Mancino, 2007). This leads to the questions: (1) What are we eating? and (2) How does this match with our basic nutrient needs? In a comparison of how Americans ate in 1909 and how they ate in 2000, Gerrior, Bente, and Hiza (2004) found some interesting data. First, we are eating a lot more fat today than we did 100 years ago, although cholesterol levels of the foods we eat are lower. We are eating more fat, but less fat from animal sources. Our total consumption of meat is slightly up recently from past years, but consumption of beef is down, and we are eating more chicken than ever before, which is good because it is leaner. So, how do we eat more fat than ever before, but less cholesterol? One answer to this is that we are eating more snacks such as potato chips and crackers, and more desserts. These all have quite a bit of fat, especially trans fats, in them. Another reason is that we are super-sizing, not only while eating out, but at home too (Cox, 2003). Children seem to be increasing portion size regardless of where they eat (Gidding et al., 2006). Recent trends in the food industry are trying to downplay this super-size mentality.

We have also changed our consumption of carbohydrates. During much of the twentieth century, we were eating fewer grains, but today we are eating more grains than we have for a number of years; however, it still does not come close to our consumption of 100 years ago (Gerrior, Bente, & Hiza, 2004). Many of the grain items we are eating today are highly processed flours, rice, and pastas, or they have added sugar, such as is found in cereals. The bran and germ have been removed from processed foods, so many of the positive factors in grains have also been removed. This has lowered the dietary fiber in our diets. This dietary fiber is essential for good health (Williams, 2006). We are not eating the recommended amount of fruits and vegetables (Guenther et al., 2006). Only 40 percent of Americans eat an average of 2½ cups of fruits and vegetables on a daily basis. American children have diets that are declining in fruits and vegetables, except for potatoes. Sugars are also considered to be carbohydrates, and the consumption of sugar in our diets is increasing. We have become consumers of lots of sugar and sweetened beverages and other foods. The consumption of sugar or sweetening products went up more than 20 percent between 1980 and 1994. At that time, each American was eating an average of almost 150 pounds of sugar and other sweeteners, such as corn syrup, each year in the foods we consumed. This increased consumption of sugar is having an adverse effect on diets of Americans, especially children (Kranz et al., 2005; DuBois et al., 2007). One of the major factors for children is the increase in consumption of sweetened beverages (LaRowe, Moeller, & Adams, 2007). The current belief is that sugar consumption is a major factor in the increase of obesity in this country.

We are eating more protein than in 1909, but we are getting it from other sources. Almost two-thirds of the protein in diets in those days was from animal sources. Today it is a balance of 50 percent from animal sources and 50 percent from vegetable sources. The consumption of meats may relate to income. People in higher-income households consume more beef and chicken than do those with lower incomes. Lower-income Americans consume

(continues)

REALITY *Check* (continued)

more pork products. Americans with higher education levels are less likely to consume beef and pork (Guenther et al., 2005). Animal sources of protein also include dairy products such as milk, yogurt, and cheese. There has been a large increase in the use of cheese. We are using it in many Mexican food products and items such as pizza, and this has increased our consumption of cheese over recent years (Cox, 2003). Studies have compared the consumption of dairy products by African Americans with that of non-African Americans. It found that African Americans are much less likely to have adequate dietary intake of dairy products than are Mexican Americans and white Americans (Storey, Forshee, & Anderson, 2006; Fulgoni et al., 2007). The consumption of milk has decreased for children over age 2. Other protein sources to consider include beans, peas, and soy products. These sources are consumed in many ways, including in a great number of ethnic products. Protein appears to be something that we eat adequate amounts of but do not overconsume as much as we do other nutrients.

It is a little difficult to compare consumption of vitamins and minerals because these were not really understood until partway through the twentieth century, and these items only began getting tracked for consumption in 1949 (Gerrior, Bente, & Hiza, 2004). Since then, our knowledge of vitamin and mineral requirements has radically changed because we are understanding more about their functions and how much of each vitamin and mineral is needed for the body to operate efficiently. Most levels of consumption for vitamins and minerals are higher today than in the past. This may be partially due to the enrichment of many food products, which puts back the minerals and vitamins taken out during processing. It is also due to the use of daily vitamins and minerals in pill form. However the levels of vitamin B_{12} and potassium consumption are lower today, perhaps due to a lower consumption level of eggs and organ meats and plant foods such as potatoes.

Consumption of water has increased greatly in the past 25 years (Sprouse, 2007b). Total sales of bottled water in 2006 were 8.25 billion gallons, which translates to 27 gallons per person in that year (Munroe, 2007). At this rate, the average American is drinking 8 ounces of bottled water every day (Arnold & Larsen, 2006). This makes it the second most popular drink in the United States behind carbonated soft drinks. The United States consumes more bottled water than any other country, trailed by Mexico, China, and Brazil. The Coca-Cola Company has complained that bottled water is beginning to erode the consumption of soft drinks.

Where do we eat? In 1909, there were few places outside the home to eat. Today there are food venues everywhere, including school cafeterias with branded kiosks of pizza, burgers, and fries (Ebbin, 2002). We are eating more and more meals away from home, and many of these meals are fast foods and therefore also high-fat foods. Average consumption of commercially prepared meals has increased to a total of 53.5 billion meals per year (Enns, Mickle, & Goldman, 2002). That is an average of almost four meals per week, per person, eaten out. It was also found that only 14 meals were prepared at home per week and an average of more than two meals per week were skipped. Another way to look at this is that an average of 57 percent of Americans, on any given day, eat away from home (Tippett, Enns, & Moshfegh, 2000). Meals eaten away from home account for about one-half of the food purchased in this country and about 32 percent of the calories that are consumed (Stewart, Blisard, & Jolliffe, 2006). The meal most likely eaten away from home is lunch, which represents about half of the commercially prepared meals consumed. Approximately 85 percent of Americans do eat breakfast, and about 20 percent of them are getting breakfast out at least once a week (Tippett, Enns, & Moshfegh, 2000). Coffee and milk are the most popular foods at breakfast. Processed cereals are also popular. Foods eaten away from home tend to be more calorie dense than

(continues)

REALITY *Check* (continued)

those prepared at home. This may correlate with the fact that obesity in this country is increasing (Kant & Graubard, 2004).

We have looked at the general population, but how do these trends compare to how children are eating? There has been a large increase in the consumption of soft drinks and a decrease in the consumption of milk by children (Enns, Mickle, & Goldman, 2002). Children ate more grains in 2002, but these were in the form of processed foods such as crackers, popcorn, pretzels, and corn chips. Children are not getting enough dietary fiber in their diets (Kranz, Smicklas-Wright, & Francis, 2006). They are eating more fried potatoes, noncitrus juices, cheese, candy, and fruit drinks. The consumption of noncitrus juices rose by 280 percent over the last 20 years (Tippett, Enns, & Moshfegh, 2000). Children are eating less bread, green peas, corn, beef, pork, and eggs.

In 2000, the most recent Healthy Eating Index was compiled. It was found that the mean score was about 64 percent, meaning that we were meeting about that percentage of our dietary needs. The newer Diet Quality Index for Preschoolers had similar findings (Kranz et al., 2006). Another way to look at this is that we were failing to meet those needs by 36 percent. If we look at overall habits, we find that 16 percent of the population have poor diets; 74 percent of the population should improve their diets; and only 10 percent of American diets are considered good (Basiotis et al., 2004). If we look at the quality of children's diets at ages 2 to 6, we find that only 8 percent were poor, and 65 percent should be improved, but 25 percent of children's diets were good (*America's children: Key national indicators of well-being, 2007,* 2007). These figures for good diets for 2001–2002 were a significant improvement over the figures from the previous studies in 1994–1996 and 1999–2000. It is also interesting to note that poor quality diets were almost equally reflected in children below the poverty line as well as those above the poverty line. The correlation of poor diets and cost does not seem to be indicated. Young children's diets are generally better than those of older children and adults, but the majority of Americans could use some improvement in their diets. The lower-quality diets of older children are related to declines in the consumption of grain, milk, and fruits, and the increase in the consumption of sodium and cholesterol. For adults there are a number of dietary factors, including too much sodium, saturated fat, and added sugar, plus too few whole grains, vegetables, and fruits (Mancino, 2007). Another factor for adults is convenience (Stewart, Blisard, & Jolliffe, 2006). It appears that adults in this country with high-quality diets are eating more low-energy-dense foods that include foods high in micronutrients and low in fats such as fruits, vegetables, and grains, as well as drinking more water (Ledikwe et al., 2006).

Dieticians, physicians, and other experts are telling us that we must change some of our diet habits. One change is that we should eat more whole grains. The new MyPyramid Food Guidance System (2005), prepared for the general population by the USDA; the dietary recommendations of the American Heart Association; and experts representing all areas of nutritional concern tell us that we should make whole-grain choices half the time. They also indicate that we should eat more vegetables, especially dark green and deep yellow ones. We should eat more fruits, both citrus and noncitrus, and we should consume more legumes. These same recommendations were also made specifically for children by the USDA in 2002 (Enns, Mickle, & Goldman, 2002) and by the American Heart Association, and were endorsed by the AAP in 2006 (Gidding et al., 2006).

CHECK*point:* **How well are you eating? Do you share some of the issues that are of concern in how Americans eat? What might you do to improve your own diet?**

Key Concept 6.2

Nutritional Guidelines

An increasing number of children rely on early childhood education programs to provide a good portion of their nutritional needs. Teachers should be knowledgeable about nutritional guidelines as they plan menus and provide food to the children in care. The MyPyramid Food Guidance System is easiest to understand and will help the teacher educate children and their parents about nutrition. Dietary Guidelines for Americans, the Daily Reference Intake Diet Quality Index for Preschoolers, Healthy People 2010, the Child and Adult Care Food Program, and The National School Lunch Program also provide helpful information for the teacher.

6.3 BASIC MACRONUTRIENTS

Each source of nutrients performs specific functions. The two major categories of nutrients are macronutrients and micronutrients.

The first major group of nutrients is the energy nutrients, or macronutrients. Macronutrients that produce energy are carbohydrates, fats, and proteins. Energy is needed to maintain life, for growth, to regulate the body, and to perform voluntary activities. We measure energy in terms of **calories**. The number of calories each body needs depends on the **basal metabolism**, **metabolism** of food, growth and physical activity, and the age of that body. Calories are supplied to the body from three major nutrients:

- **calorie** *the unit of measurement for the energy found in foods.*
- **basal metabolism** *the amount of energy used by the body while at rest.*
- **metabolism** *chemical changes that take place as nutrients are taken into the blood, processed and absorbed by the blood, and eliminated from the body.*

- Fats, which supply 9 calories per gram
- Carbohydrates, which supply 4 calories per gram
- Proteins, which supply 4 calories per gram

Carbohydrates, fats, and protein provide the energy needed to run the body and provide materials to help the body grow and maintain its functions. Although trends have been toward more energy intake from carbohydrates and less from fats, children are still not eating the balance suggested for these categories (Padget & Briley, 2005; Williams, 2006; Fox et al., 2006).

Carbohydrates

Carbohydrates are the first source of energy the body uses, and they are the major source of energy for the central nervous system. Carbohydrates are made up of carbon, hydrogen, and oxygen. Carbohydrates, protein, and fats provide energy to the body in the form of calories. If our bodies do not have carbohydrates, we cannot properly use the other energy sources of protein and fat. Carbohydrates provide a slow, steady source of energy necessary for utilization of other nutrients in the body. For example, carbohydrates supply energy so that protein can be used for growth and maintenance of body cells.

Carbohydrates come in two forms, simple and complex. Simple carbohydrates include the sugars, and complex carbohydrates are made up of strings of sugars in the form of starch or fiber. Simple carbohydrates are found in various forms including lactose, which is found in milk. Lactose from breast milk or formula supplies the major source of carbohydrates for infants. Complex carbohydrates are generally found in the Grains group in MyPyramid, which includes cereal, rice, bread, and pasta. They are also found in the Fruits category and Vegetables category, as well as the Meat and Beans category.

It is important that a child's diet have an adequate amount of carbohydrates. Many adults are on diets that stress low amounts of carbohydrates, but these diets do not have adequate amounts of carbohydrates for children to function as they should. A diet with insufficient amounts of carbohydrates causes the body to use fats or proteins for the energy it needs, thus robbing it of the functions these two nutrients provide. Having children participate in these types of diets should be discouraged. Growth and maintenance of the body will be at risk. A child needs carbohydrates to fuel the work of muscles. A child also needs dietary fiber from carbohydrates to aid in normal elimination (Williams, 2006). Many children's diets are inadequate in dietary fiber (Ralston, 2006). If a child appears listless and tired, it may be that his carbohydrate level is low. This fuel is especially important to get the day started, so a breakfast that includes complex carbohydrates is a good source to start the day with energy. Nutrient-dense diets contribute to higher fiber consumption and the types of carbohydrates that are good for a child's energy level and normal elimination (Kranz et al., 2005a).

Fats

Fats are considered to be the body's second source of energy. Fat also supplies essential fatty acids that are critical for proper growth of children. Other functions include cushioning of organs, maintaining body temperature, promoting healthy skin, and helping fat-soluble vitamins be carried throughout the body. Fat is in the membrane of every cell in the body. Fats also help regulate the metabolism of **cholesterol** in the body. Body fat also provides a good energy reserve.

- **cholesterol** *a steroid or fatty alcohol found in animal fats that is produced by the liver of the animal.*

Intake of fat is an important part of every child's diet. However, it should be carefully monitored to fall within the 20 to 35 percent range, as recommended in the Dietary Guidelines for children ages 2 to 8 years. Fat is an essential part of promoting brain development and growth in infants and young children. Infants and children younger than age 2 need greater amounts of fat than the guidelines recommend. The AAP and the Dietary Guidelines for Americans both advise against the restriction of fat in the diet for the first two years of life (USDHHS, 2005; Federal Register, 2004; Gidding et al., 2006; Rose, 2007a).

The major sources of fats are Meats and Beans and Dairy, and fats are highly represented in the minor category of Oils. Sources are both plant and animal. Primary animal sources include red meats, fish, poultry, eggs, and milk products, which account for about 58 percent of the fat in our diets. Plant sources such as corn, safflower, canola, palm, and coconut oils provide the remaining 42 percent of the fat found in a typical diet. Table 6-2 lists the different types of fats.

The DRI for fat consumption takes into consideration the risk of excess fat. Saturated fats are of particular concern because they contribute to high blood cholesterol, which influences the development of coronary heart disease. All animal fats are saturated; most vegetable sources of fat are either polyunsaturated or monounsaturated. To help lower saturated fat in the diet, it is important to choose vegetable sources of fat more often than animal fats (see Figure 6-9).

TABLE 6-2
Types of Fats

- Polyunsaturated fats

Function: Lowers blood cholesterol, decreases tendency of blood to clot

Sources: Plants and plant oils (sunflower, corn, canola) and fish

DRI: 10 percent or less of total calories

- Monounsaturated fats

Function: Neutral—neither raises nor lowers blood cholesterol

Sources: Olives, peanuts, nuts, avocado

DRI: 10 percent of total calories

- Saturated fats

Function: Raises blood cholesterol, increases tendency of blood to clot

Sources: Animals, animal fats, butter, shortening, nuts, cheese, coconut, coconut and palm oil, ice cream

DRI: 10 percent or less of total calories

- Trans fats

Function: Raises blood cholesterol

Sources: Shortening or margarine, snack foods, baked goods, and some dairy products

DRI: No recommended DRI given

Wadsworth/Cengage Learning

These children are eating a healthy lunch of pizza, milk, and applesauce, and they look happy. With a little effort, teachers in the early childhood education environment can cut down on serving meals with too many foods that are high in fat, and still provide meals that supply the fat needed for normal growth and development.

Another source of concern about fat is trans fatty acids, also known as trans fats. Trans fats occur when vegetable oils are saturated as a result of the heat and hydrogenation used to process these oils into margarine or shortening. Major sources of trans fats include baked goods and snack foods

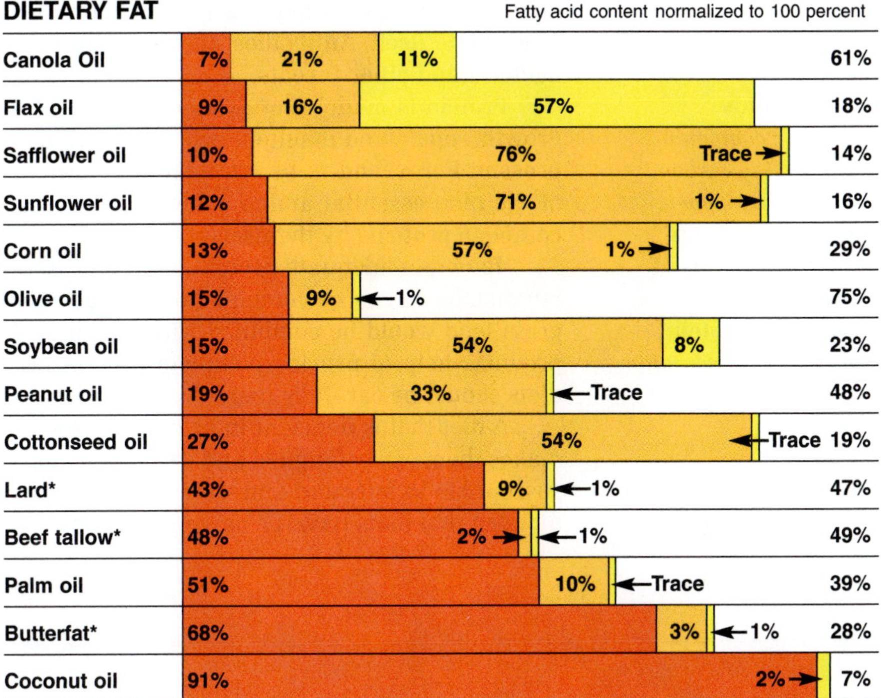

FIGURE 6-9
Comparison of dietary fats. (Courtesy of the Canola Council of Canada.)

that are made with vegetable shortening or partially hydrogenated vegetable oils. Trans fats can also occur naturally in animal products such as dairy foods. The American Dietetic Association and Dieticians of Canada have taken a position on dietary fatty acids that include trans fats. They recommend a dietary pattern high in fruits, vegetables, whole grains, legumes, nuts, seeds, and lean protein. They advocate the use of nonhydrogenated margarines and oils, which implies that dietary fatty acids should be unsaturated (ADA, 2007b). In recent years, there have been efforts to remove trans fats from foods on restaurant menus. In New York City a movement to do this in all restaurants located there succeeded (Lueck & Severson, 2006). Many fast food chains have voluntarily removed trans fats from at least part of their menu items.

Protein

Protein, the third source of energy, is the major building block in our bodies. It is found in every cell and is necessary for growth and maintenance. Any new tissue is put together from proteins. Any growth or regeneration must have proteins to accomplish the task. Protein builds new cells and aids in the repair of damaged tissue. It is used to form **enzymes** that aid in digestion and **hormones** and **antibodies** that increase resistance to infection.

- **enzymes** *organic substances produced in body cells that can cause changes in other substances through catalytic reaction.*
- **hormones** *chemical substances formed in one organ of the body and carried to another organ or tissue, where they have specific effects.*
- **antibodies** *proteins produced in the body to react with or neutralize antigens in order to protect the body.*

Enzymes, some hormones, and antibodies are all examples of proteins. Enzymes promote certain chemical reactions in the body, such as breaking down starches to aid in digestion. Hormones such as thyroxin help the body to regulate itself. Antibodies aid the immune system to prevent invasion of bacteria and other threats.

- **amino acids** *organic compounds containing carbon, hydrogen, oxygen, and nitrogen; the key components of proteins.*
- **complete protein** *protein that contains all essential amino acids.*

Protein is made of **amino acids**, nine of which are essential for tissue growth, repair, and maintenance. There are 21 different types of amino acids present. For a food to be considered **complete protein**, it must provide all of the nine essential amino acids. Foods from animal sources are the only complete proteins by themselves.

To obtain adequate protein with the essential amino acids in a vegetarian diet, foods can be combined to provide complete protein. For example, a grain food would be combined with a legume food. Additions of egg or milk products help to provide complete protein in a vegetarian diet. Vegetarian diets should be carefully monitored to ensure adequate intake of nutrients.

A diet that is deficient in protein causes stunted growth in children and makes them easily fatigued and irritable. Lack of protein also makes children susceptible to infection and slow to recover or repair a wound. It is recommended that diets have 12 percent protein to be sufficient.

Key Concept 6.3

Basic Macronutrients

Foods provide the basic nutrients needed for the body to grow, repair, regulate, and maintain itself. The macronutrients that provide energy are carbohydrates, fats, and protein. These nutrients provide needed energy through calories that help to run the body. Macronutrients also provide the materials required for growth and maintenance of the body. Protein is the major building block for the body. A diet that follows the MyPyramid Food Guidance System and takes into account the DRIs should provide the basic macronutrients needed.

6.4 BASIC MICRONUTRIENTS

- **micronutrients** *supporting nutrients, such as vitamins, minerals, and water, needed by the body.*

The macronutrients depend on the helper nutrients, or **micronutrients**, to perform their functions and to regulate the body's metabolism. Micronutrients, which are classified as vitamins, minerals, and water, must be present in sufficient quantities for the macronutrients to perform properly. Micronutrients do not contain calories. They each perform specific functions and are found in many foods. It is important for teachers to realize that children in early childhood education programs often fall short of intakes of calcium, iron, vitamin A, and vitamin B (Padget & Briley, 2005). An awareness of the need for micronutrients will help the teacher to prepare menus that provide adequate amounts.

Vitamins

Vitamins are essential nutrients needed by the body in small amounts and are categorized into two groups. Fat-soluble vitamins attach to fats to travel

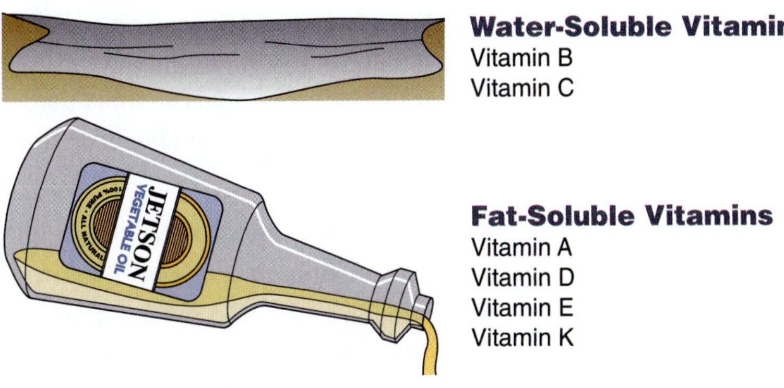

FIGURE 6-10 Fat- and water-soluble vitamins.

throughout the body and can be stored in the body. Water-soluble vitamins travel easily through the body with water and cannot be stored in the body, so they must be replaced daily (see Figure 6-10).

The fat-soluble vitamins are vitamin A, vitamin D, vitamin E, and vitamin K. These are stored in the body in the liver and build up over time, so too much can produce toxic effects.

Vitamin A

- Vitamin A is important for good vision, healthy skin and membranes in the body, and strong bones.
- Lack of vitamin A can cause poor bones, poor tooth enamel growth, rough skin, and night blindness.
- Vitamin A is most commonly found in foods in the form of retinol and carotene.
- Retinol is most commonly found in the fat of animal products such as fish, milk, eggs, and liver.
- Carotene is most commonly found in yellow, orange, and green leafy vegetables and yellow and orange fruits.
- Carotene, also known as beta-carotene, is considered to be an antioxidant that strengthens the immune system and might be a deterrent to cancer.

Vitamin D

- Vitamin D is needed to help calcium make strong bones and teeth.
- Vitamin D is produced naturally in the skin when it gets sunshine and is often referred to as the "sunshine" vitamin.
- Vitamin D is produced by a reaction of the ultraviolet rays with cholesterol in the skin.
- To ensure vitamin D consumption is adequate in all parts of the country at all times of the year, vitamin D is added to most milk.
- Vitamin D is also found in fatty fish, liver, eggs, and butter.
- Insufficient amounts of vitamin D can lead to rickets, a disease in children that stunts bone growth.

Vitamin E

- Vitamin E helps preserve cell tissues.
- Vitamin E protects red blood cells and the lungs.

- Vitamin E is considered an antioxidant.
- Vitamin E can be found in whole grain cereals, vegetable oils, and a wide variety of foods so most people get enough.
- There are no known effects of vitamin E deficiency.

Vitamin K

- Vitamin K is needed for normal blood clotting.
- Lack of vitamin K has been known to cause hemorrhaging.
- Vitamin K is found in dark green leafy vegetables and whole grains, and also made in our bodies.

Water-soluble vitamins include the B vitamins and vitamin C. There are numerous B vitamins, but the most important ones for children are thiamin (B_1), riboflavin (B_2), niacin, and folacin, more commonly known as folic acid. These B vitamins work with the enzymes in the body to release the energy from food.

Thiamin

- Thiamin is essential for carbohydrate metabolism so that energy can be released and used.
- Thiamin contributes to the normal functioning of the nervous system.
- Good sources of thiamin are lean pork, nuts, grains, and green leafy vegetables.
- Fatigue and irritability may be signs of a lack of thiamin in the diet.

Riboflavin

- Riboflavin is essential for the metabolism of all the energy sources.
- Riboflavin promotes healthy skin and eyes and clear vision.
- Good sources of riboflavin include milk products, eggs, legumes, liver, and leafy vegetables.
- Lack of riboflavin can cause skin and digestive disturbances, as well as sensitivity to light.

Niacin

- Niacin is needed for release of energy from all the energy sources, as well as for helping fat synthesis and tissue respiration.
- Niacin helps promote healthy nerves and skin and aids in digestion.
- Meat, poultry, fish, peanuts, liver, whole grains, enriched cereals, and green leafy vegetables are good sources of niacin.
- Insufficient amounts of niacin can cause pellagra or the Four Ds: dermatitis, diarrhea, dementia, and death.

Folic Acid

- Folic acid is required for normal growth, helps prevent anemia, and is an important factor in reproduction.
- Folic acid helps to form red and white blood cells and is necessary for proper cell division.
- During pregnancy, infancy, and early childhood, when rapid cell division is occurring, a sufficient amount of folic acid is crucial. In pregnant women, it can help to prevent neural tube defects or damage to the fetus.

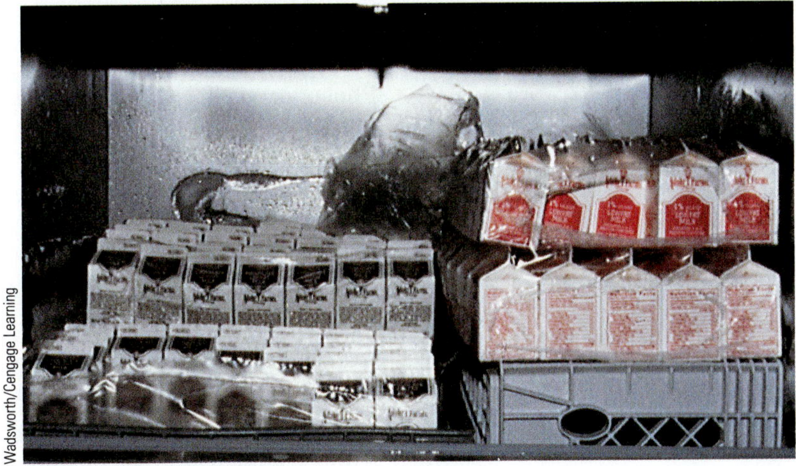
Wadsworth/Cengage Learning

Milk is a primary source of calcium, an important mineral for bone and teeth development.

- Good sources of folacin include dark green leafy vegetables, legumes, liver, and nuts.
- Anemia might be the result if there is insufficient folic acid in the diet.

Vitamin C

- Vitamin C is an antioxidant that helps fight disease and protect the body by preventing oxidation of molecules that could help create free radicals.
- Vitamin C assists with the formation and maintenance of collagen, which gives support and shape to the body.
- Vitamin C helps in healing wounds and maintaining healthy blood vessels.
- Vitamin C prevents scurvy in humans.
- Vitamin C stimulates the immune system to prevent infections.
- Good sources of vitamin C are citrus fruits, cabbage, kale, Brussels sprouts, broccoli, bell peppers, black currants, and turnip greens.

Minerals

Minerals help the metabolic process and regulate body fluids. There are 25 minerals that help the body to perform. The minerals that are especially important for children are calcium, phosphorous, iron, sodium, magnesium, potassium, fluoride, and zinc.

Calcium

- Calcium is the most important mineral because it is present in all bones and teeth. Because the childhood years are also the bone-forming years, it is critical to have enough calcium.
- Calcium helps to regulate the body systems, promotes normal nerve transmission, and functions in normal muscle contraction and relaxation.
- Major sources of calcium are milk and dairy products and dark green, leafy vegetables.

Phosphorous

- Phosphorous is combined with calcium in the bones and teeth.
- Phosphorous helps to transport fat and provides enzymes for energy metabolism.
- Phosphorous is found in milk products, meat, poultry, fish, whole grain cereals, and legumes.

Iron

- Iron combines with protein to form red blood cells and carry oxygen to the blood.
- Iron helps the immune system resist infection and helps enzymes release energy to the body.
- Liver, green leafy vegetables, whole grains, legumes, meats, and dried fruits are good sources of iron.
- A deficiency of iron causes anemia and fatigue.
- Anemia among children is one of the major health problems in the United States.

Sodium

- Sodium is important for fluid balance in the body. This balance occurs between the inside and outside of the body's cells.
- Sodium contributes to the stimulation of nerves and muscle contraction.
- Sources of sodium are salt, baking soda, celery, milk, eggs, meats, poultry, and fish. Canned foods are another source. Even if we never used salt on our foods, our diets would have sufficient amounts of sodium from all the foods that contain it.

Magnesium

- Magnesium is present in bones and teeth.
- Magnesium is important for the release of energy from the macronutrients.
- Magnesium helps transmit nerve impulses and helps muscles contract.
- Magnesium is found in milk, meat, green leafy vegetables, wholegrain cereals, nuts, seafood, and legumes.

Potassium

- Potassium is important for the metabolism of protein and carbohydrates.
- Potassium helps maintain water balance in the body and transmits nerve impulses.
- Potassium is the critical factor in maintaining heartbeat.
- During exercise or in hot weather, when sweating occurs, potassium loss can result, so it should be replaced through food or drink.
- Sources of potassium are vegetables, fruit juices, and fruits, especially bananas and tomatoes, and it is also in meats and cereals.

Fluoride

- Fluoride helps to promote bone strength and tooth structure and is important in preventing tooth decay.

- Fluoride is found in fish and fluoridated water. Many water systems in the United States add fluoride to the water to help prevent tooth decay.
- Some fluoridated water is too high in fluoride for many young children. Over-fluoridation can cause pitting and discoloration of teeth.

Zinc

- Zinc is necessary for healing of wounds, fetal development, proper growth, and to help the body properly use vitamin A.
- Zinc can be found in whole grains and meats and meat products.
- Zinc seems to be one of the DRIs that early childhood education programs have a difficult time providing in sufficient amounts (Padget & Briley, 2005)

Water

Water is necessary to sustain life and is the most indispensable nutrient we have. It comprises about 70 percent of the body and transports nutrients and oxygen. Water also protects organs, regulates temperature, and helps to eliminate waste products. How much water a body needs on a daily basis depends on body metabolism, age, and outside temperature. The brain regulates the body's intake of fluid by sending a signal that the body needs water. It is much easier for an adult to recognize the signs that she is thirsty, but it is more difficult for a young child to express thirst (Sigman-Grant, 2005).

Most of the water loss in the body is due to urination or evaporation from the skin or respiratory tract. A small amount of water is lost through fecal elimination. Larger than normal losses, such as may occur with increased sweating from exercise or heat, can be dangerous. This is especially important for infants and young children. Loss of water from fever, diarrhea, or vomiting can occur quickly and cause the infant or child to become dehydrated. This condition can turn serious very quickly, so children should be monitored for their water intake. Early signs of fluid loss include fewer wet diapers, less urination, or dark urine. The tongue may also be coated with a film instead of looking moist. There may also be nausea, clammy skin, and muscle cramping. If these occur, medical attention should be sought.

Water is present in most foods found in nature. Fruits and vegetables have it in large amounts. Fruit juices can be a major source of water for older infants and young children. Fruit juice intake should be limited to 4 to 6 ounces per day for children under age 6 and between 8 and 12 ounces for older children (Gidding et al., 2006). The source of the juice should be 100 percent fruit juice. Children should be encouraged to drink water on

Encourage children to drink water when they are thirsty. This will make them more likely to turn to water instead of sugary fruit drinks.

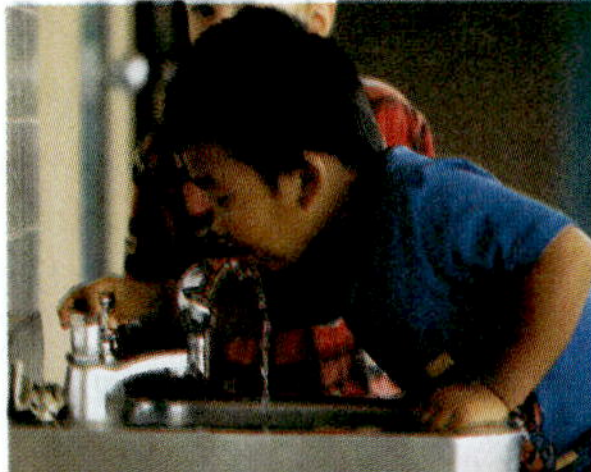

Wadsworth/Cengage Learning

Wadsworth/Cengage Learning

Wadsworth/Cengage Learning

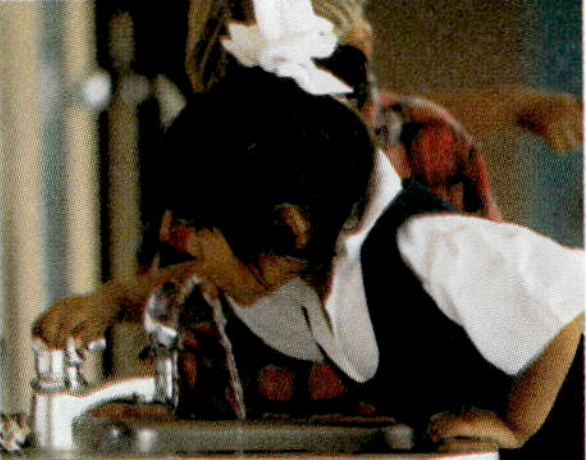

Wadsworth/Cengage Learning

a regular basis (Sprouse, 2007b; Rose, 2007b). Extra water may be needed during physical activity or in times of hot weather. Children in early childhood education environments should have an outside source of water that is safe to drink. Children who learn to drink water at an early age are more likely to turn to water to quench their thirst instead of sugary drinks.

Key Concept 6.4

Basic Micronutrients

Foods provide the basic nutrients needed for the body to grow, repair, regulate, and maintain itself. The micronutrients are vitamins, minerals, and water. These nutrients help the macronutrients run the body. Micronutrients also provide the materials needed to regulate the body's metabolism. A diet that follows the MyPyramid Food Guidance System and considers the DRIs should provide the basic micronutrients in sufficient quantities.

6.5 IMPLICATIONS FOR TEACHERS

Nutrition education for children and their parents is one of the most powerful tools that a teacher has to promote and protect the health and well-being of children. Good nutrition can help a child maintain health and fight off infections, colds, and other communicable diseases. It allows children to grow adequately and develop to the best of their potential. Nutrition information shared with parents and other family members can lead to a healthier, more protective environment for the families.

Education

Children can learn about basic nutrition and food selection early. Nutrition education activities should be prepared with the children's developmental level in mind (Bernath & Masi, 2006). Good role modeling, providing healthy food selections, and discussions about the MyPyramid Food for Kids can send children positive messages about good nutrition. Children can learn that they play a role in their nutritional well-being.

For Families

Many families are unaware of the importance of an adequate diet. Because of the pace of life in this country, regular family mealtimes are losing ground as part of a daily routine. Use of convenience foods, fast foods, and take-out meals is increasing and taking a toll on the general diet of Americans. Children in urban areas may obtain more than half their calories outside the home.

Families that are aware of basic nutrition can work to supplement the foods offered in the early childhood education environments on the days

TABLE 6-3
Good Nutrition Practices for Parent Education

- Monitor your child's growth in height and weight.
- Help children understand the difference between hunger and other needs.
- Provide only good, nutritious food choices that will lead to a well-balanced diet.
- Observe the amount and type of food consumed.
- Do not use food as a reward—choose other methods of rewarding a child.
- Help children learn to interact with others.
- Role model exercise and encourage children to exercise.
- If a child's nutritional health seems to be at risk, seek nutritional counseling.

that their children are in them (Padget & Briley, 2005). Teachers can help families do this by posting menus and the MyPyramid for Kids posters or having them available in handout form or in a newsletter for parents. They can also observe what children have eaten during a day and let the parents know what foods the child might have avoided. Table 6-3 offers more suggestions. Teachers may use other ways to involve families to build connections for nutrition like creating a welcome center for families that has nutritional information they can access (Mayer, Ferede, & Hou, 2006). In elementary school nutrition programs, input from family representatives to the federally mandated wellness/nutrition policy is a requirement (Cama, Parker, & Fitzsimmons, 2006).

Children may be bombarded by messages about food through visits to fast-food restaurants, watching television ads, and looking at food labels in the supermarkets. The messages carried by these foods make it hard for children to understand that good nutrition is not present in all foods. Children may see poor food selections at home or in early childhood education environments due to convenience and the time crush. It is important to talk about food and nutrition with children often. Early childhood education has an impact on children's developing food habits (Bernath & Masi, 2006).

Role Modeling

Nutrition and food selection are integral to achieving good health and well-being. This is an area where many centers and family care homes fall short. Nutrition is often disregarded as an important part of early childhood education. Recent studies have shown a majority of early childhood education programs do not meet the nutritional needs of the children they serve (Briley et al., 1999; Padget & Briley, 2005). Some common practices that model poor nutrition and food selection are included in Table 6-4.

These poor role modeling practices show a need for nutrition education and training in menu planning and food selection. A good background in basic

Wadsworth/Cengage Learning

Children learn about nutrition from the adults in their lives. This teacher is selecting healthy foods for her own meal, thereby role modeling good choices to the children she teaches.

TABLE 6-4
Observed Practices for Role Modeling Poor Nutrition

- There was little variety in the food presented; the same foods and menus were repeated often.
- Vegetables were generally ignored.
- Foods that were high in fats and low in fiber were served often.
- Sweets such as sugar, jelly, and honey were used moderately to liberally.
- Teachers encouraged children to eat but rarely discussed the importance of a food and why the child should eat it.
- There was not enough food served to meet the DRI requirements for energy during the time the children were in the early childhood education environment.
- Menus did not reflect the cultural diversity of the groups they served.
- Food served did not provide adequate amounts of niacin, iron, zinc, and vitamin B_6 needed in a child's diet.
- Convenience seemed to drive menu planning and included using a majority of foods that were canned or frozen.
- Staff in some centers ordered fast food instead of eating the same foods prepared for the children.

nutrition and nutritional guidelines provides the knowledge for good role modeling strategies and practices. Positive role modeling of food behaviors is a good way to help change children's nutrition habits (Parlakian & Lerner, 2007; NCCCHSRC, 2006). Some of the basic role modeling for good nutritional practice is included in Table 6-5.

TABLE 6-5
Basic Practices for Role Modeling Good Nutrition

- Provide menus and food selections that follow USDA, DRI, and CACFP guidelines, taking into consideration the number of meals and snacks a child will consume while in care. Match this consideration to the percentage of daily diet that the teacher provides for the child. Plan the menus accordingly.
- Select a variety of foods for snacks and meals while planning menus.
- Use a large number of fresh fruits and vegetables to provide more vitamins, minerals, and fiber.
- Select low-fat foods and preparations.
- Eat with the children, eating the same foods and discussing the importance of individual foods in the children's diet. This is a good place to use the MyPyramid Food Guidance System.
- Plan menus that take into consideration the regional and cultural diversity of the population at the early childhood education site. This includes children, teachers, and parents.
- Establish good communication with parents about nutrition and why it is an integral part of overall health and well-being.
- Promote and provide nutrition education for children, their parents, and staff.
- Provide parents sack lunch guidelines for the children who bring their lunch from home. The guidelines should include acceptable food selections and suggestions for meeting the child's nutritional needs. Combined with healthy snacks provided by the teacher, this will provide the child an adequate diet while in care.

Cultural Competence

Cultural competence is something to be considered when trying to impart information about basic nutrients to both children and their families. Teachers must have a basic understanding of the foods offered in the cultures the children come from. Traditional foods may be very important to families in helping continue their culture where they are now living. It is important to be aware of what foods have special meaning in the different cultures of children present in the early education environment (Zero to Three, 2007). Food patterns may be difficult to understand, but the teacher should try to gather information so that the early education environment can augment foods prepared at home to provide good basic nutrition throughout the day. One way to do this might be to involve families in creating a storybook about their family that tells what they eat and how the food is prepared (Mayer, Ferede, & Hou, 2006). Using this information might help the teacher in understanding food patterns that are being used at home. Basic nutrition information should be presented to parents in their native languages as much as possible and might be aligned to the foods of that culture. Feeding patterns of children may also vary from culture to culture, so it would be helpful to be informed. Some families encourage their children to explore their own food and feed themselves, while families in other cultures believe that children should be

Marylou, a center director, has a basic knowledge of nutrition. When the center was small, Marylou planned the menus, but as it grew, she got farther away from menu planning and food selection. Several years ago, the center became involved with the Child and Adult Care Food Program, which allowed it to be reimbursed for providing meals that met CACFP program guidelines. CACFP provided training and technical assistance and gave the center a handbook to help in menu planning and food selection. With staff turnover, menus changed only gradually, and the same foods appeared over and over—sometimes two or three times a week. When a local college dietetics class evaluating menus at several centers and family child care homes in the area asked Marylou's center to participate in their study, Marylou accepted because the staff felt they were doing an adequate job.

They were surprised to learn that not only was their menu not well balanced, but it did not even comply with the directives of CACFP. In addition, Marylou's staff had not considered the cultural diversity of the children now attending the center when planning menus. The staff looked carefully at the problems and decided to hold in-service nutrition workshops periodically and to put into practice the suggestions made by the college class. Marylou and her staff also took greater advantage of the CACFP handbook and technical assistance. The staff involved the parents in menu planning and asked for recipes that reflected the cultures present in their center.

When the center participated in the same college study the following year, the staff got a glowing report and the center was cited in the local press as being a good example of healthy nutritional practices in early childhood education.

fed and don't encourage self-feeding behaviors. Teachers should discuss the feeding patterns used in the early education environment so that the family understands how the child will be fed.

Supervision

Supervision ensures that the process of parent education, child education, and role modeling occurs. It is also helpful in examining whether the early childhood education facility, family child care home, or in-home site is practicing good nutrition habits and offering healthy food choices that are developmentally appropriate (Giosa, 2006).

Key Concept 6.5

Implications for Teachers

Nutrition education is one of the most powerful tools a teacher can use for children and their parents. By helping provide information, using cultural competency and good role modeling teachers can pass along nutritional concepts and practices that can improve the health and well-being of children and their families. Teachers should use supervision to ensure that those strategies occur.

CHAPTER SUMMARY

An increasing number of children rely on early education environments to provide a good portion of their nutritional needs. Nutritional policies that include the use of nutritional guidelines such as the Dietary Guidelines for Americans, MyPyramid Food Guidance System, and the CACFP standards should be created for early education environments. Teachers should have an understanding of basic macronutrients and micronutrients and be able to use this information along with MyPyramid Food Guidance System and CACFP standards to plan menus. Teachers should monitor children for growth and provide nutrition education. They should work with families for greater nutritional awareness so that children can have the same protective factors at school and at home. Teachers can use role modeling and supervision to manage risk and practice good nutrition.

TO GO BEYOND

Additional resources for this chapter can be found by visiting the book companion website at www.cengage.com/education/robertson. This supplemental material includes chapter objectives, internet exercises, reflection questions, quizzes, web links, glossary and flash cards, case studies, frequently asked questions, downloadable forms and tables, curriculum supplements, more reality checks, additional key concepts, references, and more.

Chapter Review Critical Thinking Applications

1. Discuss the interrelationship between nutrition and health.
2. Bring four food labels into class and analyze by serving size, DRIs, and calories. What would be the difference if this food were prepared fresh and/or from scratch?
3. As a teacher, why would you have to be careful to meet the needs of a vegetarian child in your care?
4. How would you go about cutting down on trans fats in your diet?

As an Individual

1. Record and chart your diet for three days, including one weekend day. Analyze by comparing it to the MyPyramid Food Guidance System. What could you do to improve your overall diet? What steps should you take?
2. Find a local early childhood education center that serves all the meals to children. Ask to look at their menus and evaluate them. How well do they do? What might you do to improve those menus if you worked at the center?
3. Collect two sets of nutritional labels for two similar foods—one should be healthy and the other "normal." Compare and contrast both labels. Can you see how reading labels might prove worthwhile if one were trying to eat healthier?

As a Group

1. Examine and discuss practical ways to encourage children to try different kinds of foods.
2. Gather nutritional information available in your local community. Make sure there are enough copies for your entire class, and compile the information into a portfolio for each class member to keep.
3. Separate students into smaller groups. Have each group plan a one-day menu for children in a child care center. Next, have them go to a grocery store and pick out, but not purchase, the products they selected for the menu. Have them evaluate the cost per serving and try to determine the total DRI of the foods they placed on the menu.
4. Assign each a school district in your local area, state, or nearby state. Have each student print out a school menu for that district for the same month. Have students bring menus and work in small groups to compare and contrast the information on the menus. Which districts seem to offer healthier lunches and which ones appear to need help?

Case Studies

1. Karen teaches a kindergarten class. The parents get together and take turns to provide a healthy snack, but the children bring their own lunches. Karen has noticed several children in her group have been bringing food items that are mostly empty calories. She does send reminder notes to parents, but they occasionally forget. What can she do to ensure that children get a more balanced diet at lunch than they are presently?
2. Jain is a new family child care provider who is trying to make sure the children in her care get proper nutrition. What suggestions would you have for her so that she can ensure the children in care have good nutrition?
3. Jerrod is a teacher in a class full of children from other cultures. He is trying to teach basic nutrition, but many children are not very familiar with some of the foods he is talking about. What do you suggest he do to be more prepared to deal with nutrition for children from several different cultures?

CHAPTER 7

Protecting Good Nutrition in Early Childhood Education Environments

After reading this chapter, you should be able to:

7.1 Specific Nutritional Policies

Define and discuss the nutritional challenges that pose risks for children in the early childhood education environment and the creation of policies to address these risks.

7.2 Hunger and Malnutrition

Define and discuss nutrition in regard to the challenges of hunger and malnutrition as they apply to children in early childhood education.

7.3 Obesity

Define and discuss childhood overweight and obesity in regard to the impact it may have on the provision of food to children in the early childhood education environment.

7.4 Physical Activity and Exercise

Define and discuss the importance of including physical activity and exercise in early childhood education environments.

7.5 Food Allergies

Define and discuss the issue of food allergies and how the risks for those allergies may be dealt with in the early childhood education environment.

7.6 Other Childhood Nutritional Challenges

Define and discuss the challenges of dental caries, iron deficiency anemia, cardiovascular disease, and hypertension and how to minimize risk for those conditions in the early childhood education environment.

7.7 Implications for Teachers

7.1 SPECIFIC NUTRITIONAL POLICIES

Specific policies to prevent risk for poor nutrition and nutritional challenges are important for good health and well-being of children in early childhood education environments. Indicators for the need to provide protective nutritional policies include these:

- Early childhood education environments often have difficulty achieving nutrition standards (Story, Kaphingst, & French, 2006; Briley & Roberts-Gray, 2005; Padget & Briley, 2005).
- Eleven percent of households in the United States are food insecure (Nord, Andrews, & Carlson, 2006). Children in single-parent households are six times more likely to feel this food insecurity (Nicklas & Johnson, 2004). The impact of food insecurity on a child's health can range from harmful to severe (Wilson, 2005) and normal development can be "at risk" (Rose-Jacobs et al., 2008).
- Approximately 10 percent of children ages 2 to 5 years and 20 percent of children ages 6 to 11 are overweight in this country (Anderson & Butcher, 2006). Prevention of obesity is critical to the long-term health of children (Gidding et al., 2006; Davis et al., 2007). Early childhood education environments can help children to become more physically fit (Benjamin et al., 2007; Pica, 2006; Parish et al., 2006) and provide meals that are lower in energy-dense foods (Leahy, Birch, & Rolls, 2008).
- A child's developmental outcomes can be negatively affected even if his or her nutrition is only slightly less than required (Struble & Aomari, 2003). Many early childhood environments fall short of offering meals and snacks that reflect good nutritional quality. These environments can and should offer nutritious food (Story, Kaphingst, & French, 2006).
- In the United States, diets of processed foods that are convenient and high in fat, sodium, and calories are becoming the norm for many families (Rose, 2007). Children need structure and support from the adults in their life so that they eat the right amounts of the foods that they need (Satter, 2005). Teachers can partner with families to make the necessary changes to foster good eating habits and increase physical activity (Rose, 2007; Sorte & Daeschel, 2006).
- Low physical activity and obesity in young children can increase risk for hypertension and early heart disease (Gidding et al., 2006).
- Children in care are susceptible to food intolerance or allergy because of their young age and the fact that their immune and digestive systems are not yet mature (Rose, 2005).

Social changes such as the increase in one-parent families, dual-career families, and homelessness have had a negative impact on food selection and nutrition of children in this country. Nutritional challenges that pose risks can be related to malnutrition or misnutrition, in which a person is either overnourished in low-density nutrients or undernourished in high-density nutrients (Marcon, 2003). These imbalances may appear in the form of growth retardation, hunger, obesity, iron deficiency anemia, and cardiovascular disease (Nicklas & Johnson, 2004). When children drink a lot of juices and eat sugared foods, they are at risk for dental caries. Diets high in sodium and fat can lead to the development of hypertension and high levels of cholesterol later in life. Other risk factors found in childhood are food allergies and lack of physical activity.

Some of the societal changes affecting the family are related to the lack of environmental support needed for proper growth. More than one-fourth of the children in the United States are living in single-parent households. Hunger is six times more prevalent in those households (Nicklas & Johnson, 2004). There are 500,000 children born each year to teenage mothers and more than 70 percent of those mothers are unmarried. Approximately half of the children in single-parent families are living at the poverty level (*America's children: Key national indicators of well-being, 2007*, 2007).

Other children may be at the poverty level or homeless due to unemployment or underemployment. Families with children represent the fastest growing portion of the homeless population. Children represent 39 percent of the total homeless population and 42 percent of those children were under the age of 5. It is estimated that more than 125,000 children are homeless every day.

During the past three decades the number of working mothers has greatly increased. More than 13 million children younger than age 6 have mothers who work outside the home. These families are turning to early childhood education for their children in increasing numbers (Story, Kaphingst, & French, 2006). Early education environments often fail to meet the nutritional needs of children.

Key Concept 7.1

Specific Nutritional Policies

Childhood nutritional challenges may result from lack of a balanced diet. Risks include hunger, malnutrition, obesity, food allergies, lack of physical exercise. Risk management measures should be included in nutritional policies.

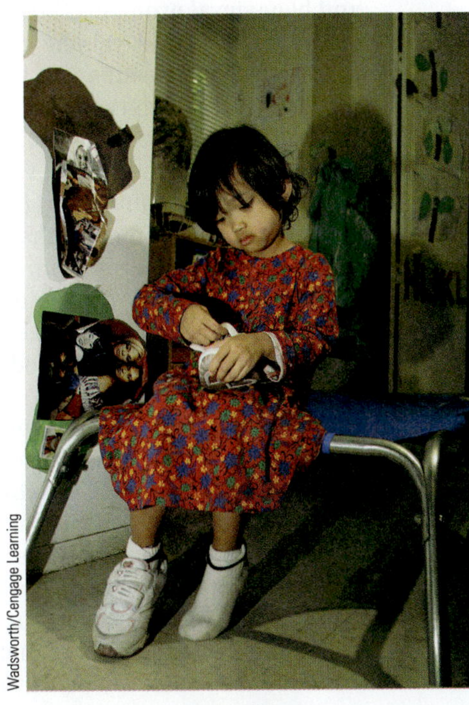

Wadsworth/Cengage Learning

Starvation and malnutrition do not happen only in other parts of the world. Children in U.S. cities are especially at risk as the number of single-parent families below the poverty level continues to increase.

7.2 HUNGER, FOOD INSECURITY, MALNUTRITION, AND MISNUTRITION

Hunger is defined as a chronic shortage of necessary nutrients caused by a recurrent or involuntary lack of food and may be a result of food insecurity. According to that definition, more than 10 million children in the United States are experiencing hunger at some point in a year. In 2005 in the United States, it was found that 11 percent of families were experiencing food insecurity, which means that they did not always have access to enough food to meet basic needs. In terms of numbers of children, it was found that almost 17 percent of all children in this country were food insecure. In 2005 more than 10.8 million children were experiencing very low food security, which indicates hunger is present (Food Research and Action Center [FRAC], 2006). As many as 14 percent of these children may be developmentally "at risk" (Rose-Jacobs et al., 2008). The prevalence of food insecurity and hunger varies throughout the United States. In all of the southern states and in some other parts of the country, large cities and rural areas were found to have a greater level of food insecurity than suburban areas (Nord, Andrews, & Carlson, 2006). Families whose incomes fall below the poverty level, those headed by single women with children, and African-American (22.4 percent) and Hispanic (17.9 percent) households were the most likely to be food insecure. Risk for hunger and food insecurity is especially high with young children in Mexican-American immigrant families (Kersey, Geppert, & Cutts, 2007; Weigel et al., 2007) and Puerto Rican-American children (Chavez, Telleen, & Kim, 2007). Children who are homeless are twice as likely to experience hunger. The average age of a homeless person in the United States is nine years old (Los Angeles Homeless Services Coalition [LAHSC], 2007).

Negative nutrient and nonnutrient outcomes have been associated with food insecurity in children (ADA, 2006a). The negative nutrient outcomes can be poor dietary intake and nutritional status, and increased risk for chronic disease and poor health. Some effects of food insecurity include depression and behavioral problems (Whitaker, Phillips, & Orzol, 2006), decreased social skills for boys, and weight gain for girls (Jyoti, Frongillo, & Jones, 2005). Other adverse consequences from food insecurity and hunger in children are higher levels of aggression, hyperactivity, and difficulty getting along with other children (Connell et al., 2005; Whitaker, Phillips, & Orzol, 2006). Food insecurity may also result in worry or sadness about the food supply and feelings of shame or fear of being labeled as poor (Connell et al., 2005). Although it may seem contradictory that a child who is food insecure or hungry would become obese, children from low-income families have shown consumption patterns of high-fat, high-added-sugar foods (Knol, Haughton, & Fitzhugh, 2005; Casey et al., 2006). Children whose families have insufficient income and who use sugar-sweetened beverages are three times more likely to be overweight at age 4 than those children whose families have sufficient incomes (Dubois et al., 2007). When money for food and beverages has to be stretched as far as possible, there are several predictable results: trading food quality for quantity and overeating when food is available, especially fresh fruits and vegetables. If a low-income family bought fresh fruits and vegetables at the levels recommended in MyPyramid Food Guidance System, they might have to spend 43 to 70 percent of their food budget on them (Cassady, Jetter, & Culp, 2007). The measurement of food insecurity has previously not looked at the quality and variety of diets for children, but it has been suggested that this should be assessed (Nord & Hopwood, 2007).

Malnutrition occurs over time and can be a result of not having enough food or from not having enough of the right kind. Malnourished children do not receive the energy needed from food in the form of macronutrients (Wilson, 2005). Weight loss may occur. Children can also suffer from micronutrient malnutrition (see Basic Micronutrients in Chapter 6). The most common micronutrient lacking worldwide is iron (discussed later). When children have diets that are too high in fats, sodium, and sugars, they may be misnourished and might even suffer from micronutrient malnutrition because of the way they eat or the foods they are fed. There may not be enough nutrient-dense foods available to them.

Hunger can disrupt the health development of children. It can lead to weight loss, growth retardation, and weakened resistance to disease, and it can cause cognitive difficulties (Olson & Holben, 2002). Malnutrition from hunger or food insecurity can be especially harmful to children in the first years of life, when their bodies and brains are developing rapidly (Marcon, 2003). Research has shown that the effects of malnutrition on brain development of very young children can be reversed (Brown & Pollitt, 1996). These studies also found that the health of children older than age 2 can be adversely affected if they become malnourished. This contradicts the former theory that malnourishment to children younger than 2 years is always permanent and that these are the only years to be concerned about.

If a child's growth is stunted by malnutrition or plagued by misnutrition, problems in other aspects of physical growth may result and can have an effect on brain growth and social development. If a child has poor nutrition in the first 3 years of life, his or her mental development can be compromised (Core, 2003; Zero to Three, 2007). This failure to thrive typically causes children to become impassive and cranky. Marcon (2003) made three points about how children's social development can be affected when malnutrition causes physical growth to be below the norm:

1. Undernourished children may reduce their social and exploratory activities because they do not have the energy to play and interact.
2. If a child is not very active, teachers may change the way they behave toward that child.
3. Children who are smaller and grow more slowly may be treated as if they were younger than they actually are.

Children with chronic health conditions, physical handicaps, or developmental delays may be at increased risk for hunger and growth retardation due to inadequate nutrition. These children may have physical feeding difficulties, alterations in bodily functions, or poor feeding behavior. Nutrition expectations and growth patterns must be carefully monitored for such children to prevent malnutrition.

Poor nutrition or misnutrition may occur because parents or teachers lack the time, knowledge of nutrition, or ability to prepare nutritious meals. Parents may rely on fast foods and convenience foods to feed their children and this pattern may also occur in early childhood education (Briley et al., 1999). Children whose daily intakes are too low in high-nutrient-density foods and too high in calories and low-nutrient-density foods will be at risk for misnutrition. The diets of most U.S. children do not meet the Dietary Guidelines for Americans and are low in calcium-rich foods, fiber, and fruits and vegetables. Their diets are high in total fats, saturated and trans fats, added sugars, and sodium (Story, Kaphingst, & French, 2006). These children are not likely to have adequate amounts of vitamins and minerals in their diets.

Ruth, a nanny, went to work for a family when the child, Mark, was 2 months old. She had no problems with Mark's diet until he was 11 months old and ready to begin eating a regular diet without baby food. His parents ate all their meals away from home and were not used to keeping much food at home. The only things they normally had in the refrigerator were salad dressing, olives, and leftovers from their latest takeout meals.

Fortunately, Ruth was a trained nanny who had taken a childhood nutrition class and was therefore aware of what Mark needed in his diet. She was able to educate the parents as to the importance of Mark's diet. They asked her to provide them with a shopping list and they bought the foods she requested. The nicest reward for Ruth was that the entire family began eating better, and the parents started preparing family meals at home to share with Mark. They were grateful to Ruth for making them realize how their habits may have caused Mark problems.

Children who are poorly nourished are more vulnerable to infection and disease, including frequent colds, ear infections, anemia, tuberculosis, and environmental toxins such as lead poisoning.

Prevention strategies for malnutrition and misnutriton include nutrition education, a balanced diet with a selection of healthy foods, and healthy food preparation methods. Because many children eat twice a day in early childhood education environments, teachers should examine their menus and compare them with the Dietary Guidelines and MyPyramid for Kids Food Guidance System to see how the selections meet the standards. Children who eat well and see good food in early childhood education environments may change their outlook on food selection as well as their nutritional status. Teachers can provide regular exposure to nutritious foods and encourage children to choose a greater variety of those foods. Children who understand that food is fuel that makes their bodies work properly may make better food choices when offered the opportunity, especially if the food is enjoyable and appetizing. It is also important to provide families with nutrition education explaining what a good diet should include as well as resource references if families need them.

Key Concept 7.2

Hunger, Food Insecurity, Malnutrition, and Misnutrition

Hunger, food insecurity, malnutrition, and misnutrition provide risks to children in early childhood. Poor nourishment lacking in the necessary nutrients may alter the growth pattern and the health, physical, and social development of children. With increasing numbers of American children in early childhood education environments and significant numbers of children experiencing food insecurity and poor diets at home, it is necessary for teachers to be aware of the importance of providing a balanced diet with healthy food selections. Teachers can help to educate children about how their bodies work and how to make better choices in their foods.

Children who are not physically active and take in too many calories can be headed for overweight and possibly obesity.

Wadsworth/Cengage Learning

7.3 OBESITY

Childhood obesity is now the most prevalent nutritional disease in children 18 years old and younger (Peters, 2004). Excess weight is basically a problem created by energy imbalance. The amount of energy taken in through foods (calories) is metabolized and then expended through the body's work, including involuntary bodily functions such as breathing and voluntary functions such as movement and exercise. If more energy is taken in than is put out, an imbalance results, and the excess energy is stored as body fat.

A child who weighs more than 10 percent above the normal weight for corresponding height, as shown on a standard growth chart, is considered overweight. A child who weighs more than 20 percent over the normal weight is considered obese. Childhood obesity is measured by the body mass index (BMI), which compares weight to height. The CDC classifies children in the 95th percentile and higher as obese and children in the 85th to the 95th percentile as overweight (CDC, 2006).

The percentage of children who are obese has tripled in the last 30 years, and it is estimated that 9 million children between the ages of 6 and 19 years are considered to be overweight (Jana & Shu, 2007). For very young children, the term *overweight* is often used instead of the term *obese*. Data suggests that 15 percent of all children ages 2 to 11 years are considered obese (Anderson & Butcher, 2006). Data also suggests that another 15 percent of children older than age 6 are heading in the direction of being overweight (Brody, 2005). One might conclude that a similar increase would occur in children ages 2 to 5 years. Obesity/overweight is considered to be an epidemic that relates to both the health of these children today and to their increased risk for adult morbidity and mortality. It has been found that children who are overweight at any time as preschoolers are five times more likely to be overweight at age 12 years than those who are not (Nader et al., 2006). It is interesting to note that when asked their perception of their child's weight status, 61 percent of mothers of overweight children did not see the child as being overweight (Hackie & Bowles, 2007). This study found that cultural and social beliefs definitely impacted this perception. When parents cannot recognize that their children are overweight, it poses risk for continued practices that might lead to obesity (Eckstein et al., 2006).

Obesity is especially prevalent among Hispanic, African-American, and Native American children (Edmunds et al., 2006; *The Role of Media in Childhood Obesity,* 2004). Studies of Mexican and Latino families have found several factors that might lead to childhood obesity (Carrera, Gao, & Tucker, 2007; Kaufman & Karpati, 2007), including cultural ideas relating to parenting and conceptions about the body and what constitutes well-being. Even when living in poverty, if a family feels it is feeding their child enough so that he or she does not look emaciated, the family feels it is providing for the child (Kaufman & Karpati, 2007). Many of the foods used are healthy, but others are very high in cholesterol and fats. Obesity and overweight have also been looked at in a geographical context. The southeastern states, especially those in the lower Mississippi area and those west of the Appalachians, had the highest occurrence of children who are overweight or at risk for overweight. The areas with the least occurrence of overweight or risk for overweight occurred in Colorado, Utah, and Wyoming (Tudor-Locke et al., 2007).

The condition of obesity has recently been linked to television viewing, sugary soft drinks, attention-deficit/hyperactivity disorder (ADHD), and portion size (Ludwig, Peterson, & Gortmaker, 2001; Cox, 2003). In fact, The Kaiser Family Foundation reported that television advertising, time spent watching television instead of being engaged in physical activity, and snacking while watching television correlated with obesity in a number of recent studies (see Table 7-1 for reasons for obesity in children).

Another study found that about one-fourth of children's daily food intake occurred while they watched television (Matheson et al., 2004). A very strong correlation between television in a child's room and obesity was also found (Dennison, Erb, & Jenkins, 2002). A number of studies have looked at the issue of food insecurity in terms of weight gain and found that there is no strong evidence linking the two, but there has been evidence that television viewing and other sedentary activities did correlate with obesity (Martin & Ferrris, 2007; Rose & Bodor, 2006; Jyoti, Frongillo, & Jones, 2005). With the endorsement of the AAP, the American Heart Association (AHA) has recommended that children limit their television viewing and not eat while watching television (Gidding et al., 2005).

Sugary drinks appear to be replacing milk as a beverage in many children's diets, and this appears to relate to later weight gain (LaRowe, Moeller, & Adams, 2007; Dubois et al., 2007; O'Connor, Yang, & Nicklas,

TABLE 7-1
Common Reasons for Obesity in Children

- Dietary excesses in foods containing fats, cholesterol, and sugar
- Excessive portion sizes
- Poor infant or child feeding practices
- Being female with a parent who is obese
- Lack of sufficient exercise
- Watching too much television
- Family genetic predisposition
- ADHD
- Using food as a comforting device or for emotional support
- Weight gain during critical developmental periods

2006). These sugary drinks include 100 percent fruit juice with sweeteners, fruit-flavored drinks or drinks that contained some fruit juice, and any sweetened soft drink. Higher consumption of these sugary drinks combined with high levels of sedentary activity and low levels of physical activity have been thought to be a factor in the overweight of young children in this country today. African-American children are more likely than white or Mexican-American children to consume fruit drinks/ades, and white children are more likely to consume carbonated soft drinks than the other ethnicities (Storey, Forshee, & Anderson, 2006). For toddlers, fruit-flavored drinks were the third most important source of energy (Fox et al., 2006). This added sugar for children this age is of concern. When these sugary drinks are consumed between meals, it more than doubles the risk of being overweight (Dubois et al., 2007).

A national survey sample of studies investigated whether or not there was a relationship between ADHD and overweight in children (Waring & Lapane, 2008). They concluded that children who had ADHD and did not receive medication were one and one-half times as likely to be obese as children with ADHD who were taking medication. They also found that children with ADHD and were taking medication were more than one and one-half as likely to be underweight as those children with ADHD who were not taking medication. This difference in risk for obesity and not taking medication in children with ADHD is being further studied.

Fisher and colleagues (2003) found that serving bigger portion sizes in preschools lead to children consuming 25 percent more than they would have normally and 15 percent more than if they had served themselves. Nutritional quality of meals and snacks offered in early childhood education environments may be poor, even if they follow the Child and Adult Care Food Program guidelines (Story, Kaphingst, & French, 2006). These guidelines have no nutrient-based standards. If the nutritional quality of the meals is poor, then serving larger portions may well lead to overweight. Elementary education environment school lunch and breakfast programs have standards that set the nutritional quality and appropriate serving sizes for children (FRAC, 2006).

There are a number of other reasons for childhood obesity, as shown in Table 7-1. It is likely that childhood obesity results from a combination of familial, nutritional, physical, economic, and psychological factors. A familial relation exists because children with obese parents are as much as 80 percent more likely to become obese (Jana & Shu, 2007). Gender appears to be a factor for overweight in food-insecure families where one parent is obese. Girls are twice as likely to be overweight as are boys in these families (Martin & Ferris, 2007). One of the major nutritional factors is the fast food and portion size of foods consumed away from home, including at restaurants, schools, and even early childhood education environments. There has been a movement afoot for fast-food outlets, schools, and early childhood education environments to stop providing so many low-nutrient-density foods and begin offering more healthy selections (Green, 2005; Coile, 2006; Simpson, 2007). This movement has opposition from the soft-drink and vending-machine industries. A congressional report has set standards for school nutrition, and it appears that state legislators are quickly building on that by enacting legislation to either limit or prevent junk food in schools. Restaurants in New York City and some other places are banning most trans fats (Lueck & Severson, 2006). This concern has even led to banning trans fat use at state fairs that have long been known as havens of fatty foods (Davey, 2007).

Effects of overweight or obesity are numerous. Childhood obesity can cause pediatric hypertension and diabetes mellitus and certain cancers (Hood, 2005). In 2008, the AAP was so concerned about obesity in children that they now recommend that children as young as two have lipid screening and if found, children as young as 8 years of age should take lovostatin drugs to keep their cholesterol level down (Daniels, Greer, and the Committee on Nutrition, 2008). Obesity can also impair the immune system and the ability to fight off infection and disease. Sleep apnea, which is a disorder that causes children to awaken many times during the night and reduces the amount of time in deep sleep, can also be a result of overweight. Children under the age of 4 years can be at risk for having their cognitive development impaired (Reeves, 2007b). Stress on the weight-bearing joints is one physical problem that may result. There are also a number of long-term effects. Mentally and emotionally, obesity lowers self-esteem and has a powerful affect on peer relationships and social acceptance. Children who are neglected are more likely to become obese (Whitaker et al., 2007). Children who are overweight may be teased or bullied or excluded from activities by other children. This can lead to serious emotional problems including depression and even rage (Reeves, 2007b). Obese children have also been found to have a slightly higher prevalence of asthma (Jacobson et al., 2008). Prevention is the key to combating childhood obesity. However, a problem in perception may result in difficulty initiating preventive measures. Many mothers of preschool children who are obese do not perceive their children as obese (Huang et al., 2007); and many mothers believe that if they are overweight, their children will be too, regardless of preventive measures (Jain et al., 2001).

The problem of childhood obesity can be improved by an increase in physical activity, diet management, and behavior modification. Physical activity alone does not seem to be effective, but the addition of diet and behavior modification contributes to successful weight loss in obese children.

Diet management should include both a doctor-recommended modified caloric intake and nutrition education. Modifying caloric intake reduces dietary fat intake, and providing three healthy meals a day can help. Nutrition education encourages children to make better choices in food selection away from home and it can help families shop for a better selection of healthy foods. The AHA feels that nutrition education in schools would be useful in providing knowledge and altering eating behaviors. Families ought to be included in the behavior modification process, which should provide problem-solving techniques. Early intervention that uses the whole-child approach has been especially effective in helping obese children lose weight and improve their level of self-esteem. The ADA has recommended that this holistic approach include families and provide nutrition education, which promotes sensible food choices (ADA, 2007). This holistic approach would include nutrition education, intervention in menu planning and foods served, increase in organized physical activities, and parental education (Gidding et al., 2006). Early childhood education environments are in a position to promote healthy changes for good nutrition selections that can address childhood overweight (Rose, 2007). Story, Kaphingst, and French (2006) also feel that early childhood education environments are good places to develop and use obesity prevention strategies. They cite the fact that Head Start can serve as a model for programs because they have performance standards for nutrition in place. Teachers can help obese children by providing a well-balanced diet that is not high in fat. Teachers can help children learn to select high-nutrient-density foods and teach them about limiting selection of low-nutrient-density foods. They can reduce consumption of sweetened beverages, including juice. Teachers can limit the use of media such as television. They can increase the amount of energy output by planning exercises and other organized physical activities and offering free time for physical play. They can also provide self-selection or age-appropriate portion sizes for all children in their care to prevent overeating (McConahy et al., 2004). They can help children to understand external food cues and opportunities to snack and to make better food choices when the occasion arises. Children need structure and support for mealtimes. If a child eats only at mealtimes and is not allowed to "graze," it is much easier to control nutritional input (Satter, 2005). It is suggested that children have three meals and two snacks per day and be allowed to eat as much as they want during those times, but eat only during those times. Teachers employing some of these measures may already be making a difference in the lives of some children. A study showed that attendance in center-based child care during the preschool years was associated with decreased risk of overweight in future years (Lumeng et al., 2005). The University of North Carolina has recognized the potential of using child care settings to assess nutrition policies and practices. They have come up with the Nutrition and Physical Activity Self-Assessment for Child Care (NPASACC) (Ammerman et al., 2007). It shows promise for promoting healthy behaviors for weight management in child care settings. Another measure being taken is to reduce the energy density in preschool lunches by 30 percent. In trials, children seemed to enjoy the lower-energy-dense meals more than the regular ones (Leahy, Birch, & Rolls, 2008). This indicates that children don't seem to mind the effects of cutting back on high-energy-dense ingredients in their foods.

Some states and a number of school districts are using school-based programs to measure the body mass index of the students who attend. This body mass index measurement is supposed to help survey for the children who are obese, overweight, or at risk for these conditions. Once these children are identified, a letter is usually sent home to the parents about the risk factors that their child may have. In addition, many of these letters include some strategies that the family can implement to help the child lose weight and lessen risks. At this point, it is difficult to tell whether these programs are effective in preventing obesity (Nihiser et al., 2007). Other measures are being tried. Canada has done a pilot study on a "healthy buddy" program where older students in fourth through seventh grade mentored children in kindergarten through the third grade for a school year. The older students taught the younger ones in three areas of healthy living including physical activity, body image, and nutrition. This pilot had positive results for both sets of children. The older students had a decrease in weight, and both that group and the younger students had an increased knowledge about healthy living (Stock et al., 2007). This may be something to consider for elementary school sites.

In 2005, former President Bill Clinton and his foundation joined with the AHA to try to cut down on childhood obesity in this country. They developed a website for older children, ages 9 to 14 years, to help them understand the seriousness of this problem. Obese children may have a three- to five-year shorter lifespan due to weight effects on their health. This interactive website can be found at http://www.americanheart.org/. It might offer some useful

When children are allowed to self-select and serve themselves, they are less likely to be hungry and less likely to overeat.

Wadsworth/Cengage Learning

tools for the teacher of younger children to adapt to the early childhood education environment. In addition, in 2007, the expert committee for obesity of the AAP came out with the recommendations for the prevention of childhood obesity found in Table 7-2.

TABLE 7-2
Recommendations for the Prevention of Childhood Obesity

- Consume adequate quantities of fruits and vegetables.
- View television no more than two hours per day.
- Consume sugar-sweetened beverages in limited quantities.
- Limit portion size.
- Eat breakfast every day.
- Limit eating out, especially at fast-food restaurants.
- Sit down and eat as a family or with adults as often as possible.

Key Concept 7.3

Obesity

Childhood obesity poses significant risk to children in the early education environment. The number of young children who are obese has tripled in the past 25 years. Some factors that contribute to obesity include overconsumption of fats and sugars and an increase in sedentary activities. Teachers can help children to make more healthy selections of food and to read their own inner food cues, and at mealtimes they can provide foods that encourage children to follow the MyPyramid for Kids Food Guidance System.

Pause for Reflection

Could your weight be improved? What types of things might you do in terms of diet and exercise to improve it? What suggestions do you have to help an overweight 4-year-old?

7.4 PHYSICAL ACTIVITY AND EXERCISE

In 2000, a new guideline was added to the Dietary Guidelines for Americans reflecting the fact that physical activity is needed to balance food intake (Johnson & Kennedy, 2000). The guideline for physical activity is still included in the most recent version of the Dietary Guidelines for Americans. Healthy People 2010 has included increased physical activity as one of its top 10 priorities (Tate & Patrick, 2000). The new MyPyramid Food Guidance System has a component for finding balance between food intake and physical activity and encourages greater physical activity among Americans. The MyPyramid for Kids goes even further. It recommends that children be physically active for 60 minutes a day on most days. The ECERS-R suggests that children participate in 60 minutes of physical activity daily (Harms, Clifford, & Cryer, 2005). The AHA, with the endorsement of the AAP, has suggested that a healthy diet and vigorous physical activity lead to normal growth in children (Gidding et al., 2006). They recommend that young children engage in at least 60 minutes of moderate to vigorous activity daily. The AAP has also created a policy statement on the prevention of childhood obesity through increased physical activity (AAP, 2006a). The National Association for Sport and Physical Education (NASPE) recommends that toddlers engage in 30 minutes of organized physical activity and 60 minutes of unstructured physical activity (Story, Kaphingst, & French, 2006).

When we consider the problem of obesity/overweight, or even when we think about fitness in children, we often focus on diet alone. Schools should offer programs that teach children how to choose healthy physical activity as well as foods (Benjamin et al., 2007; Goodway & Robinson, 2006; Parlakian & Lerner, 2007). Many efforts have been made in an attempt to include physical activity as a priority for children. The University of Missouri Extension designed a poster for physical activity intended to help children easily understand how to select appropriate activities to help them keep fit. This figure is included here as Figure 7-1. This Kid's Activity Pyramid gives children activities that they should cut down on and activities they can do by themselves or with their friends and family. NASPE has created guidelines for children birth to age 5 that will promote movement skills and healthy related fitness. These helpful guidelines can be found at http://www.aahperd.org/naspe/template.cfm?template=ns_active.html. These guidelines can be easily integrated into early childhood education environments. The Texas Women's University, in cooperation with local school districts, teachers, and families, has created a program called EASE—Eating, Activity, and Self-Esteem. The purpose of this is to create environments that promote physical activity and maintain a healthy weight through eating healthy foods (Huettig et al., 2006). Ohio State University has developed Project SKIP, which stands for Successful Kinesthetic Instruction for Preschoolers. This program, which incorporates

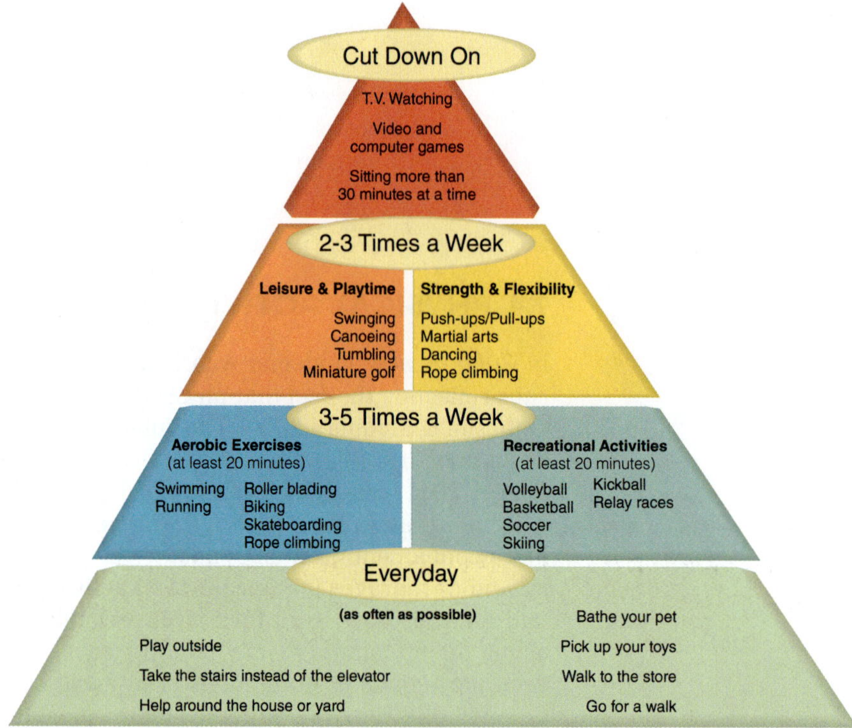

FIGURE 7-1
Physical Activity Pyramid. From Children's Activity Pyramid, by Barbara Willenberg, Associate State Food and Nutrition Specialist, University of Missouri Extension.

regular physical activity into early childhood education environments, emphasizes competency in fundamental motor skills (Goodway & Robinson, 2006). Project SKIP also has developed strategies for helping teachers understand and promote physical activities. The University of North Carolina-Greensboro created a program called Tots in Action to encourage children to see physical activity as an integral part of their lives and help increase their physical activity levels (Schilling & McOmber, 2006). Oregon State University created a project called Health In Action: Five Simple Steps to Better Health. This project works directly with families and has created toolkits for home and school to help families support better health for children. Physically active play is a key component (Sorte & Daeschel, 2006). For school-age children, Congress have enacted federal legislation that requires schools that receive federal reimbursement for school lunches to have a wellness/nutrition program in place. This includes planned physical activity (School Board Notes, 2005). The great number of programs that are being put into practice reflects the importance that has been placed on physical activity for children as a way to maintain good health and well-being.

If children are given goals for physical activity that are reachable, it is much easier to expect them to achieve a healthy level of activity as part of their fitness regime (Huettig et al., 2006). It is much easier to prevent obesity and overweight than it is to correct it. Allowing time for physical activities and exercise is a necessary part of creating nutritional policies to protect children's health and well-being. Time spent in physical activity also helps create neural connections in the brain (Rampmeyer, 2000). Activities for structured play should be planned on a daily basis. The NASPE guidelines outlined in their website give good direction. Schilling and McOmber (2006) suggest a number

A good amount of physical activity should be worked into every early childhood education environment. An evaluation of the general activity level of the class and of specific children can help the teacher identify which activities are best.

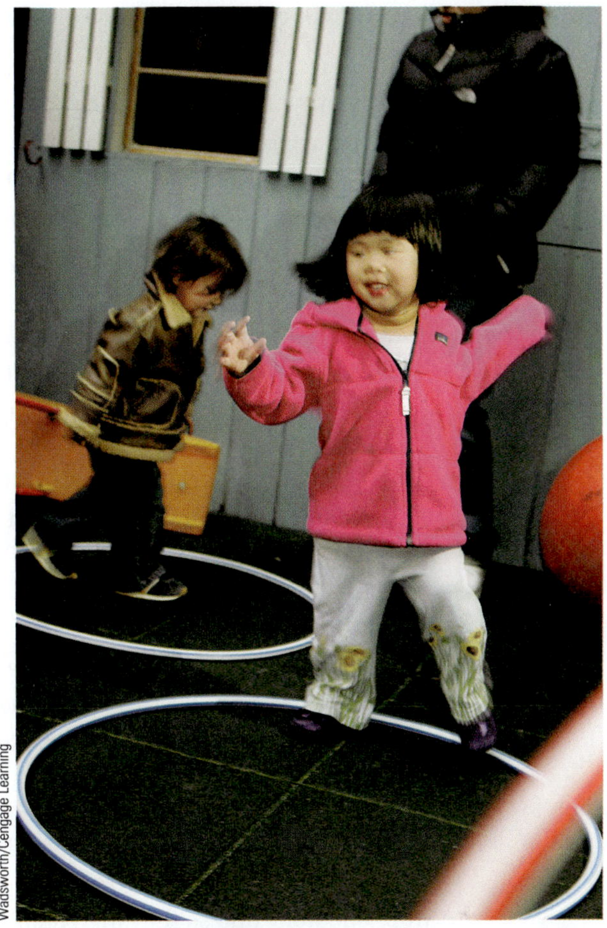
Wadsworth/Cengage Learning

of activities in *Beyond the Journal* on the NAEYC website at http://www.journal.naeyc.org/btj/200605/SchillingBTJ.pdf. The Kellogg Company provided the funding in 2003 for a booklet on young children's physical fitness activities, entitled "Kids in Action," which can be accessed online at http://www.fitness.gov. It has good suggestions for activities to do with infants, toddlers, and preschoolers to help them meet their physical fitness needs. Table 7-3 is a summary of The President's Council on Physical Fitness and Sports' *10 Tips to Healthy Eating and Physical Activity.* Although this list was originally meant for 9- to 15-year-olds, it can easily be adapted for younger children.

Preschool and school-aged children are active on a daily basis. Large motor activities offer them the exercise they need. The preschool years are especially important for gross motor or locomotor development. Running, hopping, walking, skipping, climbing, and jumping are motor activities that come naturally to young children (NCCCHSRC, 2006). They enjoy practicing these new abilities. It is also important to have children learn object control skills such as throwing, catching, and kicking. These types of activities can help children build endurance, flexibility, and strength (NCCCHSRC, 2007a). Offering opportunities for and encouragement of physical skill building will help children become physically fit. These activities don't have to be complex to be fun for children. It is important that children have at least one hour of unstructured active play every day. Infants should not be inactive for longer

TABLE 7-3
Ten Tips for Healthy Eating and Physical Activities for Young Children

- Start your day with breakfast—we all operate better with proper "fuel."
- Get moving! Fit physical activities into a daily routine—make sure you are active for at least 30 minutes per day.
- Snack smart—choose a variety of nutrient-dense foods.
- Work up a sweat—include some aerobic exercise each day, such as running or dancing.
- Balance food choices—be smart about food selections and make most of them healthy foods that are nutrient dense.
- Get fit with friends or family—activities are more fun when they are done with others.
- Eat more grains, fruits, and vegetables—they provide energy that we need to be active and vitamins and minerals needed to support growth, maintenance, and repair of the body.
- Participate in physical activities at school—structured activities help us to stay physically fit.
- Foods aren't good or bad—balance a low-nutrient-density food at one time of day with high-nutrient-density foods at another time of day.
- Make healthy eating and physical activities fun—be adventurous!

Based on information from The President's Council on Physical Fitness and Sports, 10 Tips to Healthy Eating and Physical Activity available online at http://www.fitness.gov.

than one hour unless they are sleeping. Toddlers should be provided with 30 minutes of structured play every day, in several segments, not all at once. Preschoolers should have at least one hour of structured play that allows for movement and physical activity, and should not be sedentary for more than 60 minutes except when they are napping (Hood, 2005).

Because of the federal legislation tied to the reauthorization of the School Lunch Program in 2005, a wellness/nutrition component is now required for school-aged children. Children in the early elementary years must have physical activity on a daily basis, adding up to the recommended 60 minutes per day when possible. Elementary school children are to be engaged in daily physical education activities for 150 minutes per week. The federal mandate has not yet been fully implemented. More than two-thirds of elementary schools in the United States provide a daily recess for students in all grades (Lee et al., 2007). Teachers are encouraged to plan physical activities as part of lesson plans, and children must have physical activity breaks several times a day (National Alliance for Nutrition and Activity, 2008). Many elementary schools have started running clubs and other types of sports activity groups that take place during lunch times as well as before and after school.

Active children in early childhood education programs should be encouraged to remain that way. Free play is best for active children. If some of the children are interested only in sedentary activities such as quiet play with dolls or puzzles, these children should be encouraged to be more active by providing interesting activities that use their large motor skills. Children are able to burn more calories in outdoor activities than they are in indoor activities

(Sutterby & Frost, 2002). Consider adapting children's movement activities that are normally done inside to the outdoors. Combining music with movement is a wonderful way to promote children's physical activity. Playing games together on the playground is another way to get these sedentary children involved and active. The teacher may have to guide some children into participating in more physical activities. The teacher can also plan to add a physical component to other activities, such as removing chairs from an art table for finger painting or doing activities on the floor that initiate movement. There is now a self-assessment instrument for nutrition and physical activity for child care (NPASACC) that shows promise for promoting physical activity for better healthy weight environments in preschool settings (Benjamin et al., 2007).

When children have more room to move their bodies, they can be more physically active. The early education environment should be set up to make room for children to be active and safe. Space should be planned in accordance with the age and developmental levels of the children present (Rose, 2007; Holland, 2007). When children are engaged in active outdoor play, they should be closely supervised for safety. Encouraging children to take an active part in playground play is a good way to ensure that children get enough exercise. Providing both free and structured activities, such as taking a walk or playing a game, should be part of the daily routine.

If the weather is inclement, plan indoor play as a way for children to get exercise. If there is enough safe room, set up obstacle courses or use materials such as soft balls or beanbags to engage children in physical activities (Holland, 2007). The use of exercise balls can be adapted for the indoor environment. Movement activities such as dancing to music or pretending to be animals can be easily included. If there is not enough adequate or safe room available in the early childhood education environment, and there is a nearby school, gymnasium, or community center available for use, this would be a good alternative. Have on hand a simple exercise video, or check one out from the library; having the children try to perform the exercises may be another fun way to exercise indoors on occasion. If there are school-aged children in the early childhood environment, the teacher can have them

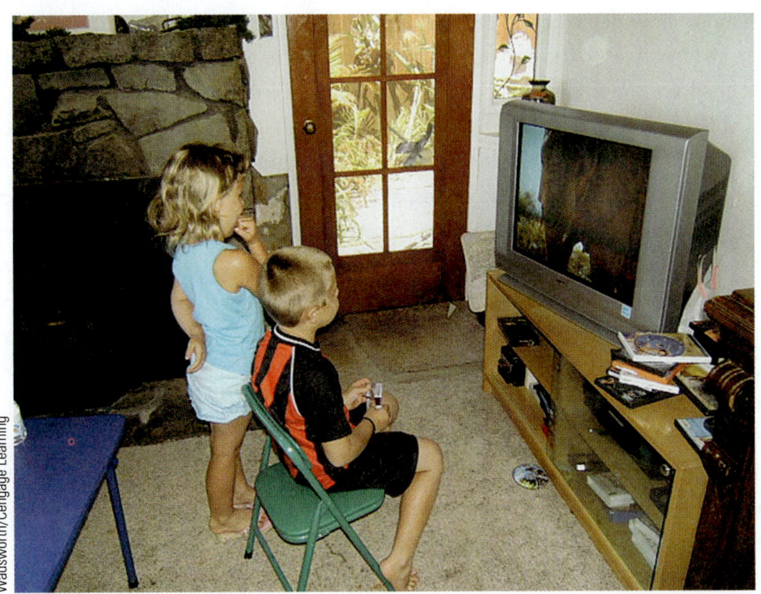

Children should be encouraged to be physically active and, whatever the early education environment, television use should be kept to a minimum and be educational.

help lead the exercises. These children also might really enjoy demonstrating exercises they have learned in school.

The teacher can also remove temptations to inactivity, such as television. This may enhance greater exercise and movement for the children in early childhood education environments. Children who watch a lot of television are likely to be less physically fit and more overweight and to have a distorted knowledge of nutrition. Use television sparingly and only for educational viewing or for use in participating in exercise. It is also important to remember that teachers are role models for children. Teachers themselves should spend some time each day in physical activities for their own fitness. Guiding children toward more physical activities and physical fitness will be more effective if teachers strive to do the same.

REALITY *Check*

Electronic Media and Its Effects on Children's Diet and Exercise

Electronic media in the form of television, videos, DVDs, computers, and the Internet have a great impact on the health and nutritional status of young children in this country. Hunger/malnutrition, obesity, dental cavities, iron deficiency anemia, lack of physical exercise, cardiovascular disease, and food allergies are basic nutritional challenges facing children. All but food allergies may be affected through the use of electronic media.

Television and other electronic media use is a part of a child's daily life. There are many television channels now dedicated to children. One is targeted for children under the age of 1 year. Twenty percent of children under the age of 2 years and one-third of children 3 to 6 years old have a television in their own bedrooms (Vandewater et al., 2007). Handheld video games, computer games, and time spent on Internet websites are becoming more common. Food advertisers have taken advantage of changing technologies and have employed highly developed methods of getting across their messages (Sigman-Grant, 2007), for example by inserting product names and logos on Internet websites and over cell phones and embedding products in television shows. Children between ages 2 and 7 watch about three and a half to four hours of television per day and spend another hour or more a day in other electronic media activity (NCCCHSRC, 2005). This means that children are watching three to four hours of advertising every week. It is estimated that children are now watching about 40,000 advertisements per year (AAP, 2006b). Of those, 50 percent are ads for food. Approximately 80 percent of Saturday morning television ads are for foods of low nutritional quality. Research has found that the overwhelming majority of food-product advertisements seen on television by children are of poor nutritional quality (Powell et al., 2007). Most children's ads are for sugared cereal, high-calorie snacks, and fast food. Put in terms of money, $2.5 billion is spent on restaurant ads and $2 billion is spent on advertising food products. Food commercials on television encourage the consumption of highly sugared and high-fat foods that are low in fiber. This is a concern to many health professionals and nutritionists. The food that is advertised is not healthy food. In 2006, only 3 percent of the foods advertised were for healthy products. Food advertising on other electronic media also encourages the consumption of low-nutrient-density foods. Internet websites advertising foods are using cartoon characters or spokes-characters to market their products. They are also using games in which the product is part of the game; this is called advergaming (Weber, Story, & Harnack, 2006).

(continues)

REALITY *Check* (continued)

Children are being bombarded by electronic media food advertising at school as well as at home. On Channel 1, an "educational" channel used in 25 percent of the middle and high schools in this country, foods of low nutrient density are commonly advertised (AAP, 2006b). Two hundred U.S. school districts have signed exclusive contracts to advertise certain soft-drink products in their schools, including on electronic "bulletin boards." Branded products from Pizza Hut are sold in 4,500 schools in this country, and in another 3,000 schools branded Taco Bell products are sold. It seems like children cannot escape this type of advertising wherever they go.

For many years, the Food Guide Pyramid was the measuring tool for our diets. It was in use until the spring of 2005, when the MyPyramid Food Guidance System replaced it, and later that year MyPyramid for Kids came out. Aronson reported in 2000 that 16 percent of children were not meeting any of the needs in any category of the Food Guide Pyramid. A more recent study found that only 10 percent of children met the DRI for the two-thirds of the day that they were in early education environments (Padget & Briley, 2005).

Television viewing is a significant source of misinformation about nutrition (Byrd-Bredbenner, 2002). Advertisers commonly use vibrant colors and packaging that lure children to want to purchase their products, such as a bright box of cereal with a prize in it, leading children to make unhealthy food choices. This is increasingly critical because children between the ages of 4 and 12 years spend about $10 billion on sweets, sweetened beverages, and unhealthy snacks (Sigman-Grant, 2007).

Food advertising geared to children usually has a particular "hook" or appeal. Children's ads have an identifiable character to relate to more often than adult ads do. These characters may be cartoon or real-life heroes and they may be used on television, the Internet, and even on videos that children watch. Nickelodeon Entertainment Company markets food to millions of children on their networks, and 80 percent of foods, beverages, and restaurant meals they market are of poor nutritional quality (Batada & Wooten, 2007). Children's advertising often has jingles or corporate logos to help children identify products. Advertisers commonly work with fast-food restaurants, toy manufacturers, and retail outlets in order to ensure their product messages are repeatedly seen by children. The number of times children request things seen on television may be an indicator of the effect of these ads. When foods are "branded" like this, children's taste perceptions are likely to be influenced (Robinson et al., 2007). The number of television ads viewed and time spent watching television directly correlates with children's requests for those foods (AAP, 2006b; Utter, Scragg, & Schaaf, 2006). The Institutes of Medicine of the National Academies (McGuiness, Gootman, & Kraak, 2006) concluded that commercial characters should only be used when advertising healthy foods. They also suggested that the food industry had the power to advertise healthy foods in the same way they were presently advertising low-nutrient-density foods.

Much of the advertising for breakfast cereals has included the phrase "part of a balanced breakfast," but this may be erroneous, considering the amount of sugar present in the cereal. Young children do not have the knowledge or sophistication to be discerning consumers. The hooks for happiness, being cool, or getting good taste or a toy may cause children watching these ads to desire many items of low nutritional quality. Cereals that are marketed specifically to children usually contain more sugar per ounce than a Hostess™ Twinkie. These cereals are usually placed at a child's eye level in the supermarket. In an effort to quell a consumer movement regarding the marketing of sugared cereals to children, Kellogg's announced it was voluntarily no longer advertising highly sugared cereals to children on television, radio, print media, or website ads (CBS News, 2007). In this voluntary restriction, they agreed not to advertise cereal that contains more than 200 calories and/or more than 12 grams of sugar per serving, excluding fruit, vegetables, and dairy. The Kellogg products that did not qualify to be advertised will have to be either reformulated or will no longer be marketed to children under age 12 by the end of 2008.

(continues)

REALITY*Check* (continued)

Many products that are labeled as fruit, such as fruit snacks, fruit ropes, or fruit leather, are highly sugared, with as much as 50 percent of their content being sugar of some form. Many so-called "fruit juices" only have a small portion of real juice in them and are highly sugared. These frequently advertised "fruit" products also have intense colors that attract children.

Besides the advertisement of food products on television, the Internet, and videos, a significant amount of food is present in television shows. Many of the characters in television shows geared to children are depicted as eating snacks instead of sitting down to a meal with other people (*The Role of Media in Childhood Obesity,* 2004). These snacks tend to be sweet or salty. Very little consumption of fruits and vegetables is shown. Modeling of good food choices is not common.

Electronic media viewing by children poses a risk to both nutrition and health. It discourages exercise, so children may become "couch potatoes" or "computer junkies." The body metabolism rate for watching television is actually 14.5 percent less than for lying down in bed. Many young children are spending more and more time watching television and videos and being on the computer, which are all sedentary activities. This increases the risk for overweight or obesity. Children who have a television in their room are at even more risk for obesity (Dennison, Erb, & Jenkins, 2002). It has been found that in one week's time, children eat more than one-fourth of their daily food intake in front of a television (Matheson et al., 2004), in the form of snacks or even "meals" with foods such as pizza, salty snacks, and sodas, which tend to decrease the intake of fruits, vegetables, and juices. The consumption of soft drinks has increased 500 percent in the last 50 years, and much of this rise may be due to television advertising. All of these dietary habits may lead to obesity, and television viewing has been directly related to increased obesity in this country (*The Role of Media in Childhood Obesity,* 2004). It appears that the trend for obesity may be rising in relationship to the amount of exposure U.S. children have to food advertising on television (Powell, Szczypka, & Chaloupka, 2007). Children in the United Kingdom also displayed this same upward trend: the more exposure to food advertising, the greater the number of children who were found to be obese (Halford et al., 2007).

Teachers can promote good nutrition by using the MyPyramid Food for Kids Guidance System to make healthier choices to serve to children. They can provide age-appropriate portions or allow children to self-select. Teachers can provide guidance to children on how to select appropriate foods, how to snack with nutrient-dense healthier foods, and how to choose activities that are less sedentary. They can offer support and structure for mealtimes and omit "grazing" behaviors (Satter, 2005). Teachers can talk about food advertisements and help children understand that although they are appealing, the food is not healthy and should be limited in their diets. Teachers should look closely at the magazines, videos, and computer learning programs in their early childhood education environment to see whether there are any materials that promote foods with poor nutritional quality (Sigman-Grant, 2007). Sigman-Grant (2007) suggests that if these are found, they should be replaced with pictures of healthy foods.

Teachers can also read food labels so they can be more discriminating in their food choices. Another way to help children is to teach them how to read their own internal cues as to when they are hungry and not to eat just because the television is on (Johnson & Kennedy, 2000). Elementary schools can also help by not allowing the sale of low-nutrient-density foods to raise money. The beverage industry recognized that selling sodas in schools was an issue for concern for many parents and legislators and agreed to halt the sale of soda in school in the United States. Only bottled waters, 100 percent unsweetened juices, and low-fat milk will be sold in school nutrition programs (AAP, 2006a).

CHECK*point:* **Considering all the information given in the Reality Check, do you personally feel that television and other electronic media such as the Internet do influence children's food choices? How about food selections when children are at the grocery store?**

Key Concept 7.4

Physical Activity and Exercise

Using physical activity and exercise as a corollary component of diet is an important measure that a teacher can provide children in early childhood education environments. Children are increasingly involved in sedentary activities. A teacher who encourages exercise in the daily early education program provides a broad base for reducing nutritional risk. By encouraging all children to be physically active and providing daily large motor activities to ensure this, teachers promote good health and well-being for children in their care.

7.5 FOOD ALLERGIES

If a child cannot eat or properly metabolize a food with important nutrients, he may be at risk for malnutrition and misnutrition. The response to food allergies may range from skin rashes and difficulty breathing to gastrointestinal problems. Foods that commonly bring on allergic reactions are milk, eggs, peanuts, tree nuts, wheat, fish, soybeans, and shellfish (Rose, 2005). Sesame seed and tree nut allergies may be related to each other and can affect children (Beausoleil & Spergel, 2006). Findings have also noted that more than half of children with peanut allergies are also allergic to eggs, and one-fourth of these children are also allergic to milk (Green et al., 2007). The difference between an allergic reaction to a food and intolerance to a food involves the immune system. A child who has food intolerance has an abnormal response to a food, but it does not compromise the general health and well-being of the child. A child who is intolerant to a food can eat small amounts of it and have little or no reaction. A child with an allergy to a food has a response that is triggered from the immune system; such a reaction may bring about a serious medical condition or may be life threatening. Only about 6 percent of children have a true food allergy (Sicherer & Sampson, 2006).

- **lactose intolerance** *inability of body to process lactose found in milk and milk products.*

A reaction to milk is most often apparent as **lactose intolerance**. Lactose is the simple sugar found in milk. When someone is unable to metabolize lactose properly, she experiences gastric distress such as abdominal pain, diarrhea, bloating, or vomiting. Infants who exhibit lactose intolerance are put on soy-based or lactose-free formulas. Care should be taken when putting a child on a soy-based formula because soy is another product that children are commonly allergic to. Lactose intolerance is fairly common in the United States. As many as 90 percent of Asian Americans and 75 percent of Hispanic Americans, African Americans, and Native Americans may exhibit lactose intolerance (*Lactose Intolerance,* 2003). This may be because non-Caucasians did not commonly include dairy products as part of their diet (National Institutes of Health, 2007). Food allergies come from both environmental and genetic factors. Diet in infancy is one critical factor. Risk for food allergy from diet can be prevented in several ways. Milk or milk products should not be introduced to children before age 1 year. Children should not have eggs until they are 2 years old. Peanuts, tree nuts, shellfish, and fish

Wadsworth/Cengage Learning

Lactose intolerance is a common allergic reaction to lactose, the simple sugar found in milk. Good communication between teachers and parents regarding a child's food allergies should be maintained.

should not be a part of a child's menu until the child is at least 3 years old and should be done so then with caution (Fiocchi, Assa'ad, & Bahna, 2006). One study has shown that children's earlier exposure to peanuts at 12 months has decreased the reaction age to 14 months since 2000, whereas in the mid-1990s the first exposure was at 19 months and first reaction at 21 months (Green et al., 2007). Other possible risk factors for allergies include maternal diet during pregnancy and breastfeeding, cesarean section, exposure to tobacco smoke, and taking multiple vitamins (Kaza, Knight, & Bahna, 2007).

An allergic reaction is triggered when the food is consumed and a person's immune system incorrectly identifies a specific component of that food as something harmful (Li, 2006). This type of reaction is most often accompanied by itching or hives and swelling of the lips. In more serious cases, an anaphylactic reaction may occur. These symptoms appear quickly and include difficulty breathing, rapid heart beating, loss of consciousness, and cardiac arrest. The following paragraph discusses treatment for this type of reaction, and Figure 7-2 shows the epinephrine auto-injector pen that would be used. If a child is suspected of having an allergic reaction to a food, use of that food should be halted immediately, and the child should be taken to a physician for diagnosis. Sixty-three percent of teachers may have a child with a food allergy in care (Wachter, 2004), and up to one-fourth of these children may not yet have had an allergic reaction (Powers, Bergren, & Finnegan, 2007). For children with known allergies, a teacher should have a Food Allergy Action Plan. The Food Allergy and Anaphylaxis Network (FAAN) created this plan for schools; a copy can be found at http://www.foodallergy.org/actionplan.pdf. This plan includes the symptoms or signs to look for in case an allergic reaction occurs, as well as the most common bodily areas where these signs of allergy may occur, such as the mouth and throat

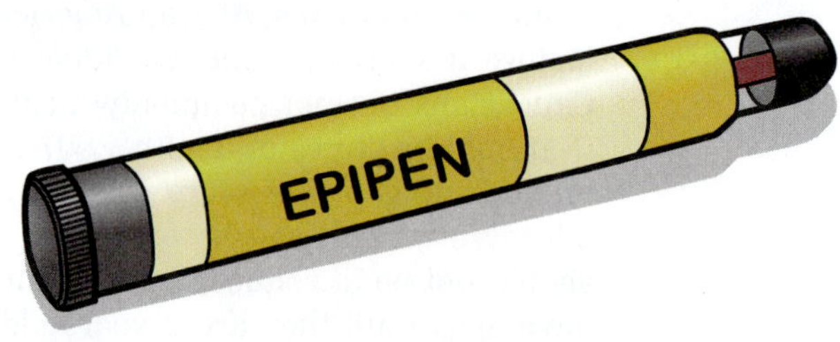

FIGURE 7-2
The EpiPen™ automatic intramuscular injection device is used to inject epinephrine for emergency treatment of anaphylaxis or shock.

(Chang, 2004). Very young children may pull or scratch at their tongue or put a hand in their mouth when they are having a reaction ("In Their Own Words," 2004). Older children might tell you that the food is too spicy or that their tongue feels prickly or strange. For children whose parents do not know they have an allergy, familiarity with common reactions is very important. Teachers can help to implement strategies to identify children at risk and increase awareness and prevention so that children who have allergic reactions can have the best possible outcomes (Leo & Clark, 2007).

The action plan also includes the steps to be taken if a serious anaphylactic reaction does occur. A medically appropriate measure, such as using an epinephrine auto-injector pen, might be necessary. Figure 7-2 shows what an EpiPen® looks like. FAAN also shows the newer double injection pen called the Twinject® and instructs how to use it. This newer device is for children whose symptoms do not go away in 10 minutes and who therefore need another dose. It is important for the teacher to know how to use these devices. There are trainer epinephrine auto-injector pens available from FAAN (1-800-929-4040). If there is a child in care who is at risk for this type of emergency, then parents should provide a regular supply of epinephrine auto-injector pens. It is important to check the epinephrine auto-injector pen regularly to make sure it is not out of date. When an emergency arises, the use of an epinephrine auto-injector pen may be critical to saving a child's life. Knowledge and use of these pen devices helps the early childhood educator to provide optimal treatment for allergic reactions (Leo & Clark, 2007; Sicherer & Simon, 2007).

Parents should inform teachers, and teachers should ask, whether a child suffers from a food allergy during the orientation. Parents should describe the exact reaction they have previously observed so that the teacher can be alert for those signs. If needed, parents should provide the early childhood educator with the pen devices in case of a life-threatening allergic reaction. Teachers should post reminders of food allergies of the children in care on the refrigerator and in other obvious places where they can be seen during both food preparation and serving. Whoever prepares the food should be careful to read labels for ingredients. Beginning in 2006, the Food Allergen Labeling and Consumer Protection Act mandates that labels for foods containing milk, eggs, fish, crustacean shellfish, peanuts, tree nuts, wheat, and soy—as well as foods whose ingredients "may contain" those common allergens—must declare the food in common language that a 7-year-old could read. If there is an allergy to foods that might be used in art projects, such as using peanut butter for a bird feeder, it is important to limit those projects to children who are not allergic or, better yet, skip those types of projects altogether. Teachers should not let children share food, especially if it is brought from home. Teachers should advise parents of all children in the early education program of any food allergies present and limit the types of foods parents can bring in for special treats, such as for a birthday or holiday. At least one teacher in the early education environment should have training in the use of equipment such as the epinephrine auto-injector pen and be able to follow directions in the Food Allergy Action Plan. A copy of the Food Allergy Action Plan and medication for allergic reaction must be carried on all field trips that include a child with food allergies, in case of exposure to allergenic foods, so that an emergency can be handled correctly. For better management of food allergies in the early education environment, Holland (2004) suggested the guidelines in Table 7-4.

TABLE 7-4
Guidelines for Risk Management of Food Allergies in Early Childhood Education Environments

- Develop written policies.
- Establish written emergency procedures, using the Food Action Plan.
- Plan menus that consider food allergies and intolerances present in the children in care.
- Make meals and snacks safe—do not allow any of the offending foods near an allergic child, and do not encourage sharing of the offending food.
- Do not share cups, utensils, or pacifiers.
- Review recipes, plans, and labels for activities such as cooking projects and art projects.
- Adopt a team approach—have everyone in care help to monitor for food allergies.

Based on information from Holland, M. (2004). "That food makes me SICK!": Managing food allergies and intolerances in early childhood settings. *Young Children,* 59(2), 42–46.

- **anaphylaxis** *reaction to an allergen that causes an attack that can result in collapse or death.*

REALITY *Check*

Peanut Allergy

In recent years, greater media focus and information has been available on allergy to peanuts. The prevalence of peanut allergy in American children doubled from 1997 to 2002 and appears to have reached epidemic proportions (Sicherer & Sampson, 2007). It is estimated that allergy to peanuts alone affects approximately 1.5 million people (MayoClinic.com, 2007). Peanut allergy is an important issue for early childhood education environments for three reasons. The first is that the most common time for food allergies is between infancy and age 3 years. The average age at first exposure has decreased to 12 months, and the average age for first reaction is 14 months for children born after 2000 (Green et al., 2007). Peanut allergy occurs in approximately 5 percent of that age group. In fact, the allergy to peanuts represents 28 percent of food allergies; it occurs before age 1 year in 46 percent of cases, and before age 15 years in 93 percent of cases (Moneret-Vautrin et al., 1998). The second reason is that many early childhood education environments often rely on peanut butter and peanut products to provide a less expensive form of protein in snacks and lunches. Other products used in daily food preparation may contain peanut oil or other peanut derivatives. These may include some Chinese, Mexican, Thai, and Vietnamese dishes, which, for cultural reasons, may have been added to the menu at the early education environment site. Traces of peanuts may also be found in some baked goods and ice creams that have been processed using equipment that may have come in contact with peanuts. The third reason is that more than 25 percent of children who are allergic to peanuts have not been identified (Sicherer, Munoz-Furlong, & Sampson, 2003). In addition to exposure to an actual food product containing peanuts, exposure to peanut dust or skin contact with someone handling a peanut product can bring on an allergic reaction.

Peanut allergies bring about more severe symptoms than any other food allergies. Approximately one-third of all emergency room visits for **anaphylaxis** are due to allergic reaction to peanuts. They are also more likely to cause death than many other food allergies. A recent study found that a peanut allergy was responsible for 80 percent of deaths due to food anaphylaxis (MayoClinic.com, 2007).

(continues)

REALITY *Check* (continued)

Anaphylactic shock occurs when one is hypersensitive to a substance and is exposed to the substance, resulting in an attack that sometimes causes collapse and death. Often this type of shock includes the constriction of the airway and consequent loss of the ability to breathe. This type of reaction to peanuts is often lifelong and severe (Sicherer & Sampson, 2007). Though research into preventive measures is being done, for now the only way to avoid these reactions is to prevent them in the first place (Fleischer, 2007).

Parents of children with a peanut allergy should inform the teacher immediately on entering their child into an early childhood education environment. Early childhood education environments are considered good places to implement strategies to provide increasing awareness and prevention of allergic reactions in young children (Leo & Clark, 2007). This enhanced awareness in the early childhood education environment may help prevent accidental ingestions for children with a peanut allergy (Yu et al., 2006). It is important for all early childhood education environments to have a plan of action prepared for reactions to food allergies. About 84 percent of children with food allergies have a reaction in school, and about one-fourth of children with food allergies have their first reaction at school (Powers, Bergren, & Finnegan, 2007).

If an early childhood setting has a child with this allergy, a plan for preventing exposure and follow-up if exposure does occur should be carefully organized and adopted and should include the following points:

- Work with the child's parent to develop a Food Allergy Action Plan for that child that includes information as to the severity of the allergy. This FAAN plan is the most reliable allergy emergency plan available (Powers, Bergren, & Finnegan, 2007).
- Inform everyone on staff, including volunteers, that this child has an allergy to peanuts and educate them as to what they are to do in case of emergency.
- Post this child's name and allergy wherever food is prepared, served, or in any place where a child could come in contact with foods, as a precautionary reminder to staff.
- Understand how to read food labels and avoid products that include peanuts and their derivatives so they are not served. Even with the new labeling law, this takes time. If this is too time consuming an issue, the teacher may wish to ask the child's parents to provide the child's lunch or snack. The teacher would still read labels and would try to keep exposure as low as possible.
- Have all food handlers wash their hands after food preparation and handling.
- As a safety precaution, have all staff and children wash their hands immediately after eating, to avoid skin contact possibilities.
- Do not allow an adult or child who may have had some form of peanut product in a recent meal to kiss or share a utensil with the child who has a peanut allergy (Maloney, Chapman, & Sicherer, 2006).
- After snacks and meals, wash the tables with warm soapy water so that any residue is removed.
- Notify all parents of children in care so that if they provide lunch or snacks, they can avoid peanut products. You might want to include a list of "safe" foods and snacks that do not contain peanuts or peanut products. This list should be updated periodically because ingredients change.
- A written emergency action plan, provided by the child's physician, should be on file. This will be the basis of the Food Allergy Action Plan that is created for the child.
- An epinephrine auto-injector, such as the EpiPen™, should be readily available, and there should be someone on staff at all times who understands how to administer it.
- If a field trip is planned, be aware of any possible exposure in the surroundings. Make sure the allergic child brings his or her own snack. Have the epinephrine auto-injector available, just in case.
- Guidelines about developing a food allergy plan for a child in school can be found at the Food Allergy and Anaphylaxis Network, http://www.foodallergy.org.

It is important to understand this allergy and be prepared to act on it, even if you do not know that there are any children in care who have it. Reactions to peanuts and their derivatives may happen on first exposure to them (Sicherer et al., 2001).

Food Allergies

Food allergies may pose great risk for some children in the early childhood education environment. It is important to identify those children with food allergies and take steps to make sure there is no exposure to those foods for children who are allergic. Risk management measures also include awareness of any form of exposure, learning how to use an epinephrine auto-injector pen, and being prepared to handle an emergency, should it exist.

7.6 OTHER CHILDHOOD NUTRITIONAL CHALLENGES

Other nutritional challenges that pose risk for children in care include dental caries, iron deficiency anemia, cardiovascular disease, and hypertension. These conditions may pose risk due to the shifts in children's diets (e.g., juice or sugared drinks replacing milk) and the prevalence of high-fat or highly sugared foods offered as snacks, advertised on television, and predominant in fast-food restaurants. More than 30 percent of a child's daily diet comes from low-nutrient-density foods (Miller, 2004).

Dental Caries

Dental caries, or cavities as they are commonly known, affect almost everyone in the population. Tooth decay causes dental caries, the most common disease in children, and occurs five times more often than the next most common childhood disease, which is asthma (Zamani, 2006). Approximately 28 percent of all children between the ages of 2 and 5 years have dental caries, and that percentage rises for African-American, Mexican-American, and poor children. Children with special needs are also at a higher risk for dental caries. Lewis and colleagues (2007) report that only 72 percent of children in the United States had a dental visit in 2003. For low-income children, this figure was even lower, at 62.5 percent. Although these numbers meet the goal of Healthy People 2010, they do not meet the dental needs of all children. Cultural beliefs and lack of knowledge about primary teeth may lead to barriers for early preventive care (Hilton et al., 2007). Hispanic and white children are more likely to have preventive dental care than are black children. A number of underlying issues may be responsible for why dental caries in children are occurring at greater rates than in the past.

Increase in soft-drink consumption has greatly contributed to the increasing risk of dental caries (O'Connor, Yang, & Nicklas, 2006; Abrams, 2007). The AAP and the AHA recommend that children limit the amount of juice consumed daily to 4 to 6 ounces of 100 percent juice and that other sugared beverages be restricted to occasional use (Gidding et al., 2006). They also encourage children to have two or more servings of calcium-rich dairy foods per day.

There may be social reasons as to why young children are not having their dental caries attended to. Some parents do not understand the importance of oral health for their children. Other parents may not have dental insurance or access to dental care. Low-income children in states with a child health insurance program are more likely to have access to dental care than those children in states without such a program (Lewis et al., 2007). Additionally, in some cultures, dental care is accessed only when it is deemed necessary, and not as a preventive measure (Lewis et al., 2007; Frank, 2004).

Zamani (2006) cites four factors that contribute to the development of dental caries: acid-producing bacteria, fermentable carbohydrates from sweet liquids including milk and juice, a vulnerable tooth, and time. Streptococcus and lactobacillus bacteria foster tooth decay. These bacteria are spread from one person to another through saliva from shared toothbrushes, cups, pacifiers, and utensils. Foods that are high in carbohydrates and sugar promote the formation of cavities. These fermentable carbohydrates in the form of starches break down as sugars, which change rapidly to acid when mixed with the acid-producing bacteria commonly found in the plaque present in the mouth. The acids produced break through the tooth's natural protective enamel barrier and form cavities in the vulnerable tooth. When sugar is ingested, the acid formation process lasts for about 25 minutes. Sticky items that contain sugar, such as honey, soft drinks, raisins, and bananas, lengthen the acid formation process. This is also true of sugars found in milk and fruit juices.

Fluoride use is the most effective method of preventing dental caries. Fluoride protects teeth by helping in tooth development and creating enamel that is more resistant to acid-causing bacteria that attack teeth (Cowling, 2007). It also helps to strengthen teeth later. Even a small amount helps to prevent cavities and tooth decay. Fluoride is added to about two-thirds of water supplies in the United States (NCCCHSR, 2007b). If the early childhood education environment is in an area with fluoridated water, children should be encouraged to drink the water. If fluoride is not in the water supply, then families should have their dentists prescribe fluoride supplements. Many family doctors include fluoride in the vitamin and mineral supplements given to babies. Twenty-five percent of U.S. children account for 75 percent of dental caries. Children who live in areas without fluoridated water, those who live in rural areas, and those who are members of minority groups are more likely than other children to have dental caries (Skinner et al., 1999). Approximately 95 percent of toothpastes today contain fluoride. It is important to note that a child receiving too much fluoride can get a condition called fluorosis, which causes white spots to form on permanent teeth (NCCCHSR, 2007b). If the water is fluoridated, infants and toddlers should not use toothpaste containing fluoride because they can easily swallow the toothpaste and may be at risk for fluorosis.

Teachers can ensure that the early childhood education environment is using good practices to prevent dental caries by providing foods with plenty of protein, calcium, and vitamins that support good oral health (Zamani, 2005a). Supporting children with meals and snacks that do not contain much sugar and eliminating "grazing" or open eating also help (AAP, 2004). Preventive methods for spreading bacteria include brushing teeth and avoiding sharing saliva contact items such as utensils, cups, pacifiers, and toothbrushes. In the national standards set forth in *Caring for Our Children,* the APHA and the AAP (2002) recommend that children should be encouraged to brush their teeth at least once a day, and infants' teeth and gums should be wiped with a clean cloth while in the early childhood education environment. Children with disabilities and other special needs may need extra assistance with brushing teeth. If a child has difficulty grasping the brush, a special brush or adaptive handle attachment can be used (Zamani, 2007).

Each child should have his or her own toothbrush that is clearly labeled. Toothbrushes should be child-sized and have soft bristles, and they should be

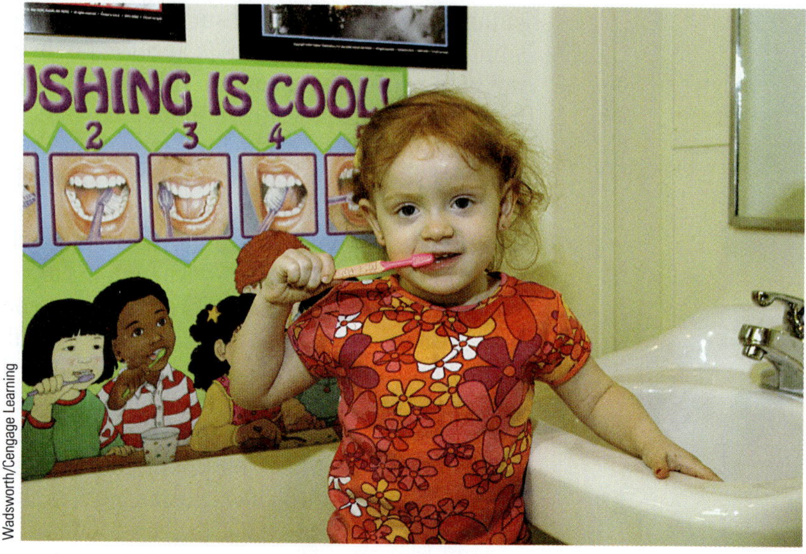

Wadsworth/Cengage Learning

Teeth brushing can be a fun and informative activity that teachers can add to their nutrition education program. Giving children the opportunity to brush after meals is another way to encourage good dental hygiene.

stored properly to prevent cross-contamination and buildup of bacteria. This should be done in open air so that bristles will dry out. Toothbrushes should have enough space between them so that they cannot drip on or touch each other. They should be changed every three to six months or immediately after a child has been ill. Toothpaste should not be shared either. A child can be given a small paper cup with the toothpaste on the rim, to put on his brush, and can then fill the cup with water for rinsing. This cuts down risk for saliva contact and the spread of bacteria.

Table 7-5 gives teachers some guidelines for helping protect children in care from dental caries.

TABLE 7-5
Reducing Risk of Dental Caries in Early Childhood Education Environments

- Encourage a mother who breastfeeds to continue.
- Never let a baby fall asleep with a bottle still in his mouth.
- Introduce a cup to a baby before the age of 8 months.
- Help to wean a baby from the bottle by the first birthday.
- Encourage children to drink water instead of juice.
- Encourage children to brush their teeth.
- Have children rinse their mouths out with water after snacks.
- Wipe out the mouths of infants and toddlers with a clean cloth or piece of gauze.
- Provide tooth brushes and a sanitary place to store them.
- Help children brush after meals.
- Do not share utensils, pacifiers, or cups.
- Provide healthy meals and snacks.
- Provide oral health information to parents.
- Provide simple oral health education to children.

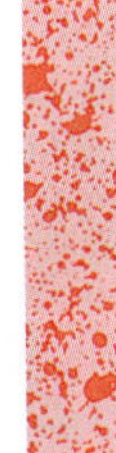

Pause for Reflection

How many soft drinks do you drink in a week? Were you aware that each 12 ounces of a soft drink contains about 10 teaspoons of sugar? Considering the amount of soft drinks you consume in a week, how much sugar have you consumed? After knowing that answer, do you intend to cut down on soft-drink consumption?

Iron Deficiency Anemia

Iron deficiency anemia is one of the most prevalent nutritional problems in childhood. Approximately 2.4 million children are affected by iron deficiency. It is two times more likely to occur among poor children than among those whose families are not poor. Older infants and young children are more likely to be at risk for iron deficiency because the iron stored in their bodies when they were born diminishes over time. African-American and Asian-American children have greater risk for iron deficiency anemia than do white or Native American children (Cusick, Mei, & Cogswell, 2007). Overweight toddlers are more likely than those who are of average weight to be iron deficient, and these overweight toddlers are more likely to be Hispanic than white or African American (Brotanek et al., 2007). Anemia due to iron deficiency may cause a shortened attention span, irritability, and fatigue. Children with iron deficiency anemia may have negative consequences for cognition, behavior, and health (Skalicky et al., 2006). The AAP recommends that babies between 9 and 12 months old be screened for anemia, as well as children ages 1 to 5 years who may be at risk (Reeves, 2007a).

The only way to avoid iron deficiency and resulting anemia is to get adequate supplies of iron in the diet or to supplement the diet with a doctor-recommended vitamin compound containing iron.

Infants receive most of their nutrients from formulas or breast milk. Most formulas provide the necessary iron (PageWise, 2001). Breast milk provides iron also, but when they reach the age of about 4 to 5 months, infants need more iron than their mothers' milk can provide. Approximately 75 percent of children in this country are breastfed for at least a while. Therefore, doctors recommend vitamin supplements that include iron to prevent iron deficiency. Baby cereals are fortified with iron to help provide the necessary iron in the diet.

As a child grows, more sources of iron, such as meats, fish, poultry, green leafy vegetables, and whole grains, are necessary to prevent iron deficiency. However, many children do not eat balanced diets. The quality of diets today, with high sugar, high sodium, and high fat and with lower than recommended intakes of whole grains, fruits, and vegetables, indicate that many children's diets may be iron deficient. Iron deficiency in lower-income children has been linked to poor compliance with nutritional feeding practices, due possibly to inadequate funds or lack of parental understanding of the importance of diet. Another cause of iron deficiency is from drinking too much milk. It is suggested that milk should be included in a child's diet but not be a major portion of it.

The best way to prevent iron deficiency and resulting anemia is through education of parents, teachers, and the children themselves. Menus at early childhood education programs were found to be lacking in foods that could help children meet their requirement for iron (Padget & Briley, 2005). Teachers who

Wadsworth/Cengage Learning

An adequate supply of iron must be provided in a growing child's diet, but frequently it is not. Teachers should try to ensure that children get enough of this essential mineral in the meals that are served in early childhood education environments.

are aware of the importance of iron can provide more balanced diets with better food selections. Iron-rich foods include green leafy vegetables, eggs, beans and other legumes, meats including poultry and seafood, raisins, nuts, and seeds. It also includes whole grain breads, cereals, and rice. In cases where supplementation is necessary, iron-fortified breads and cereals should be used.

Cardiovascular Disease and Hypertension

The diet of many Americans contains too many calories, too much fat, and too much cholesterol. It is also high in sodium. The Bogalusa Heart Study is an ongoing research project focusing on **cardiovascular disease** risk factors present in children's lives (Perry, 2004). The National Cholesterol Education Program (NCEP), sponsored by the U.S. Department of Health and Human Services (USDHHS), is also concerned with the issue of children's diet and cardiovascular risk.

- **cardiovascular disease** *disease resulting from impaired function of the heart and/or surrounding arteries.*

Early elevated levels of cholesterol can lead to the development of early **coronary atherosclerosis**. The combination of diet and genetic risk factors can trigger a higher incidence of this disease than in the normal population. Higher blood cholesterol levels can also lead to **coronary heart disease** (CHD), which is the number one cause of death in this country. Due to the increase in obesity, it is now recommended that children ages 2 and up be screened for their cholesterol levels and children who are found to have high levels of cholesterol should begin to take statin drugs as young as 8 years of age (Daniels, Greer, and the Committee on Nutrition, 2008).

- **coronary atherosclerosis** *disease of the heart resulting in degeneration of the artery walls due to fat buildup.*
- **coronary heart disease** *disease of the arteries that feed the heart muscle.*

Children who eat diets with excessive calories and too much fat tend to be overweight. This is another risk factor in cardiovascular diseases (see Figure 7-3). One recent study found that hypertension among children has increased over the past decade due to overweight (Munter et al., 2004). This is especially true for African-American and Mexican-American children. As children's weight continues to increase over time, physicians are worried that hypertension will rise too.

Excess weight and high sodium intake contribute to **hypertension**. Hypertension in children is usually referred to as secondary hypertension. In addition to obesity and/or excessive salt intake, it also occurs because of lack of physical exercise and lead poisoning (Zamani, 2005b). Hypertension causes the heart and blood vessels to overwork and over time can lead to

- **hypertension** *very high blood pressure.*

FIGURE 7-3
Risk factors for cardiovascular disease.

Risk Factors
High cholesterol
Being male
Diabetes mellitus
High blood pressure
Obesity
Cigarette smoking
Vascular (blood vessel) disease
Family members with CHD before age 60

stroke, heart failure, and damage to the eyes and other organs. The Bogalusa Heart Study found that almost all children younger than 10 years consume more than the DRI levels of sodium. High sodium intake can be linked to the later development of high blood pressure. Convenience foods and fast foods are high in sodium. Some of children's favorite foods contain too much salt, including chips, hot dogs, lunch meats, canned soups, and store-bought breads. Menus in early childhood education programs often feature these foods. The average daily intake of sodium for preschoolers was found to exceed the DRI (Padget & Briley, 2005; Story, Kaphingst, & French, 2006). Screening for hypertension is now recommended to begin at age 3 years.

The best way to improve the risk factors for cardiovascular diseases and hypertension is to modify the diet. Following the recommendations of the Dietary Guidelines for Americans, children's fat intake should contain between 25 and 35 percent of their total daily calories. Saturated fats, depending on the child's age, should be decreased to less than 10 percent of total calories, and sodium intake should be decreased. It is recommended that after age 2, children should be given low-fat or nonfat dairy products, including milk.

Children should also eat diets higher in carbohydrates, which means more fruits, vegetables, and grain products (Padget & Briley, 2005). The MyPyramid Food for Kids and the AHA recommend that, when choosing grains, at least half should be whole-grain choices. They also recommend that there be more selection of dark-green leafy and yellow vegetables. Promoting healthy eating habits by offering a well-balanced selection of foods that are lower in cholesterol, fat, and sodium can help as prevention measures. Helpful guidelines for following these recommendations are found in Table 7-6.

TABLE 7-6
Guidelines to Decrease Fat and Sodium Intake

- Provide plenty of fresh fruits and vegetables.
- Serve whole-grain breads and cereals.
- Use only lean meats, poultry, and fish.
- Choose low-fat dairy products.
- Choose fats from vegetable sources such as low-fat margarine and canola oil. Limit the intake of these fat products.
- Select cooking methods that are lower-fat alternatives to frying, such as grilling or baking.
- Avoid high-sodium foods such as hot dogs, lunch meats, and chips; if these foods are occasionally used, do so in moderation.
- At fast-food restaurants, carefully select menu items that are lower in fat and sodium.
- Moderate the use of frozen, packaged, and canned foods.
- Use margarine products made with unsaturated vegetable oils instead of saturated vegetable oils such as coconut and palm kernel oil.
- Set a good example by eating healthy foods.

Key Concept 7.6

Other Childhood Nutritional Challenges

Dental caries, iron deficiency anemia, cardiovascular disease, and hypertension also pose risks to the health and well-being of children in early childhood education environments. Teachers should provide healthy food selections that include lower fat and lower sugar choices, as well as foods that are rich in iron. Teachers can also offer children an opportunity to brush their teeth. They can model eating well for children in the early childhood education environment.

7.7 IMPLICATIONS FOR TEACHERS

Educating both children and parents about nutrition can help the teacher to protect children from the nutritional risks that are posed in childhood. Having nutritional policies that provide protective measures and manage risk are very important. Providing well-balanced meals full of healthy food selections is one excellent tool for risk management. In planning physical activity, a teacher can make sure that it is age appropriate and that some of this activity is vigorous so that children have the opportunity to be as active as possible during the recommended length of time on a daily basis. A teacher should understand the issue of food allergy, know which children have allergies to which foods, and continually survey the environment to prevent any compromise to their well-being. Nutrition information shared with everyone in the early childhood education environment can lead to an environment that will protect children's health and well-being.

Education

Children may be bombarded by messages about food through visits to fast-food restaurants, watching food ads on television and websites, and looking at food labels in supermarkets. These messages make it hard for children to understand that good nutrition is not present in all foods. Children may have poor food selections at home or in the early childhood education environment due to convenience and the time crunch. It is important to talk about food and nutrition with children often. An early childhood education environment has an impact on children's developing food habits (Fuhr & Barclay, 1998). Looking at labels and discussing the nutrition of the food being eaten should occur regularly so that children begin to understand the importance of good food in their diets. There are a number of ways that the teacher can help to educate children and parents about nutritional risk. Table 7-7 lists some of these methods.

For Families

In addition to what teachers can do for children and parents, families can play a major role in preventing nutritional risks to children. Parents can help prevent inadequate nutrition or obesity in their children. They can give teachers reports of what a child ate over a specified time period so that teachers know what the diets of children are like at home. Parents should be made aware that a permissive feeding style, where children can eat or drink

TABLE 7-7
Educational Methods for Nutrition and Nutritional Risk

Methods for Educating about Nutrition and Nutritional Risk

• Telling	Explaining and providing information
• Showing	Role modeling good nutritional habits
• Providing resources	Offering handouts and website addresses for parents
• Questions	Ask children questions to assess their understanding
• Practicing	Engaging in physical activity, making healthy food selections

Adapted from Story, M., Holt, K., Sofka, D., & Clark, E. (Eds.). (2002). *Bright Futures in practice: Nutrition—pocket guide.* Arlington, VA: National Center for Education in Maternal and Child Health.

This teacher is showing these girls about using wheat flour to improve the nutrition of the muffins they are making.

Carol had a part-time job and did not rely much on child care for her daughter Jessamyn, age 2½ years. Carol had the opportunity to be promoted into the job of her dreams and she took it. Early every morning, she dropped Jessie off at the family child care home. In the evening, when she returned to pick Jessie up, Carol was exhausted and fell into the habit of feeding Jessie cold cereal almost every night or picking up hamburgers, fries, and soft drinks. In the mornings, cold cereal was breakfast because it was easy and quick. Aleta, the family child teacher, noticed how Jessie seemed to be coming down with more colds and seemed to lack the healthy glow she had had when she first arrived. Aleta spoke with Carol about Jessie's diet, and Carol admitted that she knew it should be different, but she didn't know what she should do and had very little time to figure it out. Aleta shared some nutritional information, gave Carol a few suggestions, and provided Carol with some tips that would improve the whole family's diet. Carol was willing to make changes because of Aleta's support in providing nutritional information and tips for organizing food selection and menu planning. The entire family made a better diet their project, and it benefited the health of everyone in the family.

anything, at any time, will lead to poor diets (Rose, 2007). Families today have complex lives with full schedules and so may rely on convenience or fast foods to augment their meals. Teachers can provide nutritional information through newsletters and may even offer suggestions for quick, easy, healthy meals or provide families with nutritional tool kits, as suggested by Huettig et al., 2006. If parents know how to avoid using too many convenience or fast foods in their children's diets, then children are more likely to follow good dietary practices. When families are involved in working with the early childhood education environment to improve their child's nutrition, children are more likely to cooperate, and the effort is more likely to be successful. Families can also help children get involved in more physical activities when they are home. This may be a challenge for families who live in neighborhoods where safety is an issue; it has been shown that lack of neighborhood safety may put a child at risk for obesity because he doesn't leave the house to play outside (Gable, Chang, & Krull, 2007). Parents can look to provide space near or in the home where a child can actively play or exercise safely (Sorte & Daeschel, 2006). Teachers can work with families to come up with suggestions for safe physical activities that can be done indoors or help them find places for physical activities that are safe. The ADA has taken the position that in order to be effective in providing good nutrition and physical activities to ensure the health and well-being of children and to prevent obesity, families and early childhood education environments must work together for success (ADA, 2006b).

Some good nutrition practices for parents' education are listed in Table 6-3 (p. 247). Parents should be involved in planning menus in early childhood education environments and should work at home to complement what children are eating in care (Briley & Roberts-Gray, 2005; Rose, 2007).

Role Modeling

Role modeling takes place in numerous ways. First, by eating with children and making healthy selections from the food served, the teacher indicates that this is an acceptable way to eat. When physical activity is structured, the teacher should be a role model for participating in the activity and should show enthusiasm for movement and working toward fitness.

If television is used at all in the early childhood education environment, it should be used sparingly. Discouraging eating while the television is on is another way to model to children that this is not a healthy thing to do.

Cultural Competence

Cultural competence may prove to be a key to managing nutritional risk such as obesity, dental caries, and lack of physical activity. Understanding that food and culture are clearly related is a good starting point. In some cultures, traditional foods are a mainstay and may represent more than just something to eat. Food patterns may be difficult to change, but providing information on healthier selections or food preparation methods might help a family make some shifts away from nutritional risk. As much as possible, this information should be presented to parents in their native language.

Another method of helping reduce nutritional risk is to introduce families to the foods that children are eating in care. Some cultures may adapt to the feeding practices that they see being used by people they trust. Others are less likely to do so because of family food traditions, but they may still see that their children can enjoy other selections when outside the family environment. It would also be helpful to understand the feeding practices and foods being served in the home. Having families create a book or a journal about their lives at home would be helpful for teachers to understand food practices. This could lead to a greater understanding of what foods from other cultures could be introduced into the early childhood education environment.

A specific issue that is of concern to dieticians in the United States is the parental practice in some cultures, such as Latino, of encouraging children to eat even when they say they are full (Matheson et al., 2006; Hughes et al., 2006). Other cultures may practice the same feeding behavior. In one study, 11 out of 12 groups of parents comprised of Hispanic, white, and African-American parents all encouraged children to eat more even when full (Sherry et al., 2004). The controlling of a child's food intake appears to encourage children to become overweight (Melgar-Quinonez & Kaiser, 2004; Satter, 2005). Latino and Native American children and African-American girls are more likely to be overweight than children from other ethnic backgrounds. This issue can be related to a number of things, including food insecurity in the past, high fat content in food preparation, and drinking too many sweetened beverages. Making sure that food is given in age-appropriate portions or allowing children to self-select may be helpful. If children are encouraged to eat only until they are full, they may learn to turn down food once they are satiated.

Cultural sensitivity is important when considering encouragement of the consumption of dairy products in early childhood education environments. A number of cultures do not regularly consume dairy products. These cultures may also tend to replace the consumption of milk with beverage selections that are sugary, such as juices or sodas. Children can learn to make healthier beverage selections if their parents do not want them drinking milk. By offering water as an alternative to sweetened beverages or excess amounts of juice, a teacher may be lessening risk for obesity and dental caries.

Cultural competence should be practiced not only in the selection of meals but also in the discussions that go on while eating. This is a good time to talk to children about nutritional challenges.

Wadsworth/Cengage Learning

Supervision

Supervision is key to helping teachers manage nutritional risk by observing children and their food choices, modifying the menu for healthier food selections, and making sure children participate in the right amount of physical exercise. Being aware of a child's growth pattern can help a teacher to assess whether a child appears to be either too lean or too overweight. Table 7-8 provides some key indicators of nutritional risk adapted from *Bright Futures*

TABLE 7-8
Key Indicators of Nutritional Risk

If the child

- Consumes fewer than 2 servings of fruit daily
- Consumes fewer than 3 servings of vegetables daily
- Consumes fewer than 2 servings of dairy foods daily
- Consumes fewer than 2 servings of meat or meat substitutes daily
- Exhibits poor appetite
- Has food jags
- Eats at a fast-food restaurant more than 3 times per week
- Has a BMI of less than 5 percent
- Has a BMI of more than 85 percent
- Is physically inactive
- Has dental caries
- Has iron deficiency anemia
- Has a chronic disease or a condition that might compromise nutrition
- May be food insecure due to inadequate financial resources for food

Adapted from Story, M., Holt, K., Sofka, D., & Clark, E. (Eds.). (2002). *Bright futures in practice: Nutrition—pocket guide*. Arlington, VA: National Center for Education in Maternal and Child Health.

in Practice: Nutrition—Pocket Guide (Story et al., 2002). It is important to involve the family in helping to assess risk.

Cost may be an issue for some families in their selection of foods or the way they are prepared. Some families in care may be struggling to make ends meet. Talking to families about their food selections may help the teacher understand whether this is the case. If so, then the teacher can help the family connect to resources providing services or foods that allow families to lessen risk for food insecurity at home.

Supervision is also necessary for children with food allergies. Making sure the guidelines in Table 7-3 are followed will greatly lessen risk for reactions to food allergies. Having everybody in the environment involved in creating a protective environment for the children in care will provide good risk management for food allergies.

CHAPTER SUMMARY

Protecting good nutrition in early childhood education environments is necessary to help children avoid problems such as hunger and malnutrition, obesity, lack of physical activity and exercise, food allergies, and other nutritional risks. Teachers should create nutritional policies that help the environment support the child with protective nutritional practices. Teachers can use education, work with families, provide role modeling, and supervise to manage risk.

TO GO BEYOND

Additional resources for this chapter can be found by visiting the book companion website at www.cengage.com/education/robertson. This supplemental material includes chapter objectives, internet exercises, reflection questions, quizzes, web links, glossary and flash cards, case studies, frequently asked questions, downloadable forms and tables, curriculum supplements, more reality checks, additional key concepts, references, and more.

Chapter Review Critical Thinking Applications

1. Assess how nutritional challenges affect the teacher.
2. Define and discuss the issue of obesity and the impact it has on a child's health and emotional well-being.
3. Define and discuss the positive aspects of physical activity on the diet of a young child.
4. Describe how food insecurity might have an effect on a child's ability to learn and grow.

As an Individual

1. How does hunger affect the children in your local area? Research the issue and relate the special programs that help these children. What agencies might you contact if this issue involved children in your early childhood education environment?

2. Survey several local preschools and observe what they do to include physical activity, both structured and unstructured, in the daily routine of care. If you wish, you could do this for a kindergarten, first-, or second-grade class at a local elementary school.
3. Further research the issue of peanut allergy and create a nutritional policy to prevent risk to a child who might be allergic to peanuts and is in your care.
4. Observe Saturday morning television for one hour. Count the number of food commercials you see. Choose two of the commercials and list the methods they use to attract children to the foods advertised.

As a Group

1. Evaluate the impact that a child with a peanut allergy might have on the entire early childhood education environment. Do research on an EpiPen™ and give a basic demonstration on how it should be used. (Do not actually use the pen, but describe how it should be done.)
2. Separate into smaller groups and discuss childhood obesity. Each group should make five suggestions that would help an obese child improve her weight. Compare these with those generated by other groups, and as a class pick the seven most important strategies.
3. Hold a class potluck, with students bringing foods from diverse cultures that represent people in your local area. Compare the tastes, possible nutritional values, and cooking methods, and share ideas for healthier adaptations of the same foods.
4. Divide into smaller groups and do some research on what dental resources are available in your area for children whose parents cannot afford a dentist.

Case Studies

1. Mario is an overweight, inactive 4-year-old in your program. You notice that he eats sporadically at school, usually heading for meats and sweet foods first. He doesn't seem to like vegetables at all. His mother comes to you concerned about Mario's inactivity, which she feels does not help his ability to get along with other children. She asks for your help. What do you suggest?
2. Heidi notices that few children in her class of 3-year-olds seem to enjoy vegetables. What activities could she plan that might increase the children's interest in eating vegetables? What else might she do?
3. Debra is a kindergarten teacher who supervises the kindergartners' lunch one or two days a week. She notices that many children are bringing to school food for their lunches that isn't very healthy, and in addition, they are exchanging foods with other children. How might this impact the diets and the abilities of children to learn? What about the possible food allergies of these children? How might she tackle this problem?

CHAPTER 8

Providing Good Nutrition in Early Childhood Education Environments

After reading this chapter, you should be able to:

8.1 Specific Nutritional Policies

Define and discuss the need for nutrition policies that address growth and development to prevent risk, provide protection, and promote nutritional well-being.

8.2 Early Feeding and the Infant in Care

Discuss breastfeeding, bottle feeding, and the introduction of solids into the infant's diet, including the developmental implications and practices for the teacher.

8.3 Feeding the Autonomous Toddler

Discuss the impact of development on the feeding behavior of the toddler, and describe strategies for the teacher to redirect that behavior.

8.4 Food and the Preschooler

Discuss the food behaviors of the preschooler and strategies for the teacher to guide the child to behaviors that foster well-being.

8.5 School-Age Nutrition

Discuss the nutritional needs of the school-aged child and strategies for the teacher to meet these needs that may be compromised by outside influences.

8.6 Nutrition and the Child with Special Needs

Explain how special needs might affect the nutrition and feeding of a child, and discuss specific strategies to meet the child's nutritional challenges.

8.7 Implications for Teachers

Describe and discuss methods for education, supervision, and role modeling to ensure good nutrition for children in care.

8.1 SPECIFIC NUTRITIONAL POLICIES

The importance of providing good nutrition in early childhood education environments cannot be stressed enough. Greater numbers of children are relying on their teachers to provide a significant portion of their nutritional needs. Teachers play a significant role in the nutritional well-being of children. Creating policies to meet the changing nutritional needs of the children in care is a vital risk management tool that can affect the way children grow and learn. The following indicators reveal the need for those policies:

- Approximately 76 percent of babies are breastfed for at least a while in the United States (Gidding et al., 2006). Breastfed babies and their mothers should receive support from the early childhood education environment (Zero to Three, 2007a).
- Teachers are being asked to take on the role of nutritional gate-keeper for children (Penn State News, 2003; Story, Kaphingst, & French, 2006).
- Seventy-eight percent of children are not consuming the recommended amount of vegetables, and 63 percent are not consuming the recommended amount of fruits (Nicklas & Johnson, 2004). Most preschool age children do not get enough fiber and get far too much sugar in their diets (Kranz, Smicklas-Wright, & Francis, 2006). Menu planning for early childhood education environments should be done by someone who has training (Romaine et al., 2007).
- Children who are in the early childhood education environment eight hours or more should receive foods that provide 50 to 67 percent of their nutritional needs (Briley & Roberts-Gray, 2005).
- Providing a pleasant eating environment helps set the stage for good nutritional habits (Satter, 2005; Parlakian & Lerner, 2007; Sigman-Grant et al., 2008). Teachers can influence children's food preferences, eating behaviors, and willingness to try new foods (Bellows & Anderson, 2006). Feeding practices in early childhood education environments should be child centered (Rose, 2007).
- It is important to recognize a child's developmental abilities in respect to feeding him (Butte et al., 2004; Sigman-Grant, 2008).

Many children are in early childhood education environments for more than eight hours a day, yet their nutritional needs may not be met by the teacher. The teacher may be unaware of nutritional standards or may not know how to plan menus to meet those standards (Briley & Roberts-Gray, 2005; Story, Kaphingst & French, 2006). Many states have no regulations concerning the nutritional content of the food served in child care centers and family child care homes (Benjamin et al., 2008). The teacher's perceptions about what a child will or will not eat may also influence food choices. For example, some teachers may believe that children do not like vegetables and prefer foods that are like fast foods, so they may create menus that they think children will like and eat. Teachers may also have an unrealistic view of the developmentally appropriate portions that children should eat and often have a "clean your plate" mentality that is inappropriate (Fox, Reidy, Karwe, & Ziegler, 2006). These factors can have a negative effect on menu-planning choices and the balance of nutrition provided.

Cost is always a factor when trying to balance care with the business of caregiving. Many teachers watch for sales, buy in bulk, and look for other opportunities to cut back on cost. It may be less expensive to provide higher-fat foods like french fries and juice-based sweetened beverages than it is fresh fruits and vegetables and 100 percent juices. For toddlers, the third most common energy source in this country today is fruit-flavored drinks (Fox, Reidy, Novak, & Ziegler, 2006). Saving should never be so important as to sacrifice children's well-being. Early childhood education centers and family child care homes may be eligible to participate in funded food programs that will help defray the costs for children from low-income families.

Convenience may also be a factor in food selection in early childhood education environments. Menus in these centers have typically been in use a long time with few updates and are limited by lack of nutritional knowledge on the part of the staff (Padget & Briley, 2005). If the effort is not made to change menus or to learn more about nutrition, then choices may be limited.

Culture may also affect food choices in early childhood education environments. Cultural specific feeding practices can influence a child's diet in both positive and negative ways (Matheson et al., 2006; Gidding et al., 2006; Hughes et al., 2007; Duerksen et al., 2007). The teacher may have a cultural background that influences cooking and menu selection, and may even limit choices available (Story, Holt, & Sofka, 2000; Ziegler, Hanson, et al., 2006). For example, a teacher who is Hispanic may be more likely to serve fresh fruits and soups, but also serve fruit-flavored drinks (Mennella et al., 2006). Fresh fruits and soups are obviously very good choices, but poorer choices should be altered, for example, by serving milk or water instead of fruit-flavored drinks. Culturally competent teachers have the skills to work with diverse populations (Obegi & Ritblatt, 2005); these include knowing the diversity of the children in care and foods that represent those diverse cultures. Children may or may not eat foods from cultural backgrounds that are different from their own and may have family cultural influences that limit what they will eat. Television and fast-food commercials may have an effect on what the teacher fixes and what children will eat.

The early childhood educator who serves the family in their home may have an added difficulty providing proper nutrition. Many parents who hire nannies are focused on work and so busy that planning food for themselves and their children may be problematic. Some parents may eat all of their meals away from home and only provide what they consider to be necessities for the child or what they think the child will eat, with little thought given to overall nutritional value in the diet. Parents may have no knowledge about nutrition and how it can affect the growth and development of a child. This can make caring for the nutritional needs of a child a challenge to a nanny.

Another factor to consider is the purpose of the early childhood education environment. Briley, Roberts-Gray, and Simpson (1994) pointed out that there are three perspectives on the purpose of early childhood care and education prior to kindergarten: (1) to promote the well-being of the child, (2) to provide a service to the community, and (3) to provide a living for the provider. If the early childhood education environment is focused on the second or third perspective, the nutritional well-being of the child may be at risk. Many public school settings, such as universal preschools, kindergartens, and first through third grades, are more likely to focus on education, and nutrition may take second place. Children in such settings may be at risk for good nutrition.

Children have specific nutritional needs at each stage of their growth and development. It is essential that the teacher be aware of these nutritional requirements and create policies that will help to meet the specific needs of the children as they grow and develop.

Nutritional policies that will help the teacher meet the specific needs of the children in care are listed here:

- *Early Feeding and the Infant:* understanding the changing needs of infants, including breastfeeding, bottle feeding, and the introduction of solid foods.
- *Establishing the Feeding Behavior of the Toddler:* understanding the impact of development and changing needs on the behavior of the toddler regarding food and eating.
- *Food and the Preschool Child:* understanding the food behaviors and changing needs of the preschooler.
- *School-Age Nutrition:* understanding nutritional needs and how these needs are threatened by outside influences, including school food programs.
- *Nutrition and the Child with Special Needs:* understanding how special needs might affect the diet and feeding of a child.
- *Implications for Teachers:* understanding the need for education, supervision, support, and role modeling to ensure good nutrition.

This child is making a transition from being fed by his teacher to eating finger foods.

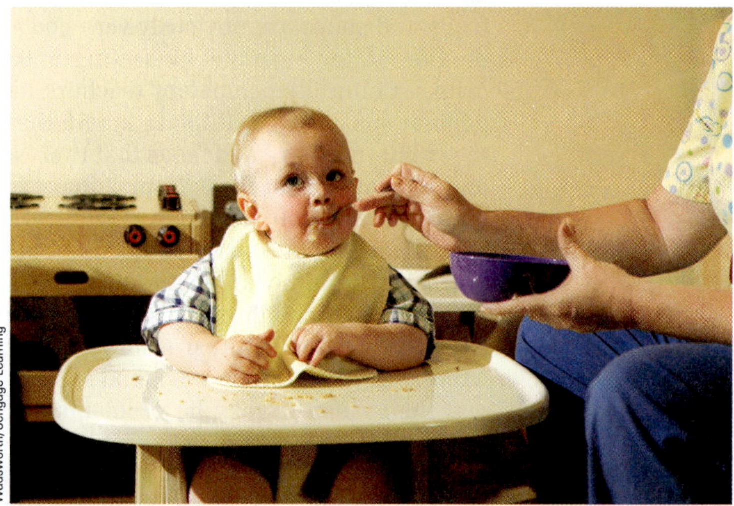

Wadsworth/Cengage Learning

Wadsworth/Cengage Learning

Key Concept 8.1

Nutritional Policies

Every teacher should practice good nutrition in the early childhood education environment. Many teachers are not meeting the nutritional needs of children in their care. Each teacher approaches the task of providing nutritious food with a perspective based on his or her own background, food practices, culture, and what the children eat or will not eat. The teacher should set up nutritional policies that cover early infant feeding, food and the toddler, the preschool child, school-age children, and special needs. The work to be done by the teacher includes education, role modeling, and supervision.

8.2 EARLY FEEDING AND THE INFANT IN CARE

The birth weight of a healthy baby will double in the first four months of life, and nutritional needs will change as a child grows and develops. An infant grows faster during the first year than at any other time of her life. This growth rate is due to the growth patterns of all the internal organs. An infant's nutrition should supply the nutrients and energy for this rapid growth.

The growth and development of an infant is directly related to nutrition. In the first four to six months of life, the only food an infant's body can accommodate is breast milk or formula that provides the necessary nutrients. As the infant grows, changes in the organs provide the ability to digest and assimilate solid foods.

At birth, newborns cannot chew or use their tongues to push food. Their kidneys are too immature to handle the wastes of solid food, and their digestive systems cannot yet handle the nutrients from solid foods. Allergic reactions, cramping, and crying are common results of introducing solid foods before the baby can assimilate them.

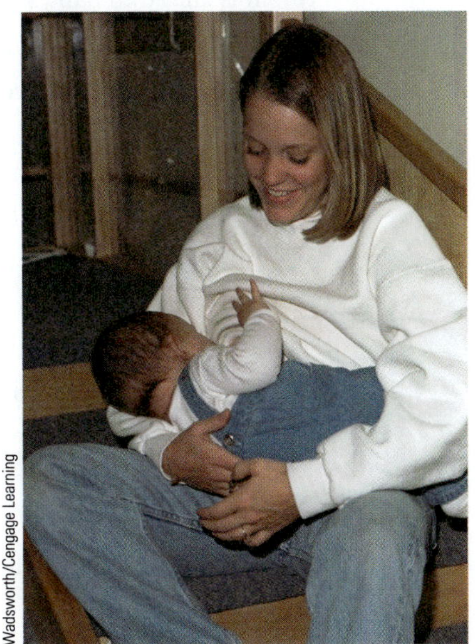

Wadsworth/Cengage Learning

Breast milk contains all the nutrients that babies need for the first six months of life. Teachers should work to accommodate the mother who wants to continue breastfeeding while her child is in care.

Breastfeeding

Historically, infants were breastfed. This changed when technology was developed to provide sanitation for bottle feeding and formulas on which babies could survive and thrive. Doctors saw bottle feeding as a way to measure the amount of milk a baby was drinking. The trend for bottle feeding of infants increased until the early 1970s, when research showed that breastfeeding offered more nutrition and immunity than bottle feeding. In the United States, 76 percent of mothers begin breastfeeding when their children are born, but only one-third are still breastfeeding after three months (Gidding et al., 2006). Today, the AAP is involved in an ongoing effort to increase the number of babies who are breastfed and to increase the time they are breastfed to the first 12 months of life (Zero to Three, 2007a). Breastfeeding varies by culture. Hispanic mothers are more likely than non-Hispanic white mothers, mothers of multiracial children, and African-American mothers to breastfeed their children (USDHHS, 2006).

Current knowledge shows that breastfeeding is preferable to provide infants proper nutrition and protection from bacteria, infections, and immunity from diseases (Walker, 2005). Breast milk cannot be replicated. There is also good cause to believe that breastfeeding actually optimizes cognitive development (AAP, 2000). Table 8-1 lists some of the benefits of breastfeeding; it is important to note that there is a public misperception of whether infant formula is as good as breast milk. Twenty-six percent of respondents in the National HealthStyles survey felt that formula was as good as or better than breast milk (Li, Rock, & Grummer-Strawn, 2007). This could have serious implications for the percentage of mothers who make the commitment to breastfeed their babies.

The teacher may be called upon to help the breastfeeding mother with quality support (Zero to Three, 2007a; Walker, 2005). This offers advantages

TABLE 8-1
Benefits of Breastfeeding

- Protein is suited to baby's metabolism.
- Provides antibodies to combat bacteria.
- Provides immunological protection from illness and disease such as polio, diphtheria, and flu.
- Contains fatty acids that are important for baby's development and growth.
- Reduces incidences of ear infection, diarrhea, pneumonia, and urinary tract infections.
- Fat and iron in breast milk are easily absorbed and digested by the baby.
- Reduces the incidence of dental cavities.
- Convenient—right temperature, sterile, and changes composition as baby's needs change.
- Psychological advantages—bonding with mother, tactile stimulation.
- Fosters optimum cognitive development.
- May provide reduced risk for SIDs, atopic, dermatitis, asthma, and Type 1 diabetes.

to everyone concerned. The baby will benefit, as Table 8-1 indicates, and the mother and the teacher will both benefit because a breastfed baby is less likely than a bottle-fed baby to become sick when left in care (Walker, 2005). Increasing breastfeeding is also a goal of the Special Supplemental Food Program for Women, Infants, and Children and of the Office of Head Start and the Early Head Start National Resource Center because of its many health benefits to babies (Carmichael et al., 2001; Zero to Three, 2007a).

Mothers can help the teacher by collecting and storing breast milk to use while they are not with the baby. Breast milk will last up to 48 hours in the refrigerator or can be frozen for two weeks. The teacher can help the nursing mother by allowing the mother to nurse the baby in the early childhood education environment (Walker, 2006). This may occur as the baby is dropped off, picked up, and even at lunch time if the mother is close enough to visit her child during the lunch break. This type of support will help mothers continue to breastfeed for the recommended time for optimum health and well-being for the infant. It is helpful to provide a quiet place for the baby to nurse and to time the baby's feedings to the mother's schedule (Walker, 2006; Zero to Three, 2007a). A sign should be posted indicating that breastfed babies are welcome in your early childhood environment (Aird, 2002). It is helpful to include fathers, as well as others in the infant's life, in supporting the mother's decision to breastfeed. When a mother feels that everyone is happy about her breastfeeding decision, she is more likely to continue (U.S. Breastfeeding Committee [USBC], 2002). A mother should be discouraged from breastfeeding if (1) she has a communicable or chronic disease such as AIDS; (2) she is taking medication that is harmful to the baby; or (3) she is a drug or alcohol abuser.

Breastfed babies usually need to be fed every two to three hours. They may have more trouble accepting the bottle because they are used to sucking the breast. It may take several tries before the right nipple is found. The teacher should not give up trying to find the right nipple for the baby to suck on while taking breast milk from a bottle!

To reinforce support for breastfeeding, it might be helpful to create a nutritional policy for breastfed infants so that you can share it with expectant parents and new mothers who are breastfeeding. Before creating the policy, teachers might have to examine their own personal feelings about breastfeeding and acknowledge that a mother makes an individual choice and should be supported in whatever she chooses. The policy should allow flexibility so that the nursing infant's needs are met, and should provide planned opportunities for teachers and breastfeeding mothers to communicate. It should also promote the early childhood education environment as being breastfeeding friendly (Walker, 2005). It could include information on recent findings indicating that breastfed babies may not be getting enough vitamin D and may need a nutritional supplement (Gartner & Greer, 2003; Butte et al., 2004). Efforts to keep babies and young children from the sun's rays may leave them vulnerable to vitamin D deficiency. Another way of supporting mothers who may be trying to decide whether to breastfeed is to provide resources that explain the benefits of breastfeeding. One of these resources is La Leche League whose website address is: http://www.llli.org/.

The teacher should apply good sanitary practices and food safety procedures when using breast milk, as listed in Table 8-2.

TABLE 8-2
Safe and Sanitary Practices for Breastfeeding

- Breast milk that has been stored unfrozen should be thrown away if not used 2 days.
- Expressed milk should be stored in single portion feedings with date and child's name clearly labeled.
- Thaw frozen milk in the refrigerator or under cold running water. Never heat in the microwave.
- Shake refrigerator thawed milk to mix cream into all the milk.
- Do not refreeze thawed breast milk.
- Dispose of any unused milk left in the bottle immediately after feeding.

Bottle Feeding

Although breastfeeding is the preferred form, many children are fed formula from the beginning or are switched to formula for a variety of reasons. Mothers may find this is easier when they work, and it allows anyone, including fathers, to participate in the feeding of the baby. A child may also be on a combination of breast and bottle feeding; for example, breast milk may be fed in the morning and at night and bottled formula during the day.

Formulas are easy to prepare and come in several forms. Powdered and liquid concentrate formulas are meant to have sterile water added to the exact directions on the can. This is very important because if the formula is incorrectly mixed, it can be harmful to the infant. The other kind of formula is ready-to-feed and merely has to be put into the bottle.

If a baby appears to be spitting up a lot or having diarrhea after being fed formula, it may indicate that the baby is intolerant to the formula. Discuss this with the family and make a determination as to how to proceed. The family may want to talk to their physician before changing formulas. Another thing that the family may want to discuss with the physician is the possibility of vitamin D deficiency if the formula is not fortified with vitamin D.

Many manufacturers make soy-protein formulas for infants who are born with lactose intolerance. These infants may suffer from diarrhea, gas, and bloating. An infant may also be allergic to the soy formula, in which case there is a formula available with the proteins already broken down by enzyme action to prevent the allergic reaction.

Formulas try to copy breast milk as closely as possible. Formula manufacturers start with nonfat cow's milk as a base and then add vegetable oil, lactose, vitamins, and minerals to approximate the energy and nutrients available from human milk. Commercially prepared formulas are heavily regulated to keep infants safe from harm.

For proper food safety and sanitation, the measures in Table 8-3 should be commonly practiced in bottle preparation using formula.

Feeding Pattern. Whether the baby is being breastfed or bottle fed, an important factor to keep in mind is that, even at this young age, the child should be able to control his own eating pattern (Rose, 2007). To accomplish

ould be held in a
evated, reclined
when feeding, to avoid
king or getting ear
s. These early feedings
te significantly to the
he child's later eating

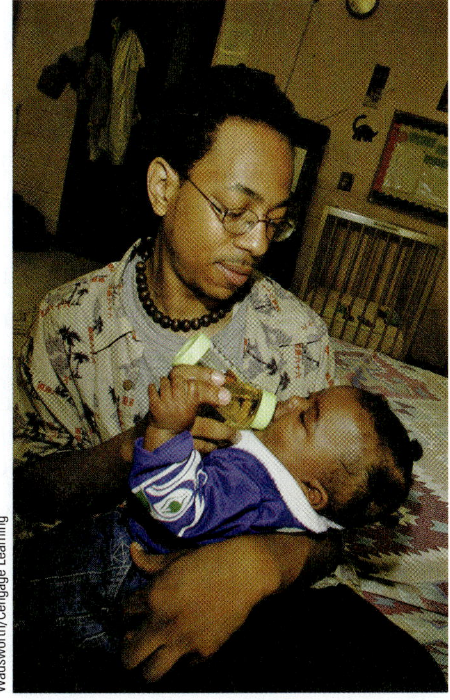
Wadsworth/Cengage Learning

formula, not air. Always burp a baby between one-third and one-half of the way through the feeding, and then again after the feeding is finished. After bottle feeding a baby a few times, the teacher should know the baby's burping "pattern." Try to always hold a baby when feeding her. Never prop a baby's bottle, and avoid giving her a bottle in the crib or on the floor, where she would be lying flat.

Infant-controlled feeding requires the teacher to be attentive to the infant's behavior and to allow the quantity ingested to vary depending on the infant's needs. Infants are capable of self-regulating the amount of food they consume (Fox, Devaney, et al., 2006; Parlakian & Lerner, 2007). Infant-controlled feeding also requires that the teacher communicate with the family about how the baby is feeding at home, including during the night (Walker, 2005). The teacher can identify the infant's cues by allowing time for pauses. This may be a good time to see whether the baby needs to be held upright to pass a gas bubble. If the baby is fussy during a feeding, it is wise to find the source of the discomfort instead of interpreting the fussiness as a sign that the baby is done eating. Helping the infant to develop a healthy feeding relationship helps to establish good eating habits later in life (Satter, 2000; Zero to Three, 2007b).

Introducing Solid Foods

Solid foods should not be introduced into a baby's diet until the baby is at least 4 months old, and not until 6 months if he does not show signs of readiness. The AAP recommendation is "about" 6 months. This is about the time it takes for the fine, gross, and oral motor skills to develop so that the child is ready to eat solid food. If foods are introduced in a child's diet too early, it can make the baby vulnerable to food intolerance or food allergies (Calder,

Babies
slightly
positio
their ch
infectio
contrib
basis o
habits.

TABLE 8-3
Safe and Sanitary Practices for Bottle Feeding

- Wash hands with liquid soap and hot water before be sterilization process.
- Wash bottles, nipples, and caps in hot, soapy water, us for hard-to-reach places. Rinse thoroughly in hot, clea
- Sterilize all bottle parts in a pan of water. Boil for 5 to Remove parts from pan with tongs and fill bottles imm
- Always buy cans of formula that are intact and have cu
- Wash the tops of formula cans before opening them.
- Prepare formula exactly to manufacturers' instruction diluted too much, malnutrition may result. If an insuffi water is added, the child's digestive system may be str
- Use clean, sterile, bottled water rather than tap water, tap water may cause digestive upsets in some infants.
- Pour formula into sterilized bottles and top with nipple if the bottle is being stored in the refrigerator. Use up a formula. Prepared bottles should be stored no longer t

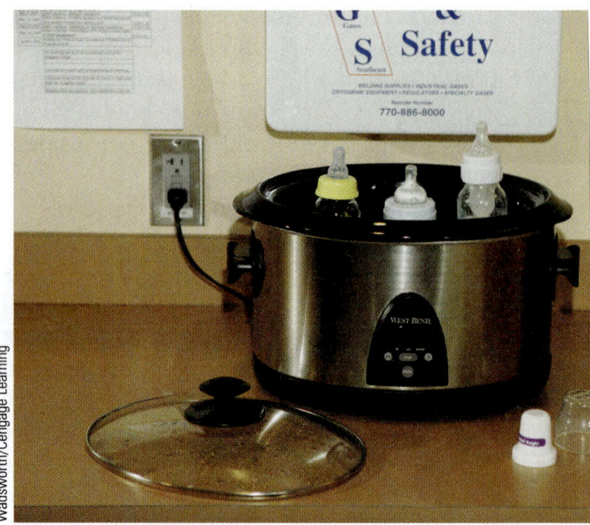

Safe and sanitary practices like this should be used to warm bottles for the infants who use them.

this, the teacher must be aware of the cues the baby gi needed or when he is full. These cues include drawing t the nipple, releasing it, spitting it out, or biting it. The i sucking or shut his mouth tightly. Changing posture or b surroundings and not the feeding are also cues that the any more breast or bottle feeding. A baby should be fed a body's schedule of food energy needs instead of an impos

It is important that a child be held correctly when b baby should not be flat on her back but should be in a s tion (Lyles, 2003). When feeding begins, make sure that

TABLE 8-4
Pattern of Developmental Skills for Eating Solid Foods

- Birth: Baby is capable only of sucking.
- 6 weeks: Baby can smile and has the ability to extrude or push things out of the mouth with the tongue.
- 8 weeks: Baby can use the tongue against the palate and can swallow semisoft food, but cannot digest the food itself.
- 3 months: Baby's gastrointestinal system is sufficiently developed for digesting starch.
- 4 months: Baby shows signs of being ready for solid foods: drinks 40 or more ounces of milk; can swallow instead of suck; and drools, indicating teeth will soon appear. Should be double his birth weight. If formula fed, iron stores may be depleted and baby will need iron from other food sources.
- 4–6 months: The baby can control head movements and can keep food in his mouth instead of pushing it out with the tongue.
- 5 months: The baby is a social creature and may be more interested in people and surroundings than in eating. She may demonstrate interest in other people's food and open her mouth to show this interest.
- 6 months: Baby can sit up in a high chair and is easily spoon fed. If breastfed, iron stores may be depleted and baby will need iron from other food sources.
- 6–9 months: Teeth begin to appear, as does the munching movement of the jaw and pursing the mouth. This allows for more biting and chewing, making it easier to eat coarser pieces of food and to begin cup feeding.
- 8 months: Baby can grasp soft finger foods with hands and put them in her mouth.
- 10 months: Baby should be able to grasp cup with both hands.
- 12 months: Baby should be able to hold an age-appropriate spoon.

2004). As long as solid food is not introduced before the recommended time, when the baby is 4 to 6 months old, it does not appear to make a marked difference in food allergies or other reactions to food from this point forward (Zutavern et al., 2008). The normal pattern of development and ability of the body to accept solid foods and the nutrients they supply is covered in Table 8-4. As shown in this table, even if he could swallow the food, a young baby is unable to sufficiently process the food in his digestive tract.

Feeding Patterns. When the infant is demonstrating developmental readiness, then solid foods should be introduced. Until this point, the protein needed for brain growth has been provided by the breast milk or formula. There is a common pattern for the introduction of solid food, and it has been developed for good reasons. Once the parent has decided to introduce solid foods, the teacher should work with the parent to do so slowly, serving only one or two servings of the food at the beginning. One new food is introduced at a time, and the teacher should wait five to seven days before introducing another new food. This waiting period allows the teacher to identify whether the food causes allergies or digestive complications such as diarrhea, gas, rashes, vomiting, or unusual fussiness. If this does not occur, move on to the next new food. It is much better to feed babies commercially prepared foods that do not have any added sugars or sodium. This food is prepared in a sanitary manner with precautions taken to prevent bacterial growth. This is not true for homemade baby food, which should be avoided because it is not as safe for the baby.

As the teacher starts the solid food routine, there are several things to keep in mind that will help the baby learn how to eat in a safe way. Utensils used to feed the baby should be small and age appropriate (Briley & Roberts-Gray, 2005). To begin with, only small amounts of food should be offered on the tip of the spoon. As the baby progresses, the amount should be increased to two or three tablespoons at a feeding. The food the teacher serves should be placed in a small bowl or custard cup with only enough for one serving, and any unfinished food should be discarded. Returning food to the jar might contaminate the food remaining in the jar and make it unsafe for the baby to eat. Table 8-5 contains the introduction pattern for solid foods.

Cereals. The first food normally introduced is iron-fortified rice cereal. Beginning with rice is a good idea because it is easily digested. The teacher should mix the cereal with some formula until it is somewhat runny. It will be easier for an infant to assimilate this experience if the food is not totally dissimilar from her liquid diet. This food should be fed to the child on a spoon, not from a bottle. It is common practice among certain cultures, including Hispanics, to introduce this food mixed with formula in a bottle in which the nipple has been cut to allow the cereal to come out. Developmentally, this puts the child back to sucking and swallowing rather than using the developing oral skills that will be needed later. This type of feeding should be discouraged.

TABLE 8-5
Solid Food Introduction Pattern

Age	Include	Exclude
0–4 months	Formula or breast milk	Solid foods, cow's milk
4–6 months	Add iron-fortified cereals	Honey, meat, eggs, sugar, powdered sweetened drink mix, cow's milk
6–9 months	Add vegetables, fruits, soft finger foods, yogurt, cheese, unsweetened fruit juices, beans	Same as above plus soft drinks
9–12 months	Add meats, egg yolks, breads, crackers, cottage cheese, pasta, rice	Egg whites, all sugared products, honey, peanuts, popcorn, low- or nonfat milk, hot dogs, high sodium meat products
24 months	Add whole eggs	

Cereals are normally fed for the first month or two of the introduction to solid foods. The child should not be fed mixed cereals or wheat-based cereal because of possible allergic reactions. It is difficult to tell which ingredient in mixed cereal may be the culprit, and wheat is often the basis for allergy among infants.

Vegetables. The next food to introduce is vegetables, one at a time. Infants may show preference for flavors and may totally reject a food. This is one reason vegetables are introduced before fruits, because sweet flavors are preferred to savory flavors. This gives the child the opportunity to learn to enjoy vegetables before being introduced to fruits. It is a good idea to stick with dark green and yellow vegetables, because they are good sources of vitamin A. Spinach and beets can cause allergic reactions, so the teacher may want to avoid these in the beginning. Offer vegetables on repeated occasions to help the child learn to eat more of the vegetable, unless there is a facial expression of distaste in response (Forestell & Mennella, 2007).

If the child rejects a food several days in a row, the teacher should respect this dislike and discontinue it. The teacher may try introducing the food again in a few months. Vegetables should be strained or pureed at this stage. The teacher may use commercially prepared baby food or make it. Remember that infants do not need salt, spices, or other enhancements to make their food palatable. It is a good habit to get a child to accept food in its natural form, so that the particular food will be acceptable later on in many forms. Infants cannot digest spices, and sweetening foods or adding salt may cause food preferences that may make it difficult for the child to follow the MyPyramid for Kids when he is older.

Fruits. Fruits are introduced next, one at a time. Many fresh fruits can be easily mashed. This is a good time to introduce soft finger food such as bananas. Most infants respond well to the majority of fruits, but certain textures such as those in pears may cause the child to reject trying a particular food. If the child rejects a food, the teacher can add the food to the list of things to try again later. When exposed to a food 8 to 10 times, children may develop an increase in preference for that food. By exposing them to new and different foods, teachers can provide opportunities for children to learn to like a variety of nutritious foods (Gidding et al., 2006; Bellows & Anderson, 2006).

Yellow fruits such as apricots and peaches are good sources of vitamin A. The teacher must be watchful when introducing items such as fresh strawberries and citrus fruits, because, although they are excellent sources of vitamin C, they also can cause allergic reactions. Fruit juices are another good source of vitamins, but the teacher should use unsweetened juices. This is the perfect time to introduce a cup to a baby. It is preferable to feed a child juice from a cup, not from a bottle (Rose, 2007). Fruit juice in a bottle can lead to baby bottle tooth decay. An infant should never be given soda or fruit-flavored beverages that are high in sugar content.

When choosing a cup, the teacher should find one that is unbreakable and weighted at the bottom. When first trying a cup, it is better for the baby to use one with at least one handle so that he has something to grasp. These cups usually come with a lid, but if the baby seems to have difficulty with sipping, you may remove the lid. Let the baby try a sip at a time, beginning with a small amount, and use a bib to protect baby from spills.

Other Foods. At this time, most children have enough teeth to do some chewing. Soft finger foods such as cheese are good beginner foods so the child can learn to feed himself. Cheese and yogurt are good sources of calcium and protein, and both are easily digestible by now. Cheese should be cut into small pieces or sliced, not cut into cubes, which the baby can choke on.

At age 9 months, meat such as chicken, beef, lamb, and fish can be added to the baby's diet. Wait awhile before serving pork, because it can cause allergic reactions. If the child has enough teeth, the meat can be chopped into very small pieces so she can pick up the pieces and feed herself. Egg yolks can also be added now, but it is best to avoid egg whites and whole eggs until the child is at least 1 year old. Cottage cheese is another addition that will offer a good source of calcium and protein.

This is the time when other finger foods such as toast and crackers can be added. They are good sources of carbohydrates, as are rice and pasta. These items can be chewed and easily digested by now. The pasta and rice should be fairly plain, not highly seasoned. The teacher should avoid serving finger foods that are not soft or will not soften in the mouth, such as carrots or celery. Infants and young children have more difficulty chewing and swallowing than do older children, so careful consideration should be given as to what foods might cause choking, and those foods should be avoided (Sigman-Grant, 2008). (See Table 8-5 for some foods to avoid.) The teacher should also avoid introducing foods without sufficient nutritional value.

Teacher Guidelines

Guidelines for infant feeding are shown in Table 8-6. As the teacher helps to establish the eating behavior of an infant as he or she goes from breast or bottle feeding to solid foods, these guidelines may assist in successful infant feeding.

This child is giving her teacher the cue that she is done eating. Does the teacher appear to understand that?

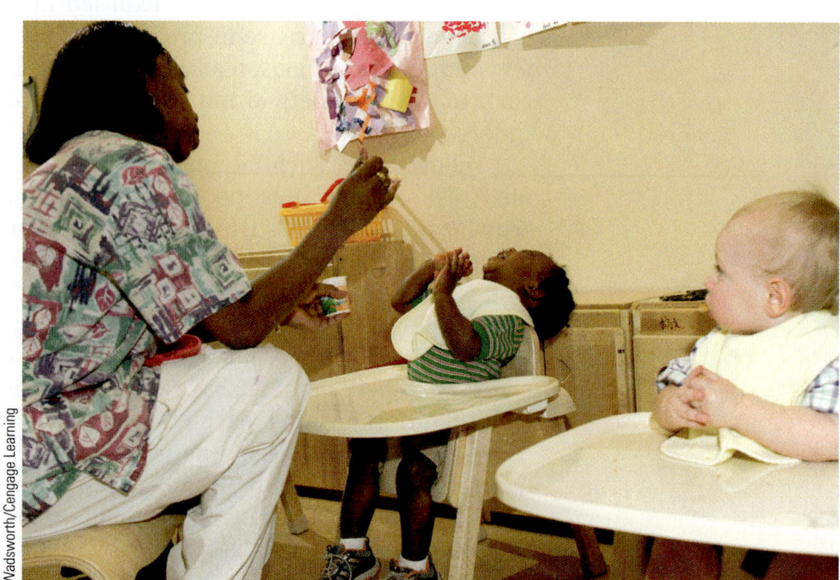

TABLE 8-6
Guidelines for Successful Infant Feeding

- Use a small spoon and age-appropriate cup.
- Watch for cues that baby is full.
- Never use food as bribery, diversion, or reward.
- Offer an assortment of healthy foods that can easily be swallowed and digested.
- Try new foods at baby's best time of day.
- Respect the child's food likes and dislikes.
- Infants may not be able to eat a great deal at a time, so serve smaller meals throughout the day.
- Let the infant be in control of how much he eats.
- Make mealtime pleasant, not distracting.
- Avoid serving foods that may choke an infant.
- Only serve foods that are soft or will become soft in the mouth.

Key Concept 8.2

Early Feeding and the Infant in Care

Infancy is a critical time for forming healthy patterns to meet the nutritional needs of a child. Whether the baby is fed by breast milk or formula, a teacher can manage health risk by using food safety behaviors. Being aware of the cues that an infant gives when he is full will help the teacher allow the infant to gain control of his own feeding behavior. The introduction of solid foods brings nutritional challenges that can be easily met if the teacher is knowledgeable about the pattern of introducing these foods. Understanding how to accommodate the infant's physical and psychological needs will allow the teacher to encourage the infant to go at his own pace. The teacher plays an important role in helping the infant and his family establish good nutrition and providing the groundwork for good feeding behaviors.

Wadsworth/Cengage Learning

This child is just learning how to feed himself and seems to be happy doing so.

8.3 FEEDING THE AUTONOMOUS TODDLER

• **autonomy**
a child's quest from ages one to two to develop a sense of self and self-rule.

The transition from infant to toddler is most apparent in a child's eating behavior. This is the first area in which a child begins to show her independence and need for **autonomy**. As part of this development a child will want to take control of things that relate to her. Eating is a good place for the child to begin to assert herself because it happens frequently. Good nutrition allows a child to grow, learn, and play. The challenge for this period is to maintain good nutrition while helping the child establish good food habits with her independence intact. As a child develops her sense of autonomy, it can also lead to frustration and a contest of wills . . . her will versus the adult's will. Creating a framework for forming good food habits is one of the most important things the teacher can do for a child to ensure good health and well-being. To help the child establish good eating behaviors, the teacher must understand how growth patterns and developmental changes affect a toddler's actions (see Table 8-7).

Food as an Issue of Control

Adults feel responsible for a child's eating habits. If the child is not eating right, we may cajole, coerce, bribe, or beg the child to eat. Without realizing it, adults have just drawn the line for the battle over food being used as an issue of control between a well-meaning adult and an independence-seeking toddler. It may be easy to fall into this trap because the great majority of

TABLE 8-7
Common Patterns of Toddler's Growth and Development That Affect Eating Actions

- Child wants and needs to be independent; child wants to control his own eating.
- Child learns to say "no" even to favorite foods.
- Appetite is sporadic as growth slows.
- Child learns by doing—wants to feed self.
- Child has food likes and dislikes. Child may develop food jags for favorite foods.
- Child is gaining more control over large motor skills and can lift food to her mouth. Because large muscle control is still developing, the child will sometimes drop or spill food.
- Child is gaining more control over fine motor skills and is able to use a spoon.
- Child is learning to manipulate objects and likes to touch and play with food.
- Child may be teething and have difficulty chewing; she will spit out or remove food from mouth.
- Child wants to master the job of eating and be successful, even if it means hiding food under plate or in a pocket to show she is done.
- Child is learning to be a social creature and may entertain others with food antics.

teachers receive little training on feeding children (Sigman-Grant et al., 2008). As a child recognizes the adult's concern over the consumption of food, the child may figure out creative ways to utilize food as a weapon in the quest for independence. It is important for the teacher to maintain clear limits and be consistent and also to provide opportunities for the child to exercise some control (Downs, 2006).

Ellyn Satter, dietitian and author of several books (1987, 2000, 2005) on the subject of feeding behavior problems, has offered some specific guidelines to help alleviate the struggle for control between the adult and the child concerning food.

- The adult is responsible for controlling what food comes into the house and how it is presented to the child.
- The adult is also responsible for making sure the child is at a meal, keeping the child on task, making sure the child behaves well, and regulating the time for meals and snacks.
- The child is responsible for how much he eats, whether he eats, and how his body turns out.

Careful examination of these areas of responsibility will change the battle into a cooperative venture. It is important for the early education environment and all those within it not to use food as a battleground (Jana & Shu, 2007). When children are allowed some control over their feeding practices, fewer issues of contention arise. If children are allowed "to eat when they are hungry, drink when they are thirsty, and refrain from doing so when they're not, you've got it made" (Jana & Shu, 2007). The early childhood education environment should avoid the "clean your plate" mentality that can cause so many negative issues (Fox, Reidy, Karwe, & Ziegler, 2006; Fox, Reidy, Novak, & Ziegler, 2006). A child who learns to self-regulate and recognize his internal cues will learn to better control food intake over his lifetime.

The way that an adult treats a child at the table may very well be a reflection of how the adult treats the child elsewhere. The feeding style of the adult can affect how the child develops eating habits (Rose, 2007; Hughes et al., 2007). A child-centered feeding style works very well. The adult can help regulate the food consumption behavior in numerous ways. Training the child to be on task in eating satisfying foods and giving the child a selection of well-prepared foods is a good first step. These foods should be nutritious and include milk, fruits, vegetables, and whole grains, and should be given in a variety of forms so that the child has a chance to have broader food preferences as he goes through life (Ziegler, Hanson et al., 2006). Offering these types of food is very important because it has been found that dietary fiber from fruits, vegetables, and whole grains are missing from many young children's diets (Kranz, Smicklas-Wright, & Francis, 2006; Williams, 2006). It also appears that only 2- and 3-year-old children are getting adequate amounts of milk in their diets (Kranz, Lin, & Wagstaff, 2007). When a child realizes that food can be enjoyable, he is more likely to be agreeable with the idea of eating and less likely to balk at the task at hand. If the child does not eat, the adult should learn to relax, stay calm, and be flexible. Erratic food intake is normal; it will support the child's growth because over time the proper balance will be achieved. Branen, Fletcher, and Myers (1997) found that when children in early childhood education environments were allowed to select foods "family style," the consumption pattern was not significantly different from being served preselected foods already portioned out by the adult. The one

Wadsworth/Cengage Learning

Eating can often become a power struggle between the adult and the child. Keeping the child on task and making mealtime enjoyable are ways that the adult can help to regulate the child's food consumption without causing undue stress.

difference they found was that although children did not waste more food, in some cases they tended to eat more because they were able to regulate their own intake. A conclusion of their study was that self-selection may help to regulate dietary intake in early childhood education environments and may offer a more healthy alternative to preselection by the teacher or food preparer. Studies since then have shown that this idea of self-selection may actually cut down risk for obesity (Fox, Devaney, et al., 2006; Gidding et al., 2006; Rose, 2007; Zero to Three, 2007b). Teachers often learn about nutrition, but how to actually feed children is not always covered in training. Only abut 42 percent of teachers have had training on feeding children, and it has been found that "family-style" meals where the child self-selects is practiced in less than half of early childhood education environments (Sigman-Grant et al., 2008). It appears that it is important for teachers to have a greater understanding that self-selection and "family-style meals" should be the norm because it is a healthier practice.

Flexibility is an important factor in allowing a child to master his self-feeding skills (Sigman-Grant, 2007). This may mean allowing a child who is self-serving food to take too much or too little at the beginning of this process. It is important for a child to learn to distinguish between feeling hungry and being full. The teacher must understand that this is a process and use patience when a child transitions to eating with utensils and a regular cup because he probably will be messy. Also, a child may not yet have the words to tell the teacher what she wants and doesn't want.

Another strategy for helping a child develop good eating habits is to make mealtimes significant for the child. Understanding the temperament of the child, his capabilities, and his tempo will help the teacher prepare for mealtime. The teacher should give the child time, attention, and awareness when meals are served. Meals are about more than food. They are a time for people around the table to connect and share. A child's eating pattern is strongly related to the physical and social environment in which he eats (Patrick & Nicklas, 2005). Sitting and talking with children while they are eating makes this time special. When children see their teachers enjoying foods, they are more likely to be adventurous and try them too. Discussing the day's events or what is happening at home, such as a visit from a grandparent, makes the child feel like he is an integral part of the mealtime occasion. The teacher should reinforce desirable behavior by paying attention to,

Judith always sits with her 2-year-old early childhood education group at lunch time. Teresa, the cook, serves the food family-style in large bowls and helps each child select foods. During this process, Judith keeps the children who already have their food on task and talks with the children who have not been served yet. When everyone is served, the group discusses the food and talks about how things taste. Judith also talks with the children about the morning activities and explains some of the things Roberta, the afternoon teacher, has planned for them. This helps the children prepare for the transition and remember what they have done that day. Also significant, every day Judith eats the same food for lunch that the children are eating. She is role modeling that the food served is just as acceptable to her as it is for the children. Judith's pet peeve is teachers who bring in fast food to eat in front of children and who do not practice what they are trying to enforce—good eating habits.

recognizing, and acknowledging good behavior. It is important to be flexible with the amount of time "scheduled" for children to eat (Lucich, 2003). Some children need more time to eat than others. Other children may not be able to sit for very long and should be allowed to get up from the table when they are finished eating (Parlakian & Lerner, 2007). In addition, food should be served in an attractive manner and should look appetizing. Sitting down to a table with a white plate with chicken, mashed potatoes, and applesauce, while nutritious, may be very unappealing to the eye. Foods should have eye appeal and be colorful and tasty, although flavors should not be too strong (Kendall & Puck, 2007).

The teacher can contribute to regulating eating habits by managing the eating environment. Setting limits makes eating more important and worthwhile. When feeding a child a snack or a meal, the teacher must make sure that eating is the only activity going on (Miller, 2004). The teacher should also limit eating to one or two appropriate places. That may be in a kitchen or patio in a home situation, not in front of a television. In center-based care, eating may occur in the classroom or on tables near the playground. The teacher should spend some time getting the children ready to eat. The transition time from another activity should be quiet and calming, to prepare children for eating time.

A child should come to the table at mealtime ready to eat. If the child is disinterested or not hungry, the teacher should not force the issue, but should have the child stay at the table a few minutes before excusing her. This removes the temptation for the child to entertain or act out. If the child complains about being hungry a few minutes later, the teacher can remind her that snack time is just a few hours away. The child made the choice not to participate and maybe next time will make a different choice. This reinforces the fact that the child made the decision and the teacher supported it. The teacher should not change the eating pattern for meals and snacks to accommodate whims, but instead be supportive of the child by being consistent. Children in early education environments should not be allowed to "graze" or to eat at any time they want. Instead, there should be meals and scheduled snacks only (Satter, 2005). In general, a child should have three meals and two snacks per day, so the amount of these available in the early education environment would depend on the time the child is present. Some younger children may need to be fed more often.

One of the issues that may be faced during this toddler stage is called a "food jag." This occurs when a child gets the idea that she wants to eat only a certain food. It might be peanut butter sandwiches, macaroni, or just about anything. These food jags occur for a number of reasons. One reason might be that very young children are much more sensitive to flavor. A child could also be bored with the foods commonly served in care and may be holding out for what she enjoys. The child may also test the teacher to see how he reacts to her demand for a specific food; this is common as the child attempts self-rule. Some children are afraid to try new things and may need as many as 8 to 12 exposures to a food before it becomes acceptable (Ziegler, Hanson et al., 2006, Jana & Shu, 2007; Bellows & Anderson, 2006). Less adventurous children may have less adventurous parents when it comes to feeding patterns (Cathey & Gaylord, 2004). A good way to introduce a new food is to serve it with a favorite food and to place the less adventurous child near a more adventurous peer. New foods should be served at the beginning of the meal, and it is better to begin with small changes (Kendall & Puck, 2007).

Food jags are just one type of picky eating toddlers may display (Tessmer, 2004). Picky eating is characteristic of this stage of development, and it may well be a definite preference for foods with certain tastes. Some foods contain a chemical referred to as PTC (phenylthiocarbamide) (Gamble, 2004). This can cause a bitter taste in the mouth of a very young child. Foods that have this compound include citrus, strawberries, green beans, apples, bacon, and broccoli. Children's preferences come as a result of trial and error (Cathey & Gaylord, 2004; Bellows & Anderson, 2006). Children may also be reluctant to try different foods because of their temperament (Zero to Three, 2007b). The best advice is to be patient because this is a normal stage of development (Butte et al., 2004). Normally, picky eating is not a threat to health. It is important not to make food an issue of control (Satter, 2005; Jana & Shu, 2007).

The teacher should keep food out of sight when eating is not the activity. Seeing food can make children think they need to eat when they are not really hungry but do not yet understand their inner food cues. Age-appropriate foods and utensils should be chosen. Finger foods and foods that are easy to eat should help toddlers learn to manipulate food more successfully. Foods such as popcorn, grapes, baby tomatoes, carrots, large chunks of meat, hot dogs, mini marshmallows and celery can cause a child to choke and should be avoided or cut into small pieces so choking is not an issue. The teacher must use utensils that a toddler can grasp easily, and small plates and cups that look as though they are full when they hold a serving of food. Pitchers for self-serving should be small and only partially filled.

Although timing the serving of food to when children need to eat may be difficult to accommodate in some center or school schedules, educators in child care homes and nannies can do so. The teacher should try to be as reliable and regular as possible in feeding children, and should not wait until they are really hungry and have behavior difficulties because of it. The teacher should not force a child to eat if he is not hungry at the moment. "Grazing" or permissive eating patterns should be discouraged.

These actions allow the teacher to establish trust with children in relationship to food. Children will act more responsibly when they can trust their teacher to provide the food and atmosphere that make them successful eaters.

Table 8-8 lists some key points about using food as nutrition and not as a battleground.

TABLE 8-8
Food as Nutrition, Not Control

- Modeling your actions and your attitudes toward food will affect how the children feel about food.
- Stay calm; do not react to negative behavior.
- Realize pressure does not work—forcing and withholding are both ineffective.
- Do not use food as a punishment or as a reward.
- Outside influences, including cultural influences, can affect your good intentions about children and their food behavior.
- Respect cultural eating differences. Expose children to foods from many cultures.
- Children learn from feeding, their first attempt at independence, what to expect from the world.
- If they are successful, the world is a beautiful place. If they fail, they may withdraw or act out.

Nutritional Considerations

Whether served as a meal or as a snack, food should be satisfying and meet children's nutritional needs. The ideal meal or snack would include a protein food, a carbohydrate food, and some fat, with some choices within that parameter. When planning meals or snacks, the teacher must be aware of empty-nutrient, high-calorie foods that have too much sugar or fat but treat their occasional use with respect. Serious thought should be given to snacks, which should be used as part of the day's nutrition. If someone has a birthday and brings cupcakes, enjoy them. The teacher should model how the food should be savored and serve it with milk or some other nutritious food to balance its nutritional effects.

The teacher should recognize that there will be variation in food consumption. A child may refuse to eat foods from a particular food group or may eat only one food to the exclusion of others. This is common. If it continues for longer than a short period, such as a week, this food should be offered only at snack time and the teacher must make sure other foods are served at regular mealtimes.

Milk is a food and should have its proper place. Children older than 6 months of age should not drink formula to the exclusion of other foods. Toddlers should not drink so much milk that they lose their appetite for other foods. Toddlers who depend on milk as their main source of energy and nutrients may have a condition called milk anemia, which is an iron deficiency caused by lack of proper food and too much milk (Rose, 2007). A toddler should drink no more than 24 ounces of milk a day. Children older than 1 year can have cow's milk, but they should never be served nonfat milk because they need the fat content for growth and development until they reach age 2 (Gidding et al., 2006). Some children may not want to drink milk by itself at this stage. Many studies have shown that in the transient pattern between infancy and toddlerhood, milk is displaced by excessive amounts of juices and other sweetened beverages (Skinner, Ziegler, & Ponza, 2004; Gidding et al., 2006; Fox, Devaney et al., 2006). The teacher must substitute yogurt, cheese, and other dairy products to be sure the child receives the necessary amounts of calcium and other minerals.

According to recent studies, overconsumption of juice can cause a child to lag in growth and development compared to children of the same age (Cathey & Gaylord, 2004). In these studies, when juice was not served, all of the observed children who had been behind the curve in growth and weight gain began making gains. Other studies have shown that over-consumption of juice directly correlates with overweight in many children (Fox, Reidy, Novak, & Ziegler, 2006; LaRowe, Moeller, & Adams, et al., 2007; DuBois et al., 2007). As previously stated, the teacher should serve juice only in a cup and should use it to enhance a meal but not to replace other foods. If a child is thirsty, water is the best choice. Some guidelines for maximizing the eating and nutritional needs of the toddler are listed in Table 8-9.

Teachers should use whatever methods are available to encourage the toddlers in care to eat good foods and be well-nourished. The teacher sets

TABLE 8-9
Guidelines for Helping Toddlers Form Good Food Habits

- Make food easy to eat.
- Cut finger food into bite-size pieces.
- Make sure some of the foods served are soft and moist.
- Serve food at room temperature. Toddlers shy away from foods that are too cold or too hot.
- Toddlers are sensitive to texture and may not eat foods that are lumpy or stringy. Let them try these foods, and if they will not eat them, try serving them again later.
- Toddlers like colorful foods and often prefer vegetables that are raw or undercooked because they are brighter in color and crisp.
- A typical toddler may like her food in different or specific shapes. You may have to cut carrots into coins before cooking them so the toddler will eat them.
- Toddlers like fun foods such as faces on pancakes or sandwiches, or other foods cut into unusual shapes.
- Provide toddlers with suitable equipment—small utensils, plastic cups, small pitchers to pour from, and plates with a lip so the food won't slip off.
- Children are still learning to control their muscle movement and need plenty of space in which to operate when eating.
- Model appropriate food behaviors and choose healthy options.
- Offer foods so that children can practice both gross and fine motor skills, such as pouring, spreading, cutting, tearing, and spearing.
- Offer age-appropriate serving sizes or, better yet, help children learn how to self-select foods.
- Help children learn to read their own cues as to when they are hungry or full.
- Never coerce or force a child to eat a food she refuses.

These preschoolers are growing and developing, becoming more physically active. They rely on teachers to provide good "fuel" for their bodies.

Wadsworth/Cengage Learning

Wadsworth/Cengage Learning

the tone for the toddler by how he patterns his food behaviors in care. Following their lead, children can be helped to learn their own body cues as to when they are hungry or full. Sigman-Grant (2003) suggested making a game of this called "Tummy Talk," where toddlers and preschoolers learn to listen to what their tummies are telling them.

Active toddlers may get hungry more often and may need smaller meals or snacks more frequently than older children. Lucich (2003) and others have suggested that children this age need to eat six times per day. If the teacher offers an additional snack, it should not be served too close to a meal. Children of this age who like quiet, sedentary activities should be encouraged to engage in more physically challenging activities in order to expend the energy they have taken in.

Key Concept 8.3

Feeding Behavior of the Toddler

The toddler is growing and developing in many ways. A number of these growth characteristics have an impact on the toddler's food behavior. If the teacher understands this, food is less likely to be a control issue. There are a number of strategies a teacher can employ to help make mealtimes pleasant and encourage the child to eat, thus meeting the toddler's nutritional needs.

8.4 FOOD AND THE PRESCHOOLER

As children reach the preschool stage, a number of developmental changes have occurred that make feeding and nourishing a much easier task. A child of 3 years knows that he is a separate person and understands acceptable and appropriate behavior. He is capable of being patient and can control impulses. If the preschooler whines, complains, or begs for food not on the table, he is capable of understanding that this behavior is unacceptable and he may be asked to get down from the table.

Outside Influences

Preschoolers are social beings who like eating with others. They are ready to learn and are willing to try new things when they are together, so they are probably more likely then to eat more servings of the basic food groups (Parlakian & Lerner, 2007). The preschooler learns much from observation and role play. She is likely to feel good about herself and enjoys cooperating, and she probably has food preferences that may have been influenced by others. Messages children receive at home from their parents and television have a great deal of influence on their attitudes about food (Cathey & Gaylord, 2004; Borzekowski & Robinson, 2001).

Teachers and friends at school also influence preschoolers. These young children feel secure eating familiar foods, but if encouraged to explore, they may try new foods. Often a preschooler may eat a food at school that she would not eat at home. This willingness to eat at school but not at home may be a result of negative messages about the particular food. A child whose parent says squash is "icky" or who makes the comment, "Jerry won't eat squash" may be keeping that behavior a fact at home. In one study, children who were offered new foods in a simple manner were more likely to try them than if they were offered a reward to do so (Wardle et al., 2003). Bellows and Anderson (2006) suggest that offering one new food at a time and not forcing a child to try a new food are good strategies. They also suggest that children like to learn about new foods and to engage them in choosing new foods to try. New foods can be thought of as a "discovery" by children, and these foods should be studied and discussed. Reading a book or conducting a cooking lesson with the new food could lead to a discussion and better understanding, and then perhaps to a greater willingness to try the food. The teacher should be a role model for trying new foods too. A teacher who is not an adventurous eater will have a difficult time convincing a child to try a new food if she is unwilling to do so herself. There are some children that may be considered to have food neophobia, which is basically the fear of trying new foods. Other children may have such strong preferences for certain foods that they may not wish to try new foods (Russell & Worsley, 2008). These children should be exposed to new foods, but not chastised if they do not try them. Positive methods of food exposure work much better.

Children of this age are easily influenced by television advertising of foods that are poor nutritional choices (Hinden, Contento, & Gussow, 2004). More than one-half of all the advertisements on television are for food, and the majority of these are for heavily sugared products. The cereal aisle of the grocery store contains an abundance of these foods. A parent may find it difficult to get through this aisle without a confrontation or without giving in to the child's demands. The cereal aisle is often the scene of the best examples of **positive reinforcement** of negative behavior for young children. An adult who gives in to the demands for a certain sugared cereal seen on television allows the child to feel that television is right about the claims made. A better alternative for the adult, whether parent or teacher, is to make positive use of the television ads and have the child help investigate the claims by reading the labels.

- **positive reinforcement** *reward given in response to a particular behavior that increases the chance of that behavior occurring again.*

Creating a Positive Environment

Just as in toddlerhood, preschool children need a positive environment that will help them eat, support their growth, and make mealtime a time that will nourish all parts of their development. Children of this age can assist with

Dawn is a teacher of older 4-year-olds in a community college preschool. The majority of children in her class have parents in the college. There is a real mixture of family types and income range. The children bring their lunches from home, and Dawn spends time every day with each child examining the lunches.

Kristin had a juice box that was full of sugar, but not much juice. After reading the label with Dawn, Kristin informed her mother that it was not really juice and enlisted her help in finding a better drink for her lunch.

Zarli's dad was new to the lunch-making business, and the first few weeks were a struggle. But after Dawn helped Zarli investigate her lunches, Zarli became aware enough to encourage her dad to read the labels and learn about good food. Her lunches became more interesting and both child and parent weer encouraged to try to understand more about healthier eating. Her father often asked Dawn for advice on new ideas for lunches. He got to be very creative.

Rashid was from a different cultural background and often had foods that Dawn did not recognize. She did recognize the drink in his lunches as a highly advertised sugared drink and helped Rashid examine the label. Dawn explained it to Rashid, and he in turn helped explain it to his mother, who spoke limited English. This exchange led to a wonderful dialogue between Rashid, his mother, and Dawn, discussing the foods that Rashid brought. Dawn learned how the foods were prepared and what healthy ingredients they had in them. Rashid and his mother learned not to believe everything one sees on television.

helping to plan meals and set the table, and can also help with meal preparation if encouraged (Rose, 2007). These tasks can help children to feel like they have a meaningful role in the mealtime experience. When meals are served family style and children are allowed to select their foods, they feel more competent. If they can use their muscles in activities such as pouring juice and spooning from a large bowl onto their own plates, they feel more independent. When children are taught to understand their own bodies' cues as to whether they are full or hungry, the teacher is helping them learn a skill they can use throughout their lives (Sigman-Grant, 2003, 2007). If the teacher provides a transition time before the meal, children will come to the table more ready to participate. Miller (2004) suggested that the teacher play soothing music at this time to help set the tone of a pleasant experience. When teachers use this time to sit down and connect with children, some of the children's important social and emotional needs are met (Patrick & Nicklas, 2005). Pleasant conversation can allow both the teacher and the children in care to get to know each other in different ways than normal classroom time might allow.

Participation

The teacher can foster good nutrition by involving preschoolers in selecting and preparing foods. Encouraging preschool children to be part of the process can empower them with the knowledge and awareness necessary to make better nutritional choices. Enjoyable activities give children confidence to try new foods and different ways of preparation. Children should have the opportunity to learn about food, nutrition, and food preparation and how they are linked to health. Reading books about new foods paves the way for greater understanding. Letting preschoolers help prepare foods and experiment with new foods helps children develop skills that will widen their food horizons. Mealtime offers genuine opportunities for conversations about food and eating behavior. This is a good time to discuss, practice, and model good nutrition and correct eating behavior (Satter, 2005; Bellows & Anderson, 2006). In addition, children should be encouraged to be physically active and participate in activities that will burn up the energy from the foods they have taken in (Rose, 2007). These strategies will help the teacher positively impact the preschooler's nutritional well-being.

Key Concept 8.4

Food and the Preschooler

A preschooler is likely to be influenced by others and by television as to his food choices. These choices have a direct effect on the health and well-being of the preschooler. A teacher can use participatory activities to bring awareness to the preschooler about best nutritional choices. Encouraging a child to be involved in food selection, preparation, and mealtime activities will give the child the confidence to make better choices.

Proper nutrition needs to be taught and reinforced at all levels.

Wadsworth/Cengage Learning

8.5 SCHOOL-AGE NUTRITION

Teachers who work in early childhood education environments may or may not be involved in care of school-aged children, depending on what age range the program or school serves. Family child care providers and nannies are commonly involved with school-aged children before and after school and during school vacations. The needs of early elementary school-aged children, ages 5 to 8, vary greatly from those of the infant, toddler, and preschooler.

Growth is slower during this period and not as observable as in the earlier infant-toddler growth spurt or the adolescent growth spurt that will occur later. However, the vigorous activity level that most school-aged children require makes the need for adequate nutrition important. In addition, good nutrition will help the school-aged child maintain resistance to infection and will ensure adequate stores of body-building materials and nutrition needed for the adolescent growth spurt.

Children of this age are not totally capable of planning a well-balanced diet each day. They may eat for social reasons, such as television viewing, when they are not really hungry. They may also have fluctuating appetites and become finicky in their eating habits. These changes may be attributed to the consumption of more and more foods that are low in nutrients and high in calories.

Snacking is easier because school-aged children are capable of preparing a variety of snacks. High-fat or sweetened foods or beverages are easy to prepare and serve. If these are available, children will probably eat them. Children can be taught about healthier snacks and when they are, they are more likely to make healthy snack choices (FDA Consumer, 2005).

Fast food has a tremendous influence on the school-aged child. All types of media, including computers, are used to sell these types of food to children (Weber, Story, & Hamack, 2006). School-age children are more mobile, and they may have their own money that allows these fast-food purchases. Many school lunch programs serve fast-type foods in order to get the children to eat what is served and cut down on waste. A significant number of elementary school campuses in the United States have fast-food outlets or serve food from these outlets as part of their lunch programs. These programs are even more wide spread in middle school and high school campuses throughout the United States. Most fast foods are high in calories or low in nutrients. For more detailed information see Reality Check: *How Does the Overall Nutrition in Elementary Schools in the United States Really Rate?* in Chapter 9 on page 341.

Good dietary habits should be focused on and practiced. Teachers can do a number of things that will help school-aged children practice better nutritional habits. First, the teacher can explain what healthy, nutritious foods are and how they work so that children will be inclined to eat them. If children have choices that are good foods and fewer choices of food of poor nutritional quality, good nutrition will be more easily attained. Second, teachers can send home a handout to parents of students who bring their own lunches to explain about the importance of food for learning and growth. This could include a list of foods that are discouraged for lunches, as well as suggestions for healthier alternatives. In this day of busy families, it may be hard to change a family's food consumption pattern. Fewer meals are prepared at home than in the past and more fast foods are eaten (Rose, 2007). Teachers can enlist families' support of healthier choices.

Supervising school-aged children in planning their own menus and preparing good food will show children that they can affect their own nutritional well-being. If the early childhood education environment, such as family child care, includes breakfast, the provider can give children a good start by preparing a meal that includes some protein. Children who have a good breakfast are better at performing cognitive skills.

If the provider's or nanny's job includes preparing or helping the child prepare a sack lunch, there are several important considerations. Children who help prepare their own lunches are more likely to eat the lunch. Typical brown bag lunches contain more sugar, sweets, and sweetened beverages and less meat, poultry, or fish than do school lunches prepared by cafeteria staff (Wohlleb, 2004). One school in Kentucky helped solve this problem by having the children bring their empty lunch boxes or sacks to school in the morning. The cafeteria workers would then fill them with healthy selections of food, and the children would pick up their lunches when it was time to eat (Wohlleb, 2004). Sack lunches usually do not contain enough fruits and vegetables and have too many convenience-type foods. If a teacher has enlisted the help of families to provide healthier selections, and the child has also had some education on healthier food selections, packing better lunches may be a positive result. Packing good food may be a challenge, especially if food safety is taken into consideration. Some creativity is in order, as well as practicing safe food handling. Some suggestions are found in Table 8-10.

Snacks are usually the main foods that most teachers provide for school-aged children. It is important that these foods are readily available when the child arrives at the site if this is an after-school care situation. Children are usually very hungry after a long school day. Offering foods prepared by the teacher as well as items that are simple for the child to prepare herself will help the child appease hunger and build self-confidence. The environment should also provide activities that allow a child to be physically active. Television and computer use should be limited, not encouraged.

TABLE 8-10
Packing Healthy Foods for Brown Bag Lunches

- Pre-cut fruits and vegetables can be stored in the refrigerator and packed in the morning.
- Sandwiches can be prepared the afternoon before, so they get thoroughly chilled in the refrigerator and will last longer in the lunches.
- Choose low-fat cuts of meat. Cut the sandwiches into interesting shapes.
- Leftovers can be frozen in small containers and packed in the morning.
- Use only 100 percent fruit juices or have the parent provide money to purchase milk.
- Avoid chips and other high-calorie, low-nutrient foods; substitute pretzels or other low-fat snack foods.
- Provide fruits that are in season, and have the child select the fruit.
- Use cool packs or other devices that will help keep the lunches cool.

Key Concept 8.5

School-Age Nutrition

Many care situations do not have school-aged children. Those teachers who do care for school-aged children face nutritional challenges that are different from those of infants, toddlers, or preschoolers. The teacher should keep in mind the school-aged children's activity levels in order to provide them with adequate nutrition. The teacher is practicing nutritional risk management by purchasing healthy foods, preparing them, and supervising the children in meal or snack preparation.

REALITY *Check*

Children of the Fast-Food Generation

The older children get, the more they eat away from home (Lin, Guthrie, & Frazao, 1999). Today half of family food expenditures were for food purchased away from home (Stewart, Blisard, & Jolliffe, 2006). In this country during the past 20 years, fast-food meals have gone from representing 10 percent of all meals consumed to almost 25 percent of all meals consumed (Jana & Shu, 2006). Approximately 75 percent of the population eats out at least once a week. The great majority of restaurant food purchases are for convenient or fast-food restaurants. In 1968 there were about 1,000 McDonald's in this country and today there are about 31,000 McDonald's located in 120 countries around the world (Schlosser & Wilson, 2006). McDonald's buys more processed meats, potatoes and apples than any other company in this country. No other company that markets food spends more money on advertising than does McDonald's. Fast food has become a way of life for everyone including our children. Bowman and colleagues (2004) reported that more than 10 percent of the energy from food consumed by children was from fast food. Americans spent more than $134 billion on fast food in 2005, compared with $6 billion in 1970.

Children's favorite fast foods include french fries, pizza, hamburgers, fried chicken, and ketchup. There appears to be a correlation between fast-food consumption and television viewing (Kaiser Foundation, 2004; Taveras et al., 2006). In 2002, in the United States, McDonald's Corporation spent more than $1.3 billion and Pepsico spent more than $1.1 billion on advertising (Linn, 2004). Eight out of 10 restaurant meals advertised on Nickelodeon are of poor quality (Batada & Wootan, 2007). The fast-food industry has grown, in part because so many mothers are in the workforce. The eating of fast food may reflect the dietary patterns of families who rarely sit down to eat dinner together and value convenience above health in their busy lives (Stewart, Blisard, & Jolliffe, 2006).

Fast food is available in malls, on main streets, in bowling alleys, at theme parks, on airplanes, and on cruise ships. Fast-food is even available at some schools, where the fast-food chains and soft-drink manufacturers "sponsor" the school in return for marketing their products on campus. Eating right at school can be problematic (Knight Ridder/Tribune Business News, 2008). One in every five public schools serves branded name fast food (Schlosser & Wilson, 2006). There is a trend beginning that is trying to stop these practices in schools (Green, 2005; Gidding et al., 2006; Coile, 2006; Woolston, 2007). Levin (2004) stated, "There is a growing awareness

(continues)

REALITY *Check* (continued)

Fast-Food Kids Meals Nutritional Breakdown

	Calories	Fats (g)	Protein (g)	Sodium (mg)	Carbohydrates (g)
Daily Total	2000	65	24	2400	300
Burger King (Source: Burger King Corporation)					
Hamburger	275	11	15	510	28
French Fries	227	13	3	161	24
Cola	190	0	0	20	16
Total	692	24	18	691	68
McDonald's (Source: McDonald's Corporation)					
Cheeseburger	305	13	15	725	30
French Fries	220	12	3	110	30
Orange Drink	230	0	0	30	59
Total	755	18	18	865	119
Taco Bell (Source: Taco Bell Corporation)					
Taco	183	11	10	276	11
Cinn. Twists	231	11	3	316	32
Lemon-lime	190	0	0	90	48
Total	604	22	13	682	91
Kentucky Fried Chicken (Source: Kentucky Fried Chicken Corporation)					
Nuggets	276	17	17	840	13
Kentucky Fries	377	18	5	215	18
Root Beer	244	0	0	45	16
Total	897	35	22	1100	46

that consumer culture influences the ideas children develop about what is good and bad. . . ." Nutritional advocates are trying hard to fight the presence of fast foods in schools.

The rise in obesity in children, in part, is attributed to less play and more consumption of fast foods (Ebbeling et al., 2004; Duffey et al., 2007). Fast foods' most clever marketing has been directed toward children (Schlosser & Wilson, 2006). Every month, 9 out of 10 of America's children between the ages of 3 and 9 visit a McDonald's restaurant, and that is just one representative of fast-food visits by children (Schlosser & Wilson, 2006).

In 2004, a movie came out titled *Super Size Me.* It was about a man living solely on McDonald's food items for 30 days. As the movie progresses, the man gets sicker and sicker, and it becomes apparent that a diet of fast-food is not healthy and can even be dangerous. Children reported that they would prefer larger portions of french fries when eating at fast-food restaurants (Colapinto et al., 2007). As a result of the movie, children's obvious preference for "super sizing," and the discussion surrounding these, McDonald's and other fast-food chains have been offering some healthier selections, especially for children's meals. Children may now choose apples with caramel dip, salad, yogurt with granola, or mandarin orange sections instead of fries at several chains. They can also choose milk or apple juice as their beverage instead of soft drinks. In addition, since

(continues)

REALITY *Check* (continued)

that movie came out, several cities have banned the use of trans fats in the foods served in restaurants (Lueck & Severson, 2007). There is a growing trend away from "super-sizing." Many chains have dropped their half-pound size of french fries and their 48- and 64-ounce size soft-drink options. Some chains are no longer asking whether their customers want to be "super-sized." The increase in portion size over the years has confused consumers about judging portion size, as they might have been able to do in the past (Mancino, 2007). Consumers are asking that fast foods be labeled for nutrition so they can see how many calories and nutrients there are in a large portion in order to make better choices (O'Dougherty et al., 2006). Consumers also want to see the more healthy food choicess clearly labeled on the menu board (Lando & Labiner-Wolfe, 2007).

A typical fast-food meal for children can provide as much as 36 percent of their daily caloric needs but falls short of basic nutrients. At a fast-food restaurant, most children have the kid's meal that includes a main item, fries, and a soft drink. Occasionally these meals include a dessert, and they almost always include a toy, which is a big draw for many children. On the previous page are some typical kids' meals with nutritional breakdown.

As this table reflects, children are getting an overabundance of fat and sodium and a large number of calories for the nutrients present in these meals. To view further nutritional breakdowns, check the fast-food chain websites: http://app.mcdonalds.com, http://www.bk.com, http://www.kfc.com, and http://www.tacobell.com.

Because children are eating out so often, it is even more necessary for the teacher to provide nutritious meals in the early childhood education environment. It is also important to avoid being caught in the fast-food challenge. Children prefer highly flavored, high-fat meals, so this may be a challenge. However, teachers can discuss these issues with children and help them make better choices when they do go out. For example, helping a child choose milk instead of a soft drink will bring the nutrients in the meal more in balance.

CHECK*point*: **How would you conduct a discussion about fast foods with 4-year-old children? What suggestions might you have to help them choose more wisely?**

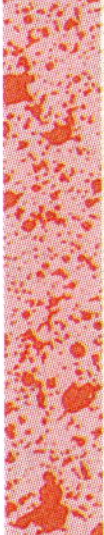

Pause for Reflection

How often do you eat fast foods? Are you doing it as a matter of time and convenience, or is cooking something you are not good at? How might you continue to eat fast food occasionally but make healthier choices? What other steps could you take to possibly cut down on eating fast foods? What types of things might you keep handy to make healthy, quick meals that are convenient so that you eat fast food less often?

8.6 NUTRITION AND THE CHILD WITH SPECIAL NEEDS

- **developmental disabilities** *physical or mental incapacities that interfere with normal progress of development.*

Some teachers care for children who have special needs. Many of these children have **developmental disabilities** or chronic illnesses that affect feeding skills, nutritional needs, or equipment needed. Some children require special feeding procedures and some require special foods or diets. Teachers caring for children with special needs may face more challenges at snack time and meal time than they would with a child who is developing in a typical manner (Holland, 2005).

Children who have cerebral palsy, Down syndrome, a cleft lip or palate, or other developmental abnormalities may have physical difficulties eating or feeding themselves. Children with metabolic disorders such as cystic fibrosis, diabetes, PKU, and maple syrup urine syndrome have special dietary limitations that prevent them from eating certain types of food and make the MyPyramid Food Guidance System less useful. Some children have conditions that require modifying their intake of sodium, protein, carbohydrates, or fats. Others may have allergies or food intolerances. Certain medical conditions may call for dietary restrictions or requirements (Holland, 2005). Children with special needs may require more time to eat; eating may be a real struggle and cause more mess than normal (Holland, 2005).

The Americans with Disabilities Act (1990) requires certain early childhood education environments and family child care homes to accommodate children with special needs as best they can. That act also has a provision that requires states to provide early intervention services to infants and toddlers. Nutrition services are included in this early intervention (National Food Service Management Institute, 2006).

There are many children whose special needs can be accommodated easily and whose nutritional needs may not be difficult to meet. Chairs, tables, and eating utensils may have to be modified for some children. Some children may need modification made in texture or calories provided. The teacher can make these accommodations without great expense or effort.

Some children have special needs that offer challenges the teacher really is not prepared or trained to accommodate. The nutritional needs of some children with chronic illness or developmental disabilities are complicated and may be compounded by eating difficulties. The average teacher should not be expected to provide this type of accommodation without outside assessment, intervention, and help. The teacher could easily train for some accommodations such as the use of a gastric tube. The Americans with Disabilities Act provides for the nutrition services the teacher may need. Contacting the state child nutrition staff is a good place to begin. Local school districts may be involved in early intervention assessment, and local regional centers may also provide some of this assessment. The American Dietetic Association supports the participation of its members in providing nutrition services to early childhood education programs that include children with disabilities and chronic illnesses. Parents of these children may be good sources of information and may be able to help the teacher to link up with the community services required to support the care of these children.

Access to these services may not provide a teacher with the skills and special handling that some children with special needs require. A referral for the child to a special care program or regional center may be all that the teacher is able to do to help the families of these children.

For the child with special needs that can be accommodated, it is important to remember to respect the child's food preferences and hunger level, just as with every other child. The child's eating pace may be slower, so more time may be necessary California Child Care Health Program ([CCCHP], 2003). Food textures may be an issue with many children with special needs, so the teacher should be sensitive to that and start with the simplest texture, working through to the ones that are more difficult. Calorie intake may also present a concern. Certain disabilities and other special needs may require greater than average calories, whereas others may require fewer calories (National Food Service Management Institute, 2006). Food allergies or food intolerance are more likely to occur in a child with special needs, so care must be taken to observe for this.

Depending on the child's specific condition, a special diet may be required. Nutritional goals for the child should be discussed with the family. The teacher should keep accurate records of feeding and should communicate often with the family. Being supportive of the family is important. The teacher will be acting as a role model for food and eating practices (Holland, 2005). All of these considerations make it important for the teacher or early childhood education environment to have nutritional policies for children with special needs who are in care.

Key Concept 8.6

Children with Special Needs

The Americans with Disabilities Act may require that some early childhood education environments and some family child care homes accommodate children with special needs as best they can. Some children with disabilities or chronic illnesses may be easily accommodated in their nutritional needs and feeding levels. Others may require special early intervention nutritional services. Those services may not be adequate to provide the level of care some children with special needs may require. Special nutritional policies for children with special needs should be developed if such children are present in the early childhood education environment.

8.7 IMPLICATIONS FOR TEACHERS

Nutrition education is an important tool for the teacher helping parents and children better understand their role in proper nutrition for good health and well-being. Education can break down barriers, provide awareness of the effects of growth and development on feeding habits, and provide strategies to parents who want to make sure their children are getting a healthy start. Education can also make children aware of their food selections and how their behavior effects their health and well-being. It can empower them to make better choices and participate in their own nutritional well-being. The teacher can carry out educational strategies through role modeling. Cultural sensitivity is essential for the teacher who has a diverse group in care. Through supervision, the teacher can help children carry out good nutritional practices.

Education and Role Modeling

Teachers and parents have a great influence on what children learn to eat. Modeling healthy eating to children of all ages can help children develop healthy eating habits themselves (Briley & Roberts-Gray, 2005; Jana & Shu, 2007). The kinds of food provided for children help to determine how the child will eat and grow. Parents and teachers model healthy food selection

Teachers who sit and eat with children and engage them in conversation can make mealtimes pleasant and can keep children on task. This measure could increase the intake of good foods, thus improving nutrition.

and acceptability to the children in their lives. If these selections are healthy choices, a child will have a positive perspective about good foods. If the selections are poor choices, this sends a negative message about good nutrition.

Good food habits are one of the greatest contributors to good health. From a very young age, a child is capable of learning these through practice and observation. Children are strongly influenced by what they see and hear. Parents and teachers are sources of behavior and information that children model and remember. Children have an influence on the shopping habits of parents. Their food preferences appear to mirror the television advertising that they see (Borzekowski & Robinson, 2001; Utter, Scragg, & Schaaf, 2006). Children have a large influence over parents' purchasing habits (O'Dougherty, Story, & Stang, 2006).

The teacher should take time out, on a regular basis, to go over the MyPyramid for Kids with the children in care. The nutritional information about what each person should be eating in a day can be assimilated over time. Regular repetition helps children understand and remember. This practice also helps the teacher keep good nutritional information in action.

Enlisting children's help with food selection and preparation encourages them to try new foods and new ways of food preparation. Readying children to help can be accomplished in several ways. The educational experience can be enhanced by reading books on certain foods, watching a video about foods, talking about what is going to be prepared during circle time, or telling a flannelboard story about the food or activity.

For Families. Families and teachers have the power to establish positive, supportive environments that allow children to develop good feeding behaviors and attitudes toward food. The teacher can help the parent understand this by providing good role modeling and some positive nutrition information. The teacher should be aware that there may be some barriers to accepting this information (Briley et al., 1998). Perhaps there are environmental constraints to good nutrition for some of the families. Cost of food, access and availability of good food, and storage space are factors that may limit the family's ability to make a wide range of good food choices.

Poverty or low income may prohibit the selection of many foods, including fresh fruits and vegetables and dairy products. These families may need assistance in accessing food programs that help families meet their food needs. The teacher may also be able to provide the parents with information on food selections as well as recipes that use low-cost fresh foods. Consequently, the teacher may find there is greater interest on the part of the family to improve their nutritional intake. Children in low-income families would qualify for both the school lunch and school breakfast programs sponsored by the federal government.

Another influence on food selection may be convenience of preparation. Some adults find it easier to open a can or a box than to prepare fresh foods. Other adults might select fast foods as a further measure of convenience (see Reality Check: Children of the Fast-Food Generation). These behaviors are an enormous barrier with middle and upper income families who can afford the convenience of packaged or fast foods. Having children help prepare foods may spark the parents' interest in preparing more fresh food. Role modeling and providing recipes as well as activities for the families to do together may encourage this behavior.

Another barrier can occur when the parent does not understand the stages and phases of growth and development as well as the teacher does. Such a parent may be unsure as to how to proceed and may wish to feed the child as he or she was fed as a youngster. Childhood food memories may influence selection or rejection of certain foods or food behaviors. A parent may model behaviors that are not productive to helping the child widen her food selections.

Adults may not realize that the social environment that is provided at mealtimes has a direct relationship to their children's dietary quality. The structure of mealtimes can contribute to a child's eating pattern (Patrick & Nicklas, 2005). Children need a positive atmosphere, companionship, and the opportunity to view appropriate adult food-related behaviors to achieve good nutrition. The children in care may be the best educators because they can model what they learned in school (Parlakian & Lerner, 2007). The teacher can help parents by explaining the different stages of growth and development and encouraging parents to observe their child's behavior. Parents may then try different ways to support their children's eating behavior. Companionship at mealtimes and a positive social atmosphere will foster healthy food selections and good behavior.

The level of written nutritional information may be another barrier for the teacher and the parent. Not all adults are literate. Approximately 60 million adults in the United States have not completed high school. Those who have completed high school may not read at the 12th-grade level. To be effective, the nutritional information provided to the parent should be at the level that he or she is capable of understanding (Busselman & Holcomb, 1994). To be fully understood, the information may also have to be presented in the native language of the family.

Wadsworth/Cengage Learning

This teacher is having fun helping children learn about food and how it is made, even if it is "green eggs and ham"!

When 4-year-old Amy came to Head Start, her mother reported that Amy did not like and would not eat most foods. Tanya, Amy's teacher, observed Amy at snack and lunchtime for several weeks. She watched as Amy refused to try new things for the first two weeks. The foods that she was most vocal about were vegetables and fruits. Of the fruits and vegetables offered to her, Amy would eat only canned applesauce and corn. Other children were eating most of the foods that Amy was refusing. One day Joelle, another 4-year-old, encouraged Amy to try some green beans. Amy tried them and ended up eating all of her beans and asking for more. Several days later, the preschoolers picked some carrots and cherry tomatoes at a cooperative garden they toured near their school. The vegetables were brought back to school, and the children helped wash them and prepare them for a snack. Amy ate both the carrots and tomatoes. She loved the carrots and was mildly interested in the tomatoes.

Tanya reported these breakthroughs to Amy's mother, who had a hard time believing Amy was eating vegetables. She explained that Amy's father, who was no longer living with them, had hated vegetables and did not even want them in the house. Amy's mother got used to serving only applesauce. Her budget was also tight, so this wasn't a sacrifice on her part. Tanya spent some time explaining the MyPyramid Food Guidance System and why a balanced diet was important. She also pointed out that there were some plots available in the community garden, so it did not have to cost too much money to increase the variety of fresh produce in the family's diet. Once Amy's mother realized the importance of a balanced diet, she signed up for a plot in the nearby cooperative garden and started trying to add more variety to the menu at home.

Cultural Competence

Cultural influences may present an obstacle to proper nutritional balance. The teacher may face a challenge in helping parents select good food. Providing food and nutrition for children from diverse backgrounds can be a real task, but it can also be rewarding. Culture influences how food is prepared, seasoned, and even how and when it is eaten. Taboos and certain cultural traits must be considered, such as the high percentage of lactose intolerance among the Asian population. Cultural differences should be taken into account when developing mealtime patterns for young children (Ziegler, Hanson et al., 2006). For example, Hispanic children are much more likely to consume fresh fruits and drink milk, whereas African-American children are much less likely to drink milk (Mennella et al., 2006; Fulgoni et al., 2007).

Understanding the cultural influence on food is important if the teacher is going to help the families provide optimum nutrition for their children when they are not in care. Incorporating home cultures by asking parents to share their culture's foods and food habits with the children in care is a good way for the teacher to find out the extent of this obstacle, if there is one. This will also encourage children to try foods from many cultures and to appreciate a greater range of food selections. Adapting food selections to cultural influences may increase the selection of foods available to the family. As the teacher understands the dietary or food limitations of a family, he may have to call on outside help, such as a nutritionist (Padget and Briley, 2005).

Another issue in cultural competence may be the teacher's own cultural perspective on the selection and presentation of foods, which may reflect the teacher's own customs, traditions, and food preferences. Not all children like foods that are different from the ones they are used to eating. These differences may be in the manner in which the foods are prepared or in the way they are seasoned. It is important for the teacher to be sensitive to the needs of the children. The teacher should present a balance of foods that represent the food selections of children from a number of cultures. Children appreciate and feel validated when their home culture is included in the early childhood environment (Volk & Long, 2005). Awareness of one's own culture in addition to the other cultures present in the early education environment is necessary (Obegi & Ritblatt, 2005). That, in combination with good communication skills to discuss nutrition and food choices with families and children, can assist the teacher in providing optimal nutrition for all.

Pause for Reflection

What is your own cultural background? How does your cultural background relate to the foods you eat and/or prepare? If you feel you don't have a particular cultural background, are there favorite family foods or food traditions that are used in celebrations such as birthdays? Do you often eat foods from other cultures? If so, what foods and what cultures?

Supervision

A teacher is likely to serve one or more meals per day to the children in the early childhood education environment, depending on the time children are present. Supervision of mealtime requires a number of skills. If the teacher provides meals to the children, the first area of supervision will be for the selection of healthy foods. Regardless of whether the food is prepared by the teacher or by someone else, meal planning should focus on healthy food choices and preparation. Food safety and sanitation should be practiced. It might be helpful to record the foods children eat by making a daily food consumption chart (Giosa, 2006). This chart can help the teacher monitor the foods children seem to enjoy and eat. It can also be helpful to track the food a child consumed in order to correlate it to his behavior. A child who exhibits challenging behaviors in the morning when he comes from home might settle down in the afternoon after a healthy snack and lunch.

If the child brings meals from home, the teacher may have to supervise which food selections are acceptable. She may also have to determine proper storage so the food remains safe. Sending a sheet of acceptable food choices for the early childhood education situation may help remind parents that the teacher is there to provide optimum care for their children. If a child brings unacceptable foods, such as highly sugared, fatty, or salted foods, these can be set aside to eat only after the good choices have been finished. If a child brings foods from another culture, the teacher should make an effort to learn about the food and how it relates to good nutrition. Reading labels with children can help make them aware of food content. This can be a powerful tool in influencing the parents to make better food selections.

Direction of mealtime behaviors helps to establish good eating habits and feeding behaviors. Observing the behaviors of children is easier when growth and developmental levels are understood. Good role modeling of mealtime practices is essential. The teacher has a great deal of influence on how the children in her care behave. Understanding the teacher's and the child's responsibilities for healthy eating will alleviate control issues over food. This helps the teacher to provide a foundation of good feeding behaviors and eating practices.

Key Concept 8.7

Implications for Teachers

The teacher has an opportunity to provide positive food practices, good food selections, and an atmosphere conducive to eating. Application of information, strategies, and practices found in this chapter and the previous chapter enables the teacher to do this. Opportunities to educate the children about nutrition will occur on a daily basis. Every time there is a meal or snack, the teacher can sit with the children and role-model good eating practices while having a dialogue about the food. Awareness of family conditions and nutritional knowledge can help the teacher be prepared to assist families in several ways. Teachers can provide education as well as connect families to resources for better nutrition for their children. Practicing cultural sensitivity by acknowledging diverse food habits and preparing foods to reflect these assists in removing barriers about food selection. Through supervising choices, the teacher can ensure that proper nutritional habits are being formed and practiced in the early childhood education environment.

CHAPTER SUMMARY

Every teacher should practice good nutrition in the early childhood education environment. Many teachers are not meeting the nutritional needs of children in their care. Teachers may approach nutrition with their own perspectives based on background, food practices, culture, and what the children will eat. Teachers should have nutritional policies that cover early infant feeding, food and the toddler, the preschool child, school-aged children, and children with special needs.

The teacher who understands how to accommodate the infant's physical and psychological needs will encourage the infant to go at his own pace. A teacher who understands that the developmental characteristics of a toddler influences how she deals with food is less likely to make food an issue of control. Teachers should use participatory activities to help the preschooler develop an awareness of the best nutritional choices. Teachers can provide adequate nutrition for school-aged children by keeping in mind their activity levels.

Some children with disabilities or chronic illnesses can be easily accommodated in their nutritional needs and feeding levels. Others may require special early intervention nutritional services or may not be able to be in the early childhood education situation.

The implications for the teacher include education, working with families, role modeling, and supervision. Opportunities to educate and role-model good nutrition to the children and adults occur on a daily basis. Cultural sensitivity can break down barriers to food selection. By supervising choices, the teacher ensures that proper nutritional habits are being formed and practiced in the early childhood education environment.

TO GO BEYOND

Additional resources for this chapter can be found by visiting the book companion website at www.cengage.com/education/robertson. This supplemental material includes chapter objectives, internet exercises, reflection questions, quizzes, web links, glossary and flash cards, case studies, frequently asked questions, downloadable forms and tables, curriculum supplements, more reality checks, additional key concepts, references, and more.

Chapter Review Critical Thinking Applications

1. Discuss how developmental levels relate to nutritional needs of children of different ages. How do the developmental levels affect the eating process for children?
2. Examine the benefits of breastfeeding. Compare and contrast these benefits to those of bottle feeding. List suggestions as to how a breastfeeding mother might be supported to continue to breastfeed her baby.
3. Describe how you would introduce solid foods to an infant.
4. Analyze how food is used as a control issue by toddlers and their parents. How would you avoid this in an early childhood education situation?

5. What barriers might families have to providing healthy, nutritious foods to their children?

As an Individual

1. Observe children and their parents in a grocery store. How do they interact in the cereal aisle? How do these interactions reflect positive rewards for negative behavior? How might food be an issue of control in these situations?
2. Observe Saturday morning television for one hour and count the number of commercials representing fast-food companies. Choose one of the commercials and list the methods employed to attract children to the products.
3. Compare your family-of-origin mealtime practices to those outlined in the rules in an early childhood education environment. Compare and contrast their similarities and differences.
4. Choose several local schools in your area that are not in the same district and look up their lunch menus. Are the menus serving items that might be found on fast-food menus, or do they offer healthier selections?

As a Group

1. During a weeklong period, watch people eating, including children, and observe their cultural patterns. Discuss these patterns in class. List the patterns observed by all students in class. How would you use this information to talk to children about eating and food? How might you use this information to adapt to the different cultures in your local area?
2. Collect menus from early childhood education centers, family care homes, and elementary schools in your area. Evaluate them and determine whether they meet the nutritional needs of children. How might these menus be changed to better meet the needs described in the MyPyramid Food Guidance System?
3. Break up into small groups and have each group write three general policies for nutrition in the early childhood education environment. Come back together as a class to discuss these. Choose the three most important policies, and discuss why these were chosen.

Case Studies

1. April is a new mother who must return to work when her son, Henry, is 10 weeks old. She has really enjoyed the breastfeeding relationship with Henry and has been pumping milk and getting him used to a bottle. As his teacher, what specific things can you do to support April? Why is it important that you offer this support?
2. Drew is a 15-month-old toddler. His mother still has him drinking formula out of a bottle and prefers to hand-feed him toddler food from a jar because it is less messy than letting him feed himself.

He wants the bottle and does not attempt to eat much of the food that you prepare for him. Drew seems to catch more than his share of colds and does not seem to be as active as he was when he was younger. How do you handle this problem? What could you say to his mother to enlist her help?

3. Jerome is in your second-grade class. You notice that, unlike other children, he sits and eats his lunch until it is gone and often asks other kids whether he can finish the parts of their lunches they are about to throw away. His mother comes to you, concerned that he is overeating at home too. She wants some suggestions for cutting down on his food intake. What action(s) might you suggest?

CHAPTER 9

Menu Planning and Food Safety in Early Childhood Education Environments

After reading this chapter, you should be able to:

9.1 Nutritional Policies

Define and discuss nutritional policies in relation to menu planning and food safety in the early childhood education environment.

9.2 Guidelines for Food Programs

Discuss the guidelines for subsidized food programs available for early childhood education environments.

9.3 Menu Planning for Early Childhood Education Environments

Indicate the importance of proper menu planning for children's well-being, including strategies for planning healthy breakfasts, snacks, and lunches.

9.4 Food Safety in Early Childhood Education Environments

Summarize the need for food sanitation and safety and practice strategies for providing it in the early childhood education environment.

9.5 Implications for Teachers

Relate the strategies for providing safe and healthy meals in the early childhood education environment through education, observation, cultural sensitivity, and supervision.

9.1 NUTRITIONAL POLICIES

An increasing number of children are being cared for in early childhood education environments. These environments appear to be the places where many children are learning their food habits because they are spending much of their day in care. In order to meet the nutritional needs of the children in care, teachers must be prepared to plan healthy menus that children will enjoy and eat. Teachers must also be prepared to protect the children from disease by practicing food safety. The following are indicators of the need for sound nutritional policies for menu planning and food safety:

- The Child and Adult Care Food Program (CACFP) standards are not nutrient-based as are the federal standards for the school lunch and breakfast meals, so "the nutritional quality of meals and snacks may be poor" in sites that participate in CACFP (Story, Kaphingst, & French, 2006). Further, in centers participating in CACFP, it was found that food actually served to the children was not the food listed on the menu 98 percent of the time (Fleischhacker, Cason, & Acterberg, 2006). Early childhood programs that participate in CACFP would benefit from a self-assessment program (Oakley, Carr, & Brainard, 2007).
- Early childhood education professionals should develop skills in maximizing the nutritional value of food so that they can appropriately select, prepare, and cook for the greatest nutritional value (Nicklas & Johnson, 2004; Droke, Kennedy, & Hubbs-Tait, 2006; Rose, 2007).
- Teachers should understand what age-appropriate portion sizes are for maximizing nutrition while children are in care (McConahy et al., 2004; Colapinto et al., 2007).
- Significant changes in the diets of children have occurred in the last 20 years. Preschool children are consuming fewer breakfast meals, fruits, vegetables, and dairy products, and are consuming more of their total calories from snacks, sweetened beverages, and fried and nutrient-poor foods. Children are not meeting the Dietary Guidelines for Americans recommendations (USDHHS, 2005; Federal Register, 2004) for nutrition (Gidding et al., 2006).
- Research has shown that only half of teachers know food sources of nutrients and portion sizes for children (Briley & Roberts-Gray, 2005; Romaine et al., 2007). Teachers can benefit from training in food and nutrition (Unusan, 2007; Sigman-Grant et al., 2008).
- Menus should be planned to meet guidelines if the early childhood education program is participating in the CACFP (Oakley & Carr, 2003b; Stang & Beyerl, 2003). By 2006, there were almost 3 million children in care participating in CACFP (FRAC, 2006).
- It is recommended that teachers provide two-thirds of the recommended daily intake for children who are in care for long hours (Briley & Roberts-Gray, 2005). Children's nutritional needs should be met during the time they are in care (NCCCHSRC, 2006).
- Early childhood education environments should have a safe and adequate food supply, provide staff training, and promote healthy eating patterns for optimal physical, social, and emotional growth and

development in the children they serve (Briley & Roberts-Gray, 2005; ADA, 2006).

- Keeping food safe to eat is one of the Dietary Guidelines for Americans (USDHHS, 2005; Federal Register, 2004). In evaluations in Texas child-care centers, there were 27 different bacteria types found on food service surfaces (Staskel et al., 2007). Food safety training is required for both directors and staff in child care centers (Enke et al., 2007).

Early childhood education centers have a number of teachers on staff. In some centers, one of them may double as the food preparer and menu planner. The director may plan the menus, whereas a food preparation person is hired specifically for the job of cooking. In some cases, there may be a centrally located kitchen, or food may be catered and prepared food distributed to several early childhood education centers. A dietician hired exclusively for that task may provide these menus.

In family child care, the care provider or the nanny is probably the menu planner and food preparer. This task, in addition to caring for children, may

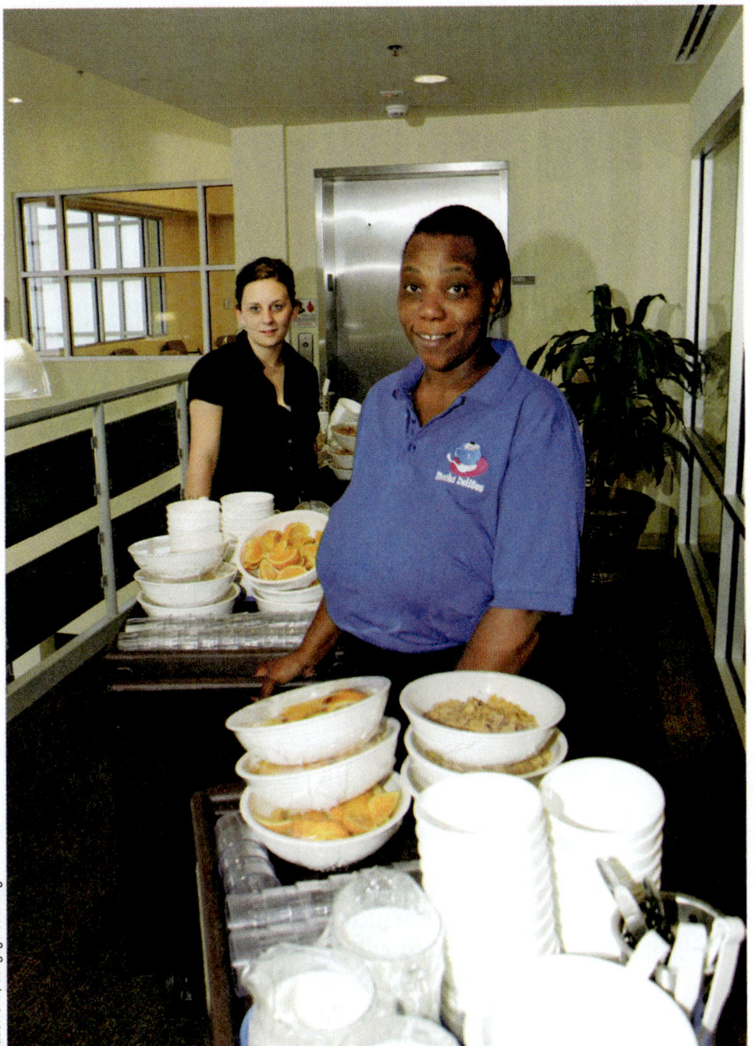

Wadsworth/Cengage Learning

Food is often prepared by cooks and then transported to the classroom, as these ladies are doing.

appear to be burdensome. With proper training in menu planning and food safety, the family child care provider may find the job easier to perform.

The early childhood education program has been examined for its potential to provide good nutritional practices and safe food handling techniques (Briley & Roberts-Gray, 2005). These can be improved through a more thorough understanding of the meals provided in care and the necessity for good menu planning as well as proper food sanitation and safety practices. Teachers will have to use education, cultural sensitivity, observation, and supervision to carry out this task.

It is recommended that policies be created for the following areas:

- *Guidelines for food programs:* understanding how the subsidized food programs' guidelines should affect the food selection in early childhood education environments.
- *Menu planning:* understanding how to plan menus that meet children's tastes and nutritional needs, as well as being cost-effective and easy to prepare.
- *Food sanitation and safety:* understanding the methods and practices for food sanitation and safety in early childhood education environments.
- *Implications for teachers:* understanding how education, cultural sensitivity, and supervision can help the teacher plan for adequate nutrition and food safety in early childhood education environments.

Key Concept 9.1

Nutritional Policies

More than 5 million children are eating meals in early childhood education environments on a daily basis. Nutrition and food safety have been found to be inadequate in many of these environments. It is up to the teacher who plans and/or prepares meals for children to be adequately trained. The teacher should have an understanding of how breakfast, snacks, and lunches affect a child's nutritional needs. The teacher should know how to select healthy foods, plan adequate menus, and prepare food that is safe. By using education, cultural sensitivity, observation, and supervision, the teacher ensures that the early childhood education environment is providing for the nutritional needs of the children in care.

9.2 GUIDELINES FOR FOOD PROGRAMS

There are a number of food programs that teachers and families can use to meet the nutritional needs of children. Several of these affect the early childhood education program directly. The CACFP, the Food Distribution Program, the School Milk Program (SMP), and the Summer Food Service Program for Children (SFSPC) help provide foods for early childhood education environments that meet the criteria. The CACFP and the Expanded Food and Nutrition

Wadsworth/Cengage Learning

The main goal of organized food programs is to provide nutritious foods for children in need.

Education Program (EFNEP) provide nutrition information and training for teachers, food service personnel, and children.

Programs that help families include the Special Supplemental Food Program for Women, Infants, and Children (WIC), the USDA's Food Stamp Program, the National School Lunch Program, and the School Breakfast program. WIC provides formula and other foods to families with children younger than 3 years old. The Food Stamp Program provides more food to children and their families than any other source. A great majority of the people who receive food stamp monies are families with children (Stang & Beyerl, 2003). Teachers should be informed about these resources in case they have to make referrals to families to help them provide adequate nutrition to their children when not in care (Stang & Beyerl, 2003).

The Child and Adult Care Food Program

The CACFP provides funding for children up to age 12 years. To be eligible to participate in this program and receive funds, the early childhood education center or home must be one of the following:

1. Nonprofit licensed or approved public or private early childhood education center
2. Family child care home that belongs to a sponsoring agency
3. For-profit private program that receives funding for more than one-fourth of the children present in care through Title XX of the Social Security Act

In 2006, nearly 3 million children were served two meals and one snack while in care, with CACFP funding (FRAC, 2006).

Funding for the CACFP is made possible through the USDA's Food and Nutrition Service (USDA FNS). Eligible early childhood education sites may be funded for up to two meals and one snack per day or two snacks and one meal. Center-based sites serve more than 2 million children on a daily basis. A sliding scale is applied at the early childhood education site that indicates how much to charge a family for meals, depending upon their income. Many children receive free meals as a result of the application of the scale.

The family child care home must have a sponsoring agency that administers the program. This may be a local early childhood education resource and referral agency, a public agency such as a USDA cooperative extension service, or another local agency willing to provide financial administration. The state child care licensing agency can provide the teacher with this information. The number of children served in family child care homes is approximately 900,000 on a daily basis. Recently, the number of children in these family child care homes has decreased by about 8 percent (FRAC, 2006). This may be due to the fact that the 1996 Welfare Reform Act states that for a family child care home to be eligible, it must be in a low-income area. This new provision allows only about 25 percent of children in family child care homes to participate in CACFP today (Report on Preschool Programs [RPP], 2004).

The CACFP provides funding for meals and nutritional training and menu planning for the teachers. In return, the early childhood education environment must meet the nutritional guidelines set by the CACFP. These are included in Table 9-1.

TABLE 9-1
CACFP Nutritional Guidelines

Infants—*Birth to 3 Months*

Breakfast, Lunch, and Snack

4–6 oz. formula or breast milk

Infants—*4 to 7 Months*

Breakfast

4–8 oz. formula or breast milk

0–3 Tbs. iron-fortified infant cereal (not snack)

Lunch

4–8 oz. formula or breast milk

0–3 Tbs. iron-fortified infant cereal (not snack)

0–3 Tbs. vegetables or fruits or both

Snack

4–8 oz. formula or breast milk

Infants—*8 to 11 Months*

Breakfast and Lunch

6–8 oz. formula

2–4 Tbs. iron-fortified infant cereal

1–4 Tbs. fruit or vegetables

Lunch or Supper

6–8 oz. formula or breast milk

2–4 oz. iron-fortified infant cereal *and/or* 1–4 Tbs. meat, fish, poultry, egg yolk, or dried beans, *or* 1–4 oz. cottage cheese, cheese spread, or cheese food, *or* ½–2 oz. cheese

1–4 Tbs. of fruit or vegetable or both

Snack

2–4 oz. formula or milk *or* full-strength fruit juice

2 crackers or ½ slice bread

Children—*1 to 2 Years*

Breakfast

½ cup milk

¼ cup fruit juice, fruit, or vegetable

Bread and/or cereal or grains (¼ cup cereal, ½ slice bread, ¼ cup grains, noodles, or pasta)

Lunch or Supper

1 oz. meat, poultry, fish, or cheese, *or* ½ egg, ¼ cup cooked dry beans, or peas, *or* 2 Tbs. peanut butter, *or* ½ oz. nuts, *or* 4 oz. yogurt

¼ cup (total) vegetables and/or fruits or 100 percent fruit juice

½ slice bread or ¼ cup cereal, pasta, noodles, or grains

(continues)

TABLE 9-1 *(Continued)*
CACFP Nutritional Guidelines

Snack (select two of four components)

½ cup milk

½ oz. meat or meat alternate (cheese, egg, beans, peanut butter, nuts/seeds), *or*

2 oz. plain yogurt or ¼ cup flavored yogurt *(do not serve yogurt and milk at same snack)*

½ cup 100 percent fruit juice, fruit, or vegetable

Bread and/or cereal (½ slice bread, ½ roll, or equivalent grain such as ¼ cup cold cereal, hot cereal, or pasta)

Children—*3 to 5 Years*

Breakfast

¾ cup milk

½ cup 100 percent fruit juice, fruit, or vegetable

Bread and/or cereal (½ slice bread, ½ roll, or equivalent grain such as ⅓ cup cold cereal or ¼ cup hot cereal, noodles, grains, or pasta)

Lunch or Supper

¾ cup milk

1½ oz. meat or meat alternate—1½ oz. cheese, ⅜ cup dry beans or peas, *or* 3 Tbs. peanut butter, *or* ¾ oz. nuts/seeds, *or* ¾ egg, *or* 6 oz. yogurt

½ cup (total) vegetables and/or fruits or 100 percent fruit juice

Bread and/or cereal (½ slice bread, ½ roll, *or* equivalent grain such as ⅓ cup cold cereal or ¼ cup hot cereal, noodles, grains, or pasta)

Snack (Select two of four components)

½ cup milk

½ oz. meat or meat alternate—½ oz. cheese, ⅛ cup dry beans or peas, *or* 1 Tbs. peanut butter, *or* ½ oz. nuts/seeds, *or* ½ egg, *or* 2 oz. yogurt

½ cup 100 percent fruit juice or fruit or vegetable *(juice cannot be served if milk is the only other snack component)*

Bread and/or cereal (½ slice bread, ½ roll, *or* equivalent such as ⅓ cup cold cereal, or ¼ cup hot cereal, noodles, grains, or pasta)

Children—*6 to 12 Years*

Breakfast

1 cup milk

½ cup 100 percent fruit juice, fruit, or vegetable

Bread and/or cereal (1 slice bread, 1 roll, *or* equivalent grain such as ¾ cup cold cereal, ½ cup hot cereal noodles, grains, or pasta)

Lunch or Supper

1 cup milk

¾ cup 100 percent fruit juice, fruit, or vegetable

(continues)

TABLE 9-1 *(Continued)*
CACFP Nutritional Guidelines

Bread and/or cereal (1 slice bread, 1 roll, *or* equivalent grain such as ¾ cup cold cereal or ½ cup hot cereal noodles, grains, or pasta)

(2 oz. meat or meat alternates—2 oz. cheese, ½ cup dry beans or peas, 4 Tbs. peanut butter or 1 oz. nuts/seeds) or 1 egg or 8 oz. yogurt

Snack (Select two of four components)

1 cup milk

¾ cup 100 percent fruit juice, fruit, or vegetable *(juice cannot be served if milk is the only other snack component)*

Bread and/or cereal (1 slice bread, 1 roll, or equivalent grain such as ¾ cup cold cereal or ½ cup hot cereal, noodles, grains, or pasta)

1 oz. meat or meat alternates—1 oz. cheese, ¼ cup dry beans or peas, *or* 4 Tbs. peanut butter, *or* 1 oz. nuts/seeds, *or* ½ egg, *or* 4 oz. yogurt

Note: All juices must be full strength. Breads, cereals, and grains must be whole grains or enriched or fortified. Yogurt may be plain, sweetened or unsweetened.

The CACFP does conduct assessments of their participants. This assessment can be a complex process. It is suggested that participants use a self-assessment tool of checklists that were designed to adhere to best practices. These checklists can help participants improve their program and document their progress, therefore making the formal assessment an easier process (Oakley, Carr, & Brainard, 2007).

National School Lunch Program and School Breakfast Program

Two programs operated by the USDA FNS impact children in the early elementary school years. One is the National School Lunch Program that provides school-age children with nutritious meals and approximately one-third of the DRI for key nutrients which include protein, iron, calcium, Vitamin A, and Vitamin B (USDA FNS, 2007a). This program was begun with the National School Lunch Act in 1946 and has gone through many evolutions since then, including adding school snacks in 1998 and a required wellness/nutrition component beginning with the 2006–2007 school year (FRAC, 2007a). All public and private nonprofit schools are eligible to participate. All children whose schools participate are included, and for those who are income eligible there are either reduced-price or free lunches. More than 30 million children in the United States participate on a daily basis (USDA FNS, 2007a). Schools are required to provide less than 30 percent of total calories from fat and no more than 10 percent total calories from saturated fats. Eighty-one percent of children who participate in this program are income eligible for reduced-price or no-cost lunches. This program funds snacks for certain after-school educational and enrichment programs.

The second program operated by the USDA FNS is the School Breakfast Program. It was initiated as a pilot program in 1966 and made a permanent program in 1975 (USDA FNS, 2007b). By providing breakfast to those children who might not get it at home, the idea was to improve children's ability to learn. More than 9 million children participate in this breakfast program on a daily basis. The School Breakfast Program provides school-age children one-fourth of the key nutrients a child needs in a day. These include protein, calcium, iron, Vitamin A, Vitamin C, and calories. The food served must keep to 30 percent or less for fats and 10 percent or less for saturated fats (FRAC, 2007b). All children whose schools participate are eligible, and those who qualify get reduced-price or free breakfast.

REALITY *Check*

How Does the Overall Nutrition in Elementary Schools in the United States Really Rate?

The health quality of elementary school nutrition in this country is a controversial subject. Those who provide school nutrition say that the nutritional quality of foods served is very healthy (Lambert & Carr, 2006; School Nutrition Association, 2007b), and those who monitor school nutrition say that it could use improvement (O'Toole et al., 2007; Stroebele et al., 2006). Schools that serve federally funded school lunches and school breakfasts must meet nutritional standards as set by the Dietary Guidelines for Americans (USDHHS, 2005; Federal Register, 2004). In 2004, the School Lunch and School Breakfast Programs were reauthorized through the passing of the Child Nutrition and WIC Reauthorization Act. It was apparent with the passing of that legislation that some changes had to be made. The adoption of that reauthorization included a statement that nutrition guidelines for school meals and for all foods available on the school campus during the day should not be less restrictive than the federal guidelines state. It also instituted a wellness component that monitors physical activity. The wellness portion also includes a wellness committee that helps to monitor both nutrition and physical activity. These components were added due to the increasing incidence of obesity in this country. With the number of obese children tripling since 1980, it was felt that this issue should be addressed, and looking at school nutrition seemed the best way to begin because it is estimated that between 35 and 50 percent of children's total calories are consumed at school (National Alliance for Nutrition and Activity, 2007). This indicates that the foods served on school campuses account for a great deal of a child's daily nutrition and therefore should be of good nutritional quality. The National School Lunch and School Breakfast Programs must both meet minimum requirements for the amount of Vitamin A, Vitamin B, protein, iron, and calcium.

Over the years, critics have claimed that these meals have too much fat, too much salt, and too many calories to be healthy. For many years, school lunches looked very similar to those found in fast-food restaurants. In fact, some schools have had contracts for "branded" foods in which they allowed fast-food franchises to supply at least part of the food served to children. With the reauthorization in 2004, many of these practices have been changed or halted altogether. The trend today for school lunches and school breakfasts is toward healthier selections. Menus have shifted to include healthier options; even those options that do not appear to be changed in fact have been. For example, healthy modifications for pizza, French fries, and chicken fingers have been created and appear to be accepted by students (Stroebele et al., 2007). These healthier versions are acceptable to children and provide greater nutritional value and fewer energy-dense calories. In addition to these healthier modifications, more focus has been put on fruits and vegetables. It is common for elementary schools to offer salad bars as a component of their lunch selections, and there is a growing trend to try to get more fresh fruits and vegetables into these menus. Affordability is the biggest issue, but some groups, like the state of New Mexico, are working to connect farmers with school districts to provide fresh fruits and vegetables while eliminating the expensive middleman so that schools may be better able to afford to offer these to their students. One of the programs that the USDA FNS has

(continues)

REALITY *Check* (continued)

initiated to encourage this is called the HealthierUS School Challenge (School Nutrition Association, 2007a). Schools are certified as "Bronze," "Silver," or "Gold" if they meet stringent criteria. To be certified, a school must meet these requirements:

- The school must be an elementary school.
- The school must be enrolled as a Team Nutrition School.
- Healthy lunches must demonstrate menu-planning practices that correlate with the Dietary Guidelines for Americans and meet USDA nutritional standards.
- Schools must provide students opportunities for physical activity and nutrition education.
- Schools must maintain an average participation rate of 70 percent for reimbursable lunches.
- Schools must follow guidelines for foods served and sold outside the bounds of the National School Lunch Program.

A "Gold" certification includes all of the above standards as well as these:

- School lunch menus must offer a fresh fruit or raw vegetable and a whole-grain food each day.
- All foods offered any time of day and anywhere at the school must meet healthy standards.

The following three-day menu is an example of one that meets the "Gold" certification standard:

Lunch

Choose 1:

Cheeseburger w/whole-grain bun
Chicken pot pie w/biscuit
Yogurt w/whole-grain Cheerios

Choose 2:

Potato tots
Mixed vegetables
Vegetable cup with dip
Fresh apple

Lunch

Choose 1:

Nacho grande w/whole-grain tortilla
Breaded shrimp
Entrée salad w/whole-grain roll

Choose 2:

Au gratin potatoes
Kale greens
Vegetable cup with dip
Fresh pear

Lunch

Choose 1:

Whole-grain cheese or pepperoni pizza

Vegetable soup and whole-grain grilled cheese sandwich

Choose 2:

Green beans
Glazed carrots
Vegetable cup with dip
Pineapple chunks

Available daily: Cold sandwiches
All menus include one milk,
1 percent or ½ percent chocolate milk

The reauthorization has changed some of the nutritional practices on elementary school campuses, but there is still room for improvement (Knight Ridder/Tribune Business News, 2008). One major issue has been that many school campuses sell foods other than those available through school lunches. These may include à la carte foods offered during breakfast or lunch, at concession stands, school stores, and vending machines. It also includes school fundraisers that help to sponsor field trips and other enrichment activities. In 2006, it was found that about a third of elementary schools had a vending machine, school store, canteen, or snack bar where students could purchase foods and beverages (O'Toole et al., 2007). Items available in these venues included soda pop or fruit drinks that were not 100 percent juice, salty snacks, candy, cookies, and high-fat ice cream. Under the criteria of the USDA, foods sold outside of meals that are "foods of minimal nutritional value" cannot be sold in the cafeteria area during meals. However, the following foods appear to be allowed in school cafeterias because they are being sold there: fruit-ades with little or no real juice added, French fries, candy bars, cookies, chips, and doughnuts (National Alliance for Nutrition and Activity, 2007).

There are several groups that routinely monitor the foods in school nutrition programs throughout the country. These include the National Alliance for Nutrition and Activity, the Center for Science in the

(continues)

REALITY *Check* (continued)

Public Interest, and the School Health Policies and Programs Study. The Center for Science in the Public Interest rates states by the overall nutrition policies in the schools in each state. These overall nutrition policies include foods sold outside the reimbursed school meals. In 2007, only Oregon and Kentucky managed an A– report, whereas 30 states including Alaska, Minnesota, Pennsylvania, and Wyoming got an F rating; the other 18 states were in between (Center for Science in the Public Interest, 2007). This group and the National Alliance for Nutrition and Activity, which is comprised of a number of organizations including the American Cancer Society and the American Heart Association, feel that nutritional science has greatly evolved since the USDA set their nutrition standards in the 1970s. These groups feel that these standards should be closely following the Dietary Guidelines for Americans for foods sold outside the school breakfasts and lunches, and at present they are not. If the nutrition standards are not high, it is difficult to teach nutrition education when the examples of food children see in their schools don't match with what they are being taught are healthy foods. The School Health Policies and Programs Study of 2006 found that some improvement has been made. The number of states that prohibit the offering of junk foods has risen to 42 percent, and the number of districts doing the same has increased to 39 percent (CDC, 2007b). More schools were trimming fat from meat (66 percent) or using part-skim or low-fat cheeses (46 percent). However, this is still way short of the goal of healthy foods on school campuses. The School Nutrition Association has agreed that eating healthily at school can be problematic. Often, candies, cakes, and sweets are a large component of fundraisers. These fundraisers often make use of vending machines and campus stores. When schools are trying to promote healthily foods but school organizations are using unhealthy foods to make money, it sends a very mixed message to children who are receiving nutrition education. As of yet, these fundraisers are not monitored, nor do they fall under any nutritional standards. It may be up to the school districts' wellness committees to eliminate these practices if legislation is not passed.

CHECK*point:* **As a teacher, how would you make sure an elementary school were following guidelines for good nutrition? What types of behaviors could you model to your students about good nutrition and lunches?**

Key Concept 9.2

Guidelines for Food Programs

A number of nutritional programs offer assistance to early childhood education centers or sites by providing funding or educational information. Other programs help children and their families access nutritional foods at no or low cost. The program that helps many early childhood education sites is the CACFP. It provides specific guidelines for the food to be served and offers menu planning and nutritional information to teachers. In return, teachers agree to follow the guidelines and provide nutritious meals to children in care. Other programs that offer education support, training, and instructional materials are the Expanded Food and Nutrition Education Program.

9.3 MENU PLANNING FOR EARLY CHILDHOOD EDUCATION ENVIRONMENTS

The ADA has set recommended standards for early education programs: the early childhood education environment should provide two-thirds of the nutritional needs for all children present for a full day (Briley & Roberts-Gray, 2005). The USDA FNS suggests that child nutrition programs should offer meals low in fats and cholesterol; plenty of fruits, vegetables, grains, and milk products; sugar and salt only in moderation; and a variety of foods (USDA FNS, 2007). These guidelines follow the most recent Dietary Guidelines for Americans (USDHHS, 2005; Federal Register, 2004).

Building a Menu

There are a number of considerations in menu planning and food preparation (Figure 9-1). The best base for good menu planning is knowledge of nutrition and children's nutritional needs and developmental stages (see Table 9-1). A teacher with nutritional knowledge is more likely to create a better atmosphere for good nutrition practices, including the planning of menus. The menu should be the focal point for nutrition education and should reinforce healthy eating habits.

This first level of menu planning also includes understanding the MyPyramid for Kids Food Guidance System, the Dietary Guidelines for Americans, and any regulations that may accompany a food program in which the early childhood education program may participate. Using the MyPyramid for Kids is relatively simple and can be a good beginning guide for planning (Kendall & Puck, 2007). Menus should be prepared to meet state licensing procedures. This level should also consider appetizing presentations. Offer

FIGURE 9-1
Factors involved in menu planning in the early childhood education environment.

Factors Involved in Menu Planning in the Early Childhood Education Environment

Level One

Knowledge of Nutrition
Children's Nutritional Needs
A Child's Developmental Stages
Dietary Guidelines for Americans
MyPyramid Guidance System

Level Two

Accessibility for Health Choices
Cost, Convenience, Storage
Culinary Skills, Economy
Seasonal Food Considerations

Level Three

Environment
Goal of Child Care
Personal History
Cultural Diversity
Perceptions of Child Food Choices
Best Practices

a variety of flavors, textures, and temperatures in the foods that are served. Young children prefer foods that they can identify. Nutritious choices in a variety of forms help children build a greater base of food preferences for life (Ziegler, Briefel, et al., 2006). One aspect of meeting the dietary needs of children is understanding proper portion size. Children might consume large portions of foods with poor nutritional quality (Fox, Reidy, et al., 2006; Colapinto et al., 2007). It is also important to realize that preschool children are less likely to eat food with high fiber density and that their diets should have more fruits and vegetables. In meal planning, an attempt should be made to provide more dietary fiber through use of fruits and vegetables (Kranz et al., 2005: Guenther et al., 2006). Whole grains should also be included on a regular basis (Sprouse, 2007; Gidding et al., 2006). Young children are likely to prefer juices and sweetened beverages and might not get enough milk in their diets if these high-calorie beverages are served too often (O'Connor, Yang, & Nicklas, 2006).The teacher must be able to apply this information to create menus that are healthy and meet the children's nutritional needs as well as fit their developmental stage. There are menu-planning tools available from the USDA even if the early education program is not a part of CACFP or any other federal food program (Ziegler, Briefel, et al., 2006). Some of these tools can be found at http://healthymeals.nal.usda.gov/nal_display/index.php?info_center=14&tax_level=3&tax_subject=265&topic_id=1374&level3_id=5180. The more knowledge, skills, and tools that the early childhood education menu planner has, the greater the nutritional quality in the meals will be (Romaine et al., 2007).

The second level involved in menu planning is based on accessibility to healthy food choices. A number of factors influence this level. The cost of food and the economics of providing adequate nutrition heavily influence the food that is purchased or the subsidized food programs that the early childhood education program may access. Spark and colleagues (1998) found that financial incentives in the form of a salary bonus were given to cooks for coming in under their food budget.

Another consideration at this level is the culinary skills of the teacher or the food preparer who will cook the meals planned in the menu. Someone with limited skills will have fewer choices and may rely on more convenience-type foods that may be less nutritional and more expensive. Menu planners must have effective resources and training for planning meals for child care centers and other educational facilities (Romaine et al., 2007). When caregivers, including teachers of preschool children, participate in cooking classes, their awareness of how to prepare simple healthful meals and their degree of comfort in preparing such meals increase (Condrasky, Graham, & Kamp, 2006). And when teachers have knowledge of nutrition and foods, they are more likely to practice good nutrition in their own lives and role-model these to children (Unusan, 2007). The literacy level and/or ability to follow a recipe of the person preparing food may also present barriers to good nutrition and may lead that person to greater use of convenience foods (Aumann et al., 1999).

Convenience itself may be a factor. Time is often limited, especially if there is only one teacher present in the early childhood education environment. This convenience factor may limit accessibility to the healthiest food choices.

Access to healthy food is also affected by seasons. Foods that are in season are much more moderate in price and more readily available. Fruits, vegetables, and occasionally meats are affected by seasonal availability.

The last factor at the second level is the amount of storage available for foods. This includes both room in a refrigerator and room in a pantry or kitchen cabinet. Maintenance of proper food temperature has been found to be a problem at many early childhood education sites (Kuratko et al., 2000). Early childhood education environments with good storage facilities are able to buy in bulk and save money. These child care environments can also purchase more fresh foods at one time and plan for more frequent use of these foods.

The third level of influence on menu planning is the environment, including the goal of the early childhood education environment. The goal will affect food selection. The menu in a setting where the goal is the well-being of children will be different from the menu in a setting where the goal is to provide an income for the staff. If mealtime is considered an important part of the day and meets some social and emotional needs as well as the physical needs of children, they are more likely to eat the foods that are available (Patrick & Nicklas, 2005).

The cultural diversity of the early childhood education environment often has an influence on menu planning. The diversity may be reflected in the teacher's cultural background and may limit choices in the menu items for planning. Cultural and regional food preparations that are deep-seated habits may be difficult to change. Teachers from different cultures have different feeding behavior, and that affects how and what children eat (Hughes et al., 2007). Attempts to change these habits by outside forces (e.g., by a director) may be looked upon as a threat to the person preparing the food (Spark et al., 1998). A positive process occurs when the menu selection is influenced by the diversity of the children in care. Children from different cultural backgrounds are served a wide variety of foods at home, depending on the culture. These food patterns should be considered when developing meals and snacks (Ziegler, Hanson, et al., 2006; Mennella et al., 2006; Jaramillo et al., 2006). Food prepared in early childhood education environments should be respectful of the culture of the children who are present (Benjamin, 2007), and parents can be involved in menu planning.

Another influence at this level is the personal histories of the teacher, menu planner, and food purchaser, who in many cases will be the same person. The person who creates the menu and/or prepares the food is going to be influenced by her own food memories, prejudices, and preferences. A teacher's feelings, experiences, and beliefs about eating and food influences what is selected. If the teacher hated lima beans as a child, they will probably never appear on the menu. How the teacher feels about her own body and eating habits at the moment can also influence the food and preparation method that is chosen (Zero to Three, 2007; Parlakian & Lerner, 2007). The teacher may have come from a background where the "clean your plate" mentality was present. It is important in menu planning to get rid of any coercive feeding patterns that may have developed (Fox, Devaney, et al., 2006) and to discuss and understand why certain types of food or food preparations should be excluded or used less frequently. It is vital that the teacher receive some type of nutritional training. With basic nutritional knowledge, it will be easier for the teacher to provide a menu that reflects good nutrition, not food prejudices. If food preparation staff is unfamiliar with recommended foods included in the guidelines, they may be resistant to including these foods or may prepare them in a less than acceptable manner.

Some teachers have a perception of what foods children will or will not eat. Many menu plans are limited by the choices that a teacher "knows" are the only things a child will eat. Food preparation staff should not be tied to

TABLE 9-2
Menu Planning Checklist

CHECK FOR:

- ☐ Menu fits budget.
- ☐ Food is seasonally available.
- ☐ Staff has culinary skills to prepare foods selected.
- ☐ There is adequate time and labor to prepare food.
- ☐ Personal history barriers are removed.
- ☐ Different methods of preparation are used.
- ☐ There is adequate storage for the food.
- ☐ Cultural and ethnic diversity are considered.
- ☐ Meal pattern meets CACFP guidelines or the Best Practices Quality Programs Checklist for Menu Planning.
- ☐ A few new foods are tried every menu planning period.
- ☐ Few foods are offered that have high fat, high sodium, or high sugar content.
- ☐ A source of vitamin C is served daily.
- ☐ A source of vitamin A is served three to four times per week.
- ☐ Whole-grain breads and grains are offered.
- ☐ Raw vegetables and fruits are served often.
- ☐ The food is chosen for sensory appeal, considering texture, color, and shape.

preconceptions about the foods they think children will not eat, or be prejudiced against foods because of their own backgrounds (Zero to Three, 2007). Children will accept 80 percent of the food offered to them at first, and with repeated exposure, they will eat most foods.

Oakley and Carr (2003a), in *Steps to Success,* have created a series of checklists for "Best Practices for Quality Nutrition" that will help early childhood education facilities that are tied to CACFP measure whether they are performing up to the standard they should. This list is a good measure for how any early childhood education program is doing in providing food and nutrition to the children they serve. There are two websites connected to this. The best practices checklists for center care and the checklists for family child care homes can be found at http://www.nfsmi.org. Table 9-2 shows a menu planning checklist for early childhood education environments.

Pause for Reflection

Looking carefully at third-level factors, examine your personal history, cultural diversity, and perceptions of foods children choose. How might these affect how you planned a menu?

Considering the influences at every level, the teacher can begin planning a menu. Care should be taken to avoid all prejudices, preferences, and perceptions or any other factor that may be an obstacle to good menu planning. The teacher should also remove any barriers to the accessibility of the healthiest food selections. This may involve applying for subsidized food programs, taking cooking lessons, and looking for easier ways to cook nutritious fresh foods.

The teacher should be equipped with the necessary nutritional knowledge and understanding of the developmental stages by reading and referencing this text. If the teacher feels more information would be helpful, further training and education in nutrition may be the next step.

Menu planning should be done on a regular basis, such as every two weeks or once a month. The menu should be reviewed and revised on a regular basis. It is not uncommon for child care centers to have had the same menu for many years. It is important to keep the menu updated and to change it so a variety of foods can be offered and seasonal availability can be taken advantage of.

By applying the meal guidelines found in Table 9-1, or following specific meal guidelines supplied by a child care licensing agency, and by respecting the cultures of the children who are present, the teacher can create menus that meet the needs of the children. Using the MyPyramid individual plan, available at http://www.mypyramid.gov/, a teacher can rate his or her own nutritional needs. Several other considerations should also be kept in mind.

Many early childhood education menus fail to meet the proper energy needs of the young child. Often, early childhood education environments do not provide enough complex carbohydrates from fresh fruits and vegetables and do not meet the daily requirements for iron and niacin. Early childhood education menus have frequently been found to provide too much fat, sugar, and salt. Studies found that lunches served provide more than 35 percent of calories from fat, 13 percent of which was for saturated fats. These both exceed the Dietary Guidelines for fat (Story, Kaphingst, & French, 2006).

Another method of making sure the menu is planned properly is to use a checklist (Table 9-2). A sample menu for a child care center or family child care home is found in Table 9-3.

Breakfast

Breakfast may well be the most critical meal of the day. USDA recommends that 25 percent of DRI should be offered at breakfast. It has been reported that

A nutritious breakfast consisting of milk, bread/cereal, and fruit meets CACFP requirements and is a healthy way to begin the day.

TABLE 9-3
Sample Menu for an Early Childhood Education Environment That Reflects the Recommended Standards for Early Childhood Education Programs

	MONDAY	TUESDAY	WEDNESDAY	THURSDAY	FRIDAY
Breakfast	Milk Cereal Fresh fruit	Milk Cornbread Fresh fruit	Milk Stir-fried rice Fresh fruit	Milk Egg burrito Fresh fruit	Milk Bagel w/cream cheese Fresh fruit
Lunch	Milk Rotelli with turkey meatballs marinara Broccoli Fresh fruit	Milk Beans Cheese Rice Tortillas Green beans Fresh fruit	Milk Tuna/Turkey sandwiches Zucchini w/ranch dressing Fresh fruit	Milk Japanese vegetables Teriyaki chicken Steamed rice Fresh fruit	Milk Cheese pizza Turkey cubes Carrots w/ranch dressing Fresh fruit
Snack	String Cheese Crackers	Fresh fruit Pretzels	Yogurt Fresh fruit	Juice Crackers	Cottage cheese Fresh fruit

eating breakfast affects cognition, strength, attitude, and endurance (Brown & Marcotte, 1999). Children who skip breakfast do not make up for the nutritional loss over the rest of the day (Nicklas, O'Neil, & Myers, 2004). People who eat breakfast are less likely to be obese because their nutritional needs are spread throughout the day. Poor nutrition among children in the United States is in part a result of skipping breakfast (Dubois, Girard, & Potvin, 2006).

As reflected in Table 9-1, breakfast should consist of milk, bread/cereal, and fruit/vegetable. Breakfasts can be built around traditional breakfast foods such as cereal, toast, fruit, milk, and so forth. Breads, cereals, and grains in adequate quantities are consistently missing from preschool children's diets (Kranz et al., 2005). Cold cereal that has been fortified with iron has been suggested as an easy way to increase this food group. (You can see this when you look at the CACFP menu guidelines in Table 9-1.) These food choices can be enhanced by making them more attractive. Fruits or nuts can be put on hot or cold cereals. A bagel can be spread with cream cheese or cottage cheese and fruit. The teacher will have to understand the food habits of the children in care. Some children do not like mixing foods. Other children may be affected by cultural tradition or practices regarding breakfast choices. This may be the reason for the recent changes in adding grains, pastas, and noodles to the breakfast component of the CACFP menu guidelines.

Other nontraditional food choices for breakfast are available, such as dried fruits, peanut butter, burritos, pizza, fruit salad, and fruit smoothies, all of which offer good nutrition and might encourage children to eat better at breakfast. Foods from other cultures, such as stir-fried rice or soba noodles, may be served as an alternative to the traditional choices.

Mati was a new director at a center in a large city where there was quite a population mix. In her area there was a large Southeast Asian community, and many of the children from that community attended her center. Over the years, that group's school population had increased. This center also ran a before- and after-school program and had a number of younger elementary school children who were present for breakfast in addition to the children who attended the center. Mati noticed that many of the children would skip what was prepared for breakfast. The normal breakfast menu often consisted of cereal and milk or yogurt and fruit. These were easy and quick and not too expensive. She sat down with Kim, the teacher who helped to prepare the menus, to see what might be done to change this pattern. They decided to call on some parents to discuss this issue and quickly found out the problem. Many of the children came from cultures that did not have dairy products in their diets, and as a result many of these children did not enjoy dairy products; some were even lactose intolerant. Kim and Mati put together some alternative breakfast menu items such as stir-fried rice, breakfast pizza pockets, and breakfast burritos. They found there was much less waste, and children ate more breakfast. In turn, with more children eating breakfast, more were ready to learn and play at their best.

Snacks

Snacks are an essential part of a child's nutritional day. Snacks should provide adequate nutrition, and there should be sufficient time between a meal and a snack for the children to be hungry, but not too hungry (Nicklas & Johnson, 2004). Snacks are a good time to begin to reflect the cultural diversity of the children in care. It is also the best time to introduce new foods. If children reject a food, there is less nutritional risk if it is served at snack time. This is also a time to help create food memories. Children enjoy food preparation, and it gives them a better attitude toward new foods (Sigman-Grant, 2005; Bernath & Masi, 2006). If fruit juice is used in the menu, it should always be 100 percent juice (Gidding et al., 2006). Children under the age of 6 years should have no more than 4 to 6 ounces and children under the age of 12 years should have no more than 8 to12 ounces of fruit juice a day (Gidding et al., 2006).

As shown in Table 9-1, snacks should consist of two of the following: a dairy or meat/meat alternate choice, a bread/grain, or a fruit/vegetable choice. Some licensing standards dictate that there be pure fruit juice served at one snack and milk at the other snack. Ideally, there should always be a protein source, either from milk, a meat, or a meat alternate. An example of this is peanut butter on celery or crackers. Protein should be spread throughout the day for optimum benefit. The fat in the meat or milk will offer satiety and help to fill up the child. Using a bread, grain, or fruit will provide bulk and flavor, and helps the children meet the MyPyramid for Kids guidelines.

Typical snacks might include bagels, tortillas, crackers, milk, yogurt, string cheese, and fresh fruit such as apples, bananas, oranges, or melons. Snacks may occasionally be more unusual, such as a vegetable soup, a yogurt sundae, a cheese crisp, a bread pudding, a fruit smoothie, or a frozen banana pop with peanut butter and coconut. The type of snack may be affected by food preparation time and cost.

Wadsworth/Cengage Learning

This girl is eating a healthy snack of fruit and milk.

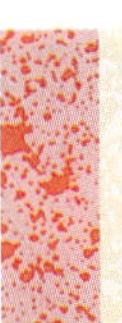

Pause for Reflection

What types of childhood food memories do you have? Did you ever help prepare foods when you were a young child, and do you remember those experiences?

Lunches

Lunches in the early childhood education environment may provide the greatest amount of nutrition in the child's day. The child's lunch should consist of milk; a meat/meat alternate; two fruits and/or vegetables; and a bread, pasta, noodles, or grain. School lunches contain more than the average amount of fats and saturated fats (Nicklas, O'Neil, & Myers, 2004). It is important to address this issue when planning menus and make efforts to keep fat content within dietary recommendations.

Some teachers limit the lunches they prepare to those things children are familiar with or those things that may resemble fast food that children will eat. Menu items such as peanut butter sandwiches, burritos, pizza, hamburgers, spaghetti, fish sticks, tacos, macaroni and cheese, and hot dogs may appear often and in some cases may be the rotating menu. Infrequent exposure to many foods as young children may limit children's range of acceptable food choices later in life. Several of these items may contribute more fat or sodium at one meal than is desired. This is a practice that should be examined and changed to better meet the nutritional needs of the children.

Early education environments that provide lunches for children should have a menu that offers less fat and sodium and a greater variety of food over time (see Table 9-3). Children who are involved in helping prepare meals may be more likely to eat a wider variety of foods (Bernath & Masi, 2006). Foods such as stir fries; baked chicken or fish; hearty soups; pita pockets; quesadillas; and different pastas, grains, or noodles can add variety and flavor to the menu. Most children will eat these foods.

Lunches from Home. Lunches may present a unique problem if they are not prepared at the early childhood education site. When children bring their own lunches to school, they are more likely to consume sugar, sweets, and sweetened beverages. They are also less likely to eat vegetables, drink milk, or have adequate amounts of meat or meat alternatives (Wohlleb, 2004). Many licensed programs prohibit the presence of these less desirable foods. Teachers should have a policy about foods brought from home, including a parent handout of unacceptable food choices such as high-fat, sugary, and calorie-laden foods that offer little food value. If children do bring lunches from home, there should be a way to refrigerate them or have parents use frozen "cold packs" to keep the food safe. That policy should also include the fact that foods from home should (1) be properly labeled with name, date, and type of food; (2) be refrigerated, if necessary; and (3) not be shared with anyone.

Children on Vegetarian Diets

Some children in care may be from families that are vegetarians. There are four types of vegetarians: vegans, whose diets consist only of plant foods—grain, legumes, fruits, vegetables, nuts, seeds, and fats from vegetable sources;

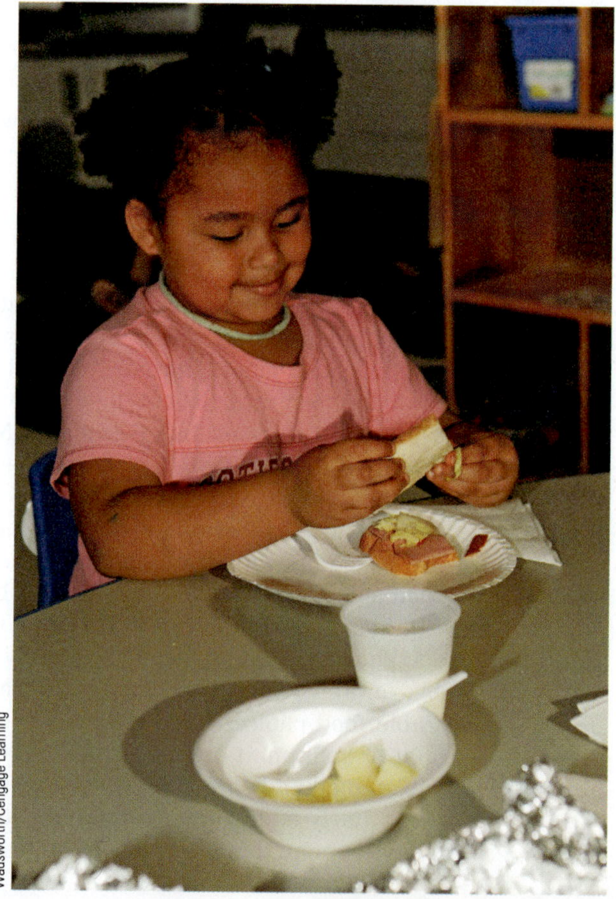
Wadsworth/Cengage Learning

Children who bring their lunches from home may not always bring the most nutritious foods. It is a good idea to set standards for acceptable nutritious foods brought from home.

lacto-vegetarians, whose diets consist of those same foods but with the addition of milk and milk products; ovo-vegetarians, who eat eggs in addition to the plant foods; and lacto-ovo-vegetarians, who eat both milk products and eggs in addition to the plant foods. It is not difficult to meet the nutritional needs of lacto-, ovo-, or lacto-ovo-vegetarian children because good sources of nutrients such as protein, iron, and calcium include milk, milk products, and eggs. Planning the menu for a vegan child can be more challenging. Well-planned vegan diets can meet the nutrient needs of children (Dunham & Kollar, 2006) (see The Vegetarian Pyramid in Figure 9-2). You may want to consult a dietician to help with menu plans for a vegan child. Another solution may be to ask the parent of the vegan child to help in planning the menu or have them supply the snacks and lunches for that child.

Vegan children should consume a wide variety of fruits and vegetables, including green leafy vegetables, which can be a good source of calcium and iron. Dried beans, peas, lentils, and soy products are good sources of protein and iron. Soy milk that has been fortified with calcium and vitamin D is a good source to help meet the child's daily calcium requirement. Nuts and seeds help give children the protein and essential fats that they require for energy and to help metabolize the fat-soluble vitamins. In addition, cooking with vegetable oil or olive oil and using a low trans fat vegetable margarine spread can help children meet their dietary need for fat.

FIGURE 9-2
The Vegetarian Pyramid.

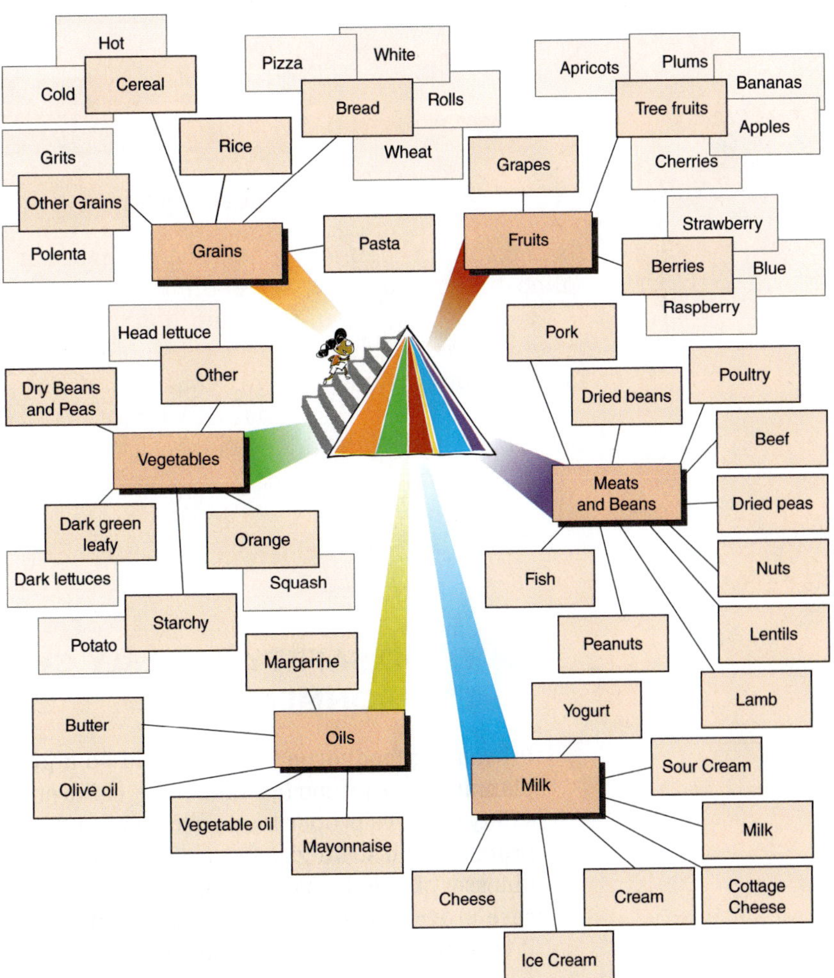

Racene was a 2-year-old girl and only child who just started preschool and whose parents were vegetarians. Her parents had requested special foods for Racene. They wanted Racene to thrive on the vegetarian diet she had been having at home before her mother went back to work. It was difficult for the program to provide the extra expense and time to provide these special food items on a regular basis. Darla, the school director, discussed this with the parents and gave them several alternatives. The parents could provide Racene's food for school or they could provide some easier alternatives to what they had requested. In the discussions, Darla found out that the parents felt they were too busy to make Racene's lunch every day and that the family did eat eggs and dairy. This made things easier for everybody. She came up with a solution that seemed to make everybody happy. She surveyed all parents to see whether they objected to have their children having more of the vegetarian foods that were already on the menu and found that very few objected. These foods included popular items such as quesadillas, egg salad sandwiches, macaroni and cheese, and pizza as well as some newer items such as red beans and rice and lentil soup. The school added at least one vegetarian choice to every meal, and Racene was able to stay on her vegetarian diet while the other children still got good protein in the foods on the menu.

Key Concept 9.3

Menu Planning

Menu planning begins with building a foundation of knowledge and eliminating barriers to accessing healthy food choices and background influences. Guidelines for meeting nutritional needs should be followed, and a variety of foods including fresh vegetables and fruits should be provided. Teachers can look at each area of menu planning and relate it to the entire day's menu choices. They should use a checklist to ascertain that all criteria for food menu planning are met. A teacher who understands the importance of breakfast, snacks, and lunch will plan more carefully to meet the needs of the children in care.

9.4 FOOD SAFETY IN EARLY CHILDHOOD EDUCATION ENVIRONMENTS

Preventing foodborne illness should be a primary task of the teacher who is planning and preparing meals for children in care (Benjamin, 2007). Food safety involves proper food purchasing, storage, handling, and cooking. These practices and strategies for providing food safety and prevention of foodborne illnesses should be carefully monitored. There is reason for concern that child care providers do not get enough training for food safety (Enke et al., 2007). It is important that the people serving food to children have good knowledge of food safety risk because children rely on them to provide safe foods. It is recommended that the teacher responsible for food purchasing, storage, handling, and cooking use the Food Safety Checklists (Table 9-4 through Table 9-7) to monitor periodically the early childhood education environment for food safety.

Food Purchasing

Food purchasing is the starting point of making sure the food in the environment is safe. Food should be of good quality, fresh, and undamaged. To ensure quality, the purchases should be made from reputable wholesalers, markets, butchers, and others who provide food to the early childhood education environment. These businesses should meet proper local and state health and sanitation codes as well as any federal regulations that apply.

Buy fresh products before the "sell by" or "use by" dates. Any products that must be refrigerated should be stored in that section of the store. Only purchase poultry and meats that have been government inspected. Do not purchase foods that should be refrigerated but are not. Avoid fresh products such as fish and poultry that have the label "frozen, defrosted." It is difficult to tell how long these items have been frozen or how long they have been sitting defrosted, or to know the manner in which they were defrosted. Purchase milk or milk products that are Grade A, and do not use any raw or unpasteurized dairy products.

When storing poultry and other meats, keep them away from fresh fruits, vegetables, and other foods that will not be cooked. This will avoid cross-contamination. Always purchase perishable and fresh foods last. Make sure that when the food is packed, fresh and frozen foods are kept together to keep them cold.

Do not buy canned goods that are dented or otherwise compromised. The few cents that may be saved could be very costly later because these can contain dangerous bacteria. Buy prepackaged foods only if the package is intact. A tear or a rip can allow the food to be contaminated. Table 9-4 lists some guidelines to ensure food safety when purchasing food.

TABLE 9-4
Food Safety Purchasing Checklist

CHECK FOR:

- ☐ Buy from sources that are inspected for health and sanitation.
- ☐ Buy only good quality, fresh, and undamaged foods.
- ☐ Buy perishable food before "sell by" date.
- ☐ Perishable foods should be refrigerated.
- ☐ Do not purchase "frozen, defrosted" foods.
- ☐ Purchase fresh foods last.
- ☐ Keep poultry and meats away from other foods.
- ☐ Do not buy damaged canned or packaged goods.

Food Storage

Proper food storage is a key to keeping food safe. This involves proper wrapping, labeling, temperature, and arrangement of the food that has been purchased.

Foods must be protected from contamination by insects, rodents, dust, coughing, sneezing, dirty utensils, and improper temperature while being stored. Proper temperature maintenance is primary. Improper temperature is responsible for 85 percent of cases of foodborne illness. Bacteria multiply rapidly in lukewarm foods.

Refrigerated Foods. Meats, poultry, and fish should be well wrapped so they do not contaminate other foods in the refrigerator. Placing the store package in a waterproof plastic bag works well. If these foods are being frozen, freezer bags or aluminum foil will help protect them from freezer burn and quality loss. It is essential that all food in the early childhood education environment be labeled by date of purchase to prevent waste and avoid risk.

All refrigerated products should be refrigerated immediately upon unpacking. Quickly freeze all frozen foods. If they have thawed, they must be used within 24 hours. This avoids any contamination. Eggs should be stored in the refrigerator, preferably in their cartons.

Clean utensils must always be used when storing food. Food must be refrigerated or stored in covered, shallow containers within two hours after cooking. Containers should be shallow and food placed in it not to exceed more than 2 inches high. If the food is planned for later use, it should be put immediately in the refrigerator. *Never store food in its cooking container!* To avoid contamination, allow only a short period of time for food to cool. Cooked food should always be dated so it will be used while still good and not be wasted or present risk. The teacher should always reheat cooked foods to a minimum of 160°F and make sure runny foods like soups have come to a full rolling boil before serving.

The refrigerator should be maintained at a temperature of less than 40°F, and the freezer should be maintained at 0°F. This inhibits growth of bacteria that can cause foodborne illnesses. There is a danger zone for contamination of foods above 40°F. Bacteria multiply rapidly between 40°F and 125°F.

The refrigerator should be arranged so that there is adequate circulation of cold air. A refrigerator that is too full may not keep the proper temperature, and foods may be at risk for contamination.

Unrefrigerated Foods. All unrefrigerated products should be stored in clean, rodent-free areas, preferably with doors that cover the storage area. These areas should also be a minimum of 8 inches above the floor. Foods should be stored so that those items that were purchased first will be used first. "First in, first out" is the recommendation for storage. This avoids waste and risk. Nonperishable items such as flour, sugar, and so forth, should be stored in airtight containers once the package is opened. Table 9-5 presents a food safety storage checklist.

Food Handling

Anyone who has any signs of illness or infectious skin sores that cannot be covered should not be handling food. It is also preferable that the food handler not change diapers. This is more practical in a center situation where there are a number of teachers. In a family child care home or in the child's

TABLE 9-5
Food Safety Storage Checklist

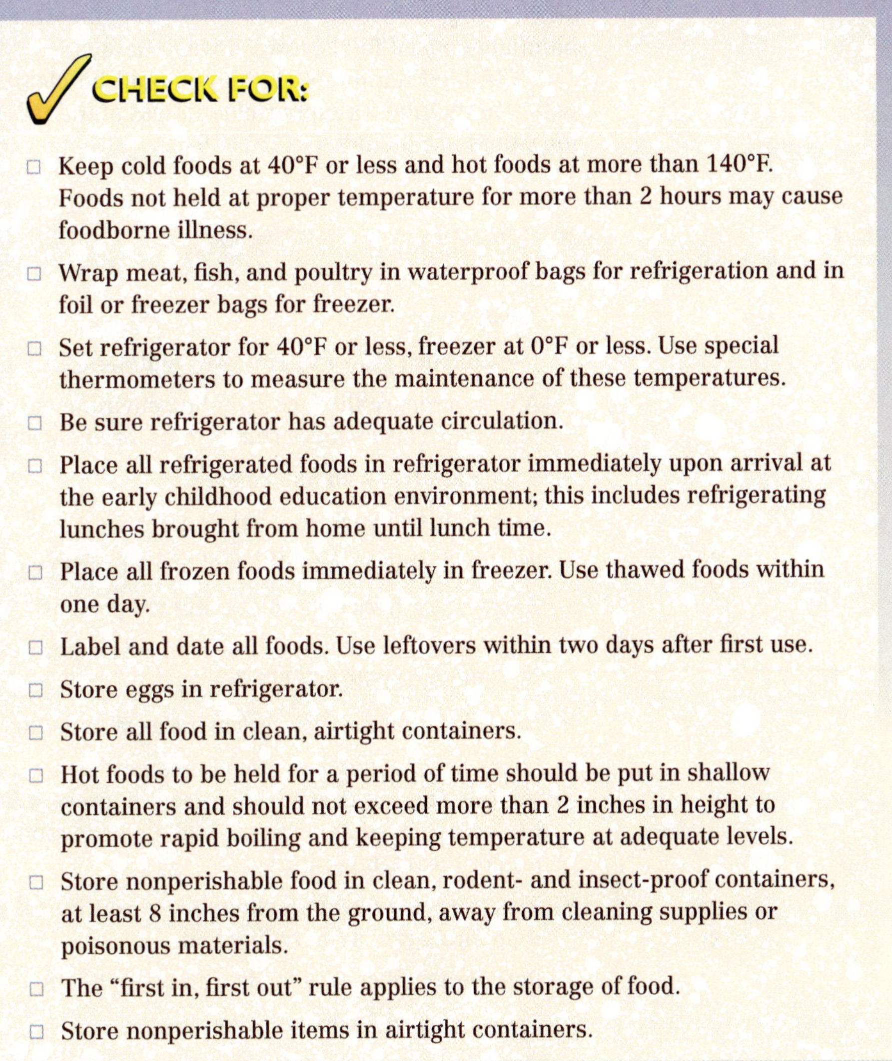

CHECK FOR:

- ☐ Keep cold foods at 40°F or less and hot foods at more than 140°F. Foods not held at proper temperature for more than 2 hours may cause foodborne illness.
- ☐ Wrap meat, fish, and poultry in waterproof bags for refrigeration and in foil or freezer bags for freezer.
- ☐ Set refrigerator for 40°F or less, freezer at 0°F or less. Use special thermometers to measure the maintenance of these temperatures.
- ☐ Be sure refrigerator has adequate circulation.
- ☐ Place all refrigerated foods in refrigerator immediately upon arrival at the early childhood education environment; this includes refrigerating lunches brought from home until lunch time.
- ☐ Place all frozen foods immediately in freezer. Use thawed foods within one day.
- ☐ Label and date all foods. Use leftovers within two days after first use.
- ☐ Store eggs in refrigerator.
- ☐ Store all food in clean, airtight containers.
- ☐ Hot foods to be held for a period of time should be put in shallow containers and should not exceed more than 2 inches in height to promote rapid boiling and keeping temperature at adequate levels.
- ☐ Store nonperishable food in clean, rodent- and insect-proof containers, at least 8 inches from the ground, away from cleaning supplies or poisonous materials.
- ☐ The "first in, first out" rule applies to the storage of food.
- ☐ Store nonperishable items in airtight containers.

own home, the single teacher must perform many roles. In these cases, extra care should be taken, including the use of disposable nonlatex gloves. In any case, it is important to remember that a key to proper sanitation is good hand-washing techniques. Proper food handling also includes keeping cooking surfaces free of bacteria. Food preparation surfaces in 36 Texas child care centers were tested and 41 percent of the swabs used for testing came back positive for bacteria. Included were 27 strains of bacteria that could pose serious health risks to children (Staskel et al., 2007). Common areas where the bacteria were found included cutting boards, sink drains, lids from garbage cans, and faucet handles. The entire food preparation area should be frequently sanitized (see Chapter 12, Table 12-8).

Teachers can avoid many risks for foodborne illnesses by handling food properly. Use of sanitary practices and healthy habits for handling food (see Table 9-6) can avoid food contamination and growth of bacteria. Food may be handled in its raw form, or it may be frozen or cooked. *Never* thaw any food at room temperature. Thawing should take place in the refrigerator, in the microwave oven, or by placing the item in a waterproof plastic bag and submerging it in cold water, changing the water every 30 minutes. When handling cooked foods, always wash hands.

The food handler's clothing should be clean, and use of a clean apron will help maintain a higher cleanliness standard. Other food handling safety measures are included in Table 9-6.

TABLE 9-6
Healthy Food Handling Tips

- Always wash hands.
- Use nonlatex gloves to improve sanitation.
- Always prepare the food-handling environment using sanitary practices. This includes countertops, bread boards, and can openers.
- Keep nails trimmed and clean.
- Keep hair tied back, in a hat or a net.
- Wash all fruits, vegetables, and tops of cans prior to use.
- Do not thaw frozen foods at room temperature.
- After cutting poultry, meat, or fish, follow sanitary cleaning procedures for cutting boards and hands.
- Never let meat, poultry, or fish juices get on other foods.
- Check internal temperature of meats using a meat thermometer before serving. This is extremely important to prevent *E. coli* or *salmonella* bacteria from contaminating food. Refer to temperature gauge for proper meat temperatures.
- Always reheat food to a minimum of 160°F, or if the food is runny, like soup, bring it to a full rolling boil.
- Refrigerate all cooked foods within two hours.
- Freeze cooked foods immediately.
- Never reuse a spoon that has been used for tasting.
- Never reuse leftover food from serving bowls used on the table, except when the food is packaged and will not spoil.
- Never prepare food when you are ill.
- Do not help children with toileting, diapering, or blowing noses while preparing food.
- Each child should have his or her own bib, and bibs should not be shared
- Keep a cloth for wiping up food for that purpose only, or use disposable cloths.
- Wash dishes and preparation tools in hot, soapy water. Rinse. Dip for one minute in bleach solution that is at least 75°F. Let air dry. Do not use a dish towel to dry.
- If using a dishwasher, thoroughly rinse dishes first, then utilize hottest, sanitizing cycle. Allow to dry before removing.

Safe, sanitary, and healthy practices should be used when cooking food for children.

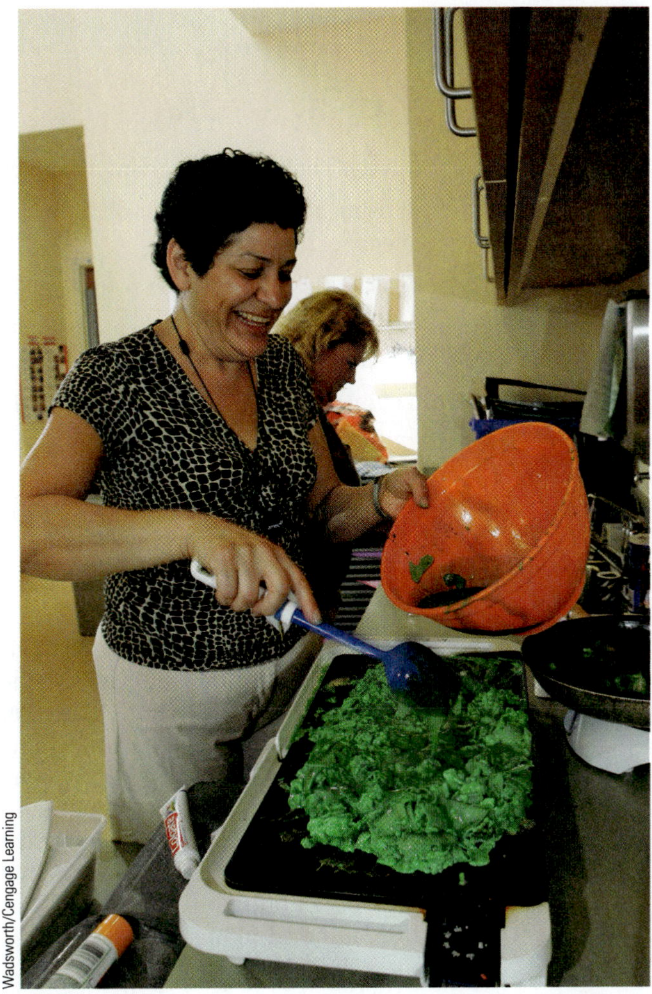

Wadsworth/Cengage Learning

An excellent way to ensure that food is handled properly is to have the person who is preparing and serving food take a food handler's course that is offered in most communities.

Always remember that the kitchen must be kept clean and sanitary. The food preparation and dishwashing areas should be kept completely separate from other centers of activity such as where children play, where diapers are changed, and toileting areas (Benjamin, 2007). All surfaces in the kitchen should be clean and free of cracks, including sinks, sink drains, faucets, and garbage can lids in addition to food preparation areas such as cutting boards. Serving dishes should not have any cracks or chips. Dishcloths to clean these areas should be for these areas only and not used in other parts of the environment. After the food has been cleared and stored properly, all areas of the kitchen and the eating area should be checked for cleanliness.

Cooking Foods

Safe, sanitary, and healthy practices should always be used when preparing foods for cooking. All kitchen and cooking equipment should be clean and safe to use. If commercial cooking equipment is used, it should be properly ventilated. All vents and filters should be kept clean and free of buildup from

TABLE 9-7
Food Safety When Cooking

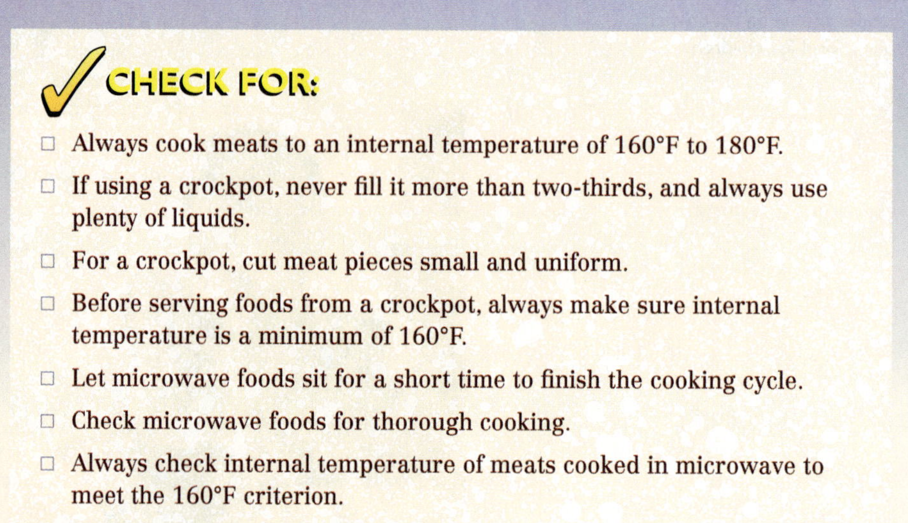

CHECK FOR:

- ☐ Always cook meats to an internal temperature of 160°F to 180°F.
- ☐ If using a crockpot, never fill it more than two-thirds, and always use plenty of liquids.
- ☐ For a crockpot, cut meat pieces small and uniform.
- ☐ Before serving foods from a crockpot, always make sure internal temperature is a minimum of 160°F.
- ☐ Let microwave foods sit for a short time to finish the cooking cycle.
- ☐ Check microwave foods for thorough cooking.
- ☐ Always check internal temperature of meats cooked in microwave to meet the 160°F criterion.

grease. As the foods are being cooked, other measures help to provide further protection. Poultry and meats should always be cooked to an internal temperature of 160° to 180°F. The minimum temperature of 160°F prevents foodborne illnesses, which is especially important when cooking for children. Outbreaks of *E. coli* bacteria have raised concern about the internal temperature of meats meeting the minimum degree criteria.

If a crockpot or slow cooker is used for cooking foods, several precautions should be taken. The cooker should never be more than two-thirds full, with plenty of liquid. If using meat, the pieces should be small and uniform, and the internal temperature must be checked before serving to make sure it meets the 160°F requirement.

When cooking foods in the microwave, the teacher should make sure the foods are cooked through and allowed to sit for a short period so the cooking process may finish. Using a microwave probe or a meat thermometer ensures all meats are at an internal temperature of 160°F. Table 9-7 contains a checklist for food safety.

Key Concept 9.4

Food Safety

Food safety in the early childhood education environment is essential to prevent the spread of foodborne illnesses. Protecting the early childhood education environment by using safe food practices and strategies will prevent risk. The teacher can use safe, sanitary food-handling practices to better manage food preparation activities to avoid bacteria and food spoilage. Good food-purchasing behaviors help eliminate foods that may pose risk. The teacher can avoid contamination of foods by understanding how to store foods and by cooking meats to a minimum of 160°F.

REALITY *Check*

E. Coli and Other Issues: How Safe is America's Food Chain?

In recent years, there have been a large number of outbreaks of foodborne illnesses coming from food that has been contaminated in one way or another. Every year, about 76 million cases of foodborne illness in the United States are reported, and a number of cases go unreported (International Food Information Council, 2007). The U.S. Food and Drug Administration (FDA) tracks *salmonella, E. coli* O157:H7, *Listeria monocytogenes,* and allergens in foods, such as nuts, dairy, soy, and fish ingredients. *E. coli* is probably the most dangerous bacteria and can cause serious illness or death, especially to young children and older adults. This pattern of outbreaks has been occurring for about 25 years and appears to be increasing due to the way food is packed and its original source.

E. coli stands for *Escherichia coli,* one of the most abundant species of bacteria in our environment. It lives in the intestines of humans and animals. *E. coli* is common and works with other bacteria within our intestines to enable us to function properly and remain healthy. The problem occurs when the *E. coli* bacteria that are present in animal intestines produce different strains that can be harmful to humans. The rare strain that has occurred recently is referred to as *E. coli* O157:H7; it causes hemorrhaging, blood loss, and dehydration ("*E. coli* infection," 2000).

The *E. coli* O157:H7 bacteria have been infected with a strain of toxin-producing virus. The toxin appears as a protein that causes severe damage to the lining of the intestines. Salt and water are lost in the intestines, and blood vessels are damaged. It can also result in hemolytic uremic syndrome, which can cause acute kidney failure (Held & Griffin, 2000). Young children and elderly persons are the most susceptible to these toxins because dehydration, blood loss, and kidney failure can easily progress to lethal conditions ("Preliminary Food Net Data," 2004).

Symptoms of *E. coli* bacterial infection may appear after several hours to several days. In a healthy adult, symptoms may appear and be gone in about a week. In young children, the time period is more likely to be short, and this disease is far more serious. It should be reported to the physician immediately if blood is noticed in the diarrhea or if the stools appear watery.

In 1982, the first outbreak of infection with the *E. coli* bacteria occurred when 47 people in two states got sick from eating contaminated hamburger meat at a fast-food restaurant ("*E. coli,*" 2001). In 1993, a serious outbreak occurred for the same reason, and three children died and many more suffered lifelong disabilities (Evans, 1995). It is estimated that as many as 20,000 cases of *E. coli* infection appear each year, and as many as 500 people die from it. In the past ten years, *E. coli* has been found in spinach, unpasteurized fruit juices, fresh cheese curds, alfalfa sprouts, dry-cured salami, lettuce, raw milk, and game meat (USDA, 2001, USFDA FSN 2006; CDC, 2007a). During the years 1996–2003, the incidence of *E. coli* infection went down by 42 percent ("Preliminary Food Net Data," 2004). This was probably due to public awareness and more careful food handling.

In September 2006, a large outbreak of *E. coli* occurred in many states with 204 cases reported, which included three deaths (United States Food and Drug Administration Center for Food Safety and Applied Nutrition [USFDA CFSAN], 2006; Chapparo, 2006). More than 50 percent of the people who suffered from the effects of this had to be hospitalized. The contaminated food was bagged fresh-cut spinach, and the contamination was caused by bacteria in the cattle feces found on the fields where the spinach was grown. The USFDA has noted that the risk of bacterial growth and contamination is increasing with the processing of fresh produce into fresh-cut products (USFDA FSN, 2007a). When fresh produce is cut, the cellular fluids that are released provide a good medium in which the bacteria can grow. Because more Americans are eating their produce in this manner, the potential for increase in these outbreaks is increasing.

Harmful *E. coli* bacteria can be found in a number of foods, the most common of which has been ground beef. *E. coli* is commonly found in cattle feces

(continues)

REALITY *Check* (continued)

and is spread by animals and people. This harmful strain is also found in roast beef, unpasteurized milk, apple cider, spinach and other greens, and municipal water.

The meat inspection system has undergone some radical changes because the most common source of these bacteria is hamburger. In 1996, the USDA announced its new four-step program to revamp the inspection system and to try to reduce the amount of *E. coli* bacteria found in meat products. Other measures have been taken to protect the public from *E. coli* bacteria. The restaurant industry has adopted the Hazard Analysis and Critical Control Point (HACCP) system and directs restaurants to cook hamburgers to a thermometer-tested 160°F. Even though *E. coli* is the most common bacterium for recalls, the largest beef recall occurred in 2008 due to concerns about animal cruelty and unhealthy animals that entered the food chain (Kim & Landsburg, 2008). Cattle who are "downer" cattle that are unable to walk on their own may have an illness or carry bacteria that could affect the food chain. Of the 143 million pounds of beef recalled, 37 million were destined for school lunch programs.

In 2008, there was a *salmonella* outbreak that was originally thought to be caused by fresh tomatoes in salsa, but that was difficult to trace. More than 1200 people in 43 states became ill after eating salsa (CDC, 2008). This outbreak did bring up the fact that federal food oversight needs to do more to protect food safety for everyone. In the past, the federal government has passed measures to regulate fruit juices and sprouted seeds. There were some positive consequences to the *E. coli* outbreak in 2006 in terms of keeping produce safer. For produce, there is now guidance to cover fresh-cut vegetables and fruits that have been minimally processed (USDA FNS, 2007a). These fruits and vegetables would be peeled, sliced, shredded, chopped, or trimmed, with or without washing or other treatment. This guidance recommends that fresh-cut produce manufacturers use the preventive measures found in the HACCP program, covering four areas that include (1) personnel health and hygiene, (2) training, (3) sanitation operations, and (4) building and equipment. The FDA also recommends that everybody in the food chain process follow the same HACCP procedures. There are new tracking systems placed on labels that follow the fresh produce from field to store (Jordan, 2007). This is supposed to ensure that any source of contamination is found quickly (Warren, 2007). Unfortunately, this is not always the case, as was seen in the *salmonella* outbreak in 2008. That source was difficult to trace in a reasonable period of time.

An objective of Healthy People 2010 is to decrease the number of *E. coli* O157:H7 cases by one-half (Healthy People 2010, 2000). An organization called STOP (Safe Tables Our Priority) provides information on the *E. coli* bacteria and how safeguards can be practiced to prevent foodborne illnesses (STOP, 2001). Their website is located at http://www.stop-usa.org/. The decrease in the numbers of these cases may be aided by a new test for *E. coli* bacteria, which was developed in Japan in 2008 (Science Daily, 2008). This new test is simple and takes only a few hours; early identification makes it easier to prevent bacteria spreading.

An increasing amount of food eaten in the United States and throughout the world is coming from other countries, which have varied standards and methods for growing and processing agricultural products. A number of the organizations that try to keep the food chain in this country safe hold a yearly Food Safety and Security Summit to write standards and discuss practices (Food Safety and Security Summit, 2008).

Different types of gastrointestinal infections occur in different parts of the world, and these may enter the food chain through contamination somewhere along the way. The FDA has recommendations for commodity-specific food safety guidelines for supply chains of other produce such as tomatoes, leafy greens, and melons.

A significant amount of processed food in our food chain comes from China, where food manufacturers carry out shoddy practices such as using industrial chemicals in products that include seafood, cooked mushrooms, preserved pears, rice cakes, juices, and candy (CNN.com, 2007; Chang, 2007).

(continues)

REALITY *Check* (continued)

Some of the issues that have come to light involve lack of safety controls, evading inspection, and excessive bacteria in processing plants. In May of 2007, China executed their former Food and Drug chief for taking bribes and ignoring safety issues. Authorities in China are pushing for greater controls on the safety of foods they produce and manufacture (Olesen, 2007).

As consumers, teachers in the early childhood environment must take measures to protect the children present from risk factors such as *E. coli*. To do so, they must be aware of what should be done to lessen risk. *E. coli* and other bacterial infections can easily be spread from one person to another in early childhood education environments and nursing homes. There are specific safeguards the teacher can use to prevent the spread of *E. coli* and other bacteria, including these:

- If a child or teacher has been infected with *E. coli* bacteria, he should not be allowed back in care until he has two negative stool cultures.
- If a teacher or child has another type of gastrointestinal bacteria that can be spread, universal safety precautions should be conscientiously practiced.
- All meat should be cooked to a temperature of 160°F. The juices should run clear and should not be pink.
- Always clean and sanitize any surface that has had raw meat on it, including utensils, before another item touches that surface.
- Do not use the plate or tray that the raw meat was on to place the cooked meat on.
- Always wash hands thoroughly before and after handling meat.
- Do not serve unfiltered apple cider, unpasteurized milk, or fresh cheese curds.
- Always handle diarrhea under strict universal hygiene conditions.
- Wash all fruits and vegetables before eating or cooking. This includes precut fresh fruits and vegetables

Those preventive measures will help curtail bacterial risk, but we must rely on government regulations, inspection, and the cooperation of governments such as China to keep our food chain as safe as possible. Future legislation may place another level of measures that will help to protect the foods that we and the children in our care eat.

CHECK*point*: Are you careful when you cook hamburger meat to make sure it reaches the proper temperature? Do you ever think of this when you go out to eat? What about raw apple juice: Do you drink it, and would you have served it to children before reading this information?

9.5 IMPLICATIONS FOR TEACHERS

As more children in this country enter early childhood education environments, teachers should understand their responsibility to meet the majority of the nutritional needs for many of these children. The teacher will have to prepare to meet those needs (Story, Kaphingst, & Fletcher, 2006; Rose, 2007).

Education

Familiarity with food programs such as CACFP will assist the teacher in accessing available funds to provide better nutrition for children from low- and limited-income families. The teacher can plan nutritious meals by using CACFP guidelines. Other programs provide nutritional training and instructional materials for children and their parents.

Wadsworth/Cengage Learning

Children can help prepare their own snacks and get involved with understanding good nutrition.

Training for food safety and sanitation is essential for teachers (Briley & Roberts-Gray, 2005; Benjamin, 2007). Knowledge is the basis of menu planning. The teacher should know the basics of nutrition, what children's nutritional needs are, and how to use the MyPyramid for Kids and the Dietary Guidelines for Americans in order to create menus that meet those needs. The teacher also should understand children's developmental stages and how they affect their eating abilities and habits. Just as there are health consultants for children's early education programs, there is a trend toward use of dieticians to provide needed information and assistance to these same programs (Padget & Briley, 2005; ADA, 2006). A teacher might want to consult with a dietician when doing nutritional planning.

The person in charge of menu planning should have an understanding of accessibility for healthy choices. This understanding allows access to be maximized. Any barriers should be removed. The teacher who plans menus should also do a personal checkup of practices, prejudices, and perceptions that may limit food selection (Zero to Three, 2007; Parlakian & Lerner, 2007).

The teacher should have knowledge of food safety practices and strategies that protect the food environment in the early childhood education setting. The teacher can prevent waste and risk to health and safety by using good food purchasing, storage, handling, and cooking measures.

With Children. The teacher can teach the children better nutritional practices by getting them to try new foods, eat a variety of foods, and consume more fruits and vegetables. Meeting a child's nutritional needs may not be as simple as providing the food and the information. Information about foods is more meaningful when the actual foods are involved (Bernath & Masi, 2006). One of the easiest ways a teacher can educate children to eat the foods found on the menu is to cook with them. Having a cooking experience involving new foods, culturally diverse foods, and fruits and vegetables is a good way to get children to participate in eating them (Sigman-Grant, 2005). Children are likely to eat foods that they helped to prepare. Having at least one cooking experience per week will encourage participation and variety. In addition, when teachers create an eating environment that is positive, children are more likely to have better eating behaviors and try more foods (Hughes et al., 2007).

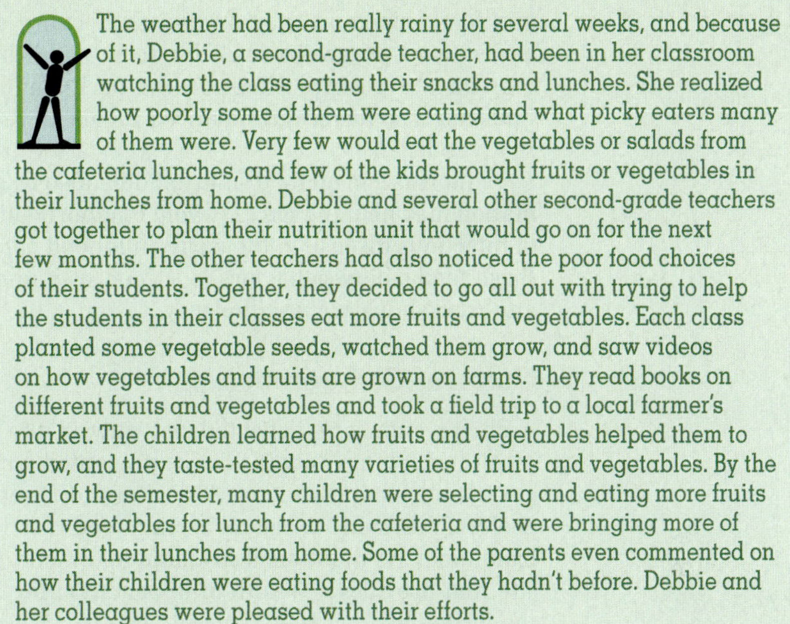

The weather had been really rainy for several weeks, and because of it, Debbie, a second-grade teacher, had been in her classroom watching the class eating their snacks and lunches. She realized how poorly some of them were eating and what picky eaters many of them were. Very few would eat the vegetables or salads from the cafeteria lunches, and few of the kids brought fruits or vegetables in their lunches from home. Debbie and several other second-grade teachers got together to plan their nutrition unit that would go on for the next few months. The other teachers had also noticed the poor food choices of their students. Together, they decided to go all out with trying to help the students in their classes eat more fruits and vegetables. Each class planted some vegetable seeds, watched them grow, and saw videos on how vegetables and fruits are grown on farms. They read books on different fruits and vegetables and took a field trip to a local farmer's market. The children learned how fruits and vegetables helped them to grow, and they taste-tested many varieties of fruits and vegetables. By the end of the semester, many children were selecting and eating more fruits and vegetables for lunch from the cafeteria and were bringing more of them in their lunches from home. Some of the parents even commented on how their children were eating foods that they hadn't before. Debbie and her colleagues were pleased with their efforts.

Snacks are a fast and easy meal for the children to help prepare. Some children may be able to make their own snacks. Simple items such as rice cakes and peanut butter are a way to begin. Children are capable of this from toddlerhood. More complicated dishes and meals can be made in stages. To prepare soups, for example, vegetables can be cut one day, and the rest of the ingredients prepared and cooked the next.

Another way to educate children is to take them on field trips to the market, vegetable stands, and even farms to see how and where food is grown. There are also excellent videos that provide this information if funding, time, and access prove to be constraints. Children who have some nutrition education are likely to choose healthier snacks for themselves (Matvienko, 2007).

There are a number of books that feature foods, many of which involve fruits and vegetables. Having those fruits and vegetables for a snack or meal the same day may encourage children to try new things.

For Families

Education for the parent is also essential. Good menu planning is not as effective if the parents are not teachers' partners. Parents may be relying on the early childhood education environment teacher to be the gatekeeper of their children's nutrition. Parents and teachers should work together instead of at cross purposes (Bernath & Masi, 2006). Posting menus is an easy way for parents to see what foods the child is eating at care. If parents are aware of the menu at school, they can plan to augment the nutritional needs that the early childhood education program has provided. Cooking and tasting demonstrations and videos are other choices for education of parents. When the parents are more educated, they are more willing to participate in planning and encouraging their children to try more variety and new foods.

Another form of education that the teacher may provide to the parents is how to access supplemental foods. Many families have low incomes, and food selections may be limited because of cost. Helping these families access food programs in order to provide them with better food at home may have a positive effect on the early childhood education environment. Children who have well-balanced meals all the time are healthier and more ready to learn.

Information on food safety should also be provided to parents. This information may help the parent avoid foodborne illnesses and prevent the spread of infectious disease in the early childhood education environment. Modeling these food safety behaviors is a good way to educate the parents; handouts and workshops are another way.

Cultural Competence

A child's culture is reflected not only in the foods served, but also in the mealtime setting, how foods are presented within a meal, and the rules that govern the meal (Brannon, 2004; Zero to Three, 2007). Each culture has food preferences, some based on certain food restrictions that may be religious or traditional. As mentioned in Chapter 6, Georgia State University has a website that provides a wealth of information for different cultures and foods in the format of a pyramid. This site can be accessed at http://monarch.gsu.edu/multiculturalhealth. This might be helpful in menu planning for the different cultures in care. Cultural competence should be practiced in menu planning. The teacher should understand the daily and special event eating patterns of the diverse children in their care. Often the foods themselves are not different from the ones used in the early childhood education environment. However, the names, recipes, method of preparation, and condiments used may make the food appear very different.

The teacher can ask families to share their recipes and talk to them about food (Mayer, Ferede, & Hou, 2006). This may be a way to discover the daily and special event choices. It is also a way to determine how food is served at home and how this environment is different from care. Adjustments may be made to accommodate these differences. Parents may also

Wadsworth/Cengage Learning

Creating opportunities for eating in different ways, like this picnic, is a good way to introduce diversity about ways to eat as well as foods from other cultures.

be involved in the planning of the menu. Another way to break any barriers to food selection is to have a potluck several times a year, so families can bring a favorite dish that represents their culture. Using their recipes for menu selections is another way to have the children try new foods and have parents feel respected. Foods from other cultures can be included and introduced at snack time, as a beginning. They can later be incorporated into breakfast or lunch. Children from all ethnic groups may have a difficult time meeting their MyPyramid for Kids guidelines for fruits and vegetables. Only 8 percent of a group of children studied for whether they met their nutritional needs in an early childhood education environment ate an adequate amount of vegetables and fruits (Padget & Briley, 2005). Using a variety of fruits and vegetables may improve this. One reason for insufficient fruits and vegetables may be families' lack of funds for purchasing these more expensive foods. The teacher may want to make sure these families get connected to some food program for resources to meet their children's needs.

Supervision

If the early education center is involved in a food program, it is up to the designated person to make sure that all rules, regulations, and guidelines are met. If the food programs supply training or instructional materials, it is up to the designated person to make sure this information is used properly and dispensed to the staff, children, and parents.

Supervision plays a key role in menu planning and food safety. Ensuring that these issues are handled correctly and properly supported is important. Using the checklists for menu planning and food safety and maintaining universal sanitary practices can ensure these processes are carried out properly.

It is up to the teacher to supervise the children's reaction to the menu and observe whether they are eating what was prepared. This supervision may lead to more frequent review and revision. It is important that the guidelines and nutritional needs of the children are being met.

Key Concept 9.5

Implications for Teachers

The teacher must meet the nutritional and developmental needs of the child. Using guidelines and information from supplemental food programs may be helpful. The teacher should be educated in how to apply this knowledge to menu planning and breaking down any barriers that may prevent healthy food choices. Education also helps the teacher to plan for safe food practices. Educating children through involving them with cooking and by other methods encourages them to eat a greater variety of foods and try new foods. Families can learn more about nutrition and better food selection at home. Cultural sensitivity provides information as well as help to remove barriers to both food selection and trying new foods. Supervision provides the method to ensure that proper menu planning and food safety are carried out.

CHAPTER SUMMARY

More than 5 million children are eating meals in early childhood education environments before elementary school on a daily basis. Millions more children are eating meals at school in the early elementary years. Nutrition and food safety have been found to be inadequate in many early education programs. It is up to the teacher who plans and/or prepares meals to be adequately trained or to get help from a dietician. There are a number of nutritional programs that offer assistance in early childhood education environments by providing funding or educational information.

The teacher whose responsibility it is for food preparation and menu planning should know how to select healthy foods, plan adequate menus, and prepare food that is safe. Understanding the importance of breakfast, snacks, and lunch enables the teacher to plan more carefully to meet the needs of the children present. Protecting the early childhood education environment by using safe food practices and strategies will prevent risk.

The teacher can use education, cultural sensitivity, observation, supervision, and can work with families to ensure that the early childhood education environment is providing for the nutritional needs of the children present.

TO GO BEYOND

Additional resources for this chapter can be found by visiting the book companion website at www.cengage.com/education/robertson. This supplemental material includes chapter objectives, internet exercises, reflection questions, quizzes, web links, glossary and flash cards, case studies, frequently asked questions, downloadable forms and tables, curriculum supplements, more reality checks, additional key concepts, references, and more.

Chapter Review Critical Thinking Applications

1. Discuss the importance of menu planning in the early childhood education environment. What are the components that a teacher must consider when planning a menu? How might these affect menu planning?
2. Examine the ways a teacher could connect to resources for help with nutrition and menu planning.
3. Discuss the CACFP program. How can it help an early childhood education environment provide better food and nutrition to children?
4. Examine how a best practice checklist might be helpful in all areas of keeping quality standards for nutrition.
5. Discuss school lunch programs at the elementary level, how they provide nutrition, and how they might be compromised by outside sources.

As an Individual

1. Using "Rate Your Plate," rate your own diet. How does this differ from the three-day charting you did the previous week? Compare and contrast the two nutritional evaluations of your diet.

2. Observe children eating at a fast-food restaurant. How much food do they appear to be eating? What types of food do they appear to favor? Record your observations and bring them to class to share with other students.
3. What food safety and storage practices have you observed in a fast-food or other type of restaurant? What types of these practices have you observed in the home? If you have observed these practices in an early childhood education facility, list them also. Compare the three. How might these practices be improved?
4. Watch parents and children in a checkout line of a supermarket for at least half an hour. What types of food are they buying? Record your findings and be able to discuss what you found in class.
5. Find an elementary school where you can go as a visitor to observe a school lunch. What were children eating if they bought lunch? What types of things did children have in lunches brought from home? Compare and contrast the two. What might be done to improve these lunches?

As a Group

1. In small groups, plan one week's menu for an early childhood education center. Be sure it is balanced nutritionally and is culturally representative of your local area. Compare it to the menus of other groups. Have the menus duplicated and distributed to the class. Evaluate the menus.
2. Divide up into groups and have each group go to two or three fast-food restaurants to obtain nutritional information. Create a scale that includes (1) how easy the information was to obtain; (2) whether lighter foods were offered; and (3) what "hook" was used to influence children. Rate the restaurants using this scale.
3. How would you help a child select better menu items for nutrition at (1) a fast-food restaurant, (2) an early childhood education center, (3) a school lunch program, and (4) home?
4. Survey the community for information about food programs that offer help to early childhood education programs. Compile the information and distribute it to the class.
5. Go online and look at breakfast and lunch menus from at least three different school districts in your area. If your school is in a rural area or smaller town and has only one school district, find some school districts that are close. Go out of your state, choose two other cities, and find school lunch menus from at least two school districts in each of these. Compare and contrast the lunches from your local area and those of other states. Draw some conclusions about these school lunches.

Case Studies

1. The director at the early childhood education program that you work at has realized that the center has been repeating the same menus for a long time. She would like the six teachers at the center to work on putting together a menu that could change frequently. She asks each teacher to prepare a week's menu that includes

snacks, breakfasts, and lunches. She also asks that you consider the cultural groups that are represented in your care. These include children of Hispanic, Asian, Southeast Asian, Caribbean-African, and European extraction. Plan a week's menu based on this information.

2. Joanna is a family child care provider who would like some financial assistance in feeding the children in her care and would like to make more profit without raising her fees. She has heard of CACFP but does not know what to do at this point. What would you tell her about the program and how to apply?
3. You are a teacher in a large early childhood education program. You have noticed some unsanitary practices occurring both in the kitchen and in the serving of food. The teacher in charge of the kitchen also happens to be the director's best friend. What steps should you take to ensure better sanitation and safety for your early childhood education environment?
4. Gabe wants to teach a unit on nutrition that involves the children in class preparing some foods. What steps should he take to make sure the food and its preparation are safe? What are five things he could pass along to children that will help them to keep the food they work with safe?
5. You are a teacher in an elementary school and you have noticed that although your school says it is trying to keep the menus healthy, they really appear to be fast-food menus. Several of your colleagues have said the same thing. Two of you have even had parents come to you and complain. What steps might you take to resolve this issue?

NUTRITION CURRICULUM SUPPLEMENT

Sample lesson plans and topic maps for subjects that concern nutrition and food safety are provided on the curriculum area of the website to help reinforce the information that is being modeled by teachers and learned by the children in the early education environment. In addition to the sample curriculum, there is a list of children's books and sources for further information. Some of this information may include songs or finger plays. This sample group is presented to help the teacher design his or her own curriculum by adding to the information provided.

SECTION IV
Health in Early Childhood Education Environments

This section discusses four areas that deal with health:

10. Promoting Good Health for Quality Early Childhood Education Environments

11. Tools for Promoting Good Health in Children

12. Prevention of Illness in Early Childhood Education Environments Through Infection Control

13. Supportive Health Care in Early Childhood Education Environments

To properly cover these expansive topics we will relate them to basic health policies that work well in early childhood education environments. These policies connect health promotion and risk management tools to each chapter's focus.

CHAPTER 10

Promoting Good Health for Quality Early Childhood Education Environments

After reading this chapter, you should be able to:

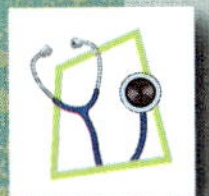

10.1 Health Policies

Define and discuss health policies and their use as a tool for health prevention, protection, and promotion.

10.2 Children's Health Records

Discuss the contents and importance of health records, including up-to-date immunizations.

10.3 Staff Health

Discuss the importance of health policies for staff, including staff health records and promoting staff health.

10.4 Providing a Mentally Healthy Environment

Indicate the importance that stable, responsive, and consistent caregiving has on providing a child with an optimum environment for good mental health.

10.5 Implications for Teachers

Discuss the importance of parent and child education, role modeling positive health actions, and supervision for providing optimum health.

10.1 HEALTH POLICIES

- **health policies** *framework for ensuring health and well-being in early childhood education settings.*

Health policies help the teacher manage risks to good physical and mental health that might be found in the early childhood education environment. These policies provide the framework for providing protection and prevention. A teacher who has health policies can improve the care of children. The following information indicates the need for improving the care of children:

- The overall quality of early childhood education programs is not good (Greenspan, 2003; Shope & Aronson, 2006).
- Children of poor or low-income families are more likely to experience substandard care (Loeb et al., 2004; Garvin, 2007; Chen, Martin, & Matthews, 2007). These children are also those most likely to be at risk for good health (Flores, Olson, & Tomany-Korman, 2005; Simon, Chan, & Forrest, 2008).
- At least one in every five children has not received one or more of the vaccinations to prevent childhood diseases, and this can lead to epidemic levels of illness (CDC, 2007a). The national goal is for 90 percent of children to be immunized. It is important that an early childhood education environment have a policy for children present who are not immunized (Salmon et al., 2005).

Wadsworth/Cengage Learning

Keeping the early childhood education environment healthy takes the cooperation of everyone, including the people who help keep it clean.

- Rates of illness for children in early childhood education environments were higher than rates of illness for children at home for the first two years of life (Shope & Aronson, 2006).
- As many as 4 out of 10 preschoolers exhibit one or more problem behaviors, and approximately 1 in 10 children are at risk for poor mental health (Collins et al., 2003). Children whose earliest experiences, environments, and relations do not include a warm and nurturing atmosphere are vulnerable to "toxic stress" (Knitzer & Lefkowitz, 2006; National Scientific Council on the Developing Child, 2007). Teachers can use a number of tools to improve the environment for those at-risk children (Lamb-Parker et al., 2008). High-quality child care can mediate the risk factor for this type of stress (Sims, Guilfoyle, & Parry, 2006).
- There are many opportunities to promote health through education for children in early childhood education environments (Gupta et al., 2005; Freeman & Feeney, 2006).
- Teachers often overlook their own health needs while taking care of children in early childhood education environments (NCCCHSRC, 2008; Arce, 2007a, 2007b; Baldwin et al., 2007). Schools can promote good staff health (Eaton, Marx, & Bowie, 2007).

Designing a Health Policy

Health policies should be developed and directed toward the children and staff. They should promote healthy practices for the child, the teacher, and the family. Basic health policies lay the foundation for the atmosphere of the early childhood education environment.

Teachers should take responsibility for providing the healthiest environment possible in the early childhood education setting. Teachers also should provide examples of healthy practices and illness prevention strategies and model them for children and their families.

The first part of the process for designing a health policy is to understand the health risks present in the early childhood education environment. Common infectious diseases, healthy sanitation practices, and health recordkeeping for both children and providers are good beginning areas for study. As the environment is examined for the risks to health, needed policies should be listed.

When the policies are created, they should be clearly written and include guidelines, limitations, and suggested methods of communication for each topic. Health policies help the teacher develop proper practices based on the knowledge of health promotion, protection, and disease prevention.

Health policies should incorporate the six major goals of high-quality child care:

- Maximizing health status
- Minimizing risk
- Using education as a tool
- Recognizing the importance of guidelines
- Practicing cultural competence
- Developing partnerships with families to provide a caring community

Basic health policies for promoting good health should cover:

1. *Health Records:* specific records for the child to be accepted and stay in care.
2. *Staff Health:* using staff health and health records to promote health and protect the environment.
3. *Protective and Preventive Practices for a Mentally Healthy Environment:* specific practices for creating a proactive and interventive environment for good mental health.
4. *Implications for Teachers:* strategies and practices for health education, cultural sensitivity, role modeling, working with families, and supervision in early childhood education environments.

Key Concept 10.1

Health Policies

Basic health policies should be designed to provide protection, prevention, and promotion of good health in early childhood education environments. These policies should include guidelines, records, and checklists. The health policy should define what is to be done and then outline the process for doing it. It should also define who is responsible and provide for follow-through. When time parameters are critical, the health policy should address them. Good health policies should address the basics of children's health records; staff health; providing a mentally healthy environment; and implications for teachers to provide education, role modeling, cultural sensitivity, and supervision.

10.2 CHILDREN'S HEALTH RECORDS

Increased risk for poor health and mental health is often associated with group care (Shope & Aronson, 2006). To reduce this risk, teachers should create a health policy for children's health records that covers certain basic information regarding each child's health and that includes guidelines for all children. The contents of each child's preadmission health history form are listed in Table 10-1. Table 10-2 lists the records that are kept for all children. It is important to note that if a family does not have access to a health care provider who can fill out the health history, give immunizations, and any other needed information, a referral to a local agency such as a county health department should be made. A child should never be admitted without the required health history because it could put the early childhood environment at risk.

- **orientation** *meeting or discussion of a child new to care regarding health, special needs, and developmental history.*

Guidelines for this health policy should include an **orientation** with the teacher for each child. Teachers should be oriented previously to this meeting with the child and the parent (Calder, 2006b). Good-quality teachers are more likely to ask detailed questions about a child's health. This may determine whether the early childhood education environment is a good match for the child and vice versa. This orientation would cover the special developmental needs of the child, dietary restrictions, and any special health or nutritional needs. Teachers can find out critical information necessary to avoid

TABLE 10-1
Checklist for Child's Health History

CHECK FOR:

- ☐ Name, address, and phone number
- ☐ Physician's name, address, and phone number
- ☐ Emergency numbers (two minimum)
- ☐ State of child's health
- ☐ Record of immunizations
- ☐ Dietary restrictions
- ☐ Allergies and other conditions that may require medication
- ☐ Any condition that requires special consideration for care
- ☐ Any special problems or fears
- ☐ TB test for children older than 1 year
- ☐ Any previous major illness or injury
- ☐ An emergency release form signed by the parent
- ☐ Any emergency instructions from family
- ☐ A list of any current medications the child is taking
- ☐ Child's health insurance information
- ☐ Duplicate emergency form for field trips
- ☐ Authorization to release child to people other than custodial parent

risk for that child and other children in the early childhood environment. For example, if a child has been adopted from a foreign country, the teacher can make sure the child has been thoroughly screened for tuberculosis. This is an example of a risk that has been identified and should be addressed (Mandalakas et al., 2007). Another example occurs when a child has recently moved or had a parent leave the household; this child may be under stress, and this should be noted. Teachers should have a developmental health history in order to know the child and provide for a holistic approach to care.

- **confidential** *keeping information private.*

Although the information found in health records is very important to the teacher, it must be a policy that this information remain **confidential** and not be discussed with anyone but the parents of the child, members of the staff, or the child's health care professional, if permitted. The parents should provide the teacher with a release to discuss medical information with the child's doctor. Discussion among staff should remain at a professional level. Certain information in the developmental history could lead to labeling a child; the professionally competent teacher understands the need for discretion and confidentiality. Staff should know necessary information to deal with the health and safety of children in care, and if there are special health concerns, they should know what these concerns entail (Walsh,

TABLE 10-2
Records to Keep for Each Child

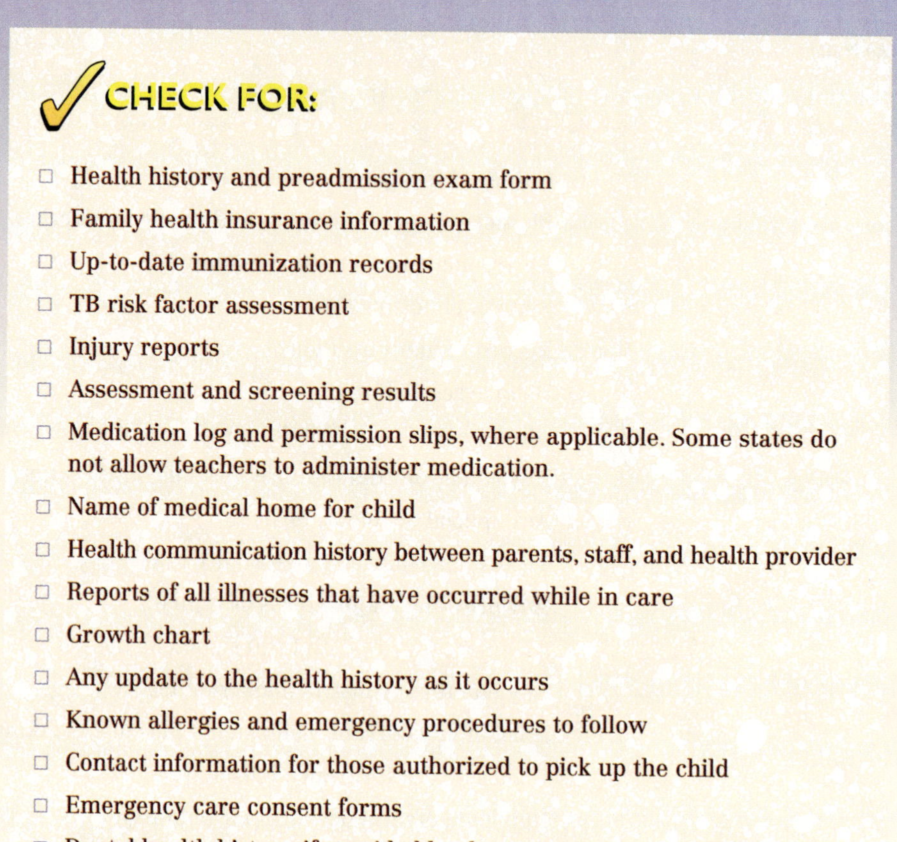

CHECK FOR:

- ☐ Health history and preadmission exam form
- ☐ Family health insurance information
- ☐ Up-to-date immunization records
- ☐ TB risk factor assessment
- ☐ Injury reports
- ☐ Assessment and screening results
- ☐ Medication log and permission slips, where applicable. Some states do not allow teachers to administer medication.
- ☐ Name of medical home for child
- ☐ Health communication history between parents, staff, and health provider
- ☐ Reports of all illnesses that have occurred while in care
- ☐ Growth chart
- ☐ Any update to the health history as it occurs
- ☐ Known allergies and emergency procedures to follow
- ☐ Contact information for those authorized to pick up the child
- ☐ Emergency care consent forms
- ☐ Dental health history, if provided by the parent

2005). An example of this would be notifying the teacher, the classroom aides, and the cook if a child has an allergy to milk. At other times, confidentiality must be expanded to include other professionals. If there is an outbreak of a reportable illness, then the public health department and licensing must be notified. If child abuse is suspected, then Child Protective Services should be notified. Another situation requiring information to be shared entails

Wadsworth/Cengage Learning

Parents should provide the teacher with a release to discuss medical information with the child's doctor. What information should be included on these forms?

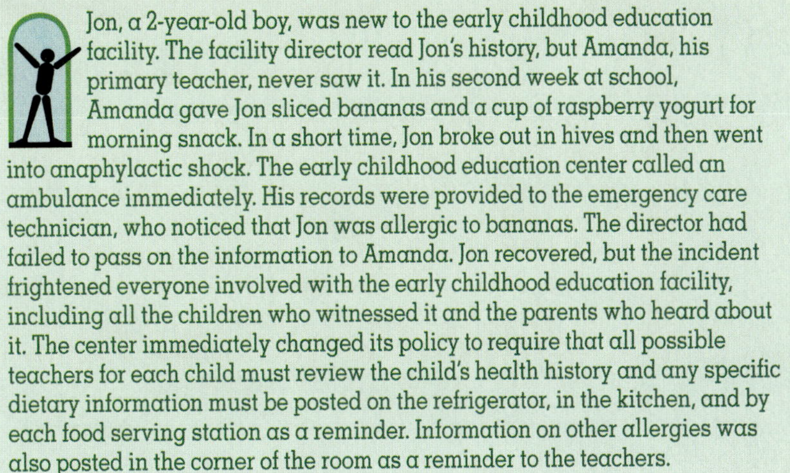
Jon, a 2-year-old boy, was new to the early childhood education facility. The facility director read Jon's history, but Amanda, his primary teacher, never saw it. In his second week at school, Amanda gave Jon sliced bananas and a cup of raspberry yogurt for morning snack. In a short time, Jon broke out in hives and then went into anaphylactic shock. The early childhood education center called an ambulance immediately. His records were provided to the emergency care technician, who noticed that Jon was allergic to bananas. The director had failed to pass on the information to Amanda. Jon recovered, but the incident frightened everyone involved with the early childhood education facility, including all the children who witnessed it and the parents who heard about it. The center immediately changed its policy to require that all possible teachers for each child must review the child's health history and any specific dietary information must be posted on the refrigerator, in the kitchen, and by each food serving station as a reminder. Information on other allergies was also posted in the corner of the room as a reminder to the teachers.

obtaining parental permission to speak with the child's health provider concerning a health or special needs issue (Calder, 2006a).

It is important that the health policy include a review procedure. Keeping records current allows for periodic review for specific warning signs, normal development rates, and immunizations.

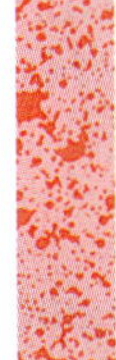

Pause for Reflection

Are you up-to-date with all your immunizations? If not, why not? What would you do if you worked in an early education environment that did not keep track of immunizations?

How can preventive and protective measures by the teacher help ensure a healthy environment?

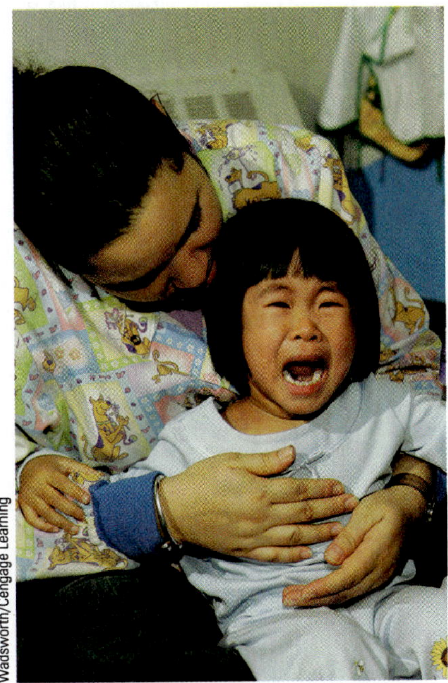
Wadsworth/Cengage Learning

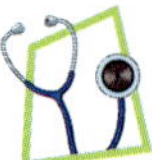

Key Concept 10.2

Children's Health Records

Health policies created for the health records of children are vitally important for the prevention of diseases and the protection of everyone involved in the early childhood education environment. Health histories that include currency information on immunizations can help teachers prevent the spread of infectious disease; knowing about special needs of some children alerts staff to possible health-related problems that may occur in the early childhood education environment. Policy procedures for orientation of new children in care as well as the management of communications and confidentiality give the teacher guidelines for conduct.

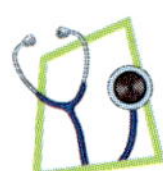

10.3 STAFF HEALTH

- **infectious diseases** *diseases capable of invading the body and causing an infection to occur; may or may not be contagious.*

The health policy that covers staff health records and health care is of primary importance. The teacher usually cares for a number of young children and the potential for spreading **infectious diseases** to other children, other employees, and her own family is great. Other occupational health hazards will be discussed later. Every teacher should be able to perform the duties of the job comfortably. The policy for health records and health care for staff should reflect preventive and protective measures. The health policy should apply to all staff members, including volunteers.

Staff Records

Before any teacher is hired or considers beginning a career working with children, he or she should have information available to complete a staff health record. The teacher's health history should include the information listed in Table 10-3.

TABLE 10-3
Checklist for Teacher Health History

- ☐ Name, address, and phone number
- ☐ Physician's name, address, and phone number
- ☐ Pre-employment examination that includes an evaluation of general health, the physical ability to perform job duties as outlined, and any condition that would create a hazard to children or other staff
- ☐ Immunization records including currency in all necessary immunizations and history of childhood diseases
- ☐ TB screening
- ☐ Hearing and vision screening

Other items that might be included in an adult health history are limitations in common situations, such as allergies to art materials, medications, and the general health status of family members residing in the person's household. Any problems with the respiratory system, such as allergies or asthma, should be reported. Some states have mandated forms that will be provided.

Before a potential teacher cares for children, he or she should have a complete physical. The potential teacher should be checked for musculoskeletal problems such as arthritis or lower back pain that might limit his or her activity or ability to perform the job (Sutton, 2003). This pre-employment health examination will evaluate general health and physical condition. It will also provide the opportunity to complete the schedule of immunizations if any of the required immunizations are missing. Any special health concerns, such as asthma, that may require more attention should be discussed with the health care provider at the time of the physical (Rose, 2006a).

After employment, regular health checkups will evaluate maintenance of good health. An orientation for the new teacher should include procedures to reduce risk for exposure to illness, including hand washing, universal precautions for blood-borne pathogens, recognizing symptoms of illness, knowledge about policies relating to exclusion from care for illness, and proper sanitation practices (Calder, 2006b).

Maintaining Staff Health

A teacher should protect the health of children and should also be a role model for good health. Schools should do what they can to promote the health of staff. This might include employee wellness programs. In about two-thirds of the states, districts or schools are provided with assistance on the development of staff health promotion activities or services (Eaton, Marx, & Bowie, 2007). Although this assistance was provided, few schools offered comprehensive employee wellness programs. Few preschool settings even offer health promotion at all. Maintaining the health of a teacher can be challenging because of the following occupational hazards:

- Exposure to infectious diseases
- Stress
- Risk for back injury
- Potential exposure to environmental hazards

Wadsworth/Cengage Learning

Staff meetings are an excellent forum for discussing the occupational health hazards that can affect teachers.

Exposure to Infectious Diseases. All teachers should have up-to-date immunizations for or have natural immunity to these illnesses:

- Tetanus (booster every 10 years)
- Hepatitis A
- Hepatitis B
- Polio
- Measles, mumps, and rubella
- Varicella (chicken pox)
- Rotavirus
- Influenza
- Pneumococcal virus (pneumonia)
- Meningococcal virus

If the teacher has had the disease, a natural immunity will have developed. Immunizations and occurrence of infectious disease should be thoroughly checked before employment. If the measles vaccine was given before age 15 months, a booster should be given to an adult, especially if the adult is a female of childbearing age. Adults' immunity to pertussis has been shown to decrease over time, so it might be important to get a booster for this disease (Burdette, 2007). Recently, the rotavirus, influenza, Pneumococcal and meningococcal vaccinations have been added to the adult list (CDC, 2007a). Teachers should be fully immunized because they are at greater risk for disease due to constant exposure to children who may have common childhood diseases and also because they have occupational hazards that expose them to disease, such as tending to children's cuts and changing diapers (Rose, 2006a). Female teachers who are of childbearing age are at special risk for certain diseases and have even greater reason to be fully immunized.

The CDC also recommends that a potential teacher be screened for tuberculosis (TB). The AAP suggests that this test should be given within one year before employment or within one week after employment. If the screening is negative, it is not necessary to repeat it periodically unless the teacher shows signs of the disease such as chronic coughing, coughing up blood, or a fever lasting more than two weeks (Kunitz, 2004); some health authorities require periodic screening. If the screening skin test has a positive reading, the teacher must provide documentation as to the status of her health (Rose, 2006b). This is often done through a chest x-ray and review of any symptoms she might have. The health provider would document that the disease, if present, was not active, and therefore the teacher would be allowed to work with children. A teacher with a positive reading might be required by health authorities to repeat the process periodically for health status with regards to tuberculosis.

Special safeguards should be in place for pregnant teachers or women with childbearing potential. Unborn children may acquire certain infectious diseases in the early childhood education environment that can cause birth defects and, in some cases, miscarriage. Five of these infectious diseases that can be prevented by proper prepregnancy immunization are measles, mumps, rubella, chicken pox (varicella), and hepatitis B. Other occupational health hazards include herpes, cytomegalovirus (CMV), parvovirus, and AIDS.

Hand washing is the number one defense a teacher uses to avoid the spread of infectious disease. Wearing nonlatex gloves helps check disease.

Special care should be made to follow all sanitary procedures, especially those that deal with children's mucous secretions, blood, and urine and bowel movements. Teachers should wear gloves each time a child's nose is wiped, after dealing with a cut or injury, for assisting in toileting or diaper changing, and before food is handled. Use of latex gloves is not recommended because of possible allergic reactions by the teachers or children. Hands should be washed immediately after removing gloves. Another supporting factor is the use of exclusion policies for ill children and teachers (NCCCHSRC, 2008).

If a teacher becomes ill, he should take a sick day. Unfortunately, too many teachers go to work when they are ill because they feel they cannot afford not to, without recognizing their part in the spread of infectious diseases (Rose, 2006c). A staff health policy should include a list of substitute teachers for the protection of the children and the rest of the staff. There should also be substitutes or backup teachers if a family child care provider or nanny becomes ill. A family child care provider may have to send the children to another provider's home. This backup care must be arranged in advance so that parents will not have to arrange for another form of care for only a day or two.

- **stress** *nonspecific response of the body to any demand put on it.*

Stress. Caring for children is a rewarding profession, but it has the potential for **stress**. Stress signals occur in two ways (Ginsburg & Jablow, 2006). First, the body makes a chemical known as a hormone and sends the stress message to the rest of the body. The signal can also come from the nervous system when the nerves send a message to the brain and rest of the body. The body's response to stress is a survival tool developed ages ago to handle emergencies and other emotionally charged situations. Teachers who are very dedicated to their jobs often don't make the time to take good care of their own health and well-being (Arce, 2007a, 2007b). There are a number of reasons why this risk factor may lead to the potential for stress in early childhood education environments:

- *Isolation from other adults:* This is more likely to occur in family child care and nanny care.
- *Long hours and hard work:* Working with children and needing to be constantly aware can be stressful. Breaks may be rare.
- *Trying to do too much in too little time:* Packing the day with too many activities or expectations of yourself or the children in care.
- *Balancing work and the rest of life:* This may include family, roommates, or school.
- *Low wages and lack of recognition:* Children and those who care for them are not adequately valued in our society.
- *Lack of training:* Teachers with more training have coping skills, organizational skills, and increased knowledge of appropriate activities for children that help them get through the day with less stress.
- *Dealing with parents and respecting their needs*
- *Dealing with individual children with a variety of needs*

- **job burnout** *inability to perform job due to excessive stress.*

Job burnout is one reaction to too much stress in life. Burnout is the combination of emotional and physical feelings of not being able to function. It results from the accumulation of stress and is a hazard for teachers and others who work directly with children (Kreisher, 2002). Studies show the job burnout rate for teachers in center-based care is at least 30 percent per year (Whitebook & Sakai, 2004). That means that for every 100 people who begin the year as a teacher, fewer than 70 are still on the job a year later. A major contributing factor to the significant turnover rate is too much stress.

It is important for the teacher to learn the warning signals and signs of stress (Crute, 2004; NCCCHSRC, 2004). A teacher must take care of her own stress level before she can really be of help to children. Awareness of stress is the first step in preventing it and protecting the teacher. Stress is the body's response to a threat. A biochemical reaction occurs within the body whether the threat is real or imagined. Stressors are people, places, or events that an individual perceives as a threat. What may be a stressor to one person may not be a stressor to another person. Causes of stress and reactions to it are unique to the individual (Table 10-4).

A person can learn how to cope with stress and may be able to reduce or eliminate it. Changing one's perception and reaction to the stressor is one

TABLE 10-4
Stress Warning Signal Checklist

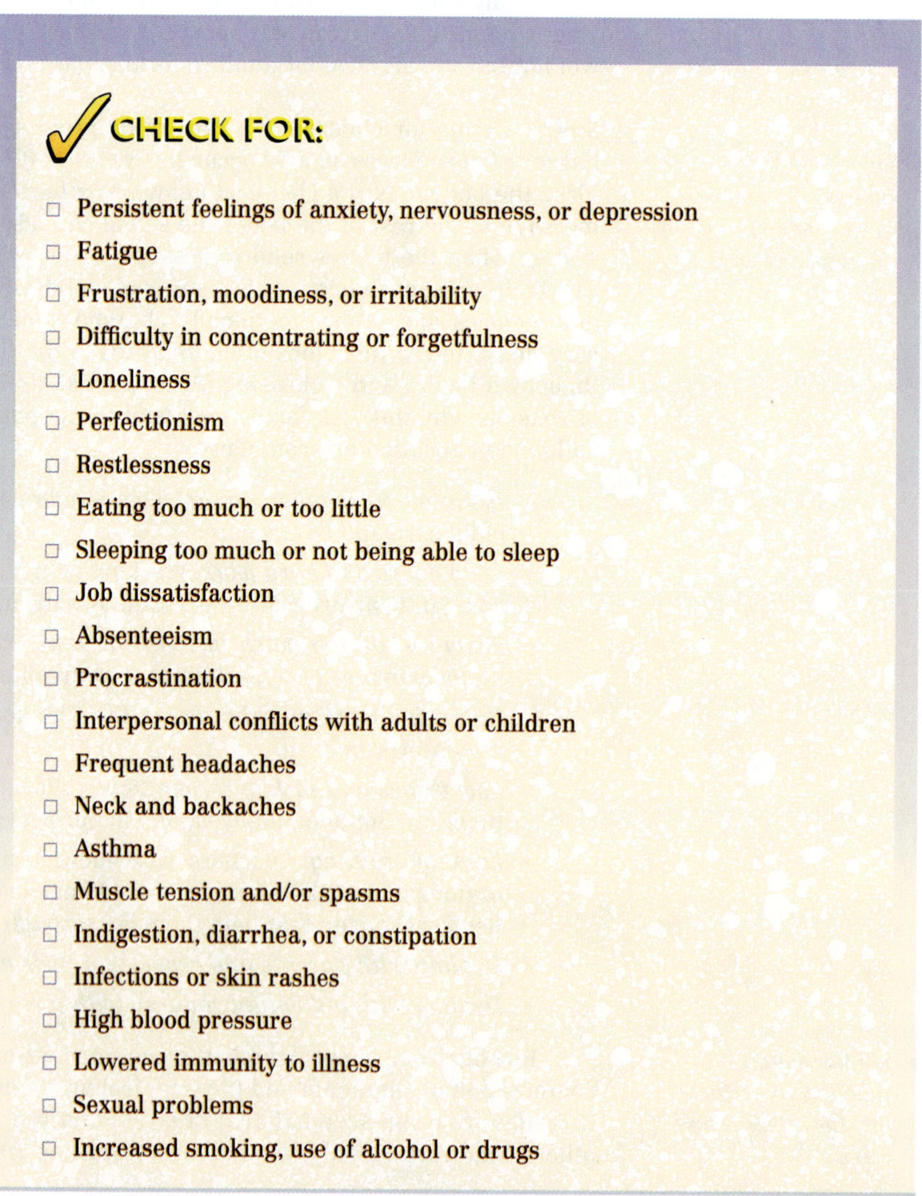

CHECK FOR:

- ☐ Persistent feelings of anxiety, nervousness, or depression
- ☐ Fatigue
- ☐ Frustration, moodiness, or irritability
- ☐ Difficulty in concentrating or forgetfulness
- ☐ Loneliness
- ☐ Perfectionism
- ☐ Restlessness
- ☐ Eating too much or too little
- ☐ Sleeping too much or not being able to sleep
- ☐ Job dissatisfaction
- ☐ Absenteeism
- ☐ Procrastination
- ☐ Interpersonal conflicts with adults or children
- ☐ Frequent headaches
- ☐ Neck and backaches
- ☐ Asthma
- ☐ Muscle tension and/or spasms
- ☐ Indigestion, diarrhea, or constipation
- ☐ Infections or skin rashes
- ☐ High blood pressure
- ☐ Lowered immunity to illness
- ☐ Sexual problems
- ☐ Increased smoking, use of alcohol or drugs

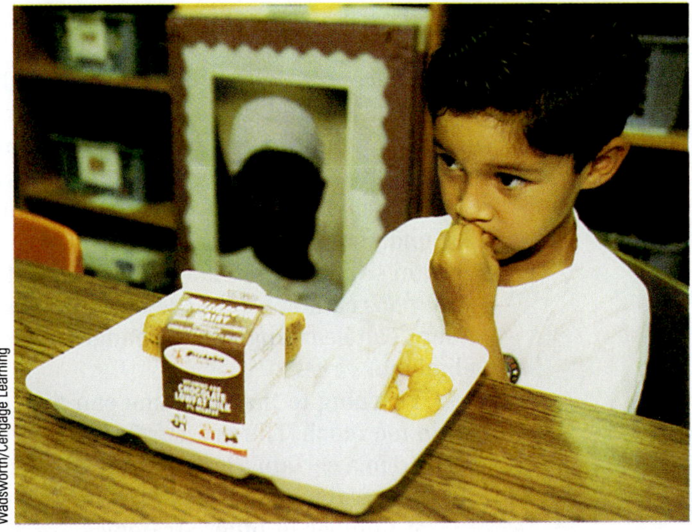
Wadsworth/Cengage Learning

A child's schedule may not always agree with the teacher's schedule, causing daily stress for both.

way to deal with stress. Another way is to eliminate or reduce the cause or source of stress. Time management is also a helpful tool to eliminate stress.

It is important for the teacher to deal early with stress and to find the best personal coping mechanisms. If a teacher does not deal with stress, it can lead to depression (Reeves, 2006a). One study found that about 9 percent of teachers had significant levels of depression (Hamre & Pianta, 2004). Teachers were more likely to be depressed if they worked in family child care or if they had little training or spent more time without other adults in the environment. Teachers should also consider their heart health in relation to

Marcus had a difficult time with transitions, especially at lunch and snack time. First, Marcus had to settle down, and then he ate very slowly. His teacher, Lavonne, worked hard to follow a scheduled routine each day. She tried to get Marcus to eat faster, but he still dawdled at each meal. Lavonne's feelings of resentment toward Marcus and frustration that she was not meeting her own expectations were causing her stress. She went to Anita, her director, to discuss her feelings. They came to several conclusions. Marcus's transitioning behavior might always be difficult at mealtimes. Lavonne would continue to try different strategies, but they agreed that in the meantime, she would try not to react to Marcus's behavior. In addition, Anita would try to give Lavonne some relief during this stressful time.

Lavonne realized that she could not fix everything, and that gave her the sense of freedom to accept the way Marcus acted at mealtime. Anita tried to provide someone to help Lavonne with the end of lunchtime as often as possible. This left the other teacher with Marcus while Lavonne was free to continue with her plan of activities. Anita and Lavonne discussed what would happen if no one were available to help relieve Lavonne at lunchtime. They agreed that Lavonne's expectation that a schedule should be or could be followed rigidly was unrealistic. Lavonne learned to be more flexible and not to feel bad if everything did not go according to her plan. Lavonne was much happier in her work, and the atmosphere of the early childhood education environment was less stressful for everyone concerned.

stress. Stress can cause high blood pressure, which can compromise heart health (Rose, 2007b).

There are several techniques for changing perception and reaction to stressors. Sharing stress with others helps one see the problem from another person's point of view. Just talking about it with a friend or family member may reduce the level of stress or even the perception that stress exists. A person who learns to recognize limitations can help reduce stress and possibly understand why stress exists in certain situations. A person who realizes certain situations are not within his control should accept the fact that these situations cannot be changed. Instead, the person should focus on which situations can be changed and change these circumstances in order to reduce or eliminate stress.

Learning to manage time can also help reduce stress. Many people try to do too much. The pressure of having expectations of what can be accomplished in a certain time frame can lead to stress. To change perception about time, several positive techniques are given in Table 10-5.

A number of other strategies are available to help reduce or eliminate stress as it occurs. These methods include both physical and mental coping

TABLE 10-5
Time Management Checklist

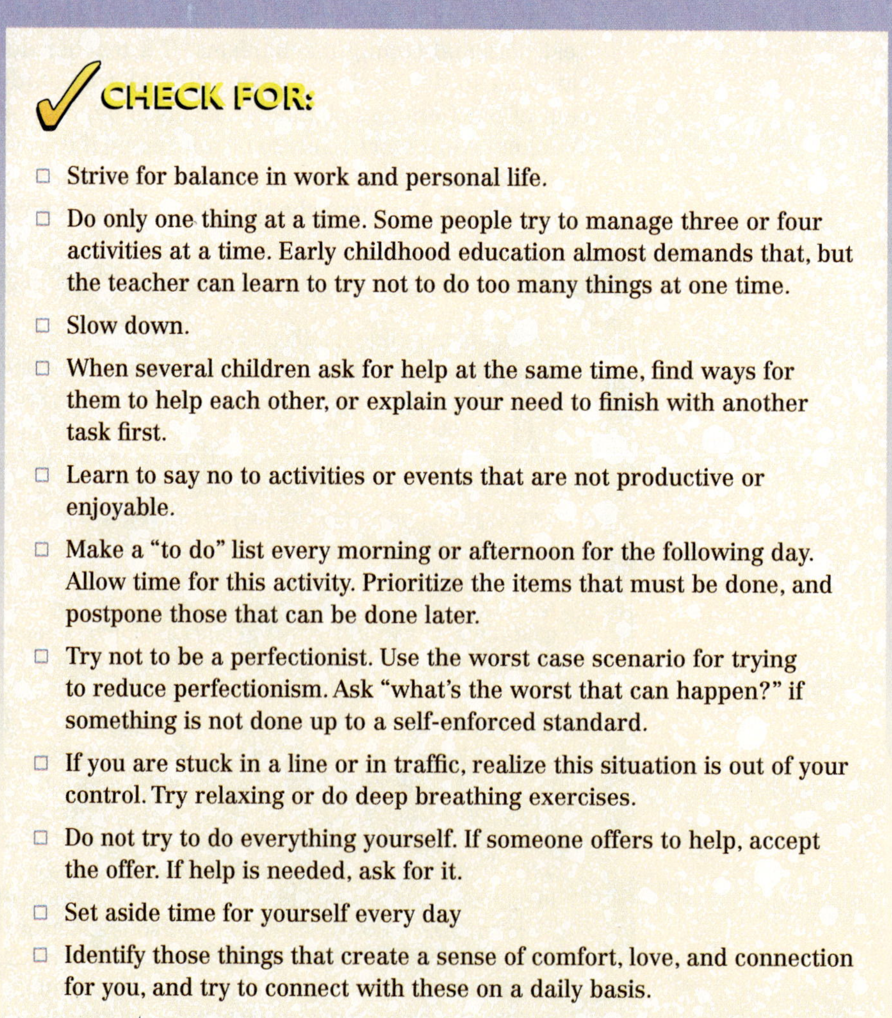

CHECK FOR:

- ☐ Strive for balance in work and personal life.
- ☐ Do only one thing at a time. Some people try to manage three or four activities at a time. Early childhood education almost demands that, but the teacher can learn to try not to do too many things at one time.
- ☐ Slow down.
- ☐ When several children ask for help at the same time, find ways for them to help each other, or explain your need to finish with another task first.
- ☐ Learn to say no to activities or events that are not productive or enjoyable.
- ☐ Make a "to do" list every morning or afternoon for the following day. Allow time for this activity. Prioritize the items that must be done, and postpone those that can be done later.
- ☐ Try not to be a perfectionist. Use the worst case scenario for trying to reduce perfectionism. Ask "what's the worst that can happen?" if something is not done up to a self-enforced standard.
- ☐ If you are stuck in a line or in traffic, realize this situation is out of your control. Try relaxing or do deep breathing exercises.
- ☐ Do not try to do everything yourself. If someone offers to help, accept the offer. If help is needed, ask for it.
- ☐ Set aside time for yourself every day
- ☐ Identify those things that create a sense of comfort, love, and connection for you, and try to connect with these on a daily basis.

skills. Some of the things one can do physically are to increase physical activity, eat a balanced diet, and get enough sleep. Getting enough sleep makes a person feel better and reduces stress levels so a person can work more effectively (NCCCHSRC, 2008). Exercise is particularly important. Exercising vigorously for 20 minutes, three times a week, can be a major stress reducer and provides for greater heart health. Hormones released during exercise help the body cope with stress. Eliminating sugar and caffeine in the diet can also help to relieve stress because both have physical side effects that may allow stress to occur more easily. Eating healthy foods, including lots of fresh fruits and vegetables, makes the body more resilient to stress and provides for greater health (Reeves, 2006a; Arce, 2007a, 2007b). If a teacher is overweight, losing weight through a healthy diet can reduce risk for high blood pressure, which can be aggravated by stress. People who care for others often find it difficult to care for themselves. Making more time for leisure, daydreaming, crying when it is needed, and learning to relax are ways that help a person's mind adjust to stress. Some people find it difficult to relax. Learn to schedule a quiet time each day to relax and reflect. Personal reflection is an excellent tool for learning about yourself and can teach you what you should recognize about your own stress. Reading, taking a bubble bath, or watching television may be relaxing. Other leisure activities such as hobbies may be more physically active, but they can be equally relaxing. Do not try the activity at a fast pace or focus on its competitive nature; this may eliminate the stress reduction quality of the leisure activity. Instead, focus on the enjoyment and relaxation benefits of the activity. Laughter is a good way to relieve stress. Watching a funny movie or doing something silly can help lower your blood pressure and suppress stress hormones (Pearson, 2006).

When stress is present, try deep breathing exercises. Breathe in slowly, hold the breath for 1 or 2 seconds, and then let it out slowly. This helps the body to come to a more neutral point. Relaxation response techniques such as holding a group of muscles taut, then allowing them to relax may also help. This process usually involves the entire body, starting with the head and moving down to the feet.

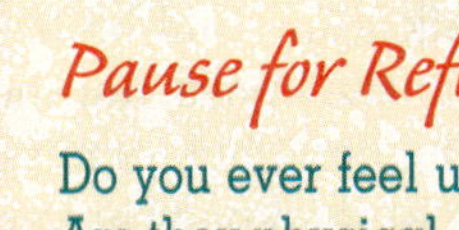

Do you ever feel under stress? What types of reactions do you have? Are they physical, emotional, or both? What types of steps do you take to relieve your stress? Are there more things you could do to relieve stress before it piles up?

Back Injury. Back problems are very common. Most people experience back pain at one time or another. Teachers may be called upon to lift and carry children many times in a day. They also bend over to play, change diapers, and feed children. Teachers may also spend time sitting on the floor and child-sized furniture. Lifting, bending, twisting, and sitting are frequent normal daily activities for the teacher. If these tasks are done correctly, problems with the back can be minimized. However, if they are done incorrectly, serious back problems can result. Many teachers are not as careful as they should be; therefore, back injury is considered an occupational hazard (Calder, 2006b).

FIGURE 10-1
How to lift a weight.

It is important for the teacher to learn how to correctly bend, lift, and sit. Lifting should be done by bending at the knees, not the waist. Bending at the knees can help relieve some stress from the back; bending at the waist adds stress to the back. When the knees are bent, the legs carry most of the load. If the waist is bent, the back carries the load. Whatever is being lifted, including a small child, should be kept close to the body, not held away from it. A firm footing is the first step to lifting. Feet should be kept apart, with one foot near the child and the other a little behind the first. During lifting, move the feet as needed, but do not twist the body (Figure 10-1). Stabilize your body against a wall or other stationary object, if possible (Kunitz, 2003). If a child is being lifted, keep the child centered on your body, and use your arms to hold and lift at the same time (Smith, 2005). For example, when a child is lifted from a crib, putting the sides down allows you to lift the child correctly. If possible, do not lift or pull heavy objects that must be moved. Instead, push the object so that the stress on the back is lessened. If carrying a child, never hold the child on one hip.

Bending over to talk to a child or to perform other common activities should also be done from the knees, not the waist. Getting at the child's level is important, but it can be done in less physically stressful ways. Position can be shifted from bending at the knees to kneeling, sitting in a chair, squatting, or even sitting cross-legged on the floor (Figure 10-2).

Surprisingly, sitting down is more stressful on the back than standing or walking. If sitting is necessary, be sure to maintain good posture and try to sit in a way that supports the curve of the back. When bending to sit or standing up from a sitting position, it is better to hang on to something stationary to remove stress from the back. Teachers often sit in child-sized chairs. This is acceptable as long as the chair is comfortable, but it should be avoided if it causes back pain or discomfort. If the teacher is holding or rocking a child, this should be done sitting down in an adult-sized chair with good back support.

Just as exercise can relieve stress, it can also build protection for the back. Regular exercise including stretching strengthens the back muscles to support the spine and keeps muscles limber (Crocker, 2003; NCCCHSRC, 2008). This will help the back withstand the teacher's daily routine. It is also

FIGURE 10-2
Sitting on a chair or on the floor at a child's level is crucial for effective teacher-child interactions, but it can result in daily back strain. To relieve pressure on the back, bend from the knees when sitting or standing.

important to use step stools to reach for things in high places, and if possible, to use adult-sized furniture when sitting for long periods of time.

Exposure to Environmental Hazards. There are numerous environmental hazards in child care (NCCCHSRC, 2005a). The most common hazards are arts and crafts materials, cleaning supplies, and pesticides. All arts and crafts materials should be examined, and labels should indicate that they are nontoxic. Throw away any materials that are not labeled nontoxic. If there are any questions, call the local Poison Control office. Some paints or other craft items can cause a harmful reaction. For example, several years ago, some early childhood education programs stopped using shaving cream as an art supply because of the rashes it caused. Others continued using it, because it did not cause rashes in their environments. If any materials are found to be harmful to the children or teachers, their use should be discontinued. It is also important always to maintain good ventilation when working with arts and crafts materials.

Cleaning supplies should also be nontoxic. Cleaning supplies may be strong enough to cause skin irritation, so gloves should be worn when using them. The gloves should be nonlatex to prevent any adverse reaction from latex by the teacher or children in the early childhood education environment. The room should be ventilated and air kept circulating during cleaning. This will help lessen any irritation to the nose, lungs, and eyes. If there should be lingering odor, continue with ventilation and air circulation until the odor lessens.

Whenever possible, it is important to use natural pesticides that are nontoxic to people (Zamani, 2007). If, for more effectiveness, pesticides should be toxic, use products that say "caution" instead of those that issue a danger warning. Try not to store any pesticides at the early education program site, but if they must be stored, keep them up high and under lock and key. When dangerous or restricted-use pesticides are necessary, they should be applied by a professional exterminator when children are not present. The area that the pesticide is applied to should be well ventilated after the application. A teacher should be present and watch the application to make sure that the pesticide does not get on food, food preparation areas, or play areas. If the teacher handles minor use of pesticides, such as spraying for ants, the same rules should apply. Nonlatex gloves should be used and discarded. These cautions will help prevent skin, nose, and lung irritations.

Arts and crafts materials are some of the most common environmental hazards in early childhood education environments. Good ventilation is essential when working with these materials.

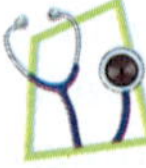

Key Concept 10.3

Staff Health Requirements

Staff health is an important factor in the prevention and protection of health in the early childhood education environment. All personnel should have a pre-employment physical examination and should meet health record requirements. Staff health should be maintained by keeping up immunizations and by washing hands frequently. The teacher should employ practices that help avoid stress, back pain, and exposure to hazardous environmental materials.

A primary teacher or caregiver for an infant or toddler provides emotional security through an atmosphere of caring and trust. This security is an important foundation for self-esteem.

Wadsworth/Cengage Learning

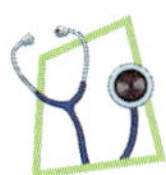

10.4 PROVIDING A MENTALLY HEALTHY ENVIRONMENT

Mental health is an area of health promotion that may be overlooked. One in every 10 children is at risk for mental health difficulties (USDHHS, 2006). Early childhood mental health is related to a child's well-being in relation to social and emotional development (Silverstein et al., 2003). The importance of providing a consistent, loving, and protective environment cannot be stressed enough. Warm, responsive, one-on-one care is essential to providing a good mentally healthy environment (Gallagher & Mayer, 2006; Goldstein, Hamm, & Schumacher, 2007; Zambo & Hansen, 2007). Longitudinal studies have shown that children in good-quality early childhood education are less likely to be depressed as adults (McLaughlin et al., 2007). Consistent routines allow children the feeling of security and a sense of trust. Children need an atmosphere where they feel that they belong. Each child needs to feel unique and have a sense of power. The child also needs to feel the freedom to express himself through play, talk, and action. Feeling comfortable enough to express negative emotions appropriately may allow the child to work through these types of emotions. This is especially true of a child with challenging behaviors (Fox & Lentini, 2006). The child's ability to deal with both positive and negative emotions may help the child deal better with life's challenges (Ginsburg & Jablow, 2006).

When a health policy is being developed for mental health, several considerations should be included. Attention to a child's family situation and cultural background is essential for developing a rapport with the child. Practicing cultural competence will help the teacher to be more sensitive to some issues that may reflect cultural differences but don't really present risk for poor mental health. Some caution signs for stressful environmental factors that a child may be dealing with and that may negatively affect health are found in Table 10-6. Notice in the list that many of these items are from the home environment. It is important that a holistic view be taken of the risk to mental health (Pachter et al., 2006).

TABLE 10-6
Caution Signs for Environmental Factors Affecting Mental Health

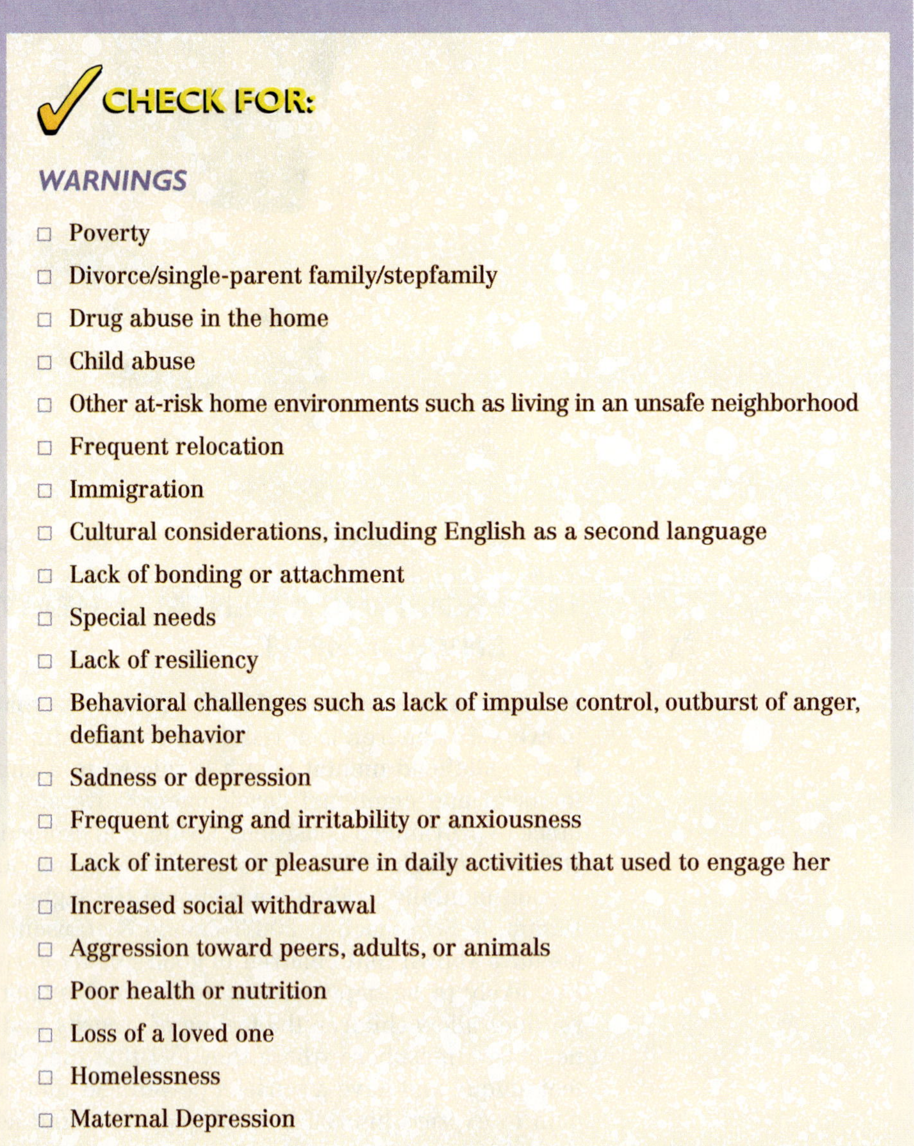

CHECK FOR:

WARNINGS

- ☐ Poverty
- ☐ Divorce/single-parent family/stepfamily
- ☐ Drug abuse in the home
- ☐ Child abuse
- ☐ Other at-risk home environments such as living in an unsafe neighborhood
- ☐ Frequent relocation
- ☐ Immigration
- ☐ Cultural considerations, including English as a second language
- ☐ Lack of bonding or attachment
- ☐ Special needs
- ☐ Lack of resiliency
- ☐ Behavioral challenges such as lack of impulse control, outburst of anger, defiant behavior
- ☐ Sadness or depression
- ☐ Frequent crying and irritability or anxiousness
- ☐ Lack of interest or pleasure in daily activities that used to engage her
- ☐ Increased social withdrawal
- ☐ Aggression toward peers, adults, or animals
- ☐ Poor health or nutrition
- ☐ Loss of a loved one
- ☐ Homelessness
- ☐ Maternal Depression

One factor to consider is the child's temperament and physical attributes (Zenah et al., 2005; Holland, 2006; Cellitti, 2006a). A child's disposition may affect how children act and whether they are more vulnerable to mental health problems (Da Ros-Voseles & Fowler-Haughey, 2007). A child's disposition also affects how he cooperates, solves problems, and how patient he is. Disposition also determines the degree of independence, self-motivation, and resilience a child shows. If the child's disposition doesn't support these factors in a positive manner, the child could have mental health issues.

Age may also be a factor in a child's adjustment to the early education environment. Older infants and toddlers may have separation anxiety and cry when a parent leaves, which is normal for many children (Cellitti, 2006c). For some young children this can lead to Separation Anxiety Disorder. This occurs when a child is excessively anxious for a month or more (Leonard, 2007). Another example of the relationship between age and a child's state of mental health would be fear. Young children have good imaginations and often take things literally. For instance, some toddlers in potty training have a fear of a toilet flushing; this is a normal fear. A deep fear based on past experience such as a child being afraid after he has been in a traumatic situation—Hurricane Katrina, for example—is very different. It is important to understand the difference between a normal emotional response of many young children and a deep fear or disorder that can lead to mental health problems.

• **self-esteem**
positive sense of self.

Self-esteem in a child is the product of a mentally healthy environment. When a child has a sense of self-esteem, that child feels both lovable and capable. A child's self-esteem evolves primarily through the quality of relationships with people in her life. Responsiveness in caregiving enables the child to feel good about herself. A teacher offering emotional security and encouragement can provide the foundation for success in later life. The quality of the relationship between the child and teacher can offer the child protective factors for later development (Zenah et al., 2005; Goldstein, Hamm, & Schumacher, 2007).

Teacher behaviors that promote a mentally healthy environment can not only provide this in the moment, but can also alleviate past problems and may help the child in the future. Table 10-7 outlines teacher behaviors that are useful in providing a mentally healthy environment. Quesenberry and

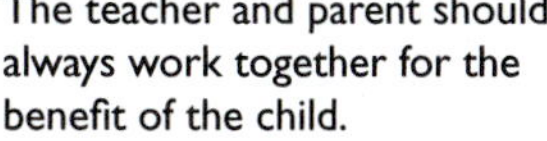
The teacher and parent should always work together for the benefit of the child.

Wadsworth/Cengage Learning

TABLE 10-7
Providing a Mentally Healthy Environment

✓ CHECK FOR:

- ☐ Establish a meaningful relationship with children and their families, including respect and mutual communication.
- ☐ Respond with consistency, predictability, and regularity.
- ☐ Establish daily routines for a sense of security.
- ☐ Provide support and emotional assurance for the child, including attention, affection, respect, and mutual communication.
- ☐ Provide a supportive environment for positive interactions among staff, children, and families.
- ☐ Allow children to explore safely and master the environment.
- ☐ Help children to express and identify emotions.
- ☐ Model appropriate emotional responses.
- ☐ Inquire as to how a child likes to be comforted when upset or afraid.
- ☐ Redirect anger and aggression through play and discussion.
- ☐ Provide a quiet area so the child can remove himself from stimulation when needed.
- ☐ Value each child's uniqueness, including cultural considerations and expressive styles.
- ☐ Promote responsive caregiving for staff and parents.
- ☐ Be flexible and reasonable in expectations.
- ☐ Provide unconditional love.
- ☐ Converse with children whenever possible.
- ☐ Listen carefully to what children say.
- ☐ Be aware of children's moods and respond appropriately.
- ☐ Extend comfort, including physical holding, rocking, and soothing.
- ☐ Have expectations for children's success and opportunities to succeed.
- ☐ Praise for accomplishment.
- ☐ Encourage children to try new things and to do them with minimal help.
- ☐ Provide access to unstructured art materials so that children can express themselves whenever they need to.
- ☐ Provide opportunities for meaningful participation.
- ☐ Encourage children to use problem-solving skills.
- ☐ Help children to accept responsibility for behaviors and consequences.
- ☐ Offer primary caregiving and, if possible, continuity of care.
- ☐ Create a pleasant, homelike environment that promotes interactions and supports relationships.

Doubet (2006) suggest that helping children with their social and emotional competencies requires a teacher to develop four skills: (1) designing supportive environments; (2) building positive relationships with children and families; (3) using effective teaching strategies for social and emotional skills; and (4) using individual interventions when needed. Another way to view helping children develop good social and emotional skills is the Teaching Pyramid (Figure 3-7) on page 120.

The health policy for mental health should include a provision for a primary teacher or caregiver for each child so that each child has one special person to bond with and form a healthy attachment to. The primary teacher can create an atmosphere of caring and trust for the child. This offers the child a sense of stability and consistency. A child who is at risk for mental health difficulties may recognize positive qualities in the teacher and may be able to seek those same qualities in other adults in the future. If it is at all possible, providing continuity of care is the ideal (Edwards & Raikes, 2002). This means that the teacher would follow the child as he or she ages from group to group through care. For example, a child begins care in the infant group, and when the group moves to toddler care, the teacher also goes with them; then when these children move to preschool care, the teacher again follows with them. When that group leaves care to enter kindergarten, the preschool teacher would revert back to infant care and follow another whole group throughout their time in care. This not only helps children feel safe and secure, but it gives families a sense of continuity, knowing the teacher will remain the same. This is a good feature of family child care, but may be more difficult to attain in center-based care. When there is a goodness of fit between the child and the teacher, the child will feel a greater sense of well-being (De Schipper et al., 2004). Stability, understanding, and consistency in the early childhood education environment may help the child to become more **resilient** in this environment (Werner & Smith, 2001; Gallagher & Mayer, 2006). (See Reality Check: *Helping Vulnerable Children to Become Resilient,* p. 563.) Another suggestion for maintaining children's mental health in the early childhood education environment is to involve mental health professionals. Head Start and Early Head Start have used this approach, which is a prevention/intervention focus (Lamb-Parker et al., 2008). Teachers are trained to work with playgroups that include children who exhibit behavioral challenges. The mental health staff supports these teachers and helps them hone their skills in the classroom.

- **resilient** *having the ability to recover after being exposed to risk.*

Lauren, a withdrawn 3-year-old child whose parents had recently divorced, lived with her father, Jim. Jim hired Julie, a live-in nanny, to help care for Lauren. Jim often traveled, sometimes with little notice. Lauren was not allowed to visit her alcoholic mother due to a court order. Julie was there for Lauren whenever a change or an unexpected event happened. Although Lauren's world seemed to have turned upside down, Julie offered comfort and security. Whenever Jim traveled, Julie stayed with Lauren, and she took Lauren home with her on her days off. Julie understood Lauren's need for stability, and she was willing to make sacrifices to ensure that Lauren knew she could depend on Julie. Julie was Lauren's nanny for almost two years. Jim remarried when Lauren was ready to attend kindergarten. Today, Lauren is a happy, outgoing 7-year-old who still occasionally talks to Julie on the phone.

REALITY *Check*

Children with Stress

Children today are dealing with many stressful events and life changes. Losses, events, or lifestyles that make the child feel she has no control may cause stress. Today, it appears that children have less time to relax and more time spent in some sort of planned activity. In addition to those risks to mental health mentioned in Table 10-6, the following items may also cause stress in a child's life:

- Birth of a sibling
- Separation anxiety
- Death of a parent, sibling, or grandparent
- Loss of a pet
- Absence of parent due to deployment, divorce, or incarceration
- Too many scheduled activities
- Living with two cultures, including their expectations
- A new care situation
- A friend leaves the early childhood education environment
- Low family income
- Financial problems at home
- Fears, real or imagined
- Observing violence in the home, neighborhood, or other real situation
- Peer pressure
- Too little privacy

Children's reaction to stress may be visible in physical, emotional, or behavioral responses. Children have limited understanding and good imaginations. When life feels out of control, the child may magnify the significance of the stressor. Children do not have the same coping skills as adults, so their reaction to stress may be somewhat different. Stress can be internalized and may not be noticeable (Reeves, 2006b).

Some children may react more to stressful situations than others. If a child is oversensitive or tends to worry, he may experience stress more easily. When a child tends to please others or does not seem to be able to assert himself, stress may have a greater impact (Foxman, 2004). When children are too young to express themselves, they may be more vulnerable to stress. Even securely attached infants and toddlers have been found to have higher levels of cortisol, the stress hormone, when adjusting to a new care situation (Ahnert et al., 2004) or when they are in an early childhood education environment that is not high quality (Sims, Guilfoyle, & Parry, 2006). Children ages 24 to 36 months were also found to have elevated cortisol levels when in all-day care (Maccoby & Lewis, 2003). Stress is also more likely for preschool age children in low-quality day care than it is for infants or older children (Geoffroy et al., 2006). The teacher should realize that stress may be part of everyday life for some children. The awareness of this may help the teacher discover ways to help manage the environment to lessen stress for the children present.

Children who react physically to stress may have headaches, stomachaches, or bouts of diarrhea. Stress in children can be associated with the reduction of hippocampal in children, which may damage the hippocampus section of the brain (Carrion, Weems, & Reiss, 2007). They may not have their regular appetites and may either not eat or constantly be eating. Children who have normal language may have some language difficulties, such as rapid speech or stuttering. Children with allergies or asthma may have reactions that appear more often.

The emotional reaction to stress can be expressed in a number of ways. The spectrum of behaviors ranges from regressive to aggressive. Children may show regressive behaviors in forms such as withdrawing or having toileting accidents. They may become clingy and too dependent or may be unable to make simple decisions, such as with what and whom to play. Children who are stressed may not laugh or smile and may cry more than usual. They may appear to escape into fantasy by constantly daydreaming or watching television. Stressed children may appear fearful and nervous; they may also become depressed.

Aggressive emotional behaviors are exhibited by acting out. This might range from throwing a tantrum to more violent behavior. Stressed children may bite or hit other children or adults. Children who use

(continues)

REALITY *Check* (continued)

aggression to cope with stress may vandalize toys, equipment, or art of their own or others. They might have difficulty with social interactions. Children under stress may become easily frustrated and use colorful language to express their anger.

An increasing number of children have exhibited challenging behaviors. This may be due to something that is referred to as "toxic stress," which is related to persistent effects on the nervous and stress hormone systems that can damage the developing brain (National Scientific Council on the Developing Child, 2007; Knitzer & Lefkowitz, 2006). This can occur in children who live under conditions of extreme poverty, family chaos, parental physical or emotional abuse, chronic neglect, substance abuse, or repeated exposure to violence. Regardless of what condition causes the stress, the one common factor is absence of a consistent, supportive relationship. When toxic stress is present, it can lead to a physiological state that disrupts the developing brain and may lead to difficulties in self-regulation.

Regardless of how it is expressed, teachers should be alert to the fact that stress can be an important factor in children's behavior. If a child abruptly changes behavior or is a constant source of regressive or aggressive behavior, stress may be a factor. If the teacher helps the child manage her stress, it will lower the risks for later physical or emotional problems (Foxman, 2004; Holland, 2006). The best way to do this is to structure the environment so that it supports the child. Allow the child to express concerns, listen to what she says, and respond in supportive ways (NCCCHSRC, 2004). The environment should be protective and prevent more stress to the child. Zenah and colleagues (2005) suggest that the teacher should have four tools to help maintain a supportive, mentally healthy environment. The first is an adequate knowledge of socioemotional development, in order to recognize the emotions of children. The second is a positive relationship with families for clear and open communication to work together for the benefit of the child. The third tool is predictable times to play, eat, and rest, and the fourth is age-appropriate behavior management techniques for children when they have problems. These factors allow children to feel secure, have a sense of control, and be more able to cope with stress and fears. The environment should be protective and prevent more stress to the child.

Providing structure through a predictable routine allows the child the comfort of understanding what comes next. The teacher can improve the quality of interaction with children by being consistent and reliable. The teacher who forms an attachment to children helps them learn to trust the teacher and the care environment (Gallagher & Mayer, 2006; Goldstein, Hamm, & Schumacher, 2007; Zambo & Hansen, 2007). This gives some children a feeling of safety and stability that they may not otherwise have.

The teacher can provide children under stress a sense of security in other ways. Some children under stress may need a quiet place to go to be free of stimulation. Providing a corner of a room that is not decorated and has a comfortable place to sit helps achieve this. Sometimes going from one activity to another can cause a child stress. The teacher can help children in their transition from one activity to another to reduce stress.

The teacher also must help children under stress learn to identify and express their emotions. Role modeling, dramatic play, reading books, and discussions with the child help. A teacher can support children by redirecting their anger, frustration, and aggression. Activities such as rocking horses, swings, and punching bags can alleviate anger. Water play and sand play are soothing and may help dissipate anger. A withdrawn child can be stimulated to act out emotions through play. Toys that encourage children to reenact things that cause them stress should be available. This might include puppets, dolls, and rescue trucks. Providing materials for unstructured art may help children express their emotions (Holland, 2006; North Carolina State University Cooperative Extension, 2007). Both organized games and unorganized play where children can be physically active might also be stress relievers. A child who feels more in control will be able to cope with stress under other situations.

(continues)

REALITY*Check* (continued)

A teacher who listens to children and responds with positive action and words allows them the opportunity to express problems and get in touch with feelings. The teacher should reinforce positive behaviors and reward them with at least a positive comment. A teacher who allows children choices where appropriate can help teach decision-making and problem-solving skills. Those actions show children that the teacher respects them, and children who feel respected have a sense of self-worth.

Each child should be treated as an individual with his own strengths and vulnerabilities (Collins et al., 2003; Gartrell, 2006). Using the context of the whole child and considering the family, the home environment, and culture is necessary to really provide the type of environment that will support good mental health and reduce stress for all children in care.

The team approach of the teacher and parents working together can also be helpful with stress. A parent may be a source of stress for the child and may choose not to participate, although most parents will be cooperative. Some parents who are under stress themselves may welcome the teacher's help. The teacher can set up times with the parent(s) to discuss the child. The teacher should show the family respect. Being consistent and predictable in all dealings with the parent can build trust. The teacher can also provide opportunities for the parent under stress to find additional help through counseling.

The teacher should employ cultural competence and acknowledge the family's feelings. By being sensitive to different values, beliefs, and expectations, the teacher can build better relationships with family partners for each child, no matter what his background (Edwards & Raikes, 2002; Zenah et al., 2005). When the teacher is consistent and predictable in all dealings with the family, trust is built. When families are under stress and circumstances are not optimal, children may be more likely to respond to stress with acting out behaviors (Greenspan, 2003; National Scientific Council on the Developing Child, 2007). The teacher can provide opportunities for the family under stress to find additional help through counseling and other community resources. When the early childhood education environment is sensitive to the needs of children and their families, the quality of care is improved. The better the quality and the more sensitive the care, the less likely a child will react in an aggressive or assertive manner to the stress he may be feeling. The more stable the care, the less stress for the child and the better the environment for the child's social development (Loeb et al., 2004).

CHECK*point:* **What do you think the stressors are for the children you know? Does this Reality Check reflect what you have observed? What other stressors would you add to the ones listed?**

Key Concept 10.4

Mentally Healthy Environment

Many children are at risk for poor mental health. Providing a stable, responsive, and consistent environment can help children acquire protective tools that will help them become more resilient to environmental factors that negatively affect mental health. Assigning a primary teacher to each child in care will help to ensure that the child can form a relationship that will provide those protective tools. Having a teacher who regards a child as unique, understands the child's temperament, and is aware of the family situation helps to individualize the care and provide the optimum environment for good mental health for each child.

This child may react differently to stress in her life than other children do.

Wadsworth/Cengage Learning

10.5 IMPLICATIONS FOR TEACHERS

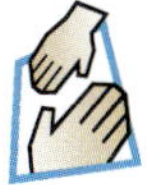

The adults they observe affect children's attitudes and behavior in relation to health. Teacher training and good practices influence the well-being of children (Greenspan, 2003). Teachers can use **role modeling**, **cultural competence**, education, and supervision to influence health.

- **role modeling** *setting a behavioral example.*
- **cultural competence** *perceptive, responsive behavior to cultural differences.*

Role Modeling

A health policy for role modeling should reflect practices that will affect the actions of children through their observation of their teachers. Good role modeling includes exhibiting awareness and practice of healthy behaviors. Teachers should display good personal grooming and hygiene and face each day with a positive mental attitude.

Good modeling uses reinforcement through observation and discussion with children. A teacher who teaches children to use healthy practices and models those behaviors can also help the parent learn. Seeing the child and teacher modeling healthy behavior may encourage the parent to adopt healthy practices.

REALITY *Check*

Secondhand Smoke

Smoking has long been an acceptable behavior in our culture. Even today, smoking is glamorized in movies, and children appear to be influenced by that (Titus-Ernstoff et al., 2008). For the last 40 or so years, medical research on the effects of smoking has found that smoking can lead to certain cancers, lung diseases, and heart disease. In the United States, 350,000 deaths occur every year because of tobacco use. Cigarettes, cigars, and tobacco carry warning labels about these facts. It has only recently been concluded that secondhand smoke may cause health problems for those exposed to a smoker's environment. Secondhand smoke refers to smoke that occurs in the burning of a pipe, cigar, or cigarettes and smoke that is breathed out from the smoker's lungs (Rose, 2007a). Almost 60 percent of children ages 3 to 11 years are exposed at times to secondhand smoke. Secondhand smoke effects are greater for young children because they breathe in more air in ratio to their body weight than do adults. Approximately 4,000 chemicals, 250 of which are toxic or carcinogenic, have been found in secondhand smoke (USDHHS, 2006) (see Figure 10-3). Secondhand smoke, or environmental tobacco smoke exposure as it is clinically referred to, is one of the most important public health hazards we face in this country (Kum-Nji, Meloy, & Herrod, 2006). Secondhand smoke has been designated as a "known human carcinogen," which means it can cause cancer. It has been estimated that if current levels of smoking persist, nearly 6.5 million children alive today will die prematurely of a tobacco-related illness (American Legacy Foundation, 2004).

Children who are exposed to secondhand smoke are more likely to die prematurely and get diseases than children who are not ("State-Specific Prevalence of Current Cigarette Smoking," 2006). Children of smokers have a greater risk for many health problems. For example, low birth weight in newborns may be caused because the mother smoked during pregnancy; it is estimated that between 20 and 30 percent of low-birth-weight babies can be attributed to the mother smoking. If smoking were eliminated, it is estimated that there would be 25 percent fewer low-birth-weight infants. As well, babies born to women who have been exposed to secondhand smoke are two to four times as likely to be low birth weight. The U.S. Surgeon General estimates that there would be a 10 percent reduction in infant deaths if smoking ceased. Studies have shown that the secondhand smoke of the pregnant mother's coworkers or family may pass blood-borne chemicals to her unborn child. These chemicals have been found to be a prelude to childhood leukemia and other cancers.

Approximately 3 million children under age 6 years are exposed to secondhand smoke at least four days a week... About 10 percent of children are also exposed to smoke while in their mother's wombs. Children from low-income, less educated families are more likely to be exposed to secondhand smoke. Children can also be exposed to secondhand smoke away from home. More than one-third of children who were not exposed at home were exposed elsewhere to secondhand smoke by other people. Much of this exposure to secondhand smoke comes from grandparents and other close relatives that the children spend time with. Some exposure to secondhand smoke may come from teachers, whether or not they are smoking in the early childhood education environment or step outside to smoke. Twelve states and many municipalities have banned smoking in public areas. The CDC is recommending comprehensive tobacco-control measures to further reduce the exposures of nonsmokers to secondhand smoke ("State-Specific Prevalence of Smoke-Free Home Rules," 2007). Only total elimination of smoking can fully protect a nonsmoker from exposure to secondhand smoke. Neither ventilating or cleaning the air or separating smokers from nonsmokers are effective ways to prevent secondhand smoke from causing health risk. In fact, routine ventilation through air conditioning and heating can actually redistribute secondhand smoke over a wider area. When children are exposed to

(continues)

REALITY *Check* (continued)

secondhand smoke indoors, it increases their risk for chronic asthma (Teach et al., 2006).

It has been estimated that exposure to secondhand smoke can account for $4.6 billion in medical expenses to treat children (American Legacy Foundation, 2004). Twenty-percent of healthy normal-birth-weight infants whose mothers smoked during pregnancy have been seen by their health care providers for bronchiolitis (Carroll et al., 2007). Between 150,000 and 300,000 cases annually of bronchitis and lower respiratory tract infections in infants and children younger than 18 months have been found to be related to secondhand smoke. Forty percent of asthma cases in children under 2 years old have been attributed to exposure to secondhand smoke (American Legacy Foundation, 2004). It has been estimated that if 1 percent of parents who smoke quit smoking, there would be approximately 19,000 fewer cases of asthma per year. (USDHHS, 2006). Exposure to secondhand smoke causes children who have asthma to experience more severe attacks more often (CDC, 2007b). In cases where secondhand smoke is a factor for asthma, a child will become symptom free if secondhand smoke is removed from the child's environment (NCCCHSRC, 2005b). Where asthma occurs as a result of secondhand smoke, there is an increased risk for a greater number of episodes as well as school absences and emergency room visits (American Legacy Foundation, 2004). More than 350,000 cases of respiratory disease are found in children each year that are directly related to secondhand smoke. Nearly 100,000 cases of otitis media (ear infection) in children under age 5 were attributed to secondhand smoke exposure (American Legacy Foundation, 2004). Chances for otitis media increase greatly if the mother smoked during pregnancy.

Secondhand smoke is a known factor in some SIDS-related deaths. In 2001, 12 percent of all SIDS deaths were attributed to secondhand smoke exposure. Infants whose mothers smoked during pregnancy had more than twice the risk for SIDS. Infants who were exposed to parental smoking before and after birth had triple the risk of SIDS than infants who were not exposed to secondhand smoke (American Legacy Foundation, 2004). Other sleeping disorders can be caused by secondhand smoke exposure. Children whose breastfeeding mothers smoked were found to have altered waking/sleeping patterns (Mennella, Yourshaw, & Morgan, 2007). When the nicotine in the mothers' milk was delivered to the infants, they would spend less time in active sleep. Children who have sleep-disorder breathing and who snore have been found to have increased negative effects from this condition if they have been exposed to secondhand smoke (Montgomery-Downs & Gozal, 2006).

Common childhood health issues of secondhand smoke include these:

- Pneumonia
- Bronchitis
- Asthma
- Middle-ear effusion (hearing loss)
- More difficulty getting over colds
- Reduced lung function
- Allergic complications
- Behavioral problems

The AAP Committee on Substance Abuse has called for a tobacco-free environment for all children (AAP, 2001; AAP, 2002). The policy statement concludes that tobacco smoke has harmful effects to the health and psychosocial well-being of children and adolescents. The policy also calls for a ban on all advertising of tobacco products. It calls on parents and health professionals to be good role models who do not use tobacco products. Because a major health function of a teacher is role modeling, smoking is a behavior that should be avoided.

Secondhand smoke has also been linked to vitamin C deficiency. Lower levels of vitamin C increase the risk for cancer, respiratory illness, and heart disease. The connection to heart disease may also come from smoking households where members tend to watch more television, eat less healthy diets, and be less physically active. Inhaling tobacco smoke may also have harmful effects on cognitive development (Park, 1999). Secondhand smoke exposure has also been related to negative behaviors in toddlers and

(continues)

REALITY*Check* (continued)

older children (Brook, Brook, & Whiteman, 2000; Gatzke-Kopp & Beauchaine, 2007). Children who are exposed to secondhand smoke may also be at risk for a decline in performance in receptive language (Lewis et al., 2007).

Secondhand smoke may be considered an environmental issue that goes beyond the home. Elevated levels of cotinine, a biomarker for nicotine, were found in 85 percent of children in one study (Mannino et al., 2001). Children between ages 4 and 6 years were the hardest hit by the exposure. They were five times more likely to have asthma than children who were not exposed. Many of these children came from nonsmoking homes. These levels of cotinine appear to increase if a child with asthma has a parent who smokes, and increase when the parent smokes more often. The cotinine level also increases if a child with asthma is involuntarily exposed to secondhand smoke in public places (Olivieri et al., 2006).

Children have also been known to eat cigarettes or cigarette butts. This can cause low blood pressure and seizure disorders (Mannino, 2003). It is important for teachers to provide a smoke-free environment (Rose, 2007a). If a teacher is going to smoke, she should lock up all tobacco products while in the early childhood education environment. She should never smoke indoors or in a car where children are present. Teachers can help to educate parents about the hazards of exposing their children to secondhand smoke. A teacher can be a role model by quitting smoking if she does smoke.

CHECK*point*: Why would smoking in an environment where children are present entail such risk? What should a teacher do to prevent this risk in the early childhood education environment?

A teacher's actions set the stage for children to learn from those actions (Zenah et al., 2005; Cellitti, 2006b; Reeves, 2006b). If a teacher encourages children to wash their hands a certain way but does not do it in the same manner himself, the children will not readily adopt those hand-washing techniques. If the teacher comes to work ill, the children will wonder why they should stay home when they do not feel well. Children often mirror what they see and hear.

Haim Ginott (1972) described the effect that a teacher's actions can have on a child:

> I have come to a frightening conclusion. It is my personal approach that creates the climate. It is my daily mood that makes the weather. As a teacher, I possess tremendous power to make a child's life miserable or joyous. I can be a tool of torture or an instrument of inspiration. I can humiliate or humor, hurt or heal. In all situations it is my response that decides whether a crisis will be escalated or de-escalated, a child humanized or dehumanized. (p. 15)

Because children view the teacher as a role model, under no circumstances should smoking be permitted at any time in the early childhood education environment. Smoking is a definite health hazard and teachers should be good role models for health. Many states do not allow smoking on the premises of early childhood education programs. Secondhand smoke has a detrimental effect on children, so they should be isolated from it as much as possible (see Reality Check: *Secondhand Smoke,* p. 400). A family child care provider might consider either not smoking or giving up the caregiving profession to prevent these effects from harming the children in care.

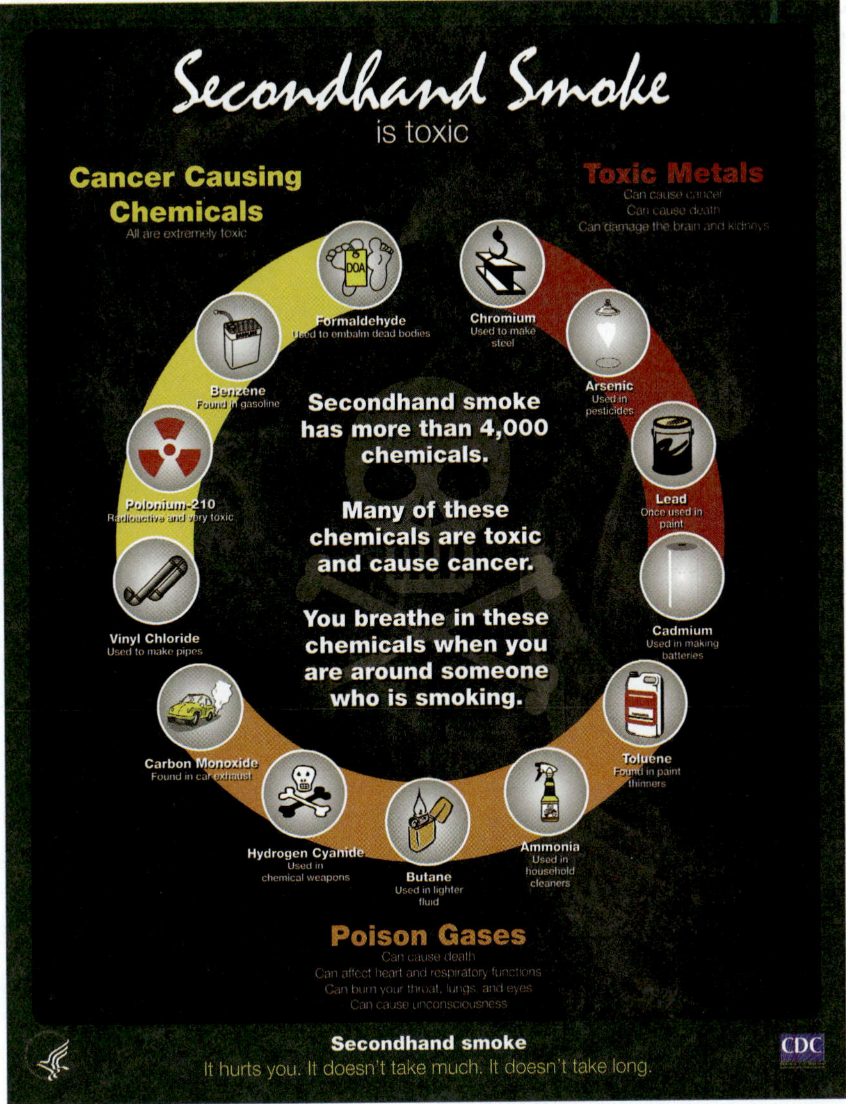

FIGURE 10-3
Secondhand smoke contains poisons. The chemicals found in secondhand smoke hurt your health, and many are known to cause cancer. You breathe in thousands of chemicals when you are around someone who is smoking.

Cultural Competence

Our country's increased cultural diversity is reflected in the early childhood education environment. It is important for the teacher to be culturally sensitive to the needs of children and families concerning health, safety, and nutrition. The teacher should learn more about the cultures of children in care. People from diverse cultural backgrounds may have different views and responses to situations concerning health. These beliefs are an integral part of cultural expression. When health behaviors are viewed in the context of culture, they may be more easily explained. When cultures are not understood, there may be barriers to communication on these issues.

Health issues may be critical, and there should always be a clear path for communication. Conflicting cultures can make immigrant and refugee children prone to psychological problems, and the children may have a difficult time forming a self-identity or feeling a sense of self-esteem (Carballo & Nerukar, 2001; Duarte & Rafanello, 2001). These children may also be at

Wadsworth/Cengage Learning

Culturally diverse early childhood classrooms provide additional challenges for teachers. It is crucial to understand critical values and traditional backgrounds to develop a bias-sensitive curriculum and effectively communicate with the children and their families.

much greater risk for illness due to their living conditions. By using a bias-sensitive curriculum and understanding cultural values and traditional backgrounds, the teacher can help provide children with the tools to maintain their health and feel good about themselves.

For Families

An open line of communication about all health issues should be set up upon the entrance of the child into the early childhood education environment. Families should provide a health history, immunization records, and all other health information needed to protect the child from risk. The teacher should be provided with this information during an orientation for the child and her family.

Families should be offered information on health matters on a regular basis. For example, families should be provided information on how to stop smoking and be made aware of the harm that secondhand smoke may cause. They should also be provided with information on developmental norms and infectious diseases. Handouts on children's stress and stress in adults will help provide useful information for the families. Teachers and families should work together if a child shows signs of stress. Offering information about creating good, mentally healthy environments may help them to provide this at home.

If there is a situation where the mental health of a child appears to be at risk, referring families to mental health resources is essential (Gartrell, 2006). The family may be reluctant or noncompliant, and if this is the case it is essential that mental health resources be consulted in order to help the family understand the need for getting help for the child. Some centers in Connecticut as well as Head Start and Early Head Start programs have used mental health consultants within their environments with good success (Waldman, 2007; Lamb-Parker et al., 2008).

Education

Education is a primary tool for promoting health. Education for current needs as well as new developments in health and early childhood education will help teachers maintain a healthy environment. Teachers should understand the importance of health records for children and staff. Sound training will offer preventive measures to avoid risk to staff health. Teachers who understand the importance of a mentally healthy environment can develop policies that provide it. Teaching children how to recognize their own feelings can help them to be better able to cope when problems occur. Using posters and brochures can be effective in helping to stop secondhand smoke.

Supervision

Supervision is an important tool for teachers to maintain healthy environments. Supervision includes the maintenance of health records for both children and staff. In situations where the teacher is in charge of staff, supervision should be used to prevent stress, eliminate environmental hazards, and prevent backaches. Gentle reminders may help the staff to alter behaviors.

Supervision is also necessary to ensure the maintenance of a mentally healthy environment. Behaviors of children and teachers should be monitored. Children may be at risk due to certain environmental factors, and a teacher who notices this early can intervene. The teacher should be providing consistent, responsive care.

Supervision may also include enforcement. It is vitally important that the teacher enforce the no-smoking regulations (Rose, 2007a). This includes no smoking in cars that transport children.

CHAPTER SUMMARY

Health policies help the teacher manage the environment for good physical and mental health. These policies should reflect the high quality of the early childhood education environment. Accurate child and staff health histories should be maintained, including immunization records. Staff should model and maintain good health by avoiding exposure to infectious diseases, stress, back injury, and environmental hazards. Teachers should be warm and responsive and give consistent care. These factors allow the teacher to provide a mentally healthy environment for children and to protect children against stress. Teachers can affect the health environment of the early childhood education program by role modeling, using cultural competence, providing education, working with families, and using supervision.

TO GO BEYOND

Additional resources for this chapter can be found by visiting the book companion website at www.cengage.com/education/robertson. This supplemental material includes chapter objectives, internet exercises, reflection questions, quizzes, web links, glossary and flash cards, case studies, frequently asked questions, downloadable forms and tables, curriculum supplements, more reality checks, additional key concepts, references, and more.

Chapter Review Critical Thinking Applications

1. Discuss how health policies affect the early childhood education environment.
2. What general health policies should be considered in the early childhood education environment? List and evaluate them.
3. Request health policies from local early childhood education programs, family child care sites, and elementary school districts. Examine and discuss the elements found in these policies. Interview teachers or school district representatives from these programs to determine the impact of these policies.
4. What is the interrelationship between the teacher's actions and a mentally healthy child care environment?

As an Individual

1. How do you as a person respond to stress? Identify your responses to stress. Identify your particular stressors.
2. List and discuss the coping mechanisms that you have to deal with stress and your stressors. How could they be improved?
3. How would you deal with a child who is distressed or suffering from outside stresses? What practices would improve the help offered to children who are feeling this way in an early childhood education environment?
4. As a teacher to infants and toddlers, what measures could you take to protect your back?

As a Group

1. Observe multicultural approaches in a preschool setting that support a bias-sensitive curriculum. Discuss how that might differ from other curriculums found in the same setting.
2. In small groups of four or five students, compare cultural health practices that may be present in your community. List those practices and cultural origins. As a class, compare the lists and create a master list. How might these practices affect an early childhood education environment?
3. How might stress be reduced in an early childhood education environment? Discuss coping skills that might be used to reduce stress in this environment.
4. Discuss the differences between a preschool and an elementary school and the use of a mental health consultant. What types of services do most preschools offer? What types of services do most elementary schools offer? Compare and contrast these.
5. What policies might an early childhood education environment have about teacher injury prevention, stress, and burnout? In small groups, design a policy for each item that the class considers important.

Case Studies

1. Molly and Margaret are teachers who work at the same center. They are both in school part-time and are single mothers whose children are in elementary school. They get along well together, although they work in different classrooms and with different age groups. Both are suffering from stress, on and off the job. What coping skills would you suggest for them. How might they help each other?
2. Mark comes from a home in which his parents just divorced and his mom is about to have a new baby. He was a happy, well-adjusted 3-year-old until these events occurred. Now he is angry and aggressive. What can you do to help him?
3. Erica is a parent in your family child care program. Her son Ronnie is 8½ months old. Erica smokes heavily, and Ronnie is having problems with colds and ear infections. How would you handle this?
4. Jordan, who is in your first-grade class, seems to have a stomachache three or four times a week; at these times, she wants to see the school health clerk, hoping she will be sent home. How do you handle this?

CHAPTER 11

Tools for Promoting Good Health in Children

After reading this chapter, you should be able to:

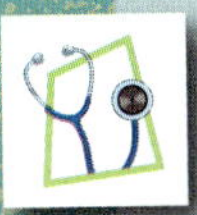

11.1 Health Policies

Define and discuss health policies for appraising, screening, and assessment.

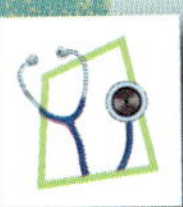

11.2 Recording Health Status of Children

Describe and detail the process of recording appraisals, screening, and assessment.

11.3 Assessing a Child's Health Status

Summarize the components of a child's health and how they are assessed.

11.4 Implications for Teachers

Relate the importance of education, observation, working with families, and the use of appraisals, screening, and assessment.

11.1 HEALTH POLICIES

Children grow and develop at different rates. They also have different levels of health and well-being. Each child must be looked at individually for accurate health assessment. Forming a health policy for appraising, screening, and assessing a child's health is a major task of the teacher. A child's health is a very significant factor in her overall well-being. The following indicators show the need for creating and implementing policies for observation, record keeping, and assessment:

- All teachers should have good tools to assess a child's development (APHA & AAP, 2002; Harms, Clifford, & Cryer, 2005; Shope & Aronson, 2006). Failure to evaluate and assess a child's progress may deprive the child of needed intervention and corrective measures (Groves-Bixby, 2007; Reeves, 2006).
- Teachers should be able to recognize developmental delay, disabilities, and other possible health problems (Lucarelli, 2006).
- A health assessment provides information on whether a child is physically, developmentally, and emotionally ready to learn in early childhood education environments (Crowley & Whitney, 2005). Yearly physical health assessments should be scheduled because of rapid growth and development that occur in young children (Cole, 2008).
- Screening children for problems can lead to early intervention and a greater chance for children to develop to their full potential. When infants who have behavior difficulties are screened for mental health, early intervention will give them a better chance for normal development (Baggett et al., 2007). When preschool children are screened for potential motor problems, intervention can lead to greater school success in later years (Bayoglu et al., 2007).
- A teacher should be aware that development takes place in a holistic manner, so that all the contexts are considered.
- The poverty rate for children in 2006 was 17.4 percent (Center on Budget and Policy Priorities [CBPP], 2007). Socioeconomic status is a predictor of children's health over time (USDHHS, 2006a; Chen, Martin, & Matthews, 2007). Chronic poverty affects child behavior in all ethnicities (Pachter et al., 2006).
- Observations about the child's health, habits, and behaviors help in the early detection of problems (Garakani, 2007). Observation helps teachers understand the needs of children from all backgrounds (Dodge et al., 2004; Christian, 2006). Many types of technology can be used to help the teacher record observations (Nilsen, 2008).

Using health policies for observing, recording, and evaluating a child's health will allow for uniformity in how **appraisals** and **screenings** are carried out. These policies will provide information for **early intervention**, if necessary, and will help protect other children from unsafe and unhealthy situations. **Assessment** provides a multitude of tools and procedures to evaluate a child's development and to signify difficulties as they occur.

According to standards of the NAEYC, a well-prepared teacher should understand the reason for assessment. This knowledge will allow the teacher to use effective assessment strategies (Harms, Clifford, & Cryer, 2005). Teachers without training, awareness, and cultural sensitivity are more likely to

- **appraisals** *regular process of evaluation of a child's health or developmental norms.*
- **screening** *to select or evaluate through a process.*
- **early intervention** *decision to modify a child's at-risk behavior or condition in an early stage in order to decrease the impact of the behavior or condition on the life of the child.*
- **assessment** *in-depth appraisal to determine whether a particular health or developmental condition is occurring.*

- **primary health assessor** *teacher who knows the children very well and can observe for health and well-being.*
- **referral** *sending a child for further testing or screening and making available resources that will intervene and avert risk that is posed to the child.*

have problems performing assessments (Santos, 2004). The teacher is often the **primary health assessor**. In an early childhood education center, the director or principal and aides may also contribute to the assessment of the child's health. In many elementary schools, there is a health clerk or nurse who takes on the role of diagnosing or counseling a child. Creating open lines of communication with the parent is essential to the evaluation of a child's health status. Successful communication begins before issues of concern appear. If an observation or other information indicates a child needs screening and **referral**, a discussion with the parent can clarify the situation, and teacher and parents can work together to decide the next step. Some families coming into care may need more services than a teacher can provide (Shope & Aronson, 2006). If the decision is for referral, then other professionals, such as a speech therapist or audiologist, will contribute to the overall assessment and any resulting intervention. Teachers who do not have training in handling specific health issues may not be able to meet the needs of a child with a chronic illness (Cianciolo, Trueblood-Noll, & Allingham, 2004).

Professional health consultants are available for early childhood education environments. These are often nurses or public health nurses who will help both to assess a child's health if problems appear and to create policies for dealing with them (Shope & Aronson, 2006).

It is important to understand that, as a primary health assessor, the teacher is a participant observer who should strive for objectivity (Garakani, 2007). In the early childhood education environment, the teacher rarely has the opportunity to stand back for long periods of time and either casually or formally observe children without interruption. In addition, the teacher brings her own perspective as an assessor. The teacher's temperament, ethnicity, culture, gender, and experience will affect how she assesses a child's health and development (Caufield & Kataoka-Yahiro, 2001).

All of the preceding factors contribute to the need for definite policies to evaluate a child's health status. These health policies include:

- *Record keeping:* specific objectives and methods of recording health information.
- *Assessing a child's health status:* procedures for translating and evaluating information to form assessment; includes using indicators of health difficulties.
- *Implications for teachers:* specific practices for observation, education, working with families, cultural sensitivity, and supervision.

Wadsworth/Cengage Learning

The teacher, as the primary health assessor, is responsible for ongoing observations of the health status of each child in his care. Recorded observations are an additional benefit of presenting a complete picture of a child's health status to parents and can aid doctors in diagnosing health problems.

Eric, an active 2½-year-old, seemed to have difficulty following directions and appeared not to pay attention during group time at the early childhood education center. Carol, his teacher, noticed this and asked the aide, Miriam, to observe Eric during those times to see whether she noticed the same behaviors. Miriam observed Eric for several weeks and documented what she had noted. She agreed with Carol that Eric had attention problems. Carol discussed the situation with Eric's father, Joe, and asked Joe to watch Eric at home. Joe agreed to do this, but he seemed to think that Eric's problem might be related to a recent divorce and living in a single-parent family situation. Joe reported to Carol after a weekend of observation that Eric did seem to have attention problems in certain circumstances. Carol, Joe, and Raoul, the director, met to discuss the situation.

Raoul suggested that they begin with a hearing assessment. Eric went to his physician, who felt further tests were needed and sent Eric to a hearing specialist. The specialist concluded that Eric had a hearing deficit that had gone unnoticed during language development but was serious enough to cause problems at his present age.

Eric was fitted for a hearing aid, and the difference in his attention was remarkable. No one had realized how much Eric had done to compensate for his problem. Now that he could hear, he was like a sponge, trying to soak up information. He asked many questions and was involved in the learning process. Eric's father was grateful that Carol had noticed Eric's problem and had pursued it.

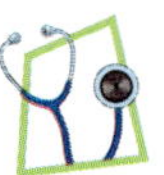

Key Concept 11.1

Health Policies

Specific health policies for appraising, screening, and assessment are necessary to enable the teacher, as the primary assessor, to accurately evaluate the health status of children. These policies include record keeping and assessing health status. Implications for teachers include practices for observation, education, cultural competence, and supervision.

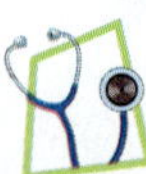

11.2 RECORDING HEALTH STATUS OF CHILDREN

Observation helps the teacher get a specific picture of an individual child's health status as well as his temperament, personality, behavioral characteristics, and abilities. What is significant and needs further deliberation depends on the teacher's insight and intuition. These insights from observation are included in the child's permanent health record by using record-keeping management tools.

Observation

Observation of children is a significant portion of a teacher's job because it allows a teacher to get to know and understand a child's temperament, personality, abilities, and limitations. Observation should be objective; the teacher observer should avoid personal feelings, interpretations, and biases. When the teacher is specifically observing a child's health and well-being, there are several goals to keep in mind.

What Is Going to Be Observed? The first goal is to decide what is going to be observed. Is the child being observed for physical well-being, how she performs physically, or how she acts emotionally? Is the teacher specifically looking for a particular health condition or communicable disease? Has the parent indicated a problem he may have observed? What is the age of the child being observed? A 3-year-old has different physical and emotional capacities than a 2-year-old. Some other considerations that may affect the observations follow:

- Are there cultural differences?
- Is the child at risk?
- Does the child have special needs?
- Has there been a recent event in the child's life that may affect his well-being or behavior (e.g., birth of a baby, loss of a pet, a move)?

These factors will influence what is observed.

How Will the Observation Take Place? A second goal is to understand how the observation will take place. The teacher needs to be aware that his own childhood, feelings, and experiences will affect the interpretation of what is observed and how it is translated. Lakin (1994) suggests that the observer go through stages of observation.

- Acting like a scientist and observing physical data
- Being the inspector and sorting out feelings from the physical data
- Behaving as an advocate and looking at the situation from the child's point of view to consider why the child acted in a certain manner
- Acting as an artist and using what is observed to take action to support the development and interests of the child (thereby enforcing a holistic approach to observation)

The "how" of observation also includes what was physically done to carry out the observation. In order to be accurate in the first stage of observation of a child's health and well-being, the teacher must use all of her physical senses. The teacher will need to:

- Look
- Listen
- Feel
- Smell

Looking at the child includes all physical aspects of the child as well as how the child is acting. Listening to the child involves hearing what the child sounds like, as well as what the child says and how it is said. Feeling the child involves touching the child to see if she is feverish, clammy, or has swollen glands or other physical symptoms to determine whether a problem exists. Smelling a child involves the teacher's awareness concerning personal hygiene as well as toileting accidents.

When Will the Observation Take Place? The teacher should also know when the appropriate time to observe is. It is very important that a health check be made daily when the child first enters the early childhood education environments. This quick check should be done before the parent leaves the child, if possible. If the child is ill and must be excluded from care or school, it should be done before other children are exposed.

At the drop-off time, the parent may share any particular concerns she has about the child's health or well-being. This helps the teacher to be on the alert for observation of that concern. This is less likely to happen in elementary school settings because parents often drop off children without accompanying them to class.

Record-Keeping Management Tools

When creating health policies for record keeping, the teacher should consider what may be implied as a result of what has been observed. Care should be taken to be as accurate as possible when taking notes and recording information (Nilsen, 2008). Teachers should remember that they are making observations, not diagnoses. A number of different types of record-keeping management tools can be used to decrease bias and to present a more accurate picture of the health status of the child.

Precise Words. The first of these tools is the use of precise words to describe the condition or event that is observed. For example, "Joey has a snotty nose" might be better recorded as "Joey's nose is constantly oozing yellow-green mucus." Children can get runny noses from colds, allergies, changes in temperature, communicable diseases, and so forth. The fact that the mucus is yellow-green and constantly oozing might infer something more serious than sniffles. If Joey's nose runs often, a comparison between precise descriptions might show a pattern for an allergy or a more serious problem. Using adjectives that clearly describe what was observed can be a way to increase perceptions about the children in care.

- **time sampling** *observervation of a particular behavior over a specific period of time.*
- **event sampling** *observation of a specific preselected behavior as it occurs, every time it occurs.*
- **anecdotal** *relating to a brief narrative account that describes a child's behavior that is significant to the observer.*
- **running records** *a detailed narrative account that describes a child's behavior in sequence, as it occurs.*

Type of Record. The next issue for record keeping is the type of record that will be kept. A number of different types of records are helpful, and there are advantages and disadvantages for each type. Table 11-1 indicates the major types of records for observing health status and the conditions in which each type would be most accurate. It would also be appropriate to use an ECERS-R scale to aid in keeping records and assessing information.

An early childhood education center might use checklists as a major source of record keeping due to the number of children assigned to each teacher. There also may be a greater need for **time sampling** and **event sampling** because of the number of children in care. **Anecdotal** and **running records** would be used occasionally as time permits or as a situation demands. Conversing with a child in order to assess the level of a child's speech and language can be a

TABLE 11-1
Types of Health Assessment Records

Type of Record	Definition	Best Used For	Limitations
Anecdotal	Brief narrative accounts that describe health conditions and behavior	Daily open-ended observation	Relies on memory of observer, can be out of context
Running Record	Detailed narrative account in sequence of health status conditions and behaviors	More comprehensive and keeps better track over time	Time consuming; teacher must have time apart from children to record
Checklist	Lists of specific health status, communicable diseases, absence of signs, symptoms; monthly, quarterly, and yearly growth and development observations	Daily scan	Specific traits and behaviors; does not describe
Time Sampling	Records frequency of health status condition or behavior occurrences	Good for over time, takes less time; objective and controlled	Does not describe condition or behavior
Event Sampling	Waits for health condition or behavior to occur, then records specific behaviors	Recurring problem; objective and defined ahead of time	Misses details of condition or behavior

Adapted from: *Observing the Development of Young Children,* by Janice J. Beaty, 2002, New York, NY: Macmillan, and *Week by Week Documenting the Development of Young Children,* by Barbara A. Nilsen, 2005, *Clifton Park, NY: Thomson Delmar Learning.*

good developmental tool. A teacher in an early childhood education program at a center would be the most likely to use all types of record keeping.

A family child care provider would more likely use a combination of anecdotal records and checklists as the major source of record keeping. A family child care home usually has children of mixed ages, so the provider has a wider age range to observe. A running record would be used only as necessary, and there probably would be little need for time sampling or event sampling unless a condition or behavior were serious enough to merit their use.

A nanny or in-home care provider would rely mostly on anecdotal records. A nanny should keep a daily log that records the child's health and developmental milestones or difficulties. A running record may be used if the nanny or parents have a specific concern about the child. Because the nanny usually has fewer children to care for and usually spends more time with each child than other types of caregivers do, there would be little need for time sampling or event sampling because the behavior recurrence or conditions leading to behavior would probably already have been noted. A nanny might use a checklist for the daily quick health check, but she would be more likely to do it mentally than to record any significant factors in the daily log.

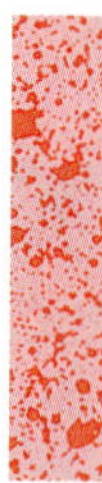

Pause for Reflection

Have you had any experience using any of the assessment tools listed? If yes, was a more accurate picture provided with the use of something this formal? What tools do you think would be most useful to you in the future?

How to Keep Records. The type of record keeping used usually determines how the record will be kept. Anecdotal notes can be kept in the child's health record, on file cards, or in a notebook, and later placed in the child's health file. Running records are usually recorded on separate sheets of paper and then filed. Checklists and time and event samples are usually printed forms that can be added to the child's file.

A teacher might use a tape recorder, digital camera, or video recorder for anecdotal notes, running records, time sampling, or event sampling. Video recordings might also be used for checklists. It is important that permission be obtained for any audio, photographic, or video record to be placed on file before these technologies are used (Nilsen, 2008). The advantages of a digital camera are that film does not need to be developed and a record can be kept conveniently on a compact disc (CD) for further use.

The child's health record file or portfolio should include all observations made. A portfolio is a record of how a child progresses through time and would include more than a health record file does—for example, how the child interacts with others and the child's work samples over time—in addition to observations and screening tests (Garakani, 2007). The file or portfolio will give a view of the child's health status, conditions, and development and may be invaluable to a health professional if a child has warning signals for specific problems. The health file or overall portfolio are tools for creating good two-way communication with the parent about the child and her development. Whichever type of file you choose, it can be used as part of the regular parent/teacher conferences to discuss the child's overall development. The actual health records might be kept on a CD, to save room and for greater convenience. If a scanner is available, all records could be scanned and added to the CD; technology can be very useful in observing children and promoting good health policies and practices.

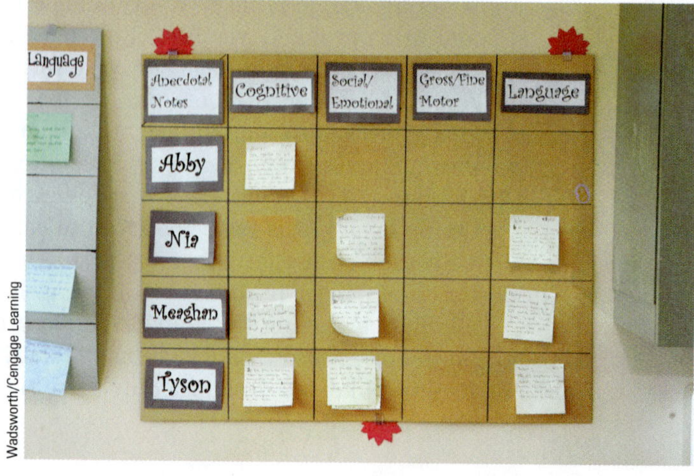

Wadsworth/Cengage Learning

This board with anecdotal notes allows the teachers to quickly identify items that may indicate a risk.

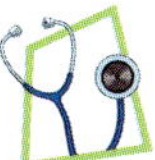

Key Concept 11.2

Health Records

Record keeping is a good tool for health management. The wording used to record observations should be accurate and descriptive. The type of record that is kept will depend on the care situation as well as the conditions or behaviors that are being recorded. The records that are kept are a valuable tool for communicating with parents and for providing information to health professionals. Technology can be a great assistance in observing and recording behaviors that may be a risk to health and in keeping health records.

11.3 ASSESSING A CHILD'S HEALTH STATUS

Appraising a child's health and well-being, screening for **developmental norms**, and evaluating the information obtained are necessary steps for the teacher assessing a child's health status. This is done at several levels, including those in the following list:

- **developmental norms** *statistically average ages which children demonstrate certain developmental abilities and behaviors.*

- A daily quick health check
- A general health appraisal
- Screening for growth and developmental norms
- A mental health appraisal
- A nutritional assessment

Wadsworth/Cengage Learning

As parents drop off children, the teacher can make an informal quick health assessment. Is the child lethargic and listless? Does the child look flushed or pale?

TABLE 11-2
Daily Health Checklist

CHECK FOR:

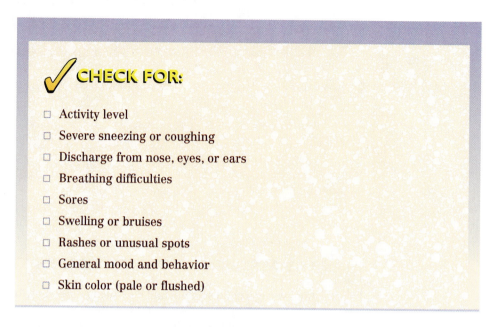

- ☐ Activity level
- ☐ Severe sneezing or coughing
- ☐ Discharge from nose, eyes, or ears
- ☐ Breathing difficulties
- ☐ Sores
- ☐ Swelling or bruises
- ☐ Rashes or unusual spots
- ☐ General mood and behavior
- ☐ Skin color (pale or flushed)

Daily Quick Health Check

The teacher needs to determine on a daily basis whether a child who is ill or has a health condition that may put other children at risk should be excluded from care. The health policy for daily appraisal is an important tool for preventing the spread of illness and disease.

It is done rapidly and is often referred to as a quick health check. The child's health condition is appraised daily when the child enters care or school (Calder, 2006). Table 11-2 shows the signs to watch for while performing the daily quick health check observation. This should be done by using all your senses to look, listen, feel, and smell if there is something that is not the norm for that child.

If a child exhibits any of the signs listed in Table 11-2, the teacher should inform the parents and discuss the observations with them immediately. If the symptoms are included in the child care exclusion policy, the parent should take the child home. If the observation does not dictate exclusion, the teacher and parent will need to discuss how the child should be managed that day and at what point the teacher will contact the parent. The discussion could reveal a simple explanation of the problem and may alleviate the teacher's concerns.

General Health Appraisal

A general health appraisal is used when warning signs of questionable health or illness are observed. It can also be used to track the recurrence of illness or health conditions. This appraisal goes into more depth as to the signs of health and illness the teacher might observe in the children in care.

If the teacher notices frequent recurring conditions or that a child is not acting normally, the teacher may want to take a closer look at the child's health. Recurring physical problems such as frequent colds or ear infections may indicate that a child has an allergy or other health problem that needs to be evaluated by a physician. The frequency of a condition will be noted in the child's health record. The parent should be consulted about the frequency before further information is gathered.

If the teacher feels more information is needed, he should seek the help of a health consultant with the parent's permission. That person can help the teacher decide whether the child needs to be seen by a physician or community health clinic. Discussions with the health consultant can assist the teacher in being better prepared to seek further cooperation with the parent about the child's specific health concern.

- **medical home** *a partnership of the family, the teacher, and a medical practitioner that ensures that all health, psychosocial, and educational needs of a child are met.*

It is also helpful if a child has a **medical home**. This medical home partnership unites the parents, teachers, and health professionals to ensure that all health and developmental needs are met (Reeves, 2002). The AAP suggests that the medical home should be family centered and culturally effective. Evaluation of a child's development and needed early intervention can be coordinated through the medical home (AAP, 2006; Crowley & Whitney, 2005). More information on the medical home can be found in Chapter 16.

Screening for Growth and Developmental Norms

Screening for growth and development is an essential component of the health status assessment process (Allen, 2004b; Crowley & Whitney, 2005). Screening identifies whether growth and development fall into the normal pattern and can indicate a potential problem or impairment. An observer should have some knowledge of the normal age range for developmental milestones (Allen, 2004b). Summaries of milestones for development are listed in this section, as are assessment tools, where applicable. A teacher who has a wide experience with children may have increased awareness of what is the norm and may be able to identify a child who is not within the norm more quickly. Through careful observation and documentation, the teacher can identify any serious concerns that should be discussed with parents.

An alert teacher can help detect whether a child falls within the normal range for growth and development. This could be vital in the child's future health status (Lucarelli, 2006). A child who is small and light for her age may have a growth abnormality and should see a physician, and perhaps a dietician. A 2½-year-old child whose speech is garbled may need a therapist or audiologist. Many different conditions that can be corrected may be uncovered through careful observation and recording. Being able to recognize the red flags for unmet developmental milestones is also important (Allen, 2004a). A policy of quarterly screening for developmental norms can aid in this process. If this periodic screening identifies a child who may have an issue, the child can be referred to his medical home for further screening and evaluation. Pediatricians and other health care providers need information from parents and teachers to better identify children who may have special needs (Hix-Small et al., 2007). The sooner a developmental delay is identified, the earlier the intervention for a child. Early intervention can be critical for many issues.

A change in a child's behavior or a child with behavioral difficulties may indicate mental health risk, a nutritional deficiency, maltreatment, or a physical health impairment. Appraising a child's physical and mental health and nutritional intake will lay the groundwork for a discussion with his parents to determine whether a referral should be made. If maltreatment is suspected, reporting the observation and showing the records that have been kept to proper authorities will be necessary. For the process to run smoothly, a health policy for appraisals and consequent discussion or referral must be in place.

The APHA and the AAP suggest that teachers have a health consultant on whom to call when they need a resource for assessing health and well-being. The consultant can be a physician, a pediatric or family nurse practitioner, or a registered nurse (APHA & AAP, 2002). The consultant should have some knowledge about nonparental child care, the community, and available resources. Many communities in this country have health consultants available through the resource and referral network or the medical community. This subject is dealt with at greater length in Chapter 13.

Screening is routinely done in early childhood education centers and can easily be done in family child care homes or in the child's own home. It is neither expensive nor sophisticated. Screening takes a closer look at specific areas and can add important information to the overall assessment process. For example, because of children's rapid growth and development, a child should be screened for physical well-being and motor development on

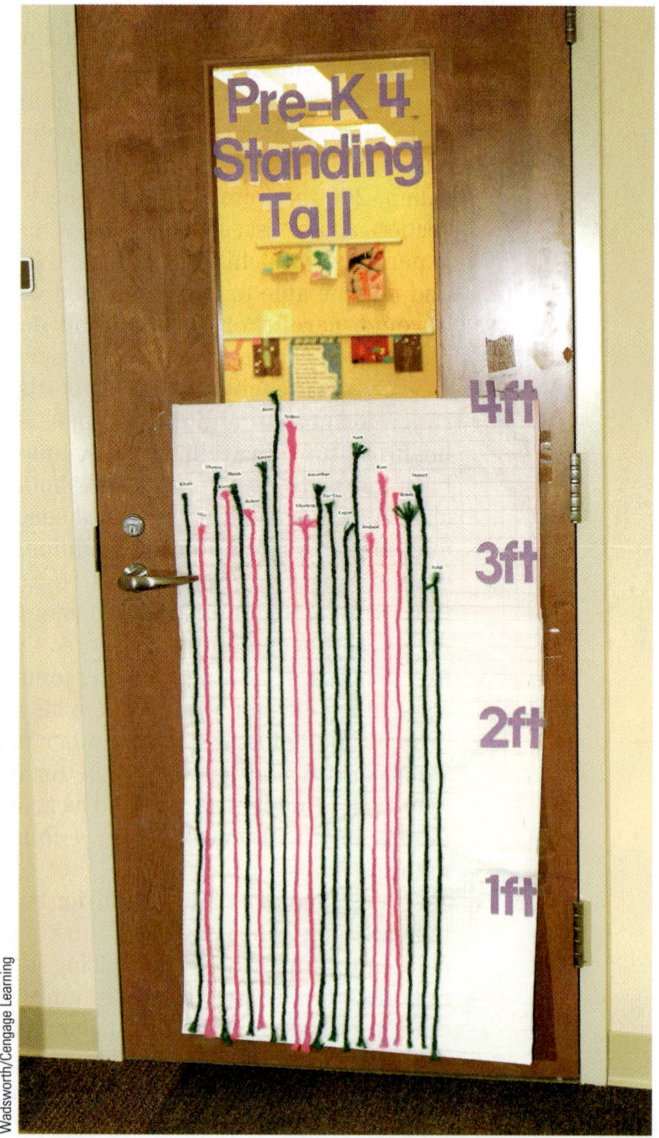

Periodic height and weight checks are exciting for children and foster pride in their own bodies. The height and weight assessment can be incorporated into the classroom curriculum by visually representing each child's height and weight (on a wall, door, or piece of poster board) at regular intervals.

Wadsworth/Cengage Learning

Karla, a healthy 3½-year-old, was very self-confident. She enjoyed having her family child care provider measure her and liked to get on the scale and see how much she weighed. Martine, the teacher, had a special place on her family room wall that was used to measure the height of children in her care. Every two months, Martine would bring out the scale and let the children stand against their spot on the wall to measure them so they could see how they were growing. One day when the children went through this process, Karla could not wait to tell her mother, "I'm 3½, and 3 (feet tall), and I weigh 34 (pounds)." She looked forward to these screening opportunities, and they helped her be more comfortable when she had to go to the doctor.

a yearly basis (Cole, 2008). The health consultant can assist with any questions the teacher may have about specific screening methods. Screening is used to

- Measure height and weight
- Appraise motor development
- Check vision
- Appraise hearing
- Evaluate speech and language
- Assess nutritional intake and deficiencies
- Appraise mental health

Measuring Height and Weight. Children of all ages are measured against a range of normal heights and weights that are calculated on a growth chart. Growth charts are easy to follow and are used to screen for body size for age that is not the norm. These growth charts are also available on the website of the National Centers for Health Statistics branch of the CDC. The address is: http://www.cdc.gov/growthcharts/. Physicians routinely use these charts to detect problems or abnormalities in a child's growth.

Recording a child's height and weight is part of the normal screening process that a teacher performs on a quarterly basis. It familiarizes children with their bodies and helps them to understand the screening process in the doctor's office. Children enjoy knowing how tall they are and how much they weigh. Even though they do not understand what the numbers mean, children seem to gain a sense of self-identification from them.

If a child seems unusually small, thin, obese, or tall for his age, there may be a good reason to compare his height and weight to the growth chart. These conditions may indicate poor nutrition, a hormonal imbalance, or a disease that causes retarded or accelerated growth. Sometimes children exhibit a condition called **failure to thrive** that indicates they are below the normal height and weight range for their age. Other children may be overweight for their height. Screening and early intervention may help prevent obesity. The results of the chart comparison should be discussed with a parent. If there is an indicator for further examination, a referral course should be planned. A discussion with the health consultant would be helpful at this point. The most common starting point for a referral of this sort is the child's

- **failure to thrive** *failure of a child to grow physically and develop mentally according to the norms. This condition may occur because of organic defects or lack of emotional bonding.*

Infancy is a period of dramatic weight and height gains. Infants should be weighed regularly to ensure that they are growing at a normal rate. A weight and height below the normal range for the infant's age could indicate a condition called failure to thrive.

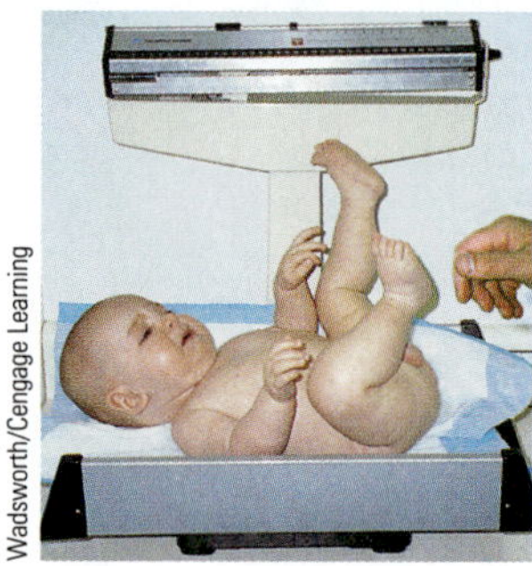

own physician. If the child does not have a primary physician, a community health clinic would be the next most likely source that the teacher could recommend to the family.

If changes in diet are indicated, the teacher can support those changes. The teacher will need to be informed by the parent or health professional what should be done to help the child. The teacher could turn to the health consultant for further assistance.

Appraising Motor Development. As a child develops, her ability to perform physical activities and use acquired motor skills are two of the most evident areas in growth and development. These skills are easily observable and fairly easy to screen. A child should be able to perform the gross motor skills and fine motor skills that are normal for her age range with a certain degree of coordination. Table 11-3 indicates the developmental motor skill norms for the first two years of life.

For children older than age 2, there are other motor skills and degrees of coordination that should be present. Between ages 2½ and 3½, a child should be able to perform the gross motor and fine motor skills listed in Table 11-4. The use of this chart can help identify preschool children who might be at risk for school problems later in life (Bayoglu et al., 2007).

Hanging by both hands is an example of a gross motor skill that children normally master between ages 2½ and 3½.

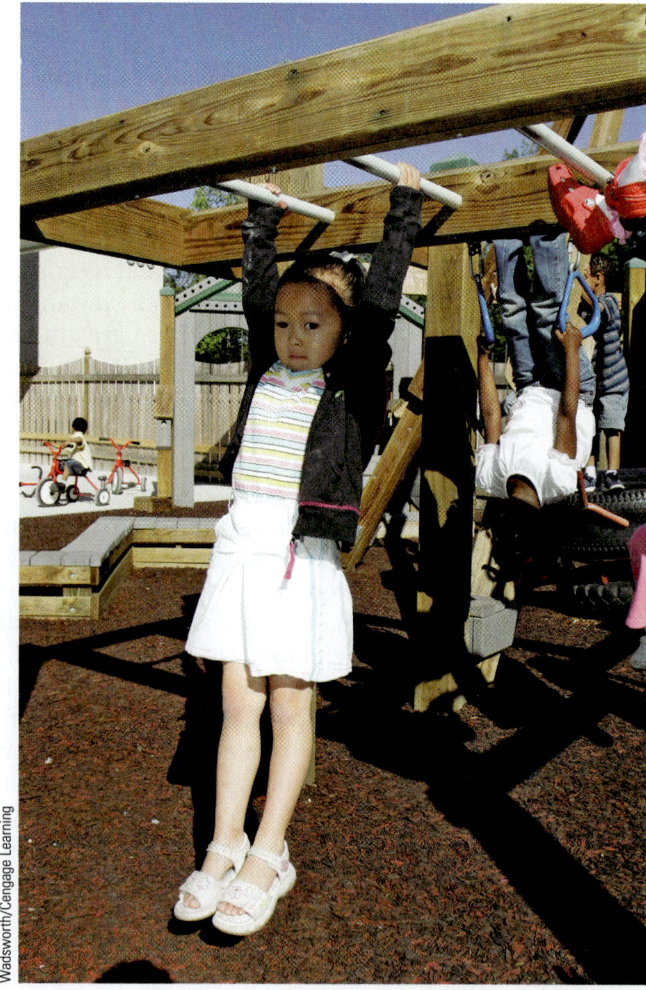

TABLE 11-3
Developmental Norms for Gross Motor Skills in Infants

Motor Skill	Months at Which 90 Percent of Infants Master Skill
Lifts head up while lying on stomach	3.2
Sits with head steady	4.2
Rolls over	4.7
Sits alone	7.8
Stands holding on	10
Walks holding on	12.7
Stands alone steadily	13.9
Walks well	14.3
Walks up stairs with help	22.0
Kicks ball forward	24.0

TABLE 11-4
Developmental Norms for Motor Skills of Children Ages 2½ to 3½

Gross Motor Skills	Fine Motor Skills
Walks well with a normal gait	Uses eating utensils well
Runs in a straight line	Copies a circle
Jumps in the air with both feet	Scribbles
Throws a ball	Stacks blocks
Reaches for objects with one hand	Manipulates large puzzle pieces
Climbs	Smears paint
Hangs by both hands	

When a child does not appear to be following the developmental norms for his age, there are usually caution signs present. The warning signals for motor development difficulties are included in Table 11-5.

Some assessment tools that can be used to evaluate a child's motor skills further are The Denver Developmental Screening Tool, The Mullin Scale, The Hawaii Early Learning Profile, the Bayley Assessment Tool, and the Gessell Assessment Tool. A health consultant could help the teacher decide which developmental tool would be most appropriate and might also assist in the administration of the assessment tool or refer the teacher to a source for help. These tools are not commonly administered by the teacher because they require specialized training.

- **regional center** *a center in a particular geographic area dedicated to helping families that have children with special needs. The center acts as a resource, a referral agency, and a source of support for families.*

If it is determined that a child appears to have a motor skill problem, the teacher and a parent should discuss the referral procedure. If the child has a medical home and the team is already working together, referral would be an easy procedure. If there is no medical home, then the child's physician, a community health agency, or a **regional center** is a good starting point. The

TABLE 11-5
Caution Signs for Motor Development

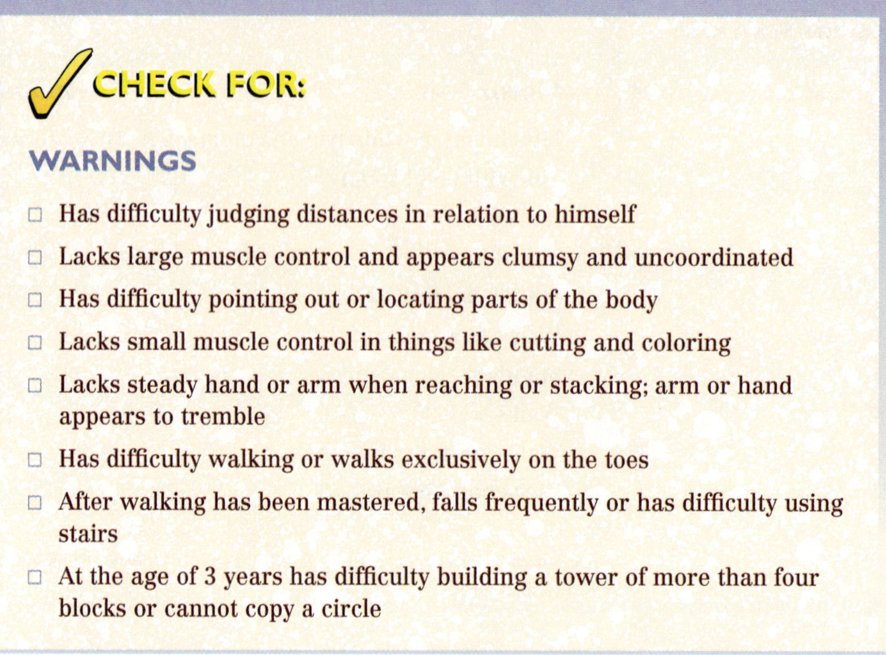

CHECK FOR:

WARNINGS

- ☐ Has difficulty judging distances in relation to himself
- ☐ Lacks large muscle control and appears clumsy and uncoordinated
- ☐ Has difficulty pointing out or locating parts of the body
- ☐ Lacks small muscle control in things like cutting and coloring
- ☐ Lacks steady hand or arm when reaching or stacking; arm or hand appears to tremble
- ☐ Has difficulty walking or walks exclusively on the toes
- ☐ After walking has been mastered, falls frequently or has difficulty using stairs
- ☐ At the age of 3 years has difficulty building a tower of more than four blocks or cannot copy a circle

National Dissemination Center for Children with Disabilities is a good source for local referrals. They can be reached by logging on to www.nich.org/staes.htm (CDC 2006a). Physical activities may be prescribed to help the child learn to cope with the motor skill difficulties. The teacher will be a source of support for both the child and the parent during this period.

Checking Vision. Children use vision to take in information about the world around them, sort it, and then make sense out of it. Visual difficulties should be caught as early as possible for correction and treatment. Children are normally screened for vision during their regular checkups with a physician. If there appears to be a problem, the physician will refer the child to an eye specialist to determine whether there is a visual deficiency. Some children may not have regular physical checkups, so vision problems may not be caught. Vision difficulties can appear over time or rapidly. The signs indicating that a child may have hidden eye problems or visual perception difficulties are listed in Table 11-6.

If the teacher observes any of the conditions listed in Table 11-6, the concerns should be discussed with a parent. The parents may have noticed the same conditions or may already have the child in care for that condition. If that is the case, it is important for the parent to share the information. If the child is not under care, it is important for the parent to understand the potential seriousness of an eye condition and refer the child to his physician or local health clinic.

The American Optometric Association advises that the optimal time for vision screening is at the age of 1 year (Groves-Bixby, 2007). If a child is treated before age 3, it is possible for him to have a 95 percent recovery of vision. Vision loss can be caused by a number of things, and the extent of the loss can greatly differ (CDC, 2006c). There are three common eye conditions found in children: nearsightedness, strabismus, and amblyopia. **Nearsightedness**,

- **nearsightedness** *lack of ability to see objects at a distance.*

TABLE 11-6
Caution Signs for Vision Problems

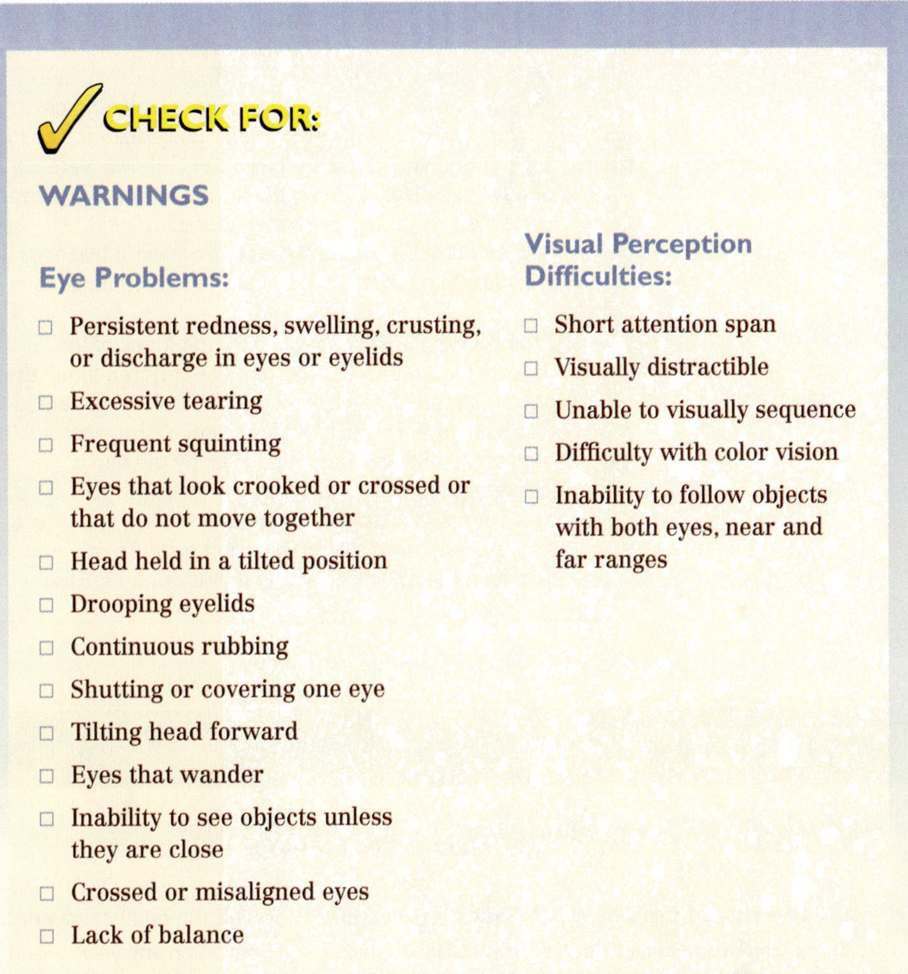

CHECK FOR:

WARNINGS

Eye Problems:

- ☐ Persistent redness, swelling, crusting, or discharge in eyes or eyelids
- ☐ Excessive tearing
- ☐ Frequent squinting
- ☐ Eyes that look crooked or crossed or that do not move together
- ☐ Head held in a tilted position
- ☐ Drooping eyelids
- ☐ Continuous rubbing
- ☐ Shutting or covering one eye
- ☐ Tilting head forward
- ☐ Eyes that wander
- ☐ Inability to see objects unless they are close
- ☐ Crossed or misaligned eyes
- ☐ Lack of balance

Visual Perception Difficulties:

- ☐ Short attention span
- ☐ Visually distractible
- ☐ Unable to visually sequence
- ☐ Difficulty with color vision
- ☐ Inability to follow objects with both eyes, near and far ranges

the inability to see distant objects clearly, is the most common visual problem in young children. Corrective lenses will enable even the youngest child to see normally. **Strabismus** is the misalignment of the eyes, which occurs because of an imbalance in the eye muscles so that they appear to be crossed. It becomes difficult for the eyes to focus on the same point at the same time. Corrective lenses, eye exercises, eye drops, and sometimes eye surgeries help to correct this problem. **Amblyopia**, also called "lazy eye," occurs when one eye does not see well or is injured, and the other eye takes over almost exclusively. Treatment of this condition is most successful when it is caught before age 3. The child wears a patch to prevent vision in the good eye, thereby forcing her to use the inactive eye.

- **strabismus** *a condition that occurs in children that causes one or both eyes to appear crossed.*
- **amblyopia** *an unequal balance of a child's eye muscles often referred to as "lazy eye." Condition is improved through the use of eye patch to enable the weaker eye to strengthen with greater use.*

Caring for a child with any of these eye conditions will take patience and assistance on the part of the teacher. A child may become easily frustrated or embarrassed over the visual difficulties she is having. It is important that other children understand and not make fun of the child.

Appraising Hearing. The CDC (2006b) estimates that hearing loss can affect as many as 3 children per 1,000. Hearing loss is caused by a number of factors. For example, a mother may have had an illness while pregnant, or there

Aaron, 2½ years old, was found to have amblyopia in his right eye. The doctor prescribed glasses with a patch on the right lens. The first day at the early childhood education center, Aaron felt awkward and embarrassed. The other children were curious; some appeared to be fearful and did not understand why Aaron had the patch. At circle time, Regina, the teacher, talked about it with the children. They talked about eyes and how it felt to see things with two eyes and how different it would be to have to use just one eye to help make the other eye see better.

After hearing the comments and questions of the children and sensing Aaron's discomfort, Regina had the children make their own patches and decorate them. Regina, and the children who wanted to, wore the patches tied with yarn during afternoon snack. They were all excited and felt rather glamorous, like a group of pirates. By the end of snack the children with patches could grasp that it was not as easy to see and coordinate with one eye. They all talked about this and asked Aaron questions. These children became helpers to Aaron and their concern restored Aaron's confidence. Regina helped defuse a difficult situation for Aaron.

REALITY *Check*

Effects of Lead Poisoning on Children

It was estimated that almost 2.2 percent of children in the United States had elevated levels of lead, which were high enough to be considered lead poisoning (CDC, 2005). Although these figures were down from record highs in the early 1980s, lead poisoning still affects a significant number of children and is a serious environmental health problem that could be prevented (Leonard, 2007). Twenty-five percent of the housing in the United States contains significant amounts of lead in lead-based paint and lead dust, so children who live in these homes are at risk for lead poisoning. Lead poisoning affects all families, but African-American and inner-city children are most likely to be affected. Twenty percent of African-American children are believed to have some degree of lead poisoning (CDC, 2004). In California, Hispanic children represent more than 80 percent of those found with elevated blood lead levels (Schilling, 2004). Refugee children have been especially vulnerable to lead poisoning in this country in recent years (Kellenberg et al., 2005). Lead poisoning has been called the number one environmental threat to children for many years—and is still considered one of the most common environmental illnesses that affect young children (Leonard, 2007).

Children between the ages of 6 months and 6 years are especially vulnerable to the effects of lead poisoning because their bodies, including the nervous system, are still developing (EPA, 2006b). The AAP has even considered lowering the acceptable blood lead levels because there appear to be problems in children who have blood lead levels lower than what was previously considered acceptable. Lead poisoning can cause mild to severe lasting effects on children. It can affect all systems in the body and does not always show definite symptoms (Leonard, 2007). Even low levels of lead are harmful; they are correlated with decreased intelligence, affecting the development of the nervous system and brain, and they can retard growth (EPA, 2006b). Low levels of lead can also be associated with behavioral problems. The damaging effects to the nervous system and brain may

(continues)

REALITY *Check* (continued)

manifest themselves as cognitive deficits, inability to concentrate, and even inability to learn. Reading, writing, math, visual abilities, and motor skills may be affected. Signs that children may have elevated levels of lead include irritability, insomnia, colic, hearing difficulties, lack of eye–hand coordination, slow muscle and bone growth, and anemia. If blood levels are high enough, a child could go into seizures and even die from elevated blood lead levels.

Lead poisoning has been found to cause learning difficulties and behavior problems. Lead in childhood lowers IQ scores, and this directly relates to behavior and cognitive impairment (Chen et al., 2007). Children with high levels of lead are six times more likely to have reading disabilities. Lead exposure can lead to mental retardation and brain damage (Wilson, 2006). Some experts believe that lead poisoning can contribute to aggression and antisocial and delinquent behaviors (AAP, 1998; Chen et al., 2007). One study found that there is a relationship between lead exposure and violent behavior in the commission of homicide (Stretesky & Lynch, 2001).

Many children younger than six years of age live in homes that have peeling lead paint or lead dust in the environment. Families from these houses are almost equally divided between lower and middle/upper incomes. Renters and homeowners are equally likely to have this problem. Children affected by lead poisoning come from all cultural and racial groups (Jaroff, 2001). Children most at risk are those who live in low-income urban areas where surfaces are deteriorating and old paint is peeling or flaking (Wilson, 2006).

More than 80 percent of houses built before 1980 have lead-based paint (NSC, 2004). Lead-based paint was banned in 1978, and lead was removed from gasoline in the 1980s. This has helped to reduce lead levels, but it has not removed it as an environmental hazard to children.

Lead poisoning is most likely to occur if leaded dust or lead paint chips are swallowed. Lead dust is the primary pathway to lead exposure (NCCCHSRC, 2005; Leonard, 2007). Children are especially susceptible to lead poisoning because they put many objects in their mouths. They may play in dirt that contains toxic levels of lead, then put contaminated fingers and toys in their mouths. Children encounter lead chips or dust on window sills, door jams, railings, radiators, and near baseboards. Lead is also found in paint on old toys and furniture and in some jewelry.

Some children have a problem called "pica," which is the act of eating nonfood items. This eating disorder causes young children to consume clay, dirt, sand, lead, paint chips, and other nonfoods. Children who have this condition are at risk for lead poisoning (Zamani, 2005).

Government programs such as those in the EPA and the CDC have cut down on elevated lead blood levels over the past 25 years. Although lead-based paint from before 1978 is still the major source, other sources that put children at risk have been discovered. Plastic and vinyl blinds and miniblinds manufactured before 1997 have also been found to contain lead for bright coloring. Secondhand smoke has also been found to contain lead (USDHHS, 2006). Lead has been found in food prepared or served in pottery that contains lead. It can be found in several types of Mexican candy and other traditional snack foods found in Oaxaca and other parts of Mexico from where they might be brought into this country (Dailey, 2006; August & Brooks, 2005). Brightly colored ethnic home remedies for illness, such as azarcon and greta, may contain lead. Lead has also been found in drinking water in homes that have copper pipes that have been soldered with lead. Another source of lead that can be an issue for very young children is keys. Some brass keys made today have been found to contain lead. Even though these levels have been reduced, lead still presents a risk for young children who put keys in their mouths (CCCHP, 2006).

Toys are another source of concern for elevated blood levels of lead in children. Crayons manufactured outside the United States and that are particularly bright may contain lead. There have been recalls of toys with lead found in them, sometimes in the paint, such as on toy cars. Other sources include toy necklaces and medallions that come in "gum ball"

(continues)

REALITY *Check* (continued)

type machines ("Death of a Child," 2006; VanArsdale et al., 2004). Children have been found to ingest these items and magnets, and they have caused serious illness ("Gastrointestinal Injuries," 2006). Metal lunch boxes are also a source of lead poisoning. In lunch boxes that were tested for lead, more than one-third tested positive for lead content (Daluga & Miller, 2007). Children who eat food stored in these lunch boxes could be at risk for lead poisoning.

Lead is absorbed into the bloodstream, then, like calcium, is absorbed by the bone. Lead can accumulate through life. It can be stored in the bone and then return to the bloodstream at any time (Jaroff, 2001). When it is built up over time, this is referred to as lead poisoning. Children's bodies are inclined to absorb more lead, especially if there is an iron deficiency. This is why a good diet is essential.

The NAEYC recommends a number of protective practices to keep children safe from lead poisoning (Kendrick, Kaufman, & Messenger, 2002; Aronson, 2002), including screening children themselves as well as paint, water, and soil for lead levels. It has been suggested that children be assessed for lead poisoning as part of the preadmission requirements (CCHP, 2006). If lead is found in the home, deleading should be done very carefully, and professional assistance may be required. The Department of Health will provide the teacher with this information. There are other precautions that can be taken in early childhood education environments. These include cleaning and disinfecting play surfaces on a regular basis. In educational programs where crawling infants are present, everybody's shoes should be left at the door and excluded from the environment. Inspections should be carried out to find any peeling or flaking paint and if found, it should be tested. Do not allow any areas of bare soil or dirt around the early childhood education environment. This can be accomplished by planting grass and shrubs and using impact absorbent materials such as bark where soil is bare. If the facility is older than 1978, professionals should be called to sand and repaint surfaces because they have been trained to remove the lead from the environment (CCHP, 2006).

The EPA (2006a) suggests five ways to protect children from lead poisoning.

1. ***Wash it out***—wash children's hands often. Toys, floors, and windowsills should be regularly washed with detergent and water. It has also been suggested to wash pacifiers and bottles often with detergent and hot water.
2. ***Eat it out***—Serve an iron- and calcium-rich diet. This reduces the amount of lead the body will hold.
3. ***Run it out***—Always run cool tap water for 2 to 3 minutes before using it to cook or drink, and never use hot tap water to drink, eat, or cook.
4. ***Keep it out***—Don't let children play in dirt—lead in soil is a hazard. People can track soil into a house, where it could become a hazard. Hire professionals do to any painting work on houses or buildings that are older than 1978. If renting a home, ask the landlord about lead hazards.
5. ***Check it out***—Have children younger than age 6 tested for lead. This is the only method to detect lead poisoning.

Washing fruits and vegetables is also a preventive measure. Preventive measures can cut down on risk for lead. For example, when houses were cleaned thoroughly 20 or more times per year, children experienced a 34 percent decrease in lead blood levels (Rhoads et al., 1999). For further information, the National Lead Information website can be accessed at http://www.epa.gov/lead; this organization may be called at 1-800-424-LEAD.

CHECK*point:* **What items would you first look for to determine whether lead is present in the environment where children are present? What dangers might these items pose? What could be done?**

may have been a genetic factor that caused an abnormal development. Or a child may have been born prematurely or may suffer from recurrent ear infections, allergies, or colds. Hearing loss has also been associated with the use of certain medications and head trauma. When a child enters the early childhood education environment, it should be noted in his health file or portfolio if hearing screening has taken place (APHA & AAP, 2002). Screening for hearing loss can be done as early as at birth. If no screening has been done, the APHA and the AAP suggest that it be done within 6 to 8 weeks of the child entering the early childhood education environment.

It is not always easy to detect a hearing loss, but the teacher may notice some warning signs. Table 11-7 contains the ages and questions recommended by the National Association for Speech and Hearing to assist the teacher in detecting whether the child may have a hearing problem. If a child's responses are not developmentally appropriate, the teacher should discuss with a parent what has been noticed and decide with the parent what action to take for a referral. A conference with the health consultant would help the teacher and the family know how to proceed. Early detection of a

TABLE 11-7
Developmental Hearing Norms

✓ **CHECK FOR:**

Age	Check for
Birth–3 months	□ Does the child listen to speech?
	□ Does the child cry or startle at noises?
3–6 months	□ Does the child smile when spoken to?
	□ Does the child try to turn toward speaker?
	□ Does the child seem to recognize mother's voice?
6–9 months	□ Does the child respond to his name?
	□ Does the child turn head toward where the sound is coming from?
	□ Does the child notice and look around for source of new sounds?
9 months–1 year	□ Does the child listen to people talking?
	□ Does the child look up when you call?
	□ Does the child look around when hearing new sounds?
1–2 years	□ Can the child follow two requests such as "go to the kitchen and get your cup?"
2–4 years	□ Can the child point to pictures in a book upon hearing the object named?
	□ Does the child understand conversation easily?
	□ Does the child hear the television or music at the same loudness level as everyone else in the room?
	□ Does the child notice normal sounds like the phone, the doorbell, or a dog's bark?
	□ Does the child hear you when you call from another room?

Adapted from Developmental Norms for Speech and Language by the American Speech-Language-Hearing Association © 2005.

hearing problem can help a child learn to cope and adapt to hearing loss or possibly have the hearing repaired. Recently, screening for hearing loss in early childhood environments was tested in Migrant and Early Head Start Programs. Teachers were trained using hand-held equipment and a screening protocol. The results demonstrated this type of screening can be effective and practical (Eiserman et al., 2007).

Hearing loss may affect speech and language and can have an impact on the development of social skills (CDC, 2006b). When hearing problems are caught early, there is less chance for an accompanying language delay (Reeves, 2006). If a hearing referral is necessary, there are several places to send the child. A visit to the family physician is a good start. Other sources would include an **audiologist**, a speech-language-hearing clinic, or a community health agency. Often, school districts have a speech-language-hearing program that will help children in that district before they enter school.

- **audiologist** *person trained to identify types of hearing losses, to interpret audiometric tests, and to recommend equipment and procedures to assist the hearing impaired.*

If a hearing loss is detected, the teacher can help the child adapt by speaking slowly and directly to the child, using hand gestures when applicable, and demonstrating more complex instructions where appropriate. Other children in care should be taught these same methods of communicating with the child who has a hearing loss. The teacher can also help to educate and support the parent in the use of these communication methods.

Evaluating Speech and Language. Speech and language acquisition come at varying ages in children. Girls tend to verbalize earlier than boys. Children in bilingual households may acquire speech more slowly (Bialystok, 2001). Some children do not acquire speech and language as rapidly as might be expected. These are normal speech and language patterns for children (Perry, 2003). Table 11-8 can help the teacher notice how children use expressive language and whether they have the ability to understand at the developmental level given. If a child does not follow this pattern, then the teacher should check the list of warning signals found in Table 11-9.

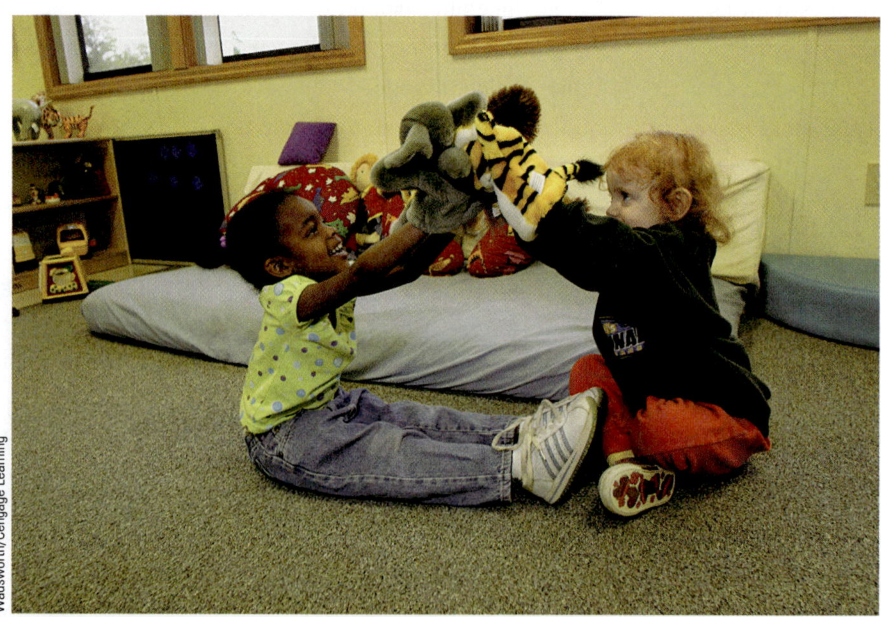
Wadsworth/Cengage Learning

Peer interaction during playtime is an ideal time to observe children's speech patterns.

TABLE 11-8
Normal Speech and Language Developmental Patterns

✓ CHECK FOR:

Age	Expressive Language	Ability to Understand
3–6 months	Babbling, vocalizing pleasure	Smiles in response to speech; seeks sound source; recognizes familiar people and objects
7–9 months	Consonants—b, d, m, t, p, z; babbling; imitates speech sounds	Responds to gestures and "no"; can play peek-a-boo, pat-a-cake, and bye-bye
10–12 months	First true word may appear; intonations begin; uses all sounds in vocal play	Relates object and name; can follow simple body action commands; always responds to own name
1–1½ years	Uses 3 to 20 single words; uses gestures	Follows simple commands; recognizes some body parts and names for objects
1½ to 2 years	Uses 20 to 60 words; combines two words in sentences; 65 percent speech intelligible	Understands 200 to 300 words; can answer simple yes-or-no questions
2–3 years	Uses 200 to 500 words; uses three- and four-word sentences; grammar emerges; 70 to 80 percent of speech intelligible	Understands 800 to 900 words; can answer what, why, where questions; can listen to short stories
3–4 years	Uses 800 to 1,500 words; uses four- and five-word sentences; asks questions	Understands 1,200 to 1,500 words; can compare (up and down); responds to two-part commands
4–5 years	Uses 1,500 to 2,000 words; very intelligible speech; uses eight-word sentences; can tell long stories	Understands 2,500 words; answers complex questions; has some color and number concepts

If a child exhibits any of the caution signs listed in Table 11-9 or is not at the appropriate developmental level, the teacher should discuss this with the parent to determine whether the parent agrees that a problem may exist. Delays or problems with motor skills can be accompanied by developmental speech and language difficulties, so this may also be a caution sign (Visscher et al., 2007). A discussion with the health consultant may help the teacher and the parent determine the best course of action. The child may have to be referred to a physician or other specialist such as a speech therapist.

A child who has a speech or language problem will need much patience and understanding. The teacher can help the child by allowing her time to speak clearly. The teacher can offer encouragement and reward the child's effort. The child needs caring and warmth. By the teacher's modeling these supportive actions, other children will begin to imitate these actions. This

TABLE 11-9
Caution Signs for Screening and Referral for Speech and Language Development

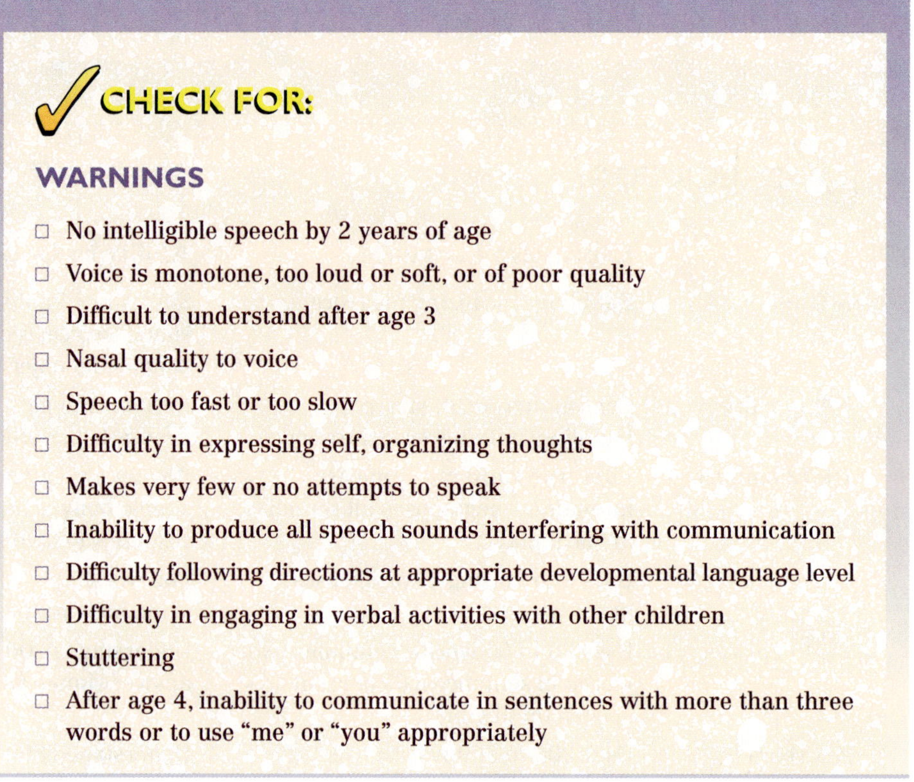

CHECK FOR:

WARNINGS

- ☐ No intelligible speech by 2 years of age
- ☐ Voice is monotone, too loud or soft, or of poor quality
- ☐ Difficult to understand after age 3
- ☐ Nasal quality to voice
- ☐ Speech too fast or too slow
- ☐ Difficulty in expressing self, organizing thoughts
- ☐ Makes very few or no attempts to speak
- ☐ Inability to produce all speech sounds interfering with communication
- ☐ Difficulty following directions at appropriate developmental language level
- ☐ Difficulty in engaging in verbal activities with other children
- ☐ Stuttering
- ☐ After age 4, inability to communicate in sentences with more than three words or to use "me" or "you" appropriately

support will make it easier for the child with the problem to practice for success. A child with a good sense of self will be less hesitant or self-conscious, enabling her to attempt to use speech and language at every opportunity.

Mental Health Appraisal. During observation, the teacher should be aware of at-risk indicators and other behavioral characteristics that may indicate poor social, emotional, or mental health. Table 11-10 shows a number of characteristics that may indicate the child is at risk. Collins and colleagues (2003) noted that partnerships between early childhood education and mental health professionals are essential to provide support for early childhood mental health services that meet the needs of young children. Early childhood education environments with preschool children who have mental health screening and employ the services of mental health professionals have demonstrated positive outcomes and good success rates (Waldman, 2007; Lamb-Parker et al., 2008). Early Head Start has used mental health screening in order to have early intervention and services for at-risk infants and toddlers in their population (Baggett et al., 2007).

There are many behaviors that may be annoying to adults but are perfectly normal and a part of a child's development between the ages of 1½ and 4 years. Children often do not pay attention and do not do what they are asked. They can be hard to reason with sometimes and may sulk or cry easily. They may not be able to sit still. Some may boss other children around and try to show off.

Younger children may not want to share and will say "no" often when requested to cooperate. They may grab toys, hit, shove, or attack others who have what they want.

TABLE 11-10
At-Risk Indicators for Children's Vulnerability to Poor Mental Health

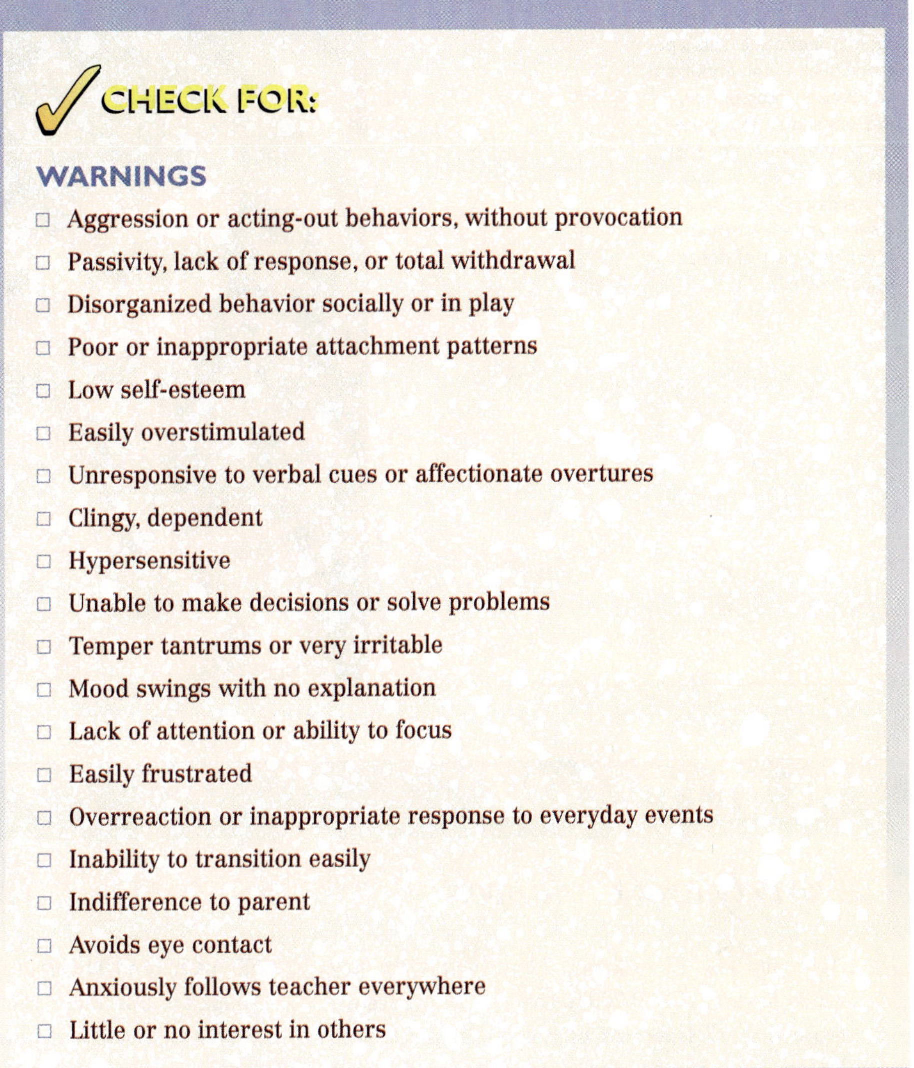

CHECK FOR:

WARNINGS

- ☐ Aggression or acting-out behaviors, without provocation
- ☐ Passivity, lack of response, or total withdrawal
- ☐ Disorganized behavior socially or in play
- ☐ Poor or inappropriate attachment patterns
- ☐ Low self-esteem
- ☐ Easily overstimulated
- ☐ Unresponsive to verbal cues or affectionate overtures
- ☐ Clingy, dependent
- ☐ Hypersensitive
- ☐ Unable to make decisions or solve problems
- ☐ Temper tantrums or very irritable
- ☐ Mood swings with no explanation
- ☐ Lack of attention or ability to focus
- ☐ Easily frustrated
- ☐ Overreaction or inappropriate response to everyday events
- ☐ Inability to transition easily
- ☐ Indifference to parent
- ☐ Avoids eye contact
- ☐ Anxiously follows teacher everywhere
- ☐ Little or no interest in others

It is not uncommon for some children to whine and complain. Other children may have a special blanket or suck their thumbs. Some children are shy and afraid of unfamiliar people and situations. Sometimes children make up stories and tell them as truths.

These typical behaviors are not necessarily indicators of risk for mental difficulties. Behaviors that may indicate children are at risk for mental health problems are found in Table 11-10. Observing children and identifying warning signals may suggest the need for outside intervention (Collins et al., 2003).

When a child shows a number of disturbing behaviors, especially with increasing frequency, it is a good idea to discuss the child's behavior with a parent. If there is no explanation or if the parent expresses concern, the teacher, with the parent's permission, may want to contact the health consultant or a medical home physician. Many conditions that cause a great deal of stress for a child may be at the root of the problem. Some children may suffer from toxic stress and may be at risk for poor mental

Identifying at-risk indicators and behavioral characteristics that may indicate a child's poor mental health is an important part of early intervention. Teachers should recognize that normal behaviors, such as crying or shyness, do not necessarily indicate a problem and may instead reflect an aspect of the child's temperament.

Wadsworth/Cengage Learning

REALITY *Check*

Poverty and Childhood

Approximately 13 million children in this country live in poverty (CBPP, 2007). This represents slightly more than 17.4 percent of children in the United States. But children disproportionately represent 35 percent of the total of the poor population. Children younger than six years of age are more vulnerable to poverty and its effects. More than 18 percent of children in this country under six live in poverty. These figures indicate a slight increase from the 2000 poverty levels. Although the figures are down from the early 1990s, they are still higher than they should be. The poverty rate in the United States is often two to three times higher than in other Western industrialized countries (Knitzer & Lefkowitz, 2006).

Poverty is more likely to affect children of color. Thirty percent of African-American children live in poverty. Twenty-nine percent of Hispanic children live in poverty, while the figure for white children is at more than 10 percent (Knitzer & Lefkowitz, 2006). Children who are represented by these ethnic groups are also more likely to have higher rates of chronic or persistent poverty, which means that a child spends most of his childhood living under the poverty level (Pachter et al., 2006). Chronic poverty leads to lower cognitive performance and more behavior problems for children (NICHD, 2005).

A correlation with the rise of poverty from the 1970s to the 1990s is the significant rise in the number of single-parent families, which has doubled during that period. In total, approximately 28 percent of children live in single-parent homes. Approximately 43 percent of children from single-parent families live in poverty, compared to 9 percent of children from two-parent families (*America's children: Key national indicators of well-being, 2007*, 2007). About one-half of children living in single-parent families will feel the long-term effects of poverty on their childhood (National Poverty Center, 2006).

(continues)

REALITY*Check* (continued)

There are many contributing factors to poverty, including family composition, parent education, and family income (Nelson, 2000; Fass & Cauthen, 2006). It is a reality that more than 70 percent of children in poverty had at least one working parent (Reid, 2006). The term "working poor" is given meaning with those figures. Although there is a higher total number of Caucasian children living in poverty, the percentage of African-American, Hispanic, and children of other ethnicities living in poverty is at a higher level. If a child is foreign born, he is almost twice as likely to be in poverty than a child born in the United States. Children living in urban areas represent one-third of the children living in poverty; those who live in rural areas represent 26 percent of children living in poverty; and those living in suburban areas represent 17 percent of children living in poverty (Knitzer & Lefkowitz, 2006). Regardless of where, the neighborhood socioeconomic conditions have an effect on young children and their behavioral outcomes (Kohen et al., 2008).

Children from families in poverty make up the largest growing segment of the homeless. More than 40 percent of the homeless are families with children (NMHA, 2005). Families with children are the largest growing segment of the homeless population. There are more than half a million young children in homeless families (Knitzer & Lefkowitz, 2006). The risk to children due to poverty is even greater for homeless children because of their lack of housing.

Impoverished living conditions can result in poor health, lack of safety, and poor nutrition (Fass & Cauthen, 2006). These conditions have long-term effects on the general health of children (Chen, Martin, & Matthews, 2007). The socioeconomic conditions of a neighborhood have an effect on young children and their behavioral outcomes (Kohen et al., 2008). Poor families are six times more likely to report that their children are in poor or fair health than families that have adequate income. Evans (2004) found that the physical environment of housing quality, noise, crowding, and air pollution affects children's health and well-being. African-American and Latino children are approximately 50 percent more likely to suffer hardships due to overcrowded housing, food insecurity, and unmet medical needs than poor children of other ethnicities (Sherman, 2006). Health problems are reflected in lower blood iron levels and higher levels of vision, hearing, and dental problems. Blood levels of lead are also higher for children living in poverty. Children in poverty have more frequent, more severe, and longer lasting infectious diseases (The National Center on Family Homelessness, 2005). Families in poverty may seek primary medical attention in the emergency room because they may not have health insurance coverage or adequate coverage. Approximately 12 percent of all children are not covered by health insurance in this country (CBPP, 2007). Homeless children are at an even higher risk. Because of living conditions, these children are also more likely to have higher levels of respiratory infections and food-borne infections. Homeless children have four times as many asthma attacks and five times more stomach problems than do other children. They are also twice as likely to have hospitalizations as other children.

Another effect of poverty on children is that they are less likely to participate in and to receive quality early childhood education (Loeb et al., 2004; Evans, 2004). Poor families are more likely to select family child care, and many of these family child care sites are unlicensed and do not follow standards of care that promote optimum growth for children. Only about 12 percent of these homes are rated as being of good quality (Kreader, Ferguson, & Lawrence, 2005). Children in poor-quality care are less likely to have optimum brain development and more likely to have numerous other health issues. Children in poverty may be eligible for public pre-kindergarten or Head Start (Barbarin et al., 2006). Good pre-K or Head Start education can ameliorate some of the issues of poverty that may affect a child's ability to learn. Quality early childhood education is correlated with positive outcomes for poor children. Poor children who are in quality early childhood education programs may experience an improvement in their lives (NICHD, 2001).

Children in poverty are also more likely to have developmental difficulties, which may be related to poor or nonexistent prenatal care for the mother. The difficulties may also relate to being born to

(continues)

REALITY*Check* (continued)

teenage mothers. Health conditions are more likely to go untreated for these children.

Poverty appears to contribute to emotional and behavioral problems for children (NMHA, 2005). Children living in poverty are more likely to be affected by substance abuse and child maltreatment, which lead to increased risk for mental health problems that result in emotional and behavioral problems. Homeless children are even more likely to suffer from emotional and behavioral problems. These children are more likely to have frequent changes of residence, be at risk for safety, and suffer from domestic conflict (The National Center on Family Homelessness, 2005).

Children living in poverty are more likely to be at risk for safety in their living conditions (Shonkoff & Meisels, 1998; Sherman, 2006). Poor housing conditions are often related to higher levels of lead and unsafe neighborhoods. The economic stress of living at the poverty level causes higher levels of domestic abuse, including neglect and physical, sexual, and emotional maltreatment.

Income level affects food consumption practices. Financial resources help families meet basic food needs. The less income, the less likely the basic needs for nutrition will be met (FRAC, 2006). Children living in poverty are far less likely to have their daily quota of fruits and vegetables. Homeless children are twice as likely to suffer from hunger than are other poor children (NMHA, 2005). Inadequate nutrition can affect cognitive development and behavior. Pollitt (1994) reported that worldwide research shows three conditions correlated with poverty and poor nutrition:

1. Effects of poor nutrition and illness on school performance
2. Relationship between poor motor and mental development and anemia
3. Positive effects of supplemental food programs

Recent evidence has shown that children need enough protein, calories, vitamins, and minerals to prevent malnutrition. Homeless children may be at greater risk for nutritional deficits because their basic food needs may depend on food programs that are not geared to children.

Teachers can have a profound effect on the lives of poor children. They are in the position to provide an environment for a significant portion of the day that will offer children greater physical safety and good nutrition (Greenspan, 2003; Shope & Aronson, 2006). Teachers can help improve the health of children through good screening and sanitation practices. They can also help families to access health care and nutritional supplement programs. Teachers can offer children emotional stability that may help to counteract the problems that poverty brings to their lives (Werner & Smith, 2001; Goldstein, Hamm, & Schumacher, 2007).

CHECK*point:* **How does poverty relate to a child's risk for inadequate health and well-being? What efforts might a teacher use to help decrease these risks?**

health because of it (National Scientific Council on the Developing Child, 2007). Collaboration on the part of the teacher, the family, and a health professional, as in the medical home partnership, may detect the problem and enable early intervention to alleviate the difficulty. Identifying mental health issues is less likely to be done by the physician alone, because most parents do not realize that there is an issue and hence do not bring it up with the physician. That is why collaboration is important and has been found to work well (Hix-Small et al., 2007). A referral to a physician or mental health counselor or psychologist may be necessary if the difficulties are not easily solved.

Nutritional Assessment. Assessment of a child's nutritional status may be warranted for a child whose growth is different from the norm, such as children who appear obese, have a food intolerance, or show an increased susceptibility to infections or illness. Assessing a child's food intake pattern may be very helpful in determining whether there is a physical or organic difficulty that is affecting a child's growth, health, or well-being. The types of foods a child eats, how much food is eaten, and when and where the child eats may be pertinent information. Charting a child's eating patterns can also lead to greater understanding about behavior difficulties. When food consumption is tracked, a teacher can also note behaviors (Giosa, 2006). If necessary, the teacher and the parent can work together to provide this information for a health professional who may further assess the child's condition.

The nutritional assessment will reveal this information:

- What types of foods and how much food the child eats
- When and under what circumstances the child eats
- Parental knowledge of nutrients and adequacy of nutrition provided to the child
- Why the child eats what she eats and why the child refuses to eat certain foods
- Any behavioral difficulties that may be related to particular foods or poor nutritional intake

Nutritional screening is usually accomplished in several ways. The first is the 24-hour dietary recall method. This information is relatively easy to obtain and can be done in several ways. With this method, the parent and teacher create a list of foods eaten, including an estimate of how much food is eaten. This can be done for either a one-day or a three-day period. Because any one day may not reflect the child's normal diet, a three-day record may be more beneficial. Some difficulties with this method are that the estimates may not be accurate, and gaining the cooperation of the parent to record more than one day's intake may be difficult. The recall method may reveal potential patterns of consumption that put the child at risk for nutritional deficiency. See the sample in Table 11-11.

As far as diets for children are concerned, the sample given in Table 11-11 might be a typical diet for a 3-year-old. If this sample diet is compared to the MyPyramid Food for Kids Guidance System with regard to the recommended daily allowances, there are definite indicators that the diet is lacking in grains, vegetables, and fruits and that there is overconsumption in the dairy category.

Another method of nutritional assessment is the food frequency questionnaire (see Table 11-12). This tool will show how often foods are consumed in the four food groups plus the "other" group in the period of one week. This questionnaire relies on the parent for recall, but it might be easier to use it to find out whether the child is lacking in or excessively consuming certain food groups. This tool may also establish a cultural or ethnic eating pattern that may put the child at risk for nutritional problems. A third type of nutritional assessment, which is relatively new, is the direct observation for food intake. This type of assessment trains field staff to observe children's nutritional

TABLE 11-11
24-Hour Dietary Recall

Name: Dane Leonard	**Age: 3 years, 2 months**
G = Grains, bread, and cereals	MM = Milk and milk products
V = Vegetables M = Meat	F = Fruits
Breakfast	*Snacks*
½ cup sugared cereal (1 G)	1 apple (1 F)
1 cup milk (1 MM)	2 chocolate chip cookies
1 banana (1 F)	1 cup grape juice (1 F)
Lunch	1 cup milk (1 MM)
1 corn dog (1 M)	*How many servings of each in one day?*
chips	Grains, Breads, and Cereals
punch	(G)—1
½ cup pudding (1 MM)	Fruits (F)—3
Dinner	Vegetables (V)—2
1 chicken leg (1 M)	Milk and Milk Products (MM)—4
peas (1 V)	Meats (M)—2
mashed potatoes (1 V)	
1 cup milk (1 MM)	

Assessment: Low on grains, breads, and cereals; high on milk and milk products

intake in child care centers (Ball, Benjamin, & Ward, 2007). It will become more readily available with time.

All of the nutritional assessment tools require understanding and cooperation between the parent and the teacher, working together to establish what the child's eating patterns are to make changes that help the child follow the recommended diet pattern. Establishing respect and forming an alliance between the teacher and the parent are of primary importance. Care should be taken to practice cultural competence if the diet of a particular culture appears to present nutritional challenges for a child. Discussing the dietary pattern with the health consultant or a dietician might be helpful if a problem is indicated. A referral to the child's physician or local health clinic may be recommended.

If you were to do a 24-hour dietary recall right now, how would you do? Would you have met your dietary needs, or would you need to change some things?

TABLE 11-12
Food Frequency Questionnaire for Children

Name ______________________ **Age** ________

Indicate how many times on average your child eats the following foods in a week by marking down the number of times in the category that most describes your child's eating pattern.

D = Daily O = Often S = Sometimes R = Rarely

Food	Frequency **D**	**O**	**S**	**R**
Milk and milk products: cheese, milk, yogurt, ice cream, and pudding	☐	☐	☐	☐
Meat, meat products, and meat substitutes: beef, chicken, pork, lamb, fish, egg, lunch meat, bacon, dried beans, peas, and peanut butter	☐	☐	☐	☐
Grains, breads, and cereals: rice, pasta, tortillas, grits, breads, cereals	☐	☐	☐	☐
Fruits and vegetables	☐	☐	☐	☐
Other: fats, oils, sweet bakery goods, fast foods, and candy	☐	☐	☐	☐

What type of milk does your child drink?

skim	1% lowfat	2% lowfat	whole	formula	breast
☐	☐	☐	☐	☐	☐

How many meals, including snacks, does the child eat in one day? ______

Also, explain the child's eating habits: ______________________

____

____

Are there any dietary restrictions or limitations practiced by your family? If yes, please explain. Yes ☐ No ☐

____

____

Key Concept 11.3

Health Status Assessment

Assessing a child's health status is a major task for the teacher. Daily health checks, general health appraisals, screening for developmental norms, screening for good mental health, and assessment of nutrition are the tools that the teacher can use to detect any problems or deficits that a child may have. Early detection may lead to early intervention to correct the problem.

Wadsworth/Cengage Learning

Teachers need to communicate with families about a child's health and development, and practicing cultural competence is essential.

11.4 IMPLICATIONS FOR TEACHERS

Teachers are a key link in promoting good health for children. Teachers have the opportunity to contribute to the health and well-being of children in care. These areas include observation, education, cultural sensitivity, and supervision.

The first appropriate time to observe is the quick daily health check. In addition, a child should be observed for physical and mental health on an ongoing basis. If there has been an outbreak of an infectious disease, special care should be taken to observe for that particular disease.

A plan and health policy for monthly, quarterly, and yearly observations for health and nutrition in regard to assessment and screening for growth and developmental norms should be created and carried out.

For Families

Assessment facilitates communication between the teacher and the parent and can lead to collaborative practices that involve all key players in the child's environment: the child, the teacher, the parents, the school, the child's physician or a health consultant, and the community. Information about the child's growth and development is collected and recorded at certain intervals. The teacher must be trained to perform basic assessments. Another good practice is to discuss concerns with a health consultant before talking to the parent so that you are better informed as to the implications of those concerns. The health consultant can also be a source for referrals for the child.

The daily appraisal need not be discussed unless there is a problem or concern. All other forms of assessment should be discussed thoroughly with the parent. The parent may need to be educated as to the importance of any assessment. Any difficulty with the child's health and well-being should be addressed early in the process.

When a referral is made, the teacher should follow up. If there is a problem, the teacher should be aware of it and should be given instructions on how best to help the child cope with any difficulty. A discussion with the parent and the person to whom the child was referred would be most helpful to give the child the continuity of care that he might need.

Education

The use of assessment tools can help decrease developmental risk for the children in the early education environment. The teacher needs to be educated in the use of these tools and learn to work with a health consultant to provide as much information as possible to promote intervention when it is needed.

Cultural Competence

A child whose first language is not English may appear not to follow developmental norms. A child who is exposed to two languages may have difficulty switching from the home language to the language used in the early childhood education environment. Patience and understanding are important. It is helpful to have a teacher or someone that the teacher can call upon who speaks the same language as the child to make the shift between the two languages easier.

If the teacher notices real difficulties in hearing, speech, or language, she might want to have a discussion with the parent to see whether the child seems to have these same difficulties in the native language. If the child seems to have a problem, discussions with the parent and then referral should be approached with cultural sensitivity. Many cultures view any problem with a child as an imperfection that is a source of guilt and shame for the parent. An understanding of the child's native culture helps the teacher relate better to the parent.

Dietary patterns are greatly influenced by cultural and ethnic considerations. Certain cultures such as Southeast Asian and Indochinese rarely consume milk products. Other cultures may not have a varying menu that allows for the meats or fresh fruits and vegetables that a child needs in his diet. When assessing the child's diet, it is extremely important to have some knowledge of the family's customs. This will allow the teacher to be culturally sensitive when talking to the parent. A health consultant, dietician, or family member who speaks both the child's and the teacher's languages can help alleviate any problems that a language barrier might cause. It may be a challenge to help a family from a different cultural background adjust to dietary allowances recommended for the child. A medical home that is headed by a culturally competent physician can be an invaluable source of support for both the teacher and the family.

Supervision

The teacher needs to supervise the early childhood education environment to make sure that record keeping and assessments are carried out on a regular basis. A director in an early childhood education center usually supervises the assessments and makes sure that the records are kept up to date. In family child care or in-home care situations, there may be only one teacher present. It is up to this teacher to make sure that children's health is supported through regular use of record keeping and assessment.

A communication system should also be established within the early childhood education environment. Teachers must work together to collaborate on promoting the good health of the child. A family child care provider may have an aide or a substitute who could assist in appraisals and assessment. In an early childhood education environment, the child may see several teachers and aides in one day, as well as the director and perhaps a kitchen helper. All of the staff should be trained to cooperate in appraising and assessing a child's health status.

Key Concept 11.4

Implications for Teachers

The teacher must promote the good health and well-being of the children in care by using observing children, working with families, education, cultural competence, and supervision as tools to promote health and prevent risk.

CHAPTER SUMMARY

Children must be observed as individuals to assess their health and well-being. Teachers can appraise and assess children for physical health, mental health, and nutrition. They can screen children for growth and developmental norms, documenting their observations through several forms of records. If there appears to be a difficulty in any area, they can discuss it with the parents and offer a referral, if necessary. Teachers need to employ observation, communication with families, education, cultural competence, and supervision to provide adequate assessment measures for children in care.

TO GO BEYOND

Additional resources for this chapter can be found by visiting the book companion website at www.cengage.com/education/robertson. This supplemental material includes chapter objectives, internet exercises, reflection questions, quizzes, web links, glossary and flash cards, case studies, frequently asked questions, downloadable forms and tables, curriculum supplements, more reality checks, additional key concepts, references, and more.

Chapter Review Critical Thinking Applications

1. Explain the interrelationship of assessment and early intervention. How might this affect a child's later success in school?
2. Compare the differences between observing children and diagnosing them. Discuss how to observe without making judgments or diagnoses.
3. Discuss how homelessness can affect a preschool-age child. What benefits would that child receive if he or she attended a preschool? What local resources in your community might help this happen? How would homelessness affect an elementary school child? Would the resources in the community be the same?
4. How might technology help in observing, assessing, and recording the development of children?

As an Individual

1. Assess your own physical health by self-observation. Record how you feel physically for a period of three days. Be sure to use precise

words. When you are done, evaluate whether you have been observing or diagnosing your health.

2. Observe two children in an early childhood education situation, if possible. If that option is not available to you, go to a local playground or park. Use the anecdotal type of record to document your observations. Write two paragraphs explaining how you felt documenting and what you learned from it.
3. Find two articles on lead poisoning and compare and contrast them. Be able to report on these articles in class.
4. Choose one item to assess from the following: motor development, dental, vision, and hearing. Find one article and one website that discuss developmental delays in this area. Compile a short list of warning signs for this item.

As a Group

1. Bring several 2-year-olds to class. Provide a number of toys and books for them. Watch them and observe their actions and interactions. Compare observations for developmental norms for speech, language, and gross motor skills. Discuss how each child develops at his or her own rate.
2. Examine mental health indicators that put children at risk. Select the indicators that are most likely to lead to mental health risk. How could a teacher help to ameliorate these risks? How would you get a mental health counselor involved in a school with limited funds? Answer this by doing research on available resources in the local area.
3. In small groups of four or five, go out into the community and collect information about resources that offer help to people in poverty. Share the resource information in a class discussion. Why does poverty greatly affect the development of children?
4. In small groups of students, survey the community for resources available to help children with health issues. One group will cover motor difficulties; another group will research vision problems; a third group will find resources on hearing; a fourth group will seek out nutritional services; and a fifth group will cover speech and language services that are available. After everyone has gathered the information, put together a resource file to be placed in a classroom or library so that all students have access to it.

Case Studies

1. Steve has observed 3-year-old Jerrod having a difficult time during circle time. He seems to fidget, play around, and not really pay attention, especially if he sits farther away from Steve. Bridget, the assistant, notices that Jerrod is more attentive if he sits closer to Steve. She thinks that it might be that Jerrod has trouble with his hearing. What is the next step that Bridget and Steve should take? If they feel Jerrod does have a hearing difficulty, what should they do?
2. Emma has been in your care since she was 8 months old. She was happy and loved to explore. She is now 13 months old but does not

seem to be growing as fast as she should and seems more listless than she used to be. Her mother doesn't want Emma to get too fat, so she has replaced milk in her bottle with half apple juice and half water. She wants Emma to have as much juice as she wants, not only at meals but at naptimes. How would you handle this?

3. Jose is a quiet 2½-year-old boy. He uses a few garbled words and seems hesitant to speak. His family speaks only Spanish at home, but you are not sure that is why he does not talk much at school. You are concerned that he may have a language difficulty that is not tied to English being his second language. What course of action do you take?
4. Harry is in your kindergarten class. He seems hyperactive in the morning when he comes to school, then settles down later. During those times when he is so active, it is difficult to teach the rest of the children because he is so distracting. You notice that when he eats breakfast at the school breakfast program, he begins his day a little calmer and everybody's day goes better. What might you say to his parents? How could you find out what his typical breakfast at home is, then suggest some changes?

CHAPTER 12

Prevention of Illness in Early Childhood Education Environments Through Infection Control

After reading this chapter, you should be able to:

12.1 Health Policies for Infection Control

Define and discuss health policies for the prevention of childhood infectious diseases.

12.2 Mechanisms of Infectious Disease Spread

Explain the mechanisms of communicable disease spread.

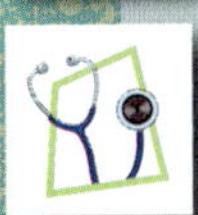

12.3 Immunizations for Disease Prevention

Relate the importance of immunizations in the prevention and reduction of communicable diseases.

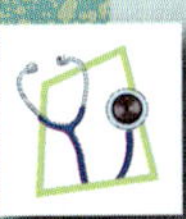

12.4 Universal Sanitary Practices for the Early Childhood Education Environment

Summarize sanitation methods used in the prevention of spread of disease in the early childhood education environment.

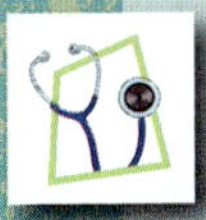

12.5 Environmental Quality Control for Disease Prevention

Discuss factors in the environment for which quality control can help to curb the spread of disease.

12.6 Implications for Teachers

Describe the importance of education, supervision, working with families, and role modeling in the prevention of communicable diseases.

12.1 HEALTH POLICIES FOR INFECTION CONTROL

- **infection control** *control of infectious agents by sanitary practices.*
- **immunization** *vaccines given in order to protect individuals through the development of antibodies against specific infectious diseases.*
- **hygiene** *protective measures and sanitary practices to limit the spread of infection and to promote health.*

Policies for **infection control** are essential to maintain health and prevent serious illness among children. Children in early childhood education environments are more likely to become ill than children who stay at home. **Immunization** and **hygiene** can provide barriers to the spread of infectious diseases and illness among children who are in early childhood environments. The need for infection control policies is reinforced by the following:

- Early childhood education centers that have detailed routines to clean and disinfect can significantly cut the number of illnesses reported because the cycle of germ transmission is interrupted (Gonzalez, 2005).
- Children in early childhood education environments with more than six children have a higher incidence of infections than children in smaller groups (Shope & Aronson, 2006). Children in infant and toddler care may be more vulnerable to infections because children put almost everything in their mouths (Smith, 2003).
- Approximately twelve percent of all children in the United States, or 8.7 million children, do not have health insurance (CBPP, 2007). Preschool children without health insurance or public health insurance are less likely to be up-to-date with their vaccinations (Santoli et al., 2004; Kohen et al., 2008).
- Less than 30 percent of teachers in early childhood education environments are familiar with the infectious disease guidelines published by the APHA and the AAP (Copeland et al., 2006). Teachers should receive training in infection control for early education environments (AAP, 2003).
- Policies for the control of the spread of illness should be developed (NCCCHSRC, 2004; Shope and Aronson, 2006).
- In order to protect all children in care and prevent illness, the child care day should start with a health check (APHA & AAP, 2002; Calder, 2006).

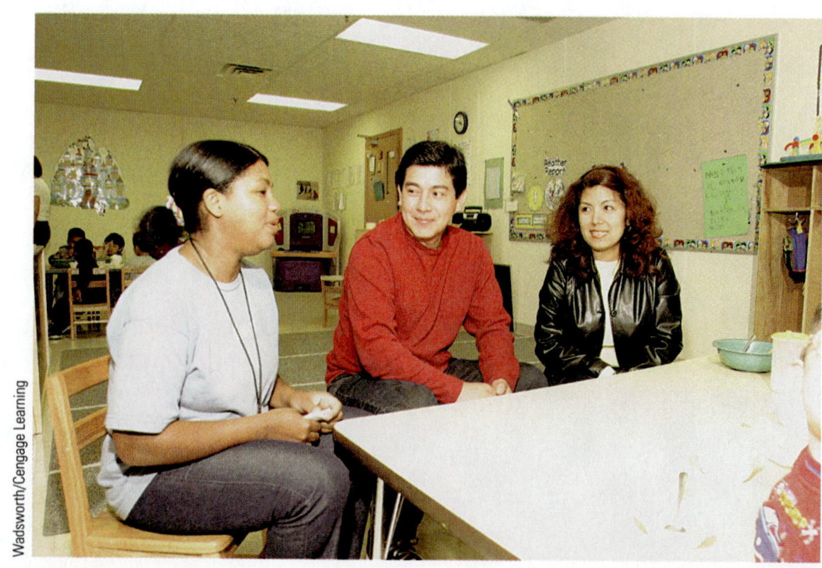

Wadsworth/Cengage Learning

Developing health policies is essential for the control of infection and the spread of diseases. Even more important is communicating these policies to teachers and parents. The distribution of written policies, meetings to articulate and reinforce the written policies, and new staff and parent training sessions are ways to communicate health policies.

- A "no-nit" policy for lice in early childhood education environments should be abandoned (Pollack, 2007; Mumcuoglu et al., 2006; Lebwohl, Clark, & Levitt, 2007).

The key tools of risk management for health are prevention, protection, and promotion. To utilize these tools properly, there must be an understanding of how disease is spread and how it is controlled. It is also important to know that educating teachers, parents, and children can help prevent the spread of disease.

As discussed throughout this text, protection is an important key for the management of risk and the greatest degree of well-being. Keeping healthy includes protective measures such as getting enough sleep, exercising often, eating well, and lessening stress levels; these can help both children and adults optimize their health so risk is lessened.

There are many people involved in the early childhood education environment, both directly and indirectly. The potential for the spread of infectious diseases is increased as these numbers increase. There are the teachers, the children, and the families whose interactions with each other make them more vulnerable than the general population. An added risk is present for a teacher who is pregnant. A fetus is particularly vulnerable to certain infectious diseases. Health policies for the control of infectious diseases are critical for all people involved in the early childhood education environment. These health policies should include:

1. *Mechanisms of communicable disease spread:* understanding the mechanisms that spread disease and practices that will prevent the spread of disease.
2. *Immunizations for disease prevention:* understanding the importance of immunizations for protection and prevention and implementing strategies to be sure that children and adults are properly immunized.
3. *Sanitation for disease prevention:* practices for sanitation, hygiene, and cleanliness that offer protective and preventive measures.
4. *Environmental quality control for disease prevention:* strategies that help prevent the spread of disease in the rest of the early childhood education environment.
5. *Implications for teachers:* methods and practices that provide minimum risk and maximum health protection for the early childhood education environment.

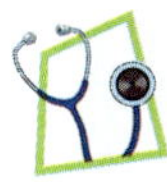

Health Policies for Infection Control

Health policies for the control of infection and the spread of disease are essential in early childhood education environments. These policies should cover the mechanisms of disease control, the immunizations, and sanitation required for disease prevention. Health policies should also address environmental quality control and education for disease prevention. The teacher must understand the methods and practices that provide protection and prevention.

12.2 MECHANISMS OF INFECTIOUS DISEASE SPREAD

To many people, the early childhood education environment is thought of as a barrier to good health. Infectious diseases are common there. Some teachers often complain about frequent illnesses. What most people do not understand is that the frequency of infectious diseases and the potential for disease spread can be greatly reduced through use of sanitary practices.

- **germs** *microscopic organisms that can cause disease.*

In order to place barriers against infectious diseases and to control them in the early childhood education environment, one must fully understand how disease is spread. In child care, in an office, or in a home, **germs** are always present. The fact that they cannot be seen does not mean they are not there. This may be especially important in the event that a pandemic type of flu should occur. If this should happen, it is important that the barriers and preparation for prevention be put into place as mitigating factors. A matrix for this information may be found at http://www.state.gov/m/a/os/c17204.htm.

There are several major reasons why the spread of infectious diseases is more likely in the early childhood education environment. The young children present have not yet learned good hygiene practices, and germs multiply in warm, moist places. The early childhood education environment and the children present offer germs many warm, moist places in which to grow. Diseases are spread through the air and by person-to-person contact.

Certain practices in the early childhood education environment greatly contribute to the spread of infectious diseases. Table 12-1 lists those practices.

Wadsworth/Cengage Learning

Early childhood education environments present a challenge for germ control. The frequent exchange of toys among children who have not yet mastered personal hygiene is one example. Important prevention measures include regularly disinfecting mouthed toys and frequent hand washing.

TABLE 12-1
Practices That Contribute to the Spread of Infectious Disease in the Early Childhood Education Environment

WARNINGS

- ☐ Failure to wash hands as needed and to wash hands properly
- ☐ Presence of children in diapers who put toys in the mouth
- ☐ Mixed ages where older children play with children in diapers
- ☐ Large numbers of children present, especially if within a contained area
- ☐ Improper diaper-changing procedures, including disposal and cleanup
- ☐ Staff who have dual duties, such as preparing food and working with children
- ☐ Lack of facilities, such as not enough bathrooms, small rooms, or diaper area not separated from rest of care
- ☐ Water tables or wading pools that are not sanitized or do not have the water changed frequently
- ☐ Pets in the environment that are handled by children or teachers
- ☐ Not requiring or checking immunization records for completion or update for all children in the early childhood education environment
- ☐ Not requiring or checking immunization records for all staff
- ☐ Failure to perform daily health check
- ☐ Not excluding ill staff
- ☐ Not having a good backup substitute list for replacing ill teachers
- ☐ Not having a policy for exclusion of ill children
- ☐ Not properly informing families when the children are exposed to a communicable disease
- ☐ Lack of proper sanitation and cleaning, especially of toys and food preparation, bathroom, and sleeping areas
- ☐ Improper storage of food
- ☐ Lack of hygiene in food handling
- ☐ Inadequate circulation of air
- ☐ Children sharing sleeping space or equipment
- ☐ Failure to have a policy for unimmunized children
- ☐ Lack of multiple sinks for different tasks to prevent cross-contamination

For greater understanding of why the practices in Table 12-1 are so careless, it is helpful to know exactly how germs are spread to cause infectious diseases. There are four basic ways diseases are spread:

1. Respiratory tract transmission
2. Fecal-oral transmission
3. Direct contact transmission
4. Blood contact transmission

Respiratory Tract Transmission

- **respiratory tract transmission** *germs that are passed through the air from the respiratory tract of one person to another person.*

Respiratory tract transmission is perhaps the most common method of disease spread in the early childhood education environment. Tiny droplets from the eyes, mouth, or nose get into the air when a child sneezes, coughs, drools, or even talks, and these droplets are transmitted to other people through the air they breathe. This is referred to as "droplet spread," and it is the main way that these illnesses are spread (Abrams, 2007). These droplets can also land on toys, food, and other things in the environment. Germs can live for many hours and activate once they come into contact with the mouth, nose, throat, lungs, or eyes of an uninfected person. When germs come into contact with an uninfected person, they can multiply and cause illness. Colds occur more often in the fall and winter when children spend more time in a confined environment, and most are caused by viruses and bacteria (NCCCHSRC, 2007). The cold germs are spread by sharing of tissues, food, and cups. They can also be spread by coughing or sneezing without covering the mouth. The common cold accounts for 75 percent of all infant illnesses. The most common infections in early childhood education environments are colds and flu. There have also been common outbreaks of another respiratory tract disease known as respiratory syncytial virus (RSV) in early childhood education environments (Abrams, 2007). RSV is an infection in the lower respiratory tract, and it is the most common viral infection in infants and young children. An outbreak of the rarely seen respiratory disease tuberculosis was found in a family child care in children whose parents were foreign born (Dewan et al., 2006).

The best ways to prevent germs from spreading are to disinfect often all toys that are put in the mouth, wash hands at appropriate times and in the appropriate manner (see page 463), and teach children to protect others when they cough, sneeze, or blow their noses. The number of active germs on a surface can be reduced by 80 to 90 percent if a child sneezes into a tissue instead of in the open or on his arm or shirt (Tierno, 2003). It is important to remember to throw the tissue away after it has been used and to wash hands properly. Even sneezing or coughing into the crook of an arm is better than sneezing or coughing into the open (HCCP, 2008). Many teachers have found it easy to teach children to do this when coughing, instead of coughing into their hands, which, if not washed, can easily spread the disease (see Figure 12-1). Children under age 3 are more likely to have respiratory tract infections, and they are also more likely to mouth toys and other objects. It is important to note that children with chronic diseases or other health conditions as well as a respiratory infection are more likely to develop severe illnesses than those who do not have these health conditions. Infants at high risk may have to be restricted from care during the RSV season, and children at high risk may be given monthly injections of antibodies during this time (NCCCHSRC, 2007).

Fecal-Oral Transmission

- **fecal-oral transmission** *passing of germs from an infected person's bowel movement via the hand into another person's system via the mouth.*

Fecal-oral transmission occurs when the germs from one person's feces get into another person's mouth and then are swallowed and introduced into the digestive tract of that person. The most common way for germs to spread is when hands are not properly washed after toileting, before eating, or before preparing food. Diseases that are spread by fecal-oral transmission can affect a number of children. Children in early childhood education settings

FIGURE 12-1
Cover your cough.

have increased risk for diarrhea (Ethelberg et al., 2006). Rotavirus is a type of fecal-oral disease that is commonly found in the early childhood education setting (HCCP, 2007a, 2007b), as is norovirus, which is commonly referred to as "stomach flu" (Rose, 2007a; Calder, 2007a). Another less common disease that has had outbreaks in child care centers is cryptosporidiosis (Turabelidze et al., 2007). This disease may begin with a child being exposed to it via tap water or pool water, but it can spread in the normal fecal-oral manner.

- **sanitized** *removal of bacteria, filth, and dirt that makes transmission of disease unlikely.*

In the early childhood education environment, another common way that germs are spread is through the water. Water tables that are not **sanitized** and do not have the water changed frequently are hosts to germs that are transmitted from unwashed hands. The AAP and APHA do not recommend water tables in the early childhood education environment for this reason. However, many teachers feel that the benefits of having a water table outweigh the risks. In addition, if the early childhood environment wants an ECERS-R rating, a water table must be included. Therefore, special care must be taken to maintain these water tables so they are not good hosts to germs and do not encourage the spread of disease. This includes properly washing hands before and after water play. If a child has a runny nose, an open sore, a rash, or diarrhea, he should be given an individual water bin and should not share with others (NCCCHSRC, 2004). Water tables should be cleaned and sanitized after use. Sand boxes may also pose risk for fecal-oral transmission. Proper hand washing should occur after sand play.

Germs are also found on rugs, furniture, tables, and toys. If the early education environment has infants that spend any time down on the floor, everyone in the environment should leave their shoes at the door so that they do not track in germs that may have come from animals outdoors. Hand washing at proper times, proper care of a water table, and proper food safety can help prevent the spread of disease through the fecal-oral route.

Direct Contact Transmission

- **direct contact transmission** *passing of germs from one person's body or clothing to another person through direct contact.*
- **secretions** *saliva, mucus, urine, and blood produced by the body for specific purposes.*

Direct contact transmission occurs when one person has direct contact with **secretions** from an infected person. Secretions can be left on toys, doorknobs, or other objects that come in direct contact with the uninfected person. Direct contact transmission also occurs when a person picks up parasites from infested objects such as bedding, toys, clothing, or combs. Diseases can spread easily through direct contact among children and teachers in an early childhood education environment if precautions are not taken to curb them. Some of these diseases such as methicillin-resistant staph aureus (MRSA) may be resistant to antibiotics, so they should be carefully monitored (Rose, 2006b, 2007a). Good hygiene, including hand washing, sanitizing, covering cuts and scrapes, not sharing personal items such as bedding, and proper food handling can help block the spread of disease through direct contact. In addition, other good practices include avoiding sharing cups or silverware, keeping door handles clean, and wiping down toys and books after play (Reeves, 2007).

Lice, and its accompanying nits, is a controversial subject and whether to exclude children from care is a topic of debate. Amanda was sent home with lice, which her mother treated, so Amanda returned the next day. Amanda's teacher found nits still in her hair and took her to the director to see what should be done. Sherry, the director in the college laboratory school where Amanda attends, felt that, because head lice was not life threatening and Amanda's mother desperately needed the support of the early childhood education program to stay in school and work, she was willing to bend. Without communication, this situation could have created real animosity among staff. If the teachers were trying to enforce the "no-nits" policy while Sherry was allowing the child to stay in care, they would not present a united front. What Sherry and the teachers at this center did was to sit down and review the policy and make some changes.

Amanda's mother had a very difficult time getting rid of the head lice. Through cooperation, either Sherry or a teacher, Damaris, would spend 10 minutes at the beginning of each day with a lice comb, combing through Amanda's hair as she played a computer game in the director's office. After three weeks, the lice were eradicated, and Amanda's family and the early education center had developed a trust that still exists to this day. Amanda has graduated from the center, but her parents still come by to volunteer and to help in any way to support this early childhood education program.

REALITY *Check*

The Issue of Head Lice in Early Childhood Education Environments

Head lice infestation among children between the ages of 3 and 12 years is reportedly common in the United States. It is estimated that there are between six and twelve million cases of infestation every year (Bazar, 2007). Lice are small parasitic insects about the size of a sesame seed and are spread through direct contact. Historically, the appearance of head lice on a person has been associated with lack of cleanliness and low socioeconomic class. This is one of the reasons that parents may be offended or defensive when their child appears with a lice infestation. Because of these historical connotations, parents whose children have lice often feel guilty or embarrassed. Head lice are common among all socioeconomic levels. Because children are more frequently affected than adults, head lice can have a significant effect on the early childhood education environment that is basically unwarranted. Communication is the key to keeping this situation and the emotional reactions to it in check, whereby directors, teachers, and parents work together to solve the problem.

Head lice survive by feeding on a person's blood via the scalp and cannot survive for more than 24 hours without access to a host. It takes eight days for a single louse to hatch from the egg, and that louse begins to feed somewhere around 10 days after hatching. Each fertile female can lay as many as 100 eggs over a period of more than a month. Left unchecked, this can cause an infestation, which can spread to others via *direct contact*.

More than anything, a head lice infestation is annoying. It is not life-threatening, nor does it carry disease, and the potential for epidemic spread is almost nonexistent. But it can cause a lot of itching, and if that itching is out of control, an infection may occur. The biggest threat to a person with head lice is overexposure to the toxic substances used to eliminate the lice (Pollack, 2007).

Most early childhood education centers and elementary schools in this country have a "no-nits" policy, which states that, if children are found to have an active head lice infestation, they will be sent home and must not return until all signs of infestation are gone. The Harvard School of Public Health and many others feel that this "no-nits" policy is archaic and unwarranted given the basic lack of threat or risk (Pollack, 2007; Sciscione & Krause-Parello, 2007; Lebwohl, Clark, & Levitt, 2007; Mumcuoglu et al., 2006; Hill, 2006). Sciscione & Krause-Parello (2007) feel that the no-nits policy may have been based on fear and misinformation instead of good scientific evidence. The AAP and the National Association of School Nurses (NASN) have moved to discourage a "no-nits" policy (Sciscione & Krause-Parello, 2007). Frankowski and Weiner (2002) found that, of 1700 children with lice, the ones that had only nits were only 20 percent likely to develop mature head lice. A "no-nits" policy is by no means a guarantee of stopping outbreaks of lice. Most schools lack expertise and tools to distinguish an active from an inactive infestation. Mass screenings are misguided and fail to honestly identify infested children. Many inactive or nonexistent infestations have been erroneously found to be "active." It is estimated that two-thirds of so-called infestations were not active and therefore misidentified. Pollack (2007) suggests the presence of nits on the hair should lead to the use of photos on the Harvard School of Public Health site (http://www.hsph.harvard.edu/headlice/photos.html) for identification. If lice are crawling on a child's hair, then at the end of the day the parents should be notified. This notification should also include providing information on head lice and methods that can be used to eliminate them. Exclusion, notification of all parents, and mass screenings are unjustified responses (Pollack, 2007).

(continues)

REALITY *Check* (continued)

Much of the information about head lice has been based on anecdotal evidence, not scientific principle (Pollack, 2007). In fact, many researchers have found the surrounding hysteria much more disturbing than the infestation itself. A child who has a head lice infestation is more than likely to have had it for at least a month (AAP, 2002). Lice cannot hop or jump around from person to person. Most transmission occurs by direct contact of one person's head to another's. The AAP and NASN have agreed that after proper treatment a child should be allowed to return to school. If an old infestation where there are only hatched eggs is found, there is no reason for treatment.

The "no-nits" policy can lead to another concern, which is that many products that are supposed to get rid of lice seem to be ineffective. It has been suggested that head lice may have developed an immunity to those products (Pollack, 2007). Overuse of such products can have toxic effects, so other ways to rid a child of head lice have been studied. Here are the general guidelines to eradicate head lice:

- Use a shampoo that contains active ingredients that will kill the lice; pemethrin has previously been found to be the most effective but has also shown increasing resistance (Lebwohl, Clark, & Levitt, 2007).
- If there appears to be no improvement after two treatments, then use of a lindane or malathion insecticide may be the next course; malathion appears to be the best chemical choice (Zamani, 2007).
- Hot dry air produced by a hand-held dryer may be used as an effective tool, but with caution, as too much heat can scald the hair and scalp (Goates et al., 2006).
- Use a special lice comb to remove lice after shampooing, and comb daily until no live lice are discovered for about two weeks.
- Machine wash all possibly infested items such as bed linens, nightclothes, and towels, using hot water.
- All nonwashable items should go into a hot dryer for 20 minutes or in a freezer for several days.
- Soak combs and brushes in a bleach solution for an hour and then clean daily as long as infestation exists.
- Items such as stuffed animals should be placed in sealed plastic bags for a period of 3 to 4 weeks.
- Do not use spray-on lice killers, because the toxicity cannot be controlled.

If a parent has followed the above guidelines and head lice are still found on the child, frustration may ensue. Many directors and teachers have become very discouraged because they have complied with all guidelines, yet nits remain. Some researchers have suggested applying isopropyl (rubbing) alcohol so that the hair is wet, then rubbing with a white towel for about 30 seconds (CHA, 2003). The lice will become intoxicated, release the hair shaft and show up on the towel. A number of home remedies have been presented, but none is scientifically effective, and some may actually be very toxic. The only home remedy that may be effective, according to the Harvard School of Public Health, is the use of olive oil, which they do not endorse because of lack of scientific evidence (Pollack, 2007). Some early childhood education center directors and teachers have found that this treatment seems to be effective in those cases that appear to be resistant to the "normal" head lice shampoos.

Another solution is the use of a really good lice comb and magnifying tool to examine for nits thoroughly, instead of a visual examination, which may not be as accurate. Mechanical removal of lice and nits can be an effective, yet time-consuming method, and it poses no risk (Zamani, 2007). Still another suggestion has been the use of a nontoxic lotion, Nuvo®, which is placed in the hair and then dried with a hair dryer (Pearlman, 2004). The cure rate for this product has been found to be 96 percent, though other health professionals question this product and method.

Directors and teachers have often been at odds over the "no-nits" policy. In many cases, teachers

(continues)

REALITY *Check* (continued)

trying to follow the exclusion policy for lice have tried to send the child home or not allowed the child to return if head lice or nits (even dead ones) were found. Directors, understanding the parents' frustration, have tended to be more lenient and allowed the child to stay in school. There are a number of factors against a "no-nits" policy. These include (1) a child without a live infestation may be unnecessarily excluded; (2) families that cannot comply may be penalized; and (3) exclusion can cause stigma or hysteria (Pollack, 2007).

Many authorities suggest removal of a "no-nits" policy. It is best for each early childhood education environment to make its own determination. It is also suggested that children not be excluded immediately or sent home early (Pollack, 2007). Parents should be informed that their child must be treated properly before returning the next day.

It is best that each early childhood environment evaluate whether to enact a "no-nits" policy. A "no-nits" policy puts the responsibility for removal of nits on the parents. Another guideline for exclusion could be the degree of risk, using a scale to determine whether the risk is high or low, and in the case of lice the risk is almost non-existent (Pollack, 2007). This issue should be discussed at length, and a consensus among teachers should be reached so that everyone is comfortable.

Communication and consensus on the issue is critical. It is important that the teacher provide accurate information on the treatment and prevention of head lice. This should be done for all children in the environment, so the information may have to be translated into the languages of all children present. Translators may be available through the local health department.

CHECK*point:* **Why might the "no-nits" policy for early education environments be changing? With all the information at hand, would you have a policy like this in your early childhood education environment?**

Blood Contact Transmission

- **blood contact** *passing of germs through the blood from one person's circulatory system to another person's circulatory system.*

Transmitting disease through **blood contact** occurs when the infected blood of one person enters the bloodstream of another person. The infected blood can be transmitted and absorbed easily. For example, spread can occur when an infected person has a cut, scraped skin (such as from a skinned knee), or a bloody nose and is treated by a person with a hangnail, chapped hands, or a small cut. Spread also can occur when mucous membranes such as the inside lining of the mouth, eyes, and nose come in contact with another person's blood through a broken surface. The major risk for this would be child biting. Teachers should wear nonlatex disposable gloves when caring for a child with an open wound and any secretions. Any child biting should be handled immediately (see Table 3-9 in Chapter 3).

Following guidelines set up in the remainder of this chapter, the teacher should be able to forestall or deter the spread of disease in the early childhood education environment, as shown in Table 12-2. Figure 12-2 shows the five most effective ways to prevent the spread of disease in the early childhood education environment.

TABLE 12-2
Infectious Disease Spread in the Early Childhood Education Environment

Method	How Spread	Diseases
Respiratory tract	Infectious droplets from the mouth, nose, and eyes get in air via talking, sneezing, coughing, and blowing nose	Colds Strep throat Bacterial meningitis Chicken pox Measles RSV Flu, Hib flu Tuberculosis Pneumococcol and viral pneumonia Bronchiolitis Bronchitis Adenovirus Whooping cough Croup Ear infections Fifth disease Sixth disease
Fecal-oral	Germs from stool of one person get in mouth of another person and are swallowed. Not washing hands after toileting, before preparing food, and before eating, and not disinfecting toys that have been put in the mouth. Also handling pets such as birds, snakes, and lizards can spread bacteria from salmonella.	Hepatitis A Giardia Shigella Salmonella Cryptosporidiosis Pinworms Diarrhea
Direct contact	Infected articles or secretions from infected area. Spread through touching toys, faucets, food, tables, or bedding touched by infected person. By parasites through bedding, clothing, shared hats, combs, brushes, or dress-up clothing.	Impetigo Lice Scabies Cold sores Pink eye CMV MRSA
Blood	Infected blood from one person entering bloodstream of another person. Infected blood can come in contact through cuts, chapped hands, a hangnail, and other broken skin, or lining of mouth, eyes, nose, and rectum. In the early childhood education environment, common transmitters are child biting, bloody noses, and skinned knees.	Hepatitis B HIV-AIDS

Five
Fabulous
Forestallers
1
IMMUNIZATIONS
SUE
JOE
KAY
Keep immunization requirements and records up to date.
2
Use proper hand washing.
3
DIAPERS
Use universal sanitation procedure for diapering.
4
DISINFECTANT
Bleach with hypochlorite.
5
Carry out daily health check.

FIGURE 12-2
Five fabulous forestallers of disease spread in early childhood education environments.

Key Concept 12.2

Mechanisms of Disease Spread

Infectious diseases are common in the early childhood education environment. In order to protect children's health, barriers must be in place. The teacher must understand how diseases spread. The four methods of transmission are respiratory tract, fecal-oral, direct contact, and blood. This knowledge will provide a foundation for the teacher to construct barriers to disease spread.

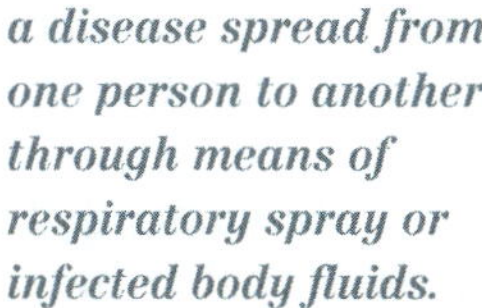

- **communicable disease** *a disease spread from one person to another through means of respiratory spray or infected body fluids.*

12.3 IMMUNIZATIONS FOR DISEASE PREVENTION

One of the major deterrents of **communicable disease** spread is immunization against those diseases. Immunizations can protect children from diseases that cause epidemics. These outbreaks could make children violently ill, disable them, and even kill them. Through medical science, a number of these diseases have been controlled by a regular schedule of immunizations for children at particular ages (see Table 12-3 for an immunization schedule).

TABLE 12-3

Recommended Childhood and Adolescent Immunization Schedule, United States—2008

Vaccine ▼ / Age ▶	Birth	1 month	2 months	4 months	6 months	12 months	15 months	18 months	19–23 months	2–3 years	4–6 years	7–10 years	11–12 years	13–18 years
Hepatitis B	HepB	HepB				HepB							HepB Series	
Rotavirus			Rota	Rota	Rota									
Diphtheria, Tetanus, Pertussis			DTaP	DTaP	DTaP		DTaP				DTaP		Tdap	Tdap
***Haemophilus influenzae* type b**			Hib	Hib	*Hib*[4]	Hib								
Pneumococcal			PCV	PCV	PCV	PCV				PPV			PPV	
Inactivated Poliovirus			IPV	IPV		IPV					IPV		IPV Series	
Influenza								Influenza (Yearly)					Influenza (Yearly)	
Measles, Mumps, Rubella						MMR					MMR		MMR Series	
Varicella						Varicella					Varicella		Varicella Series	
Hepatitis A							HepA (2 doses)			HepA Series			HepA Series	
Meningococcal										MCV4		MCV4	MCV4	MCV4
Human Papillomavirus													HPV (3 doses)	HPV Series

This schedule indicates the recommended ages for routine administration of currently licensed childhood vaccines, as of December 1, 2007, for children through age 18 years. Additional information is available at www.cdc.gov/vaccines/recs/schedules. Any dose not administered at the recommended age should be administered at any subsequent visit, when indicated and feasible. Additional vaccines may be licensed and recommended during the year. Licensed combination vaccines may be used whenever any components of the combination are indicated and other components of the vaccine are not contraindicated and if approved by the Food and Drug Administration for that dose of the series. Providers should consult the respective Advisory Committee on Immunization Practices statement for detailed recommendations, including for **high-risk conditions:** http://www.cdc.gov/vaccines/pubs/ACIP-list.htm. Clinically significant adverse events that follow immunization should be reported to the Vaccine Adverse Event Reporting System (VAERS). Guidance about how to obtain and complete a VAERS form is available at www.vaers.hhs.gov or by telephone, 800-822-7967.

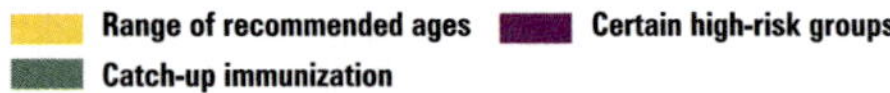

Catch-up immunization

The Childhood and Adolescent Immunization Schedule
Advisory Committee on Immunization Practices www.cdc.gov/nip/acip
American Academy of Pediatrics www.aap.org
American Academy of Family Physicians www.aafp.org

- **vaccinations** *inactivated, dead, or weakened live organism of infectious diseases to which the body builds resistance.*

Immunizations or **vaccinations** are available for a number of diseases that are associated with children and early childhood education environments. Diseases that can be prevented include measles, mumps, rubella, whooping cough (pertussis), diphtheria, Hib (Haemophilus influenza type B—meningitis), chicken pox, hepatitis A, hepatitis B, and influenza. The AAP in conjunction with the CDC have a list of recommended immunizations that is updated on a yearly basis. Immunizations for these diseases are recommended by the AAP and are required for entrance into elementary schools. The local health department in your area is one of the recommended sources for new immunizations schedules, as well as the website at http://www.cdc.gov/nip/recs/child-schedule.htm. The AAP is now recommending a pneumococcal conjugate vaccine that can prevent meningitis, pneumonia, and serious infections transferred by blood for children as young as 6 weeks who are at high risk and for healthy children ages 24 to 59 months (AAP, 2008). They are also recommending a meningococcal vaccine for high-risk children between the ages of 3 and 10 years. The influenza vaccine is now recommended for all children as young as 6 months and as old as 18 years unless they have an allergy to eggs (Calder, 2007b; Stobbs, 2008). Hepatitis A vaccines have now been approved for children as young as 12 months (AAP, 2007a). In 2007, a three-dose rotavirus vaccine was added for children ages 2 to 6 months and a second dose of the varicella vaccine was added to the list for children from ages 4 to 6 years ("Recommended Immunization Schedule," 2007).

Immunizations against disease are effective as a preventive measure only if they are administered according to schedule. Parents do not always realize that many serious childhood diseases still pose threats and they must prevent those threats through immunization. In recent years, whooping cough and measles have greatly increased because enough children have not been vaccinated against them (AAP, 2004). Adult teachers should make sure that boosters are administered as scheduled.

With funding from the U.S. Department of Health and Human Services, the AAP and Healthy Child Care Pennsylvania have created a software tracking system for immunization records to be used in early childhood education environments, called *WellCareTracker*™. This risk reduction tool allows teachers to keep track of immunizations and screening tests. It flags missing immunizations and continues to check for updates. This allows teachers lead time to notify families when children must have their immunizations updated. This is a web-based service (https://www.wellcaretracker.org) with continuous updates as needed. At the time of publication of this text, the service was available for $1.50 per year per child in care, plus a $25 one-time setup fee. This is an inexpensive way to keep track of immunizations for children in care and keep them up to date (HCCP, 2007a, 2007b).

Children in early childhood education environments must have protection not only from the classic childhood diseases, but also from those diseases that seem to flourish in early childhood education environments if proper precautions are not practiced. Recent outbreaks of childhood diseases seem to be traced to child care situations (AAP, 2004; Dewan et al., 2006; Tomlin, 2007). These outbreaks include hepatitis B, hepatitis A, and Hib, which is a flu-like form of meningitis. Vaccines available for each of these diseases will help protect children in care. Table 12-3 shows the recommended immunization schedule that was most current when this text was submitted for publication. The CDC now updates this chart twice a year. For the most current schedule, go to www.cdc.gov/nip to link to the most current immunization schedule for children under 6 years old. This page will also link you to the latest adult schedules for teachers working in the early childhood education environment.

Children in care who are not immunized can jeopardize others who have been immunized or are too young to have received the immunization (Offitt, 2007). Diseases that can be prevented with immunizations remain a threat, can be difficult to treat, and can be deadly if there are children in early childhood education programs that have not followed the immunization schedule. An example of this is the recent outbreaks of measles in 2004, 2006, and 2008 (CBS News, 2008). These outbreaks did not begin in this country, but rather were brought back to the United States by a child who was traveling out of the country. The outbreak in 2008 in San Diego began with a 7-year-old child who traveled to Switzerland and came back with the measles. He spread it to two siblings, two playmates from school, and four children in the pediatrician's office. It continued to spread until 17 children were identified with this disease ("Outbreak of Measles," 2008). Several of the infants were hospitalized.

As a teacher, it is imperative to protect the children and everyone else in the early childhood education environment by requiring the completion of the immunization schedule (Rose, 2006a). Parents must provide an immunization record filled out by a physician or local health clinic on the form provided by the state in which the child resides. A copy of this record should be on file with each child's health record and should be periodically updated if the child is in the process of receiving a series of vaccinations. Better still, at a minimal price the teacher can have Well-CareTracker™ software that will provide this information on an ongoing basis. In addition, the teacher should provide information to all parents about the importance and benefits of immunizations (see Reality Check: *At Risk for Preventable Disease,* p. 461). Handouts and articles for parents are good ways to keep the importance of immunization in everyone's thoughts.

Children who have not followed the immunization schedule and have missed a particular vaccination will not be protected from that particular disease. If a child has not met all of the requirements of an immunization schedule, he must do so immediately (see Table 12-3). A quarterly check of children's records can help keep them up to date. To simplify record keeping, the teacher can place a "red flag" or special sticker on the file of each child who must still complete the immunization schedule. In the case of the 2008 outbreak of measles, the children who got measles were either too young to have the immunization, did not complete the immunization schedule, or had parents who had personal reasons for not getting their children immunized ("Outbreak of Measles," 2008).

If a child in the early childhood education environment has not completed the schedule and the parents do not have any plans to complete it, the child should be excluded from care until the process of immunization is resumed. An exception to this would be a child who, for medical reasons, religious, or personal beliefs, may be exempt from the immunizations. For example, a child with a medical reason such as an allergy to eggs would be exempt in all 50 states. The CDC estimates that approximately 38,000 children in the United States have been exempted from receiving the recommended childhood vaccinations (National Network for Immunization Information [NNii], 2005). In two states, those with children whose parents who follow religions whose documented beliefs do not allow immunization can be refused enrollment (in 48 states, children of parents with a religious reason must be admitted) (NNii, 2005; Tomlin, 2007). Twenty states allow exemption for personal or philosophical reasons. Many physicians are calling for states to reexamine their exemption policies in relation to nonmedical reasons (Omer et al., 2006). The measles outbreak in 2008 involved a number of children who were exempt. If an outbreak of a disease were to occur, excluding these children from care might be an important preventative measure.

Teachers in the early childhood education program should be familiar with state requirements. A medical release form must be on file and kept confidential (CCHP, 2004). If the state allows a religious or personal belief exemption, then an affidavit of religious or personal belief must be on file and kept confidential. This allows the teacher to identify these children without immunizations so they can be quickly excluded if an outbreak of a disease occurs. This is important because it has been found that unimmunized children are as much as 35 times more likely to catch diseases such as measles than were those children who were in immunization compliance (NNii, 2005). This exclusion policy should be made clear to the parents of the unimmunized children. Other parents in care should be notified that there is or may be an unimmunized child in care, without revealing that child's identity, to maintain confidentiality. This information may be included in the parents' handbook if one is available at the early childhood education program. The Pennsylvania Chapter of the American Academy of Pediatrics (PAAAP, 2003)

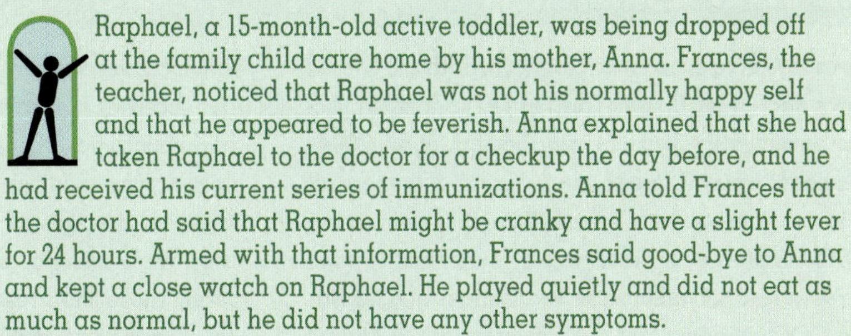

Raphael, a 15-month-old active toddler, was being dropped off at the family child care home by his mother, Anna. Frances, the teacher, noticed that Raphael was not his normally happy self and that he appeared to be feverish. Anna explained that she had taken Raphael to the doctor for a checkup the day before, and he had received his current series of immunizations. Anna told Frances that the doctor had said that Raphael might be cranky and have a slight fever for 24 hours. Armed with that information, Frances said good-bye to Anna and kept a close watch on Raphael. He played quietly and did not eat as much as normal, but he did not have any other symptoms.

Frances was glad to have the information because when she had first started her child care business, a mother had dropped off a child whose fever had become elevated later in the day. Frances had not been able to reach the mother and had been worried for several hours until the child's doctor returned her call. The doctor told Frances that the girl had had an immunization the day before and that the girl's reaction was normal.

REALITY *Check*

At Risk for Preventable Diseases

Table 12-3 shows the recommended childhood schedule of immunizations to protect children from communicable diseases. Recent studies show that large numbers of children are at risk for these preventable diseases because they have not been immunized. There has been an increase in reported cases of measles and mumps. (AAP, 2004). Recent outbreaks of whooping cough and measles have also been reported (Offitt, 2007). These outbreaks were traced to unimmunized carriers. It was thought that whooping cough had been eradicated, but that is obviously not the case because since first reports in 1993, the number of whooping cough cases has been growing.

The Centers for Disease Control and Prevention (2007b) reported that in 2006 the vaccination coverage for children was at an all-time high, with 77 percent of children in the United States receiving their basic recommended vaccinations. This reflected a strong increase in the pneumococcal and varicella (chicken pox) vaccines and the increased availability of other vaccines. There are no results reported for the new additions of the rotavirus vaccine and the influenza vaccine or the second dose of the varicella vaccine. Even though there has been an increase, we are still lower in vaccination coverage than the Healthy People 2010 national health objective for 90 percent of the children in the United States to be vaccinated. There may be several reasons for this.

The first reason is that some children have less access to immunization coverage than others. Santoli and colleagues (2004) found that children with private insurance were more likely to be up to date in their immunizations than those with public insurance or no insurance. Access to immunization may be more difficult for some families. There is now a Vaccines for Children Program, which is a partnership between health care providers and public health agencies that provides uninsured children and those who are in Medicaid with vaccination coverage. More information from the CDC about this program can be found at http://www.cdc.gov/nip.

The second and more controversial reason for some children not having their immunizations up to date is the alleged relationship between an increase in autism and the MMR (measles, mumps, rubella) and DTP (diptheria, typhoid, pertussis) vaccinations, which

(continues)

REALITY *Check* (continued)

has caused concern among parents in both the United States and Great Britain. This has led to a fall in vaccine coverage in Great Britain (Smeeth et al., 2004). The controversy is due to the inclusion of thimerosal, which is a derivative of an ethyl-mercury compound, in the vaccines as a preservative. Some studies have shown a link between these vaccinations and autism. The CDC reported that in some areas of the United States the rate for pervasive developmental disorders or autism has been as high as 1 of every 150 children (CDC, 2007a). Twenty years ago, that figure was 1 child in 2500. However, several studies have proved no relationship between autism and vaccinations (Destefano et al., 2004; CHA, 2004; Smeeth et al., 2004; NNii, 2006a). Other researchers are not convinced and are continuing to study this controversy (Parker-Pope, 2004; U.C. Davis M.I.N.D. Institute, 2007; Zamani, 2008). It has been suggested that there may be a genetic link and that genetically susceptible children, when exposed to thimerosal, may develop autism (Hornig, Chian, & Lipkin, 2004). There is emerging evidence that some children who may be immunologically compromised may have an adverse response to vaccinations (U.C. Davis M.I.N.D. Institute, 2007). Today, all vaccinations for universal immunization of infants less than 6 months no longer contain thimerosal. The only vaccine routinely recommended for children in the United States that contains thimerosal is the influenza vaccine. Influenza vaccines with low doses of thimerosal are available as trivalent inactivated influenza vaccine (NNii, 2006b). Benefits for influenza vaccination appear to outweigh the risk of not receiving it as part of the recommended schedule of immunizations because in February 2008 the CDC began recommending influenza vaccine for all children between the ages of 6 months and 18 years, unless they were allergic to eggs (Stobbs, 2008). Vaccines rarely cause life-threatening or life-changing reactions. (A child is at far greater risk if she is not immunized properly [U.C. Davis M.I.N.D. Institute, 2007; Zamani, 2008]). Risk ranges from common and minor effects to less common and severe effects that can even be life threatening. Benefits to immunization include protection from illness, prevention of disease outbreaks, and prevention of death. It has been found that, when more children were vaccinated with the varicella vaccine, fewer children in early childhood education environments without the vaccination actually got chicken pox (Clements et al., 2001). A child who has not followed the schedule for MMR vaccination is between 22 and 35 times more likely to have measles and spread them than is a vaccinated child (NNii, 2005). Teachers can help eliminate these childhood diseases by requiring up-to-date immunization schedules before children enter care and by educating parents about the need for keeping with the schedule (Tomlin, 2007). They should track the children's records for immunizations that must be updated for compliance to the immunization schedule. The WellCareTracker™, discussed in the text, is an effective tool. Teachers should also have a policy for excluding children from care who are not exempt from immunization.

CHECK*point*: **Why might children be at risk for preventable diseases?**

suggests grouping unimmunized children together and away from the infants in care that are too young for immunizations and from toddlers who may not have finished their immunization schedule. Parents of unimmunized children should be told of this policy if the early childhood education environment decides to follow this recommendation.

The more children in the early childhood education environment who are properly immunized, the less the risk for the spread of childhood diseases (Rose, 2006a). Teachers should also verify their own immunity to childhood diseases and should follow the vaccination schedule for Hib, hepatitis A, and hepatitis B. Staff may not be required by state licensing laws to get certain immunizations such as the influenza vaccine, but they should be given incentives to do so (Rose, 2007a). See Chapter 10 for further details on teacher immunizations.

Key Concept 12.3

Immunizations for Disease Prevention

Immunizations are a major deterrent to disease. In order to be effective, they must be administered according to schedule. Both the children and the teachers in the early childhood education environment should meet the immunization requirements.

12.4 UNIVERSAL SANITARY PRACTICES FOR THE EARLY CHILDHOOD EDUCATION ENVIRONMENT

- **sanitary practices** *practices that remove bacteria, filth, and dirt to cut down on disease transmission.*
- **viruses** *small microorganisms that are produced in living cells and that can cause disease.*
- **otitis media** *infection of the middle ear.*
- **disinfecting** *procedures to eliminate all germs through use of chemicals or heat.*

One of the most effective tools you have to create a healthy environment for the child is to incorporate universal **sanitary practices** to keep the environment as clean and germ free as possible. These protective and preventive actions can greatly reduce risk for infection or disease. Proper sanitary practices can help prevent the spread of **viruses**, bacteria, parasites, respiratory diseases, and **otitis media** common in early childhood education environments (Kotch et al., 2007). Training and education in hygienic practices can reduce the occurrence of diarrhea in children older than 2 years and respiratory illnesses in children younger than 2 years in early childhood education environments (Shope & Aronson, 2006).

Cleaning, sanitation, and disinfection procedures should be the main points of a health policy for a sanitary environment. These procedures should include

- Hand washing
- Diapering
- Toileting
- Cleaning and **disinfecting**

It is very important that a written explanation of the sanitary practice policy be sent home with children so that parents understand that an effort is being made to keep the environment healthy and germ free. Cooperation may also be elicited to encourage children to use these sanitary practices in the home by providing parents with a flyer on correct hand-washing procedures.

Hand Washing

Washing the hands is perhaps the single most important thing the teacher can do to prevent illness personally and to keep it from spreading to and among the children in care (Aronson, 2003) (see Table 12-4). Hand washing can help to interrupt the germ transmission cycle. The use of antibacterial soap has been found to produce a 50 percent decline in both absenteeism and respiratory illness. The use of antibacterial soap does not appear to be harmful nor to make bacteria resistant with its use (Sprouse, 2007). It is essential that the teacher develop the habit of frequent hand washing. Often, when the pace of life is hectic, it is easy to forget that hand washing should be done. If it is developed into a routine and becomes a habit, hand washing will be second

TABLE 12-4
Universal Sanitary Hand-Washing Practices

When:

Both the Child and the Teacher

- Upon arrival at child care
- Before eating or drinking
- After touching a child who may be sick
- After using the toilet or changing diapers
- After sneezing, coughing, or using a tissue
- Before and after playing in water that is used by more than one person
- Before and after playing in sandboxes
- After handling pets

Teacher

- After handling body secretions (vomit, mucus, and so forth)
- Before and after handling or preparing food
- After cleaning
- Before and after giving medication, if applicable
- After cleaning and handling garbage
- After helping a child use the toilet
- Before and after changing diapers
- After handling toys that have been mouthed
- After moving from one care group to another

How:

- Before starting, make sure there is a clean, disposable paper towel available. If a dispenser is used, make sure the paper towel is pulled down and made readily available.
- Use running water that drains. Do not use a stoppered sink or container.
- You must use soap. Liquid soap is preferable because germs can grow on soap bars.
- Use **friction**. Rub hands together for germ removal for at least 20 seconds. Rub between fingers and around nails. It has been suggested that children sing the song "Happy Birthday" twice while washing their hands so enough time elapses for good cleaning.
- Rinse thoroughly in running water. Dry hands with paper towel.
- Turn off faucet with paper towel. Touching the faucet can recontaminate your hands.
- If using a bathroom with a door, use the paper towel to open the door.
- Throw paper towel away.

Adapted from *Control of Communicable and Infectious Diseases: A Manual for Child Care Providers*, California Child Care Health Project.

- **friction** *rubbing together.*

nature and will be done regardless of the pace. When hand washing becomes routine, fewer infections and fewer cases of common childhood diseases that maybe be found in child care, such as common colds, asthma, gastroenteritis, and dermatitis, are reported (Dunder et al., 2007; Green & Lee, 2007a).

The times for routine hand washing shown in Table 12-4 reflect when the teacher should wash hands and help the children wash their hands. By observing this modeling of hand-washing behavior, children can easily follow the teacher's direction. Children can learn to wash their hands correctly if they are presented with interactive experiences when being taught (Tousman et al., 2007). Children who watch their teachers model hand-washing behaviors and then participate themselves can learn at a very early age to wash their hands in the correct manner. Some teachers offer extra helpful tools such as singing a song that lasts the right amount of time for good hand washing to occur. Teacher hand washing should be part of training as well as monitoring the environment. The combination of training and monitoring leads to a very significant decrease in diarrhea in children in early childhood education environments (Holland, 2006). Another issue that could be looked at from a hand-washing viewpoint is the presence of long or artificial nails in the early childhood education environment. Nurses with long or artificial nails were found to cause illness in young babies that they worked with; after they got rid of the nails, the rate of infection and illness decreased (Moolenaar et al., 2000). It has also been suggested that elaborate wrist and hand jewelry should not be used in the early childhood education environment because it too could harbor germs that good hand washing will not catch (Aronson, 2003). It has been found that rings can hide bacteria that cause disease (Trick et al., 2003). Removal of rings should be considered when working in an early childhood education environment.

The same sink should not be used for hand washing after toileting or diaper changing and for hand washing before food preparation or before eating (Harms, Cryer, & Clifford, 2003). The only exception to this would be if children are ready to sit right down after washing their hands. If an adult turns off the faucet with a paper towel and children do not touch the faucet,

Teachers can model correct hand-washing procedures to the children even as they go about their regular duties.

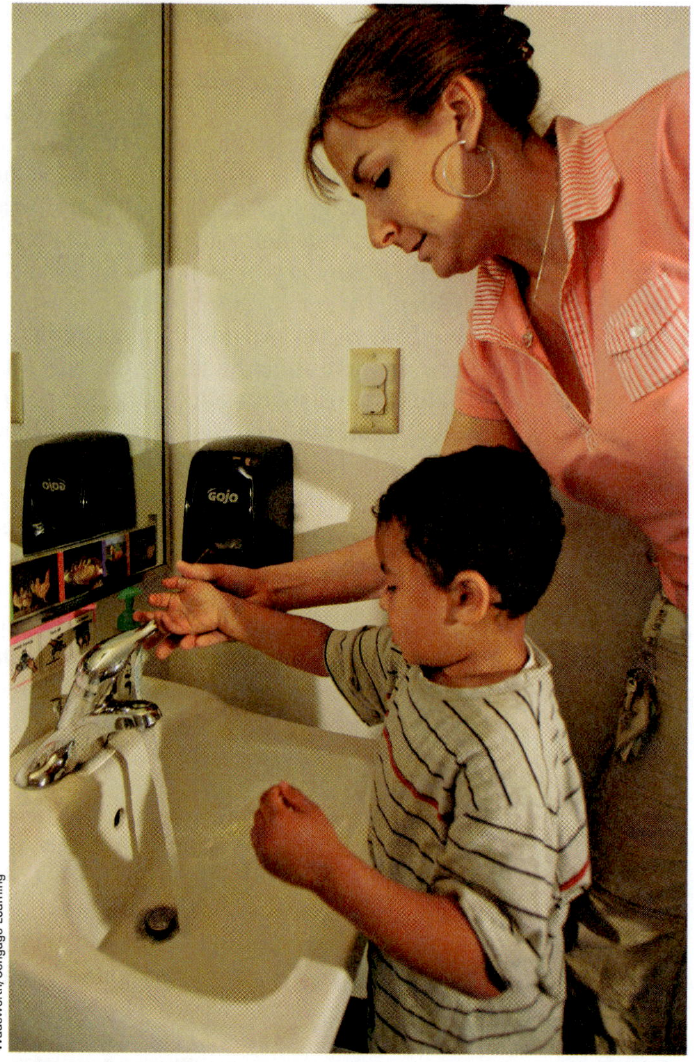

Wadsworth/Cengage Learning

Routine hand washing should be a part of training in the early childhood education center for any child. It is important to have sinks at a child's level, or safe footstools, so the child can comfortably wash.

this is acceptable. Faucet handles have been found to be one of the most contaminated sites in early childhood education environments (Kotch et al., 2007). Child care facilities that have special hand-washing and diapering equipment have been found to reduce disease among children greatly (Kotch et al., 2007).

In 2002, the CDC published recommendations for hand hygiene in health care. These can be translated to the early childhood education environment (Aronson, 2003). The recommendations advocate the use of alcohol-based hand sanitizers in health care. This is less ideal in the early child education environment because of the ingredients in the sanitizers. The use of these types of products will cut down on disease spread, but care should be taken if they are used (Sprouse, 2007); they should be used only in areas where they are inaccessible to children because if swallowed, they are toxic for children. If they are in an area used by children, they should be used only if sinks are not available, such as on a field trip (Allen, 2005). These sanitizers should be used according to the manufacturer's instructions, and the dispenser systems should be checked on a regular basis They should be stored carefully because they are flammable.

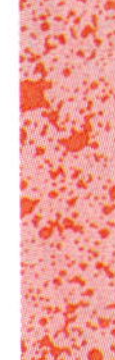

Pause for Reflection

Do you always wash your hands when you should? If not, why? What could you do to encourage yourself and others you know to wash hands when needed?

Diapering

- **fecal contamination** *contamination occurring through exposure to feces.*

Fecal contamination in the early childhood education environment leads to the spread of infection from the carrier to others. Containment of fecal matter, use of disposable changing table pads, use of disposable diaper wipes, proper hand washing, use of disposable gloves, and use of a clean plastic bag for soiled clothes are protective measures that control the risk of contamination and spread of disease. Bacteria can also be spread through urine, and the same protective measures help to manage this risk. Gloves may have small defects, so it is important that hands be washed after changing a diaper, even though gloves may be worn (Aronson, 2003; Harms, Cryer, & Clifford, 2003). Using just a baby wipe is less than ideal because, although it cleans, it does not stop the transmission of disease. Therefore, it is important to remember to wash hands, not just use a baby wipe alone. This is also true for the children. Use of gloves helps to prevent hands from being soiled with urine and fecal matter, but it does not prevent contamination. Teachers should remember that whatever they handle with gloves could be contaminated by those same gloves.

The area where diapering occurs should be isolated and equipped for cleanliness and safety (Table 12-5). A correct procedure for changing diapers should be developed and posted above the diaper-changing area. Following the procedure as well as maintaining a clean and sanitary area to change diapers greatly reduces risk (see Table 12-6). In a recent study, the use of commercially available diaper-changing and hand-washing equipment was experimentally tested to see whether it cut down on the spread of bacteria in this area. In the experimental intervention group, it was found that there were fewer reported diarrhea illnesses and absences in both children and

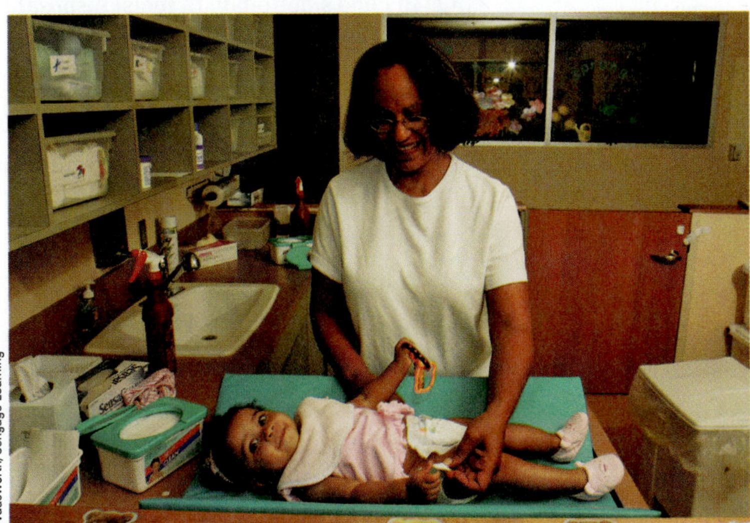

Wadsworth/Cengage Learning

Proper diapering procedures should be followed to avoid the spread of infection. A sanitary diapering area and the use of disposable gloves are examples of proper diapering procedures. What's wrong with this picture?

TABLE 12-5
Creating a Sanitary Diapering Environment

- Use area for diapering only.
- Provide running water to wash hands before and after diapering.
- Put the diapering area as far away from food preparation area as possible.
- Surface should be flat, safe, and preferably 3 feet off the floor.
- Make sure surface is clean, waterproof, and free of cracks. Use disposable covers such as squares, rolls of paper, paper bags, or used computer paper. Throw away immediately after use.
- If a child is holding a toy or other object during the diaper change, it should be sanitized afterward.
- For safety, keep all lotions out of the reach of children. Restrain child. Never leave child unattended.
- Remember, before handling clean diapers or other items, that the gloves are soiled and therefore could contaminate the clean diaper or other objects.

Adapted from *Control of Communicable and Infectious Diseases: A Manual for Child Care Providers*, California Child Care Health Project.

TABLE 12-6
Universal Sanitary Diapering Procedures

- Have area and supplies ready. This includes cleaning and sanitizing the changing table and washing hands properly.
- Put on disposable gloves.
- Pick up child. If diaper is soiled, hold child away from you.
- Lay child down on diapering surface. Remove shoes and socks if necessary to prevent their contamination.
- Remove soiled or wet diaper. If clothes are contaminated, remove them.
- Place disposable diapers in a plastic bag and throw it away in a lined, covered trash can.
- Clean child's bottom with moist disposable wipes. Wipe from front to back, using towelette. Use another towelette if needed.
- Pat dry with paper towel.
- Dispose of towelette and towel in lined, covered trash can with lid.
- Wipe your hands with moist towelette and dispose of it in lined, covered trash can with lid.
- Diaper and dress child.
- Wash the child's hands.
- Remove disposable covering from diaper surface.
- Wash area and disinfect with bleach solution.
- Remove disposable gloves.
- Wash your own hands thoroughly.

Adapted from *Control of Communicable and Infectious Diseases: A Manual for Child Care Providers*, California Child Care Health Project.

teachers (Kotch et al., 2007). The major limitation of this study is the expense of the special commercial equipment, which may be prohibitive to many early childhood education environments. Regardless of equipment, the study shows that increased awareness of sanitation practices in diapering can cut down on diarrhea illnesses in early childhood education environments.

If a child uses cloth diapers, the diapers should be placed in a second plastic bag and sent home with the child. There is too much risk of spreading disease by rinsing or laundering diapers at an early childhood education environment. Also, if the diaper soils the child's clothing, the clothing should be bagged in a clean sealable plastic bag.

If an infant has more than three episodes of diarrhea in one day or if blood or mucus is present, the parent should be notified and a physician should be consulted (Lyles, 2003). Having a medical home for a child makes this a much easier task. When a policy for diapering provides a safe and sanitary method, then illness and disease spread can be reduced.

Toileting

Toileting in a center is easier to control than toileting in a family child care home or the child's own home. The initial risk prevention is to have good supervision. The toileting area should be conveniently located to both indoor and outdoor play space (Gonzalez-Mena, 2004). An adult should accompany children to the toilet and be able to see the child using the facility. If the teacher is alone, then all children should accompany her to the bathroom so that all children can be supervised (Reeves, 2006). The facility should include child-sized toilets and access to sinks with running water. Most centers have child-sized toilets that should be cleaned and sanitized daily. If the toilet is contaminated with diarrhea, it must be cleaned and sanitized immediately. When training children to use the toilet, they should be taught about the importance of washing hands. Instruction in hand washing should be given before and after toileting. Observing the children when they wash their hands will help the teacher know which children need assistance in thorough hand washing. Miller (2003) suggests the use of a hand-washing song to help children wash their hands for the minimum of 10 seconds that is necessary. This

Toileting is a good opportunity to teach children about the importance of hand washing. Some states require that teachers use disposable gloves when helping children with toileting.

TABLE 12-7
Sanitary Procedures for Potty Chairs

- Use gloves.
- Wash child's hands.
- Empty contents into toilet.
- Rinse potty chair with water. This should be in a sink used for no other purpose. If children use it for hand washing, clean and sanitize the sink after toileting.
- Wash chair with soap and water in a utility sink, not a bathroom sink. Empty water into toilet.
- Rinse again and again empty contents into toilet.
- Spray with bleach solution.
- Air dry.
- Sanitize the utility sink.
- Wash hands.

Adapted from *Control of Communicable and Infectious Diseases: A Manual for Child Care Providers,* California Child Care Health Project.

makes the event more fun, and it helps reduce the spread of disease if the hands are washed properly.

Toileting in a family child care home environment often involves a potty chair. The USDHHS, APHA, and the AAP indicate that the use of potty chairs should be discouraged (Reeves, 2006). Ideally, if they are used, each child learning to toilet should bring his own potty chair to the provider, which would decrease the risk of spreading germs. The potty chairs should be stored clean and kept out of the reach of children and away from other surfaces that may have germs. Table 12-7 reviews sanitary procedures for potty chair use.

The use of disposable gloves is necessary to reduce the risk of spreading disease. The teacher should understand that this is just a stopgap measure and is not a substitute for washing hands. Teachers should check the

Wadsworth/Cengage Learning

A standard solution of bleach and water should be used to clean and sanitize the classroom, toy surfaces, and floors. What other surfaces should be sanitized?

requirements of their state licensing agencies, as some require the use of disposable gloves for helping with toileting. Consider the use of nonlatex gloves due to the increasing frequency of allergies to latex.

Cleaning and Disinfecting

The first line of defense against germs in the early childhood education environment that involve spills of body fluid, drainage from wounds, changing tables, counter tops, floors, and other surfaces is cleaning with soap and water followed by the disinfecting process (Gonzalez, 2005). The best way to stop the spread of germs is to both clean and disinfect. Neither is adequate alone. Cleaning gets rid of dirt and some surface germs, while disinfecting rids the surface of the remaining germs through the use of a sanitizing solution. In child care, the most common effective and least expensive sanitizing solution is bleach. According to the CDC's latest standards, liquid bleach should contain a 5.25 percent hypochlorite solution for maximum sanitizing (Hendricks, 2003).

Several strengths of the sodium bleach solution are necessary for disinfecting different surfaces or contaminants. Figure 12-3 shows a general-purpose sanitation mix.

The solution is placed in spray bottles and used in the bathroom, kitchen, and diapering area and on other surfaces and toys. This solution is also used on floors and to clean sleeping mats. See Table 12-8 for frequency of cleaning and disinfecting required in the early childhood education environment.

One area of concern in early childhood education programs is the lack of sanitation in sinks, which allows germs to thrive. Sinks that are used for multiple purposes, such as diapering, toileting, washing hands, food preparation, and brushing teeth, can increase the transmission of fecal-oral bacteria (Kotch et al., 2007). The recommended practice is to have multiple sinks—one for each purpose in each area (such as the kitchen, the bathroom, and the program area) (Kotch et al., 2007; Harms, Cryer, & Clifford, 2003).

For cleaning more infectious items such as blood, blood spills, and body fluids, including vomit, a stronger solution is required. This stronger solution

Cleaning and Disinfecting Sanitizing Solution

- Mix 1/4 cup bleach with hypochlorite in 1 gallon of water or mix 1 tablespoon bleach in 1 quart of water.
- Place in labeled spray bottles out of reach of children in the bathroom, the diapering area, and the kitchen.
- Wash surfaces first with soap or detergent and water.
- Spray on sanitizing solution and allow to air dry.
- Replace solution daily.

FIGURE 12-3
General purpose cleaning solution used in the bathroom, the kitchen, the diapering area, and on toys.

TABLE 12-8
Cleaning and Disinfecting Guidelines

Cleaning and Disinfecting Procedure:

- Clean objects and surfaces with detergent and water first.
- Next apply bleach solution by spraying from bottle or dipping object in bleach solution and allowing it to air dry.

Cleaning and Disinfecting Schedule:

Object or Area	Frequency
Diaper-changing area, toilets, and potty chairs	Clean after every use. Spray with sanitizing solution after cleaning.
Bathroom	Clean thoroughly one or more times daily.
Kitchen	Clean thoroughly one or more times daily.
Play areas	Mop or vacuum daily. Teachers and children remove or replace shoes worn outside if children are infants and toddlers. Remove litter or food immediately. For carpet, vacuum daily. For flooring, mop, cleaning first, then rinsing and sanitizing.
Cribs and cots	Change linen when wet or soiled; otherwise, weekly. Disinfect weekly.
Toys	Clean and sanitize all mouthed toys after each use. Machine wash stuffed toys and all play items at least once a week and when visibly soiled. Sanitize water tables and wading pools after each use. Throw away mouthed play dough or clay immediately. Change frequently. Dress-up clothes in the dramatic area should be laundered weekly. Books, headphones, and computer keyboards should be quickly wiped with an alcohol-based wipe (not a baby wipe) as needed/used.

Cleaning: All-purpose liquid detergents and water are used to remove dirt, urine, or vomit by washing and scrubbing.

Sanitizing: Soap, detergents, and abrasive cleaners are used to remove filth, soil, and a small amount of bacteria. To be considered sanitary, surfaces must be clean and germs must be reduced to a level at which disease transmission is unlikely.

Disinfecting: A solution of bleach and water is used to eliminate practically all germs from surfaces. For normal disinfecting, a general-purpose solution is used. When working with blood or stools from bowel movements, a contamination solution is used.

FIGURE 12-4
Contamination cleaning solution. Use to clean blood, body fluids, and vomit.

Contamination Cleaning Solution

1 tablespoon of bleach with hypochlorite
3/4 cup of water

is shown in Figure 12-4. The contamination cleaning solution is also used for regular cleaning when outbreaks of infectious disease occur.

When a child has soiled her clothing with fecal or bodily fluid, the item should be removed immediately and placed in a plastic bag for the parent to take home and launder. Parents should be informed of this policy when the child enters care. A reminder note should be attached to the soiled clothing bag. Younger children in early childhood environments should always have an extra set of clothes in their cubbies for times like this.

Clothing and hats used for dress-up in play areas should be laundered frequently with bleach. Hats should be sprayed frequently with a disinfectant such as Lysol™. If an outbreak of lice or a skin infection such as scabies occurs, these clothes should be temporarily removed, laundered, and placed in airtight plastic bags for at least two weeks.

Toys that children have mouthed should be picked up immediately after they are discarded or dropped, and placed in a container that is out of children's reach (Smith, 2003). These toys should be later sanitized before going back into the children's toy environment. Toys that cannot be washed or sanitized should not be present in early educational environments (Green & Lee, 2007c). The teacher should always wash hands after handling mouthed toys.

Each child should use his own bedding only (Rose, 2007b). These items should be stored separately in bins or boxes labeled with the child's name. Regular weekly laundering can keep bedding fresh and clean. Never share sheets. If one child uses them, remove sheets before another child uses the same crib. If bedding becomes contaminated with mucus, feces, urine, vomit, or blood, send it home with the child to be washed. Cots or napping mats, cribs and crib mattresses should be covered with nonporous, wipeable surfaces and should be used only by one child or cleaned and sanitized between uses by different children (Green & Lee, 2007c).

When soiled or contaminated items are sent home with the child, a reminder note accompanying the items is an effective communication tool. It will explain to the parents why the item was not rinsed and alert them that they should closely observe their child for illness. The prevention, protection, and control of infectious disease are not always easily understood, but they are very necessary in maintaining a sanitary environment.

It is possible to sanitize the early childhood environment without using bleach (Gonzalez, 2005). Some teachers prefer not to use bleach because they are bleach sensitive or because the solution must be made daily. Alternative solutions include alcohols, phenols, and quaternary ammonium compounds. It is best to read labels as to application and contact time necessary to kill germs and for the safety of the product in relation to children. The teacher should consider the safety aspects of using the product on items children may mouth, and also whether the product would be effective against blood-borne diseases.

Good hand washing and disinfecting of commonly touched surfaces has been proven to reduce illness greatly and promote safety in the early childhood education environment (Shope & Aronson, 2006).

Key Concept 12.4

Universal Sanitary Practices

Universal sanitary practices are some of the most effective risk management tools a teacher can employ to create a healthy environment. A clean, sanitary environment will help curb the spread of germs and infectious diseases. Proper techniques for hand washing, diapering, toileting, cleaning, and disinfecting are the main tools the teacher uses to provide a healthy environment.

12.5 ENVIRONMENTAL QUALITY CONTROL FOR DISEASE PREVENTION

There are certain other areas of the early childhood education environment that may contribute to the spread of disease. These special areas of consideration include water play, play dough, air quality, and contamination.

Water Play

Water play occurs in a container that, if not properly cleaned, can be an environment where germs multiply. If the water becomes warm, it offers a warm, moist place where germs thrive and rapidly multiply. Few measures, including the one below, work for cryptosporidiosis, a diarrheal disease common in child care settings. It is resistant to chlorine so it is tougher to kill than the majority of diseases that are found in child care settings. For optimal use of a water table in the early childhood education environment, follow the water table health tips found in Table 12-9.

Play Dough and Clay

Play dough and clay are also good hosts for germs because they are moist and get warm through frequent contact with children's hands. Safety tips for having play dough and clay in the early childhood education environment are included in Table 12-10.

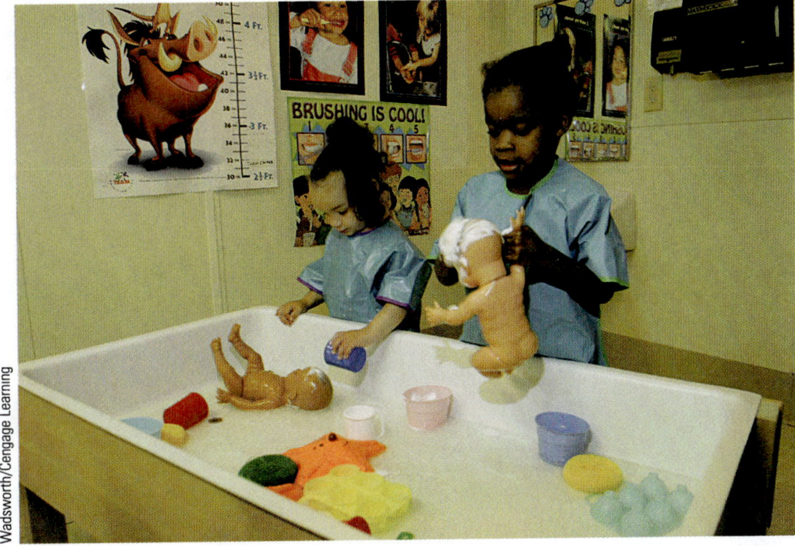

Wadsworth/Cengage Learning

Water play is an engrossing and enjoyable activity for young children, but a playing field for germs is opened up if the table or container is not properly cleaned.

TABLE 12-9
Water Table Health Guidelines

- Clean and sanitize the water table with the general-purpose sanitation mix daily.
- Change water at least daily; more frequently, if it gets warm (over 72°F). Use fresh, cool water.
- Children should wash hands before and after playing in water table.
- Wash water-play toys daily either with general-purpose solution or in the dishwasher.
- Use plastic throwaway items when possible.
- Use an individual water bin for any child with a condition, such as a runny nose, that might spread germs.

TABLE 12-10
Play Dough and Clay Health Guidelines

- Children must wash hands before and after playing with the play dough.
- Do not use scents in play dough, because it encourages mouthing.
- Replace play dough frequently and always throw it away if it has been mouthed or appears dirty.
- Store play dough in the refrigerator.
- Keep clay in a cool, dry place and make sure it is well covered.
- Clean and sanitize tables before and after play dough or clay is used.
- Allow only a small amount of clay at a time so it can be replaced more often and the expense will not be as great.
- Do not use play dough or clay for a day or two if a fecal-oral disease has been identified in the environment.

Wadsworth/Cengage Learning

Play dough is a classroom staple, but health precautions should be taken to make this fun, manipulative molding clay germ free and safe for children.

Air Quality

Air flow in the early childhood education environment is especially important to help control the spread of germs. Crowding of children contributes to poor air quality (Rose, 2007a). If the air is not moving or if there are too many children in one area, the air will not flow as well as it should, resulting in a better environment for germs. Air fresheners do not help air quality but merely mask odors. They may also pose a threat to some children with allergies or asthma and may trigger a reaction. To avoid poor air quality, follow the air quality health guidelines in Table 12-11. If the air in the early childhood education environment is dry and hot due to heating, everyone in care may be more vulnerable to colds and other respiratory problems. Placing a cool air humidifier or vaporizer adds moisture to the air and can reduce the likelihood of illness (Ware, 2004). Air should be kept as free of triggers for asthma as possible.

TABLE 12-11
Air Quality Health Guidelines

- Keep air temperature cool; under 72°F helps prevent disease spread.
- Circulate fresh air as much as possible—open windows as daily weather permits.
- Make sure children get outside to breathe fresh air daily, weather permitting.
- Heating and cooling equipment should be checked several times a year and should be cleaned every three months. Any filters should be replaced when serviced to prevent buildup of molds and dust.
- Arrange your environment so that there is plenty of open space. This discourages the spread of germs.
- Keep at least 3 feet of space between cribs and cots in the sleeping area.
- Follow guidelines of indoor space per child so that there is no crowding.
- When placing children on cots, alternate placing heads and feet toward the front. This helps avoid airborne transmission.

TABLE 12-12
Health Guidelines for Disease Prevention

- Minimize the number of people who handle contaminated materials.
- Use disposable gloves and paper towels to clean up spills from diarrhea, blood, urine, or vomit.
- Clean and disinfect surfaces involved with contamination sanitation mix.
- Dispose of cleanup materials, disposable gloves, and so forth in a plastic bag that is covered, tied, and placed in an outside trash can immediately.
- If any contaminated materials soil the child's or teacher's clothes, they should be changed immediately.
- Wash hands immediately.
- Place contaminated clothing in a plastic bag with tie. Double-bag it in another plastic bag and send it home with child or teacher to be laundered at home.

Contamination in Child Care

Special precautions should be taken to minimize the effects of contaminants such as blood, vomit, urine, and loose stools or diarrhea in the early childhood education environment. For proper health precautions see Table 12-12.

Key Concept 12.5

Environmental Quality Control for Disease Prevention

There are special areas of need for environmental quality control for infectious disease spread found in the early childhood education environment. These areas include water tables, play dough and clay, air quality, and contamination. Using preventive strategies and techniques for these items can help the teacher control the spread of infectious disease.

12.6 IMPLICATIONS FOR TEACHERS

Teachers must use a number of tools to prevent the risk of infectious disease spread. These tools include education and role modeling, cultural competence, and supervision to make sure protective measures are carried out.

Education and Role Modeling

Education is one of the best preventive tools a teacher has to help control the spread of infectious disease in the early childhood education environment. The effort to prevent the spread of germs and disease should be a cooperative venture. Teachers should model proper health behaviors. Children should be taught to perform proper health practices. Parents must understand the need for these practices and help children remember to carry these out at home so they get into the habit of good hygiene.

Wadsworth/Cengage Learning

Hand washing at scheduled intervals throughout the day can be a fun activity and teaches the children good hygiene.

Children should focus on several things to play their role in prevention. Good hand-washing techniques at the right times is the most important tool for children to prevent the spread of disease. This can be done in a number of ways. Modeling the hand-washing techniques is important.

Modeling hand washing should include

- Showing
- Helping
- Telling
- Feedback

When the teacher is washing her hands or helping a child to wash his, the teacher should talk about what is happening and why. Reinforcing the conversation and hand-washing method with feedback is important for the teacher to see that the child is grasping (1) why hands are being washed; (2) when hands should be washed; and (3) how hands should be washed.

Reminders should be given throughout the day at times when hand washing is a must. A poster or line drawing showing proper hand-washing procedures placed by the hand-washing sink offers a visual reminder when the teacher is not present.

To ensure a healthy environment, one of the teacher's most important tasks is to help children form the good hygiene habit of hand washing. If hand washing is made a fun task, the children will more likely participate and remember when and how to use the hand-washing techniques. Teachers who develop or use songs that focus on hands while in circle groups or at the sink at hand-washing times may make it easier for some children to grasp good hand-washing behaviors. Using books that focus on hands or good hygiene will also help. There is also a good website called Henry the Hand: Champion Handwasher that focuses on four principles of hand washing. This website is located at http://www.henrythehand.com/.

For Families

Parents have a significant degree of responsibility in preventing the spread of disease in the early childhood education environment where their children attend. Parent education is critical in the prevention of outbreaks such as chicken pox, Hib, and meningitis. Parents can make sure their children are immunized according to schedule. They can reinforce the hygiene practices that children learn at school, and they can make sure not to send their children to school when they are ill. Some of the supportive behaviors that are essential on the part of the parents may require some special effort on the part of the teacher.

Cultural Competence

Cultural competence may be necessary, especially when dealing with the issue of immunization. A parent may be unaware of the need for immunizations or may lack access to immunizations. Recent immigrant families may not be aware of the need for immunization or tuberculosis screening, or may even feel these are unnecessary. Some children from culturally diverse or immigrant, low-income working families may not have ready access to health care (Flores, Abreu, & Tomany-Korman, 2006). These families have higher rates of infectious diseases as well as chronic illnesses (Duarte & Rafanello, 2001). Resistance to participation in immunization and screening may also result from culturally defined acceptable behavior or language difficulties (Carballo & Nerukar, 2001). It is important for the teacher to help the parents understand how vital it is to follow the immunization schedule and get regular health care for their children. Teachers can provide resources to help these families connect with public funds for low-cost health insurance for low-income families. It is important for the teacher to help the parents understand how vital it is to follow the immunization schedule. Following this schedule is critical to the child's own health as well as that of others in the early childhood education environment (Omer et al., 2006).

Supervision

Children from many different backgrounds may come to the early childhood environment. It is up to the teacher to supervise the environment so that children come into the program as risk free as possible. There are five basic commandments for infectious disease control that must be monitored by the teacher.

- Prevent the spread of disease
- Require and monitor immunizations
- Report some illnesses to public health officials and to parents
- Exclude some children
- Be prepared to deal with an ill child, if necessary

Key Concept 12.6

Implications for Teachers

The effort to prevent the spread of infectious disease is a cooperative venture. The teacher can educate and model behaviors to the children. Modeling will also help the parent reinforce these behaviors at home. The teacher must be especially culturally sensitive about the need for immunizations and help the parents understand the necessity of a current immunization schedule for children. The teacher must supervise the early childhood education environment to make sure sanitary practices are carried out.

CHAPTER SUMMARY

Health policies for controlling infection maintain health and prevent some illnesses in children and adults present in the early childhood education environment. Two practices that contribute to this are good hygiene and sanitary practices. Checking the immunization schedule is another preventive practice. Food safety and storage are other practices that help manage the spread of disease. The four methods of infectious disease spread should be understood and proactive measures should be taken to reduce the spread.

TO GO BEYOND

Additional resources for this chapter can be found by visiting the book companion website at www.cengage.com/education/robertson. This supplemental material includes chapter objectives, internet exercises, reflection questions, quizzes, web links, glossary and flash cards, case studies, frequently asked questions, downloadable forms and tables, curriculum supplements, more reality checks, additional key concepts, references, and more.

Chapter Review Critical Thinking Applications

1. Discuss the four methods of transmission of infectious diseases. Relate these methods of transmission to sanitary practices that could be performed to prevent spread.
2. Debate the question of whether children with lice should be allowed to stay in care or school or whether they should be excluded from care or school.
3. Examine the importance of immunization schedules. How much have these schedules changed in recent years, compared to when the students were young children?
4. Discuss how a teacher would handle the acceptance of a child into care who has not been immunized.

As an Individual

1. Observe hand-washing practices in an early childhood education environment. Next, observe hand-washing practices in a public restroom. Compare and contrast these two environments. Were universal hand-washing procedures used at appropriate times? Record your observations.
2. Research and report on the programs in your state and local area that help low-income children and their families gain access to health care.

As a Group

1. Discuss environmental quality control in the early childhood education environment. What further measures might be taken to improve the health of that environment? Discuss the impact of children's cots or sleeping pads being placed close together.

2. In small groups of four to five students, design health policies for (1) lice, (2) long nails on teachers, and (3) hand washing.
3. Research the topic of the present controversy over immunizations. Divide the class in half and debate the issue. What are your conclusions? Should a child be allowed in care without immunizations?
4. Discuss how diversity in early childhood education environments might affect health policies or health practices. List measures that may help culturally diverse families understand these policies and practices.

Case Studies

1. Chloe came into care on an emergency basis, and her parents did not fill out the health history completely. She has been in care for a month, and the family child care provider still does not have the immunization record. What should be done?
2. As a teacher, you have been trying very hard to keep your environment as healthy as possible. You try to wash your hands at the appropriate times, change diapers properly, and clean on schedule. You notice, however, that the 2-year-olds seem to be passing colds back and forth and there have been several cases of scabies. What might you be overlooking?
3. You work in an early childhood education facility that has several rooms. During waking hours, the children are spread throughout the center. However, during nap time they are placed on cots in the largest room, for convenience purposes. There is hardly any room between the cots to even walk. How would you approach your director about this issue and how it affects air quality?
4. You are a teacher in a second-grade classroom. It is winter and children seem to be coughing and catching colds. What universal procedures and strategies could you use in order to keep the germs from spreading?

CHAPTER 13

Supportive Health Care in Early Childhood Education Environments

After reading this chapter, you should be able to:

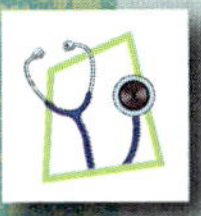

13.1 Health Policies

Describe and discuss health policies for the identification and management of childhood communicable diseases.

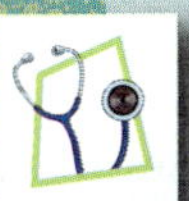

13.2 Identification of Infectious Diseases

Describe the methods and means of identifying childhood infectious diseases for early interventions and prevention of disease spread.

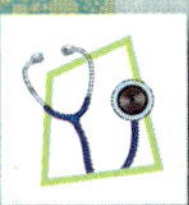

13.3 Managing Infectious Diseases

Describe the methods and practices for managing childhood infectious diseases for early identification and prevention of disease spread.

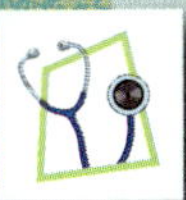

13.4 Managing Care for Mildly Ill Children

Summarize and indicate the importance of policies and protocols for care of mildly ill children in early childhood education environments.

13.5 Children with Chronic Illnesses

Describe and discuss special considerations for caring for children with chronic illnesses.

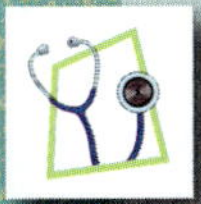

13.6 Optimizing Health in Early Childhood Education Environments

Describe and discuss the inclusion of a health consultant in the early childhood education program and the advantages of having a medical home for every child.

13.7 Implications for Teachers

Indicate the need for and importance of education, observation, and supervision for early intervention to manage childhood communicable diseases in the early childhood education environment.

13.1 HEALTH POLICIES

Policies for health care in early childhood education are essential to keep children as healthy as possible, to prevent disease spread, and to care for mildly ill children. The following are indicators of the need for good health care policies for child care:

- Children under age 3 years are more vulnerable to infectious diseases because their immune systems are not fully developed (Roder, Borte, & Herbarth, 2006). As children grow older they become more immune to common diseases (Green & Lee, 2007).
- The chances of diseases being transmitted depend on three things: (1) the characteristics of the children in the group; (2) the nature of the disease; and (3) the health policies and practices of the child care facility (Kendrick, Kaufman, & Messenger, 2002).
- Children in early childhood education environments are more likely to have a respiratory illness than those children who are at home (Hagerhead-Engman et al., 2006). But by age 3, the rate of illness was found to be the same in both settings (Shope and Aronson, 2006).
- Reported cases of pertussis or whooping cough are at a 40-year high (Knight, 2007). Teachers should understand that whooping cough and some other childhood diseases can be very serious and may even require emergency assistance (Tomlin, 2007).
- Early childhood education environments should have an exclusion policy and know the difference between what should be excluded and what should not (Copeland et al., 2006; CCHP, 2006; Leonard, 2007).
- If the state allows medication to be administered in early childhood education environments, there should be a plan to ensure that medications are given safely and correctly (Calder, 2004).
- Accepting a child with a chronic condition into care requires planning by the family and teacher so that the child's needs will be properly met and risk will be reduced (NCCCHSRC, 2005a; Rose, 2006a). Teachers often serve as gatekeepers of children's health (Sailors, 2004; Tomlin, 2007). Children with asthma and their caregivers or teachers can be taught asthma education and can reduce emergency department visits for asthma (Coffman et al., 2008).
- Formal written policies for infection control and training in infection control practices have proven to be valuable (Brady, 2005). Control measures are indispensable (Nesti & Goldbaum, 2007).
- Dealing with health in early childhood education is complex, and a health consultant could help a teacher optimize management of the health of children in care (NAEYC, 2004; Farrer, Alkon, & To, 2007). A medical home for all children in care is beneficial, and that medical home should work with early childhood education teachers to help identify children with chronic diseases or special needs (Benedict, 2008; AAP, 2002, 2006).

Health care in early childhood education environments is a complex issue requiring many considerations. A teacher must be able to identify the signs and symptoms of illness and parasite infestations. The identification process helps put an exclusion policy into operation. The exclusion policy enables the teacher to separate those children who are very ill or contagious and must leave the early childhood education environment from those children who are not contagious or very ill and may remain. The exclusion policy should include how to communicate with parents (CCHP, 2006). If children are not excluded from the early childhood education environment, the teacher must manage the care for mildly ill children without putting others at risk. Chronic illness in children requires continued treatment and vigilance for things that might trigger responses or cause symptoms to worsen. Children with special health care needs such as those with chronic illness should have policies created for them that provide the most protective and healthy environment.

Parents and teachers have to work together to help identify and manage risks to the health of the children in care. When a teacher uses a health consultant and encourages a medical home for every child, the health environment in care will be optimized. Teachers must supervise the environment to intervene and minimize risk and to help maintain the health of all of the children in their care.

To provide the early childhood education environment with the optimum health care, there should be policies for the following:

- *Identification of childhood infectious diseases:* practices for recognizing signs and symptoms of infectious disease for early intervention.
- *Management of childhood infectious diseases:* practices for managing childhood infectious diseases, including exclusion.
- *Managing care for mildly ill children:* strategies and practices for managing the care of mildly ill children.
- *Children with chronic illnesses:* understanding coping skills and strategies needed to provide the most protective and preventive environment for these children in early education programs.
- *Optimizing health care in early childhood education environments:* rationale for using a health consultant and encouraging a medical

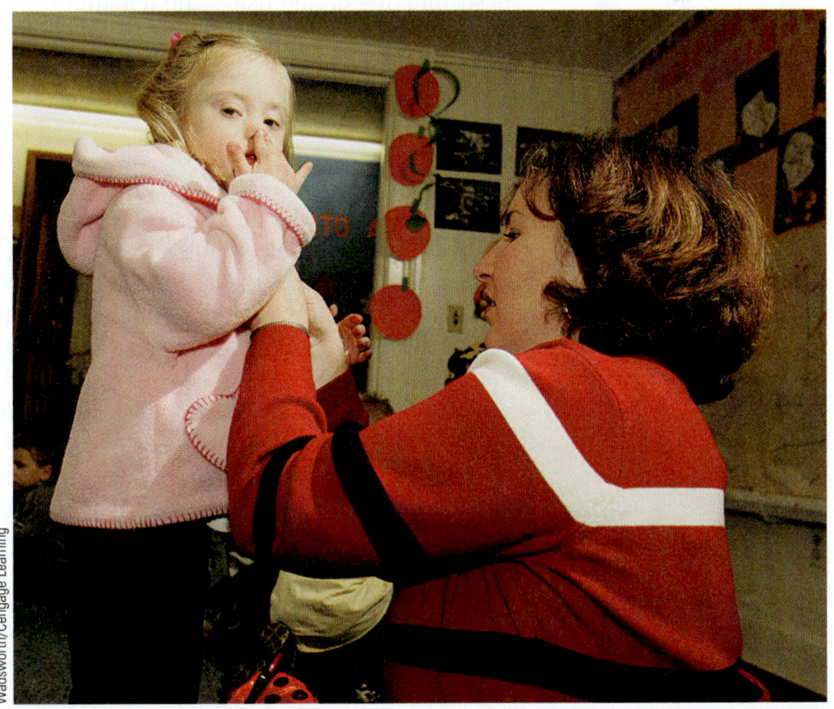

Wadsworth/Cengage Learning

A program's health policy should specify that, if a child exhibits signs and symptoms of a contagious disease or infection, the parents must be notified and an authorized person contacted to come pick up the child.

home for all children in care to maximize the health of everyone in the early childhood education environment.

- *Implications for teachers:* methods and practices to provide minimum risk and maximum protection for health in the early childhood education environment through education, observation, working with families, and supervision.

Key Concept 13.1

Health Policy

Managing health care in the early childhood education environment may be a challenge to the teacher because it includes a number of aspects. The teacher must learn how to identify infectious diseases and know when to exclude children from care. She must understand how to prevent the spread of infectious disease and protect the health of the children in care. The teacher should be prepared for dealing with chronic illness. The use of a health consultant and the encouragement of a medical home for all children will help optimize health in early childhood education.

13.2 IDENTIFICATION OF INFECTIOUS DISEASES

The first line of defense for illnesses in the early childhood education environment is the control of infectious diseases through good hygiene and sanitary practices.

Identifying Infectious Diseases and Illness in Children

The second line of defense is the teacher's ability to identify illness as quickly as possible (Bradley, 2003; Green & Lee, 2007). Many illnesses may be present several days before signs or symptoms appear. Guidelines for helping a teacher recognize signs and symptoms provide a barrier to the spread of an infectious disease.

Signs and Symptoms of Illness. Children may show few signs of illness, then suddenly appear to be ill. The teacher has to observe for certain signs and symptoms that will help identify an ill child (Figure 13-1). Observation can help determine whether the illness is the type that may spread rapidly and necessitate excluding a child from care. Some signs and symptoms are serious, and others should have special consideration because they might signify an oncoming illness.

Conducting a daily health check as the child arrives is the first time in the day to watch for caution signs for health or illness. The health policy for the early childhood education environment should state that any child who exhibits infectious disease signs and symptoms be excluded. These signs and symptoms should be thoroughly understood and the policy should be strictly enforced. (Table 13-5 presents the conditions for exclusion.)

The child who appears to be below the normal level of mood or activity should be monitored for further symptoms. Signs or symptoms may not be exhibited in the first stages, yet the child may indeed be ill.

FIGURE 13-1
Head to Toe Signs and Symptoms of Disease or Infection

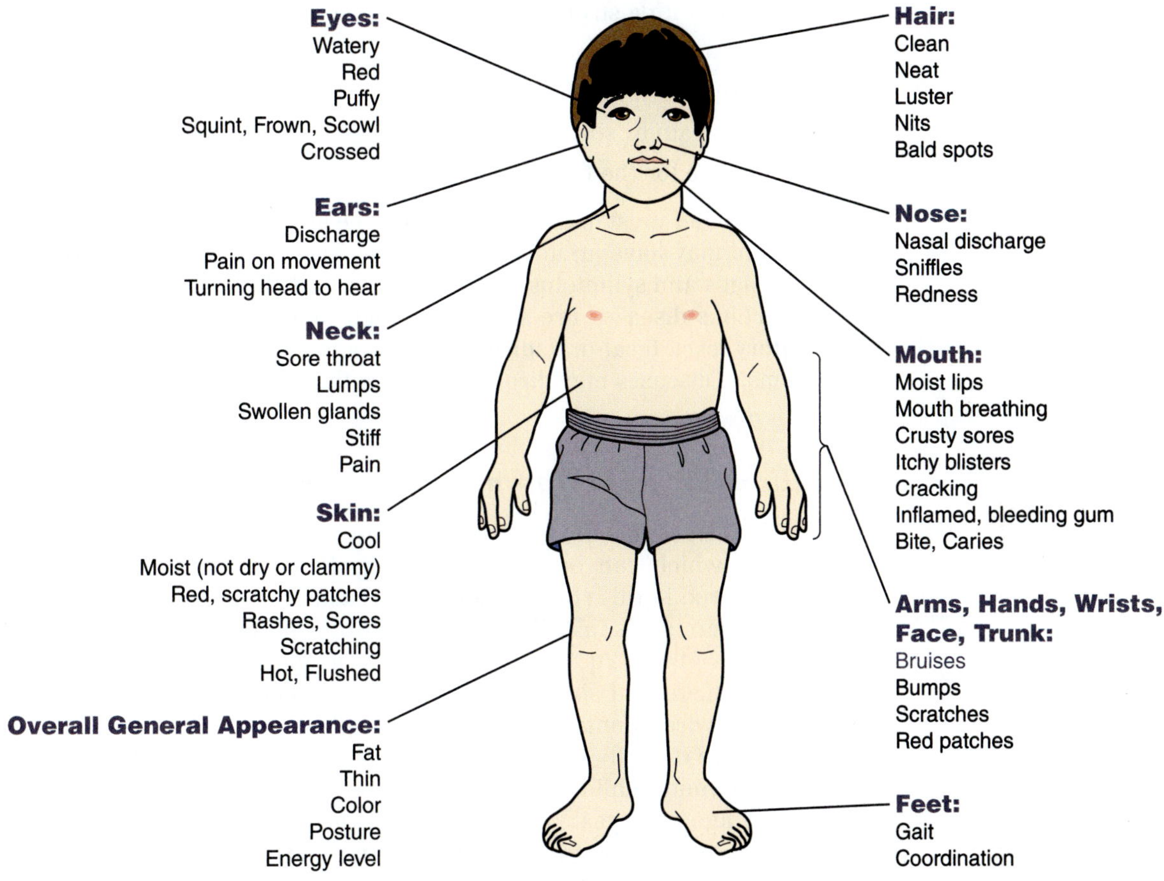

The following are some common primary indicators of whether a child is ill:

- Unusual crankiness or listlessness
- Complaint of sore throat or difficulty swallowing
- Runny nose (clear discharge indicates allergies; green or yellow indicates infection)
- Complaint of stomachache or cramping
- Diarrhea
- Complaint of headache or earache
- Red, watery, or draining eyes
- Unusual rashes or spots
- Infected skin lesions

More serious indicators of illness that must have *immediate attention* include the following:

- Fever
- Vomiting

- Severe coughing
- Breathing problems
- Urine with a strong odor
- Unusual drowsiness
- Excessive crying
- Neck pain or stiff neck
- Seizure for the first time

The teacher must determine whether the child is just under the weather or is ill and may have an infectious disease. The teacher can identify illness with the signs and symptoms listed in Tables 13-1 through 13-4.

Infectious diseases are spread through four methods of transmission: respiratory tract, fecal-oral, direct contact, and blood contact. The signs and symptoms of diseases may directly relate to the method of transmission.

Infectious Diseases Transmitted Via the Respiratory Tract

Respiratory tract infectious diseases range from a mild cold to bacterial meningitis, which can be life threatening. Pertussis or whooping cough has reappeared in this country and is increasingly reported (Knight, 2007). Cases of tuberculosis in children adopted internationally have been found (Mandalakas et al., 2007). Tuberculosis was found in 12 percent of the children studied, and some of these children may attend early childhood education environments. Many of the respiratory tract transmitted diseases that are described in Table 13-1 affect all age groups. RSV illness is common in young children and can cause serious problems for children under the age of 2 years 9 months (Abrams, 2007b; NCCCHSRC, 2007). Other diseases are also more common in children, such as Hemophilus influenza type B (Hib), pneumonia, and influenza, for which there are now preventative immunizations.

Whooping cough is on the rise, which the teacher should keep in mind, although it is not common (AAP, 2004; Omer et al., 2006). Teachers should also be prepared to look for unusual illness such as Avian Flu because stopping the spread of it quickly can avoid a pandemic (Rose & Nevraumont, 2006).

Infectious Diseases Transmitted Through the Fecal-Oral Route

Diseases spread by the fecal-oral route are caused by bacteria, parasites, and viruses that grow and spread in the intestines. The stool is the main vehicle of disease spread to others. Early childhood education environments that have infants and toddlers in diapers are especially at risk for these types of diseases. The best course for preventing the spread of disease is always to use special precautions. Table 13-2 relates how to identify and manage diseases transmitted through the fecal-oral route. Hepatitis A and rotavirus are good examples of fecal-oral diseases that appear to be linked to child care; vaccines for these diseases are now recommended for children. Another common childhood disease related to fecal-oral transmission

TABLE 13-1
Identification and Management of Diseases Transmitted Via the Respiratory Tract

Disease	Signs/Symptoms	Teacher's Role
Colds	Sneezing, runny nose, stuffy nose, watery eyes, sore throat, fever Most contagious 2 to 3 days before and 3 to 5 days after symptoms appear	Wipe runny noses; use gloves. Wash hands often. Do not share food, drink. Disinfect mouthed toys. Teach children to cover mouth when coughing. Ventilate environment to keep germs at a minimum
Influenza	Fever, chills, headache, drowsiness, muscle aches, nausea, vomiting, sore throat, lethargy	Follow procedures listed under Colds. Should be immunized with flu vaccine. Call parent if fever or vomiting is present.
Strep throat	Painful, scratchy throat, tender/swollen glands, fever, spots on throat	Wash hands often. Do not share food, drink. Disinfect mouthed toys. Call parent if fever is present or child is unable to swallow. Can lead to rheumatic fever Notify all parents if strep throat is present. Be alert to outbreak. Exclude child from care until 24 hours after antibiotic treatment has begun and no fever is present.
Scarlet Fever	Same as above Red, sandpapery rash on trunk, neck, groin Red tongue, flushed cheeks	Wash hands often. Do not share food, drink. Disinfect mouthed toys. Call parent if fever is present. Be alert to outbreak. Exclude child from care. Notify all parents.
Chicken Pox	Fever, runny nose, blistery rash, cough	Exclude if chicken pox is suspected until doctor confirms. Readmit after the sixth day or after rash is crusted and dry Follow procedures listed under Colds. Children in care should be immunized.
Fifth Disease (Parvovirus)	Headache, body ache, sore throat, fever, chills, lacy rash	Follow procedures listed under Colds. If pregnant, report to doctor.
Sixth Disease (Roseola)	High fever, lacy rash	Follow procedure listed under Colds.

(continues)

TABLE 13-1 *(Continued)*
Identification and Management of Diseases Transmitted Via the Respiratory Tract

Disease	Signs/Symptoms	Teacher's Role
Meningitis	Fever, lethargy, poor feeding, fine red rash, stiff neck, headache, irritability, vomiting, decreased consciousness	This is considered a medical emergency that can lead to brain damage or death. Exclude if suspected. Exclude adults and children exposed by close contact. Must begin rifampin or ciproflozone antibiotic treatment in 24 hours. See doctor immediately if symptoms appear. Report to local health department. Notify all in contact with child immediately. Follow procedure listed under Colds.
Hib (Haemophilus Influenza type B)	Same as meningitis, earache, rapid onset of difficult breathing, red/swollen joints, red/purple area of skin	Report to local health department. Notify all in contact with child immediately. Follow procedure listed under Colds. All should be immunized. See doctor immediately if symptoms appear.
Measles	Brownish/red rash beginning on face, fever, white spots in mouth, runny nose, cough	Exclude if suspected. Allow to return 6 days after rash appears. Report to public health. Notify parents. Wash hands often; use gloves. Do not share food, drink. Disinfect mouthed toys. All children in care should be immunized.
Rubella (German measles)	Joint pain, red rash, enlarged lymph glands	Follow procedure listed under Measles. If teacher is pregnant, notify doctor. All children in care should be immunized.
Mumps	Fever, at least one swollen salivary gland near jaw, earache, headache	Exclude if suspected. Allow to return after 9 days. All children in care should be immunized.
Whooping Cough	Coughing spells with whoop sounds, vomiting, runny nose	Exclude if suspected. Notify local health department. Notify parents. Allow to return 5 days after antibiotic therapy has begun or 3 weeks after onset of cough. Do not share food, drink. Disinfect mouthed toys. Wash hands often; use gloves. All children in care should be immunized.

(continues)

TABLE 13-1 *(Continued)*
Identification and Management of Diseases Transmitted Via the Respiratory Tract

Disease	Signs/Symptoms	Teacher's Role
Otitis media (ear infection)	Fever, difficulty hearing, pain, drainage from ear	Wash hands often; use gloves. Do not share food, drink. Children with frequent ear infections should be monitored for speech or language difficulties.
Tuberculosis	Cough, fever, weight loss, or no symptoms present	Exclude anyone with active TB. Allow to return when no longer contagious. Notify the health department. Notify parents. All children in care should be tested before entrance to care, then every two years.
Pnemococcol Pneumonia	High fever, cough, shortness of breath, rapid breathing, chest pain, nausea, vomiting, headaches, muscle aches, fatigue	Follow procedure listed under Colds. All should be immunized. Can cause meningitis and bacteremia.
Bronchiolitis	Begins with stuffy, runny nose, cough and low fever. Can progress to rapid, shallow breathing, rapid pulse, lethargy	Follow procedures listed under Colds. Elevate the child's head for sleeping.
Bronchitis	Fever, cough, headache, difficulty breathing, wheezing, tightness in chest	Flu and pneumonia vaccines can prevent some infections. Follow procedures listed under Colds. If it is bacterial bronchitis, child should be excluded and returned when fever is gone and child feels good
Croup	Noisy difficult breathing, low fever, cough that sounds like a barking seal	Follow procedures listed under Colds.
RSV (respiratory syncytial virus)	Runny nose, fever, cough (often severe), bronchiolitis, wheezing, rapid breathing Children with asthma may be more prone to this disease Can lead to pneumonia Most contagious one or two days before symptoms appear and as long as two weeks after	Exclude only if child does not feel well. Infection spreads rapidly, so use procedures listed under Colds. Disinfect toys child has played with.

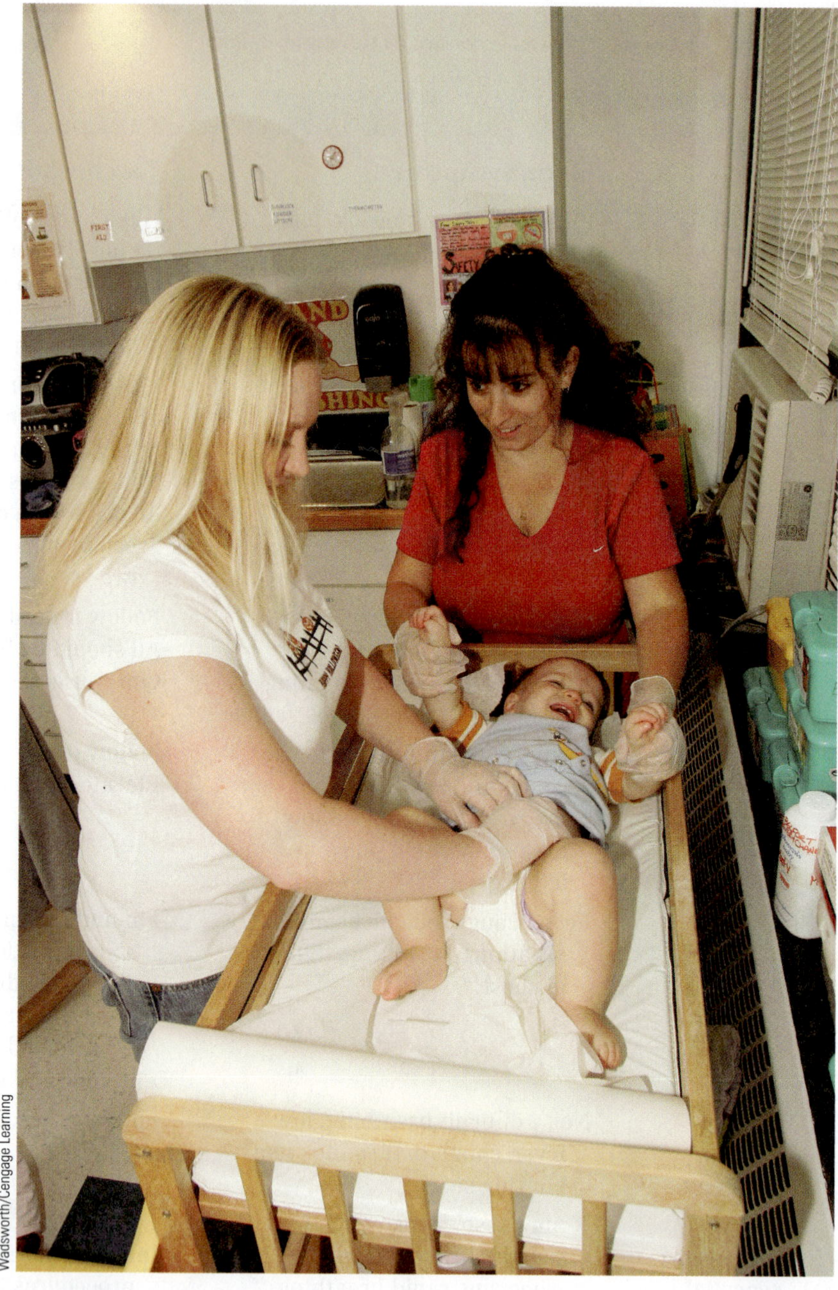

A clean and sanitary diapering area, as well as disposable gloves, is essential in preventing fecal-oral transmission of disease.

is norovirus, often referred to as the stomach flu but actually viral gastroenteritis, which is very contagious (Calder, 2007). One more recent fecal-oral disease linked to child care is cryptosporidiosis, which is a diarrheal disease associated with tap water and swimming in public pools (Turabelidze et al., 2007).

Infectious Diseases Transmitted by Direct Contact

Diseases transmitted by direct contact are spread from the secretions of one person that penetrate through the skin or mucous membranes of another person. These germs may be in the form of bacterial infections, parasites, or

TABLE 13-2
Identification and Management of Diseases Transmitted Through the Fecal-Oral Route

Disease	Signs/Symptoms	Teacher's Role
Giardia	Diarrhea, gas, poor appetite, weight loss, cramping, bloating	Frequent hand washing according to schedule. Use sanitary procedures and gloves during diapering and toileting and before handling food. Exclude child if diarrhea is uncontrolled. Allow child to return once diarrhea is gone.
Shigella	Diarrhea, fever, pain, mucus or blood in stool, vomiting, headache, convulsions	Wash hands following schedule. Use sanitary procedures and gloves during diapering and toileting and before food handling. Exclude if fever is present. Call parent immediately if convulsion occurs.
Salmonella	Stomach cramps, diarrhea, fever, fatigue, poor appetite	Wash hands following schedule. Use sanitary procedures and gloves during diapering and toileting and before food handling. Notify local health department and all parents. See doctor if diarrhea occurs.
Hepatitis A	Fever, jaundice, nausea, poor appetite, dark-brown urine	Wash hands following schedule. Use sanitary procedures and gloves during diapering and toileting and before food handling. Exclude child; allow him to return one week after onset if fever is gone. Notify local health department and all parents. All exposed persons should have immune globulin treatment.
Campylobacter	Fever, vomiting, stomach cramps, diarrhea or severe bloody diarrhea	Wash hands following schedule. Use sanitary procedures and gloves during diapering and toileting and before handling food. Notify local health department and all parents. See doctor if diarrhea occurs.
E. coli	Diarrhea or bloody diarrhea	Wash hands following schedule. Use sanitary procedures and gloves during diapering and toileting and before handling food. Cook all hamburger meat to 155°F. Notify local health department and all parents. Exclude child until diarrhea is gone and stool specimen is negative.
Cocksackie virus (hand, foot, and mouth disease)	Fever; stomach pain; sore throat; rash with tiny blisters on hands, feet, and mouth; diarrhea	Wash hands following schedule. Use sanitary procedures and gloves during diapering and toileting and before handling food. Notify parents. Notify staff.

(continues)

TABLE 13-2 *(Continued)*
Identification and Management of Diseases Transmitted Through the Fecal-Oral Route

Disease	Signs/Symptoms	Teacher's Role
Pinworms	Anal itching, worms that crawl out during sleep or no symptoms present	Follow procedure listed for Cocksackie virus. Each child should have own crib, mat, or cot. Exclude child until first dose of medicine has been given; check with family to make sure second dose is taken in two weeks.
Rotavirus	Fever, nausea, vomiting, and watery diarrhea Fever and vomiting usually stops after two days Diarrhea may continue for five to seven days	Exclude child if diarrhea cannot be contained by diaper or toilet use. Child can return after diarrhea stops. Notify parents. Notify health department only if there is an outbreak. Wash hands following schedule. Follow universal/standard precautions for diapering and toileting. Clean and disinfect surfaces.
Cryptosporidiosis	Diarrhea may come and go for up to 30 days	Exclude child until diarrhea has stopped. Instead of disinfection with bleach, use a 3–6 percent concentration of hydrogen peroxide and clean surfaces and objects daily. Leave disinfectant on surfaces for 20 minutes. Disinfect high chairs, tabletops, and toys more frequently. Notify parents.
Norovirus	Fever, nausea, vomiting, and watery diarrhea Fever and vomiting usually stops after 1–2 days Diarrhea may occur for 1 to 2 days	Notify health department only if there is an outbreak. Exclude child if diarrhea cannot be contained by diaper or toilet use. Child can return after diarrhea stops. Notify parents. Notify health department only if there is an outbreak. Wash hands following schedule. Follow universal/standard precautions for diapering and toileting. Clean and disinfect surfaces.

viral infections. Contact may be made directly through the infected or infested skin areas or by touching an infested article of clothing, a brush, or bed linens. Conjunctivitis or "pink eye" is probably the most common direct contact infection found in early childhood education environments, and it is highly contagious (CCHP, 2007; Reeves, 2007). There has been recent concern about MSRA because of its resistance to antibiotics. It is usually spread through direct contact with hands, skin, or secretions from a wound or the nose (Rose, 2006b, 2007). The teacher should provide protective measures to prevent the spread of these diseases. Two methods of protection through identification and management are offered, as shown in Table 13-3.

TABLE 13-3
Identification and Management of Infectious Diseases Transmitted by Direct Contact

Disease	Signs/Symptoms	Teacher's Role
Conjunctivitis (pink eye)	Mucus in eye, watery eyes, red/pink eyes, painful eyes, red eyelids, itchy eyes	Keep eye wiped free of discharge. Always wash hands after wiping. Teach children to wipe eyes and wash hands. Clean toys well. Have child see doctor. Exclude child only if white or yellow discharge is present. Allow child to return 24 hours after start of antibiotics. Notify parents and staff.
Impetigo	Red/cracking/oozing pimples, scaly rash, often on face or a sore that will not heal	If suspected, wash area and cover rash with a bandage or gauze. If child scrapes or cuts another area, clean thoroughly. Follow good hand-washing procedures. Have child see doctor. Exclude child until oozing stops. Follow sanitary cleaning schedule. Notify parents and staff.
Ringworm (Tinea)	Flat, growing, ring-shaped rash, often scaly; may be in between toes, on scalp, or on body	Keep environment clean, cool, and dry. Wash hands thoroughly. Follow sanitary cleaning schedule. Have child see doctor. If more than one case is in care, notify parents and staff.
Head Lice (see Reality Check on p. 453)	Lice (sesame seed-sized insects) on scalp or hair, nits (eggs) behind ears or nape of neck	Learn to identify nits and regularly check children's scalps (see Figure 13-2). Notify parent with handout concerning procedures. Machine wash all possibly infested items using hot water. All nonwashable items go in dryer for 20 minutes. All other items placed in sealed plastic bags for 30 days or in freezer for several days. Soak all combs and brushes for one hour in bleach solution and wash daily.
Scabies	Very itchy red bumps or blisters, often between toes or fingers, head, neck, feet	Wash and dry all items contacted by the child 72 hours before outbreak; use hot cycle wash and dry. Vacuum play area carefully and dispose of bag, if there is one. Have child see doctor. Child may return after treatment. If a serious problem exists, all children and teachers need treatment. Notify parents.

(continues)

TABLE 13-3 *(Continued)*
Identification and Management of Infectious Diseases Transmitted by Direct Contact

Disease	Signs/Symptoms	Teacher's Role
Cytomegalovirus (CMV)	Often no symptoms, fever, swollen glands, fatigue, jaundice	Always wash hands after contact with urine, saliva, or blood. Do not share food or drinks. Do not share utensils or glasses. Do not kiss children on mouth. Have child see doctor. Can cause problems for pregnant teachers; notify doctor if pregnant.
Herpes simplex (cold sores)	Fever; painful, small blisters on lips, mouth, or gums; may ooze	If blisters are oozing and child bites or is drooling, exclude child until sores are crusted over. Do not share food, utensils, or glasses. Do not kiss children on mouth. Wash hands often. Follow sanitary cleaning schedule.
Methicillin-resistant staph aureus (MRSA)	Skin infections like boils, pimples, spider or insect bites, or infected wounds	Exclude child until oozing stops, and is dry. Have the child see doctor. Hand washing is the most effective method of prevention. Cover infected wounds with clean bandages and keep covered until healed. Wear nonporous gloves when changing bandage. Follow sanitary cleaning schedule. Notify public health department, parents, and staff.

FIGURE 13-2
Here are the relative sizes of the three forms of lice compared to a penny. (From the CDC website at http://www.cdc.gov/lice/head/factsheet.html)

Bloodborne Infectious Diseases

Infectious diseases are spread through the blood when a person's blood containing the infectious organism enters the bloodstream of another person. This usually occurs if the infected blood comes in contact with broken skin or mucous membranes such as the inside of the nose, mouth, eyes, anal area, or sex organs. The two diseases that are transmitted in this manner are hepatitis B and HIV/AIDS. These viruses may be present without any symptoms. It is important that all blood and body fluids contacted in the early childhood education environment be treated as if they were contaminated. Prevention of these diseases is critical. All blood spills should be cleaned up immediately and the area disinfected.

All surfaces should be thoroughly disinfected with the bleach solution for contaminated items. If the teacher is aware that another adult or child in the early childhood education environment has hepatitis B or HIV/AIDS, then the stronger solution should be used in all cleaning and disinfecting tasks. Table 13-4 lists blood-borne infectious diseases.

TABLE 13-4
Identification and Management of Blood-Borne Infectious Diseases

Disease	Signs/Symptoms	Teacher's Role
Hepatitis B	Fever, loss of appetite, nausea, jaundice, pain in joints, skin rash	All present in care should be immunized. All blood and bodily fluids should be cleaned up immediately and treated as if contaminated. All disposable items with blood should be thrown out in plastic bags, then placed in covered trash cans. Everyone washes hands often. Do not share personal items that could be contaminated. Send home contaminated personal clothing with instruction for parents to wash them with bleach and hot water. Discourage aggressive behaviors. Children infected with hepatitis B who demonstrate behaviors such as biting, have no control over bodily secretions, or exhibit other risky behaviors must be supervised closely. If this is not possible, the child may have to be excluded from the early childhood education environment. Consult with health department and health consultant. If someone is bitten by an infected person, contact doctor.
HIV/AIDS	Failure to grow and develop, enlarged lymph nodes and glands, frequent infections, illness	Follow procedures as in hepatitis B except for immunization. Protect those with HIV or AIDS from infectious disease outbreaks by exclusion; allow to return when outbreak is over. Maintain confidentiality of child with HIV or AIDS. Provide staff with information.

Disease Note: There is another childhood disease for which the cause is unknown called Kawasaki disease. Children of Asian descent are most likely to have it, but it can affect young children of all races. The symptoms include a fever that lasts for several days, a rash—often in the groin area—red eyes, bright red swollen lips, "strawberry" spots on tongue, swollen hands, feet, and lymph nodes. It is important to catch this disease early and refer the child to a physician because long-term consequences can occur if the disease is not dealt with quickly (Minich et al., 2007).

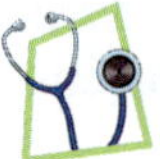

Key Concept 13.2

Identification of Infectious Disease

It is an important task of the teacher to be able to identify infectious diseases. Teachers must have a base of knowledge to recognize signs and symptoms of infectious diseases. They must be able to identify symptoms that are serious for the child and that indicate the presence of a contagious disease.

13.3 MANAGING INFECTIOUS DISEASES

Teachers who use universal sanitary practices and can recognize and identify signs and symptoms of illness protect the environment and prevent disease from spreading. An additional way to provide management of infectious diseases is to require that everyone involved in the early education program be immunized for those infectious diseases that have vaccines and immunization schedules (Zamani, 2008) (see Table 12-3 in Chapter 12). Children's records should be kept current and checked for compliance on a regular basis. The same process should be performed for staff. No one should be hired or should care for children if they do not comply with all of the required immunizations in Chapter 10 (*Exposure to Infectious Diseases*) on page 382.

Certain symptoms in children, such as fever, may not necessarily indicate an illness. A fever may be a result of too much activity, warm weather, teething, or the body overheating due to other circumstances. If the child does not appear to be ill, a fever may not be a problem. The teacher must learn how to take a temperature, how to read it, and how to evaluate whether it is a serious indicator of illness (see Figure 13-3).

The teacher who recognizes serious symptoms knows when to call a parent and when to exclude the child from the early childhood education environment. This is an issue because it has been reported that less than 30 percent of early childhood education teachers are familiar with the

FIGURE 13-3
Guide to thermometers.

Mercury	Digital	Tympanic
	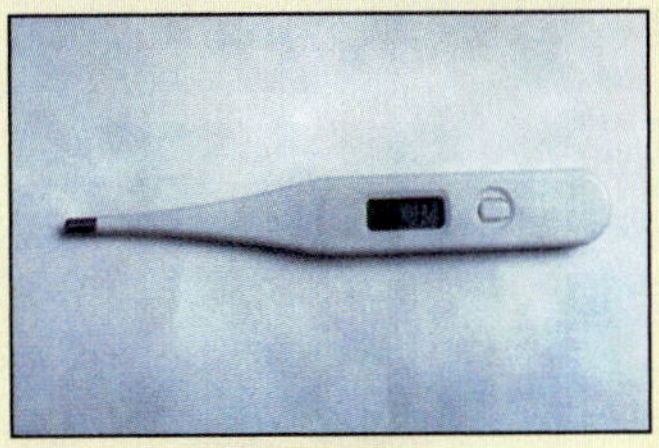	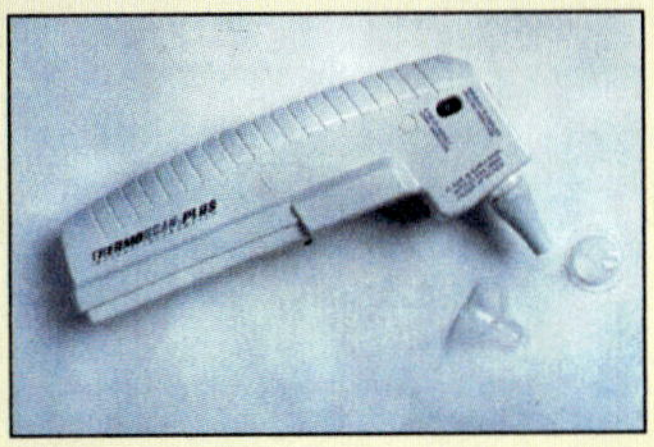
Positives • Lowest cost • Accuracy	**Positives** • Easy to read • Beeps when ready • Temperature reading is recorded digitally	**Positives** • Quick reading • Easy to use with fussy children
Cautions • Hard to read • Delicate • Child must be still	**Cautions** • Child must be still • Battery powered	**Cautions** • Must be placed correctly in ear canal for accurate reading • Battery powered • Highest cost
Methods A. Shake until mercury line falls below 96 F (30.6C). B. Clean with soap and water or alcohol. Rinse with cool water.	**Methods** A. Clean with soap and water or alcohol. Rinse with cool water. B. Switch on (it beeps at child's highest temperature).	**Methods** A. Place new plastic covering over end. B. Set for rectal or oral temperature equivalent. C. When small window reads "ready," position the end gently into the ear canal and press the start button. After one second, a digital readout of the child's temperature will appear on the small window.
Rectal: (children under 3 yrs) 1. Coat bulb with petroleum jelly. 2. Place child stomach down. 3. Insert bulb end first 1 1/2 inches into anal canal.	**Rectal:** Use with nonpetroleum lubricant (K-Y jelly).	
Oral: (children 5 and older) 1. Slowly insert thermometer under tongue. 2. Child closes lips for 2–3 minutes.	**Oral:** Place far under tongue for one minute.	
Underarm: (any age, any type—oral or rectal) 1. Snugly bury bulb under armpit for 3–4 minutes.	**Underarm:** Keep tight under arm.	

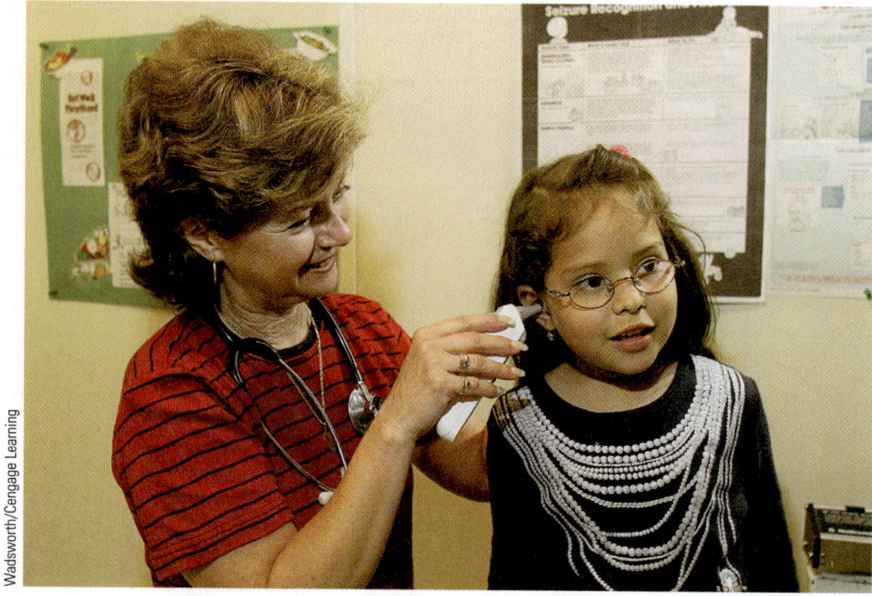
Teachers should have the training and proper equipment to take a child's temperature if necessary.

Wadsworth/Cengage Learning

AAP/APHA guidelines for exclusion (Copeland et al., 2006; Copeland, Duggan, & Shope, 2005). Teachers were more likely to exclude than is necessary and might be more likely to exclude due to perception of risk (Shope & Aronson, 2006). The ability to identify serious symptoms and know exclusion guidelines will help the teacher determine when to notify parents that children in care have been exposed to an infectious disease. Parents can monitor children for further signs and symptoms. Children who need medical attention should go to the doctor immediately. Certain infectious diseases must be reported to the local public health department. This information is available at the health department that has jurisdiction over the area in which the early childhood education environment is located.

When a child shows some signs of illness, the teacher should observe the child and write down the symptoms. Do not draw conclusions. Report measurable facts, such as "Joanna has a temperature of 101°F and looks flushed." If the symptoms are mild and do not affect the child's ability to participate, continue observing the child, and go on with regular activities.

Exclusion

An exclusion policy should be carefully created for the early childhood education environment. This policy should be given to both teachers and parents and should also be posted. It is much easier to enforce a policy that is widely known beforehand. One of the reasons for exclusion would be that the early childhood education environment cannot provide the care and comfort an ill child would need. A child also might not feel well enough to engage in normal activities. And any child who shows symptoms that are on the list of reasons for exclusion should be sent home (AAP & APHA, 2002).

As previously discussed, many children have been unnecessarily excluded (Shope & Aronson, 2006). This is often due to the part of a policy that would exclude children who have fevers but do not show any other symptoms. Fever by itself is rarely a condition for exclusion (AAP & APHA,

2002; Dailey, 2006). The exception to this would be infants from 7 weeks to 4 months of age with a rectal temperature of 101°F or a temperature taken in the armpit of 100°F (Sears, 2003). Any child with a fever of 105°F should have the parents called and see a physician immediately (AAP & APHA, 2002). Use of newer types of thermometers, such as a tympanic thermometer that measures temperatures in the ear, can be a more accurate tool for taking a temperature. Figure 13-3 shows these types of thermometers. If a child has a fever with no other signs, the parent should still be notified. The decision as to what to do should be made with the parent and the child's physician, if possible (Shope & Aronson, 2006).

Another reason for exclusion may exist. If a child in a family child care, center program, or elementary school is without immunizations, for whatever reason, and that child becomes exposed to an infectious disease, she may be excluded until the incubation period has ended and it is established that she does not have the disease. This exclusion is important because it has been found that unimmunized children are as much as 35 times more likely to catch diseases such as measles than those children who have had proper immunizations (NNii, 2005). This exclusion policy should be made clear to the parents of the unimmunized children when they enter the school. Several recent outbreaks of measles can be traced to unimmunized children who spread these diseases at school, at the doctor's office, and in public places.

If a child shows symptoms that are serious or that indicate a high risk of contagion, the child should be isolated from the rest of the children in care (Sailors, 2004). The teacher should set aside an area that will allow for isolation. Once serious symptoms are recognized, the parents should be notified immediately (Dailey, 2006). If the parents cannot be reached, there should be backup or emergency contacts in the child's permanent health file who can be called next. The teacher should ask the parent on a regular basis whether the emergency information is still current. While the child waits for the parent or other emergency contact person, it is important to reassure the child.

Shelly was a teacher at a church center preschool that also provided infant/toddler care. There were several older students who had not been immunized. Grace, one of the unimmunized students, had an older brother, Erik, who had gone to visit their grandmother in another state and came home exposed to the measles. A few weeks later he got them. Shelly felt badly, but she told Grace's parents that it was unfair to the other children at the preschool to let Grace stay and potentially expose the children at the preschool to a measles outbreak. Grace would have to stay home until all potential exposure was over. This was the school policy on unimmunized children, and Shelly and her director felt they had to protect the other children, particularly those who were under a year old and hadn't had all their vaccinations. This move, although difficult, was the right thing. In the period that Grace was out, no one came down with the measles except for Grace. However, at Erik's school, in their neighborhood, and at Grace's physician's office, a number of children had been exposed and a mini-epidemic of measles was reported in their area. By having an exclusion policy for these unimmunized children, Shelly and her director prevented a real problem.

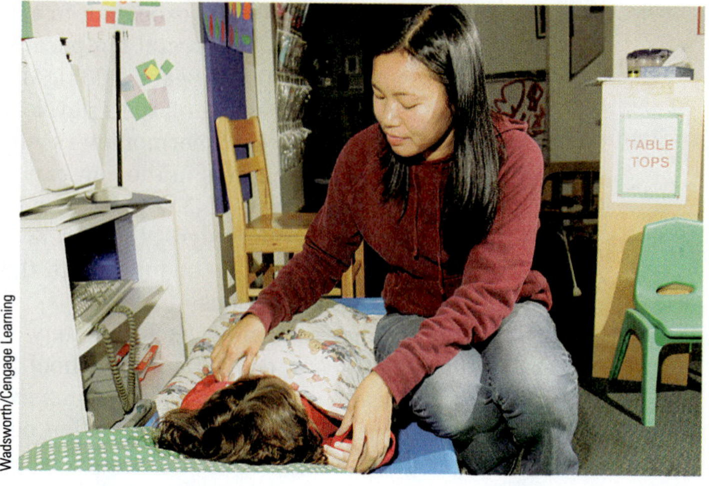

Wadsworth/Cengage Learning

Sick children who are isolated from the group need a comfortable place to rest and, if possible, the company and reassurance of a teacher until the child's parents or emergency contacts arrive.

In addition to any serious signs or symptoms of illness, conditions such as uncontrolled diarrhea, a yellowish tint to the skin, and discharge of the eyes also indicate the need to isolate the child immediately and call the parent.

Table 13-5 indicates the guidelines for exclusion of ill or infected children. It relates the type of illness or disease, gives the signs and symptoms, and describes the conditions for return to the early childhood education environment. These guidelines are a major tool for the teacher to manage the spread of infectious disease in the early childhood education environment and are the basis for the health policy for exclusion.

Adults in the early childhood education environment must also be consideraed for exclusion. If a teacher has any of the signs or symptoms in Table 13-5, he or she should also be excluded from participating in care and return only when the conditions for return are met.

TABLE 13-5
Guidelines for Exclusion of Ill or Infected Children

Illness or Infection	Sign or Symptom	Return
Temperature	Oral temperature of 101°F or more; rectal temperature of 102°F; should be accompanied by behavior changes or other symptoms	Until doctor releases child to return to care
Symptoms of severe illness	Unusual lethargy, irritability, uncontrolled coughing, wheezing	Until doctor releases child to return to care
Uncontrolled diarrhea	Increase in number of stools, water, and/or decreased form that cannot be contained in a diaper or underwear	Until diarrhea stops
Vomiting illness	Two or more episodes in 24 hours	Until vomiting stops and child is not dehydrated or doctor determines illness not infectious

(continues)

TABLE 13-5 *(Continued)*
Guidelines for Exclusion of Ill or Infected Children

Illness or Infection	Sign or Symptom	Return
Mouth sores with drooling	—	Until condition is determined to be noninfectious
Rash	Rash accompanied by fever or behavior change	Until doctor determines it is noninfectious
Conjunctivitis	White or yellow discharge in eye(s) accompanied by eye pain and/or redness around eyes	Until 24 hours after treatment has begun
Head lice, scabies, or other infestations	Infestation present	Until 24 hours after treatment has begun; no remaining lice on hair or scalp
Tuberculosis	Cough, fever, chest pain, coughing up blood	Until doctor or health official allows child to return to care
Impetigo	Rash-blister to honey-colored crusts; lesions occur around mouth, nose, and on chin	Until 24 hours after treatment has begun
Strep throat	Fever, sore throat, throat drainage, and tender lumph nodes	After cessation of fever or 24 hours after antibiotic treatment
Chicken pox	Sudden onset of slight fever, fatigue, and loss of appetite followed by skin eruption	Until 6 days after eruption of rash or until blister eruption has dried and crusted over
Whooping cough	Severe, persistent cough	Until 5 days after antibiotic treatment to prevent infection
Mumps	Tender/swollen glands and/or fever	Until 9 days after onset of gland swelling
Hepatitis A virus	Fever, fatigue, loss of appetite, abdominal pain, nausea, vomiting and/or jaundice	Until 1 week after onset of illness or as directed by local health department; immune serum globulin should be administered to staff and children who have been exposed
Measles	Rash, high fever, runny nose, and red/watery eyes	Until 6 days after onset of rash
Rubella	Mild fever, rash, swollen lymph nodes	Until 6 days after onset of rash
Unspecified respiratory illness	Severe illness with cold, croup, bronchitis, otitis media, pneumonia	Until child feels well enough to participate
Shingles	Lesions	Until doctor allows child to return to care or if child can wear clothing that covers lesions
Cryptosporidiosis	Diarrhea	Until diarrhea no longer present
Herpes simplex type 1	Clear, painful blisters	Until lesions that ooze, involving face and lips, have no secretions

When a child is excluded from care, there are several things the teacher must do. The parents should be provided with information on the infectious disease that caused the child to be excluded; this is usually in the form of a letter or handout. The information includes the exclusion policy for that disease, the period of time the disease lasts, and the conditions for return to the early childhood education environment. The teacher should remove and sanitize any toys the ill child has been playing with or mouthing. Make sure hands are carefully washed and that the hand-washing policy is strictly enforced. The illness and any teacher actions should be documented and added to the child's health record.

Information on how to care for the disease or condition should also be included. For example, if the child has lice, the information given to the parent would include consulting the physician for the type of shampoo to use, how often to use it, and what else must be done to rid the child's home of lice so that the process does not repeat itself.

The teacher should discuss the return-to-care policy for that particular disease or condition at the same time. Parents like to know the time parameters of a child's illness, if possible, so that necessary work or backup care arrangements can be made.

Notification of Public Health Officials

A number of infectious diseases must be reported to the local health department so they can track the disease for patterns of outbreak. This helps to prevent the spread of infectious illnesses in the community. The types of disease typically requiring reporting are those that can spread rapidly and may cause serious illness. Table 13-6 gives a list of infectious diseases that most health departments want reported. It is also a good idea to notify the health

TABLE 13-6
Checklist of Commonly Reported Childhood Infectious Diseases

CHECK FOR:

- ☐ Chicken pox
- ☐ *E. coli*
- ☐ Giardia
- ☐ Hepatitis
- ☐ Hib (haemophilus influenza type B)
- ☐ Measles (rubeola)
- ☐ Meningitis
- ☐ Methicillin-resistant staph aureus (MRSA)
- ☐ Mumps
- ☐ Polio
- ☐ Rubella (German measles)
- ☐ Salmonella
- ☐ Shigella
- ☐ Tuberculosis
- ☐ Whooping cough (pertussis)
- ☐ AIDS

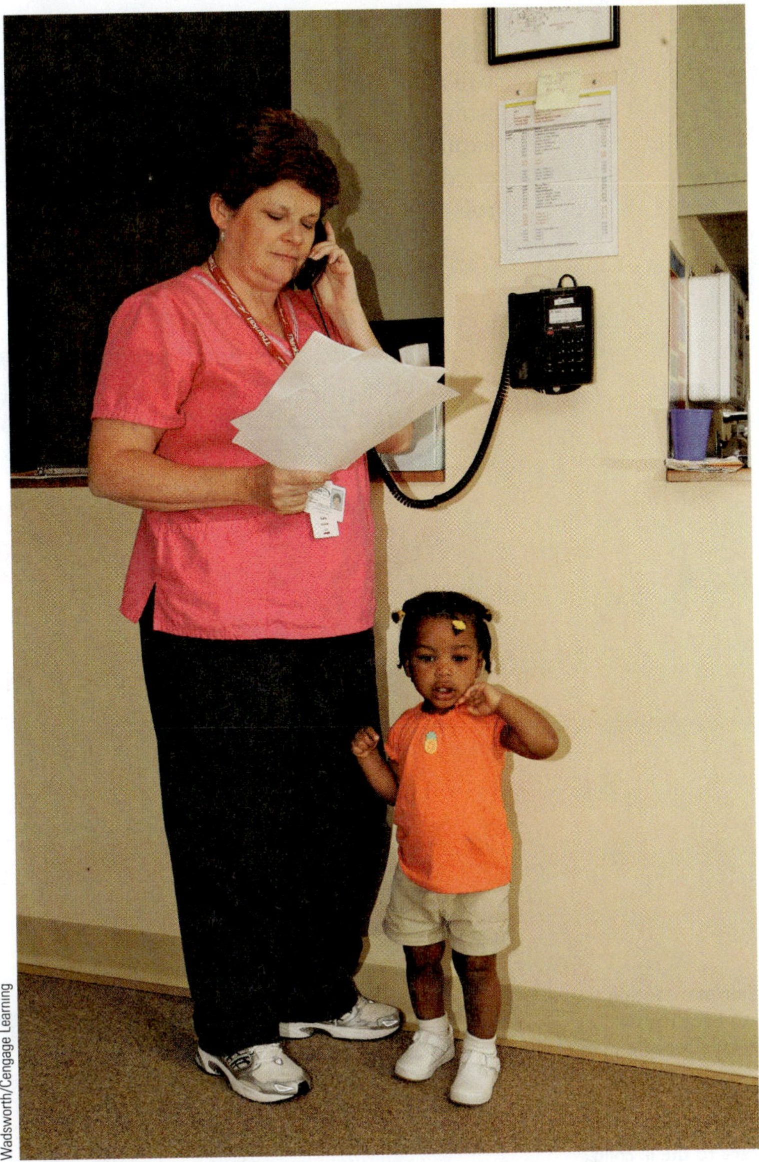
Parents need to be called when children are too ill to stay in care, and health officials need to be notified if a child has a communicable disease.

Wadsworth/Cengage Learning

department if a large number of cases of an infectious disease not requiring reporting occurs at the early childhood education site.

The teacher should be familiar with the reporting procedures of the local public health department. The teacher who is the on-site health advocate should be the person to contact the health department.

Notification of Parents

It is important to notify all families in case of infectious disease occurrences that will cause exclusion or will require a follow-up by the parents. This notification provides them with information such as signs, symptoms, and incubation period.

Letting parents know ahead of time about exclusion policies, for example, by placing them into the parent handbook, is also beneficial. It is much easier to handle the management of ill children if these communication guidelines are in place (CCHP, 2006; Nesti & Goldbaum, 2007).

If the infectious disease is serious and is one that has preventive measures, such as hepatitis A, the teacher should notify the parents (Brady, 2005). This will allow the parents to take the child to the family physician, who may administer a course of treatment. It is critically important for the parent of a child exposed to a serious infectious disease to understand the need for taking the child to a physician. The teacher must make sure that parents understand the role they play in the prevention of disease and preserving the child's health.

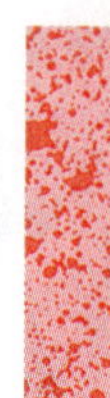

Pause for Reflection

How would you handle a situation in which a parent shows up with an obviously ill child and tells you that she has to go to work because she has a presentation to give that her job depends upon?

Key Concept 13.3

Management of Infectious Diseases

The role that the teacher plays in managing infectious diseases must be clearly perceived. The first line of defense is the use of sanitary procedures for hand washing and the use of gloves. The next step is to make sure immunizations are current for everyone in the early childhood education environment. The teacher must understand the procedures and policies for exclusion from and return to the early childhood education environment. The teacher must recognize when to notify the public health department and when to notify the parents of children in care.

Wadsworth/Cengage Learning

The teacher must decide whether to keep the mildly ill child in care, based on the risks to the child, the staff, and the other children in care and the ability of the teacher to provide care to the ill child.

FIGURE 13-4
Three questions to ask to determine whether exclusion is appropriate.

Three Questions

1. Is it a highly infectious or communicable disease?
2. Does the child feel well enough to participate?
3. Can the teacher provide the mildly ill child adequate care?

13.4 MANAGING CARE FOR MILDLY ILL CHILDREN

A number of tools will help the teacher make the decision as to whether to care for a mildly ill child. The most effective tool for managing care for mildly ill children are three questions that the teacher should ask (AAP & APHA, 2002) (Figure 13-4).

Three Questions

The first question a teacher should ask is: *"Is the child's infectious disease highly infectious or communicable at this time?"*

There are certain childhood infectious diseases that do not pose a health threat. Some of these may be viral diseases that are no longer contagious once the symptoms appear, or the infectious disease might be one that is not highly contagious. For example, colds are very common in young children (Zamani, 2005). Most children average 6 to 10 colds in the period of a year. Ear infections are not easily spread and therefore should not cause a child to be excluded from care. The teacher should be familiar with those diseases that are not easily spread and that will allow the child to participate in care.

The decision-making process proceeds to the next step once it has been established that the infectious disease is not highly communicable or does not pose risk to others in care. The question, *"Does the child feel well enough to participate in the early childhood education environment?"* addresses the issue of whether the child feels well enough to be in care.

Families are busy, and parents may have deadlines or have difficulty missing work. It may be tempting to take a child who is ill but not contagious to school. The daily quick health check is an effective tool for the teacher to help prevent this from happening. Parents must understand their responsibility to keep a child who does not feel well at home.

A child-centered approach focuses on the child's individual needs.

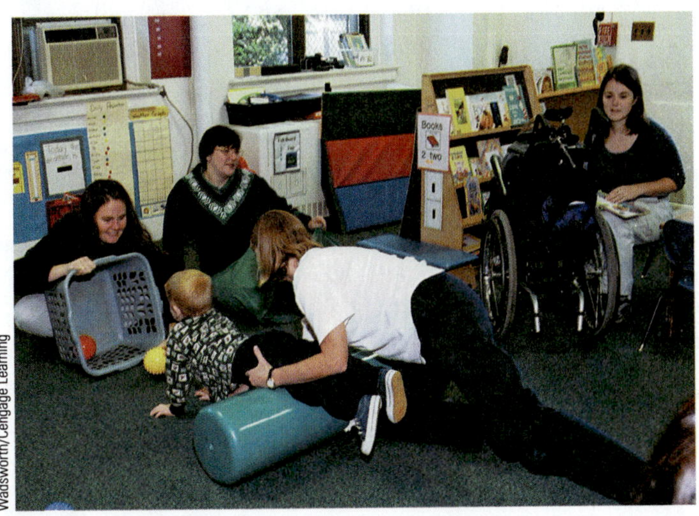

Wadsworth/Cengage Learning

The final question in the decision-making process is, *"Can the teacher provide the mildly ill child adequate care?"* This question addresses several issues:

- Is there a place for the child to rest or play quietly?
- Is there a teacher who can be responsible for caring for the mildly ill child?
- If not, are the parents willing to pay extra for care so that the teacher can hire a helper?

There may be a number of additional tasks that have to be performed, and the teacher should agree to provide care for the mildly ill child only if the quality of care is consistent with that usually provided in the early childhood education environment.

If the answers to any of the three questions indicate that the teacher would have difficulty caring for the child, the parent must take responsibility for caring for the ill child. There may be an alternative care site that specializes in caring for mildly ill children. Contact the local resource and referral agencies for information.

Special Considerations for Care of Mildly Ill Children

If the decision to care for the mildly ill child is made, the teacher should be prepared to provide the necessary degree. Table 13-7 provides a checklist of strategies that will help the teacher meet the needs of the mildly ill child.

If the illness requires the administration of medications, there are special procedures that should be followed. In some states, administering medication is prohibited. Teachers should check with the local licensing agency. Figure 13-5 shows how easily children can mistake medication for candy and how it is important that an adult be the one to dispense it to a child without comparing it to candy. Table 13-8 gives specific instructions that should be followed (Palmer, 2005). The most common errors with medications in the

TABLE 13-7
Care Checklist for the Mildly Ill Child

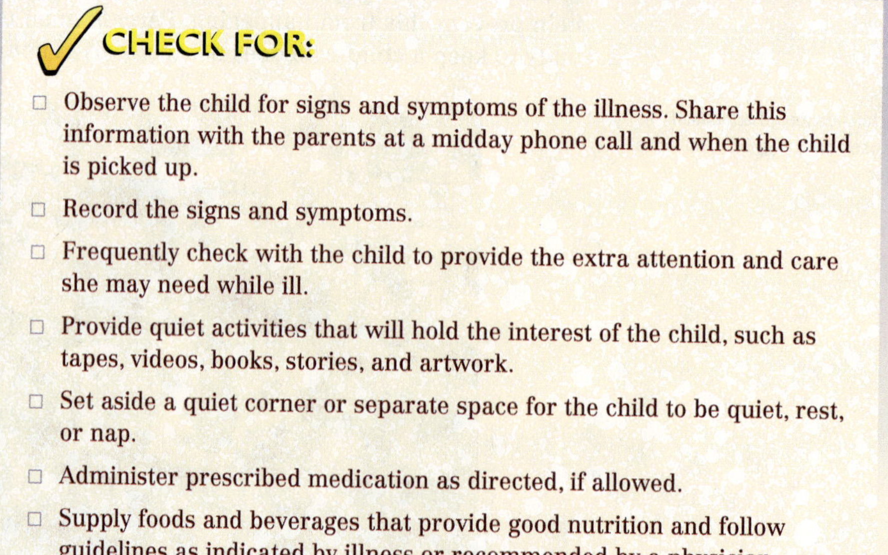

CHECK FOR:

- ☐ Observe the child for signs and symptoms of the illness. Share this information with the parents at a midday phone call and when the child is picked up.
- ☐ Record the signs and symptoms.
- ☐ Frequently check with the child to provide the extra attention and care she may need while ill.
- ☐ Provide quiet activities that will hold the interest of the child, such as tapes, videos, books, stories, and artwork.
- ☐ Set aside a quiet corner or separate space for the child to be quiet, rest, or nap.
- ☐ Administer prescribed medication as directed, if allowed.
- ☐ Supply foods and beverages that provide good nutrition and follow guidelines as indicated by illness or recommended by a physician.

TABLE 13-8
Procedures for Administering Medication in Early Childhood Education Environments

- It is a good idea to have one teacher per group of children to be the consistent administrator of medicine. This person should be the most knowledgeable about how to do this and should be known to the child.
- Any medication, whether over-the-counter or prescribed, must have the child's name and date on it and be clearly labeled.
- All medications should be in original containers and not transferred to other containers.
- Medications should be administered according to the label direction.
- Parents must include a written note for permission and the instructions and dose for each medication.
- The medication label and parent's instructions should not conflict. The instructions should be photocopied and one set placed in the child's folder. The other set of instructions should be kept with the medication.
- Use accurate medical measuring devices, such as dosage cups or vials, when administering medicine. Do not use common kitchen utensils such as a teaspoon. This can affect proper dosage.
- Parents' instructions should be provided every time a child is ill or a new prescription is provided for a chronically ill child.
- Always wash hands before and after administering medication.
- Explain to the child what medication you are giving and why. NEVER refer to medicine as candy (see Figure 13-5).
- Teachers should administer medication exactly as prescribed. This includes method, dose, time, and frequency prescribed. If the prescription says to give it until medication is gone, as with antibiotics, then this should be done regardless of how the child feels. There is a reason for dosage dates.
- Teachers should always keep an accurate written record of medication given, including time and dosage, in a medication log. This way other teachers in the environment can check and not repeat a dose unnecessarily. Copies of the medication log for the child should be provided to the parent whenever medication is given, even if on a daily basis.
- Medications should be kept at proper temperatures, as directed on the label. If the medication must be refrigerated, it should be kept in a plastic zip bag to keep it away from food items.
- Always watch for reactions. Have a list of possible side effects for each medication given.
- Store all medications out of the reach of children, preferably in a locked cabinet, on a high shelf, or in the back of the top shelf of the refrigerator.

FIGURE 13-5
Children can very easily mistake medication for candy. Medications should be stored in a locked cabinet at all times. (Courtesy of Payless Drug Store.)

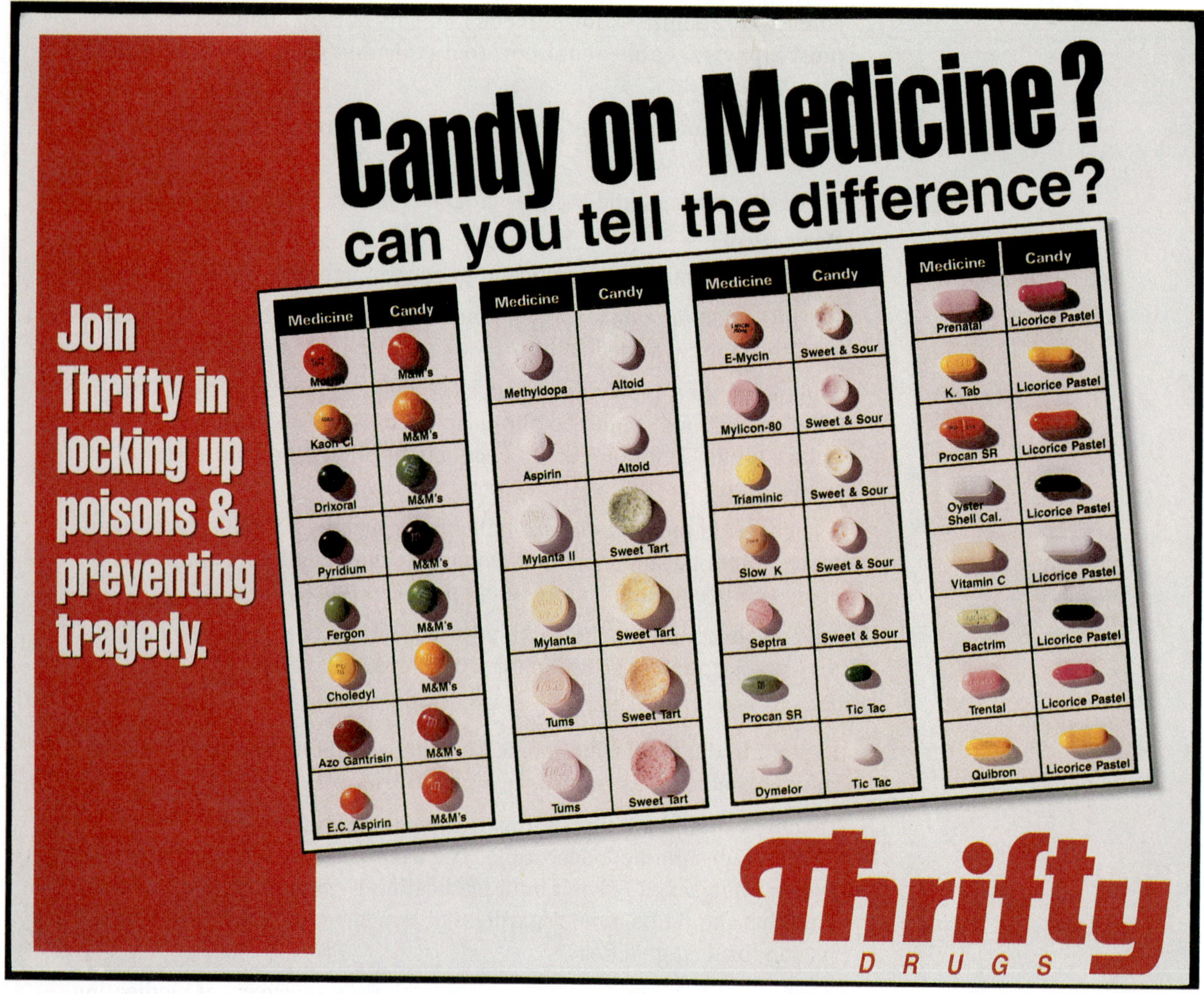

early childhood education environment are missing the dose and medications not being brought back to the care site so that it can be administered after the first day (Sinkovits, Kelly, & Ernst, 2003). The most common medications given in early childhood education environments are

- Antibiotics
- Acetaminophen, such as Children's Tylenol™ (fever reducer)
- Cold medications
- Analgesics/antihistamines (for allergies)
- Bronchodilators, including inhalers and nebulizers
- Decongestants
- Medications for chronic conditions

Antibiotics top this list. Parents often ask physicians for these medications even if the child has a virus that is not helped by the use of antibiotics (NCCCHSRC, 2005b). Antibiotic resistance appears to be occurring among

REALITY *Check*

Special Care for Mildly Ill Children

Many companies experience high absenteeism rates from their employees because their children are ill. A child's illness causes missed deadlines, parents who feel guilty, and coworkers who must do extra work because of the absent worker (Sears, 2003). This situation can cause many problems for the parents and discomfort for the child. Children are most comfortable in a familiar setting with familiar people when they are ill. This familiarity offers emotional support for the ill child. It is not always possible to provide this familiar comfort, so parents may have to settle for physical care alone.

Care for mildly ill children may take place in several ways.

- Care in the child's own center, family child care setting, or in-home care
- Family child care homes or centers that specialize in caring for mildly ill children
- Corporate on-site care for ill children of employees
- In the child's home by specialized teachers
- At a hospital site that contracts with corporations and/or the general public

Many centers and family child care homes provide this care within their regular programs. Most states permit early childhood education centers to offer get-well care for mildly ill children. Some centers provide a designated teacher to care for these mildly ill children. Some teachers specialize in the care of mildly ill children.

To address this situation, many corporations are cooperating by providing care for mildly ill children. One example of this is TLC for Mildly Ill Children, which is located in the Virginia Mason Hospital in Seattle, Washington. It contracts with local corporations and businesses and also provides services to the public (Virginia Mason Team Medicine, 2004). University of Illinois employees can use home-based care provided especially for their mildly ill children (Unger, 2004). Another example is the Chicken Soup Room at the ABC Child Care in Temecula, California, for children who are already in care at the site. Johnson and Johnson provides on-site care for mildly ill children at their headquarters in New Brunswick, New Jersey. This is offered at their early childhood education center in an infirmary. The Get Well Place is a subsidiary of the Rainbow Stations child care facilities and is located in numerous states on the East Coast, in Washington, DC, and in Texas. In order for a child to qualify for being admitted, only a current immunization card is required. The Get Well Place is staffed with full-time nurses.

There are centers specifically designed for the care of mildly ill children. These centers must meet licensing standards that are more stringent than those for regular care sites. They must also be very careful to prevent the spread of infectious diseases. The APHA and APA suggest that these special centers have the following for each child:

- Information concerning the diagnosis and the attending physician's name
- Prognosis for illness, including activity level, diet, and so forth
- Health care plan
- Open communication line with parents

Caring for mildly ill children can be challenging (Polyzoi & Babb, 2004). Mildly ill children can still be relatively active. Care should include provision of toys, games, and other activities that provide these children stimulation as required.

The licensing regulations should be determined for the local area and state where the care will take place, if the teacher intends to provide this type of care for mildly ill children.

CHECK*point:* **Does your local area have a "chicken soup" child care facility for mildly ill children? If not, what special regulations do you think your local area would have to meet to establish a care center for mildly ill children? Would these regulations be so prohibitive that it would be impossible to have this type of facility?**

children who are given too many antibiotics (Calder, 2004). It is more common for parents to pressure physicians for antibiotics than it is for teachers to ask parents to get them because parents often believe that antibiotics will speed up their child's return to care (Friedman et al., 2003).

There should always be a policy on administering medication, and it should be shared with the parents if it is appropriate in the state where care is taking place. If the parent asks for herbal remedies or other natural medicines to be given to the child, it is a good idea to ask the parents to give these to the children at home because they are not regulated.

Key Concept 13.4

Special Considerations for Care of Mildly Ill Children

Taking care of mildly ill children is not something all teachers or early childhood education situations are prepared to do. Determining the ability to handle this type of care will be based on three questions:

1. Is the infectious disease contagious or will it put others at risk?
2. Is the child able to participate in care?
3. Can the teacher accommodate the needs of the mildly ill child?

When the determination is made, the teacher will have to understand the issues of the special care he or she will be providing for the child. One of the special considerations is the administration of medication. The teacher should follow exact procedure for this.

13.5 CHILDREN WITH CHRONIC ILLNESSES

- **chronic illnesses** *medical conditions requiring continuous treatment.*

Chronic illnesses or conditions affect between 15 and 18 percent of the population younger than age 18 (Laundy & Boujaoude, 2004). The number of children with a chronic illness has quadrupled in the past 30 years (Zimm, 2007). A chronic illness requires continuing treatment. The range of the condition can be from mild to severe. Asthma is the most common chronic illness in childhood, with 9 percent of children reported to have this condition (Perrin, Bloom, & Gortmaker, 2007). The second most common chronic disease in children is diabetes mellitus (Lipton, 2007). Teachers are most likely to be confronted with children who have a mild or moderate form of a chronic illness.

Each chronic illness has its own unique causes, indicators, and medical responses. Most chronic illnesses have organizations that can provide the teacher with a wealth of resources. The following chronic illnesses are covered in this text: allergies, asthma, diabetes mellitus, HIV, seizure disorders, and sickle cell anemia. These are the most common chronic illnesses found in early childhood education environments. Whatever chronic condition presents itself, the teacher should gather as much information and resources on the condition as possible (CCHP, 2006). He should know what constitutes an emergency for that condition, and be prepared to act in an emergency. Practice for that emergency can reduce stress and affords a course of action should the emergency occur.

The following information will help a teacher provide care for a child who has one of these chronic illnesses. Each description of a chronic illness

Teachers need to be aware of allergies or potential allergies for all children in their care.

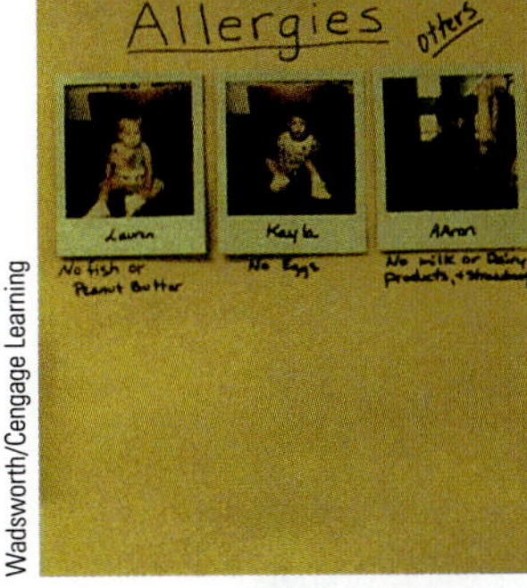

Wadsworth/Cengage Learning

provides the definition, significance, and how the disease occurs. This gives the teacher a background in order to understand the rest of the information. The remaining details inform the teacher about triggers, identifiers, and strategies for care of a child with the particular chronic illness. It is important to note that some states do not allow teachers to administer medication. If this is the case, a health professional should be close by if help is needed, or the family of the child with a chronic illness should make provisions for emergencies.

Allergies

Definition. An allergy is a heightened response to a substance.

Significance. Some children have known allergies; many others may have undiagnosed allergies. Symptoms depend on the organs that are affected (Williams, 2007).

How Does It Occur? The person who is allergic to a substance is exposed to it by ingestion, touch, or breathing.

When Does It Occur? An allergy occurs when the person is exposed to a substance that causes the response. Common allergy **triggers** are

- **triggers** *substances or conditions that activate a response.*

- Foods such as peanut butter, nuts, wheat, chocolate, milk, fish, citrus
- Pollen from flowers, grasses, hay, weeds, or trees
- Mold spores
- Dust
- Animal fur, feathers, or dander; this may be on a live animal, feathers in a comforter, or an animal skin on a wall
- Insects, including stings or parts from dead insects such as cockroaches

Identifiers of Reaction. Allergic reaction may take the form of sneezing, hay fever, asthma, swelling/hives, eczema, or cold-like symptoms when the respiratory system is affected. Digestive tract symptoms may include nausea, vomiting, and diarrhea.

Support. Be alert to the signs of allergic reactions of children in care. Discuss any allergies with parents, and avoid those triggers that are observed to cause a response. It is very important to work hard to keep the early childhood education environment or family child care home clean and free of dust mites and other allergens such as pet dander, cockroaches, and certain molds (Abrams, 2007a). Environmental triggers include very cold air and tobacco smoke. Forty percent of early childhood education environments have been found to have levels of allergens high enough to cause a reaction in an allergic child ("Do Child Care Centers Contribute," 2002). For more serious allergic reactions, the child may require medication. If an epinephrine instrument such as an EpiPen™ is needed, there should be written permission from the parent for a teacher to administer it. It would be most helpful for the teacher to work with a health consultant and the child's physician in order to be better prepared to do this.

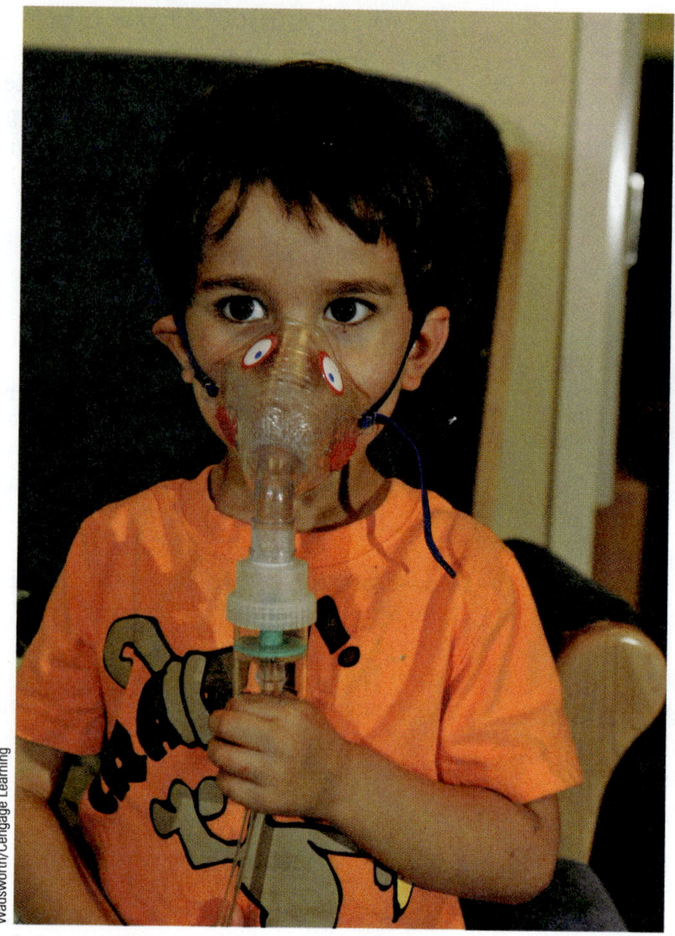

A child like this one who has asthma may need treatment while in the early childhood education environment.

Asthma

Definition. Asthma occurs when there is a narrowing of the small airways in the lungs called bronchi and bronchioles. Muscles around the airways tighten and, when mucus clogs these airways, breathing difficulty results.

Significance. Asthma affects about 6.3 million children younger than 18 years old (Abrams, 2007a). Rates of asthma are continuing to rise rapidly (NCEH, 2005; Perrin, Bloom, & Gortmaker, 2007). Boys are more likely to have asthma than are girls at a younger age. Girls are more likely to have it as they enter puberty (Almqvist, Worm, & Leynaert, 2008), unless they have been prenatally exposed to tobacco smoke (Jaakkola & Gissler, 2007). African-American children are more likely to have asthma than are non-Hispanic white children (McDaniel, Paxson, & Waldfogel, 2006).

How Does It Occur? Most asthmatics have persistent bronchial irritation. Environmental irritants trigger reactions that lead to an attack or episode.

When Does It Occur? The asthma episode or attack may occur if the child is exposed to one or more of the following triggers:

- The same items found on the allergy list
- Household products—vapors, deodorants, sprays, cleaning solvents, paints

- Pesticides
- Dust from clothes, broom, furniture, or filters on furnaces and air conditioners
- Weather—humidity, cold, wind
- Exercise—overexertion
- Infections such as colds, bronchitis, or other viruses
- Smoke—cigarette, pipe, or cigar
- Strong emotions—fear, laughing, crying, anger
- Aspirin
- At the end of the day when tired and lying down and mucus accumulates

Identifiers of Reaction. Tightening of airways and muscles causes difficulty breathing. In addition to shortness of breath, an increase in breathing rate can occur, and the child may be either irritable or listless. The child may also have a more rapid speech pattern, dark circles under the eyes, and a fever (Getch & Neuharth-Pritchett, 2004). Wheezing, coughing, and spitting up of mucus may also occur.

Support. Be aware of asthmatic reactions, especially after exercise, emotional display, or exposure to allergens. When children and teachers have education about asthma, they can reduce the number of emergency room visits (Coffman et al., 2008). The teacher should keep the child free from infection by providing a healthy, safe environment (Rose, 2006a). It might be helpful for the teacher to use "A Checklist for Parents and Providers," available at www.asthmaandallergies.org. This comprehensive list would be extremely helpful in providing the healthiest environment for a child with asthma or allergies. It is a wise idea to use the Child Care Asthma Action Card, which can be downloaded from http://www. schoolasthmaallergy.com, as a further tool. This card is part of the Asthma Action Plan and provides important information on how the early education environment can help a child in trouble (Pulcini, DeSisto, & McIntyre, 2007). The Action Card should be filled out by the health professional and the parents and kept on file. Wheeler and colleagues (2006) suggest that elementary schools take the following actions: (1) Build strong links to asthma care clinicians; (2) identify students most affected by asthma at school; (3) choose the right mix of resources to use; (4) coordinate a multicomponent and collaborative approach to the problem; and (5) conduct an evaluation of the program that is used to see whether it works sufficiently.

A teacher may not be totally comfortable handling an asthma emergency (Getch & Neuharth-Pritchett, 2004). An older child may be able to let the teacher know she is having an incident before it gets serious enough to warrant an emergency (Olson et al., 2007). If an inhaler or nebulizer is to be used for an asthmatic child, the directions found in Table 13-9 should be followed. If there is ever any question about a child's ability to breathe comfortably, emergency services should be called. If an episode does occur, the teacher should make sure the child is sitting up and is calm, and should encourage the child to focus on slow, deep breathing. Follow procedures if medication should be given.

Diabetes Mellitus

Definition. Diabetes mellitus occurs when insulin is not produced in the pancreas at the rate the body needs it. Insulin is involved in the process that

TABLE 13-9
Administering Inhaled Medications in Early Childhood Education Environments

Contact your local licensing agency to determine whether you are allowed to administer inhaled medication for the children that need it. If you are allowed, then the following should be done for each person who may administer the medication to the child:

- Obtain written permission from parent or guardian to administer the medication via the inhaler or nebulizer.
- Obtain written permission from parent or guardian to contact the child's physician. If the child has a medical home, this relationship will already be established.
- Contact the child's physician and get written instructions on what the specific child needs with the administration of the medication.
- Obtain training from the parent, guardian, or health consultant on how to administer the inhaled medication.
- Keep a written record in the medical log each time this type of medication is administered. Prepare a copy for the parents whenever the child has the medication administered, even if on a daily basis.

Adapted from "Administration of Inhaled Medications in Child Care," available through the Child Care Law Center, San Francisco, CA.

stores and uses glucose for energy. There are two types of diabetes: type I, which is insulin dependent, and type II, which is noninsulin dependent.

Significance. Type I diabetes is often referred to as juvenile-onset diabetes; it is the most common type among children. Approximately one in every 400 to 600 American children have type I diabetes (CDC, 2006a). Type 2 diabetes is increasing due to widespread obesity (Jones, 2008). This type of diabetes requires insulin injections at least twice daily. Food and exercise levels must be controlled, and blood sugar should be tested several times throughout the day.

How Does It Occur? Because adequate insulin is not present, the body cannot absorb excess glucose. Glucose levels build in the blood and spill into the urine. Sugar not used for energy is stored in fats; when broken down, the resulting chemicals, ketones, can poison the blood if they are allowed to accumulate.

When Does It Occur? Diabetes reaction is triggered when there is

- Too much exercise
- Not enough food
- Too much sugar
- Too much insulin

Identifiers of Reaction. Lack of insulin can cause numerous reactions. Among them are these:

- Disorientation, confusion, blurred vision
- Excessive sweating
- Dizziness, poor coordination

- Irritability, behavior change
- Excessive thirst or sudden hunger
- Coma

Support. The teacher must be educated and trained in what to watch for and provide and how to handle emergencies when caring for the diabetic child (American Diabetes Association [ADA], 2003). Glucose levels are affected by diet and exercise, so those activities should be carefully monitored. Children ages 4 years and younger are not usually capable of being involved in their own care and treatment. The ADA (2003) suggests that a child in care have a Diabetes Health Care Plan. This plan should be individualized for the child and should be prepared by the parents working with the teacher as a team (NCCCHSRC, 2005a). This process is simplified if there is a health consultant available or if the child has a medical home; these entities can also be involved in the plan.

The family should provide the materials, equipment, and training necessary for diabetes care tasks. The family should also discuss the diet and meal schedule of the child with the teacher. In addition to their own telephone numbers, the family should provide emergency numbers for the child's diabetes care team so they can be contacted if necessary.

There should be at least one teacher and one backup adult on site who is trained to perform the fingerstick blood glucose monitoring and record the results. They should also be able to test urine or blood for ketones. These teachers should know how to react to the results. The early childhood education environment should provide an area where there will be privacy for the child to be tested and to have insulin administered, if necessary. The child's diet should be carefully tracked and recorded.

A diabetic child may also have episodes of hypoglycemia, when his blood sugar is low, or hyperglycemia, when his blood sugar is high. Again, the same basic tenets of care apply: The teacher should be trained on how to handle an episode and the parents should provide the proper supplies (NCCCHSRC, 2005a).

HIV/AIDS

Definition. Human immunodeficiency virus (HIV) is a viral infection that threatens the immune system's ability to fight off infection. It can lead to acquired immunodeficiency syndrome (AIDS), which is a combination of illnesses that may become life threatening.

Significance. Ninety-one percent of children with HIV/AIDS had it passed from mother to child. HIV/AIDS in children in the United States has declined from 1800 new cases in 1996 to only 122 new cases in 2004 (CDC, 2006b). Even with this decline, the seriousness of this blood-borne disease should not be minimized. The teacher should be aware of the implications and protect all children in the early childhood education environment from this risk.

How Does It Occur? The methods of transmission that affect children are in utero transmission via blood from a mother who has the disease; breast milk from an HIV-positive mother; sexual abuse by a person with AIDS; and exposure to blood or blood products from an infected person through a cut or sore or by blood transfusion.

When Does It Occur? Exposure to infection or normal childhood diseases can trigger an immuno-suppressed response. Chicken pox is especially dangerous.

Identifiers of Reaction. Some symptoms found in children with HIV/AIDS are listed here:

- Multiple bacterial infections
- Enlarged spleen and liver
- Abnormal growth pattern
- Frequent illnesses

Support. The teacher should be supportive in two areas. The first area is protecting the child with HIV/AIDS from exposure to childhood diseases, especially chicken pox. The second is to protect all other children and teachers from HIV/AIDS. Universal precautions should be followed. These include hand-washing and sanitary procedures and wearing gloves when in contact with blood or other bodily fluids. Everyone with sores, scratches, or lesions should keep them covered. The teacher should also attempt to prevent and handle immediately any biting by any child in the early childhood education environment.

Seizure Disorders

Definition. Seizure disorder is a neurological condition that is not usually diagnosed until after a child has had at least two seizures from an unknown cause (Leonard, 2007). Seizure disorders can be another term for epilepsy and febrile seizures. There are 20 types of seizure disorders that may occur when there is temporary overactivity in the electrical impulses in the brain.

Significance. One in every 100 persons has some form of seizure disorder on the continuum from rare to frequent displays.

How Does It Occur? Seizure disorder can result from head injuries, infections, high fevers, or lead poisoning, or it may be hereditary.

When Does It Happen? Possible triggers include these:

- Fast-rising fevers
- Fatigue
- Disorientation from outside source, such as flashing lights or rapid movement

Identifiers of Reaction. Because there are 20 different types of seizure disorders, the reaction range is wide. The following list demonstrates the range:

- Dazed behavior
- Unusual sleepiness and irritability
- Unexplained clumsiness, falls
- Feeling strange, disoriented
- Rapid eye movements, eyes rolling up

- Head appears to move involuntarily
- Involuntary, unnatural movements of body
- Unconsciousness, drooling at the mouth

Support. The first thing a teacher should do is to become familiar with the type of disorder the child has and how to handle the reaction of that disorder. When the reaction occurs, remain calm. If a child is having a seizure that includes unconsciousness, place the child on the floor and turn him on his side. Remove glasses and any harmful objects that are close to the child. Place something soft under the child's head. Loosen clothing around the head and neck. Comfort the child with a soft voice. Clarify what is happening to other children. Do not put anything in the child's mouth, restrain his movements, or give anything to eat or drink until the child is totally awake and aware (Leonard, 2007). Patiently wait until the seizure has finished, and then help the child in the transition to normal activity. If the seizure lasts longer than 10 minutes, call the parents or physician.

Sickle Cell Anemia

Definition. Sickle cell anemia is a hereditary disease that affects the red blood cells. It is most often found in African-American children and young adults.

Significance. Sickle cell anemia occurs in 1 of 400 African Americans.

How Does It Occur? An abnormality in the red blood cells causes them to change shape and decrease the amount of oxygen that they deliver to all parts of the body. When this causes blockage to tissues of an organ or joint, pain occurs, and tissues in that location may be damaged.

When Does It Happen? Sickle cell anemia can be triggered by these conditions:

- Fatigue
- Overexertion from exercise
- Stress

Identifiers of Reaction. There may be no apparent triggers. When a reaction happens, there may be intense pain in arms, legs, back, or chest.

Katy went to a special school that mainstreamed healthy children with children with chronic diseases. Both she and her friend Paul had diabetes and required urine testing and sometimes shots of insulin. Many of the other children watched their teacher, Charles, test Katy's and Paul's urine to check their insulin levels. This process evolved into an activity for all the children. They would all gather around, and most could identify what the insulin test result was. They often watched Katy and Paul get shots. Everyone was involved so there was nothing really "different" about Katy and Paul that the other children considered to be a problem.

Support. A teacher should be aware of the disease and watch the child for shortness of breath and fatigue. If a crisis occurs, the teacher should remain calm, call the parents, and support the child until she is picked up. A preventive measure would be to protect the child from infection by offering a sanitary environment.

Working as a Team

Many of the issues that occur when caring for a child with a chronic illness are similar to those of a child with special needs. Some children with a chronic illness qualify as children with special needs under the Americans with Disabilities Act. Regardless of whether the child qualifies, using the strategies developed for children with special needs will help the teacher meet most of the needs of the chronically ill child.

The team for a chronically ill child may consist of the parent, the physician, and the teacher. This supports the idea of a "medical home" for the child. The teacher should ask questions and access any other resources available (such as a health consultant), to support care for the child. The teacher should have a plan for care for each child with a chronic illness in the event that a reactive or crisis episode should occur. It is vital that the teacher learn to recognize and identify reactions that may lead to crisis and be prepared to handle an emergency that may result from the crisis. This includes understanding what constitutes an emergency that requires outside help. The teacher who possesses the knowledge of how to handle a crisis can remain calm and do what needs to be done.

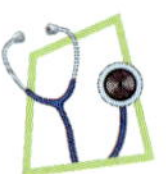

Key Concept 13.5

Chronically Ill Children

Many teachers will find themselves caring for one or more children with a chronic illness. A teacher should have general knowledge of the chronic illness—especially the reactions leading to a crisis episode. She should also have understanding of what to do should this occur. Many of the strategies used for children with special needs can be applied to the child with a chronic illness.

13.6 OPTIMIZING HEALTH IN EARLY CHILDHOOD EDUCATION ENVIRONMENTS

As has been mentioned frequently throughout this chapter and the other chapters in this section, the use of a health consultant and a plan for every child to have a medical home can optimize the health environment in early childhood education programs. The health consultant can provide training, information, and resources the teacher may otherwise not have available. The medical home can provide a natural team effort for each child.

Child Care Health Consultants

It is unrealistic to assume that each teacher will know how to handle every health issue that may come up (Cianciolo, Trueblood-Noll, & Allingham, 2004). A teacher can easily provide comfort, but she may not always know how to handle chronic illness or emergencies that deal with health. The idea of a child care health consultant originated in the late 1990s in the Maternal and Child Care Bureau, and support of this issue has been continued by the AAP (Gupta et al., 2005). Child care health consultants can provide assistance in a number of areas (Aronson, 2002; Farrer, Alkon, & To, 2007). See Table 13-10 for some of the ways that a health consultant might provide help.

A health consultant for the early childhood education environment may be a public health nurse, nurse, nurse practitioner, or other health professional. The health consultant should have specialized training for the early childhood education setting. A National Training Institute for Child Care Health Consultants has been federally funded at the University of North Carolina (Cianciolo, Trueblood-Noll, & Allingham, 2004). The use of health care consultants is Action Step Nine of the Healthy Child Care America arm of the AAP. Both entities see the health consultant as a positive step to providing the maximum environment for good health and safety in early education.

The health consultant may be assigned through a local resource and referral agency, a health clinic, health agency, or children's hospital. If none of those provide health consultation for the local area, the teacher might try contacting the AAP representative in the state in which care is performed.

TABLE 13-10
Duties of Health Care Consultants

- Train teachers on health and safety issues.
- Perform on-site assessments of health and safety in the early childhood education environment.
- Provide technical advice on improvements for health and safety.
- Work with teachers to provide families with information on health and safety issues and concerns.
- Help create policies for health, safety, nutrition, and food safety.
- Provide telephone consultation to teachers as issues arise.
- Help link teachers, families, and medical home for greatest communication on issues of health.
- Help link teachers, families, and children to community resources.
- Provide referrals for families and children who require services.
- Review staff and children's health records.
- Support the idea of a medical home.
- Provide assistance, training, and information for managing care of children with chronic illnesses and/or special needs.

The map for this information can be obtained through Healthy Child Care America and is available online at http://www.healthychildcare.org.

A Medical Home for Every Child

As described in Chapter 11, a medical home is a partnership of the family, the teacher, and a medical practitioner that ensures that all health, psychosocial, and educational needs of a child are met. This care should be provided in a culturally effective way to remove any barriers that might be present (Cooley & McAllister, 2004). The medical home for a child should be of good quality (Benedict, 2008). As a child enters care, his immunizations should be up to date. This is the first contact that the teacher has with the child and the family about health. It would be a good time to ascertain whether the family has a regular health care provider. If the family does not have one, then the teacher can encourage the family to find one (AAP, 2002).

A number of families do not have a single source of medical care, and some lack access to medical care altogether (Chen, Martin & Matthews, 2007). The ability to access a medical home is affected by education and income (Nageswaran & Farel, 2007). The lack of consistent medical care can result in delays in diagnosis and treatment, missed immunizations, and trips to the emergency room that may not have been necessary (Reeves, 2002). In turn, this situation has an effect on the health of the children in these families. When these children are in early childhood education programs, it can also affect the health of everyone in that environment.

Lack of insurance may be one barrier to a consistent source of medical care. Families with insurance are more likely to have a medical home (Starfield & Shi, 2004). Children from Latino families represent a significant number of uninsured children, and they were found less likely to have a medical home (Flores, Abreu, Tomany-Korman, 2007). Today, many states offer free health insurance through Medicaid or low-cost health care plans to families who qualify. Other barriers include location, cultural practice patterns, and other social forces. The teacher can assist families in finding a medical home by providing information about access to no-cost or low-cost medical insurance and to the possible sources of medical care. Medical homes may be private physicians, hospital outpatient clinics, public health services, community health centers, public health departments, health maintenance organizations, and even school-based clinics or clinics linked to schools.

If the barrier of access is removed, families are more likely to have regular medical care. When the health provider is culturally competent, all families are more likely to use services (Flores, Abreu, & Tomany-Korman, 2007). A child with a medical home is more likely to be provided care on a consistent basis, including intervention if needed. Children with chronic illnesses and special needs, in particular, need a medical home (Cooley & McAllister, 2004; AAP, 2006). These children may require therapeutic or supportive services, and a good quality medical home will provide these needed services (Benedict, 2008). The teacher who is caring for a child with a chronic illness or special needs will feel greater support if a medical home is present. A team consisting of the family, the teacher, and the health care provider can promote better health for all children in care and optimize the environment for health, safety, and well-being.

Key Concept 13.6

Optimizing Health

The use of a health consultant and encouraging each family to have a medical home for their child will optimize the environment for health and safety. A health consultant can provide training, assist in creating policies, and provide assistance in many other ways. A child with a medical home can have consistent medical care, and intervention can take place as soon as it is needed. Having a team of the family, the health care provider, and the teacher can promote better health for children in care.

13.7 IMPLICATIONS FOR TEACHERS

Teachers must have the tools of observation and supervision in order to provide and maintain a healthy environment. Education and cultural competence also help them to manage the spread of disease as well as to handle care of the mildly ill child. This endeavor can be aided by the use of a health consultant and the provision of a medical home for each child.

Observation

Observation provides the teacher the ability to recognize any symptoms of infectious disease early. The daily quick health check allows the teacher to monitor the health of a child on a regular basis. Recording any signs, symptoms, or irregular behaviors can give the teacher indicators of illness. When a child is observed, the question "Is the child able to participate?" can be answered more readily. A teacher who knows a child well will recognize whether the child is acting in a normal enough manner to be in the early childhood education setting.

Supervision

Supervision is a powerful tool that helps the teacher to manage health care in the early childhood education environment. Supervising the setting for proper immunizations and sanitary hand-washing and cleaning procedures can reduce the number of infectious diseases spread. Supervising for exclusion and return policies helps keep contagious diseases away from the early childhood education environment.

Notifying the public health department allows the teacher to help manage the spread of infectious diseases both in and out of the early childhood education environment. When the health department is able to track infectious diseases, another child care setting may benefit from the notification. This may prevent further outbreaks.

Teachers must notify all parents when a child in care has an infectious disease that is highly contagious and/or can cause serious problems. The parents can observe for the signs and symptoms and can prepare for follow-up care after exposure to the infectious disease.

Education

Education provides a wonderful tool for the promotion of healthy habits and the prevention of disease (Gupta et al., 2005). All participants in the early childhood education environment should be educated to avoid exposure to and reduce the spread of infectious diseases (Brady, 2005).

Education offers teachers the base of knowledge and training required to carry out their daily task of creating a healthy environment. Teachers who have the ability to identify the signs and symptoms of infectious diseases protect the environment against any further spread of these diseases.

Health education in early childhood education environments should incorporate several strategies. The first educational tool the teacher will use is sharing the importance of hand washing along with the "how-to's" and "when to's." Teaching children to recognize when they feel ill may help the teacher identify an infectious disease before outward symptoms appear. This may provide another level of protection for all the children in care. Teaching children at their own level about an infectious disease that is present in the early childhood education environment may reinforce the information sent home concerning that disease.

For Families

Working with families in the early childhood education environment is essential to maintain health and well-being of children at all times. Education for parents allows them to work with the teacher as a team. It also allows the family to offer a more protective environment in the home. Teaching parents about hand washing and the importance of immunizations will help them understand their own responsibility to protect their children and to prevent disease (Zamani, 2008). Parents who understand proper procedures for the care of a child with an infectious disease may be able to reduce the seriousness of the disease.

It is suggested that every child should have a medical home. This is a primary health care provider who takes care of both well care and screening measures in addition to treating illnesses (Shope & Aronson, 2006; AAP, 2006). A medical home allows for regular visits and should help prevent serious health problems. Today, most children are eligible for some type of health care insurance. A website to check is http://www.insurekidsnow.gov. The teacher should cooperate with parents by providing information about medical homes and available resources so that each child can have a medical home.

Cultural Competence

The teacher should understand that early access to health care for ill children is perhaps the major issue for cultural competence. This may be especially true for recent immigrants. Certain cultures may have had little access to health care. Parents of these children may not understand the health care system or may come from countries where health care was readily available and used regularly. For example, there appears to be a pattern of delayed care for Latin-American children who are children of immigrants and are from low-income families (Flores, Abreu, & Tomany-Korman, 2006). Emergency medical services may be the primary care for many of these children.

When a child becomes ill, the teacher may have to help the parent access health care. Many cultures use the emergency room as their first contact of

Parents may not have children immunized because of fears, cultural beliefs, or lack of understanding of the importance of immunizations. Although teachers need to respect the beliefs of different cultures, the "No immunization, no care" rule must be enforced whenever possible as dictated by state laws in order to protect all children in care.

Wadsworth/Cengage Learning

care. This is dangerous for the child and it is not protective for the early childhood education environment. It may take extra effort on the part of the teacher to help parents from other cultures provide the health care required for these children (Sokol-Gutierrez, 2000). This is one of the reasons that a medical home for a child can be a boon to early childhood education environments. The medical home should be culturally effective (Cooley & McAllister, 2004; Farrer, Alkon, & To, 2006).

Immunization may be another culturally sensitive issue. Many families do not understand the need for immunization. If the child is from a country where immunizations are not readily available, the thought of having a child stuck with needles may cause fear (Gonzalez-Mena, 2004). The need for immunization should be dealt with when the child enters care. The rule "No immunization, no care" must be understood by both the teacher and the parents. No exceptions should be made. The teacher may have to educate parents who want to enter their child in care about the need to adhere to the immunization schedule. When a child is in care, it is up to the teacher to follow up and make sure that immunizations occur (Brady, 2005).

The teacher should understand the sanitary habits of the various cultures that are represented in care. The teacher may have to provide extra education or acquire interpreters to inform parents of their responsibility in keeping their children well. This task can be greatly assisted if there is a health care consultant for the early education environment.

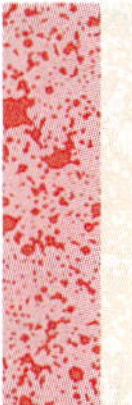

Pause for Reflection

Are there any superstitions related to health from your own culture or others you are familiar with that might be helpful to know so that you are more culturally competent? How might you work with a parent who believes one of these superstitions?

Key Concept 13.7

Implications for Teachers

The implications for the teacher are the tools of observation, supervision, education, working with families, and cultural competence that help the teacher create the holistic approach required to deal with the many issues raised. Through observation the teacher can identify infectious diseases early and thus provide some protection for others in care. Supervision will give the teacher the tools needed for exclusion and notification. The teacher must be educated and must educate parents and children in methods that will forestall the spread of infectious diseases. Teachers should work cooperatively with families to provide healthy environments both at home and at school. Cultural competence should be practiced by the teacher in order to include all children and parents in providing the best preventive environment possible. The use of a health consultant and provision of a medical home for the children in early childhood education programs optimizes the health environment.

CHAPTER SUMMARY

Teachers must prevent disease spread and also care for mildly ill children. They must form exclusion policies and understand reporting procedures. Teachers have to determine whether they have the ability to care for noncontagious children who become ill as well as for chronically ill children. Observation and supervision will help the teacher identify and manage infectious diseases and chronic illnesses. Education will help the teacher impart healthy habits to children and their parents. By working with families and using cultural competence, the teacher can provide the optimal health environment.

TO GO BEYOND

Additional resources for this chapter can be found by visiting the book companion website at www.cengage.com/education/robertson. This supplemental material includes chapter objectives, internet exercises, reflection questions, quizzes, web links, glossary and flash cards, case studies, frequently asked questions, downloadable forms and tables, curriculum supplements, more reality checks, additional key concepts, references, and more.

Chapter Review Critical Thinking Applications

1. Discuss the identification and management of infectious diseases. How should these be applied in these early childhood education situations: (1) family child care, (2) center-based care, and (3) an elementary school?

2. Describe the particular skills required to manage infectious diseases. How well prepared are you for these skills? What could you do to improve these skills?
3. How might early childhood education in your area be improved if there were a facility that specifically dealt with mildly ill children?
4. Discuss the presence of children with chronic illnesses in the early childhood education environment. Should a teacher have more qualifications to work with these children?
5. Examine how a health consultant and a medical home for all children can affect a teacher's job.

As an Individual

1. Obtain the local licensing or public school guidelines for exclusion. Compare and contrast those with the ones in this text. Should they be more thorough?
2. Describe the type of early childhood education environment you intend to participate in, then ask the three questions about caring for ill children. How do they relate to the particular care situation you have in mind?

As a Group

1. Discuss exclusion policies. In small groups, design an exclusion policy for center-based care and one for family child care. How are they different? Why? Why might elementary school be different?
2. Examine the idea of "medical home." Does this make sense, or are there other solutions that might more effectively help keep children well? How does this work in your own community?
3. In small groups, design a center for mildly ill children. Describe what this type of center would look like and what type of training might be necessary to run it. Is this a possibility for your own community?

Case Studies

1. Charley has arrived at school and seems to have a runny nose. Upon further inspection, because the mucus is clear, Lauren, his teacher, allows him to stay. She keeps a careful eye on him and notices at about 11:00 A.M. that he seems to be feverish. By noon, Lauren notices a blistery rash on his torso. She immediately suspects chicken pox. What actions should she take?
2. Kevin and Kyle, 3-year-old twins, were rubbing their eyes a great deal. Kevin also had a white discharge coming from his left eye. Donna, their family child care provider, noticed this and suspected that both boys had conjunctivitis (pink eye). She informed the boys' mother when they were picked up. The next morning, Donna woke up with red, watery eyes. How should Donna proceed with the day? If Kevin and Kyle arrive at care that morning, should she let them stay? How would you handle this?

3. Four-year-old Taylor did not eat much of her lunch. Connie, her teacher, noticed that this was unusual behavior for Taylor. She decided to keep an eye on the child. Within an hour, Taylor began to have diarrhea, and shortly after that she began vomiting. How should Connie proceed? What should she do for Taylor?
4. Paula is a 6-year-old who has diabetes that is controlled by insulin injections. The diabetes is pretty well under control because her urine is tested several times a day when she is in school. She still needs help to test it. A few of the other children in your class are very curious about this. How should you handle this situation in a way that will assist Paula as well as answer the curious children?
5. Blanca is in your first-grade class and has asthma. Your class runs laps for 10 minutes every morning. Some mornings this seems to bring on a bout with asthma for Blanca. It is not too bad, but it is a concern. What might you do to prevent this?

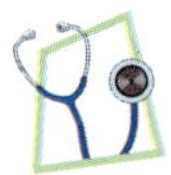

HEALTH CURRICULUM SUPPLEMENT

Sample lesson plans and topic maps for subjects that concern health are provided for the teacher on the website under "Building Curriculum" to help reinforce the information that is being modeled by teachers and learned by the children in the early education environment. In addition to the sample curriculum, there is a list of children's books and sources for further information. Some of this information may include songs or finger plays. This sample group is presented to help the teacher design his or her own curriculum by adding to the information provided.

SECTION V
Current Issues in Early Childhood Education Safety, Nutrition, and Health

This section discusses three current issues:

14. Child Maltreatment

15. Children with Disabilities or Other Special Needs

16. Creating Linkages

These topics will prepare the teacher to deal with sensitive issues; create linkages with children, families, and the community; and develop curriculum for safety, nutrition, and health in the early childhood education environment.

Wadsworth/Cengage Learning

CHAPTER 14

Child Maltreatment

After reading this chapter, you should be able to:

14.1 Policies for Child Maltreatment

Define and discuss policies for child abuse that may affect the early childhood education environment.

14.2 Preventive Measures for Child Maltreatment

Describe and discuss measures for preventing child maltreatment.

14.3 Protective Measures for Child Maltreatment

Describe and discuss how to recognize, document, and report child maltreatment, and methods for caring for an abused child.

14.4 Working with Children from Substance-Abusing Families

Describe and discuss the common problems and their solutions that may arise in early childhood education environments when working with children from drug-abusing families.

14.5 Implications for Teachers

Describe and discuss the importance of education, observation, role modeling, and supervision in dealing with special topics issues.

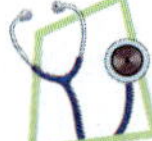

14.1 POLICIES FOR CHILD MALTREATMENT

A teacher may encounter a child who has been maltreated in some way. Child maltreatment is defined as "all intentional harm to or avoidable endangerment of anyone under 18 years of age" (Berger, 2009). This includes neglect, physical abuse, sexual abuse, and emotional abuse. Child maltreatment is a serious threat to the health, safety, and well-being of children in this country. It is up to the teacher to offer preventive and protective measures to all children in the early childhood education environment. The following facts show the need to create policies that deal with child maltreatment (see Figure 14-1):

- Over 3.3 million cases of child maltreatment, involving 6 million children, were reported in 2005. More than 899,000 incidents of child maltreatment were substantiated (USDHHS, 2007). Child care providers and teachers should be trained to spot the symptoms of child abuse (NAEYC, 2004; Foster, 2007).
- Children younger than age 6 are the most at risk for being abused and neglected. Most victims are younger than 1 year old (Knitzer & Lefkowitz, 2006; USDHHS, 2007).
- Seventy-seven percent of abuse and neglect fatalities are younger than 4 years old. Forty-two percent of the fatalities are children younger than 1 year (USDHHS, 2007).
- With help, parents can learn to recognize behavior patterns that may develop into abusive behaviors and can produce positive parent–child relationships instead of the cycle of abuse (CSSP, 2004; Prevent Child Abuse America, 2007).
- A supportive adult can make a difference in the life of a child who is in an abusive family (Rice & Groves, 2005; Kersey & Malley, 2005; Werner & Smith, 2001).
- Eighty-four percent of perpetrators were found to be parents either acting alone or with someone else (USDHHS, 2007). Fathers are more likely to inflict physical injury than are mothers (Starling et al., 2007).
- Substance abuse can lead to physical harm and neglect of a child (Landsman & Hartley, 2007). Approximately 40 to 80 percent of all cases of child abuse and neglect involve substance abuse by the

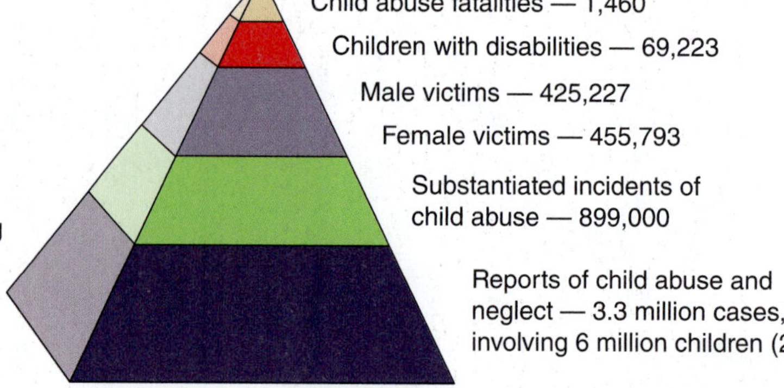

FIGURE 14-1 Child maltreatment statistics, 2005 (USDHHS, 2007).

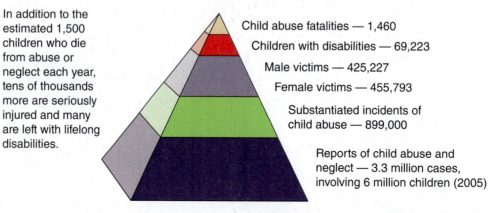

parents (CDF, 2005). In all but five states, parental drug use where children are exposed to the drugs in some form is now considered child abuse (Child Welfare Information Gateway, 2007).

- Children over age 3 can learn abuse prevention concepts (Crosson-Tower, 2002). Children should have safety education to protect them from violence (Renshaw, 2006).

The teacher should provide an environment that supports the children's well-being. The environment and the actions of the teachers must be beyond reproach. Methods for preventing accusations must be used.

The teacher should learn to recognize any indicators that a family may be at risk for child maltreatment. Intervention methods and strategies must be used when necessary. The teacher is mandated to report any maltreatment that may be observed. He should learn to recognize the signs and symptoms of maltreatment. The teacher needs to know how to document and report any indicators of maltreatment that have been observed (CCHP, 2006). Teachers should know the methods and strategies used to provide for the well-being of a child in care who has been maltreated.

The following are areas in which policies should be created for child maltreatment prevention and protection:

1. *Preventive measures:* understanding how to prevent accusations and how to intervene to protect children in care from maltreatment.
2. *Protective measures:* practices to recognize, document, and report all forms of child maltreatment and methods for working with abused children.
3. *Working with children from substance-abusing families:* understanding the common problems and their solutions that may arise in early childhood education environments when working with children from drug-abusing families.
4. *Implications for teachers:* practices that use the tools of education, cultural sensitivity, observation, and supervision to provide children with protection and prevention from harm and to offer an environment that fosters well-being.

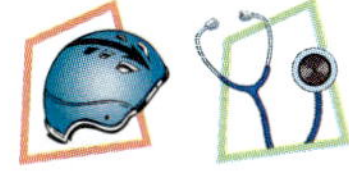

Policies for Child Maltreatment

Child maltreatment affects as many as 5 million children annually. Teachers should learn preventive, protective, and promotional measures that will help provide for the well-being of children. Policies should be created to help the teacher provide intervention and prevent accusation. These policies should offer the teacher methods and practices needed for recognition, documentation, and reporting of child maltreatment. The teacher should understand protective strategies to provide the child who has been maltreated with an atmosphere of support and a sense of trust in the teacher. The teacher should understand the effects that substance-abusing families have on children and how to help them.

A good policy for hiring new teachers is to screen them carefully, including an in-depth interview and checking all references.

Wadsworth/Cengage Learning

14.2 PREVENTIVE MEASURES FOR CHILD MALTREATMENT

Child maltreatment is an issue that affects approximately 1 million children yearly. Those are the substantiated cases, but for another 5 million children a year there are reports of maltreatment that go unsubstantiated. There are several basic development issues that can affect these maltreated children throughout their lives. Neurodevelopment may be impaired and can cause decreases in brain size and function. This can, in turn, lead to lower IQs and poor school performance (Putnam, 2006). Psychosocial development can also be affected. Children who are abused often have either too little or too much control over their emotions, which limits their ability to interact effectively with others. Too often, those who have been abused as children turn to drugs and alcohol to mask their pain, anger, and confusion. Early intervention can save many children a life full of social difficulties, diminished capacity, and lowered emotional competency (Knudsen et al., 2006). Teachers have a particular insight to children they are with on an almost daily basis. Prevention of child maltreatment can be effective and is less costly in terms of human suffering as well as the financial cost required to remedy it (Putnam, 2006). Policies should be in place to deal with prevention, intervention, recognition, documentation, and reporting of child maltreatment.

Child maltreatment is a very sensitive issue that needs to be handled carefully. It can be complex when it surfaces as an issue in early childhood education environments. The teacher has a number of responsibilities for handling this issue. Prevention, protection, and promotion of child safety are essential. Children should never be harmed (NAEYC, 2004). One of the basic indicators of quality in early childhood education is the absence of abuse (Shope & Aronson, 2006).

Teachers can offer preventive measures by cooperating with their state licensing agency. Many states screen teachers for a history of child maltreatment. The director or teacher who employs others can make sure all prospective employees are screened for child abuse and neglect and conform to the licensing regulations (Palmer & Smith, 2006a). This screening would include teachers, janitors, secretaries, cooks, substitutes, and volunteers. If it is difficult to get local licensing or screening information, NAEYC recommends using the screening decision model instrument developed by the American Bar Association, which is very thorough (Wells et al., 1995). Other screening methods might include checking with the state department of motor vehicles for driving records, running a credit check, and obtaining educational transcripts. It is important that at least three professional and personal references be checked.

In addition to the licensing process, each prospective employee should be carefully interviewed, and all referrals from previous employment should be checked. Table 14-1 provides a sample of questions the teacher might ask prospective employees. If there are any doubts about the person after the interview, the teacher should listen to her intuition. There is no room for doubt when it comes to the safety of children in care. New employees should go through a probationary period so that the employing teacher may carefully observe them as they relate to the children. If the new teacher does not meet the standards of behavior on or off the job, a policy should be in place to terminate him.

Proper teacher–child ratios also act as a preventive measure. If the ratio is followed, teachers are able to best meet each child's individual needs. Check your state for regulations on ratios. If your state does not have them, NAEYC accreditation suggests the following:

- 1 teacher for 6–8 for infants
- 1 teacher for 8–12 toddlers
- 1 teacher for 14–20 preschoolers
- 1 teacher for 16–20 kindergartners
- 1 teacher for 20 primary grade-school children

TABLE 14-1
Sample Interview Questions to Screen for Abuse Potential

- Why do you want to work with children?
- How would you describe your own childhood?
- What is your viewpoint on discipline?
- Do you believe in corporal punishment (hitting a child)?
- Does child behavior ever make you angry?
- Do you suffer from a lot of stress in your everyday life?
- How do you express your anger?
- What would you do if . . . ? (a series of questions that relate to anger, discipline, and so on)
- What are some coping skills you have to alleviate stress?

Preservice orientation and in-service training should be given to keep teachers up to date about child maltreatment in a group setting. This should include the definition of child maltreatment, identification of signs of maltreatment, and how to document and report child maltreatment. Many cases of maltreatment are either erroneously reported or go unreported because the teacher does not understand what constitutes maltreatment and how it should be reported (NAEYC, 2004). All staff should be educated so that they clearly understand the common behaviors, signs, and symptoms of child maltreatment.

Another preventive measure is to set up the early childhood education environment so that children and teachers are never isolated from view of others (Palmer & Smith, 2006a). Some centers use video equipment that promotes high visibility for the parents to see all angles of the early childhood education environment. Restrooms should have an open-door policy that requires the door to remain open so that there is no opportunity for privacy. Supervision should be provided to support this. Establish policies to discourage maltreatment, such as never using physical punishment even if the state in which the early childhood education program is located allows it. Understand what emotional maltreatment entails, and be aware of it so that it does not occur. For example, never belittle a child. If the teacher feels angry and may hurt a child, she should take a break and have a coworker take over, or at least talk to someone.

Preventing Accusations

- **mandate** *an order by law.*

Teachers should inform parents who sign their children up for care that there is a policy that covers child maltreatment. The teacher must be sure the parent understands that any suspected maltreatment must be reported. All states and U.S. territories **mandate** that teachers report any suspected child maltreatment. More than 55 percent of the cases in 2005 were reported by mandated reporters such as educators, child care providers, and social workers (USDHHS, 2007). The parents should also be informed of the steps the teacher uses to prevent maltreatment from occurring in the care situation. The teacher should make sure the parents understand the philosophy of discipline, guidance, child care, and the policy about suspected child abuse.

Routine quick health checks should be done daily. During this time, in addition to observing for health, take time to observe bruises, scratches, or any other injuries that you note. If the child comes to care with an unexplained bruise or physical injury, the teacher should ask the parent about it. The report of the bruise and the explanation should be recorded and added to the child's file. Use injury incident reports any time an accident or injury occurs in your care. Discuss these daily with the parents as they pick up the children. Save a copy of the report in the child's file to document each accident or injury. Any injury incident report should include the date, time, nature of the injury, and any comments by the parent. Documentation is the teacher's best defense (Figure 14-2). Visitors to the early childhood education environment should be required to sign in and out. A clear directive should be given by parents concerning who is allowed to pick up their child or children in care. If a substitute or new volunteer is present or will be coming later in the day, the parents should always be informed before they leave children in care (NAEYC, 2004).

FIGURE 14-2
Injury Incident Report

Injury Incident Report

Child's name: ______________________________

Date: ______________ Time: ______________

Where did the incident take place? ______________________________

Description of incident: ______________________________

____

____

____

Teacher's initials: ______________________________

Action taken by teacher: ______________________________

____

____

____

Observations of behavior changes, if any: ______________________________

____

____

____

Parent notified: ______________________________

Teacher's initials: ______________________________

Teacher's signature ______________ Parent's signature ______________

Intervention

Intervention strategies such as observation, discussion, and action may prevent maltreatment. The teacher should learn to identify when parents or their children are under stress. He should work closely with parents to establish a good, communicative relationship (NAEYC, 2004). NAEYC suggests that the teacher take an active part in preventing abuse and neglect. The Center for the Study of Social Policy (CSSP, 2004) suggests that the presence of a teacher in a child's life is a new, effective, and affordable strategy that may help to prevent child maltreatment. They noted that teachers can offer five protective factors (see Table 14-2). Developing trust and respect keeps the line of communication open between teacher and parent. The teacher may observe a parent or child under stress over a period of time. Talking with the parent may help to relieve the stress or open up other avenues to relieve stress. The teacher can inform the parent that there may be coping skills or outside help for this stress. Information regarding stages of child development and effective ways to handle guidelines and discipline should be made available to families. Children from the age of 3 years can be taught preventive strategies and concepts. They can easily learn about what abuse is, what the body parts are, and the types of touching (Crosson-Tower, 2002; CCHP, 2006). This may provide the action needed to impede the progress of maltreatment.

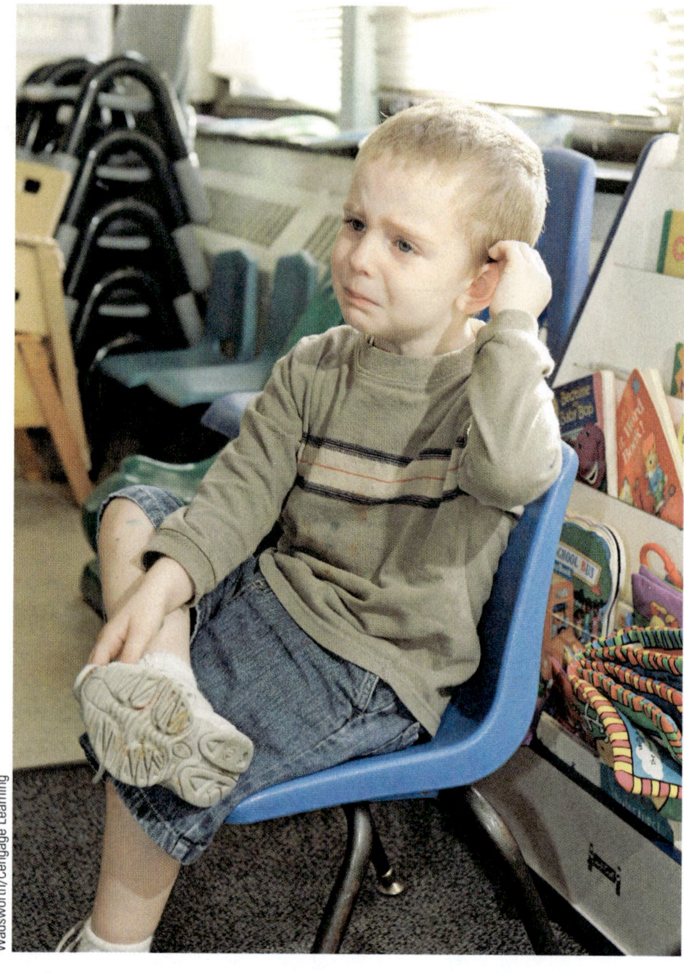
Wadsworth/Cengage Learning

Teachers are in a good position to identify possible maltreatment. In most states, they are mandated to report suspected abuse.

TABLE 14-2
Five Protective Factors for Helping Families Prevent Child Maltreatment

1. Establish trusting relationships with families in order to provide the parents greater resilience. Teachers that are trained to look for early warning signs of distress are better able to intervene if they have positive relationships with families.
2. Help to provide a sense of community for the families in care through social events, potlucks, cultural competence, and other measures.
3. Pass along knowledge of child development and parenting through daily communication, newsletters, handouts, libraries, and support groups.
4. Respond to family crises by offering real support and connections to resources for families. Families may be suffering from unemployment, illness, or housing difficulties, and may not have the coping skills or strategies to seek the help they need.
5. Offer children support so that they can develop their social and emotional competence. Providing protective measures, helping children identify their feelings, and teaching problem-solving strategies will make the children more resilient. This, in turn, may help parents look at their children in a more positive light.

TABLE 14-3
Parental Factors That May Lead to Abusive Behaviors

- Significant changes in lifestyle: death of family member, divorce, unemployment, marital difficulties, or a recent move
- Poor knowledge of child development and unrealistic expectations of the child's capabilities (e.g., the child is a little adult)
- Apathy toward child
- Denial of a child's difficulty at school
- Parenting a child with a disability
- Isolation from support; little or no contact with extended family, neighbors, and friends
- Low self-esteem
- High levels of stress
- History of abuse
- Domestic violence
- Few coping abilities
- Poor impulse control; gets angry for even minor things
- Questionable communication behaviors; may appear to feel threatened or defensive when ordinary questions are asked concerning the child or children
- Lack of bonding or attachment to a child or children
- Under the influence of alcohol or drugs
- Teenage parent
- Poverty
- Adult in home unrelated to child
- Unemployment
- Lacking a high school diploma
- Cultural acceptance of violence toward children
- Belittling or berating the child
- Involved in intimate partner violence, either as victim or perpetrator
- Overprotective of the child, limiting child's interaction with other children

Table 14-3 relates some factors that may exhibit potential for abuse. These behaviors may be exhibited to greater extent when a parent is under stress. Several of these factors are common. Children who come from disadvantaged neighborhoods are more likely to be exposed to punitive parenting behaviors (Kohen et al., 2008) and to suffer child maltreatment than those who do not live in this type of neighborhood (Coulton et al., 2007). Parents of children who are below the poverty level are 22 times more likely to abuse or neglect them than families with incomes of $30,000 or more (CDF, 2005). When people's economics improve, the risk for neglectful parenting diminishes (Zolotor & Runyan, 2006). Parents who are active substance abusers are three times more likely to abuse their children and four times more likely to neglect them. Parents who were maltreated, felt vulnerable, and were involved in partner violence appeared more likely to have cases of substantiated child abuse than parents who did not (Wekerle et al., 2007). Children who have disabilities are at greater risk for maltreatment from their parents (Hibbard & Desch, 2007; Kellogg & The Committee on Child Abuse and Neglect, 2007). The more types of risk a child is exposed to, the greater the chances for maltreatment (Appleyard et al., 2005; Flaherty et al., 2006; Sidebotham & Heron, 2006).

A child's behavior may not always be consistent due to temperament and developmental changes. The teacher will, however, probably be able to find a pattern of behavior for most children. When a child increasingly exhibits poor behavior or appears sad or withdrawn, he may be experiencing stress in his life. The teacher can talk with the child about his feelings and alert a parent to these changes. Children can also use coping skills to relieve stress.

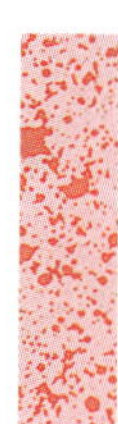

Pause for Reflection

Have you ever been a victim of child maltreatment, or do you know someone who has? What are some of the effects of maltreatment on children? Do you feel you could help a child who has been maltreated?

Key Concept 14.2

Preventive Measures

Preventive measures such as screening teachers and having an open-door policy can help prevent undue accusations against responsible teachers. Teachers should always document any accident, injury, or illness that a child has while in care. The teacher should be aware of the indicators of social circumstances and behaviors of children and parents that could escalate into child maltreatment. Intervention may help prevent maltreatment from occurring.

14.3 PROTECTIVE MEASURES FOR CHILD MALTREATMENT

It is imperative that every teacher be aware of the physical and behavioral indicators of maltreatment. Child maltreatment has been defined by the U.S. Congress (2003) as "any recent act or failure to act on the part of a parent or caretaker, which results in death, serious physical or emotional harm, sexual abuse or exploitation, or an act or failure to act which presents an imminent risk of serious harm." Identifying child abuse is usually not based on one indicator or incident, but rather a series or group of indicators.

Recognition

A teacher needs to know how to recognize the indicators of child maltreatment. Child maltreatment is divided into four categories: physical, emotional, sexual, and neglect (CDC, 2007). Each type of abuse has signs and symptoms

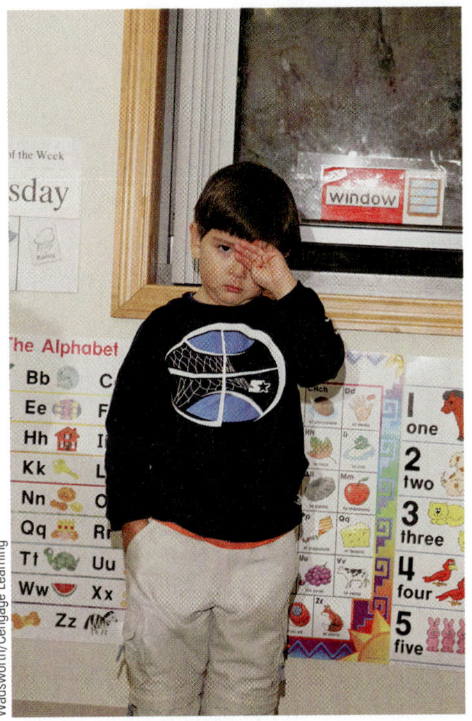

Wadsworth/Cengage Learning

Each type of abuse has signs and symptoms that a teacher should be on the lookout for.

that may indicate that child maltreatment has taken place. A child may suffer from maltreatment in one or more areas.

It is essential that the teacher have an awareness of the indicators of maltreatment. All states mandate that people who care for children are to report suspected abuse. In most states, failure to report brings penalties, including a monetary fine. Some teachers may feel reluctant to report because they believe that the parents may retaliate or that their relationship with the parents may be compromised. Regardless of reluctance or feelings of guilt, a teacher who suspects child maltreatment must report it. The report may make a lasting difference in a child's life. It may prevent death or injury and may help the family to access resources and assistance. In some states, the only follow-up to the maltreatment report may have to come from the early childhood education center unless the children were removed from parental custody. This places the teacher in an awkward situation. All states protect teachers from criminal or civil liability due to reporting of maltreatment.

Physical Abuse. Physical abuse is any act that results in a nonaccidental physical injury. This type of maltreatment may result from severe corporal punishment or from intentional injury by deliberate assault. Table 14-4 includes many physical and behavioral indicators of physical abuse. Physical abuse accounted for 16.6 percent of the substantiated child abuse cases in the United States in 2005. It is thought that the actual prevalence for this type of abuse is actually larger than the substantiated cases (Kellogg & The Committee on Child Abuse and Neglect, 2007).

Emotional Abuse. Emotional abuse includes placing unrealistic demands, excessive yelling, and unnecessary criticism that results in emotional harm or mental suffering. It is perhaps the most difficult type of child maltreatment

TABLE 14-4
Indicators of Physical Abuse

Physical

- Bruises—in linear markings, clusters, on several different areas at a time, and at various stages of healing; may appear after absence, weekend, or vacation
- Burns—cigarette or cigar, immersion burns (on buttocks and genitalia), patterns (iron, grid, rope), or infected burns for which treatment may have been delayed
- Unexplained bite marks
- Lacerations or abrasions—typically around mouth, eyes, and external genitalia; may be in various stages of healing
- Internal injuries
- Unexplained broken bones
- Head injury or whiplash—from shaking the child, known as shaken baby syndrome

Behavioral

- Tells you parents or other adult hurt him
- Overcompliant
- Poor self-concept
- Wary of adult contact; may be frightened of parent or parents or other adults
- Does not want to leave the early childhood education environment
- Extremes in behavior
- Feels deserving of punishment
- Vacant, withdrawn, or detached
- Indiscriminately seeks affection
- Chronic ailments—stomachaches, headaches, vomiting
- Clothing that is not appropriate for the weather but covers body parts
- Describes reason for physical injury not in keeping with developmental level

to prove, but it may be observed when the interaction between a child and parent is seen. See Table 14-5 for a list of indicators of this type of abuse. Emotional abuse accounted for 7.1 percent of the substantiated child abuse cases in the United States in 2005.

Sexual Abuse. Child sexual abuse can be sexual exploitation as well as sexual assault upon the child by an adult or older child. Sexual exploitation includes fondling, mouth to genital contact, exhibition, and showing or using the child for obscene materials. The offender is known to the child in almost 70 percent of the cases of child sexual abuse (USDHHS, 2007). Sexual maltreatment is a reality in the United States. It is estimated that as many as one in five adult

TABLE 14-5
Indicators of Emotional Abuse

Physical

- Failure to thrive
- Withdrawn or depressed
- Disruptive or hyperactive
- Speech or language disorders
- Repetitive rhythmic movements
- Little facial affect—no signs of emotional response
- Bedwetting or toileting accidents for older children

Behavioral

- Rigid in conformity to authority
- Withdrawal
- Overly responsible due to demanding and unrealistic parental expectations
- Destructive or antisocial
- Sleep disorders
- Unusual fears
- Fear of parent or teacher
- Behind in mental or emotional development
- Vacant facial expression
- Aggressive or compliant behavioral extremes

REALITY *Check*

Shaken Baby Syndrome

Shaken baby syndrome is a form of child maltreatment involving forceful or violent shaking of a child from birth to 5 years of age (National Institute of Neurological Disorders and Stroke [NINDS], 2004). Many children in the United States are shaken every year, and of those children at least 1300 are forcefully shaken to the point of harming the child (Zamani, 2005). Between 25 to 30 percent of those children die (Ianelli, 2007). Shaken baby syndrome is the leading cause of death and accounts for the majority of permanent damage or disability to infants and children who are physically abused (Carbaugh, 2004a). The AAP (2001) declared shaken baby syndrome as a serious form of child abuse. Approximately 15 percent of child maltreatment deaths are due to shaking, and it is possible that another 15 percent may be due to shaking (Massey-Stokes, 2006). It is often difficult to believe that children are maltreated, and especially by shaking a baby (Reece, 2004). It most commonly occurs in children under age 2, especially in those between 6 and 8 months of age (Ianelli, 2007).

Children up to age 5 have been violently shaken resulting in shaken baby syndrome (Zamani, 2005; Ianelli, 2007). It is much more common for males to be shaken than females, perhaps due to societal

(continues)

REALITY *Check* (continued)

expectations of males (Carbaugh, 2004a). Children with disabilities are more likely to be shaken than those without disabilities. Shaken baby syndrome may also occur as a result of tossing a small child into the air, but this is much less likely. The violent type of shaking makes infants and young children especially vulnerable to injury because their heads are larger, their neck muscles are not well developed, and their brain and surrounding tissues are very fragile. Violent shaking of a baby is usually done in anger and frustration. When this type of shaking occurs, it multiplies the force to between 5 and 10 times that which occurs when a child trips or falls. Anyone who witnesses this type of force can easily see how the child is in a life-threatening situation (AAP, 2001). The sudden movements occurring with this type of force can cause some parts of the brain to pull away. The result is torn brain cells and blood vessels (American Humane Association [AHA], 2001b). Babies' brains have a high water content, and the nerve cells in their brains are less likely to have a high level of myelination. Often a young child's brain rotates much more than an adult's brain would.

Shaken baby syndrome does not occur with short falls, seizures, or because a child has been vaccinated. It only occurs through violent shaking, which does not have to last more than 20 seconds or 40 to 50 shakes to do damage that can be fatal (National Center on Shaken Baby Syndrome [NCSBS], 2007). Twenty-five to 30 percent of babies who die from child maltreatment die from being shaken. The common triad of injuries for shaken baby syndrome is water on the brain, with swelling and subdural and retinal hemorrhages (Harding, Risdon, & Krous, 2004). These are commonly accompanied by other injuries such as broken ribs. One baby in four dies as a result of shaking. Very few babies escape permanent injury, and most survivors suffer brain damage (AHA, 2001b). Permanent injury for the majority of these babies can range from partial to complete blindness and hearing loss, as well as seizure disorder, cerebral palsy, developmental disabilities, autism, behavior problems, and sucking and swallowing disorders. It can also result in a permanent vegetative state.

Adult males in their twenties who are the father of the child or the boyfriend of the mother are the most common perpetrators of shaking a baby (Carbaugh, 2004a). Estimates that adult males are the perpetrators range from 65 to 90 percent. Often they are involved in domestic violence and substance abuse (AAP, 2001). The most common risk factors for shaken baby syndrome are listed here (NCSBS, 2005; Carbaugh, 2004a):

- Depression, anxiety
- Substance abuse
- Low income
- Social isolation or lack of social support
- Diminished satisfaction with relationship
- Poor family function
- Loss of perceived control, feelings of frustration

Females who shake babies are more likely to be babysitters or teachers than mothers. Several recent sensational cases across the nation have focused on caregivers who were accused of shaking a baby and causing death or permanent damage.

Immediate medical help can reduce the impact of shaking. Many people who do shake an infant put the child down, thinking he will sleep and later wake up and be fine (AAP, 2001). Any opportunity for recovery may be lost during this time. People who shake an infant often claim to have no knowledge of how the child got injured. This claim prevents vital care because medical tests that take a great deal of time are used to determine the cause of the injury before proper care may be initiated.

Babies who have been shaken exhibit signs that indicate they have been seriously shaken (Carbaugh, 2004b), among them these:

- Poor feeding
- Hard to wake up
- Throwing up
- Breathing problems
- Dilated pupils; pooling of blood in the eye
- Weakness
- Seizures
- Coma

(continues)

REALITY *Check* (continued)

If these symptoms are exhibited, it is important to call 911 or the local emergency rescue number. When a child is brought to the emergency room with these symptoms and no other apparent reason for this condition, there will always be an investigation by the social agency in charge of child protection (Blumenthal, 2002).

Frustration with a crying child seems to be the biggest cause of shaking. Most people are unaware that this type of shaking can cause permanent damage or death to a child. A normal baby spends between 2 and 3 hours a day crying. Approximately one-fourth of infants cry much longer than that. There may be no apparent reason for the crying. Infants in the 1- to 4-month-old range are most likely to display this excessive crying (NCSBS, 2007). Recently, Dr. Ronald Barr described his discovery called "The Period of PURPLE Crying" (NCSBS, 2007; Wells, 2007). He found that babies may tend to cry increasingly from birth until they are about 2 months old. There is no pattern to the crying, and when the baby cries she may resist any effort at soothing. The infant may look as if she is in pain, even if she isn't. This type of crying typically occurs in the late afternoon and evening and may last at least half an hour or more. For more information about this type of crying, as well as more links for teachers, visit the website, http://www.dontshake.org/index.php. A book out now titled *The Period of PURPLE Crying* is available from this website (Wells, 2007; NCSBS, 2007). This information may make someone dealing with a crying infant feel better, knowing that it is normal.

A parent or teacher who is easily frustrated or angered may respond by shaking the baby in an attempt to get him to stop crying. Shaking may stop the crying, but it may also kill the baby or injure him to the extent that he will never fully recover. It is very important for teachers of young children to understand this and never, ever, shake a baby.

Some methods have worked to help stop a baby from crying. The first step would be to calm down and try to figure out what is making the baby cry. Is he crying because she is hungry, wet, too hot, too cold, or overtired? Does the baby have a fever or is she in pain? The next step is to try to help the baby to relax (Carbaugh, 2004b). Running a vacuum cleaner near the baby, giving her a pacifier, or cuddling the child gently may help to alleviate the crying (AHA, 2001b). Swaddling a baby or rocking her gently, turning down the lights, or even playing some calming music might help. If none of those suggestions work, realize that a baby can be left in a safe place to cry. Walk away after putting the baby in a safe place. This third step keeps the baby safe. Listen to music or call someone for support or advice. If the crying continues, call the doctor. After you have calmed down, resume trying to help the baby. If you become desperate, call the parents to come get the child and then call CHILDHELP (800-4-ACHILD) to talk to someone while you wait for the parent. If crying is difficult for you to hear, you may want to consider working with older children, who may be less frustrating for you, or not working with children at all.

Parents should also be educated about shaken baby syndrome (Massey-Stokes, 2006). When parents are educated, the incidence of shaken baby syndrome can be significantly reduced (Dias et al., 2005). Obtain brochures to hand out, and put up a poster warning about shaken baby syndrome. Find these by visiting the National Center on Shaken Baby Syndrome at http://www.dontshake.org/index.php or by faxing 801-627-3321. This information will help a parent better understand and may prevent shaking at home. It will also help the parent to understand that it is best for the teacher to call the parent when help is needed. As an infant or very young child enters care, have a handout for the family on how to cope with crying babies. Display this handout on the bulletin board.

CHECK*point:* **What are the steps to take if a baby has cried and cried, and you can't seem to stop it and you are getting frustrated?**

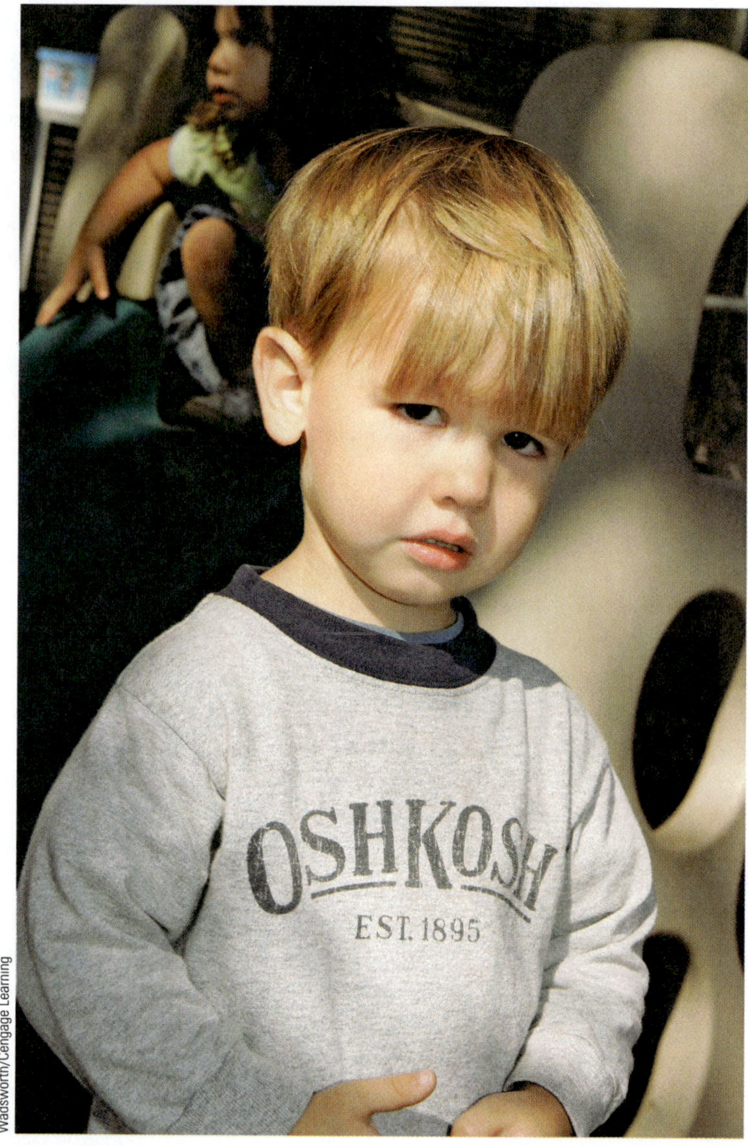

Wadsworth/Cengage Learning

A consistently vacant, withdrawn, or detached child may be a victim of emotional abuse.

women were abused as children (Bono, 2004). Table 14-6 includes indicators of sexual abuse. Sexual abuse accounted for 9.3 percent of the substantiated child abuse cases in the United States in 2005.

Neglect. Neglect causes death more frequently than any other type of child maltreatment (CDF, 2005). While cases of physical and sexual abuse in the 1990s decreased, the cases of neglect remained the same or increased slightly (Jones, Finkelhor, & Halter, 2006). In 2005, approximately 36 percent of fatalities due to child maltreatment were found to be from neglect (USDHHS, 2007). Neglect of a child includes depriving the child of food, shelter, medical care, supervision, or education (Theodore, Runyan, & Chang, 2007). Negligence occurs both in actions and in failure to act on behalf of the child. Severe neglect includes intentional failure to provide for a child and allowing danger to the child's person or health. Table 14-7 lists the indicators of neglect. Neglect accounted for 62.8 percent of child abuse cases in the United States

TABLE 14-6
Indicators of Sexual Abuse

Physical

- Torn, stained, or bloody underclothing
- Pain, itching, or swelling in genital areas
- Bruises, lacerations, or bleeding in genital, vaginal, or anal area
- Discharge in vaginal/genital area
- Venereal disease
- Difficulty in walking or sitting
- Pain when urinating or defecating

Behavioral

- Withdrawn, fantasy, or infantile
- Poor self-esteem and self-image
- Poor peer relationships
- Depression
- Abrupt changes in behavior such as eating, sleeping, or school performance
- Excessively clingy or inappropriate attachment
- Excessive bathing or need to be clean
- Exceptional fear of a person or place
- Draws scary pictures that include plenty of black and red coloring
- Inappropriate sexual knowledge or behavior
- Reporting of abuse by parent or other adult
- Neglected physical appearance

TABLE 14-7
Indicators of Neglect

Physical

- Always hungry, dirty, or inappropriately dressed
- Lacks medical or dental care
- Lack of supervision, especially for long periods of time
- Unsanitary home
- Abandonment
- Underweight, poor growth
- Consistently absent from school
- Signs of hunger
- Long, dirty fingernails

(continues)

TABLE 14-7 *(Continued)*
Indicators of Neglect

Behavioral

- **Stealing or begging for food or money for food**
- **Parent bringing child early and picking up late**
- **Inappropriate attachment or affection**
- **Shows or expresses no emotions**
- **Parent abusing drugs or alcohol**
- **Overly responsible; assumes adult role**
- **Does not want to leave school**

Julena was a happy 4-year-old who had been at the center she attended for more than two years. In the past few months, however, she had been more withdrawn at times and at other times more aggressive. Gayle, her teacher, noticed that Julena spent a lot of time in the bathroom and would rub private areas at nap time. This eventually led to the observation that Julena was masturbating. This greatly disturbed Gayle, who spoke with her director, Rose. They discussed the issue and spoke to Julena's mother, Traci, about it. She was shocked and somewhat in denial. But, as the discussion progressed, Traci admitted that she had left Julena a lot with her new boyfriend, George, because her mother had been ill and in the hospital. George had picked up Julena a number of times in the past month or so. Gayle and Rose both suggested that Traci more closely observe Julena, take her to the doctor's for an examination, and not allow her to be alone with George for a while to see whether that helped the situation. They also documented Gayle's observations and the conversation with Traci and were ready to report it. After a few days, Traci came back to inform them that George was no longer in her life. The doctor confirmed that Julena had been molested. Traci had discussed the matter with George, and he got very angry but did not deny that he had sexually molested Julena. Gayle and Rose reported the incidents to Child Protective Services, who in turn opened an investigation on George. Apparently, George had been reported several years earlier by a previous girlfriend who had a young child and suspected George might be molesting her daughter. Nothing could be proven, so nothing happened. This time, the previous suspicion, the documentation from Julena's physician, and the observations from Gayle led to George's arrest. Gayle and Rose did what they could to support both Julena and Traci through this difficult time. They referred both to counseling, which did help. Julena eventually became a relatively happy child again, but was somewhat hesitant around men she did not know. Traci felt great guilt, but through counseling saw that she had been put in a position where she needed someone's help and George had conveniently been there. She also knew the next time she was in a bind that she would find a more reliable and less threatening source to help her with Julena.

Children who are unsupervised for long periods of time (a sign of neglect) are at a higher risk for death than children who are physically abused.

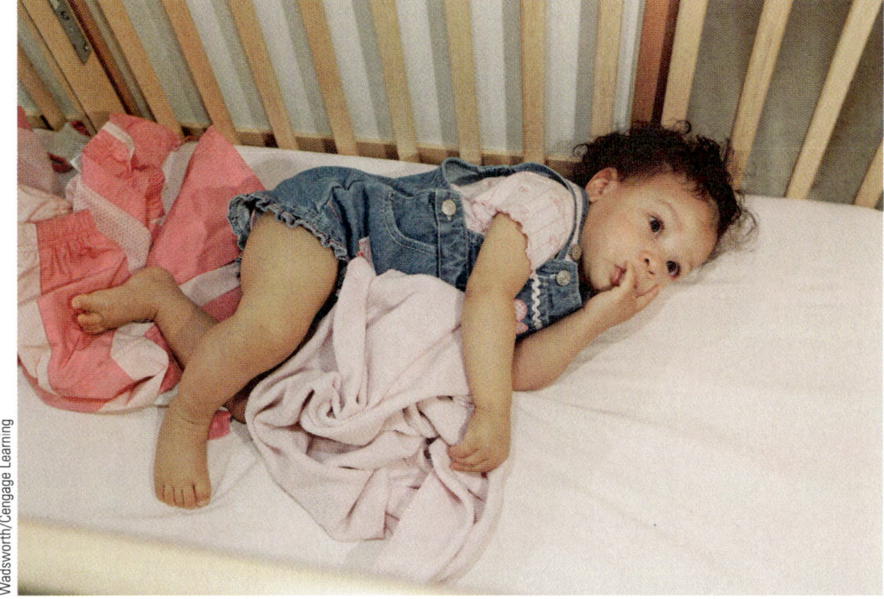

Wadsworth/Cengage Learning

in 2005, and medical neglect accounted for 2 percent. The remaining child abuse cases were counted as "other," which includes abandonment, threats of harm, and congenital drug addiction.

A form of neglect that affects children under the age of 3 years is called failure to thrive. There is an organic form of this condition, but that can be traced to physical factors such as inability to process certain enzymes or other problems. The form of failure-to-thrive that is traced to neglect is directly caused by environmental factors such as not feeding enough food, not attending to the child when he cries, and leaving the child alone for long periods of time with no interaction. These children appear emaciated, have a vacant expression, and apparent lack of energy.

Documentation

If the teacher suspects or has reason to believe that maltreatment is occurring, then it must be reported. The teacher does not have to witness the maltreatment personally or have positive proof that it occurred. Teachers need to understand how to document suspected child maltreatment and how to report it (Palmer & Smith, 2006b).

Observing children is one of the major jobs of a teacher. The teacher needs to be aware of the indicators of maltreatment in order to notice a problem. The teacher should observe the child at different times of day and in different settings and record the observations in note form.

The teacher should record behavior, conversation, and physical signs. This type of anecdotal record may signify a pattern that indicates maltreatment is present. It may also indicate that there is no pattern present and what the teacher noticed about a bruise and limp might have been the result of a fall. The records should be kept in the child's health record in case there is need to refer to them again. If a teacher is still uncertain, he should talk to others on the staff to see what they think. In the end, if the teacher reasonably suspects that maltreatment has occurred, it must be reported.

Reporting

If the teacher needs to report child maltreatment, the reporting process should be clear. In most states there is a Child Welfare Office or Child Protective Services. If the teacher is unsure, the local Department of Social Services or law enforcement agency should be contacted, well before any suspected maltreatment is observed, because each state has its own individual laws governing the reporting of abuse. There may be forms that the teacher must keep on hand. The teacher should also inquire whether there is a 24-hour hotline so the number may be posted. For many states, making a phone call is the first step.

In some states, the phone call is not the first step unless it is an emergency. The first step may be to write a written report filled out on the proper form. When a report is filed, the child's name, address, and age must be included. The parents' names and address or addresses (if they have separate homes) should also be given. The teacher's name and address should be given as well. Anonymity for the teacher will be provided. The teacher should realize that the parents might be able to tell who reported the maltreatment because it is likely that the teacher has more information about the child than anyone else. The action by the Child Protective Services or police department will follow in one or more ways. A case may be dismissed as unfounded, or it will be officially opened. Services will be offered to the family, which may be refused. An in-home inspection may take place or a visit to the early childhood education environment may occur. If the agency feels there is just cause, the child may be placed in protective custody. If allegations appear to be grave, criminal charges may be filed.

The teacher may want to talk to the parent before reporting the maltreatment. Some parents may be relieved that help is available, although anger and hostility are another common reaction and the parents may remove the child from the early childhood education environment. If the teacher decides to tell the parents before the report, once again, she should explain the requirement to report any suspected maltreatment. As difficult as it may be to tell the parents before reporting the suspected maltreatment, it may be better that they still trust the teacher for her honesty. The best course is for the teacher to plan to help the parents through the process. Supporting the family after reporting maltreatment is often a center-based responsibility and includes referrals to meet the needs of the family.

A roadblock that a teacher may run into is her own reluctance to report maltreatment. Human emotions enter into matters that are this grave. Reluctance may be based on the teacher's personal background, lack of support from supervisory personnel, or family rights issues. In some cultures, a family's rights over their children are deeply held beliefs (Zamani, 2000, CCHP, 2006), and this may be even more true if the family has recently immigrated from another country. The teacher may feel nervous or emotional about this because of her own family experiences. She may be concerned that although a report was made, there will be no proper follow-up to it. She may fear that the parents will retaliate or that they will pull their child out of the early childhood education environment. The teacher may even fear that she will lose her job. Often, the teacher may feel she is betraying the child and the family by reporting suspected maltreatment (CCHP, 2006). "Knowing how, when and what to report about child abuse and neglect may make a life or death difference for a child" (AHA, 2001a).

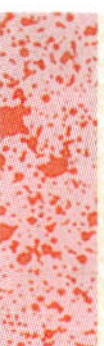

Pause for Reflection

Could you easily report suspected child maltreatment, or would that be a roadblock for you? If so, why?

Caring for the Maltreated Child

If maltreatment is blatant and puts the child in real danger, the child may be removed from the family. If this is the case, the courts, foster families, or other family members who gain custody of the child may wish to continue to keep the child in the early childhood education situation so as to maintain some consistency in the child's life. The teacher will be working with a team to help support the child and to create solutions to any behavioral difficulties that may have arisen as a result of his maltreatment (Blanchard, Gurka, & Blackman, 2006). Many times, one of the major effects of child maltreatment is a sense of shame that children feel (Deblinger & Runyon, 2005). In addition to the shame, they may also feel anger (Bennett, Sullivan, & Lewis, 2005).

The maltreated child may have a number of outward symptoms or behaviors that manifest due to the circumstances. He may exhibit one or more behaviors as listed in Table 14-4 through Table 14-7. He may have varying degrees of posttraumatic stress disorder (PTSD). In some cases, these children who show PTSD may be quick to react emotionally, especially when something scares them (Masten et al., 2008). Maltreated children may also have a harder time making friends. They may be either disliked because they are physically or verbally aggressive or shunned because they are withdrawn and not very social (Anthonysamy & Zimmer-Gembeck, 2007).

Teachers need to understand how to support a child and his family or custodian after maltreatment has been established. The first step in this process is for the teacher to examine her own confidence level, her knowledge of human development, and how she feels about the maltreatment. How the teacher

Domestic violence is a problem for families of all languages and cultures.

Wadsworth/Cengage Learning

REALITY *Check*

Domestic Violence and Its Effect on Children's Lives

The home can be a more dangerous place than the streets. Intimate violence is a widespread issue (Dubowitz et al., 2008). Women are nine times more likely to get hurt in the home than on the streets. Three-quarters of domestic violence occurs in the home (CDF, 2005). Domestic violence usually involves a pattern of assaultive and/or coercive behaviors toward an intimate partner. This can be physical assault, sexual assault or coercion, or psychological or economic abuse (Rose, 2005). It is estimated that at least 20 percent of women have been beaten at least one time in an intimate relationship (Child Witness to Violence Project, 2007). Studies indicate that the number of children that witness domestic violence and the maltreatment of their mothers ranges from 3 to 10 million (Family Violence Prevention Fund [FVPF], 2004; Kolar & Davey, 2007). Witnessing domestic or intimate partner violence includes hearing it, seeing it, and knowing about it. It is estimated that at least one-third of children in the United States witness violence between their parents (Child Witness to Violence Project, 2007). A child may not have seen or heard the act occurring, but he may indeed be able to see the results by observing cuts, bruises, and broken bones. Domestic violence ranges from insults, to beatings, to homicide (Osofsky, 1999). Experts believe that domestic violence is the single major precursor that leads to child abuse and neglect. Studies have found that in homes where domestic violence is present, children are 15 times more likely to be physically abused or neglected than in homes where it is not present. Many studies have indicated that there is a co-occurrence between domestic violence and child maltreatment at least 40 percent of the time (Zero to Three, 2005a; Child Witness to Violence Project, 2007). The more often domestic violence occurs, the more likely the children are to be abused. Nearly half the men who abuse their female partners will abuse their children (Child Witness to Violence Project, 2007). A woman who is a victim of domestic violence may be less able to protect her children. Even though this is true, many child welfare workers appear to be more likely to give responsibility for child maltreatment to the mother who could not protect her child than to the father who was the designated domestic violence batterer (Landsman & Hartley, 2007).

Changes that have occurred in family systems in recent decades have led to greater stress in families. Some of these changes include poverty, social isolation, low educational levels, substance abuse, marital discord, and lack of coping abilities. All of these can lead to child maltreatment. Families are no longer like those that were portrayed on television in the 1950s and 1960s. Divorce affects almost one in two families, and more than one in four families are headed by a single parent. Parents may not be able to stay at home with children due to economic stresses, so younger children may be in nonparental care and older children may become latchkey children. More families with children live in poverty, and there is a greater degree of drug and alcohol abuse than we have previously seen in this country. All of these factors contribute to stress that can manifest in domestic violence. The more of these factors present, the greater the risk for domestic violence (Wekerle et al., 2007; Appleyard et al., 2005).

Domestic violence occurs at every socioeconomic level and in every racial, cultural, religious, and ethnic group (Moore et al., 2007). Men are more likely than women to commit domestic violence. Men who had witnessed domestic violence in their homes as they were growing up were found to be twice as likely to abuse the women in their life as men who had not (FVPF, 2004). Women who commit domestic violence usually do so in self-defense or in retaliation for abuse.

Even if children themselves are not maltreated, witnessing abuse can have traumatic effects on them. The basic sense of trust that should be present in a child's life may be damaged or destabilized.

(continues)

REALITY*Check* (continued)

Witnessing violence may lead to fear, discipline problems, depression, poor social interaction, and drug abuse among children (Zero to Three, 2005a; Kolar & Davey, 2007). Both internalizing and externalizing behavioral problems may be present if a child has witnessed severe domestic partner violence (Hazen et al., 2006). For some children, the witnessing of violence towards their mothers puts them at risk for emotional and behavioral problems and for reproducing violent behavior (Cater, 2007). Long-term effects may include PTSD and personality disorders (Rice & Groves, 2005; Child Witness to Violence Project, 2007). Physical problems can be present as well as cognitive developmental delays (National Clearinghouse on Child Abuse and Neglect Information [NAIC], 2004; Rice & Groves, 2005). Younger children may be more vulnerable to the effects of domestic violence than children who are older (Sternberg et al., 2006). Witnessing violence may lead to children's performing violent acts as they get older (Garbarino, 2001; Mersky & Reynolds, 2007; Hanson et al., 2006).

It has been reported that 79 percent of children in institutions for violent behavior have witnessed violence. Boys who witness violence are more likely than girls to act out (Bauer et al., 2006). Children who have been exposed to intimate partner violence are more likely for increased levels of physical aggression and acting out. They are three times more likely to become abusive to their domestic partners later in life. Girls are much more likely to allow abuse to occur to them as women. Both behaviors perpetuate domestic violence.

Many professionals believe that witnessing domestic violence is the most harmful type of violence that a child could experience (Groves, 2003; Zero to Three, 2005a). When children see violence in their own homes with their own families, they realize that they have no safe place. Even a child under the age of one year can still have memory of when domestic violence or child maltreatment occurred (Gaensbauer, 2004). If a child cannot feel safe at home, he is less likely to develop trust and later explore his environment. Without trust and exploration, achieving autonomy as a normal course of development is difficult. Children may also feel guilty that they could not prevent the act or that they did something to trigger the act (Farmington, New Mexico, Police Department [FNMPD], 2001). Children who witness domestic violence may become anxious and fearful under most conditions. The health of these children may also be at risk (Flaherty et al., 2006; Bair-Merritt, Blackstone, & Feudtner, 2006). Children who witness domestic violence may have physical complaints like headaches and stomach aches. They may worry about danger, have sleep disturbances, or separation anxiety (Rose, 2005).

Children who have an adult they can trust are likely to cope better. Frequent positive interactions can help a child feel safe (Adults and Children Together [ACT], 2001). The most protective factor for a child who does not feel safe at home is the existence of a strong, positive relationship between the child and a competent and caring adult (Kersey & Malley, 2005). Teachers can provide this type of relationship and can develop trust among themselves and the children in their care. Teachers can help to foster resiliency and teach children conflict resolution. Providing these types of supportive relationships for vulnerable children is being encouraged for inclusion in the early childhood education environment (Kersey & Malley, 2005).

Teachers can model prosocial behaviors and help children have a greater sense of acceptance and self-esteem. Children can be praised and recognized for good behaviors and redirected away from aggressive behaviors. The early childhood education environment can provide predicable routines and teach nonviolent ways of problem solving. Teachers can also provide a safe haven from a difficult home life for a few hours a day.

CHECK*point*: What protective factors could a teacher provide for a child who has witnessed domestic violence?

feels about herself will affect whether she can offer support. If the teacher has a low confidence level, it will be difficult to help the child raise his.

The teacher needs to determine her level of understanding about what is normal behavior. She needs to understand what behaviors need to be redirected. These factors will determine the skill level the teacher has to do the job. The child may have to address factors of his social and emotional development process. Can the teacher help a child learn to trust and live within safe boundaries? Judging the maltreatment can impede the teacher's ability to perform. Placing blame and being angry will not help the teacher perform her job.

If the teacher has personally suffered from abuse in some form as a child, there may be unresolved feelings. Will these feelings hinder the relationship with the child or parent?

If the teacher determines that she is capable of helping and supporting a maltreated child, there are several critical things that she can provide:

- Trust
- Predictable routines
- Consistent behavior
- Safe boundaries
- Confidence
- Good communication skills
- Model healthy ways to relate to others

These will offer the child the sense of well-being needed to progress beyond the maltreatment.

Key Concept 14.3

Protective Measures for Child Maltreatment

Protective measures such as recognition of maltreatment, documentation, and reporting give teachers the tools needed to protect children from maltreatment. The teacher should be able to recognize the physical and behavioral indicators of physical abuse, emotional abuse, sexual abuse, and neglect. The teacher should understand the procedures for documenting and reporting maltreatment, and know the practices and strategies that will offer care to a maltreated child.

14.4 WORKING WITH CHILDREN FROM SUBSTANCE-ABUSING FAMILIES

It is estimated that 30 percent of drug abusers are women of childbearing age. An estimated 10 percent of young children live with a parent who is substance-dependent (Knitzer & Lefkowitz, 2006). Between 40 and 80 percent of families who have Child Protective Services interventions have difficulties with drugs and/or alcohol (CDF, 2005). Methamphetamine use alone accounts for large numbers of rural children who are taken into Child Protective Services custody (Lester, et al., 2006). Parental substance abuse can be a predictor of maltreatment and subsequent foster care placement (Smith et al., 2007). Prenatal exposure to drugs can cause developmental difficulties in several areas, and this risk increases if there are also environmental factors such as continued substance abuse (Messinger et al., 2004; Linares et al., 2006). Difficulties may include the ones listed here:

- Children may be unable to organize their own play.
- Sporadic mastery is common.
- Learning strategies and problem solving may be hindered by a lack of organization of inner states.
- Communication and language development may be impaired by delayed acquisition of words and gestures, inability to express feelings, and speech difficulties.
- Difficulty with motor skills may be exhibited in both gross and fine motor skills.
- There may be subtle deficits in cognitive development.
- Acquiring a sense of self may be hampered by lack of attachment or inconsistent or negligent care.
- A range of disorders, from oppositional defiant disorder to AD/HD, may be present.
- Problems with aggression, externalizing behaviors, and total behavioral problems may exist.

All of these vulnerabilities can be assessed through observation and the use of assessment tools. Women who enter drug treatment programs often have custodial children and few economic resources (Hanson, 2002). More than 80 percent of the perpetrators of child maltreatment are parents (USDHHS, 2007), and almost half of parents who maltreat children have some substance abuse problems (ChildHelp USA, 2004). These families may present a great challenge to the teacher. The families may be represented in several ways:

- The recovering family, who may be feeling vulnerable
- The addicted family living in chaos, who may be emotionally unavailable or negligent
- The foster family or kinship caregiver (related to the child), who may feel overwhelmed

The Recovering Family

The recovering family may be in or out of a recovery program. The parent or parents may have few coping skills. They may have little knowledge about nutrition, what to do about a child's behavior and discipline, how development occurs, or the basics of how to take care of a child. The parents may be developmentally "frozen" at the stage of their own development when they began abusing drugs. They may be emotionally unavailable and struggling with attachment issues. They may be struggling to remain clean. The environment may be chaotic. These parents may also feel aware for the first time in a long time, especially if they have been in recovery for a while. This may make them feel ashamed and guilty for what they have put their children through. Many of these parents could benefit from the teacher's role modeling how to treat children. They may need extra help in caregiving skills. The teacher should try to create a sense of trust so that information about parenting can be passed along through conversation and other measures found in Table 14-2.

The Actively Abusing Family

FIGURE 14-3
Downward Spiral of Addiction

- Distrust
- Unhappiness
- Denial
- Irritability
- Loss of interest
- Self-defense
- Depression
- Self-neglect
- Loss of self-respect
- Dishonesty
- Isolation
- Indefinable fears
- Hostility
- Blames others
- Escape
- Chronic depression
- Increased drug use
- Suicide attempts or admits defeat
- Bottoming out and into recovery or death

The addictive family brings a whole series of problems. As people who abuse drugs go through the cycle of abuse, there is a tendency to get hostile when dealing with people in authority. Figure 14-3 shows the feelings that the downward spiral of addiction can cause in an active substance-abusing family.

Substance-abusing families live in an extremely chaotic environment. Children from this environment may have difficulty getting their physical needs met. There may not be food or clean clothes available for them. They may suffer great stress from negligent or inconsistent care at home. As of 2007, all but Alabama, Connecticut, Delaware, New Jersey, and Vermont have laws on their books that consider the exposure of children to their parents' substance abuse as child maltreatment and grounds for involvement of Child Protective Services (Child Welfare Information Gateway, 2007).

A child cannot count on a substance-abusing parent to meet her needs. Behavioral problems with a child may directly relate to active drug use in the home (Delaney-Black et al., 2000). An active substance abuser may have sudden mood swings that display the person as being either really up or really down and depressed. It is difficult to predict whether the person will show up when expected for appointments, including bringing the child to care. An addict may lose track of time or suffer from a hangover. Another common characteristic of an active abuser is the avoidance of contact with concerned persons. Isolation is at the core of addiction, and that in itself can cause many problems. A parent who is actively abusing drugs or alcohol may have difficulty forming a bond of trust with anyone and may be emotionally unavailable to the child or the teacher. Abusing families put their children at risk. They may fear that if help is sought, the child will be removed from the home. The family addictive system may discourage any behavior changes.

Pause for Reflection

Do you know the statistics for substance abuse in your community? Do you know the drug most commonly abused? Have you ever known someone with a substance abuse problem? Can you relate to the section on "The Actively Abusing Family"?

The Foster or Kinship Family

More than 500,000 children are in foster care at any one time in the United States (CDF, 2005). Of those in foster care, 58 percent are children of color. Foster families may be dealing with children of a different racial/ethnic background and some children who do not speak the same language. Children who go into homes where the family does not speak the same language or follow their cultural traditions may feel a sense of isolation and fear, which

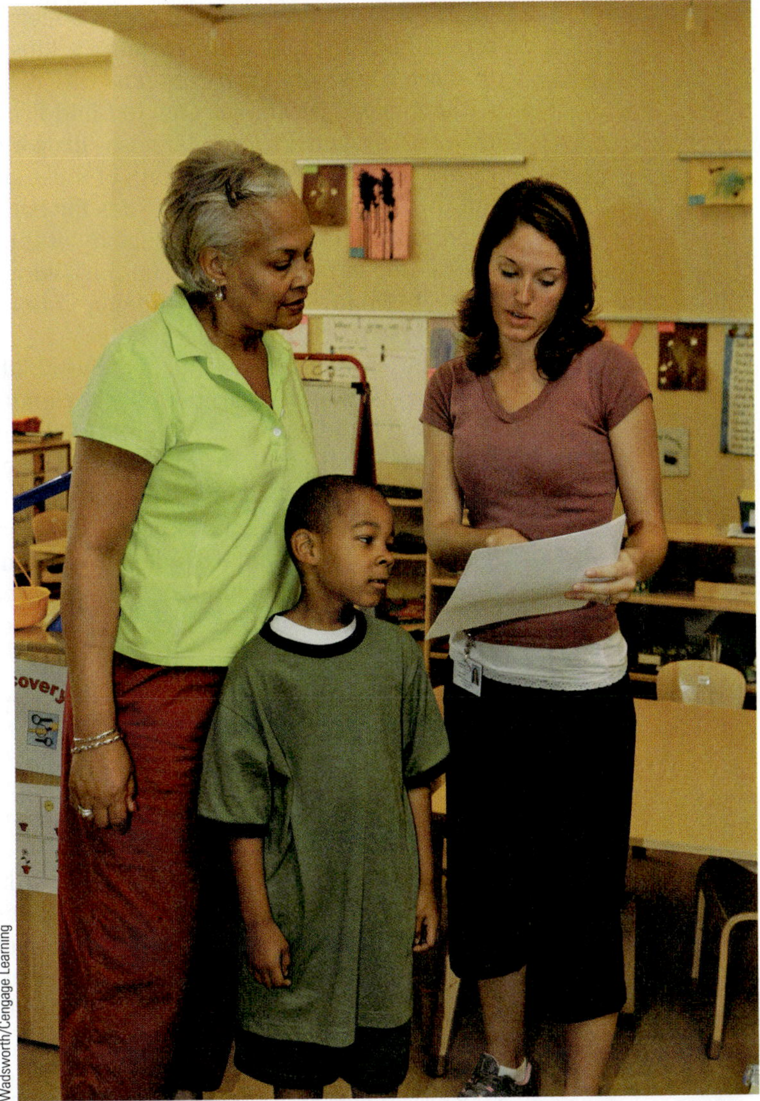
Wadsworth/Cengage Learning

Many grandparents are actively involved in their grandchildren's lives. As many as 10 percent are helping to raise these children, and the majority of these children have at least one parent with a substance abuse problem.

the foster family must deal with. The average length of time a child is in foster care is about 2½ years. Federal law requires that parental rights be terminated if children have been in foster care for more than 15 months of the most recent 22 months (CDF, 2005). Many children in the foster care system are there due to their parents' substance abuse and may have issues including cognitive difficulties and behavioral problems as a result. Foster families may be dealing with issues of culture and law in addition to any special needs of the children in their care. These foster families may need services or resources that should be provided by the system in which they operate, but which are not always immediately available. They may need extra help in coping with these children. Having a teacher to talk to may be of help. Teachers might also help with referrals, if needed.

By 2000, more than 2.5 million children were living in households headed by grandparents or other relatives where no parent was present. These kinship families may have their own difficulties. Almost half of those children are there because of their parents' substance abuse. More than

50 percent of these children are younger than age 6 (Egyptian Area Agency on Aging [EAAA], 2004). Becoming a kinship family usually happens in one of three ways. The most common way is for families to take the children in without reporting the parents to Child Protective Services and thus avoiding the court system. Parents can also "drop off" their children for a visit and not return for months or years. Both of these situations usually help the children, but they do offer some legal issues for both the teacher and the kin that will need to be addressed. Legal custody of the child may be in flux. The parents may still have legal custody. The third way is for kin to be given guardianship through the juvenile or dependency court system. In this case, they do have custody, so there are no legal issues.

The circumstances that led the child to this caretaker situation may have an effect on the caretakers. They may be sad, angry, depressed, or overwhelmed. If the parent of the child is around and wants to participate in the child's life, that can cause difficulties. There may be legal boundaries that have been or need to be mandated. The teacher will need to be aware of these or any other legal custody issues. Teachers can also assist these families by recognizing that extra help may be needed both in the early childhood education environment and in the home. Teachers can help the family access social services to support them through the difficulties they may encounter.

Establishing a Relationship with the Family

Establishing a relationship with the family is a crucial step in the intervention process to help a child from a substance-abusing family. Providing a safe and secure environment for the parent and family is almost as critical as providing that type of care for the child. As difficult as it may be, the teacher should try to establish communication with the parent concerning the child. If the family is a foster or kinship family, it should be easier to have an open channel of communication. The teacher should be consistent and predictable in these relationships, and should use cultural competence if applicable. The teacher who tries to show respect to the family, whichever type it is, is more likely to be accepted by them.

Families where the parents are in recovery or actively using substances may present greater challenges. Many teachers try to avoid difficult situations involving parents. They may also avoid difficult parents (Boutte et al., 1992). Children in this situation need the support of the teacher. The teacher should avoid arguing with the parent, getting angry, being taken in by the parent's defensiveness, and becoming an enabler. The teacher should model good coping skills, be flexible, remain calm and nonjudgmental, and be culturally competent. It might help the teacher to practice possible parent responses and be prepared to answer them. If none of these suggestions work, respect the limitations of your abilities (Gonzalez-Mena & Stonehouse, 2000). You may need outside help in the form of a counselor or drug counselor in your area.

Foster or kinship families may be much more receptive and appreciative of the teacher's role in the child's life. The major focus of most of these families is to provide a safe, caring environment for the children in their charge. The foster families may have been in the system for many years or they may be relatively new to it, and that will determine how much help or understanding they will need from the teacher. Foster families who have been providing care for children for many years may be connected to resources and information that would be helpful to the teacher. They are usually most happy

Frances had been a postal worker and was retiring in a couple of years. She had custody of her granddaughter Emma, who was 2½ years old. Frances' daughter Betsy had been on drugs for many years as had Betsy's husband and they were not doing well parenting Emma. The courts had taken Emma from her parents and placed Emma with Frances. Neither Frances nor her husband Mark were sure how they felt about doing this, especially since they had upcoming retirement plans. They weren't sure they were up to the task. Frances had already been paying for a part-time preschool experience for Emma to get her out of the environment she had been in, at least for a few hours a day. Hillary was Emma's teacher and had noticed how withdrawn Emma had been in the few months she had been in her class. When Frances got custody she had to extend Emma's time at school due to her full-time employment. Hillary gave Frances some suggestions for helping her give Emma the support she needed at home for the changes that had happened in her young life. Frances and Mark spent time going to classes and support groups for grandparents raising grandchildren. Frances shared much of what she had learned with Hillary. Between Frances, Mark, and Hillary doing what they could to support Emma, slowly but surely Emma came out of her shell. After a year, it was hard to tell that this was the same child. Emma was happy, active, and appeared to be very bright. Emma was fortunate enough to be in a place that supported her situation and that also helped Frances and Mark with that early time. The courts had taken parental rights away from Emma's parents, and Frances and Mark had decided they would adopt Emma and raising her would become their retirement "project."

to share what they know with others, so the teacher should take advantage of this knowledge. Kinship families may be more likely to be struggling and so any form of help the teacher can give will be appreciated. As with the children in this situation, it is important to be calm, nonjudgmental, and culturally competent with the families they are in.

Working with the Children

The teacher needs to provide a safe and protective environment. Good child development techniques are essential. A child at risk can be a challenge. The teacher may need to add some protective and facilitative factors to his skills. The best thing that the teacher can do is to provide consistent, predictable, and reliable care. These measures can improve the quality of interaction with the child and help to form an attachment bond. For a very complete list of good practices, the Center on the Social and Emotional Foundations for Early Learning Curriculum at Vanderbilt University have prepared the Inventory of Practices for Promoting Emotional and Social Competence. This 28-page inventory is available at http://www.vanderbilt.edu/csefel/modules/module1/handout4.pdf. This list should help the teacher set up the best environment for helping children to be more competent to deal with their emotions and issues that may stem from child maltreatment. The inventory would be helpful for dealing with emotions of all children.

The child at risk may need to be protected from overstimulation. The teacher can help the child by creating a quiet, safe place to retreat. Transition times may stress the child at risk. The teacher can provide structure and clear limits to help make the transition more manageable. These measures also allow the child to understand boundaries and acceptable behaviors. Recent studies have shown that if the child at risk is able to find someone with whom to develop a secure attachment, that child is likely to be able to overcome nonmedical behavioral and developmental difficulties (Groves, 2003; Rice & Groves, 2005; Putnam, 2006). A child at risk from a substance-abusing environment will have to find reliable bonds with other people. The teacher who helps a child in this way may give the child the tools needed to find other adults to rely on Zero to Three (2005b). If children are in a better environment with caring people, their cognitive, social, and emotional development will be less at risk (Knudsen et al., 2006).

If the situation at home with parents is intolerable, the teacher may have to report the situation to the local Child Protective Services office. If the child or children are removed from the home environment, it is possible that Child Protective Services will work with the foster family or relative caring for the children to continue in the early childhood education situation. The consistency of the teacher and the early childhood education environment will be a very important source of support to the child.

Key Concept 14.4

Children from Substance-Abusing Families

Many teachers may find themselves working with children from substance-abusing families. They should learn to recognize the indicators for this condition. Teachers who understand the family situation are more likely to be able to help. Families may be in recovery, may be active abusers, or may be a foster or kinship family that has complex issues to address. Teachers can work more productively by developing good communication and trust with these families and their children.

14.5 IMPLICATIONS FOR TEACHERS

Teachers need to see that policies are created for child maltreatment. These policies should include the processes needed to help prevent child maltreatment and protect the children in care. The methods and strategies should include education, working with families, cultural competence, observation, and supervision. Education for the teachers, as well as the parents and children, offers prevention and protection. Cultural competence is crucial, because in some cultures child maltreatment may not be seen as a problem but a parental right. Observation helps the teacher to recognize and document maltreatment. Supervision maintains a set of checks and balances to provide protection for the children in the early childhood education environment and prevent some maltreatment from occurring.

Education

It is essential that the teacher understand what child maltreatment is and how to recognize it. Awareness and familiarity with the indicators of abuse in four areas—physical, emotional, sexual, and neglect—is necessary for a teacher to be able to observe for them. Teachers must understand the process to report maltreatment because they are the mandated reporters of child abuse. State laws regarding the reporting must be carefully followed. The teacher must know how to report maltreatment, and in order to do so he must know how to document for accuracy and support. Failure to do so could be breaking state law, for which there is a penalty.

With Children. The teacher can help to educate the child about what is and is not acceptable behavior between the child and an adult. The teacher can promote safety from sexual abuse from an early stage. At 18 months, children can learn about body parts. From ages 3 to 5, they can learn about the body parts and what parts are unacceptable for others to touch. At each age and stage, there is something children can learn in order to identify "bad touches" they should avoid. A child who learns to use the word "no" will be empowered to help protect herself. A child can also learn that what feels aggressive may vary by culture (Gonzalez-Mena & Shareef, 2005). A child should know what physical or abusive behavior looks like and that in our society it is not allowed.

A child who learns to achieve mastery in her life by making choices may be more prepared to act if she is abused. A teacher can provide opportunities that allow the child choices.

A teacher can model self-control, verbalize feelings and fears, and provide a predictable, stable environment. These actions will offer the child a protective environment where she feels safe enough to talk. A child who experiences this environment may be more willing to share difficulties in her life.

For the Families

Education can also be a tool to help the teacher to prevent maltreatment. Having methods and strategies for working with children and parents can help the teacher offer greater protection for the children. The teacher can educate the parents and children to help prevent maltreatment (Knitzer & Lefkowitz, 2006). Parents can be educated about normal child development and the behaviors that can be expected at each point of development. Parents who have an understanding of the capabilities of their children may have more realistic expectations. The teacher should keep an open line of communication with the parents. They can share common concerns about the child or about stress in the family environment. This can help to form a partnership. The teacher can also support the parent during times of stress or other difficulties by providing referrals or resources. Teachers can help reduce the likelihood of child maltreatment by family members. Working with families and giving them support may help to break the cycle of abuse (NAEYC, 2004).

- **immigrant**
  one who leaves a country to settle in another.
- **migrant**
  a transient who travels from place to place to find work.

Cultural Competence

Cultural competence is a preventive measure. The process of child rearing may be culturally defined. What is normal and acceptable in one culture may not be considered normal or acceptable in another. The United States has large **immigrant** and **migrant** populations that are ever increasing. In 2005, there were 15.7 million children living in these families in this country (Annie E. Casey Foundation, 2007). A teacher who cares for children from a culture other than his own should try to learn about the child-rearing practices and behavior of that culture. Some of the diverse cultural practices that may be seen as child maltreatment include female circumcision; coining, cupping, scarring, and burning of the skin; and use of poisonous herbal remedies (Zamani, 2000).

The family's view on discipline and punishment may be in conflict with the laws of this country. Some cultures believe in children's unquestioning obedience and use corporal punishment as a consequence for violating a rule; they may also hold unrealistic expectations about a child's developmental level. A family can easily fall into the Child Protective Services system if they are unaware of the laws and customs of this country. The teacher can ask a family about their cultural customs to determine whether this is the case. If so, the teacher may need to begin a dialogue with the family. The teacher should show respect about differing cultural beliefs of the family but should also clearly inform them about the law (Gonzalez-Mena, 1997). The teacher can also help the parents to have a better understanding of appropriate developmental expectations for children.

Families who recently immigrated or migrated may have experienced a great deal of stress (Duarte & Rafanello, 2001). Stressful events related to the relocation of families may affect their psychological well-being. Strange customs, lack of support networks, economic challenges, and inability to speak English may all contribute to the stress of a family and its children.

Observation

Observation is the most important tool that a teacher has to protect a child from maltreatment. Careful observation for signs and symptoms of child maltreatment can make the teacher aware of the possibility that the child's safety and well-being are in jeopardy. Observation is also the key tool for documentation of suspected maltreatment. A good observer will use the tools of the senses to report what was seen, heard, felt, and smelled.

Observation also plays a part in preventing maltreatment. It is important to observe the early childhood education environment for practices that offer prevention of maltreatment. The teacher can observe for behaviors of families and possible stressors because the teacher can intervene before maltreatment takes place. Many of the tables in this chapter provide good tools for observation.

Supervision

Everyone employed in the early childhood education environment must be trained to recognize, document, and report maltreatment. Employees should learn to recognize their own stress. The teacher should supervise the early childhood education environment to prevent any situation or practice that does not offer protection from, and prevention of, child maltreatment. Discipline should be supervised to make sure it is correct and that all teachers offer good guidance and discipline and do not cross the line into punishment.

The teacher should supervise to make sure all protective measures such as recognition, documentation, and reporting of child maltreatment are

REALITY *Check*

Helping Vulnerable Children to Become Resilient

Some children manage to thrive despite much stress and turmoil in their lives. Other children who have very little stress and turmoil in their lives may not manage as well. Researchers refer to a child's ability to cope with stress as resiliency and the opposite is **vulnerability**. (Osofsky, 1999; Ginsburg & Jablow, 2006).

A child who is vulnerable may be so due to a variety of factors. These factors may be inborn and include genetic abnormalities, malnutrition, preterm birth, prenatal stress, or drug exposure. Temperament may also be a factor (Boles et al., 2005). Difficult children have a harder time adapting and getting into a rhythm in life. Parents may have a more difficult time coping with and attaching to a difficult child. Children who are at risk may also have lower levels of stress responsive hormones that may make them more vulnerable (Cicchetti & Rogosch, 2007). The greater the number of risk factors, the greater the chance a child will be vulnerable (Knitzer & Lefkowitz, 2006). On the other hand, a resilient child is one who is able to buffer against circumstances that may normally make a person unable to cope (Stewart & McWhirter, 2007).

Outside circumstances that may make a child more vulnerable are usually related to significant relationships. The bonding process is extremely important. Children who are maltreated have been found to have disorganized attachments (Cicchetti, Rogosch, & Toth, 2006). Parents who are depressed often find attachment difficult. Children who are insecurely attached may be more vulnerable to outside environmental stresses such as poverty, abandonment, or chaotic living. If a child gets little or no response from or is afraid of the parent this could lead to increased risk for psychological or social difficulties (Dozier & Peloso, 2006). A child whose physical circumstances may make him vulnerable is liable to be less so if he has a secure attachment to a significant person in his life (Hamre & Pianta, 2005; Colbert, 2006). First-born children who begin life with no physical difficulties and who are easy in temperament are thought to be most resilient (Werner & Smith, 2001).

Child abuse or neglect can also be major factors in making a child vulnerable. We know that resiliency can be fostered and that there is no special timeline for it. Children don't become resilient on their own. They must have a connection to someone who has faith in them (Breslin, 2005; Colbert, 2006). They need to feel good about themselves and their capabilities. Children need help in trying to cope with difficult situations or traumatic events (Zero to Three, 2005b).

There are protective factors that can foster resilience in children. These include having caring and supportive relationships, positive and high expectations, and opportunities for meaningful participation (Kersey & Malley, 2005; Hamre & Pianta, 2005). Grotberg (1999) has described a resilient child in the framework of three factors:

1. I HAVE (strong relationships, structure and rules at home, role models, encouragement, access to services).
   Building block = TRUST
2. I AM (lovable and my temperament is appealing, proud of myself, a person who has hope and faith and cares about others).
   Building block = AUTONOMY, IDENTITY
3. I CAN (manage my feelings and impulses, seek trusting relationships, communicate with others, solve problems).
   Building block = INITIATIVE, INDUSTRY

Breslin (2005) also identified four major characteristics that resilient children appear to have: heightened sensory awareness; high, positive expectations; a clear and ongoing understanding of their strengths and abilities; and a well-developed sense of humor. If a teacher is armed with this knowledge, Breslin believes that she can enhance and support those particular resilient behaviors.

Emmy Werner and Ruth Smith (2001) have done a 40-year study on resilience in children as they grow into adulthood. They have found that children

(continues)

REALITY *Check* (continued)

who begin life as vulnerable can be helped to become resilient. The most important factor they found was that, if a child has one significant, trusting relationship with an adult, he will be able to seek out that type of relationship with others. If that trusted person can help foster social competence, the child will be more likely to be able to communicate, respond with caring, have a sense of humor and the ability to attract others, and identify those who can be resources. A trusted person can help a child learn problem-solving skills, foster her imagination, and teach about initiative. A child with those capabilities will be able to organize and have greater coping skills. A trusted person who gives a child a sense of autonomy fosters the child's sense of self-esteem and feeling more in control of life. This can give a child a sense of purpose and optimism for the future.

Resilient children find it much easier to develop key trusting relationships with an adult. Goleman (2005) suggests that resilient children can increase their degree of emotional intelligence by being helped by an adult to improve their self-awareness, confidence, and self-regulation. In turn, the increased degree of emotional intelligence and positive emotionality can make a real difference in a child's degree of resiliency (Curtis & Cicchetti, 2007). This adult can be a parent, grandparent, other relative, or a teacher. This relationship allows the resilient child the freedom to know that she is significant. The child can laugh and be silly or be serious and it won't matter to the caring adult. As long as the resilient child has someone who cares for her, she can handle almost any situation that comes along.

Both vulnerability and resiliency are significant to the teacher. The teacher may watch a vulnerable child who is insecurely attached have great difficulty coping with life. She may observe a resilient child cope with problems that seem insurmountable. The more supportive the environment is for either of these children, the less the stress.

The vulnerable child may need extra support from the teacher through responsive and stimulating care (Levin, 1999; Colbert, 2006). He may need the teacher to adapt to his needs. The vulnerable child will definitely benefit from a secure attachment with the teacher. This factor can help the child deal with other factors in his life.

The teacher can help to foster resiliency in the vulnerable child by providing:

- Unconditional love
- Comfort, including physical holding, rocking, and soothing
- Consistency
- Clear limits
- Stability
- Security
- Expectations of success and opportunities to succeed
- Praise for accomplishment
- Encouragement to try new things and to do so with minimal help
- Opportunities for meaningful participation
- Acknowledgment and labeling of the child's feelings so that he can identify those feelings and be able to recognize them in others
- Encouragement to use problem-solving skills
- Support for increasing persistence
- Help for children to accept responsibility for behaviors and consequences
- Acceptance in times of error, behavior difficulties
- Materials that allow the child to use and develop her imagination
- Materials and opportunities to explore new things
- Activities that will allow the child to make decisions and solve problems

The teacher can also model confidence and optimism, good self-esteem, and flexibility. By communicating verbal expressions of caring and calming and by sharing positive feelings, a teacher can reassure the child of her value.

The resilient child will need the care and support of the teacher, much as a cheerleader helps a team play a game. Teachers can enhance children's resilience (Knight, 2007). Although this child is already equipped for success, he will need the secure attachment of an

(continues)

REALITY*Check* (continued)

adult to remain successful. If a secure attachment with an adult is unavailable elsewhere but is found at the early childhood education environment, the child may retain his resiliency to the problems and stresses that life may bring (ACT, 2001; Hamre & Pianta, 2005).

It is important to remember that dealing with a vulnerable child is not easy. The teacher needs to remember not to get enmeshed in the family's life while helping the child. Not everything can be easily fixed. The teacher should accept what is not in his control and learn to control only that which can be controlled. He should share feelings with others and not bottle up frustration, anger, or sadness that might come when working with a child who is vulnerable. If outside help is needed, then resources should be used. The teacher needs to remember to take time each day for herself so that she does not become vulnerable to the situation.

CHECK*point:* Name what you consider to be the five most protective factors you could offer to a child who might be vulnerable.

- **vulnerability** *inability to protect from risk.*

done when necessary, in the right way, and in a timely manner. It is important for the teacher to supervise the care of a maltreated child and to make sure the child is being offered a supportive environment. The teacher should make sure the child's health, safety, and well-being are promoted by healthy interactions. Everyone in the early childhood education environment who is dealing with a child who has been maltreated should also be supportive of each other. Dealing with child maltreatment can cause depression, stress, and burnout, so it is important for all the teachers to take care of themselves (Knitzer & Lefkowitz, 2006; Rice & Groves, 2005). In addition to stress management, peer support is essential (Zero to Three, 2005b).

Key Concept 14.5

Implications for Teachers

The teacher can promote a safe environment by using tools that prevent and protect children from child maltreatment. The tools of education, working with families, cultural competence, observation, and supervision can help the teacher to offer a safe environment for the well-being of the children in care. Education helps the teacher recognize abuse-related behaviors and the four types of abuse. It helps the teacher understand how to document and report maltreatment. Education gives the teacher strategies to help the maltreated child. Cultural competence may offer an intervening measure to prevent children from being maltreated. Observation is the major tool used to recognize, document, and report maltreatment. Supervision provides the necessary checks to make sure the environment is offering protection and prevention of abuse.

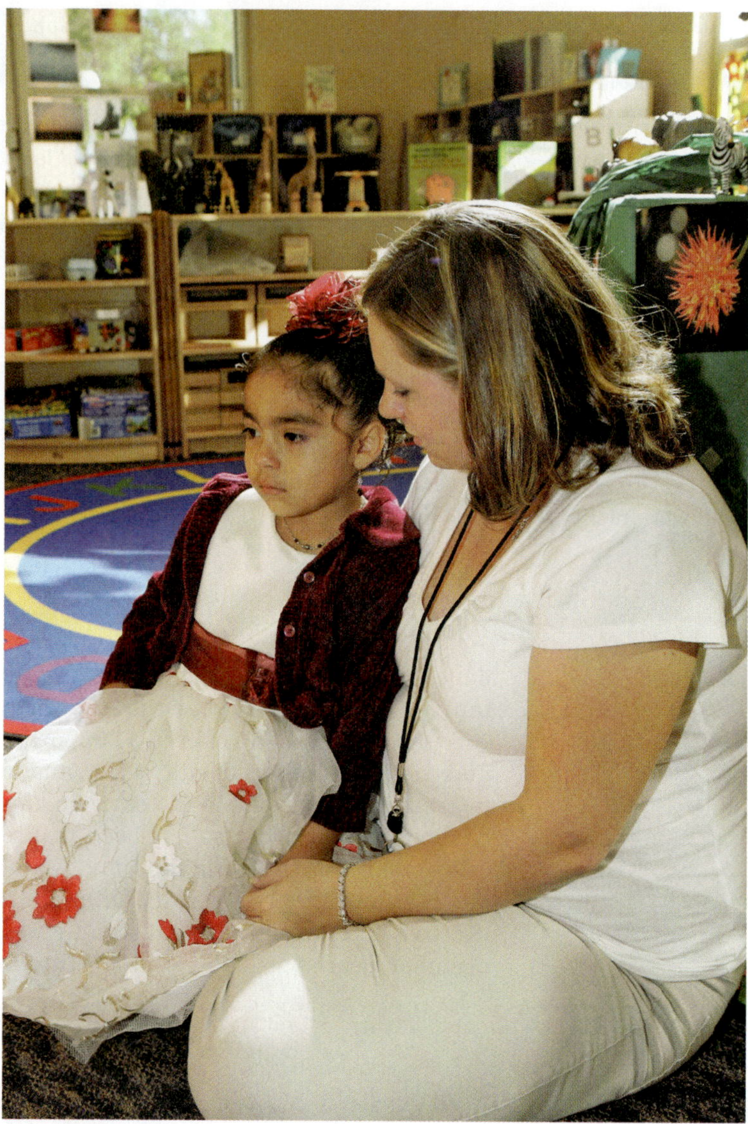

A trusted teacher is one of the best protections that a child at risk for maltreatment can have.

CHAPTER SUMMARY

Considering the large number of children who are abused or neglected each year, teachers should learn preventive, protective, and promotional measures that will help provide for children's well-being. Policies should be created that will help the teacher ensure preventive measures such as freedom from accusation and the ability to intervene. Protective measures such as recognizing maltreatment, documentation, and reporting give teachers the tools needed to protect children from maltreatment. The teacher should know the practices and strategies that will offer care to a maltreated child. The tools of education, working with families, cultural competence, observation, and supervision can help the teacher to provide an environment that offers safety and well-being to the children in care.

TO GO BEYOND

Additional resources for this chapter can be found by visiting the book companion website at www.cengage.com/education/robertson. This supplemental material includes chapter objectives, internet exercises, reflection questions, quizzes, web links, glossary and flash cards, case studies, frequently asked questions, downloadable forms and tables, curriculum supplements, more reality checks, additional key concepts, references, and more.

Chapter Review Critical Thinking Applications

1. Define and discuss the different forms of child maltreatment.
2. Describe some of the factors that are involved in child maltreatment, including what might lead an adult to abuse a child.
3. Explain how child maltreatment is recognized.
4. Describe how a teacher would report child maltreatment.
5. Explain how you would prevent shaken baby syndrome.

As an Individual

1. Collect information about child abuse services available in your community.
2. Research shaken baby syndrome, finding at least two articles on the topic. Write a one-page paper on the subject and be prepared to discuss it in class. Why is it important to understand this topic?
3. List ways that cultural differences might affect child maltreatment. Be prepared to discuss in class.

As a Group

1. Watch a film or video that describes child maltreatment. Compare the film with the reality of child maltreatment. Was the film/video realistic?
2. Invite a speaker from the local child abuse hotline to talk about reporting child maltreatment.
3. Invite a local physician who deals with child maltreatment in the emergency room to speak and describe what is occurring in your own community.
4. Examine some factors in today's society that might lead to child maltreatment. In particular, discuss domestic violence and its effect on the family.
5. Discuss the conflicting feelings that a teacher who suspects abuse has in making the decision to report. What should be done to ensure the right decision is made?
6. Create a policy for child abuse reporting for child care.

Case Studies

1. Thomas, a 3-year-old, bites Lordes when she won't give him the ball she is playing with. Angela, the lead teacher at your site, grabs Thomas by the arm and, while she is screaming and yelling at him

for having bitten Lordes, she bites Thomas and says, "Here, let's see how you like it when someone bites you!" Of course, Thomas starts to cry, and then Angela yells, "Stop it right now, you big baby, or I'll really give you something to cry about!" With that, Angela storms off the playground and leaves you with this situation. What will you do now and what will you do later?

2. The D'Amigo family has a new baby daughter. Their 3-year-old, Emilio, is in your class. Emilio used to be a happy, outgoing little boy, but now he is withdrawn and anxious. He clings to you every day when his father drops him off, and he cries when it is time to go home. He seems to be exhausted and each day sleeps soundly at naptime. What do you think?
3. One day while you are observing during free play, Duran, Micah, and Devonne are in the dramatic play area. Devonne and Duran are twins. Devonne is pretending to be the mom and Micah is the child and Duran is the dad. You hear Devonne say, "Micah, you are a bad little boy and I am going to send you to bed without any supper." Duran then says, "Come here, you bad boy, I am going to give you a whipping." At that point, Duran takes a belt and pretends to hit Micah with it. How should you proceed?
4. While you were supervising on the playground during recess, you see Derek, who is in your second-grade class, aggressively hit his friend Shawn in the face. Shawn ends up with a bloody nose and is sent to the school health clerk. A little later you sit down with Derek and ask him why he hit Shawn. He answers that he was angry about something Shawn had said, and tells you that's what his dad does when he is mad at him; he doesn't understand the big deal. You are concerned and talk to him, but the next morning Derek arrives at school with a black eye. He says he ran into a door. How should you proceed?

CHAPTER 15

Children with Disabilities or Other Special Needs

After reading this chapter, you should be able to:

15.1 Policies for Children with Disabilities or Other Special Needs

Define and discuss policies for children with disabilities or other special needs that may affect the early childhood education environment.

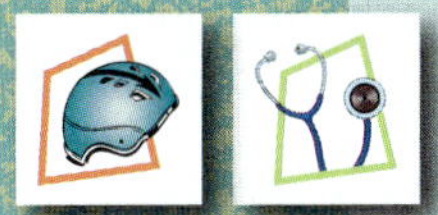

15.2 Inclusion of Children with Disabilities and Other Special Needs in Early Childhood Education Environments

Describe and discuss the process of including children with disabilities or other special needs in the early childhood education environment.

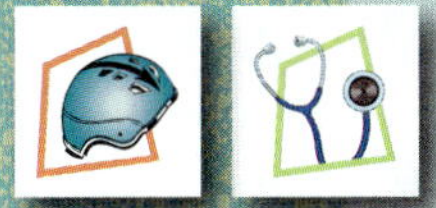

15.3 The Team Approach

Describe and discuss the forming of a team to create an optimal environment for a child with disabilities or other special needs.

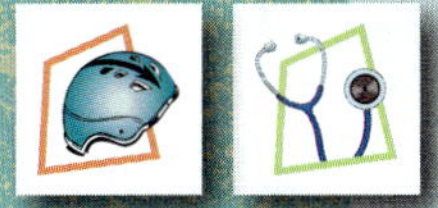

15.4 Supporting the Child with Disabilities or Other Special Needs

Describe and discuss the best practices for the support of children with disabilities or other special needs.

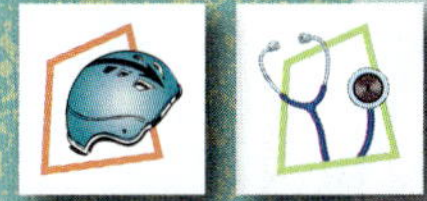

15.5 Supporting Families Who Have a Child with Disabilities or Other Special Needs

Describe and discuss the best practices for the support of families with children with disabilities or other special needs.

15.6 Implications for Teachers

Describe and discuss the importance of education, observation, role modeling, working with families, cultural competence, and supervision in dealing with children with disabilities or other special needs.

15.1 POLICIES FOR CHILDREN WITH DISABILITIES OR OTHER SPECIAL NEEDS

Policies must be developed for children with disabilities or other special needs who may be included in the early childhood education environment. The teacher may deal with numerous issues presented by accommodating a child with disabilities or other special needs and should be prepared to do so. These issues must be examined in order to provide the maximum protection, risk prevention, and well-being for these children in the early childhood education environment. The following are reasons for development of policies for children with disabilities or other special needs:

- All teachers will work with a child with special needs at some point in their careers (Huffman, 2006).
- Children who have disabilities and are in early childhood education programs with nondisabled children show more advanced play than if they were in special care for disabled children alone (Diamond, Hestenes, & O'Connor, 1994). For children with disabilities or other special needs, inclusion is meant to allow them to participate fully and actively, not just to be present (NCCCHSRC, 2006).
- Support and training should be provided for preschool teachers to promote integration of service providers in the early childhood education setting (Legal Update Newsletter, 2004; Shope & Aronson, 2006).

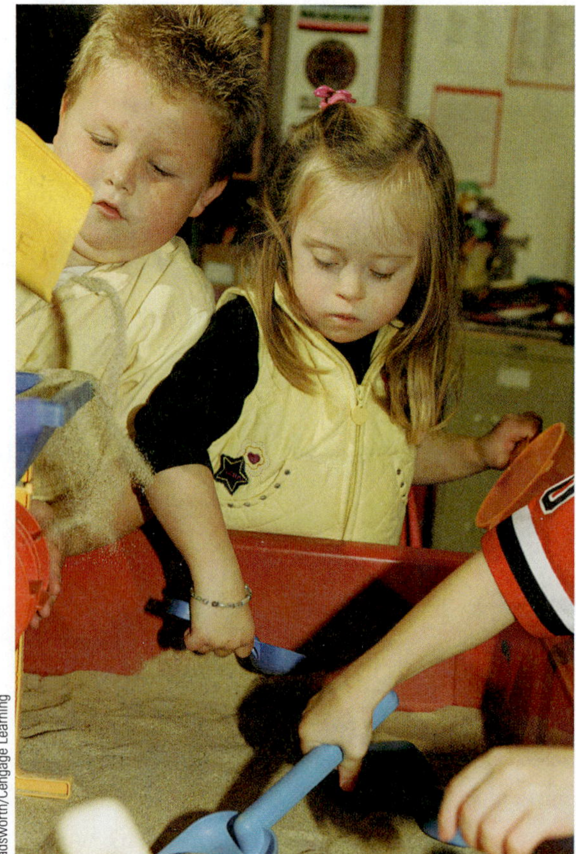

Wadsworth/Cengage Learning

All children can benefit from play in an inclusive environment.

- An increasing number of young children are being diagnosed with a disability or special needs. An estimated 9 percent of children have asthma and approximately 24 percent of children under the age of 19 years have diabetes. (Zimm, 2007). There are 2.4 million children (8.7 percent) who meet the criteria for ADHD (Froelich et al., 2007). ADHD is likely to co-exist with other disorders (National Resource Center on AD/HD, 2007; CDC, 2006a). Approximately 5 percent of children have serious emotional or behavioral difficulties (*America's children: Key national indicators of well-being, 2007*). Children with challenging behaviors should have early intervention (Division for Early Childhood [DEC], 2005).
- The Americans with Disabilities Act requires that all public accommodations, including family child care homes and early childhood education programs, must provide access to children with disabilities (Child Care Law Center [CCLC], 2007).
- Children with disabilities or special needs are children first, and therefore each is unique regardless of the presence of any disability (Mickel & Griffin, 2007).
- Almost 13 percent, or one in eight children in the United States, have special health care needs (USDHHS, 2004). Boys are 50 percent more likely to have special health care needs (van Dyck et al., 2004). One in six children may need more specialized care than children who follow developmental norms (Aronson, 2000).
- "Key to success in collaborating with families of young children with special needs is a commitment to coordinated planning and communication between teachers and early interventions staff" (Kaczmarek, 2006). There is a need for the medical home to work with childhood educators to provide the most favorable outcome for infants and young children with developmental disorders (AAP, 2006; Nageswaran & Farel, 2007).
- As the diversity of families' cultural backgrounds increases in the United States, teachers of children with disabilities and special needs will be increasingly called on to be culturally competent (Bradley & Kibera, 2006; DEC, 2002).

Some children may come to the early childhood education environment with no issues that affect their health, safety, and well-being. Preventive measures can help these children remain risk-free in care. Other children may have disabilities or other special needs that affect them and their care (USDHHS, 2004). An individual with a disability is defined as "a person who has a physical or mental impairment that substantially limits one or more major life activities" (USDOJ, 2002). Children with special health care needs are defined as "those who have or are at increased risk for a chronic physical, developmental, behavioral, or emotional condition and who also require health and related services of a type or amount beyond that required by children generally" (USDHHS, 2004). Quality early education environments respond positively to differences in children's abilities and support the special health care needs these children may have (Shope & Aronson, 2006). To provide the most protective and healthy environment, policies must be created to deal with some of the issues that might arise when caring for children with disabilities or other special needs. Here are the issues that are most likely to emerge as the teacher performs care:

1. *Inclusion of children with disabilities or other special needs:* Teachers should understand the effects of accommodation on early childhood education environments.
2. *The team approach:* Caring for the child with disabilities or other special needs should not be done alone; it requires help and support. Strategies for creating a team must be used.
3. *Supporting the child with disabilities or other special needs:* Each child with a disability or other special needs has differing abilities. The teacher can use strategies to successfully include these children.
4. *Supporting families who have a child with disabilities or other special health care needs:* Families who have a child with disabilities or other special needs may have needs of their own that the teacher can help them to address.
5. *Implications for teachers:* A teacher may take care of children with disabilities or other special needs. These children need a holistic approach to care, using education, cultural competence, and supervision.

Key Concept 15.1

Policies for Children with Disabilities or Other Special Needs

Many children in care have no special issues in their lives that will affect the early childhood education environment. However, the teacher who accommodates children with disabilities or other special needs may have to deal with a number of issues. The teacher must have policies that will help maximize the care environment for those children.

15.2 INCLUSION OF CHILDREN WITH DISABILITIES OR OTHER SPECIAL NEEDS INTO EARLY CHILDHOOD EDUCATION ENVIRONMENTS

The Federal Americans with Disabilities Act (ADA) of 1990 was enacted to protect people with physical or mental disabilities from discrimination. If a person has a physical or mental impairment that limits how he lives his life, he is considered disabled. The ADA defines disability as "a physical or mental impairment that substantially limits a major life activity." Title III of this act states that public accommodations must make reasonable modification to accommodate people with disabilities. Under the law, privately operated early childhood education environments are considered public accommodations. Under Title III, a public accommodation must comply with basic requirements that do not allow discrimination in excluding, segregating, or unequally treating a person with a disability. This act also applies to transportation services that are provided. Title III allows for reasonable accommodation to be made to policies, practices, and procedures of the entity (early childhood education program). Barriers in architecture that are inexpensive or easy to change must also be removed or altered (USDOJ, 2002). Title II of the ADA applies to early childhood education programs that are operated by state or local government agencies such as school districts or municipalities. These programs fall under ADA and also the Individuals with Disabilities Education Act (IDEA), which was originally passed in 1975 (CCLC, 2004). This act was renewed in 2004 (National Dissemination Center for Children with Disabilities [NICHCY], 2004).

The ADA basically applies to all early childhood education situations except for a nanny caring for children in her home and church-operated programs. A teacher cannot discriminate against a child because of a disability. This nondiscrimination policy might be included on any promotional literature the teacher offers and should be included in the teacher's health care policies. A teacher should be willing to make reasonable adjustments or adaptations in order to accept a child with special needs into care. Any teacher who does not attempt to make these adjustments or adaptations can be held liable for nonaccommodation and may be at risk for a lawsuit from the Department of Justice. The determination of whether the teacher has made a reasonable effort to accommodate the child may be found by following the chart in Figure 15-1, which was created by the Child Care Law Center.

The first step is to determine whether a child's condition poses a direct threat to the early childhood education environment. If this threat cannot be eliminated through reasonable accommodation, then the child cannot be accommodated. If there is no direct threat posed, then the teacher would identify how he might accommodate care to the needs of the child. Other considerations include removing barriers, using auxiliary aids and services, and modifying policies, practices, and procedures. A thorough investigation should be made so that it is clear whether the child can be accommodated or whether, at this point, the early childhood education environment cannot accommodate the child. If this is the case, then it is possible to set long-term goals to accomplish the accommodation of children with disabilities or other special needs. Figure 15-2 makes this process easy to understand. The ADA does not require any "undue burden" (significant difficulty or expense) on the part of the accommodator.

The IDEA may also affect public schools, but in a different way. It is used to determine whether a child has a disability and then to learn what the special needs are (Legal Update, 2005). Once these needs are determined, special educational intervention would occur. IDEA contains four parts and two deal directly with young children. Part B ensures that all children with a disability who are between the ages of 3 and 18 years shall have "free and appropriate public education" in the "least restrictive environment" (Legal Update, 2005). Part C ensures services for early intervention in a child's natural setting for infants and children up to the age of 3 years. This would generally mean where other children of the same age who do not have disabilities gather, such as in a preschool. This intervention is usually accomplished by local education agencies (LEA), for example, a school district or regional center. The regional centers often deal with children under the age of 3 years, whereas the school district takes over after age 3. This depends entirely on how each state or county sets this up. If a particular school district does not have the ability to provide the special education intervention needed, an interdistrict transfer to a school that can handle the special needs of the child may occur.

FIGURE 15-1
When are you required to admit a child with a disability? The evaluation process ender the ADA, Title III: Public Accommodations. (Copyright © 1995, 2002 Child Care Law Center. Reprinted with permission.)

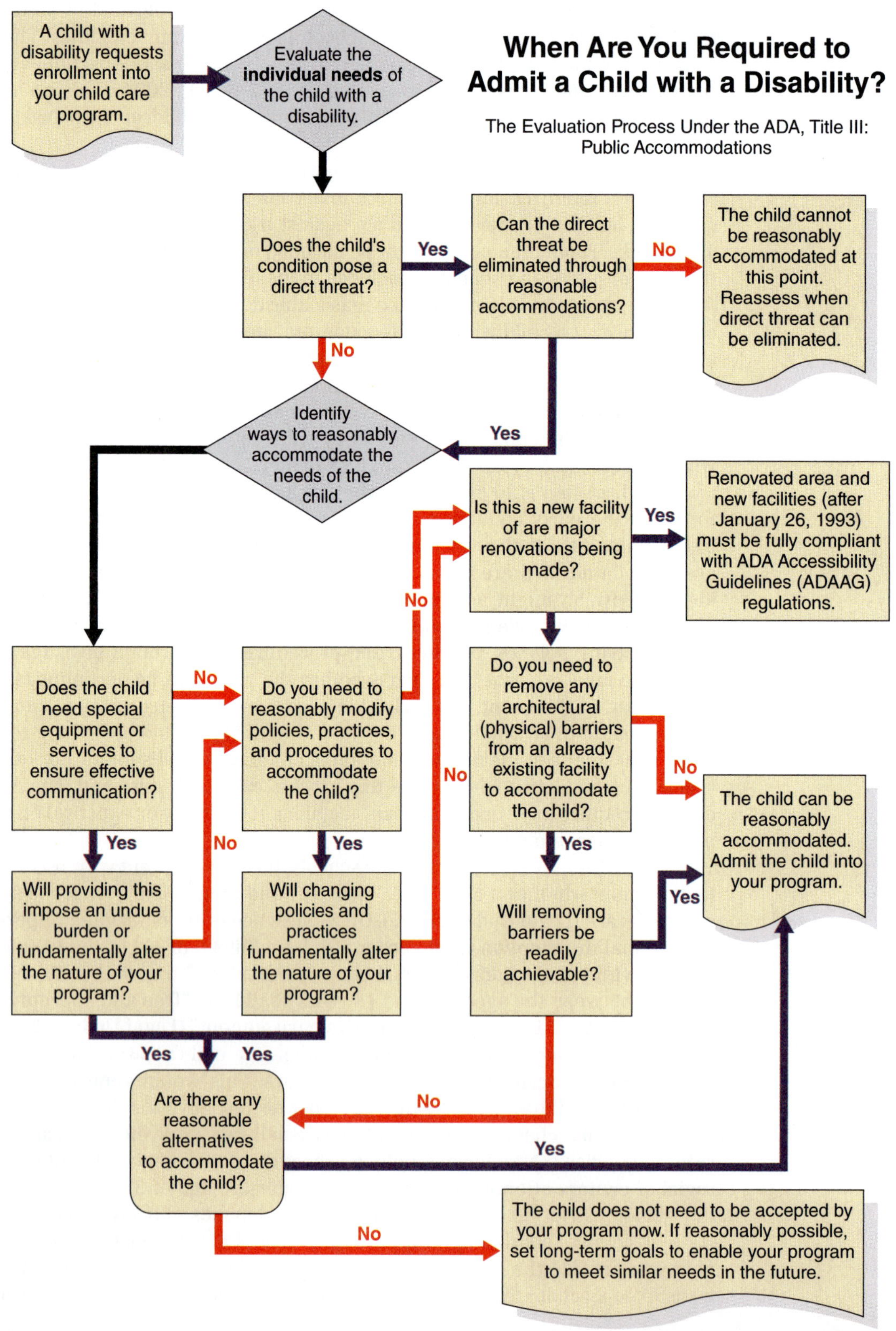

FIGURE 15-2
The Americans with Disabilities Act (ADA). A New Way of Thinking: Title III. (Copyright © 2002 Child Care Law Center. Reprinted with permission.) This figure is accurate as of 2003, but the law changes often so it may not be up to date.

The Americans with Disabilities Act (ADA)
A New Way of Thinking: Title III

ADA GOAL:

To *make reasonable accommodations for* individuals with disabilities in order to *integrate* them into the program to the extent feasible, given *each individual's* abilities.

ADA PRINCIPLES:

- INDIVIDUALITY
  the abilities and needs of *each* individual;
- REASONABLENESS
  of the modification to the *program* and to the *individual;*
- INTEGRATION
  of the individual *with others* in the program.

TYPES OF MODIFICATIONS:

- AUXILIARY AIDS AND SERVICES
  special equipment and services to ensure effective communication;
- CHANGES IN POLICIES, PRACTICES AND PROCEDURES;
- REMOVAL OF BARRIERS
  architectural, arrangement of furniture and equipment, vehicular.

REASONS TO DENY CARE:

- ACCOMMODATION IS UNREASONABLE, and there are no reasonable alternatives.
  - ☐ For **auxiliary aids and services,** if accommodations pose an ***UNDUE BURDEN*** (will result in a significant difficulty or expense to the program) or will fundamentally alter the nature of the program;
  - ☐ For **auxiliary aids and services,** or **changes in policies, practices or procedures,** if accommodations ***FUNDAMENTALLY ALTER*** the nature of the program;
  - ☐ For **removal of barriers for existing facilities,** if accommodations are ***NOT READILY ACHIEVABLE*** (cannot be done without much difficulty or expense to the program). Childcare facilities built after January 26, 1993 must comply with ADA Accessibility Guidelines (ADAAG)
- DIRECT THREAT
  The individual's condition will pose or does pose a significant threat to the health or safety of other children or staff in the program, and there are no reasonable means of removing the threat.

Children from birth to age 2 years may need this early intervention because without it they may experience delays in the following areas:

- Cognitive development
- Physical development, including vision, hearing, and fine and gross motor skills
- Communication development
- Social or emotional development
- Adaptive development, regarding how children take care of themselves
- Developmental delays resulting from a diagnosed mental or physical condition

Those same categories apply to children ages 3 through 9; for these children, one is allowed to use the term "developmental delay" without specifying which area of delay is involved. These delays are defined by states and must be measured by appropriate diagnostic procedures and instruments. A child age 3 years or older who has been previously diagnosed with one of the following conditions would be eligible for services (NICHCY, 2002):

- Autism
- Deaf-blindness
- Emotional disturbance
- Hearing impairment (including deafness)
- Mental retardation
- Multiple disabilities
- Orthopedic impairment
- Other health impairment
- Specific learning disability
- Traumatic brain injury
- Visual impairment (including blindness)

It is possible for a child to come into an early childhood education environment prior to being identified as having a disability or special needs. Parents may not realize that a child isn't developing in a normal manner. They also may have concerns but not know where to turn. The help the early childhood education environment can provide is invaluable. A teacher can suggest that the parent contact the child's physician or the regional center or LEA for screening. The parents or guardians of the child are the only ones who can initiate such a request (Garakani, 2007b). The physician or medical home would refer the child to the early intervention agency in the local area. The parent can also go directly to the agency. The most effective way to make contact with the regional center or local education agency is to write a letter with specific concerns, and this could include observations that the teacher has made. It would be helpful to have a copy of the letter in the child's health file or portfolio. There is usually a reasonable time period in which the agency must reply to the request. At this time, the parent would sign an assessment plan and authorize the release of any information, as needed. It is a good idea to make the authorization bidirectional so that the agency can communicate to the early childhood education environment as well as receive communication from it. Once screening has been completed and the child is eligible for special education, a plan will be developed for the child.

The concept of IDEA is to include these children in a program designed to help them to be educated, from kindergarten on, at the greatest level possible in a public school. Before that, for children under school age, intervention and special educational services may be offered on site at a public state preschool or may be offered to an individual child at the early childhood education environment, depending on the LEA plan. By the time a child reaches 30 months, he must have an individualized education plan (IEP) in place. Between the ages of 30 and 33 months, a transition plan must be developed. The service agency that has jurisdiction over the child will coordinate this. At this time, a child may be moved from a preschool or family child care home to a special education program run by the LEA, if appropriate. If it is determined that a child is making progress, the child may remain in the early

Inclusion of children with special needs has many benefits.

Wadsworth/Cengage Learning

childhood education environment she is in. Special education professionals will work directly with the teacher to offer intervention to the children who need it. The impact of the ADA on the IDEA is that children are now included within the same classroom as children without disabilities or other special needs, and special education services are delivered in that venue. There are many benefits to inclusion.

Benefits of Inclusion

The ADA legislation was created to encourage acceptance and decrease discrimination. Some children with disabilities or other special needs can easily be accommodated in care, whereas admitting others may require some adaptation. Some children may have disabilities that are beyond the teacher's abilities to accommodate. These decisions should never be made automatically. Rather, a decision as to whether a child can be reasonably accommodated should be made on a case-by-case basis. It is important for the early childhood education environment to create an inclusion policy for children with disabilities or other special needs. This policy should include how the environment plans to implement inclusion, and it should meet all legal responsibilities required by the ADA and IDEA. This policy may then be used to determine whether the environment can accommodate a particular child's needs. All teachers and staff should be familiar with the policy and understand their commitment to children with disabilities and other special needs. The policy should be shared with the family before the child enters the early childhood education environment so that they can be confident as to the degree of commitment that exists. Including children with special needs in the early childhood education environment has many benefits for everyone involved (NCCCHSRC, 2006).

For the child with special needs, the early childhood education environment offers opportunities to play and grow. These children make better developmental progress when they are mainstreamed with children with no disabilities or other special needs, and their play is more advanced (Brault, 2004a). Children with special needs learn better interaction skills and become more self-reliant. Being included allows the child with disabilities or other

When children with and without disabilities or other special needs are accommodated together in the same setting, they learn acceptance and self-esteem.

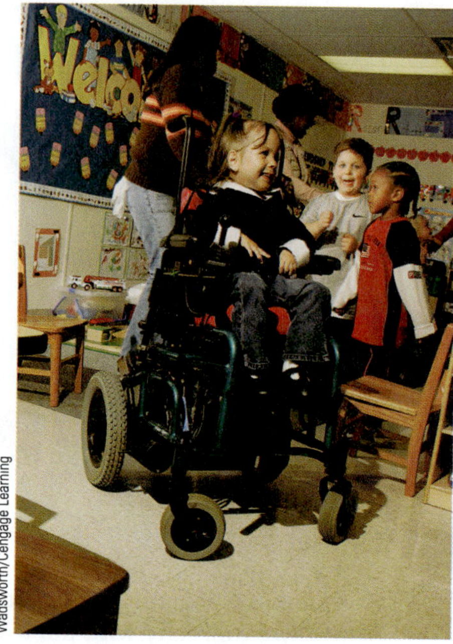
Wadsworth/Cengage Learning

special needs to learn to cope and figure out appropriate social skills. This provides the opportunity to make friends and build a positive self-concept (Buysee, Goldman, & Skinner, 2003).

Children with no disabilities or other special needs benefit from being around children who have them. They can learn empathy and see that diversity is not something to be afraid of because the children with disabilities are more like them than they are different (NCCCHSRC, 2006). Opportunities for interaction between children with disabilities or other special needs and other children reinforce this concept. Children can gain an awareness of how

Richard, a bright, cheerful 3-year-old, attended a campus early childhood education center three mornings a week. Two full days a week he attended a special school for children with developmental difficulties. Richard was born with a problem with his tongue that was not detected until he was almost 2 years old.

Having surgery and going to the school helped Richard begin to learn how to verbalize. He attended the campus early childhood education center to help him acquire language from his interactions with other children who had good language skills. In the beginning, Richard was hesitant to speak and somewhat withdrawn. Cathy, his teacher, read several books to the children that dealt with characters who were different. These books helped bring about a realization that there were more similarities than differences among these characters. After this, Richard seemed less hesitant to speak and began to relate to the other children. The children observed how Cathy listened to and spoke with Richard and began to follow her lead. The inclusion was a success for both Richard and the other children. Richard's language became more intelligible, and the other children learned that differences are not threatening.

REALITY *Check*

Attention-Deficit/Hyperactivity Disorder

Attention-deficit/hyperactivity disorder is a condition that has two basic symptoms: inattention and/or a combination of hyperactivity and impulsive behaviors. It is estimated to affect 8.7 percent of children in the United States (Froehlich et al., 2007). The behavior patterns that typify ADHD usually begin appearing between the ages of 3 and 5 years. Most children of this age are more active, more impulsive, and less able to focus their attention than are adults. Children are also more likely to be unaware of time frames and future events, living instead in the here and now as concerns their wants and desires. However, if these behaviors seem to be out of hand or occur more often for one child in comparison to others, that child may be exhibiting the beginning behaviors of the hyperactive/impulsive type of ADHD. If a child exhibits the inattentive type of ADHD he may be more easily distracted, appear not to listen, and struggle to follow through on instructions. Some children have a combination of the inattentive and the hyperactive/impulsive type of ADHD (National Resource Center on AD/HD, 2007). Boys are much more likely to exhibit these behaviors than girls (Froehlich et al., 2007). In fact, some studies show that boys may be as much as nine times more likely to suffer from ADHD because they are more likely to have genetic nervous system irregularities than are girls (Shaw, 2003).

Typical ADHD behaviors listed by the American Psychological Association (Nadeau & Dixon, 1997) include these:

- Failure to give close attention to details of "work" at school or other activities
- Difficulty in focusing attention on play activities or tasks
- Difficulty in listening when spoken to
- Apparent inability to follow through on instructions
- Difficulty in transitioning from one activity to another
- Avoidance of activities that call for concentrated mental activity
- Apparent inability to organize himself/herself for activities or tasks
- Easily distracted by stimuli in the environment
- Talks when inappropriate, often interrupts conversation
- Easily loses things and seems forgetful
- Difficulty in awaiting his turn for activities
- Difficulty sitting still, squirms with hands or feet
- Leaves group when expected to remain
- Runs around excessively at inappropriate times
- Difficulty participating in quiet activities
- Talks excessively
- Appears to be active at all times

Not all children who have some or many of these symptoms have ADHD. There are other conditions and problems that may cause these behaviors. It is very important to have the child diagnosed so that corrective measures can take place to assist the child in coping and overcoming some of the obstacles of this condition. If a child in care is exhibiting a significant number of these behaviors, the parent should be asked to have the child screened for this condition. Careful consideration should be made in discussing this with the parents. Historically, it was believed that this condition was caused by dysfunction in the home. Another belief for the cause of ADHD has been that the child's diet was high in sugar and food additives. Recent studies have shown that neither of these issues is related to ADHD, so parents may feel relieved to know that their parenting is not the cause for the child's condition.

What has been found to be linked to ADHD are neural connections and brain chemistry. In new research, lower levels of attention activity have been found in the brains of people with ADHD, as well as lower levels of glucose. An iron deficiency shown in lowered serum ferritin levels appears to relate to ADHD (Konofal, et al., 2004). There is a possibility for relationship between environmental toxicants and many disabilities such as ADHD (Hussain et al., 2007).

(continues)

REALITY *Check* (continued)

Other studies have investigated neural connections and causal factors for interruption, including genetics and prenatal exposure to chemicals, drugs, alcohol, and tobacco. Brain cells developed during pregnancy enable the transmission of neural signals from the eyes, ears, and skin and allow for the control of responses to the environment. Some research has focused on vision problems affecting information that is taken in and organized. A number of studies have looked at the correlation between watching television and later attention problems (Christakis et al., 2004; Landhuis et al., 2007; Johnson et al., 2007; Zimmerman & Christakis, 2007). These researchers felt that watching television might shorten children's attention span. The conclusion was that a significant number of children studied had problems with attention and that the effects may be long-lasting; however, the fact remains that it is not known what causes ADHD.

The National Resource Center on AD/HD reports that it is possible that two-thirds of the children with ADHD may have another coexisting condition (Children and Adults with Hyperactive Attention Deficit Disorder [CHADD], 2003). From their estimates, about 40 percent of children with ADHD may have oppositional defiant disorder (ODD). ODD includes factors such as losing one's temper, refusing to follow rules, being angry, and annoying others. Conduct disorder (CD) is another common occurrence in children with ADHD. This includes aggression and destruction of property. Between 10 and 30 percent of children who have ADHD may also be depressed or anxious, and children with ADHD commonly have learning disabilities (CHADD, 2003).

For a child to be diagnosed, there are several areas that will be checked. First, the child has a physical examination that includes a thorough family medical history. The parents and perhaps the child's teacher are interviewed and complete a behavior rating scale. The child is observed in several situations, and a variety of psychological tests may be given. If the parents cannot afford this type of diagnostic screening, the early childhood education center should help the parent link to helpful community resources. Often, a child's school district may be of assistance, even before the child enters kindergarten. Many school districts feel that early diagnosis of conditions such as ADHD will help them manage the situation for the school-age child.

Teachers and directors can help these children even before a diagnosis is made by controlling and monitoring the environment so that the child can be more successful (Shaw, 2003). Listed here are some of these helping strategies developed for the U.S. Office of Special Education within the U.S. Department of Education:

- Anticipate events and help with transition from one event to another. This includes informing the child of the change before and during the transition.
- Break tasks down into smaller, more manageable steps.
- Use immediate rewards for completed tasks and positive behaviors. For older preschool and school-age children, this might include a special chart for a child and the use of stickers to show the child how well she is doing. It is better to focus on a few tasks at a time, in order to allow the child greater success.
- Keep this child near you when working on tasks so that you can maintain eye contact.
- Use gestures to emphasize directions.
- Eliminate unnecessary materials, so that the child can focus on the task at hand.
- Provide a quiet area for the child to go to if he is feeling overloaded. Distractions can cause the overload and exacerbate the problem.
- Have a special place for the child's belongings and tools and ask the parents to do the same for the child at home.
- When speaking directly to the child, use her name and focus attention, including eye contact with the child, until the signal to communicate has been received.
- Communicate often with the parent as to how the child is doing in the early childhood

(continues)

REALITY *Check* (continued)

education environment, and inquire about behavior at home so that a partnership in helping the child is created.

- Establish clear rules with immediate consequences so that the child understands that the behavior exhibited is not acceptable. This might included a time-out area for the child to go to when she cannot control her behavior.

CHECK*point:* **List five protective strategies you might use for a child with ADHD in your classroom.**

to express compassion, concern, and care (Brault, 2004b). They may actually help the adults in the environment reach a good comfort level with children with special needs. Children usually ask a few questions about a disability, then focus on the child and not the disability (Grechus, 2000). Teachers can learn from them.

Teachers can also benefit by realizing that all children are more alike than different. By focusing on the child's strengths, not weaknesses, a teacher can be more successful. The teacher working with a child who has a disability or other special needs will learn patience and self-confidence in his ability to care for the child. The teacher can learn techniques for supporting a child with disabilities or other special needs by offering individualized activities (Huffman, 2006; Katz & Schery, 2006.). Children have the same basic needs, and every teaching skill that is strengthened is shared with all the children in care.

The parents may learn that the child with special needs is more like other children than they expected, and this awareness may allow them a comfort they had not experienced before (Kaczmarek, 2006). The parents of children with disabilities or other special needs will receive support from the teacher to carry on everyday life. When they share the responsibility with the teacher to help the child learn, families are expanding their own understanding. The family whose child with special needs is in early childhood education can become aware of more resources and can experience a connection to a caring community.

Key Concept 15.2

Inclusion of Children with Disabilities or Other Special Needs in the Early Childhood Education Environment

Children with disabilities or other special needs may be included in the early childhood education environment. The Americans with Disabilities Act (ADA) discusses public accommodations. The Individuals with Disabilities Education Act (IDEA) provides the intervention. Teachers should be aware of these laws and how to determine whether they are able to take a particular child with disabilities or other special needs into the early childhood education environment. While doing so, they should consider the potential benefits for everyone.

15.3 THE TEAM APPROACH

Caring for a child with disabilities or other special needs should not be done without help and support. The parents who approach a teacher about providing care for their special child should provide contact to a number of professionals who are dealing with the child. Some typical members of this group might be a physician, an audiologist, an occupational therapist, a nutritional consultant, a speech pathologist, and a counselor. If the parent comes without these resources and a child is defined as having a disability or other special needs after he is already enrolled, then the early education environment can help provide community links and resources for the family (Kaczmarek, 2006). Key practices for this are looking at the family's priorities for the child, providing services where possible, and supporting the child to transition into the educational environment (DeVore & Russell, 2007).

The Health Resources and Services Administration of the Maternal and Child Health Bureau is working in conjunction with Healthy People 2010 to support children with special health care needs. They suggest that care be coordinated through a medical home (see Chapter 13). Children with disabilities and special needs should have access to a medical home so the child can receive necessary medical and therapeutic support (Nageswaran & Farel, 2007; Houtrow et al., 2007). The Health Resources and Services Administration of the Maternal and Child Health Bureau also suggest children be screened early and often so that if intervention is required, it can be given immediately. A major goal is a community-based service system where families, teachers, health practitioners, and other community resource people work together for the benefit of the child. The timeline for this to be in place is by 2010 (AAP, 2002). Olson, Murphy and Olson (1999) suggest that such an inclusive community empowers parents, gives teachers the training and support they need, and provides necessary support services. The AAP (2006) introduced a policy to help identify infants and young children with screening tests at routine doctor visits at ages 9, 18, and 30 months. They also stated the need to work closely with early childhood educators to provide the optimal environment for young children who may be identified with a developmental disorder.

Each child has unique needs, and the people who will help the child are selected to meet those needs. In the classroom, additional assistance may be required depending on the particular needs of the child. For example, a child with a hearing impairment may need a sign language translator; or a child with cerebral palsy may need an occupational therapy technician to visit regularly to help the child reach her maximum potential for physical movement and coordination.

The IDEA provides special education and other services related to disabilities or developmental delay in children. It offers the means to create a team for each child with disabilities or other special needs (CCLC, 2004). This team approach supports the child and offers everyone involved a common sense of purpose. Everyone on the team works together to help the child reach his maximum potential developmental growth level. It is essential that those involved participate in the team on an equal level.

Each professional may have ownership in part of the process and may tend to see that part as the most significant. Each member of the team has a key ingredient to help the child. Often, when a professional works with a teacher, the professional gets a greater understanding of child development

The cooperative team should work together, each bringing to the system his or her unique expertise to benefit the child.

Wadsworth/Cengage Learning

(Brault, 2004a). With this knowledge, when the professional sees children in groups and how they interact, he may have a better grasp on how to help a child with disabilities or other special needs. Each player on the team must contribute and cooperate to make this holistic approach work.

The Individualized Family Service Plan

- **individualized family service plan** *plan that coordinates services to meet the special needs of the child and his or her family.*

The team should work together to prepare what is called an **individualized family service plan** (IFSP). The IFSP provides for an organized goal and delivery of services to the child and the family. The plan should be made up of measurable outcome objectives, which help guide the team to provide what the child needs. It is much easier to assess the success of a plan based on whether the objectives have been met.

Usually one person is designated as the coordinator of the service plan. This is often the representative of the group that has financial responsibility. It can be a professional who represents the Department of Health or the Department of Education, and this varies from state to state.

There should be one contact person who coordinates the care of the child with special needs in the early childhood education situation (Allred et al., 1998). For a center, it might be the director or the child's primary teacher. In a family day care home, it would most likely be the care provider. In an in-home care situation, it would be the nanny who has agreed to care for the child with special needs.

Families are also an integral part of the IFSP. They know their children best and can help by sharing knowledge and information (Vakil, Freeman, & Swim, 2003). The IFSP is based on the unique needs of each child, but it also focuses on the family. Families play an important role because they are the bridge between the child and the early childhood education community and all the service providers.

If a child with disabilities or other special needs is accepted into the early childhood education environment, the teacher should be prepared to accept the responsibilities that go along with caring for that child. The team effort continues at the early childhood education site (NCCCHSRC, 2005). All people involved in the care of the child should be privy to what is planned for the child. The IFSP should be shared and the objectives reviewed to identify the progress of the child. If any training is required to provide care for the child, all members of the caregiving team should receive it. The early childhood education program that accepts a special needs team should provide the skills necessary to help the child reach maximum potential (CCLC, 2004).

Key Concept 15.3

The Team Approach

Children with disabilities and other special needs may be included in the early childhood education environment. The Individuals with Disabilities Education Act provides the intervention and means to create a team. The individualized family service plan (IFSP) is the vehicle for the team. The teacher is an integral part of this team that works to support the child with disabilities or other special needs.

15.4 SUPPORTING THE CHILD WITH DISABILITIES OR OTHER SPECIAL NEEDS

Each child with a disability or other special need has his own particular needs requiring support. Support can be offered to all children with special needs in some general ways. The teacher and the special needs team should develop goals that match the needs and abilities of the child. The teacher is the one who will carry out these goals on a daily basis and should be involved in the process.

The Environment

Adjusting the physical environment to adapt to whatever special needs are present is a good starting point. Removing obstacles is helpful for children who are visually impaired or who have physical disabilities that may require a walker or a wheelchair. For children with emotional disabilities, the teacher may have to provide a quiet corner. The area needed for adaptive equipment should be in a place that does not interfere with other activities.

The toys that are present in the environment should be safe and durable for the sake of all children. They should provide opportunities for learning, interaction, exploration, and engagement. Modifying toys as necessary may help the child with special needs use the toy for its intended purpose. For example, the ring in a ring toss game may have to be cut larger; wooden knobs or spools can be attached to puzzle pieces to make them easier to manipulate; and paintbrushes, markers, and crayons may be wrapped with clay or foam to make them thicker and easier to handle (NCCCHSRC, 2007–2008). After a child with special needs has been in care for a while, the teacher may notice what types of toys that child is most likely to choose and use. Selecting

A least restrictive environment should be provided for all children with disabilities or special needs.

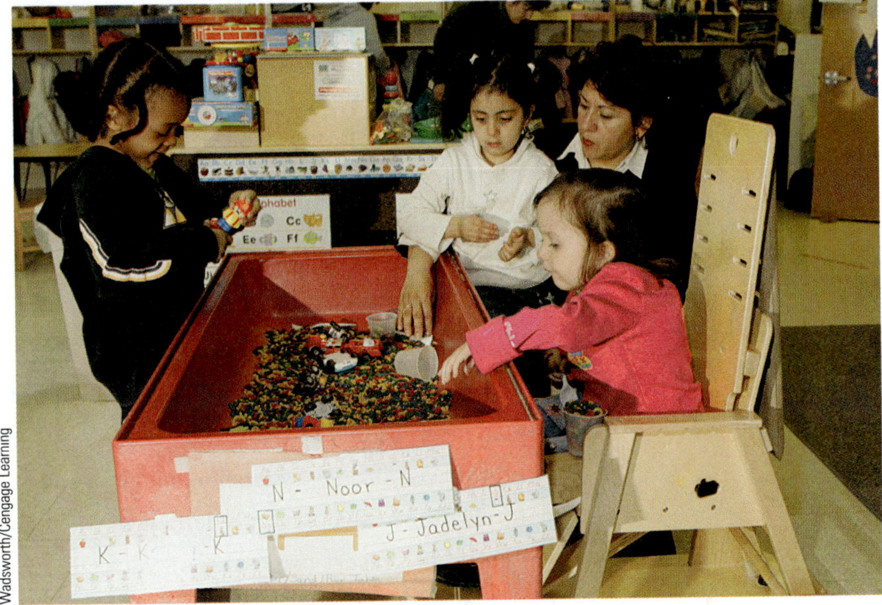

Wadsworth/Cengage Learning

new toys that have similarities will offer new challenges or things to explore. Table 15-1 includes strategies for the successful inclusion of children with differing abilities in the early childhood education environment. Whatever goals are chosen for the IFSP should be incorporated with routine care. To help reinforce this, signs might be posted as reminders (Allred, 1998). Daily routines help reinforce the skills and competencies of a child with special needs. When you create a nurturing, supportive environment, all children will benefit (Greenspan, 2003; Bakley, 2001).

Flynn and Kieff (2002) suggested three guidelines for promoting outdoor play. The first is to consider the quantity and quality of the multisensory activities available for children. These involve moving, hearing, tasting, touching, and seeing. The second is to promote independence for all children. By considering a child's abilities and needs, modifications of activities and materials can be made. The final guideline is to use cooperative learning groups in which a few children work together in a meaningful way. This promotes positive interaction and allows for communication (Hess, 2003) and also supports the creation of friendships and good social skills (Buysee et al., 2003; NCCCHSRC, 2006). Physical space should be structured to promote play, active movement, interaction, and interest.

Assistive technology can also be used to support the participation of children with disabilities or other special needs (Mulligan, 2003; Sandall et al., 2005). Table 15-1 indicates some recommended practices for use of assistive technology developed by the Division for Early Childhood (DEC) of the Council for Exceptional Families (Mulligan, 2003).

Music can also be used as an inclusive participatory activity in the early childhood environment (Moore, 2004; Humpal & Wolf, 2003). It is a fairly unrestricted part of daily activities and can offer a host of experiences for all children, especially those with disabilities or other special needs. The level of engagement in music activities can vary from child to child and can range from observation to complete participation. Music can open doors to social experiences, teach social skills, and help facilitate friendships.

TABLE 15-1
Strategies for Inclusion of Children with Disabilities or Other Special Needs

Instructional Adaptation

- Establish realistic goals.
- Describe task or activity.
- Model task or activity.
- Adapt task or activity to child's ability for time allotted.
- Give child time to practice new things that she is learning.
- Teach in small segments.
- Sit close to child or stand near to provide assistance.
- Plan for transition times.
- Provide visual clues by labeling pictures and objects.
- Be clear and use descriptive language when giving directions.
- Encourage sensory experiences such as tasting, touching, and smelling.

Physical Adaptation

- Learn to position a child in the most comfortable way for him to work and play (this may take the help of a physical therapist).
- Clear pathways.
- Organize access and physical spaces as necessary.
- Keep doors shut, if necessary.
- If adaptive equipment is required, provide and use.
- Know about and use assistive technology as necessary.
- Promote health and safety—adapt for activities such as hand washing, as necessary.

Communication

- Address child directly so that she knows you are speaking to her.
- Be a good listener and observer.
- Use everyday activities such as books, music, and play to foster language development.
- Expand language by repeating what the child said and then extending it with other words.
- Model correct language and pronunciation.
- Make directions easy to understand.
- Praise child for attempts at communication, even if not perfect.
- Facilitate play in developmentally appropriate and age-appropriate activities.
- Teach children to understand nonverbal responses of child with a disability or other special needs.
- Use assistive technology where applicable.

(continues)

TABLE 15-1 (Continued)
Strategies for Inclusion of Children with Disabilities or Other Special Needs

Social Interaction and Peer Support

- Teach peers to assist friends.
- Encourage peer partnerships (i.e., "buddies").
- Encourage interaction and meaningful participation.
- Teach peers to understand nonverbal responses.
- Teach peers to repeat or rephrase words for better understanding.
- Answer peers' questions honestly.
- Model respect.
- Model warm and accepting manner.

Environmental Support

- Be familiar with the IFSP or IDEA for the child.
- Utilize support of other team members of the IFSP or IDEA when necessary.
- Have a clear line of communication with the family, including suggestions or information that may help the child adapt.
- Recognize the child's strengths.
- Create and maintain a setting for children of all abilities to thrive and develop.
- Model desired behavior.
- Support the child with an organized schedule and structure in a safe, nurturing environment, and allow for flexibility.
- Provide time and support for transition, with clear and consistent signals.
- Provide realistic, reasonable consequences for unacceptable behaviors.
- Use visual cues on cubbies, equipment, and materials.
- Provide positive support for persistent attention.
- Ensure health and safety.

Emotional Support

- Recognize each child's uniqueness.
- Recognize the similarities among all children.
- Show respect, acceptance, and warmth.
- Help children to learn to express feelings in acceptable ways.
- Establish a positive relationship with families.

Sandall and colleagues (2002) proposed eight types of modifications that can be made for children with disabilities or other special needs to optimize the early childhood education environment:

1. Environmental support
2. Materials adaptation
3. Simplification of the activity
4. Using a child's preferences (materials, activity, person)

5. Special equipment
6. Adult support
7. Peer support
8. Invisible support (naturally occurring events)

Adapting the environment for the child with disabilities or other special needs by using this list, providing opportunities with music, and using the specific strategies found in Table 15-1 will help the teacher maximize the environment for optimal development.

Intervention

If the teacher observes that the child is having difficulty playing with certain toys, games, and other materials, she may have to intervene. The teacher may help the child learn how to play with a toy or adapt the toy to play. She may have to show the child how to use or adapt for use other play materials. Modeling appropriate play behavior may help the child learn how to be a player. The teacher's goal should be to facilitate the child's engagement with his environment and give the child confidence to initiate activities for himself.

The teacher may also encourage other children to assist the child. The children who are not disabled may need help in learning how to understand and accept the child with a disability or other special needs. The teacher may teach specific skills such as eye contact or appropriate language. The children in the group can learn to help the child with a disability or special need to accomplish tasks on her own, as well as learn specific helping behaviors when appropriate. They might show a child how to do an activity such as playing with blocks or hold a book for a child who cannot. The teacher can also model acceptance and show understanding. Her actions and words with the child with special needs are the most effective tools she has to teach the other children about interaction. The nondisabled child can role model and provide opportunities for positive interaction with the child with special needs.

Pause for Reflection

How might you use assistive technology and music to help children with disabilities? Which appeals to you more, and why?

- **activity based** *activities that promote adaptive behavior.*
- **functional skills** *skills that allow children to adapt to their environment.*
- **generalizable skills** *common skills that can be practiced and used in different settings.*

Teacher intervention should be **activity based** and occur in a natural manner. Opportunities for this type of intervention occur in everyday activities. The objective of activity-based intervention is to help develop two different skills for the child with special needs (Vakil, Freeman, & Swim, 2003). The first skill is referred to as **functional skill** and offers the child opportunities to adapt to the physical and social environments in care. The child receives personal satisfaction and a sense of accomplishment that helps him gain confidence.

The other type of skill is referred to as **generalizable skill** and transfers from one setting to another. An example of this would be a child with a speech or language disorder learning how to name a particular object; a ball is a ball, whether it is at the early childhood education environment, at home, or in the park.

The teacher should recognize the strengths in all children in the early childhood education environment. The holistic approach to early childhood

Tamara, an autistic child, was acquiring some sign language capabilities. She spent part of her morning in a special school and then went to Kate's family day care before lunch. Her favorite food was watermelon, and whenever Kate served watermelon, Tamara could sign the word *more*.

Kate felt that there was an opportunity for learning here, so she went to the special education teacher at Tamara's school and learned how to sign the word *watermelon*. She used it at every opportunity when she gave Tamara watermelon for lunch or a snack. Eventually, Tamara learned how to sign the word. Her mother was very excited when she informed Kate several days later that Tamara had asked through signing for watermelon for dinner. It was a real milestone in Tamara's limited language.

education focuses on the whole child. Activities and opportunities that focus on strengths and support, and minimize difficulties should be provided. All children want to feel capable, successful, and confident. A teacher who is aware of this can provide the environment a child needs.

Intervention may also include the teacher being able to identify a child who is already in care. As previously discussed, some children may have special needs that have not been detected and must be addressed. The teacher should look for help to identify the behaviors or characteristics that appear to indicate a special need and then pass the information along to the parents. Regional centers, maternal and child health services, and other resources are helpful sources for this information.

REALITY *Check*

Autism Spectrum Disorder

Autism spectrum disorders (ASDs) have a wide range of symptoms and characteristics ranging from mild to severe. Autism is typically thought of as a disorder that presents difficulties in verbal and nonverbal communication, as well as an inability to carry out normal social interactions and play activities (NICHD, 2005; CDC 2006b; Garakani, 2006; First Signs, 2007a). Each person can exhibit unique combinations of these behaviors in various degrees of severity. Many children are diagnosed as having Asperger Syndrome, which is a form of autism in which the person is high functioning in most ways but may exhibit idiosyncrasies in social skills and play. People with this condition are quite verbal and intelligent but can be self-absorbed.

Many researchers today believe that the major defect or deficit in autism has to do with theory of mind, which enables us to realize that we have our own thoughts, perceptions, and emotions, but so do others. We grasp the fact that, when we interact with others, we may not share the same perceptions, but we are able to adapt and adjust. In normal development, by age 4 theory of mind is present in children. The autistic child appears not to have this same capability. Self-absorption and the inability to consider others are major characteristics in most autistic people. This factor may also account for the fact that autistic children do not imitate others as normal children do, which offers the foundation for much of a child's learning process.

(continues)

REALITY *Check* (continued)

Problems beyond communication and social difficulties found in autistic children include sensory disturbances, gastrointestinal problems, depression, food allergies, ADHD, and obsessive-compulsiveness. Research appears to connect these characteristics with the genes that may be causing the major defects (First Signs, 2007b).

Why has autism appeared to increase? Until recently, it was believed that only 1 child in 10,000 might have this rare disorder. The latest research concludes, however, that as many as 1 in every 150 children younger than age 10 may have some form of autism or a related disorder (Leonard, 2007). If adults are included, as many as 1.5 million people in the United States may be afflicted with an autistic disorder, which makes this condition five times more common than Down syndrome. The incidence of autism appears to be increasing at an annual rate of 10 to 17 percent (Autism Society of America [ASA], 2002). It is unclear whether estimates are due to increases in ASDs or in improved reporting methods (CDC, 2007; Rudy, 2007b). In 2002, a U.S. congressional committee declared ASDs a national health emergency.

To understand the difference between a normally developing young child and a child with autism, look at some of the following characteristics from the National Institute of Mental Health brochure on autism (1999) and information from First Signs for infants (2007b), CDC (2007), and U.C. Davis M.I.N.D. Institute (2007):

A Normal Infant or Child

Studies mother's face and interacts through smiles and so forth
Hears normally, reacts to sounds
Learns to speak and gains in vocabulary
May get frustrated when hungry or tired
Has normal social interaction with others
Moves from activity to activity
Uses body with normal motor skills
Explores toys and plays with them in a normal manner
Enjoys pleasure, avoids pain

An Autistic Infant

Has no happy expressions or big smiles by age 6 months
Does not interact with smiles, facial expressions, or sounds by 9 months
Does not babble by 12 months
Does not use interactive gestures such as pointing, reaching, or waving by 12 months
Does not respond to his or her name

An Autistic Child

Avoids eye contact and has little interaction, if any
Has no reaction or hyperreaction to sounds, smells, textures, or tastes
Has no words by 16 months, no meaningful phrases by 2 years
Begins to develop language, then abruptly ceases development
Has no apparent attachment to anyone
May be overly aggressive with no reason
Is zoned out/tuned out—little interaction
Fixates on an activity and is repetitive
Exhibits strange motor actions such as flapping, rocking, and banging head
Licks, sniffs, or mouths toys beyond toddlerhood
May echo or repeat words instead of normal language use
Does not regularly want to cuddle
Prefers to play alone
May not appear to know how to play with toys
Self-inflicts pain
Has difficulty expressing needs in a normal manner
Has difficulty transitioning from one activity to another

Autism appears to have no specific single cause, nor is there a cure (First Signs, 2007a; Leonard & Garakani, 2006). In many families, there seems to be a genetic link because there is a pattern of autism in the family. No particular genetic link has been found as yet. A number of researchers believe it is a combination of genes—as few as 3 or as many as 20—that may yield this condition. It is suspected that some of the genes regulate neurotransmitters and/or control brain development. Some researchers feel that risk for autism may be tied to increased parental age, low birth

(continues)

REALITY *Check* (continued)

weight and duration of gestation (Kolevzon, Gross, & Richenberg, 2007).

Another belief, which has been highly publicized in Britain, is that autism is caused by combination vaccines such as the MMR and DPT vaccinations (Smeeth et al., 2004). (See Reality Check: At Risk for Preventable Diseases in Chapter 12, for more information.) These vaccines in the past contained thimerosal, a mercury-based preservative (AAP, 2004). Many parents of children who later developed autism have reported that their child was normal before this vaccination and then began having problems that were later diagnosed as autism. This link is unsubstantiated, and no evidence has been found to explain how these vaccines might cause autism ("MMR Vaccine and Autism," 2004; Smeeth et al., 2004; NNii, 2006). Even though there has been no concrete evidence, there is a major debate over whether this vaccination may, in fact, be linked to autism (Park, 2002). Congress is in the process of investigating to see whether any link may actually exist (Groppe, 2004). There are cases in courts across the country, labeled as "Vaccine Courts," which will put to the test whether vaccinations are related to autism. The three scenarios they examine are (1) the combination of MMR vaccine and thimerosal, (2) thimerosal alone, or (3) MMR vaccine alone (Rudy, 2007a). Manufacturers of most vaccines have removed thimerosal from all but one of the vaccines. The one exception is the influenza vaccine, which the AAP recommended that all children receive between 6 and 23 months of age as an annual vaccine (AAP, 2006).

There is emerging evidence that some children's immune systems are compromised, and these children may be more susceptible to infections (Rosen, Yoshida, & Croen, 2007). This deficient immunity may also make the child more vulnerable to having a negative reaction to vaccinations. If a child has difficulty fighting off infections or there is a family history of immune disorders, consulting with a physician to explore the safest options for vaccinations is recommended (U.C. Davis M.I.N.D. Institute, 2007.)

The University of California at Davis is studying mercury, PCBs, and other heavy metals to see whether they may be causing autism. These researchers believe that some children are more genetically susceptible to these and other agents. The University of Rochester is investigating how ingestion of certain teratogens might lead to autism. They are specifically looking at a gene that is turned on only briefly during the first trimester of life. The premise is that a teratogen at this time may affect the developing brainstem. Other theories posit that brain structure, brain activities, and brain chemicals may play a factor in the development of autism. Brain studies have shown that the autistic brain grows at a more rapid rate between the ages of 12 months and 3 years and then slows to a normal rate. Brain imaging studies have shown that the autistic brain does not process information in the same manner as the normal brain. Some chemicals in the brain that allow for normal transmission of neurons may not be at a normal level in the autistic brain and may cause faulty processing of information (Rudy, 2006).

There is no basic medical testing for autism. Accurate diagnosis of autism is generally based on intense observation of a child's communication, developmental level, and behaviors. This includes input from parents and a developmental history of the child. Behaviors associated with autism are also often found in other medical disorders; medical tests for those behaviors may be possible to rule out autism. In an ideal world, diagnosis should be made by a multidisciplinary team that may include a speech/language therapist, a psychologist, a neurologist, a developmental pediatrician, and any other professional with expertise in autism and its characteristics. One thing is certain: Early diagnosis is critical because the sooner intervention and treatment occur, the better chance the child has of functioning at the highest level possible (Gupta et al., 2007; Pivalizza, 2007). More than half of the children diagnosed with ASDs don't get diagnosed until they are 4¼ to 5½ years old (CDC, 2007); this misses critical early intervention time. A number of successful approaches can result in great differences in children before and after assistance. Emphasis on helping autism always includes early intervention (Garakani, 2007b). If interventions occur at the stages where normal children pick up

(continues)

REALITY *Check* (continued)

their learning skills, it is much more helpful to autistic children than "catching up."

Developmental appropriateness, a great degree of structure, behavior-based interventions, and training of parents and others to work with children are the most successful foundations for helping an autistic child. With proper intervention strategies, many autistic children can grow up to lead productive lives.

Dr. Temple Grandin (2001), an autistic adult, has shared how the world is viewed by an autistic person. She suggests using the following key points in understanding the autistic child and creating strategies to help that child:

- Autistic people think in pictures, not in language. Pictures are their first language; words are their second language.
- Avoid long strings of verbal language. Make language short and succinct.
- Many autistic children are good at computer skills, drawing, and art. Encourage these skills.
- Use fixations to teach. If a child likes trains, use trains to teach him how to count or to read.
- Use visual objects and other visual methods to help teach a child about numbers and number concepts.
- Be sensitive to sounds in the surrounding environment; many autistic children and adults are sound sensitive.
- Some autistic children are bothered by fluorescent and other types of lighting, so be aware of this.
- Some autistic children sing better than they speak, so singing instructions to them may improve their understanding.

The child with ASD can be given assistance in becoming more functional by teachers who have good strategies to help them. Using actions and objects with words gives a child a better picture of what is being communicated. Help the child concentrate on communication skills by asking him for something, even if it is in sign language. Assist the child in pointing out events or objects so he can share with others (Leonard & Garakani, 2006). Provide opportunities to interact with other children, such as singing songs or drawing together. Create a predictable environment and routine, and label as many things in the environment as possible with pictures. Offer the child opportunities for experiences in a variety of ways.

Teachers can use the suggestions presented in this list to offer more strategies for helping the autistic child in the early childhood education environment. They can also understand that mothers of these children may be under a great deal of stress (Montes & Halterman, 2007). Teachers may be able to help parents by being part of a team and by providing resources for families.

CHECK*point:* **What are five strategies to use to assist a child with autism?**

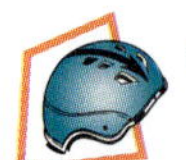

Key Concept 15.4

Supporting the Child with Disabilities or Other Special Needs

The teacher should provide a safe, protective environment and do whatever possible to both challenge and support the child with disabilities or other special needs. Through modification and intervention, the teacher can provide the help these children need.

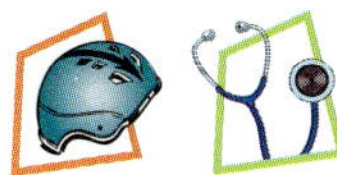

15.5 SUPPORTING FAMILIES WHO HAVE A CHILD WITH DISABILITIES OR OTHER SPECIAL NEEDS

Families who have a child with disabilities or other special needs will come to the early childhood education environment with an extra set of issues that other families do not have (Gonzalez-Mena, 2004; Kaczmarek, 2006). Some parents are in denial that their child has a disability. Other families may feel guilt. Cultural issues may affect both of these if the family is from a culture that does not easily accept children with exceptionalities or does not perceive them as healthy. It is important that there be a plan for special care and that the teacher work closely with the family to create that plan (Walsh, 2005; Kaczmarek, 2006). For these families, maximizing their involvement will not only support the child and the teacher, but the parents as well. Parents may gain a new confidence level, and their stress level may be reduced.

Children living in poverty are at the greatest risk for disabilities or other special needs (Peterson et al., 2004: USDHHS, 2006). These families may have less perceived access to intervention services or lack of awareness in regard to developmental delays in their children (Oswald et al., 2007). The degree of knowledge that a family has about their child's special needs can range from very little to a great deal of expertise. Regardless of where the family is on this continuum, they are going to need a greater degree of support than many families in care (Legal Update Newsletter, 2004; Huffman, 2006).

Parents whose child is developing in an atypical manner may be surprised to see what typical development is and may feel saddened to realize that their child is so far behind or will never reach that point of development. It is important for the teacher to offer these families the ability to come and participate if they choose. Some family members may find it difficult to relate to their children with disabilities or other special needs. One of the reasons for the IFSP is to involve the entire family (Rump, 2002; Garakani, 2007c). An environment that is welcoming for all family members allows them to get more involved with these children and to observe how to nurture them successfully. In any communication that is sent home to the families, be sure to include fathers as well, if they are present.

Families' parenting skills may be limited if they spend a great deal of time providing physical care for their children with disabilities or other special needs. As their children participate in the early childhood education program and they observe the role modeling of the teacher, parents can hone their parenting skills and feel more like typical parents than they may have previously. Families provide the emotional connection to the children that can help the teacher interact at a greater degree with both the children and the families. Teamwork and cooperation are essential to provide the greatest number of opportunities for these children to grow and develop to their highest potential (Walsh, 2005).

Having an orientation meeting for the family of a child with disabilities or special needs is a good way to get off to the right start. This will allow the family to meet the teachers and perhaps other families who are also dealing with the same type of issues. If the parent doesn't attend, then a follow-up phone call should be made. If there are communication difficulties due to language, these must be solved. Encourage parents to visit the classroom, and hand out newsletters that discuss what is happening in the early childhood education environment. Create a communication notebook for the family so they can be aware of what is occurring on an ongoing basis (Kaczmarek, 2006). This will encourage greater interaction.

Cultural Differences

Cultural differences must be addressed (Legal Update Newsletter, 2004; Bradley & Kibera, 2006). As much as possible, it is important to accept how families from different cultures care for their children with disabilities or other special needs. It is crucial to keep lines of communication open and to remove language as a barrier. If the parent and the teacher cannot speak the same language, it is important to get an interpreter. The IFSP may provide those services for both the family and the early childhood education environment. In general, communication is a vital link uniting all segments of the team effort. It is useful for both the teacher and the family to look at their own differences. They may have different communication styles, and they may process information differently (Greenspan, 2004; Sandall et al., 2005). One place to begin is to examine the strengths of the cultural community in which the family operates. This can help both families and the early childhood environment tap into resources of these communities. Useful strategies may come from understanding these various perspectives. This will enable families to appreciate their differences and to empathize with their child who is also different in her own way. A home visit might be a useful strategy to gain a greater understanding for the teacher. The early childhood environment should recognize that supporting the whole family is an essential element of helping a child (Bradley & Kibera, 2006).

Strategies to optimize communication in the early childhood education environment are found in Chapter 16. Programs that are culturally competent and promote effective communication with families can offer the greatest degree of support.

Key Concept 15.5

Supporting Families Who Have a Child with Disabilities or Other Special Needs

Supporting families who have children with disabilities or other special needs is challenging because these families have more issues as their children enter care. Providing access and support that includes both parents, if present, is essential for the child. Modeling parenting skills, being culturally competent, and communicating effectively are other strategies to use to support these families.

15.6 IMPLICATIONS FOR TEACHERS

The teacher must understand that some children in the early childhood education environment have disabilities or other special needs that can be challenging. Children with disabilities or other special needs may have extenuating circumstances. The teacher should use tools such as education, supervision, working with families, and cultural competence to help these children and their families by providing an environment that will support the safety, nutrition, health, and well-being of the child.

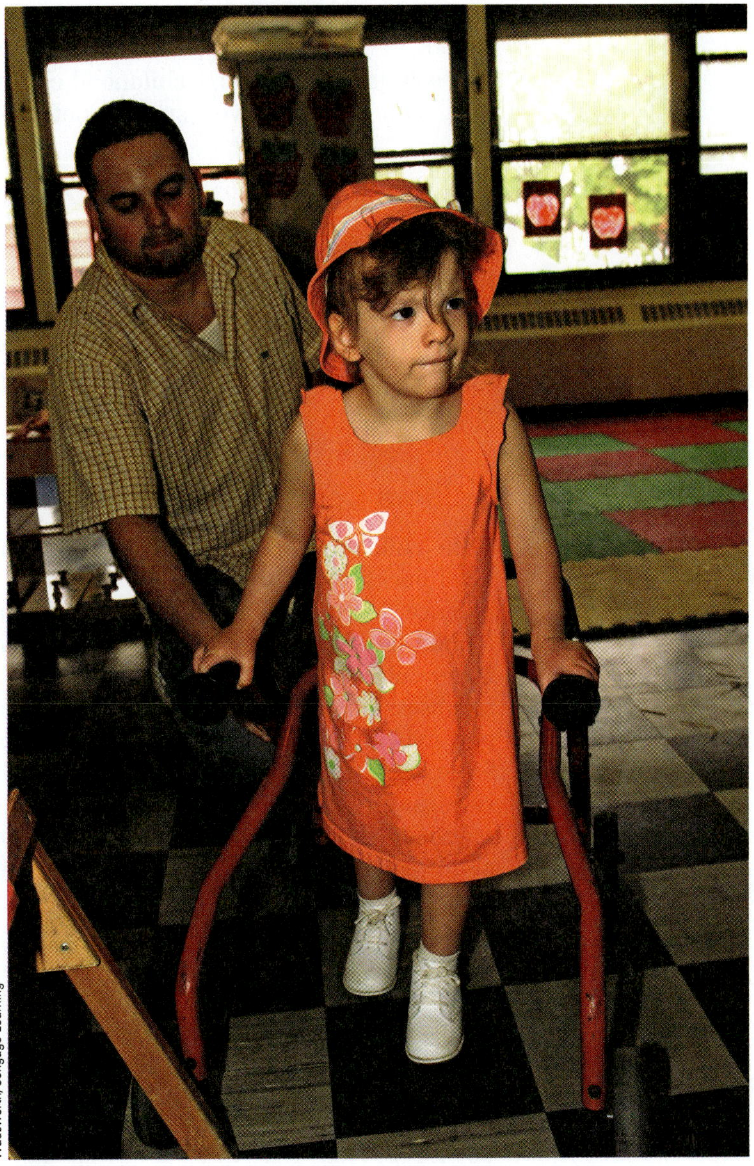
Wadsworth/Cengage Learning

Many modifications can be easily made to help a child with special needs adapt to the early childhood education environment.

Education

When children with disabilities or other special needs are included in care, some modifications to the early childhood education environment may be necessary. These may include toys, equipment, or nutritional requirements. Teacher intervention may be required to help the child interact and engage in exploration of the environment. The teacher may have to use natural situations for activity-based learning. All of these situations require teacher knowledge and awareness. The teacher may need special training by the other IFSP team members in order to be fully able to support the child.

It is important for the teacher to remember that he is not alone in dealing with these issues. Outside support and resources are available from local and national organizations and agencies. Child care resource and referral services might be a good source of support. Another source would be professionals in the community, who are often willing to help by discussing issues and solutions. Local early childhood education organizations can offer support and may even have a support network in place.

For Families

The teacher should try to do whatever is possible to support the family of a child with disabilities or other special needs. A team should be created, and a clear line of communication must be in place. It is important to help parents access any resources they may need, and to cooperate with resources. The teacher can model parenting skills and cultural competency.

Cultural Competence

If the child with disabilities or other special needs is from a different cultural background, the teacher may need an additional tool: cultural competence. Many cultures have the tendency to either ignore or deny that a child has a problem and may not respond to the issues surrounding it. Other cultures may focus on the problem to such a degree that it becomes an obsession. Values, child-rearing practices, family roles, and outside support may all have an effect on how a disability is perceived and acted upon. State departments of maternal and child health, departments of social services, and regional centers may be good resources for this information. The reactions and tendencies on the part of families whose children have disabilities or other special needs may also be true of families with chronically ill children. Figure 15-3 discusses the cultural dimensions of families and provides information that can assist both the teacher and families to communicate and to remove any barriers that may be present. This is especially important when dealing with children who have disabilities or other special needs.

Supervision

The teacher who cares for a child with disabilities or other special needs must carefully supervise the early childhood education environment because these children are more at risk for health and safety issues as well as nutritional well-being. It is up to the teacher to observe these children with a holistic approach. The teacher may have to observe more often, to make certain that the child's special needs are met and relief is offered through supportive behaviors.

Medication and nutritional needs must be maintained through careful supervision. Some states have laws regarding the administration of medications and these laws should be carefully followed. The timing and frequency of medication administration for a child with disabilities or other special needs may be critical. These needs may have to be met by an outside source if the teacher lives in a state where he is not allowed to offer medication. Nutritional needs may also be significant. In addition, the teacher will have to supervise any team created for a child from the early childhood education viewpoint in order to reinforce that child's goals.

FIGURE 15-3
Cultural Dimensions of Families. (From Bradley, J., & P. Kibera. 2006. Closing the gap: Culture and the promotion of inclusion in child care. *Young Children* 61 (1): 34–40. Reprinted with permission from the National Association for the Education of Young Children.)

Cultural Dimensions of Families

Four dimensions of culture are listed here with questions that encourage early childhood professionals to further explore the influences of culture in their work. The questions can be modified for individual self-assessment, for use as a tool to explore differences among staff, or as the basis for discussing cultural issues with families.

Dimensions	Questions for reflection and/or discussion
Values and beliefs	How is family defined? What roles do adults and children play? How does the family make sense of a child's behavioral difficulties? How does culture inform the family's view of appropriate/inappropriate ways of dealing with problem behavior and guiding children? What is most important to the family?
Historical and social influences	What strengths and stressors does the family identify? What barriers do they experience?
Communication	What is the family's primary language? What support is required to enable communication? How are needs and wants expressed? How is unhappiness, dissatisfaction, or distress experienced and expressed?
Attitude toward seeking help	How does the family seek help and from whom? How do members view professionals, and how do professionals view them?

Key Concept 15.6

Implications for Teachers

A teacher may take care of children who have disabilities or other special needs. These children need a holistic approach to their care and education. The tools that the teacher will use are education, working with families, cultural competence, and supervision. The teacher must have a knowledge base for these. Children who do not have these special circumstances may have to be taught to understand and support the children who do. Cultural competence should be practiced because of the actions and reactions of other cultures to children with disabilities or other special needs. Supervision will provide an environment that offers maximum well-being for all children.

CHAPTER SUMMARY

Some children in care may have disabilities or other special needs that affect the early childhood education environment. If these children are included, the teacher should work as part of a team with the families and service providers who are part of the child's special care plan. Teachers can help support the child by using strategies that maximize the child's abilities while in the early childhood education environment. Teachers can support the family by keeping a clear line of communication and by understanding cultural issues. Teachers should be prepared to offer stability and support to all children in the environment. Teachers are most effective in meeting children's needs when they use a holistic approach that includes education, working with families, cultural competency, and supervision.

TO GO BEYOND

Additional resources for this chapter can be found by visiting the book companion website at www.cengage.com/education/robertson. This supplemental material includes chapter objectives, internet exercises, reflection questions, quizzes, web links, glossary and flash cards, case studies, frequently asked questions, downloadable forms and tables, curriculum supplements, more reality checks, additional key concepts, references, and more.

Chapter Review Critical Thinking Applications

1. How does the Americans with Disabilities Act affect early childhood education environments? Describe the process of accommodating children with disabilities or other special needs.
2. Describe and discuss the Individuals with Disabilities Education Act and how it offers a team approach.
3. Describe and discuss autism and its implications for early childhood education environments.
4. Describe and discuss ADHD and its implications for a teacher.

As an Individual

1. Research children's books that deal with the issues discussed in this chapter. Create a list of 10 "special subjects" books and report to class on one of these books. These lists will be collated, duplicated, and distributed to the entire class.
2. Examine how individualized family service plans (IFSPs) are handled in your community. List the agencies that handle the IFSP and deliver the services needed for the family and the child with disabilities or other special needs. Do these agencies offer any type of support to teachers who care for the child with special needs?

As a Group

1. Divide the class into small groups and send them into the community to gather information on what help is available for children with disabilities or special needs. Collate the information, distribute it to the class, and discuss your findings. Was there any specific help available for teachers of these children?
2. Discuss how cultural differences might affect working with families who have children with disabilities or other special needs. List measures that would help the teacher bridge these differences.
3. In small groups of four or five, create a policy for an emergency situation related to a child's disabilities or special needs. Evaluate what extra support might be required for this type of an emergency.
4. Discuss ADHD and how a child with this condition might affect the early childhood education environment. What measures could a teacher use to support a child with ADHD?

Case Studies

1. Mimi is a 3-year-old who is hard of hearing and has limited speech. She has recently joined Lin's family child care. What steps could Lin take to help Mimi transition into the care environment? What should Lin do to help the other children help her to support Mimi?
2. Kamryn is new to the early childhood education center, and Mandy is her teacher. Kamryn is two years old, and her mother has recently been told that she has autism. The mother has not yet contacted the school district. How would you help her to get an IFSP started for Kamryn?
3. Malin has come to care with some serious vision difficulties. He is almost three and has great physical control. What could you do to help him adjust to your center and maximize the environment for him?
4. Isaac has Down Syndrome and has just entered your kindergarten class. He is very friendly, but he also has outbursts of screaming when he gets overstimulated. What might you do in your classroom environment to accommodate this?

CHAPTER 16

Creating Linkages

After reading this chapter, you should be able to:

16.1 Policies for Creating Linkages

Describe and discuss policies for creating linkages for better health and well-being within the early childhood education environment and the community.

16.2 Toward Better Communication Skills

Describe and discuss how to develop good communication skills for working with parents, children, and coworkers.

16.3 Cultural Competency

Describe and discuss the importance of understanding issues regarding diversity and how they may affect safety, nutrition, and health in early childhood education.

16.4 Accessing Community Resources

Describe and discuss the importance of accessing and developing community safety, nutrition, and health resources for helping the teacher, the child, and the parents.

16.5 Developing Effective Advocacy

Describe and discuss the advocacy role the teacher plays in linking the child, the family, the community, and beyond.

16.6 Creating a Caring Community for Families

Describe and discuss how to create a caring community environment that provides the maximum protection for a child's health and well-being.

16.1 POLICIES FOR CREATING LINKAGES

- **linkages** *connections that unify the teacher, child, family, and community.*

Linkages should be formed within and without the early childhood education environment in order to offer the maximum in protection and prevention for issues dealing with children's safety, nutrition, and health. The teacher must secure the cooperation of coworkers, parents, and community resources to create these linkages. The following indicators reflect reasons for linkages to offer support to the child care environment:

- More frequent communication between teachers and families may bring about a greater knowledge for both sides and improve the care given to the children in the early childhood education environment (Ghazvini & Mullis, 2002; Dambro & Lerner, 2006). A foundation for constructive relationships is built on many forms of communication (Greenberg, 2006).
- Frequent positive communication between teachers and staff within an early education environment is a good practice to prevent conflict (Bruno, 2007).
- Communication skills that are well developed and backed by knowledge of one's own perspective and those of other cultures can help the teacher negotiate conflicts based on culture (Obegi & Ritblatt, 2005). "Learn to identify and challenge stereotypes, prejudices, and discriminatory practices" (Derman-Sparks & Ramsey, 2005).
- Teachers who are culturally competent have the ability to value diversity, know what their own cultural perception is, can manage the differences between the two, and can adapt to the cultural context of the community they serve (Volk & Long, 2005; Chang, 2006; NCCC, 2007).
- Twenty percent of the children in the United States have an immigrant parent, many of whom speak a language other than English at home (Parker, 2006). If the language and culture of a community is valued,

Wadsworth/Cengage Learning

Communicating with the child is the first step toward learning how to communicate with parents, coworkers, and directors regarding a child's safety, nutritional, and health needs.

families are more likely to become involved with their children's school (Riojas-Cortez, Flores, & Clark, 2003; Simons & Curtis, 2007).

- Early childhood education programs are becoming family-centered organizations that reflect the changes going on in society (Hamilton, Roach, & Riley, 2003). Parents are the real experts about their children, so teachers should tap this knowledge (Greenberg, 2006; Christian, 2006; ChildWelfare, 2007). Involving parents as partners is a key to good early childhood education (Henrich & Gadaire, 2007).
- The biggest challenge that teachers have in trying to make sure good public policy for early childhood education environments exists is to be "at the table" and advocate for what is good care for children (CCW, 2002; Meyer, 2005).
- Teachers and parents who work together as a caring community can improve the quality of child care (Baldwin, DaRos-Voseles, & Swick, 2003; Collins et al., 2003; Williams & Cooney, 2006). The quality of relationship among children, parents, and teachers impacts every aspect of development of those children (Goldstein, Hamm, & Schumacher, 2007; Knopf & Swick, 2007).
- Increasing numbers of children have challenging behaviors (Kaiser & Rasminsky, 2007). Creating inclusive communities and linkages of resources for these at-risk children can lead to more positive outcomes (PBS Parents, 2007; Edwall, 2007).
- Forming community partnerships for keeping children safe, healthy, and active can offer everyone involved important support (Dickinson, Lothian, & Jonz, 2007).

- **synergy** *combined effort or action.*

Synergy, or combined effort, is much more effective than individual effort. This is especially true in the early childhood education environment. Policies should be in force to help teachers develop approaches using synergy as often as possible. The holistic approach to early childhood education allows the teacher to realize that one person is less effective than the combined effort of a team. A teacher is called upon to be many things to a child. The physical, emotional, and cognitive care and education of a child is a very large task. Most teachers are involved in this task on a daily basis for a number of children.

The teacher can make this job easier. The teacher who learns to communicate about the child's safety, nutritional, and health needs can be more proactive in the care of children. This effort will involve communicating to the parents as well as all those present in the early childhood education environment. Coworkers, directors, assistants, and food preparers should all be involved in the effort to promote and protect the health and well-being of children in care. An important part of this communication is to let the parents know, in advance, what the policies are for safety, nutrition, and health (Lucarelli, 2002).

The communication effort eases the transition from the early childhood education environment to the home environment so that the child can feel the sense of well-being as a constant. Many parents do not realize how much they can actively affect their own environment. A teacher who passes on knowledge about safety, nutrition, and health can help parents create a better environment at home.

A teacher who is culturally competent is more effective in preventing problems and protecting the well-being of the child. The many cultures, races, and other diverse conditions of people in this country are causing rapid change, and this diversity should be understood instead of ignored. The teacher who learns to celebrate the differences and understand the similarities will be more effective in offering the children in care an optimal environment. The teacher who approaches situations from a broad viewpoint will be more likely to pick up nuances of how families approach safety, nutrition, and health. A teacher should be comfortable knowing his limitations (Gonzalez-Mena & Stonehouse, 2000; Kaczmarek, 2006).

In addition to the parents and families, the teacher also should seek help from outside the early childhood education environment. A teacher is rarely a qualified health or nutrition professional. There will probably be instances when the teacher will have to call on outside resources and professionals to deal with a situation that presents a challenge. An example of this might be the challenging behavior of a child or children that may seem insurmountable. The teacher may have tried a number of strategies that do not work. It may be time to call in a mental health professional (Waldman, 2007).

It is getting more difficult to remain in the early childhood education environment without acknowledging that the teacher must be an advocate for the health, safety, and well-being of children, not only within the environment and by providing an example for the parents, but also in the greater community. The difficulties that communities are seeing with violence, poverty, homelessness, child maltreatment, and other family situations may have a residual effect in the early childhood education environment. The teacher may feel the need to take a leadership role to help improve the community or the situation (Meyer, 2005).

The best way to provide families with a caring community is to use the synergistic approach by creating teams made up of people within the early childhood education environment, parents, and others in the greater community. A teacher who makes the most of the people and the resources available will offer the children in the early childhood education program the best environment possible.

To provide the maximum benefit to the child, policies should be set in place that include the following considerations:

1. *Communication skills:* practices for supporting better communications among teachers, parents, children, and others.
2. *Cultural competency:* understanding diverse cultures, races, and health conditions in order to recognize differences and similarities that will help maintain the well-being of children.
3. *Accessing community resources:* understanding how to recognize and access community resources that will help the teacher be more effective in providing for safety, nutrition, and health.
4. *Developing effective advocacy:* understanding the importance of advocacy and how to perform it.
5. *Creating a caring community for families:* understanding that, when families are more involved in the early childhood education environment, the quality of health and well-being of children will be improved.

Key Concept 16.1

Policies for Linkages

Early childhood education is an important part of many children's lives. Its quality is greatly improved if there is good communication with parents and if cultural competence is practiced. The quality of care is promoted by accessing and using community resources. The teacher who is an advocate for the child with the parents, other key figures in the child's life, and the greater community is offering maximum protection and prevention. Creating a caring community for families uses synergy for greater safety, nutrition, and well-being both at the child care site and at home.

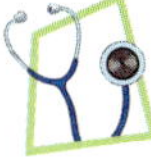

16.2 TOWARD BETTER COMMUNICATION SKILLS

Development of good communication is critical for the early childhood education environment. Families come in many different forms. There may be two parents present, or only a single parent. There may be families where one parent is a stepparent or where both parents are of the same gender (Rowell, 2007). Grandparents, aunts, uncles, and foster parents are becoming increasingly responsible for raising children. Mutual communication with the parent or guardian concerning the child should show respect and acknowledge feelings about certain situations. This helps both parties feel more comfortable. Keeping parents informed about the child's activities and any concerns you have helps families learn to trust you and provides a basis for communication (Gonzalez-Mena, 2004; Gillespie, 2006).

Developing Trust and Respect

The teacher who is consistent and predictable in the relationship with parents develops a bond of trust. If the teacher shows the child and the family respect, they are much more likely to be responsive and to participate actively in the safety, nutrition, and health of the child (Figure 16-1).

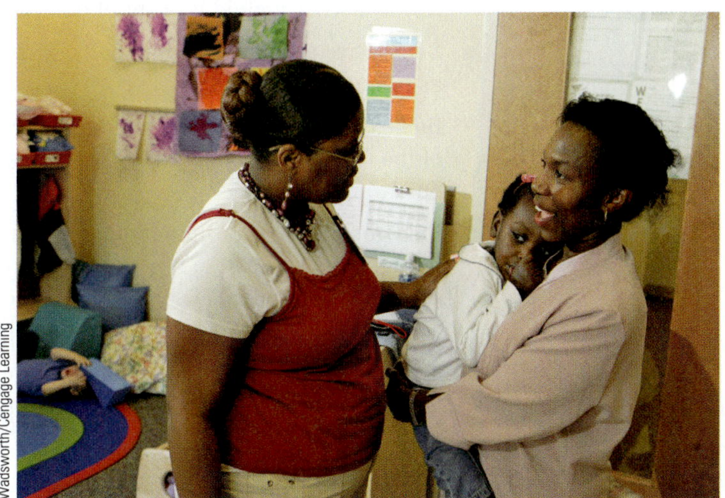

Wadsworth/Cengage Learning

A bond of trust between teacher, parent, and child is formed by consistency and respect.

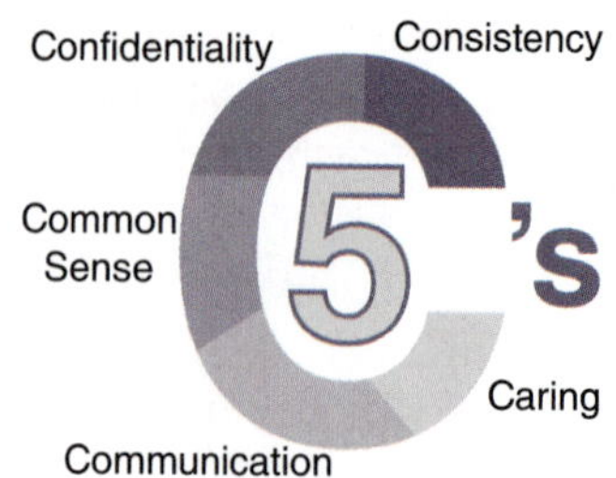

FIGURE 16-1
The five Cs of parent relations.

The teacher should be supportive and responsive to concerns about a child. This should be established at the beginning of the relationship with the child and parent or guardian and should be continued on a daily basis. Establishing and continuing the communication relationship is often a matter of common sense, as listed in Table 16-1. Gillespie (2006) suggests four simple steps for active listening in order to cultivate good relationships with families:

TABLE 16-1
A Dozen Ways for a Teacher to Communicate Successfully

- Show a genuine interest in the child, and ask the parent to share feelings and concerns about the child.
- Encourage the parent to ask questions, to visit the early childhood education environment, and to participate whenever possible. Seek parental input.
- Be an active listener. Focus on the parent or guardian, not on how to respond. Assume nothing. Clarify any confusion or misunderstanding by repeating what was heard.
- Provide parents with verbal and written information about the child and the concerns or information that will help address the safety, nutritional, and health needs of the child.
- Think before speaking. What is it that must be communicated? What is the best way to do it? Practice through role play if necessary.
- Any concern about the child should be dealt with immediately and not allowed to go unchecked.
- Never discuss a child in front of other children or adults.
- Be positive and discuss good behaviors and accomplishments as well as problems.
- Be flexible. Each family is unique and has different needs. Be aware of the family situation, the cultural background, and the child's home environment.
- Be a good observer. Often it is what is not said or done that may be significant. Learn to read nonverbal cues such as body tension, avoidance of contact, a sense of chaos, or other vulnerabilities.
- Never compare the child or situation with others. This never accomplishes anything and can cause resentment and guilt.
- Always keep whatever is communicated in confidence. Use the information to help the child and family find resources or get any help necessary.
- Remain calm; do not argue or be defensive. Model good coping skills.

(1) Stop what you are doing and give the parent your undivided attention. (2) Look at the parent and make eye contact if culturally appropriate, and observe nonverbal cues. (3) Listen to what the parent is saying, including how he or she says it. (4) Respond during the conversation with gestures that indicate that you are listening, and when the parent is finished, restate or summarize what was said for clarification. This can be established through questions and statements. This validates the fact that you heard what the parent said, how she said it, and that you understood what she meant. These easy four steps can help to avoid a lot of problems in communication and can help form a good relationship.

Make sure that you do not make any assumptions about the child or the family culture (Gonzalez-Mena, 2004; Derman-Sparks & Ramsey, 2005). Ask questions and, where applicable, be aware of cultural issues. If culture may be a part of the issue and a relationship has already been established, you might want to ask direct but sensitive questions about the culture or ethnicity to help you to understand (Kaiser & Rasminsky, 2003; Chang, 2006). Before you begin, you should become aware of your own culture so you can understand your own behavior and interactions with others. There may be communication barriers on both sides—not created by language, necessarily, but by cultural differences (Obegi & Ritblatt, 2005). There may also be a language barrier. With the help of the health consultant or other parents in care, a translator can be found if language appears to be a barrier to communication between families and teachers about the needs of a child.

Remember, when you are engaging in communication with parents, you should be sure to respect their comfort zone as well as your own. Communicate thoroughly and ask questions about anything that might be relevant to the issue at hand. It is important to realize that "one size" or one solution does not fit all situations and people. Each child, each family, and each issue is different, and the teacher should be considerate of that fact (Kaiser & Rasminsky, 2003; Derman-Sparks & Ramsey, 2005). You can ask parents for their opinions and ask them to clarify what they have said (ChildWelfare, 2007). A family's values should be supported, but both the teacher and the family should realize that there are different perspectives. Always keep in mind that the goal is the well-being of the child (Gonzalez-Mena, 2004; Chang, 2006). Without clear discussion, communication may break down, and both the parent and the teacher may become frustrated. Clear communication must occur in order to understand differences, whether they be cultural, religious, or socioeconomic. Gonzalez-Mena and Bhavnagri (2000) suggested that when you are trying to communicate about a practice or policy that the family may not understand or agree with, some questions should be asked. Those questions are found in Table 16-2.

Developing a System of Communication in Early Childhood Education Environments

Good communication skills are necessary for the early childhood education staff. It can affect the quality of care (Lucarelli, 2002; Shope & Aronson, 2006). During a day, the same child may have more than one teacher. These teachers must communicate with each other as to the child's safety, nutritional, and health needs. The quality of any interactions concerning the child affect the care of the child. Children need to feel that their environment is constant and that the care is consistent. The degree of communication among staff members can affect the morale of the early childhood education environment.

TABLE 16-2
Questions for the Teacher to Clarify Perspective

1. Is the family's cultural perspective on this issue different from mine?
2. How does the family's cultural perspective relate to its care practices for their children such as feeding, napping, and toileting?
3. Am I aware of the child-rearing differences in that particular culture? How does this culture deal with a child who cries, is angry, or is curious? What gender differences between boys and girls do they enforce?
4. What goals do the family have for the child, and how do those goals relate to the cultural perspective of the family? Do they want the child to be independent or interdependent?
5. Are the policies of care particularly suited to one culture and not all? What might have to be changed to adapt to more than one culture?
6. Have I attempted to understand the family's perspective and the complexity of the issues that may be present?
7. Have I tried to explain to the family my own rationale based on my perspective, and have I looked at my own perspective from my background and values and how culture may have affected it?
8. How might I work with the families to construct an environment that meets their needs and the needs of early education and brings resolution between the two? This may take a little education on the part of both the teacher and the parent to understand each other's perspective.

Wadsworth/Cengage Learning

Face-to-face verbal communication between teachers and supervisors is the most effective way to communicate, but it is also good to have a parent board for all types of information for the parents.

There can be problems if any one person feels that she is not being heard or her opinion is not respected. If there is miscommunication, it can lead to indirect communication such as gossip and may cause power struggles within the early childhood education environment between teachers, or the teachers and the director (Bruno, 2007). A peer resolution process should be in place to make sure that communication within the system is positive and direct and that there is resolution. When the communication within the early childhood education environment is consistent, the children can also learn to communicate at a higher level.

Communication is most effective when it is verbal and face to face. However, the nature of the early childhood education environment may not always offer the opportunity. A system of communication through notes, after-hours telephone conversations, and regular staff meetings can help to maintain an open line of communication about concerns and issues concerning the well-being of the children in care. If the early childhood education environment includes a director, he or she should model good communication and help others on the staff to resolve any conflicts that may be present.

Another area that might be further developed in the early childhood education environment is communication with preverbal infants and toddlers. Recent research has shown that very young children can reduce their communication frustration level by learning simple signs to represent language ("Signs of the Times," 2004). Early childhood education centers all over the United States and Great Britain are employing this method of communication for the preverbal children in care ("Signs of the Times," 2004; Fawcett, 2001). The idea is that children know what people are saying to them before they can talk, but they cannot reciprocate in spoken language (Helms, 1999). Children younger than 12 months are capable of learning and mastering simple signs (Baca, 2001; Fiedler, 2002). Signing can encourage communication at least six months before children begin to form basic words (Acredolo, Goodwyn, & Abrams, 2002). The ability to learn to communicate gives preverbal children the opportunity to participate and decreases their frustration level. Signing has been found to be a major source of reducing tantrums and stress for very young children. Another benefit has been that children who use signs at this early stage of development can increase their cognitive abilities (ABCNews, 2005). Communication like this has also shown to increase the bonding level of the child and the person communicating with the child. In fact, when babies communicate by using signs, they are much more likely to engage those they are communicating with to form a reciprocal relationship (Moore, Acredolo, & Goodwyn, 2001). Children who engage in reciprocity through language develop the ability to become more rational in their thinking, can problem-solve both on their own and with others, and can learn to be more reflective (Greenspan, 2003a).

Opinions differ as to which signs should be used with preverbal children. Some believe that using American Sign Language (ASL) is the best way. Others have been successful in making up signs that, when consistently used, seem to work fine. Videos such as *Baby Signs* and *Sign with Me* are available to help parents and teachers understand this important communication pattern. Good communication between the child and the teacher can affect the child's cognitive and language development (Loeb et al., 2004). The quality of communication between a child and a teacher affects the overall quality of care. A teacher who gets down to the child's eye level when talking or listening is more attentive to the child's needs (Sherry, 2004). When a child

Mia had worked as a preschool teacher for several years and really liked working with young toddlers, but also found it frustrating when they couldn't tell her what they wanted. The children would throw temper tantrums when they couldn't get what they wanted because they couldn't communicate. Mia moved to a different town and a new school to work with 3-year-olds but found she missed working with the younger children. This new school used signing for the older infants and younger toddlers, and she decided to take a class to learn how to use this type of signing. Mia also went through some other special training for working with infants and toddlers. When a position opened in the infant/toddler classroom, Mia got the job. She was very excited to be able to put some of what she had learned to use and was curious to see whether working with these younger children would be as frustrating as it had been. She spent a great deal of time teaching the infants and young toddlers how to sign their basic needs and felt her work was much less frustrating than it had been before. When the very young children could use the signs she taught them, she found that their basic needs were met without the normal frustration at not being understood. She was very pleased she had taken this step because it not only helped the children but also made her job more rewarding and less frustrating.

feels that someone is listening to what he says and cares about it, he is better able to develop a sense of self (Greenspan, 2003b). A preverbal child also needs to be "listened" to in other ways. Watching for verbal and nonverbal cues is important. The teacher should ask himself what the cue meant, and then verify with the child what is being asked for. He should watch how the child responds to his actions and modify them according to that response. A teacher who creates activities or has available materials that encourage interactions among children in care will also foster language among children. Using stories to engage children in conversation can be beneficial (Whaley, 2002; Zambo & Hansen, 2007) as it provides an opportunity for children to interact with each other, the teacher, and the story. Storytelling can help extend the language of the children.

Key Concept 16.2

Good Communication Skills

Communication is a key factor in the success of an early childhood education environment's effort to provide for the safety, nutrition, and health of the children present. Communication with the families of the children is vitally important and should be a priority. Asking for input and listening to parents are key to consistency and optimum care. Communicating with others who participate in the early childhood education environment affords the highest levels of protection and prevention.

  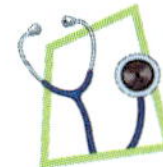

16.3 CULTURAL COMPETENCY

• **diversity** *differences; variety often related to culture.*

Culture is defined as parameters of behavior. Regardless of the culture of a home environment, when one steps into the outside world, **diversity** is everywhere. Diversity is represented in race, ethnicity, handicapping conditions, language differences, age, religion, class, gender, and more. One of the greatest effects on the diversity of early education programs is culture. The increasing population of different cultural groups has had an impact on the United States (Lundgren & Morrison, 2003; Parker, 2006). The society we live in is multicultural and multifaceted. Being culturally sensitive is no longer enough. To be a successful, effective teacher, one must be culturally competent (Obegi & Ritblatt, 2005; Chang, 2006). This should not be just a "tourist approach" where culture is brought up only on special occasions, but an integral part of the environment for all (Williams & Cooney, 2006; Derman-Sparks & Ramsey, 2005). "Culture is a fundamental building block in the development of a child's identity" (Gonzalez-Mena & Shareef, 2003). Diversity of culture cannot be taught directly; it is not a lesson plan, a curriculum, or a holiday celebration with costumes and food (Wardle, 2005). Understanding and appreciating cultural diversity is a concrete experience in which children can develop a sense of being included when they see themselves, their families, their cultures, and their communities reflected in the environment.

Everyone should learn how to appreciate this diversity, and this is especially true for people who care for children. The teacher has the opportunity to teach children positive values about gender, race, ethnicity, class, and disabling conditions. The teacher will also be dealing with families of children who may represent differing cultures, social classes, ethnicities, and other variations of background and experiences. Early education offers children and their families opportunities to share their cultural heritages with others who are present.

Creating a cultural consistency between the home environment and the environment in care is important (Gonzalez-Mena, 2004; Greenberg, 2006). If there is no representation for a child's culture in toys, language spoken, language in books, foods, or other people around her, then she is likely to feel that she is in "stranger" care (Cronin & Jones, 1999; Joshi, 2005). Children who experience conflicting child-rearing practices may feel confused (Joshi, 2005). Children who are uncomfortable in care are less likely to play and learn, and more likely to be at risk for safety, nutrition, and health problems. When a child is exposed to diversity in culture and cultural practices, he is more likely to become comfortable and to see differences as normal (Derman-Sparks & Ramsey, 2005). When a child is comfortable in care she is more likely to develop a sense of identity (Gonzalez-Mena & Shareef, 2003). The awareness of cultural diversity and differing values has the potential to improve the early childhood education environment significantly. It will also allow the teacher the ability to best meet the needs for safety, nutrition, and health for all children in care.

Preparing for Cultural Competence

Cultural competency is about how we learn to value diversity in many ways and how we come to situations with open minds about other cultures and diverse backgrounds. Valuing this diversity is the first step in the process of building a framework for cultural competency (NCCC, 2007). The second step is for the teacher to recognize her own cultural background, attitudes, beliefs, and guidelines for behavior (Obegi & Ritblatt, 2005; Im, Parlakian,

FIGURE 16-2
Cultural competency continuum.

CULTURAL COMPETENCY CONTINUUM

Cultural Destructiveness
(Intentionally deny, reject, or outlaw any other culture)

↓

Cultural Incapacity
(Accept the existence of other cultures but unable to work effectively with other cultures)

↓

Cultural Blindness
(Assume that all people are basically alike; universal approach and services for all people)

↓

Cultural Precompetence
(Willing to learn about and understand other cultures)

↓

Cultural Competency
(Able to work effectively in cross-cultural situations; develop standards, policies, practices and attitudes that value diversity)

↓

Cultural Proficiency

(Proactive in promoting cultural diversity; seeks opportunities to improve cultural relationships)

Reprinted with permission by Carol Ann Brannon, MS, RD, LD "Dietetic Diversity" a Continuing Education Course published by Nutrition Dimension, Inc. April, 2005. (www.nutritondimension.com)

& Sanchez, 2007). This can be done as the teacher carefully looks at Figure 15-3 on page 597 and answers those questions for her own experiences. People can break down barriers to accept those who are different if they understand their own biases and ways of operating (Derman-Sparks & Ramsey, 2005). Figure 16-2 shows the cultural competency continuum, and a teacher can place himself on the continuum when looking at biases and methods of operating. Each person should appreciate his own uniqueness as well as similarities to others.

The next step is to create a balance within the dynamics of difference. Today, early childhood programs of all kinds reflect the cultural, ethnic, and

Wadsworth/Cengage Learning

Diverse classrooms present the immediate need for understanding and nurturing diversity. Teachers play an important role in creating an unbiased environment in which children can grow and learn about their own and others' uniqueness.

racial differences found in the greater society (Daniel & Friedman, 2006). Duarte and Rafanello (2001) suggested that "best practices recommend that environment and instruction practices reflect the language and culture of the children they serve." Many others have agreed (NAEYC, 2005; Bowman, 2006; Volk & Long, 2005; Williams & Cooney, 2006). Culturally informed teaching takes the information required to welcome children from diverse cultures and create a learning environment that is comfortable for all (Im, Parlakian, & Sanchez, 2007). Teachers must work actively to get families involved so that there are no barriers between the two environments and children will be able to get the best possible care and education from both of them. Families from other cultures may want and need help with parenting skills and other care issues (Bornstein & Cote, 2004). Routines, practices, and procedures in care may be unfamiliar to or misunderstood by families (Walker-Dalhouse & Dalhouse, 2001). Teachers should be happy to provide information and should appreciate creating this type of consistency between the two environments. Working toward this balance enables the teacher to create an environment where all children are able to accept who they are and value their backgrounds (Wardle, 2005; Chang, 2006). The teacher should seek to acquire and increase knowledge about other cultures (NAEYC, 2005); this also entails cultural sensitivity. When learning about another culture, the teacher should recognize subtleties that may not be readily apparent and should accept a

An understanding of different cultural backgrounds provides a deeper understanding of parenting strategies. Socioeconomic differences are also an important factor.

person from another culture in the many ways he may express his cultural background. The teacher should take care not to apply a group label, making the assumption that all individuals within a group are alike (Early Childhood Teacher [ECT], 2004). For example, Asians are not all alike; China, Japan, Vietnam, Malaysia, India, and the Philippines may all be classified as parts of Asia, but their cultures are very diverse. Cultural competence is something that is gained in informal and natural ways by observing, asking for or seeking out information, and being involved with the children and families in care (Joshi, 2005; Moore, 2004). A teacher cannot know everything about all cultures, but knowledge about one culture at a time can be acquired through exploration of that culture (Huber, 2004). Some techniques for developing cultural competence can be found in Table 16-3.

A teacher who is trying to understand diversity should learn how families behave on an ongoing and everyday basis (see Table 16-3). Values and beliefs regarding items such as family roles, child-rearing practices, gender differences, and communication styles are reflected in how families live their lives on a daily basis (Greenberg, 2006). Focusing on a child and his family life, language, traditions and other practices may provide excellent insight into that child's culture.

Personal Interactions

Personal interactions are the best way to adapt to the issues of cultural diversity (Okagaki & Diamond, 2000; Burchinal & Cryer, 2003). As diversity is explored and understood, it allows the teacher to be more able to communicate, more sensitive, and more willing to change and adapt (Seefeldt, 2002). Having an open dialogue can break down misconceptions and fears on the parents' part and help to establish trust.

In some cultures, there are distinctive differences that can be observed, and communication style can be adjusted. In low-context cultures such as Western Europe and the United States, great value is put on independence. Communication is precise, direct, and logical. In cultures that are high-context, such as Latino, African-American, Asian, Native American, and Southern European cultures, interdependence is valued. Communication is more likely to include nonverbal cues, and tradition, history, and social status play a large role (Kaiser & Rasminsky, 2003). There are other indirect ways to communicate as well, such as pauses and silences. See Table 16-4 for some strategies to help with cross-cultural communication.

Differences in backgrounds may elicit necessary responses in order to maintain the safety, nutritional well-being, and health of the children in care. Parents develop their philosophy of how to parent based on their own culture, socioeconomic background, personality, and family experiences.

Studies have shown that, even though parents may come from diverse cultural backgrounds, it is the socioeconomic level that most greatly affects parenting styles (Collins & Ribeiro, 2006). These and other studies have found few differences in parenting based on culture alone. Low-income status may bring with it emotional stress and decreased abilities of parents and families to provide the necessary support for the children (ChildWelfare, 2007). Social conditions such as large households, lack of access to health care, language barriers, and unemployment were found to have an effect on the health of children of Mexican immigrants (Duarte & Rafanello, 2001; Collins & Ribeiro, 2006).

TABLE 16-3
Techniques for Developing Cultural Competence

- Develop a dialogue with parents about their own cultures. Invite them to share their culture with others in the early childhood education environment. Express a desire to learn from the parents. Ask for their opinions, and encourage them to participate. This might include having them help plan curriculum and participate in activities.
- If language barriers exist, try to find someone who can translate and break down any barriers to teacher–parent communication.
- Have family evening potlucks where families bring dishes representing their backgrounds and share some of their histories with other families.
- Research games, songs, and so forth, from other cultures in books on child care curriculum and histories. If there are children in care who have disabilities, this can also be researched. Incorporate these into the curriculum.
- Attend cultural fairs to get a greater understanding about the cultures represented in the early childhood education environment. Learn everything you can about a child's home culture.
- Create a support group with other teachers. Use this collaborative effort to share information, resources, and hold open discussions. This is a good way to remove barriers that the teacher may have.
- Observe children who are from diverse cultures, socioeconomic levels, or abilities. Watch the child with parents and family members. Do this without judgment. Watch how they communicate in verbal and nonverbal ways.
- Talk to others in the community who represent the diverse group to find out about the group.
- In larger early childhood education situations, encourage the hiring of diverse staff.
- Acknowledge with parents that a topic may have many points of view and, when necessary, reach a consensus for the well-being of the child.
- Create a family book where families of the children in care talk about the people in their families, their customs, their home, and their lives. Ask children to bring pictures from home to go in these books; if the family has no camera, have the children draw the pictures to go in the book. If the care environment has a digital camera or video recorder available, it could be loaned to families to accomplish this task.
- Create a regular time every week or two to invite parents to sing songs from their culture or share stories. Have them talk about cultural traditions. If a translator is needed, try to have one in attendance.
- Put up pictures of famous buildings or places around the world and of children and families from all over the world.
- With prior parental permission, use digital cameras and video recorders to take pictures of the children to place on the wall.
- Provide some distinctive cultural clothing and props, such as product boxes, for the dramatic play area.
- Provide children's books about other cultures and in the prevailing language. A number of books from many cultures are now available.
- Incorporate storytelling from other cultures into activities. If possible, bring in bicultural storytellers.
- Incorporate music from other cultures.
- Plan cooking projects for foods from other cultures, maybe even recipes brought in by children to represent their family's culture.

TABLE 16-4
Keys to Cross-Cultural Communication

- Be open, honest, and respectful.
- Understand and respect personal space. Individuals of different cultures have varying degrees of comfort about the amount of personal space between them and another person.
- Establish a rapport in the common interest of the child.
- Express interest and pay attention by listening carefully.
- Respect silence. It may be a cultural norm or the result of taking time to understand what is being said in a nonnative language.
- Watch how, when, and if eye contact is made. In some cultures making eye contact shows lack of respect.

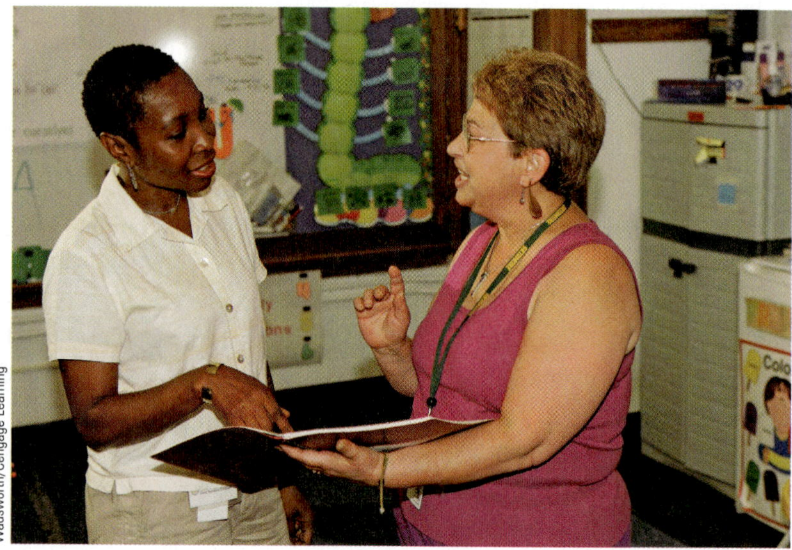
Wadsworth/Cengage Learning

The teacher can gain insight into diversity issues by talking with parents individually or in groups.

The realization by the teacher that families are more alike than different breaks down further barriers to providing care. The effects of low income may be more easily understood than a cultural difference. As the teacher recognizes the similarities to families of other cultures, the ability to discern differences may increase.

Understanding Family Actions

- **acculturated** *adopting attitudes and beliefs.*

There may be cultural differences that account for the actions of families. These are most likely to occur in families who are less **acculturated** to the social values commonly accepted by American society. Families who perceived difficulties in adapting to the patterns of social integration were more likely to place greater demands on children and were found to practice more strict control over them (Julian, McKenry, & McKelvey, 1994). Families that operate from the viewpoint of their own culture alone are more likely to have bicultural conflicts. These conflicts may include how children are expected to behave, how health is perceived, whether safety is seen as an issue, and how children are fed (Gonzalez-Mena, 2004).

Integrating Diversity into the Early Childhood Education Environment

It should be understood that differences between the early childhood education environment and the home environment may become an issue. Children develop their attitudes and identity through experiences in their environments and with their bodies as they pass through developmental stages. When children are infants and toddlers, they become self-aware. As they grow and explore their world, they begin to identify differences as well as similarities. They will also begin to question differences. Teachers should be able to respond appropriately. For example, color is an integral part of a person, and children of color should be made to feel good about who they are (Derman-Sparks & Ramsey, 2005; Poussaint, 2006).

A teacher should show appreciation for diversity and be aware of the dynamics involved when diverse cultures interact. She should be sensitive to group differences but should not stereotype or minimalize the differences. This can lead children to form prejudgments (Wardle, 2005). A teacher should teach respect and tolerance for everyone in the early childhood education environment. Tolerance should include people who are diverse culturally, racially, ethnically, or in abilities. Biracial, biethnic children may need extra support in this respect (CCHP, 2001). Increasingly, these children are present in the classroom. Children with racial or ethnic differences should be empowered to stand up for themselves (Wardle, 2005).

The best way to manage diversity is on an ongoing basis. The teacher should continually interact with children and other adults with diversity in mind. The early childhood education environment should integrate diversity into all aspects of providing for the safety, nutrition, and health of children. The management of the environment for diversity should include the physical setup, a culturally sensitive pattern of interactions, and encouraging participation of children from many cultures (Im, Parlakian, & Sanchez, 2007).

Children who learn about diversity in a positive manner are less likely to develop biases as adults (Derman-Sparks & Ramsey, 2005; Williams & Cooney, 2006). Children learn from what the people around them think, say, and do. Table 16-5 offers some suggestions to help integrate diversity into the curriculum for safety, nutrition, and health.

Key Concept 16.3

Cultural Competency

A teacher has to manage diversity on an ongoing basis. Children in early childhood education environments represent a wide array of family structures, ethnic and cultural backgrounds, and experiences. The teacher who employs techniques that encourage understanding of diversity is better prepared to interact with children and their parents. This is essential for the teacher who wants to offer an environment that provides the best in safety, nutrition, and health for the child. The teacher can initiate activities that promote the integration of diversity into the early childhood education environment.

TABLE 16-5
Activities that Integrate Diversity

- Create a nonjudgmental atmosphere. Avoid isolating any child.
- Focus on the diversity of the children in your own early childhood education environment. This includes not only culture, but also lifestyle and socioeconomic differences.
- Weave different cultures into the curriculum themes. This allows for greater depth of understanding.
- Provide materials that depict diverse images. This might include pictures on the wall of children from all backgrounds and toys that are nonsexist and representative of the different cultures in your early childhood education environment. Dolls should be anatomically correct. Books and stories should be from a cross-section of society, including those in different languages represented by children in your care.
- Include staff from diverse backgrounds at all levels of responsibility. It is important to have this representation reflect the diversity of children in your care.
- Actively involve parents. Have parents and teachers from diverse cultures share their knowledge of their home cultures.
- Encourage participation by community helpers from diverse backgrounds for special circle times or programs that deal with safety, nutritional, or health issues. For example, a visiting nurse may be Filipino; a police officer may be African American; and a dietician may be in a wheelchair.
- Initiate activities that help provide self-esteem, self-identity, and well-being for mental health. Help children learn to value the differences and similarities among themselves. This will help break down stereotypical viewpoints that may impair how a child feels about himself or others.
- Encourage children to develop critical thinking skills to resist prejudice and develop acceptance.
- Respond positively to children's questions about issues concerning diversity. A child who asks about a disabled person should be answered instead of being ignored or having the question sidestepped. What is not discussed becomes the foundation for bias. These are the teachable moments.
- Discuss and try to find ways to support the differing values of the families in your care.

Pause for Reflection

What cultures are you personally familiar with? Are you from a distinct culture that is different from the "American" culture of the early settlers from Europe? What might you do to become more culturally competent about a culture you are not familiar with?

  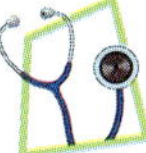

16.4 ACCESSING COMMUNITY RESOURCES

The teacher may have to access a host of resources to help in meeting the safety, nutritional, and health needs of the children in care. The number of resources available may depend on the type of community where the care is provided. With any type of care, if there is a health consultant available, that person can act as a key or conduit to all available resources. The same is true for the medical home of each child. These health professionals can connect the teacher with myriad resources. If neither of these is available, then the community should be surveyed to find them.

Surveying the Community for Resources

Larger urban communities, such as major cities, are more likely to have a number of resources that the teacher can access. Smaller urban or suburban communities may offer a more limited number of resources, and rural communities may have even fewer. The teacher will have to attempt to access resources to determine the number available in the local community.

Community size is only one determining factor. Another is the degree of commitment that the local governments have to the well-being of children. Some cities, counties, and states have a higher degree of commitment and, therefore, more resources available for teachers. An example would be those cities that have a specialist on staff to help the area organize for early childhood education programs. However, other states, counties, and cities may have less commitment or fewer of their own resources, which limit the information that they are able provide. Many states, counties, and cities have community child care resource and referral agencies. These agencies provide much-needed information that the teacher should attempt to access.

The federal government provides many resources that the teacher can access. Government agencies such as the U.S. Department of Health and Human Services and the U.S. Department of Agriculture provide a great deal of information to promote safety, nutrition, and health. The information is

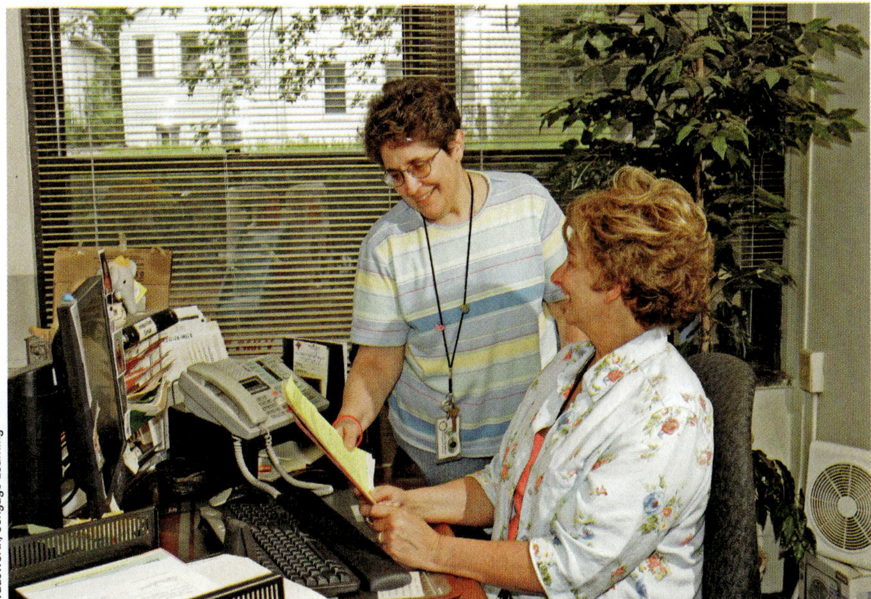

Wadsworth/Cengage Learning

Child care resource and referral agencies are a good source for parents to find quality, licensed child-care that meets their individual needs.

readily available to all consumers and is easy to access through mail or the Internet. Some information may be available locally at government offices or through programs such as the WIC program and Head Start.

Many national organizations have offices that provide information to promote the health and well-being of children. Some have state and local affiliates that provide easier access to information. Examples of these are the American Red Cross and the American Cancer Society.

Colleges and universities are resources for information. The departments most likely to have important information are child development, nutrition, human services, family studies, nursing, and schools of medicine. Both public and private institutions of higher learning are usually happy to share their information. Some might even be willing to share expertise, if time permits. Many child care health consultants come from this resource. Some universities offer extension services that are excellent sources of all types of information concerning children, families, nutrition, and health. Pennsylvania State University and Iowa State University are good examples of this type of support.

Hospitals, clinics and health centers, and poison control centers may also be good resources. They have information readily available that concerns the health, safety, and well-being of children. These types of facilities may also offer speakers for specific information such as immunizations. These speakers can be used for special topic programs that the teacher provides for families. Also remember the health consultant and medical home, as previously discussed in several chapters; these are both excellent resources for you to tap into to get many services for the children in your early childhood education environment (Cianciolo, Trueblood-Noll, & Allingham, 2004).

Many common local resources exist for teachers regardless of their location. These resources are included in Table 16-6.

Organizing and Using the Resources

It is vitally important that the teacher have resources organized should need for access occur. The APHA and the AAP recommend that a teacher create a community resource file that includes written information on a number of topics dealing with safety, nutrition, and health. These resources are for the teacher and the parents of children in care. If the information is available in the parent's native language, it should be provided; as an alternative, a translator should be used, whenever possible. These organizations also recommend that the teacher use consultants from available local resources. Consultants might include people from the fields of health care, nutrition, safety, mental health, or child abuse prevention. Because the teacher's time is often taken up with the business of care, the consultants can offer an invaluable service.

The Internet—A Resource Beyond the Community

There are many excellent resources on the Internet. Some are especially tailored to early childhood education teachers such as Healthy Child Care Magazine at http://www.healthychild.net/articles/. Childcare Health Program at http://www.ucsfchildcarehealth.org/; North Carolina Child Care Health and Safety Resource Center at http://www.healthychildcarenc.org/; and Healthy Child Care Pennsylvania at http://www.ecels-healthychildcarepa.org/ are also good sources. These all have numerous articles and publications that would

TABLE 16-6
Common Local Resources for Safety, Nutritional, and Health Information or Assistance

- Department of Public Health
- Hospitals, children's hospitals
- Health centers and clinics
- Fire and police departments
- Child care licensing/foster care licensing
- Child care resource and referral agencies
- Children's protective services
- Gas and electric companies
- Colleges and universities
- Medical societies (e.g., American Academy of Pediatrics)
- Local chapters of national organizations such as American Red Cross, American Dietetic Association, Girl Scouts, American Cancer Society, American Heart Association, and March of Dimes
- Poison control centers
- Libraries
- Head Start
- Department of Social Services
- Dental societies
- Family day care associations
- State and local affiliates of the National Association for the Education of Young Children
- Schools and school districts (for screening, school nurses, and special education resources)
- Humane societies
- County extension services
- WIC
- Visiting nurses associations
- Department of Parks and Recreation
- Pharmacies and pharmacists
- Department of Environmental Protection
- Associations for cultural and ethnic affiliations

be very helpful for the teacher. Good resources for information also come from child care resource and referral agencies such as Bananas whose website is at http://www.bananasinc.org/. Other Internet sites deal with a single issue that this book has covered such as cultural competence at http://www11.georgetown.edu/research/gucchd/nccc/documents/fcclcguide.pdf, where an excellent resource for this topic can be found. Surfing the web by the topic or specific detail is relatively easy and can help a teacher gather resources.

REALITY *Check*

Creating Linkages for Children's Challenging Behaviors

About 10 percent of children in this country have moderate to severe socio-emotional difficulties (USDHHS, 2006). Between 10 to 25 percent of young children display challenging behavior, and that disruptive behavior is the biggest issue confronting early childhood education teachers (NCCCHSRC, 2007). A significant number of children get expelled from preschools due to their challenging behaviors (Kaiser & Rasminsky, 2007; Brault & Brault, 2005). Challenging behavior may be defined as "any repeated pattern of behavior, or perception of behavior, that interferes with or is at risk of interfering with optimal learning or engagement in pro-social interactions with peers and adults" (Center for Evidence-Based Practice: Young Children with Challenging Behavior, 2007).

There are a number of reasons why children come to early childhood education environments with these behaviors. Children may have issues in their families or have health conditions or disorders such as ADHD that directly contribute to behavioral difficulties. These behaviors may relate to children's young age and developmental capabilities, or lack thereof. A child with a difficult temperament may have a hard time coping in groups. A child may not be getting enough sleep (Kurcinka, 2007) or may be competing for attention, even if it comes from negative behaviors (Logue, 2006). Children may have attachment issues or be affected by the degree of time spent in early childhood education environments (Kaiser & Rasminsky, 2007), or they may have dispositions that lead to these behaviors (Da Ros-Voseles & Moss, 2007). They may also be experiencing stress regarding issues of cultural differences and lack of social supports in their early childhood education environment. Regardless of the reason, these behaviors seem to serve a purpose for the child who has them. The challenging behaviors are a form of communication (PBS Parents, 2007). The child is trying to tell us something. The impact of these behaviors is great both on the early childhood education environment and the children themselves. The disruption in the environment can affect the comfort and education of other children (Lamm et al., 2006). Children with challenging behaviors have a difficult time with other children and haven't developed the social and emotional skills required to get along with peers (Center for Evidence-Based Practice: Young Children with Challenging Behavior, 2004). This can have a lifelong effect on the mental health and behavioral actions of the child (DEC, 2005). A child who has these issues resolved with early intervention can learn to function well now and prepare for success in the coming years (Funk, 2006). The more help early education environments have from outside sources, the more likely they are to deal with these behaviors and help the children who are exhibiting them. Creating linkages for this issue is essential in most early childhood education environments.

There are three levels from which to approach these linkages. Looking at the Teaching Pyramid (Fox & Lentini, 2006) in Figure 3-6 on page 112 can help you determine which level you are in and what types of linkages you may need. First-level linkages are made through the early childhood education environment by working with colleagues, families, and children to create positive, supportive relationships. This is also the level where preventive practices can be put into play by altering the environment in ways to make it more positive and functional for those children who have challenging behaviors. Linkages at this primary level are people and preventive practices. A major preventative practice is good observation (Parker, 2007).

At the second level are teaching strategies for positive social and emotional behaviors. These strategies can provide good methods and coping skills to shift behaviors. These linkages are generally from outside community resources. One such link might be resources and referral agencies. The idea of resource and referral began in 1973 in Oakland, California, when three women, calling themselves "Bananas," organized a support group for other mothers who did not have extended families in their

(continues)

REALITY *Check* (continued)

area. There was a clear lack of child care funding, and they set out to change that. They motivated legislators to introduce and pass the legislation that created the first resource and referral network in the nation. Bananas found themselves in business as they became the first resource and referral agency in the country. Today, Bananas has evolved into one of the most effective linkages in the nation. Their mission is to help parents and teachers in any way they can. They have handouts in 10 languages and videos in 6. A number of these handouts and videos deal with challenging behaviors and discipline for both at home and in group settings. There is also a good newsletter. Check out the Bananas website at http://www.bananasinc.org/.

Other good sources of linkages at this level might be college classes, seminars, or workshops that deal specifically with this issue. Resource and referrals may be a source for workshops. These classes may even be online such as the ones at Eager to Learn from Minnesota Child Care at http://etl.mnchildcare.org/classes.cfm. There may also be strategies and ideas from Internet sources as those mentioned on page 620 in this chapter or ones specifically dealing with this issue such as those at Center for Evidence-Based Practice: Young Children with Challenging Behavior at http://challengingbehavior.fmhi.usf.edu/. Another excellent source is the Minnesota Association for Children's Mental Health (2005), which collaborated with the Minnesota Department of Education to create a packet of teaching strategies, *Unlocking the Mysteries of Children's Mental Health: An Introduction for Future Teachers,* which can be found at www.macmh.org. PBSParents also has good information on and strategies for this issue at http://www.pbs.org/parents/inclusivecommunities/challenging_behavior.html.

To address the third level, which deals with intensive individual interventions, linkages should be specific to the individual child and should be professional in nature. Linkages for this level will require parental permission. This may not always be easy because many parents do not understand the degree of the problem or the fact that young children may be at risk for good mental health (Edwall, 2007). A child care health consultant might be of value to help parents understand the urgent need to deal with these behaviors before they become a lifelong pattern. When parents agree, a mental health consultant would have to be called upon. In some states, such as Connecticut, these professionals are available through an early childhood education partnership (Waldman, 2007). In other states, it may be a regional center for children under age 3 or a school district for children who are older that could provide this link. Zero to Three at http://www.zerotothree.org/site/PageServer?pagename=homepage may have information on how to find professionals to help. The professionals from any source identified may administer a screening tool such as the Ages and States Questionnaire to parents. This can offer reassurance to parents as well as establish whether there is further need for evaluation (Edwall, 2007). If that is the case, one of several screening tools would be used. For children under age 3, this would be the Diagnostic Classification for Zero to Three Revised (DC:0-3R), which was created by the organization Zero to Three (2005) to help in early identification and intervention. For children over age 3, the professional might administer the diagnostic and statistical manual of mental disorders (DSM) or the International Classification of Diseases (ICD) (World Health Organization [WHO], 1992). These tools will help the mental health professional to determine the diagnosis and implement practices and strategies for early intervention. Efforts to bring mental health consultants into early education environments to deal with challenging behaviors have been very successful (Waldman, 2007). Creating linkages at three levels may be what many early educational environments need to act upon to ameliorate the challenging behaviors presented by many young children.

CHECK*point:* **What is the most challenging behavior you have personally seen? How would you go about creating linkages for that challenging behavior?**

There are many resources found on the Internet that can be accessed by visiting the Online Companion at www.cengage.com/education/robertson listed under this text. Another excellent database source is http://www.sunflowered.com/hsn, which is the author's database for safety, nutrition, health, and other topics.

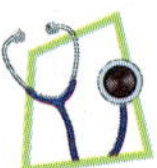

Key Concept 16.4

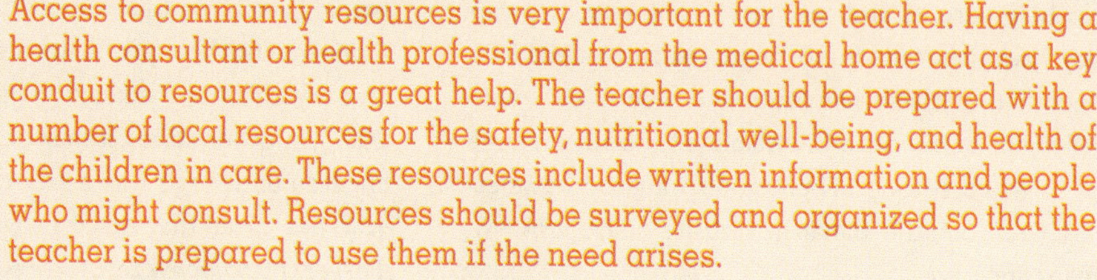

Accessing Community Resources

Access to community resources is very important for the teacher. Having a health consultant or health professional from the medical home act as a key conduit to resources is a great help. The teacher should be prepared with a number of local resources for the safety, nutritional well-being, and health of the children in care. These resources include written information and people who might consult. Resources should be surveyed and organized so that the teacher is prepared to use them if the need arises.

  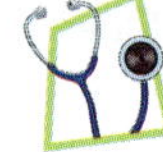

16.5 DEVELOPING EFFECTIVE ADVOCACY

- **advocate** *to support or speak on behalf of another.*

The majority of people who become teachers do so because of care and concern for children and their welfare. Regardless of the type of care the teacher is supplying, opportunity may present itself to **advocate** on behalf of a child. It is an inherent part of the job of a teacher to make sure the children in care are supported for optimum health, safety, and well-being. This may require the teacher to talk to parents, health professionals, and other sources of community resource and support. There are organizations that can help a teacher get involved and learn to advocate (Meyer, 2005). The Center for

Wadsworth/Cengage Learning

Teachers, by the nature of their profession, also become child advocates to ensure that children in care are supported for optimum health, safety, and well-being.

Child Care Workforce (CCW), The NAEYC, and the National Association for Family Child Care are just a few that could help the teacher to get involved, learn to advocate, and gain leadership skills.

For the Early Childhood Education Environment

Center-based care may already anticipate this need. It may even be part of a director's job description. Teachers in center care may have to advocate to the director about problems or issues about children or the environment of care. In turn, directors may represent the early childhood education center to the parents and others. Directors should be prepared for this through their education, training, and experience. They should help the teachers in their facilities to learn to do the same. Staff meetings, daily consultation, and mentoring will help teachers learn to best represent the children in care. Education and training will provide added support for teachers.

Elementary school teachers may find a different social structure for advocacy. In these settings, a principal and a district superintendent might provide support for advocating for children. In addition, there may be some type of intervention mechanism provided for children who need extra help, for example, from a social worker or school psychologist. The school district may have one or both of these on staff. School districts often provide ongoing training to their teachers in a wide range of areas. Elementary teachers would also benefit from staff meetings, daily consultation, and mentoring.

Helm (2007) suggests that building communities of practice for early childhood professionals, where they can come together for sharing concerns and gaining support, is a powerful tool to improve the quality of early childhood education environments. The teachers in these communities of practice can meet regularly face-to-face or exchange information via email. The communities of practice can help inspire and make creative changes to improve all facets of the early childhood education environment (Helm, 2007).

For the Family Child Care Provider

New family child care providers may not anticipate the need to intercede on behalf of a child. Veteran providers report a great deal of advocacy on behalf of the children in care. Approaching parents is usually the first line of communication. However, community resources and support may be necessary to help the provider approach a situation with the parents.

Support from others in the same profession might prove to be very valuable to the family day care provider. National organizations have local chapters that may provide this support. Local child care resource and referral agencies may also help the family child care provider to find others to share concerns and solutions. Local licensing may also be a source of connecting with other family day care providers. Education and training facilities are also a source of support and learning to advocate on behalf of children.

For the Nanny

The in-home care provided by a nanny may appear to be an ideal situation. With a lower nanny-to-child ratio, one might think there would be few problems. However, very few people performing the job of a nanny are trained, and

The APHA and the AAP recommend that early childhood education programs designate a "health advocate" to receive additional training in the areas of safety, nutrition, and health.

Wadsworth/Cengage Learning

difficulties are present here too. Two issues raised by many nannies are home safety and nutritional needs. The families that employ nannies are not always aware of what is safe or healthy for children. It may be awkward for the nanny to approach the family because of the employer–employee relationship. Nannies should understand the importance of advocacy for the children in care. Community resources and support can provide the foundations needed.

Nanny support groups are good sources of resources and solutions for advocacy. Local placement agencies may know of support groups in the area. Placing an ad in the local family press or newspaper to start a nanny support group has been effective in many parts of this country and in Canada. A list of support groups can be found on the National Association of Nannies website at http://www.nannyassociation.com or on the National Association for Nanny Care at http://www.nannycredential.org/page/page/4225838.htm.

The Health Advocate

The APHA and the AAP (2002) would like to see health advocacy in early childhood education taken one step further. They recommend that early childhood education facilities and large family child care homes should have one person who is designated as the health advocate. In many cases, this might be the child care health consultant who works with the early childhood education environment to advocate and educate on issues concerning the health and well-being of children in care. In other cases, it would be an assigned teacher, director, or other staff on whom people can rely to call attention to issues concerning safety, health, and nutrition (Healthy Child Care Pennsylvania, 2006). This designated person would receive more training in these issues. In cases of small family child care home providers and nannies, the health advocate is usually the teacher, and therefore it would be her duty to keep current in all issues that deal with the safety, nutrition, and health of the children in the early education environment. The designated health advocate could also be an outside community resource such as a health professional who is in the facility on a frequent basis and knows the children well. This may be a health professional from a medical home. Many resource and referral networks and agencies have added a health consultant to their staff. These health consultants are generally available to teachers in the local area for questions and can act as a resource. The California Child Care Health Program is a pioneer and innovator in the area of health consultants for child care. They offer a bimonthly newsletter that is available at http://www.ucsfchildcarehealth.org.

Leadership

Leadership may go beyond advocating for the children in the early childhood education environment to the parents and others. Some issues may be of real concern, and the teacher may want to pursue the issue at another level. This may involve working to make changes at the local level or even more sweeping changes at the state or national level. The NAEYC (2005) suggests that teachers get connected to state and local groups, get informed in three areas of interest, and get involved in many advocacy efforts. They also suggest that these efforts to become advocates be intentional with a goal in mind. A teacher will have to understand all the ramifications of the goal that has been set for advocacy, including political, economic, and social implications.

Grassroots advocacy or leadership begins at the local level. Local affiliates of national organizations that represent the early childhood education programs or children may be a good starting point. The national office can provide the local contact. Some cities and counties have a child care coordinator. This office may be able to provide good information and may be willing to help change local ordinances, laws, and other matters affecting the care of children. Other local places of support for advocacy are the local health department, children's hospitals, school districts, and medical societies.

Some states and local areas have child law advocacy groups, and some have a child care lobbyist who can provide valuable information and assistance. These can be found by contacting the local or statewide legal societies.

The teacher may have to take a greater leadership role if these types of support for advocacy are not available. Pursuing the issue may call for directly working with townships, city councils, county board of supervisors, or aldermen. If the issue goes beyond local assistance, the teacher may have to contact state legislators, the governor, individual representatives, or senators who represent the area in state or national matters. Professionals in the early childhood education environment can participate in the political process through advocacy and activism in both local and national arenas, and they can play a role in determining the policies impacting their profession (Freeman & Feeney, 2006; Cunningham, 2006).

Whatever reason may exist for advocacy or leadership, many teachers feel it is their responsibility to go beyond just providing daily care. The issues involved in safety, nutrition, and health for children have a tremendous impact on the well-being of children and their future.

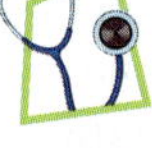

Key Concept 16.5

Advocacy for Children

Teachers may have to advocate for children in care on issues concerning safety, nutrition, and health. The teacher can do this in all areas of child care. Early childhood education centers, family child care homes, and nannies may all require advocacy at some point in time. The advocacy contact may be with parents, community resources, or other sources of support. Some issues may cause the teacher to seek local, state, or national assistance to make changes.

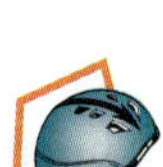

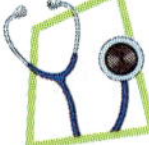

16.6 CREATING A CARING COMMUNITY FOR FAMILIES

For a caring community to exist, the families in care must be involved. The early childhood education environment should develop a program philosophy or policy that is family friendly and encourages family involvement (Halacka Ball, 2006; Knopf & Swick, 2007; Henrich & Gadaire, 2007). When there are high levels of family involvement, early childhood education is of higher quality (Michael, Dittus, & Epstein, 2007). We must begin as we did in the first chapter, when we looked at the holistic care of children. Looking at the whole child includes all the aspects, such as historical, cultural, and economic. Families and family systems are an integral part of the lives of children in

FIGURE 16-3
Creating a Caring Community.

Team Members

Family

Teacher

Community Resource

care (Hamilton, Roach, & Riley, 2003; Levinson, 2007). We must also consider what constitutes a family. According to many dictionaries, a family is two or more people who share goals and values, have long-term commitments to one another, and usually live in the same residence. As mentioned in the first chapter, the family may take many forms. It may be headed by a married couple, an unmarried couple, or a single parent. Grandparents may be the head of families (Birckmayer et al., 2005), or a gay or lesbian couple may be the parents (Rowell, 2007). Foster parents may be the head of the family. Children may be related by blood, by marriage, by circumstances, or by adoption. However the relationship exists, it is important that the family be valued, respected, and accepted in the early childhood education environment.

The first objective for creating a caring community for families is to create a plan. Teachers must develop mutual trust and understanding to work with families in a partnership. There may be barriers to this of culture, language, or communication style that will have to be addressed; these may bring with them misperceptions about parental roles (Ahnert & Lamb, 2003). Some teachers may not see parents as partners because they feel they have more knowledge about child development and are therefore the "experts." They may feel that parents do not care or have the time or motivation to be involved (Knopf & Swick, 2007). Parents may lack confidence because they don't believe in their own capabilities. Parents may work and may feel guilty about having their children in care so many hours. Whatever the reason, the barriers must come down.

One of the standards of the NAEYC is to "build strong relationships with all families in all communities" (Hyson, 2002). Early childhood education environments that are based upon relationships are of the highest quality. Preschools, public schools, family child care homes, and nannies that generate meaningful family involvement will be able to provide the optimum experience and ensure greater health, safety, nutrition, and well-being of the children. A beginning step is to use communication in many forms to connect with the families. Frequent communication provides more opportunities to create a balance between the early childhood education environment and home environments (Ghazvini & Mullis, 2002; Greenberg, 2006). Making communication in all forms an integral part of the plan is a step toward creating a caring community. Using bulletin boards to post information, having a notebook or notepad available to parents to communicate with the teacher, and sending home positive notes about the child are all great ideas. In the case of the family child care provider or nanny, a daily log could be used to keep communication lines open. Where appropriate and if possible, provide communication in the parents' native language if the family is unfamiliar with English. A translator could be an older child, friends, other family members, or even other children in care who are native speakers. A newsletter for all parents talking about the early childhood education environment and events could be offered on a regular basis—as frequently as weekly or as infrequently as monthly. Label pictures in the environment to help parents who do not have English as a first language to see simple words that describe the pictures. Communication is the beginning of collaboration.

Another way to engage families is to involve them in a variety of special communication processes and let them choose the ones that fit them best (Halacka Ball, 2006). Ask families to select a storybook that shares something about their family, and persuade an adult family member to come and read these stories (Lee, 2006). All children can be asked to share how their

REALITY *Check*

Relationship-Based Care in Early Childhood Education Environments

Infants and toddlers are entering early childhood education environments in increasing numbers. Approximately 40 percent of infants under age 1 year, 53 percent of 1-year-olds, and 59 percent of 2-year-olds are in some form of nonparental care (Mulligan, Brimhall, & West, 2005). Physical care is not enough. Beginning with these very young children and continuing throughout the early education process, the quality of relationships among teachers, children, and parents influences all phases of a child's development. From the very beginning, it is important that the relationships between parents and their children and those children and their teachers be consistent and responsive (Goldstein, Hamm, & Schumacher, 2007). These relationships should also be culturally responsive, and the teacher should practice cultural competence. When there is a caring community in early childhood education environments, it is easier to form the necessary partnerships between the parents and teachers so that teachers can form positive relationships with the children in their charge (Zero to Three, 2005). In this type of early education community where parents are respected and valued, there is less likely to be competition or conflict with teachers (Dombro & Lerner, 2006). If the teacher consciously works to connect the child's home experience with the early childhood education environment, this is reflected in the cohesion of the caring community.

Relationship-based care focuses on the child and "a continuous, individual relationship with one particular adult in an environment that provides security and closeness" (Leonard, 2006). This would be the parent when the child is not in the early childhood education environment and the teacher when the child is present in that environment. A child's attachment to a parent occurs during the first few months of life and is secure if the care is responsive to his needs. If the care is not sensitive and responsive, strong attachments may not be formed and babies may not learn how to organize their world or control their emotions (Zambo & Hansen, 2007). If the parent–child relationship is missing a secure attachment, a more secure relationship can be fostered if the parent has good role modeling by teachers. A teacher who is sensitive and responsive to the needs of an infant or young child is more supportive to both the child and his family.

When a child enters an early education environment as an infant, he is just learning to respond in relation to others. A child needs a sensitive teacher to respond to his cues and temperament (Loeb et al., 2005). This is especially true in group care (Leonard, 2006). This teacher sensitivity and her consistency of care are predictors of secure attachment (Ahnert, Pinquart & Lamb, 2006). The smaller the group, the easier it is to offer each child this type of sensitive, responsive care. Staff-to-child ratios and recommendations for group size should be adhered to. Each child should have a primary caregiver or teacher who is familiar to him and with whom he can form an attachment. It would be ideal if these teachers could offer continuity of care and move up with the children they have developed close relationships with as the children grow older and transition to other classes (Leonard, 2006).

Curriculum for this relationship-based care is predicated on what interests and motivates each child (Lally & Mangione, 2006; Dodge, Rudick, & Berkee, 2006). This will afford a holistic development of each child's sense of self and will allow children to go at their own pace (Friedman & Soltero, 2006). The Program for Infant Toddler Caregivers suggests a three-step approach for the responsive process (WestEd, 1997). First, the teacher should watch the child for both verbal and nonverbal cues. Next, the teacher should ask himself what messages the child is sending and what the child might want at that moment. This might also include directly asking the

(continues)

REALITY*Check* (continued)

child what she wants. The final step is to adapt actions to what are believed to be the child's needs. Then the teacher should observe how the child responds to those actions and, if necessary, modify them.

This responsive process can be used in every situation all through the day and will provide the teacher insight into what the child is most comfortable with. In addition to the watch/ask/adapt/respond process, the teacher should ask families about how children prefer to interact with them at home. This recognition of the child's preferences in both environments will allow the teacher a deeper knowledge of the child's ability and how she operates (Gallagher & Mayer, 2006). When a teacher is familiar with a child's needs, actions, and reactions, she can appreciate and respect the child in a holistic manner and use this knowledge to provide the type of curriculum that will be most beneficial to the child's development (Friedman & Soltero, 2006).

As the child becomes a toddler, there may be some challenges in responsive care. Toddlers want to explore their environments, so these environments should be safe. The toddler will want to go out and explore the environment independently, then come back to the teacher for the affectionate interactions that are familiar (Gallagher & Mayer, 2006). The key to this, again, is to watch for the child's cues. Knowing a child's interests and abilities will help the teacher to encourage new experiences and further explorations. Children of this age enjoy these types of activities, but they also need the predictability and consistency that routines and a familiar teacher can give them. This helps children to self-regulate (Gillespie & Seibel, 2006).

When a child reaches preschool age, he is prepared to be a real partner in the relationship between himself and his teacher. He is capable of healthy social relationships and interactions. He has enough language that he can verbalize his needs and wants. The child is capable of following rules and seeing another perspective than his own (Gallagher & Mayer, 2006). As a child goes through the stages of relationship-based care, he expands his socio-emotional, intellectual, and language-based skills and abilities; these will positively impact all areas of his development. Everyone will benefit: the child in his developmental outcomes; the family in the quality and consistency of care their child has had; and the teacher in knowing that she has had a real impact on the child's life.

CHECK*point:* **What are the benefits of relationship-based care for the child? The family? The teacher? How might this affect the relationship of all involved?**

own families may be similar (Mayer, Ferede, & Hou, 2006). These storybooks can be a focal point in the welcoming area of the early childhood education environment so families can become familiar with them and understand how to choose a story that represents their perspective or experience. Create opportunities for families to discuss their beliefs about children by having them participate in a storytelling project (Curenton, 2006). Listening to their childhood stories will help the teacher understand more about the values and traditions that the parents have experienced, which may in turn clarify their present positions. Stories could be told in person or recorded on a video or audio recorder.

Teachers can encourage families to read at home to their children. A family member who reads or tells stories is also a teacher for his child, whether he realizes it or not. Reinforcement by the teacher can acknowledge the importance of this role, making the family aware that they play a large role in their child's educational experience. When families participate at this level, they are more able to recognize their children's strengths and their own. Teachers could construct journals that are bi-directional. Families can include pictures of their own family and extended family for children to share. The journal could also contain photographs of the children, pictures they have drawn, and notes the teacher puts in about an accomplishment or a special day. Teachers can also send home pictures of children engaged in activities of their school day so that the families can see what the children are doing. Emailing messages back and forth about the journal can engage parents and teachers in a different format and bring about important communication (DeBey & Bombard, 2007).

A caring community should offer some protective factors to help strengthen families; there are some specific protective factors that an early childhood education environment can offer to families (ChildWelfare, 2007). The first of these factors is to help families build a close bond with their children. Teachers can model responsive care and help families to better understand their children's needs. Early childhood education environments can provide knowledge of effective parenting skills and offer strategies through workshops, newsletters, and support groups. They can help parents to be more resilient by helping them to recognize stress and offering coping skills through many forms of communication. Teachers can help families to forge social connections with other families in care through support groups, potluck dinners, and informal gatherings. And finally, early childhood education environments can offer families concrete support by helping them access resources to meet basic needs so their families can feel more secure. Connecting families to community resources and strategies helps to strengthen families (Dickinson, Lothian & Jonz, 2007; Olson, 2007). Research has shown that when children are helped in good quality care, they grow up to be happier, more productive adults (McLaughlin et al., 2007).

The early childhood education program or family child care home should be family friendly. If there is a comfortable welcoming place provided for the parents to sit while they talk with the teacher or other parents, or watch their children, their level of comfort will be high. Before the families and children even enter the early childhood education environment, it would be nice to post "Welcome" signs in all languages represented by the children in care (DiNatale, 2002; Halacka Ball, 2006). Again, the use of translators who are familiar with the families or live in the community could help. When the physical environment is welcoming, it shows a strong sense of respect for the families and the capabilities of the children (Edward & Raikes, 2002). Early childhood education environments that support the families and children in creating new friendships and being open to learning about each other will create a safe haven for all. This safe haven will promote the emotional well-being of everyone and will support greater interaction and communication.

Family events such as potlucks or field trips involve families and help them make lasting connections with everyone in care so that a sense of community is felt. If education of parents through workshops or classes is available in the early education center, this too can offer families a sense of community. All early childhood education environments could offer information about available classes, as well as news articles and magazine articles that deal with child development and parenting. A number of centers in educational systems such as colleges and universities have created "parent rooms," where student parents can go to study, be sociable, and connect with others. Many students have economic difficulties, and some of these centers have even provided mini food banks for the families so that nutrition for the children and their families is consistently healthy.

As a member of a caring community, the teacher represents the issues dealing with safety, nutrition, and health that concern the early childhood education environment. The teacher may have solutions to some of these issues. It is important for the teacher to determine the areas in which she is well-informed, has had experience, and has received specialized training. This will allow the teacher to form the base from which to seek help from outside sources.

By creating a file of safety, nutritional, and health information, the teacher will have a great deal of necessary information available as it is needed. Keeping a current list of community resources will also help the teacher function as a team member. Networking with other teachers will also provide information.

Marissa and Kathryn were co-directors of a college child care center. In the past several years, they had made it a very family-friendly place, with a welcoming foyer and a parent room where the parents who were students could study and fix a quick meal in the microwave or put their food in the little refrigerator. As more parents began to "hang out" in the center, Marissa and Kathryn began to have a better focus on the individuals within the families and could also see some of the problems these parents were having. They could see how some of these problems were affecting the children in the family. A number of the students were single parents, and two of these families, due to finances, ended up homeless for part of the semester. Another mother had been a victim of domestic violence; one of the fathers was suffering from depression; and several other parents had other difficult issues that they were dealing with. Marissa and Kathryn found themselves spending more and more time trying to help these families and their children get the resources and help they needed and ended up spending less time doing what their job descriptions stated. Finally, they decided something had to change. Neither woman was willing to go back to the way the center had been before becoming a family-centered school. They decided that what they needed was a part-time social worker who could counsel the families and help them find the necessary resources. They did some investigating and found several grant funds that could help their situation. They applied for three grants and got two of them, and were able to get a social worker 20 hours per week. This offered the families what they desperately needed—someone who was trained to deal with their issues and could counsel them and help them connect to the resources they needed. Several of the children who had had issues of their own seemed to have fewer problems now that the parents were getting help. Many of the children who needed it were also getting helped. It was a win-win for all concerned. Kathryn and Marissa were so glad they had taken the step to make their center family friendly and were amazed at differences in the center and the families when they put in the extra effort that was required. Their center is now considered a model family-centered school, and teachers from all over the area come and see what they have done.

The health records, daily observations, and assessments of a child will assist the teacher in establishing whether the child has an issue or problem that may affect the child's health or well-being. Involving the family every step of the way will help them to feel a part of the early childhood education environment. In some cases, because of cultural perspectives or denial, the family may not want to discuss certain issues. Establishing trust and having a caring community as an integral part of the early childhood education environment may make it easier for teachers to approach the more delicate matters. Parents want to feel a sense of control, and if the issue is approached in a manner that leaves the parent feeling empowered, the family may be more likely to respond to any intervention attempts made to help the child.

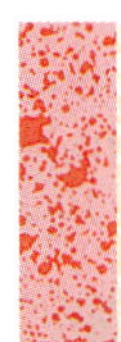

Pause for Reflection

What might you personally do to see that a caring community is created in your early childhood education environment?

Providing an Atmosphere for Teamwork

If a teacher connects effectively with families, it will be easier to see the goals, hopes, and dreams that the families have for their children (Greenberg, 2006). Outreach to families is the key to creating caring communities. As a family partner, the teacher represents the issues. The teacher can provide an atmosphere for teamwork that will encourage the parents to participate. Responsiveness to parental concerns, trust, modeling respect, and good communication skills provide the basis for a parent–teacher relationship. Parents appreciate warmth, positive attitudes, and accessibility of the teacher. When this type of climate is available to parents, they are more likely to participate. If parents are comfortable, they may be open to volunteering in care if it is asked of them. The needs and interests of the parents are important. These may be examined through surveys, conferences, parent information centers, parental involvement in the program, and home visits.

The teacher should survey the parents and other adults in the early childhood education environment on a regular basis to find out where help is needed on issues concerning safety, nutrition, and health of the children. Parents often respond to a call for information solicited by the teacher. The survey might form the basis of special topics for newsletters, parent handouts, speakers, videos, or even field trips including both parents and children.

The survey could begin a dialogue between a parent and the teacher relating to a specific issue with a child. Teacher and parent conferences help to continue this dialogue. For example, one of the answers you might find in your survey is that some families have no access to health care for their children. This also means that there is no "medical home" for those children. A teacher can inform a family about available no- and low-cost public health insurance policies in the local area and can help them navigate the health care system to advocate for their children (Sokol-Guiterrez, 2000). Parents may recognize a problem but be unwilling to admit that it exists if the teacher approaches them first. Asking the parents for input may put the parent at ease and may help the parent to acknowledge the problem. If this approach does not work, soliciting the help of a community resource may be necessary.

Annie was a family child care provider who was very organized and really tried to help the parents of the children in her care. She printed a weekly newsletter telling parents what the children did that week and reminding them of future events. She included any new safety, nutrition, or health information she received from the local agencies that she was linked to.

One day, a mother came to her, worried and stressed. Lisa, a first-generation Vietnamese American, was concerned that her extended family wanted to "coin" her son Vu when he was sick. Coining involves placing a hot coin on the child's neck that causes red streaks in this area. Usually, Lisa would have gone along with tradition, but she had read in the paper that this practice was dangerous. She wanted Annie to help her with this problem. Annie called several local health care agencies and confirmed that "coining" was indeed dangerous. The agencies mailed information to her that she gave to Lisa. Lisa was able to go to her family and tell them that, although she appreciated their traditions, she could not allow her son to be put in danger with that particular tradition. She told them that whenever Vu was ill, she would take him to the physician for care.

Parents may also feel the need for specific help dealing with parenting issues that could affect the health and well-being of children. For example, linkages can be created for the issue of challenging behaviors, which are occurring with greater regularity in early childhood education environments (see Reality Check: Creating Linkages for Children's Challenging Behaviors on page 622). Posting a list of topics to be considered may help parents decide which issues are most pressing to them so they can request information. Creating a parent center, even if it is just a tabletop or rack for providing information, may help engage the parent in a mutual effort (Kaczmarek, 2006). A database for the issue can be created and either posted or sent to families in an email. A parent who is used to accessing information may be better prepared to participate as a team member. If there are a significant number of non-English speaking families in care, the teacher should attempt to provide information in the language of the family. Community support may be needed to accomplish this.

Home visits allow the teacher to view the child in a more holistic manner, with all the environments considered (Shaw & Zehaye, 2000). Some parents and families are more than happy to encourage the teacher to visit their homes, but this may not be possible due to time constraints. However, if an issue is creating difficulties, a home visit may provide a better picture or elicit more cooperation from the parents involved. A home visit should be handled carefully, and it might be a good idea to consult with community resource professionals before visiting the family. Some families may refuse to participate in this strategy. The nanny may have an advantage in creating a partnership based on this aspect, because the care is provided in the family's own home and the teacher is privy to most of what is occurring.

Providing Linkages to the Community

All of the strategies used to create a caring community in the early childhood education environment may also help to promote the inclusion of a third

The team of teacher and parent can be expanded to include a resource and referral worker.

party, the greater community and its resources. Teachers should have access to a number of people who are resources for community support. Successful early childhood education programs and family child care homes are those that involve community agencies and support networks (Lovejoy, 1998). These people may include health professionals, nutritionists, and those employed in safety professions such as police and firemen. Social workers, occupational therapists, family counselors, speech therapists, and child abuse prevention specialists are all good sources of community support. Partners may also be secured from organizations such as the American Red Cross, Head Start, community health services, resource and referral agencies, and special interest groups such as the March of Dimes.

Prevention is one of the primary goals of the teacher to protect the children's health, safety, and well-being. Providing linkages for families to many of the community resources can help prevent problems concerning these issues. Collaborating with people to whom parents can turn for guidance might help integrate the information into the early childhood education environment, thus making the information more accessible and saving time on taking action on an important issue (Lally, Lerner, & Lurie-Hervitz, 2001). These linkages may occur by simply providing brochures and access information; they can also happen if the teacher invites these community resources to speak at special programs for parents. Linkages may also occur through referrals to specific professionals to provide extra help or care to children who may need it. If a teacher understands the community system for a specific need of a child, he can help families get needed information and services (Olson, 2007). A parent must participate for this linkage to be successful. Earlier groundwork for establishing good communication should make getting parent participation easier. A family who is involved in a caring early childhood education community is more likely to be involved. The more the family is involved, the more valuable are all the linkages. This will allow for the greatest protection, prevention, and assurance of well-being for the children in care.

Key Concept 16.6

Creating a Caring Community

Teachers must have the help of parents and community resources in order to provide the optimum environment for good safety, nutrition, and health for children. Providing an atmosphere for a caring community can engage parents and create a linkage between the early childhood education environment and the home environment. Providing families a linkage to community resources can help the teacher to create a team that will help protect and provide the best for the children's health, safety, and well-being in and out of the early childhood education environment. Providing an atmosphere for creating a caring community for families will create a linkage between the early childhood education environment and home environments.

CHAPTER SUMMARY

A teacher should provide an environment that meets the safety, nutritional, and health needs for the children while they are in the early childhood education environment. Communication with the families is vitally important and should be a priority.

The teacher should practice cultural competency on an ongoing basis. Children in care represent a wide variety of different family structures, ethnic and cultural backgrounds, and experiences. The teacher can initiate activities that promote the integration of diversity and cultural competence into the early childhood education environment. Teachers should access and use community resources that will help provide a greater degree of health and well-being for the children and families they work with.

Teachers may have to advocate for the children in the early education environment on issues concerning safety, nutrition, and health. Teachers need the help of parents and community resources in order to provide a caring community and the optimum environment for good safety, nutrition, and health for children.

TO GO BEYOND

Additional resources for this chapter can be found by visiting the book companion website at www.cengage.com/education/robertson. This supplemental material includes chapter objectives, internet exercises, reflection questions, quizzes, web links, glossary and flash cards, case studies, frequently asked questions, downloadable forms and tables, curriculum supplements, more reality checks, additional key concepts, references, and more.

Chapter Review Critical Thinking Applications

1. Discuss the importance of communication in the early childhood education environment. Include all the elements.
2. How does diversity affect early childhood education environments? What steps should be taken to be culturally competent?
3. How would you go about creating a caring community for parents? What would you do to get parents really involved and feeling comfortable?

As an Individual

1. List the resources in your area that a teacher could use.
2. Research the topic of preverbal communication by finding two articles on signing with infants. Write a two-to-three paragraph paper and be prepared to discuss in class.
3. Survey the community for culturally diverse health and safety practices. Create a list to share with the class.
4. Go to your local resource and referral agency and find out what measures they are taking to advocate for the children in your community. List these measures and discuss in class. What more might be done to help children in the community?

As a Group

1. Working in small groups, create a list of resources for teachers that is compiled from the lists that individuals have collected. Do any of these deal with diversity or advocacy?
2. In these same groups, create a team of teachers, parents, and resources. Role-play these different roles.
3. Discuss the best methods to create a "cultural consistency" between the early childhood education environment and the home.

Case Studies

1. You are a new teacher in an inner-city elementary school with a number of children from different cultures. You love your job, but you are overwhelmed by the issues that you are facing that seem culturally oriented, particularly communicating with several parents whose first language is not English. What should you do to help manage the diversity in your environment and acquire a greater degree of cultural competence?
2. Cort is a 3-year-old boy in Keela's class. He appears to be having some difficulty with his vision. His mother, Janice, is struggling to keep her family clothed, fed, and sheltered, and she does not have health insurance. Janice knows Cort has a problem, but she does not have any resources to help him. What steps should Keela take to help Cort and his mother? What resources in the community could she call?

3. Su Yen was opening an early childhood education program in an urban area. She had no worries about the number of children that might attend because there was a real lack of that type of program in that area. She was concerned about creating a climate in which parents would participate. She wanted to create a caring community that would help to meet children's and parents' needs. How would she go about creating this type of climate at her school? What suggestions might you give her to help her?

  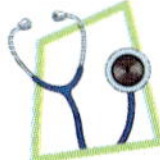

CURRENT ISSUES CURRICULUM SUPPLEMENT

Sample lesson plans and topic maps for subjects on current issues related to health, safety, and nutrition are provided on the website for the teacher to help reinforce the information that is being modeled by teachers and learned by the children in the early childhood education environment. In addition to the sample curriculum, there is a list of children's books and sources for further information. Some of this information may include songs or finger plays. This sample group is presented to help the teacher design his or her own curriculum by adding to the information provided.

Credits

Chapter 1. 6: Wadsworth/Cengage Learning **11:** Wadsworth/Cengage Learning **20:** Wadsworth/Cengage Learning **29:** Wadsworth/Cengage Learning

Chapter 2. 43: Wadsworth/Cengage Learning **47:** top, Wadsworth/Cengage Learning **47:** bottom, Wadsworth/Cengage Learning **48:** Wadsworth/Cengage Learning **51:** Wadsworth/Cengage Learning **57:** Wadsworth/Cengage Learning **59:** Wadsworth/Cengage Learning **63:** Wadsworth/Cengage Learning **66:** Wadsworth/Cengage Learning **70:** Wadsworth/Cengage Learning

Chapter 3. 80: Wadsworth/Cengage Learning **84:** Wadsworth/Cengage Learning **85:** left, Wadsworth/Cengage Learning **85:** right, Wadsworth/Cengage Learning **90:** Wadsworth/Cengage Learning **92:** Wadsworth/Cengage Learning **95:** top, Wadsworth/Cengage Learning **95:** bottom, Wadsworth/Cengage Learning **96:** left, Wadsworth/Cengage Learning **96:** right, Wadsworth/Cengage Learning **100:** Wadsworth/Cengage Learning **106:** Wadsworth/Cengage Learning **116:** Wadsworth/Cengage Learning **118:** Wadsworth/Cengage Learning

Chapter 4. 130: Wadsworth/Cengage Learning **134:** Wadsworth/Cengage Learning **136:** Wadsworth/Cengage Learning **139:** Wadsworth/Cengage Learning **141:** Wadsworth/Cengage Learning **150:** Wadsworth/Cengage Learning **153:** Wadsworth/Cengage Learning **156:** Wadsworth/Cengage Learning **159:** Wadsworth/Cengage Learning

Chapter 5. 168: Wadsworth/Cengage Learning **173:** left, Wadsworth/Cengage Learning **173:** right, Wadsworth/Cengage Learning **174:** Wadsworth/Cengage Learning **177:** Wadsworth/Cengage Learning **184:** Wadsworth/Cengage Learning **186:** Wadsworth/Cengage Learning **194:** Wadsworth/Cengage Learning **199:** Wadsworth/Cengage Learning

Chapter 6. 216: Wadsworth/Cengage Learning **228:** Wadsworth/Cengage Learning **232:** Wadsworth/Cengage Learning **238:** Wadsworth/Cengage Learning **243:** Wadsworth/Cengage Learning **245:** left, Wadsworth/Cengage Learning **245:** center left, Wadsworth/Cengage Learning **245:** center right, Wadsworth/Cengage Learning **245:** right, Wadsworth/Cengage Learning **248:** Wadsworth/Cengage Learning

Chapter 7. 255: Wadsworth/Cengage Learning **259:** Wadsworth/Cengage Learning **264:** Wadsworth/Cengage Learning **267:** Wadsworth/Cengage Learning **269:** Wadsworth/Cengage Learning **274:** Wadsworth/Cengage Learning **280:** Wadsworth/Cengage Learning **282:** Wadsworth/Cengage Learning **285:** Wadsworth/Cengage Learning **288:** Wadsworth/Cengage Learning

Chapter 8. 294: top, Wadsworth/Cengage Learning **294:** bottom, Wadsworth/Cengage Learning **295:** Wadsworth/Cengage Learning **299:** Wadsworth/Cengage Learning **300:** Wadsworth/Cengage Learning **304:** Wadsworth/Cengage Learning **305:** Wadsworth/Cengage Learning **308:** Wadsworth/Cengage Learning **313:** left, Wadsworth/Cengage Learning **313:** right, Wadsworth/Cengage Learning **316:** Wadsworth/Cengage Learning **324:** Wadsworth/Cengage Learning **326:** Wadsworth/Cengage Learning

Chapter 9. 335: Wadsworth/Cengage Learning **337:** Wadsworth/Cengage Learning **348:** Wadsworth/Cengage Learning **351:** Wadsworth/Cengage Learning **352:** Wadsworth/Cengage Learning **359:** Wadsworth/Cengage Learning **364:** Wadsworth/Cengage Learning **366:** Wadsworth/Cengage Learning

Chapter 10. 374: Wadsworth/Cengage Learning **378:** Wadsworth/Cengage Learning **379:** Wadsworth/Cengage Learning **381:** Wadsworth/Cengage Learning **385:** Wadsworth/Cengage Learning **390:** Wadsworth/Cengage Learning **391:** Wadsworth/Cengage Learning **393:** Wadsworth/Cengage Learning **399:** Wadsworth/Cengage Learning **404:** Wadsworth/Cengage Learning

Chapter 11. 411: Wadsworth/Cengage Learning **416:** Wadsworth/Cengage Learning **417:** Wadsworth/Cengage Learning **420:** Wadsworth/Cengage Learning **422:** top, Wadsworth/Cengage Learning **422:** bottom, Wadsworth/Cengage Learning **430:** Wadsworth/Cengage Learning **434:** Wadsworth/Cengage Learning **440:** Wadsworth/Cengage Learning

Chapter 12. 446: Wadsworth/Cengage Learning **448:** Wadsworth/Cengage Learning **465:** Wadsworth/Cengage Learning **466:** Wadsworth/Cengage Learning **467:** Wadsworth/Cengage Learning **469:** Wadsworth/Cengage Learning **470:** Wadsworth/Cengage Learning **475:** Wadsworth/Cengage Learning **476:** Wadsworth/Cengage Learning **478:** Wadsworth/Cengage Learning

Chapter 13. 485: Wadsworth/Cengage Learning **492:** Wadsworth/Cengage Learning **500:** Wadsworth/Cengage Learning **502:** Wadsworth/Cengage Learning **505:** Wadsworth/Cengage Learning **506:** Wadsworth/Cengage Learning **507:** Wadsworth/Cengage Learning **513:** Wadsworth/Cengage Learning **514:** Wadsworth/Cengage Learning **525:** Wadsworth/Cengage Learning

Chapter 14. 534: Wadsworth/Cengage Learning **538:** Wadsworth/Cengage Learning **541:** Wadsworth/Cengage Learning **546:** Wadsworth/Cengage Learning **549:** Wadsworth/Cengage Learning **551:** Wadsworth/Cengage Learning **557:** Wadsworth/Cengage Learning **566:** Wadsworth/Cengage Learning

Chapter 15. 570: Wadsworth/Cengage Learning **577:** Wadsworth/Cengage Learning **578:** Wadsworth/Cengage Learning **583:** Wadsworth/Cengage Learning **585:** Wadsworth/Cengage Learning **595:** Wadsworth/Cengage Learning

Chapter 16. 602: Wadsworth/Cengage Learning **605:** Wadsworth/Cengage Learning **608:** Wadsworth/Cengage Learning **612:** Wadsworth/Cengage Learning **613:** Wadsworth/Cengage Learning **616:** Wadsworth/Cengage Learning **619:** Wadsworth/Cengage Learning **624:** Wadsworth/Cengage Learning **626:** Wadsworth/Cengage Learning **628:** Wadsworth/Cengage Learning **636:** Wadsworth/Cengage Learning

Section Opener 1. 1: Wadsworth/Cengage Learning

Section Opener 2. 39: Wadsworth/Cengage Learning

Section Opener 3. 211: Wadsworth/Cengage Learning

Section Opener 4. 371: Wadsworth/Cengage Learning

Section Opener 5. 529: Wadsworth/Cengage Learning

Index

Note: Page numbers referencing figures are followed by an "*f*." Page numbers referencing tables are followed by a "*t*."

A

B

C

E

F

G

H

I

J

K

N

O